Leviticus

OPENING THE SCRIPTURES

Opening the Scriptures is neither a new series of technical commentaries, nor is it a collection of sermons. Instead it offers devout church members a series of popularly accessible primers so that the average churchgoer can easily grasp them.

The organization of this series follows the four main sectional divisions of Holy Scripture: the Torah, the many prophetic books, the Psalms and wisdom books, and the New Testament. The authors of *Opening the Scriptures* show throughout that Holy Scripture is from A to Z the Book of God's covenant with his people.

Leviticus

OPENING THE SCRIPTURES

CORNELIS VONK
Nelson D. Kloosterman, Translator

WIPF & STOCK · Eugene, Oregon

LEVITICUS

OPENING THE SCRIPTURES

Copyright © 2024 Paideia Press Ltd. All rights reserved. Except for brief quotations in critical publications or reviews, no part of this book may be reproduced in any manner without prior written permission from the publisher. Write: Permissions, Wipf and Stock Publishers, 199 W. 8th Ave., Suite 3, Eugene, OR 97401.

Wipf & Stock
An Imprint of Wipf and Stock Publishers
199 W. 8th Ave., Suite 3
Eugene, OR 97401

www.wipfandstock.com

PAPERBACK ISBN: 978-1-6667-8222-6
HARDCOVER ISBN: 978-1-6667-8223-3
EBOOK ISBN: 978-1-6667-8224-0

04/23/24

Unless otherwise indicated, Scripture quotations are from the ESV® Bible (The Holy Bible, English Standard Version®), copyright © 2001 by Crossway, a publishing ministry of Good News Publishers. Used by permission. All rights reserved.

Scripture quotations marked (NIV) are taken from the Holy Bible, New International Version®, NIV®. Copyright © 1973, 1978, 1984, 2011 by Biblica, Inc.™ Used by permission of Zondervan. All rights reserved worldwide. www.zondervan.com. The "NIV" and "New International Version" are trademarks registered in the United States Patent and Trademark Office by Biblica, Inc.™

Contents

Translator's Introduction		vii
1	You shall be holy unto me	1

PART 1 | THE SACRIFICIAL TORAH: GENERAL PRINCIPLES

2	Reconciliation through death	15
3	The requirements for sacrificial animals	42
4	The general procedure for sacrificing an animal	46

PART 2 | THE SACRIFICIAL TORAH: SPECIFIC REQUIREMENTS

5	The burnt offering (Lev 1)	63
6	The grain offering (Lev 2)	68
7	The peace offering (Lev 3)	84
8	The sin offering (Lev 4:1–5:13)	96
9	The guilt offering (Lev 5:14–6:7)	123
10	The second section of the sacrificial Torah (Lev 6:8–7:38)	136

PART 3 | THE PRIESTHOOD

11	The "installation" of Aaron and his four sons (Lev 8)	149
12	The "inauguration" of Aaron and his four sons (Lev 9)	159
13	The "deposition" of Nadab and Abihu (Lev 10)	166

CONTENTS

PART 4 | THE PEOPLE OF YAHWEH

14	General observations	179
15	Torah instruction with regard to eating clean and unclean animals (Lev 11)	188
16	Torah instruction with regard to the uncleanness after childbirth (Lev 12)	202
17	Torah instruction with regard to the uncleanness of leprosy (Lev 13–14)	211
18	Torah instruction with regard to uncleanness through discharges of males and females (Lev 15)	228
19	"Zealots for the Law"	236
20	The Great Day of Atonement (Lev 16)	246
21	Be careful with the blood! (Lev 17)	268
22	No pagan lifestyle! (Lev 18–20)	282
23	Keeping priests and sacrificial gifts holy (Lev 21–22)	333
24	Observe my Sabbaths! (Lev 23–25)	353
25	Conclusion and transition to Numbers (Lev 26–27)	441

Bibliography   477
Subject Index   479
Scripture Index   513

Translator's Introduction

THIS VOLUME IS PART of the original multi-volume Dutch commentary series entitled *De Voorzeide Leer*, which means "the aforesaid doctrine," a phrase found in the Reformed liturgical form used in connection with the baptism of infants. In their responsive vows, the child's parents promise to teach their child "in the aforesaid doctrine," referring to the teachings of the Bible, the ecumenical creeds, and the Reformed confessions. We have chosen to entitle the series *Opening the Scriptures* as an encouragement to readers to take in hand these commentaries as handbooks for working through portions of Scripture that may be unfamiliar.

Opening the Scriptures is not a new series of technical commentaries that explain the Bible word for word, although this series of volumes does rest upon careful exegesis. Nor is it a collection of sermons, although now and then the authors shine the light of Scripture on our modern world. Actually, there is no familiar category of Bible studies that serves as a suitable classification for *Opening the Scriptures*. This series has a unique character. It offers devout church members a series of popularly accessible primers, with no display of scholarly expertise, so that the average churchgoer can easily grasp them.

As far as their approach is concerned, these volumes begin by telling you about the structure of the biblical book that you want to study. This is because an overview of the whole enhances insight into the parts. After all, Scripture is neither a loose-leaf assortment of essays nor a collection of isolated texts. The ABC guidelines of the authors of this series is this: pay attention to the text, the context, and the canonical place of the biblical book (or the other way around). What is the scope of a particular book, and how is it organized? What is its place in the totality of Scripture? For example, what ties Joshua, Judges, Samuel, and Kings together? In short, *Opening the Scriptures* resembles a museum guidebook that opens your eyes to the beauty and meaning for today of the treasures, large and small, being exhibited.

TRANSLATOR'S INTRODUCTION

The organization of this series follows the four main sectional divisions of Holy Scripture (Luke 24:44). For the Holy Spirit has joined together all the books of the Bible into an imposing edifice. The Torah, or the five books of Moses, is the foundation upon which the entire Scripture rests. Therefore this section of the Bible is discussed most extensively in *Opening the Scriptures*. The many prophetic books form the walls. The Psalms and Wisdom books are the windows. Over all of this the Holy Spirit has laid the golden dome roof of the New Testament. The authors of *Opening the Scriptures* would like to guide you through this immense building. They will ask, "Have you seen this, and did you notice that?" And when you respond, "Surely the Bible is a wonderful book, and I would like to know more about it!" then they will have achieved their purpose.

These concluding translator comments may be helpful.

First, in the original Dutch volume, each chapter concludes with "notes," endnotes referring the reader to commentaries and other relevant studies, most of them in Dutch or German. The usefulness of these endnotes to the English-language reader is dubious. Where substantive explanations of the main text appear in these notes, they have been incorporated into the main text in English.

Second, because of both their content and their interruption of the flow of the exposition of Leviticus, sections of the original Dutch edition dealing with the immortality of the soul (pages 49–161 in the original) and with Judaizing (pages 397–477 in the original) have been omitted from this English-language edition.

Finally, throughout the commentary, the author engages in somewhat incidental discussions relevant to his own ecclesiastical history and tradition. A number of these have been omitted simply for the sake of brevity and relevance.

1

You shall be holy unto me

IF THE PENTATEUCH IS a necklace with five sparkling jewels, then Leviticus is the carnelian.

It is as red as a carnelian because of so much blood, so much that the book overflows with blood.

For in this book we hear more about that foundation of the (Israelite) world that we discussed in the closing pages of our commentary on Exodus. Here we will learn more about the basis upon which Israelite society was established by God.

The first stone of that foundation was laid with the announcement of the ten words of the covenant from Mount Sinai.

The next action was the erection of the tabernacle as the palace of Israel's king among his people at Horeb. That was what Exodus was about.

Leviticus talks about the ministry with which this people were to please their God with and around that palace, that sanctuary.

A ministry of blood.

Daily, weekly, annually.

Does not that impressive river of blood call out for the once-for-all sacrifice of Christ?

"For Christ has entered, not into holy places made with hands.... Nor was it to offer himself repeatedly, as the high priest enters the holy places every year with blood not his own, for then he would have had to suffer repeatedly since the foundation of the world. But as it is, he has appeared once for all at the end of the ages to put away sin by the sacrifice of himself" (Heb 9:24–26).

1. THE PLACE OF LEVITICUS

No one reading through the book of Leviticus right after reading Exodus receives the impression of suddenly entering a totally different world.

The transition is almost invisible.

The last chapter of Exodus, chapter 40, was just telling us about the tabernacle, occupied by God as his home.

Now immediately following, Leviticus 1 begins by speaking about the sacrifices that would have to be brought to that newly erected sanctuary (Lev 1–3), all the way to Leviticus 7. A rather lengthy explanation. Commentators often call Leviticus 1–7 the "sacrificial Torah."

Next follows a narrative about the appointment of those who would have to serve in that sanctuary in the sacrificial ministry. We read about the appointment of Aaron and his four sons in Leviticus 8–10.

The next section, Leviticus 11–15, is about cleanness and uncleanness, and is closely related to the tabernacle. For in a camp that was stationed around the tent of Yahweh, nothing was allowed to enter that hinted of . . . death. If such a hint appeared, it must be removed. Removed from the presence of God and the people of life.

Leviticus 16 deals with the great day of atonement.

This too was inconceivable apart from the tabernacle.

And the book continues in this line.

Everything focuses on God who wants to occupy a palace and ascend a throne in the midst of Israel. That is all well and good, but then everything surrounding it must comport with his will and command. As the sanctuary, so the people.

That is what Leviticus teaches us.

That is its special place among the first five books of the Bible. This is what we indicated in our earlier commentary on Exodus:[1]

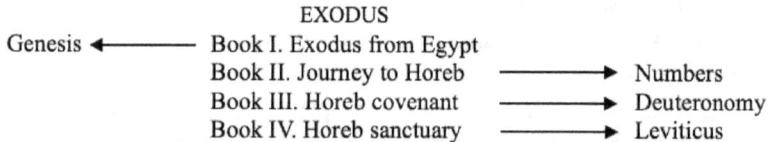

After becoming acquainted in Genesis with the background of the exodus, we open the Pentateuch in Exodus to learn that the same Yahweh who had led Israel out of Egypt was the one who had created heaven and

---

1. Vonk, *Exodus*, 33.

earth, and had saved Abraham. Only to discover next that Leviticus begins where Exodus ended. With the sanctuary in which the king of Israel had taken up residence.

2. THE TIME OF LEVITICUS

After the tabernacle was constructed, Israel did not remain long at Mount Sinai, no longer than a month, in fact. In that time period God had revealed to Moses what we now read in the book of Leviticus.

How do we know this?

In our commentary on Exodus we calculated a number of dates,[2] which we can now supplement. As the reader may recall, we call the year of the exodus Year 1.

Month 1, Day 15, Year 1	Exodus out of Egypt (Exod 12:17; 13:4)
Month 3, Day 15, Year 1	Arrival at Horeb (Exod 19:1)
Month 1, Day 1, Year 2	The tabernacle was constructed (Exod 40:2, 17)
Month 2, Day 1, Year 2	Census with a view to marching against the Canaanites (Num 1:1)
Month 2, Day 20, Year 2	Departure from Horeb (Num 10:11)

Not only will this list help us later when we read Numbers, but it can help us now already as we read Leviticus. We can see clearly that there must have been one month between the completion of the tabernacle and the census of the fighting men that preceded the departure from Horeb.

During that month God must have revealed to Moses and commissioned him with what we now have in the book of Leviticus. That fact is evident from Leviticus itself. Let's look at a few passages.

First, Lev 1:1: "The Lord called Moses and spoke to him from the tent of meeting."

To what does "the tent of meeting" refer here? Perhaps the tent in which God occasionally talked to Moses during the intermezzo after Israel's sin with the golden calf?[3] There was no reason for that. Was it then perhaps the tabernacle? There is every reason for thinking so. For that had been promised earlier. God would not only live there among Israel, but he would also speak from there to Moses. That had been promised in Exod 29:42. That could now occur. Apparently it occurred frequently. We should probably have in mind such meetings between God and Moses even when

---

2. Vonk, *Exodus*, 304–307.
3. See Vonk, *Exodus*, 127–45.

no mention is made of the tabernacle as the place of revelation (Lev 8:1, Yahweh spoke to Moses; Lev 11:1, Yahweh spoke to Moses and Aaron; Lev 16:1, Yahweh spoke to Moses; Lev 17:1; 18:1; 19:1; 20:1; 21:1; 22:1; etc.).

Some Bible readers might perhaps think of a different place of revelation, when, for example, we read several times about "Mount Sinai" (Lev 7:38; 25:1).

With Lev 7:38 we should probably see this as a notation written by the person who organized and collected the parts of Leviticus. The verse reads like this: this is the law for such and such sacrifices "which the Lord commanded Moses *on Mount Sinai*, on the day that he commanded the people of Israel to bring their offerings to the Lord, in the wilderness of Sinai." It is evident that the person who later collected the various parts wanted to tell the readers that the laws that had just been narrated all dated from the time when Israel was staying at Horeb. The only question is: During which time? From the time when Moses was still receiving revelation from God on top of Mount Sinai, regarding the covenant and the construction of the tabernacle? It is not obvious that we should think that this referred to that period, for that has already been described in Exodus, in great detail. No, when Lev 7:38 speaks about laws that Yahweh had commanded Moses "on Mount Sinai," we should not suppose this refers to those earlier revelations of God to Moses, but to the later ones. Not on the mountain per se, but in the tabernacle. Could we not date what God had said to Moses in that tabernacle as occurring during Israel's stay at Horeb, all of which Lev 7:38 is referring to as "on Mount Sinai"? Though it is stated in more general terms, Lev 1:1 was more accurate: "The Lord called Moses and spoke to him *from the tent of meeting*." This is the heading above Leviticus to which all the subsequent passages are referring that we mentioned earlier. All of these conversations happened at Horeb, but after the tabernacle had been built and consecrated. Which means that these conversations happened near the end of Israel's stay at Mount Sinai. So as we review our list of dates, we conclude that these occurred during the month between Month 1, Day 1, Year 2 and Month 2, Day 1, Year 2.

All of Leviticus, its entire *content*, was revealed during that single month.

We arrive at that conclusion with the help of the verse with which the book closes: "These are the commandments that the Lord commanded Moses for the people of Israel on Mount Sinai" (Lev 27:34).

Here again we encounter the words "on Mount Sinai." We discussed them above, in connection with Lev 7:38, and it is our view that when they surface again at the end of the book, they do not prevent us from connecting this to the specific month when Yahweh gave Moses various commandments, speaking from the ark. The conclusion of Lev 27:34 is casting a backward glance toward that event.

But people are generally of the opinion that the last chapter of Leviticus does not really belong to the book, but was added to the book as an appendix.

Even so, if the actual book of Leviticus ended one chapter earlier, with Leviticus 26, its final verse closely resembles the last verse of chapter 27. In Lev 26:46 we read: "These are the statutes and rules and laws that the Lord made between himself and the people of Israel through Moses on Mount Sinai." As you can tell, this verse also has the appearance of a concluding verse. It is speaking in general terms. It does not mention any specific laws, like particular sacrificial prescriptions, as we find in Lev 7:37–38. No laws about specific impurities, like we find in Leviticus 11, 13, 14, and 15. Nothing specific. The entire content of Leviticus is summarized, concerning which we are told—once more, since this was repeated earlier with other sections—that all those statutes, ordinances, and laws had been given at Horeb by God to Moses. The phrase "on Mount Sinai" should not be interpreted to mean "on the top of Mount Sinai," but to mean "at Horeb, after God had taken up residence in the tabernacle."

When we say that "*all* of Leviticus was given by God to Moses within that month," we are not excluding the possibility that the hand of someone other than Moses had written down, arranged, annotated, and collected what had been revealed to Moses. In Deut 17:8–13 we read that Moses himself had incorporated the labor of others.

And don't forget especially the language. Let's assume that ancient Near Eastern life was more stable than our own, that mores and customs continued the same for centuries. Let's also assume that in religious affairs, the language showed little development. You have only to think of our own formal ecclesiastical language. Nevertheless, it need not be the case that the language of the Israelites had remained so unaltered since the time of Moses that centuries later it could have been read with ease as a document written in the language of Moses and his contemporaries. Just like most Dutch people today would not be able to read a Dutch book from the 1500s. The Hebrew of Moses' day would have shown considerable Egyptian influence, judging by the second half of the book of Genesis. Living for so many centuries in a strange environment would not have left the language of such a small group unaffected. Even if the majority of the Israelites had lived in isolation in Goshen, others had certainly lived among Egyptian neighbors (Exod 3:22), had even married Egyptian husbands or wives (Gen 41:45; Lev 24:10), and Moses himself was raised in an Egyptian palace and instructed in all the wisdom of the Egyptians (Exod 2:10; Acts 7:22), so that in his notes written at Horeb, he would not have used the language of the Canaanites. Thanks to the significantly enlarged understanding today of the languages of Canaan from the time surrounding Israel's exodus and entrance, we may conclude that some terms found in the sacrificial Torah of Leviticus strongly resemble those commonly used among the Canaanites of that time. That points to a later translation, revision, alteration, or whatever one might term it. The adapting of the ancient linguistic garment in which Israel received its inheritance through Moses, to the language of their new land. For even if a shared Babylonian past had likely played a role, it appears certain that in the case of Israel in Canaan, the conquerors adopted much of the language of the vanquished.

Possibilities galore for editorial consequences.

Even though there are still all those sentences in Leviticus that speak repeatedly about Moses. "Then Yahweh said to Moses . . . ." Would a person write this way about himself?

For this and other reasons, we would not dare to insist that the book of Leviticus *as we have it before us* dates from the time of Moses. This is something that in fact is not reported to us in the book itself.

We suggest the following course of events.

Just as had happened earlier, before the construction of the tabernacle (Exod 24:4), Moses would have made a record of everything that God told him during that particular month. Then (exactly when, we don't know) someone other than Moses grouped portions and documents and provided titles and summaries. Why could that not have been done by someone like Joshua or Eleazar? We can only guess about when the later linguistic revisions may have occurred.

In any case, with this view we are maintaining the conviction that the *content* of Leviticus came from God to Moses, so that our Savior could say about Moses, both on formal as well as material grounds, in terms of the book of Leviticus: He has written of me (John 5:46).

3. LEVITICUS: A FENCE

In the month preceding the census and preparation for marching, the book of Leviticus, at least in terms of its content, came into being at Horeb.

Leviticus was given before the march against Canaan.

Like a tank.

For God did not want his Israel to go into battle unprotected.

For we must recall that initially God had not intended that Israel would have entered the land of Canaan after forty years. Entering Canaan could have been a matter of months. But we will say more about this in connection with our commentary on the book of Numbers.

Leviticus was given with a view to Canaan. That land of Canaan against which Israel would be marching in 1.5 months. Read the warnings concerning the Canaanite wickedness in Lev 18:3 and 20:23. The book of Leviticus had to serve as armor against the filth of Canaan, to keep Israel what she was: the holy congregation of Yahweh. For otherwise . . . .

Let us look now at the other side of the coin.

The laws of Leviticus had a double purpose. Not only to protect Israel against Canaan, but also to preserve Israel against . . . her own God, Yahweh. This is what I mean:

If there is one word we encounter repeatedly in Leviticus, it's the word *holy*. We find this word in the richest variety of contexts. It's a word that defies definition. We repeatedly hear Yahweh say about himself that he is holy. Naturally, no mortal possesses the same holiness as Israel's God, the One who now is our God. "With whom will you compare God?" Isaiah asked (40:18). Even though God was free to declare as holy whomever he chose, and *whatever* he chose. In Leviticus you will frequently be astonished that objects, things, like the tabernacle, are called holy. The "utensils" of the tabernacle as well. Although one thing may be more holy than another. In addition, those performing the sacrifices were holy. But this did not mean that everything was "most holy." To say it reverently: the word *holy* is used with considerable variation in meaning. Finally, we would not fail to mention that in Leviticus the entire people of Israel is called holy. This is something that, with their arrival at Horeb, appeared at most to be a task laid upon Israel (Exod 19:6): Holiness as "calling." But in Leviticus we hear Yahweh announcing *his* holiness as a gift that served as the foundation for Israel's existence, it was granted to Israel so that Israel would be holy. Both are true. The "calling" first and then the "gift." First, you shall be holy before me. For I, Yahweh, am holy, and I have separated you from the nations to be mine (Lev 20:26).

What then does *holy* mean?

Language studies provide no useful answer to that question. The etymology of the Hebrew word *qadosh* is uncertain. As one commentator notes, behind the holiness of Yahweh there probably lies the notion of the awesome appearance of his majesty. In the Babylonian Assyrian language, the root of the Hebrew word possesses the meaning of "to be awesome," as well as "to be of glorious appearance." He is "majestic in holiness, awesome in glorious deeds, doing wonders" (Exod 15:11). When God reveals himself as the Holy One, he displays his power among the nations in the deliverance of Israel (Ezek 20:41–42). But it was especially the consuming side of God's holiness that was described, as in Lev 10:1–7: when Aaron's sons brought "strange" fire on the altar, a consuming fire came forth from Yahweh, and he said: "Among those who are near me I will be sanctified, and before all the people I will be glorified" (Lev 10:3).

Holy . . . and holiness . . . of God, of people, and of objects. Leviticus supplies us with no concrete definition, but we must discover it by reading the book. Or stated better: we must seek an impression by reading and more reading.

As we read through Leviticus, we will come to see that the laws of this book were given to Moses, and to Israel, so that it might be possible for those two—God and Israel—who had been so closely related through the covenant and the tabernacle, *to continue together*.

Yahweh was so very holy, and therefore Israel had to be just as holy.

As you might imagine, no amount of money in the world could induce us to denigrate the Torah. That lovely Torah, that Law of Yahweh for Israel, given so that people might come to know him as their faithful covenant God.

But also to learn from the Torah how to interact with God. For in the midst of an entire world of nations wandering about in darkness and succumbing to death, Israel was permitted to be the people of life. But she was also commanded to be the people of life. Otherwise God could not dwell among his people as Yahweh, the One who is near. This explains the massive complex of measures given to enable the continued interaction between those two. For ultimately Israel was nothing but one nation among others, whose ancestry and character were no different from those other nations. How easily Israel would slide back down to that former level from which she had been graciously delivered. That deathly level. Something that entailed the risk of destruction through the pouring out of God's holiness against the entire nation or against individual members of the nation. This explains the manifold measures designed to rescue Israel from abandoning or even unintentionally slipping off the foundation on which she had been placed at Horeb. This explains why we find later in Numbers an important chapter about the mediating place of the tribe of Levi in Israel's encampment. Like a guardrail between the congregation and the tabernacle. This explains why in Leviticus we find numerous "statutes and rules and laws that the Lord made *between* himself and the people of Israel through Moses on Mount Sinai"—as we read once more in the closing verse of Lev 26:46.

We already discussed the phrase "on Mount Sinai." Here we have italicized the word *between*. Should we not interpret this as referring to the fence at the foot of Sinai for the safety of people and animals when God descended on the mountain? The laws of Leviticus would form a permanent isolating railing between Yahweh and his people.

The men of Beth-shemesh later complained: "Who is able to stand before the Lord, this holy God?" (1 Sam 6:20). And in Isa 33:14 the sinners heard people crying out: "Who among us can dwell with the consuming fire? Who among us can dwell with everlasting burnings?"

Nadab and Abihu had scarcely been consecrated as priests before they were killed in the presence of Yahweh. For God said: "Among those who are near me I will be sanctified, and before all the people I will be glorified" (Lev 3:10).

At this point we must recall that the mediator between God and people, the man Jesus Christ, was permitted by this God, whom he himself had called "holy Father" (John 17:11), to enter into the holy of holies above. And this when he had taken upon himself the entire burden of our sins. When he had stood before God as sin itself (2 Cor 5:21). But he had died to sin once for all, and death no longer has dominion over him (Rom 6:9–10). Like a sponge absorbs water, like a tissue soaks up the spilled ink, and like the lightning rod attracts the fire of heaven to itself, so too he has borne God's wrath in his suffering and death.

Anyone who has read Leviticus and been impressed with God's awesome aversion to sin and death will catch his breath when he sees Jesus Christ, in the Gospels, ascending the path as our substitute, the path leading him to the mount of God's holiness. We can only stagger when we behold him with pierced hands breaking down the wall between Yahweh and the congregation, the wall that Leviticus describes for us.

He was successful.

The church today is free from the law. It was a good law. Certainly. Of course. But in many respects it was a harsh custodian.

Coming after this advocate and surety, we too may now appear before God without fear, along this living way, Christ Jesus. We are fervently exhorted not to throw away our "proof of access" (Heb 10:35). In the paradise that will descend to earth, the church of glory will receive an access much freer than Aaron and his sons ever received in terms of the shadow of that access known as the tabernacle. As kings and priests, for the purpose of "worshiping" the Holy One, "they will behold his face." It is the privilege of priests (Rev 2:7; 21:2; 22:3–4).

4. THE STYLE OF LEVITICUS

Things occur in Leviticus that would have never been permitted in our textbooks and law books today. Here are a few examples.

As we mentioned earlier, Leviticus 1–7 deals with sacrifices. In fairly broad strokes, seven chapters are devoted to that. Nowadays many people would surely think that that was rather exhaustive. Space enough, and then some, so that the author would not have needed to return later to the subject with supplemental comments. Such comments could have easily been included in those seven chapters.

But not in Leviticus.

When we find seven chapters devoted to that subject, we encounter all the way at the end, in Lev 22:17–25, various regulations about . . . inadmissible defects in sacrificial animals. Defects that rendered an animal unusable for slaughter at Yahweh's sanctuary.

This was something that, according to the style of writing—of articles, brochures, books—as would be considered by some in our day as absolutely correct, would not have occurred. Sloppy, incomplete, we will have to accept the fact that the Holy Spirit did not take into consideration their style in Leviticus. If they did that, perhaps they could learn from Leviticus, also when it involved that so-called "dry material," to put forth some effort to avoid boring their readers.

Leviticus is the kind of book about which a heartfelt Christian once honestly admitted to us that he had skipped over in family devotions. Leviticus is a wonderful book. Especially for Christians. For everywhere in this book you meet the costly suffering and genuine death, but especially the resurrection from the dead unto life, of our Lord Jesus Christ.

You need not fall asleep while reading Leviticus. It does not consist of a collection of police regulations, static narratives, financial statements. Nor does it consist of a bunch of dry sermons, the kind that resembles dry minutes of a meeting instead of the lively proclamation of the words of eternal life.

Of course Leviticus does require careful attention on the part of its readers. Especially at those points where you come into contact with the unsavory aspects of the law applied to the church of Israel. People need to be careful. Anyone who had touched a dead animal at work early in the morning would be unclean for the rest of the day and was not allowed to set foot in the forecourt. And if there were a leper or a corpse in the tent, the uneasiness was great. When Leviticus talks about such things, we can understand that some people might get the impression that they were reading a manual for priests. Indeed, those priests had to give Israel significant *torah*, or instruction about God's ways.

But Israel possessed in rich measure something that is unfortunately missing among us.

Sensitivity for *symbolism!*

Thanks to that rich symbolism, Leviticus contains a lot that requires explanation, but it is on that account that makes it all the more stimulating. It is a book full of variety.

In that connection, *story* plays a very important role in Leviticus as well. Where would you find in a modern law book or manual such doctrinal teaching? And what reads more interestingly than a good story?

Part 1

The Sacrificial Torah:
General principles

2

Reconciliation through death

WE HAVE SAID IT more than once already. The first seven chapters of the book of Leviticus are all devoted to one and the same subject, namely, the sacrifices. That much is obvious, in view of what preceded and what followed this section. We have already discussed what preceded. That Moses' account of what God revealed to him about the required sacrificial ministry obtained a place of prominence is obvious. In this way we have a suitable coupling with the conclusion of Exodus, regarding God's accepting of the tabernacle from Israel's hands. That tabernacle would be the place where the sacrifices would later need to be brought.

Concerning what followed, we see that after the instruction about sacrifices in Leviticus 1–7 we find the story about the census of the priesthood in Leviticus 8–10. This would apply to various sacrifices. In fact, later in Leviticus various sacrifices would be discussed with a view to different occasions. Thanks to the placement at the beginning of the large section about the sacrifices, every reader would be able to know accurately what kinds of sacrifices were involved.

This is indeed a large section. It carries extra significance because of its introductory character. Therefore we believe it would be helpful to do what we did in connection with the tabernacle, namely, arrange our discussion in terms of a general section and a particular section. In the first section we will discuss things related to all, or at least most, of the sacrifices. Once we've completed that, we will be able in the next section to discuss each sacrifice separately and more briefly.

PART 1 | THE SACRIFICIAL TORAH: GENERAL PRINCIPLES

I. GENERAL SECTION

Israel knew more than one kind of sacrifice. We can surmise that by skimming over the first seven chapters of Leviticus. God talked with Moses about burnt offerings, grain offerings, peace offerings, sin offerings, and guilt offerings. But all those offerings had something in common, for example, they were all brought to God. Some sacrifices belonged to a distinct group and shared something special. You should understand that these matters are more general in nature, so we will discuss them as follows:

A. Reconciliation through death

B. The theory of an immortal soul (chapter 3)

C. The requirements for each sacrificial animal (chapter 4)

D. The general procedure for sacrificing an animal (chapter 5)

A. Reconciliation through death

1. The origin of the sacrifice

Nowhere in Holy Scripture do you read one word about God explicitly instituting sacrifices in earlier times. Not even at those points where we might have expected it, like Genesis 4, the first Scripture passage where we encounter the word for sacrifice (*minchah*).

True enough, we do not find there an explicit narrative about the instituting of any sacrifice. But from the silence of Scripture concerning this subject we should not deduce that such an instituting of sacrifice by God did not occur. We should certainly not conclude that sacrifice was therefore something that people invented. That would be a completely illegitimate conclusion drawn from the silence of Scripture. We would mention the following matters, which point us in an entirely different direction.

In the story about Cain and Abel, Genesis 4 talks directly above sacrifices as though they were the most familiar practices in the world, without any introductory explanation of them. We are not surprised by that when we recall that Genesis 4 did not receive its place in Holy Scripture, first of all, for us, but for Israel, for people who had grown up with sacrifices.

Furthermore, however, we notice that Israel consequently knew good and well—in Leviticus we will see this repeatedly—that sacrifices were very important to God. Therefore we have the strong sense that when reading Genesis 4, no Israelite would have thought the first people, including Cain and Abel, would have invented sacrifices from their own imagination. Certainly not. Otherwise an Israelite would have been unable to comprehend that back then already God looked upon sacrifices with approval, which is what in fact had happened, and what is narrated in Gen 4:4. This points to the divine origin of sacrifice.

In addition, even though we admit that in Scripture we are told very little about the first human beings, we nevertheless know for certain that after the rebellion of Adam and Eve, God did not immediately break off all contact with them. Not even with Cain. The gospel of compassion and salvation arose historically in that earliest period. We know about God's ancient prediction that one day the great enemy of the human race would be destroyed, although that victory would be achieved in no other way than at a high cost (Gen 3:15). From where else than from that prediction can we explain the international rise of hope in the resurrection of the dead, though that hope was often defective? Surely primitive humanity had knowledge of God's intention and desire to dwell one day in peace among the people he created. The cherubs in the tabernacle appealed to the memory of that among Israel and the nations. We will not repeat what we have written in our commentary on Exodus about the paradise-longings of the patriarchs connected with the tabernacle. We believe that entire portions of God's revelation concerning that high cost had been preserved among the nations, a price that ensured, come what may, that a resurrection to glory would occur, along a route of suffering and death. From where else can we explain the international sense that there was no possibility for restoring the disrupted fellowship with the offended deity apart from the shedding of blood? Would pagans have heard the apostolic gospel of Heb 9:22—no forgiveness without the shedding of blood—with surprise as though this were something unheard of? What nation did not know about blood sacrifices?

We believe that no one would be guilty of holding to an inappropriate fantasy if they assumed and accepted the claim that God instituted sacrifice, and this institution lay behind the sacrifices of Cain and Abel, the sacrifice of Noah after the Flood (Gen 8:20), and the innumerable sacrifices mentioned in very ancient extra-biblical accounts. These were the kind of sacrifices that provided people an opportunity to confess their faith in God's promise of restored fellowship with him along the route of surrendering to him the best that people could offer, for putting to death. Apparently from early on, God had permitted the symbolizing of that terrible death of a human being through the sacrifice of an animal. Primitive humanity received no explicit permission to put an animal to death for any other purpose than sacrifice. That is clear from the post-Flood account of God permitting the slaughter of animals for consumption as well (Gen 9:2–4).

PART 1 | THE SACRIFICIAL TORAH: GENERAL PRINCIPLES

So primitive humanity possessed both word and sacrifice, truth and seal, instruction and symbol.

However, we have not received as much information as we might wish concerning these two treasures. We can point to a twofold reason for this. First, the wisdom of God, who apparently determined that what Holy Scripture would tell us about this matter would be sufficient. Second, the sin of those who, with Cain, began already to suppress the truth in unrighteousness (Rom 1:18). According to Genesis, Cain immediately had many followers in this practice. Nevertheless, here as well.

The truth is so powerful. For liars, the truth is indispensable. For just as without iron there would be no rust, no lie could exist without the truth. Every lie contains an element of truth. The world religions must be explained fundamentally on the basis of their distortion of the truth, their bastardization of the tradition. Concerning specifically the constant flowing of blood that has been shed throughout the centuries among the innumerable sanctuaries of Eastern and Western hemispheres, their source and origin must be found in the tragic mangling of the paradise gospel of salvation from the power of the great executioner of humanity, and especially of the pagans (Acts 26:18; Eph 2:2; 1 John 5:19), along the route of bloody struggle, all the way to death (Gen 3:15).

For centuries humanity has undergone a terrible *process of apostasy*. In addition to the testimony of Scripture, we have the testimony of remarkable remnants of the original knowledge of God and of his commands among the nations. Everywhere we encounter remnants of the ruins of knowledge about creation and "a golden age," rebellion and punishment, atonement and peace, resurrection and judgment. Even though by the time when Abraham lived, it had become very, very dark.

Nevertheless, in the pagan religious customs of that time God himself found so much that was useful that he took things over into his service from the religious sphere of Abraham's idolatrous ancestral home. When we read in Gen 12:7 that Abraham built an altar at Shechem, "to the Lord, who had appeared to him," that report appears without any commentary. Apparently because for both Abraham and Israelite readers, for a long time altars and sacrifices had been the most usual phenomena ever.

Notice: for Israel as well.

Just as the fact that God established a covenant with Israel at Horeb and gave two identical tablets as a testimony of this was hardly surprising, so too Israel would not have been surprised when on the day when that covenant was established, Moses had to build an altar, on which God commanded him to present *burnt offerings* and *peace offerings* (cf. Exod 24:5). The terms for these (*oloth* and *zevachim*) were not introduced or described with a word of explanation, neither for the initial participants in that ceremony nor for the subsequent (primarily Israelite) readers of the story. That was thought to be unnecessary.

In arranging the tabernacle construction, God made use of so many parallels of pagan sanctuaries with their furnishings and priestly garments, that in connection with the tabernacle, we could speak of God's "great annexation" at Horeb.[4]

We will encounter such striking parallels as well when we discuss the sacrificial *cultus* that God gave to Israel through Moses.

For at Horeb, Yahweh did not want to exhaust his people by removing them entirely from their context as an Eastern people. He did not overwhelm Israel with a flood of novelties. What could be retained was retained, although it was purified, and reunited to the genuine, ancient gospel of Genesis 3–4, with its preaching of God's hatred of Satan, sin, and death, and of his compassion toward people. Those people he was prepared to save, at any cost. Through the surrender, from his side, of the highest and most beloved gift humanly possible, surrendered to that same terrible death.

Today we would say: all of this extended to the Mediator's death.

2. Blood sacrifice was central, bloodless sacrifice was incidental

We hasten to add a correction to the preceding. We have repeatedly used the word *sacrifice*, by which we were continually referring to *bloody* sacrifice.

But not all sacrifices that Israel brought were bloody. We see that from the general term for sacrifice, the word *corban*.

This term was so general that it included gifts not intended at all to be laid on the altar to be burned. *Corban* referred, for example, to gifts of wine for the sanctuary, mentioned with respect to the princes of Num 7:3 and the generals in Num 31:50 (wagons for transporting the tabernacle and military plunder that consisted of gold armlets and bracelets, signet rings and earrings).

Corban referred as well to every gift brought to Yahweh as Israel's Landlord, including first fruits and tithes.

Finally, *corban* also referred to what for us would be identified as a sacrifice, namely, a gift to be laid on the altar, to be entirely or partially consumed by fire. As the reader can see, people generally use the word *corban*, sacrifice, far too narrowly.

---

4. Cf. Vonk, *Exodus*, 299–304.

PART 1 | THE SACRIFICIAL TORAH: GENERAL PRINCIPLES

Moreover, those altar sacrifices did not always consist of an animal. In addition to bloody altar sacrifices there were bloodless altar sacrifices. People placed flour, bread, loaves, wine, oil, incense, and salt on the altar.

What then did that general word, *corban*, mean with reference to sacrifices?

This word *corban* would be most familiar to Bible readers from Mark 7:11. There we read how our Savior had criticized how the Jewish scribes had neutralized the simple word and command of God with their complicated doctrines. Because, after all, God was more than a human being, they approved the practice of prosperous children failing to care for their needy parents by declaring their gift to be *corban*, set aside as a gift for God's temple. The Hebrew word *corban* is translated into Greek in Mark 7 with the word *doron*, a word that generally means *gift*. It is used for a gift that one person gives another, such as the gift of the Eastern wise men to baby Jesus (Matt 2:11), and for the presents mentioned in Rev 11:10. But it appears also in the combination of "gifts and sacrifices" to God (Heb 5:1; 8:3; 9:9). This might lead people to suppose that the fundamental meaning of the Hebrew word *corban* was *gift*, *present*, even when referring to altar sacrifices, including bloody altar sacrifices.

In our commentary on Exodus, we saw that this is not accurate. We saw that in the word *corban* we are reminded of the work of the priests whom God had given to Israel, according to their own request. For actually Israel should have consisted entirely of priests. But at Horeb, God approved the substitution of separate individuals to whom had been committed the special task of coming near to God. Accordingly, they were called *kerobim*, the one approaching. Similarly, their work was called *hikrieb*, causing to bring near. Both of these words, referring to *sacrifice* and *bringing sacrifice*, are used for sacrifice in general in Lev 1:2, and for each kind of sacrifice individually (for the burnt offering, Lev 1:3; for the grain offering, Lev 2:1, 4, 12; for the thank offering, Lev 3:1, 7, 12; for the sin offering, Lev 4:13, 14, 23; and for the guilt offering, Lev 7:3; 14:12).

In this way, Israel was being taught, by that general term used in Scripture for sacrifice—quite apart from whether it referred to a bloody or a bloodless sacrifice—about the need for mediation between God and them. Even a grain offering—a non-bloody sacrifice—could not be placed on the altar by the hands of just any Israelite, but exclusively and only by the hands of a priest. Even though the grain offering had no atoning significance whatsoever, for example, even for that sacrifice the mediation of the priesthood was required.

The result is that everyone senses that this mediation in cases where a bloody sacrifice was being brought was absolutely indispensable. Whereas with a bloodless sacrifice no restoration of broken fellowship occurred, such restoration always occurred through the bloody sacrifice. Every bloody sacrifice was reconciling, restoring, mediating in the most fundamental and indispensable sense.

This explains why the question about the mediating character of all the sacrifices can best be answered if we pay attention to the preaching that was tied to the bloody sacrifice. For that reason we will turn to this matter in our general section. Not, of course, from a lack of appreciation for the beautiful grain offering, which we will discuss in due course. But here we think it is important to pause to look at the background as we inquire into the meaning of Israel's sacrificial system. In that connection we must surely place the bloody sacrifice in the foreground, since most kinds of sacrifices among Israel by far involved not plant sacrifices, but animal sacrifices. The grain offerings were merely incidental, compared with the bloody sacrifices, though they too were indispensable.

3. The key to the teaching of the bloody sacrifice

We did not invent this heading. We are borrowing it, more or less, from K. C. W. F. Bähr, *Symbolik des Mosaischen Cultus*,[5] whose work we mentioned with appreciation and followed with agreement in our commentary on Genesis. Bähr supplied this heading to a particular passage in the book of Leviticus, namely, Lev 17:11, which reads in the KJV: "For the life of the flesh *is* in the blood: and I have given it to you upon the altar to make an atonement for your souls: for it *is* the blood *that* maketh an atonement for the soul." Bähr has written excellent things about this verse. But he has also made comments that give us pause, comments that lead us to use Bähr's explanation of the sacrifices with great caution. We want to interact with him for the benefit of our readers, since we can learn some things from this exercise.

Just as we have done, so too Bähr took as his starting point for explaining Israel's sacrificial ministry the bloody sacrifice. We need not say anything further about that. (We will discuss in due time the manner in which Bähr viewed the relationship between the blood sacrifices and the grain offerings.)

Virtually every Bible reader knows from youth onward that the blood of the sacrificial animals was sprinkled on the altar, by the priest, not by the one bringing the offering. The latter could lead the animal, with his hand on the animal's head, could slaughter the animal, skin it and cut it into

---

5. Bähr, *Symbolik*.

pieces, but that was the extent of his task. Only the priest, who had collected the animal's blood and sprinkled this on the altar, could place some of the animal pieces very specifically on the horns of the altar of burnt offering in the forecourt, and on certain occasions on the horns of the altar of incense in the holy place of the tabernacle. A place where the laity were not allowed to enter. In the forecourt, the one bringing the offering was not allowed to perform every task with respect to the animal. The primary sacrificial action, sprinkling the blood, was exclusively the work of the priest.

Concerning this sprinkling of blood Bähr argued emphatically that this was the central, most essential action connected with the sacrifice. Can we not read this clearly in Lev 17:11 (cited above)? Bähr called that verse "the key to the entire Mosaic sacrificial instruction."[6] And according to Bähr, what was remarkable about that verse? That it didn't say a word about killing the animal. It said nothing about slaughtering the sacrificial animal. It talked only about the blood of the animal, and about what was supposed to be done with that blood.[7]

What must we conclude, according to Bähr?

That according to Scripture, it was not the death that brought reconciliation, that the means of atonement was not death, but the blood. So it was impermissible to thoughtlessly confuse and equate death and blood. This was the mistake the people made who emphasized the juridical or forensic view of sacrifice. They thought they had found in the notion of sacrifice a *satisfaction vicaria* to God (rendering a substitutionary satisfaction). According to them the person bringing the sacrifice symbolically placed his sin and guilt on the animal, which was then a substitute for him and bore the punishment in his place. In the course of time, this interpretation had acquired its most ardent defenders among Christians, but it contradicted Scripture. For Scripture sharply distinguished putting to death and sprinkling blood. The former could be performed by the one bringing the sacrifice, but not the latter. That was exclusively the work of the priest that Lev 17:11 taught with emphatic wording, that sin was covered not by the slaying and putting to death, but by blood and sprinkling. "For it *is* the blood *that* maketh an atonement for the soul." Literally: blood *covers*. So you see, that was the purpose and result of the sacrifice. Not the removal of punishment, but the communication of life. For how was the sacrifice a means of reconciliation? By functioning as a means of sanctification. The blood of the sacrificial animal, symbolic of the blood of the one who was bringing the sacrifice, was put on the altar, its horns and atonement covering, and

---

6. Bähr, *Symbolik*, 2:199.
7. Bähr, *Symbolik*, 2:201, 293.

thereby came into contact with sanctuary and life. In this regard, according to Bähr, the "Mosaic system" corresponded with pagan religions. Pagan antiquity knew nothing of a process of punishment and a juridical execution in connection with the one bringing the sacrifice. As Bähr put it, "A person gave life to the deity, the source of all life, with the intention of receiving his life back and entering into living fellowship with the deity; that is the heart of all religion, and of sacrifice, but not the *permutatio personarum* (exchange of persons) and punishment."[8]

How did Bähr come up with this?

Unfortunately we are unable to supply an answer that is absolutely verifiable, but we do have a hunch.

The kind of notions like those Bähr defended above remind us of one of his older contemporaries, the German theologian F. Schleiermacher. He lived from 1768–1834, when the two volumes of Bähr's work now under discussion appeared, in 1837 and 1839. Late enough to have been written under the influence of Schleiermacher. In the doctrinal system of this dogmatician there was little attention given to the justification of sinners on the basis of Christ's substitutionary suffering and death, but more attention given to human sanctification through contact with God. The saving work of Christ consisted, according to Schleiermacher, in Christ including us within his powerful consciousness of God and in the fellowship of his undisrupted salvation. Logically this salvation of the sinner occurred first, followed by reconciliation between God and the sinner. What was needed first was to be included in the life-communion with Christ. In that sense he was our substitute. Justification consisted in the inclusion of a person in life-communion with Christ. Through this union with Christ, conversion was brought about. This converted individual was then justified, and received forgiveness. Christ's voluntary surrender unto death was merely a proof of his readiness to include individuals in his life-communion.

We assume that there was affinity between Schleiermacher and Bähr. The latter would have been strongly influenced by the former. Regrettably so. For in his work on Israel's worship according to the Torah, he constantly pointed to God's holiness, and he never tired of pointing out to us in the Torah God's aversion to death and his love for life. These features of his work were very helpful to us. But when we have to observe that according to Bähr, the forgiveness of sins came to expression symbolically through touch, through contact, through the fellowship of the blood that was sacrificed by the one bringing the offering and poured out by the priest, with such holy places of divine revelation as the altar, horns of the altar, and

---

8. Bähr, *Symbolik*, 2:283.

atonement covering, then we fear that Bähr's otherwise clear insight in reading the Torah was clouded over by the teachings of Schleiermacher or something similar.

Even when he was alive, Bähr's views were not universally accepted. In our commentary on Exodus, we saw this especially with respect to his views on the tabernacle. But what he wrote about Israel's sacrificial ministry aroused still greater opposition.

The most famous opponent of Bähr's explanations about Israel's sacrifices was J. H. Kurtz (1809–90). He was well-known as a church historian. But he earned his stripes especially in the field of Old Testament interpretation. Of his numerous writings relevant to our discussion, we mention only the larger ones, viz., *Sacrificial Worship of the Old Testament*[9] and *Der Alttestamentliche Opferkultus nach seiner gesetzlichen Begründung und Anwendung* (*The Old Testament Sacrificial Worship according to its Legal Justification and Application*).[10] It was not that Kurtz had no appreciation for Bähr's work on the Torah, since he often cites him with approval. But in one respect, and a very important one at that, he did not withhold his criticism. For Bähr had trivialized the *death* of the sacrificial animal. He had eliminated from the law of Moses the gospel of substitution, of the vicarious bearing of punishment and substitutionary death.

Naturally our readers would have noticed the great importance of this critique for our time as well. We are immediately drawn into this debate between Bähr and Kurtz. For we sense that this pertains to the death of Christ. Scripture is one, and the gospel is one. If according to the Old Testament, specifically, according to the Torah, there was no mention of a symbolic vicarious suffering and dying of the sacrificial animal for the one bringing the sacrifice, then according to the New Testament there would not have been a real suffering and dying of the sacrificial Lamb, Jesus Christ, for us.

In what follows, when we trace the dispute between Bähr and Kurtz with careful attention, we will do so not for entertainment, not even intellectual entertainment. We do consider the contest of minds stimulating, as we watch the well-formulated arguments of one scholar being wrestled with in the equally well-constructed arguments of another scholar. But what truly stimulates us is our own interest in the truth of the gospel as it has been taught to us from our youth: there is no peace with God except through the *death* of his Son.

From Kurtz we have some biographical information about Bähr. He tells us, for example, that he had expected the kind of discussion of Israel's

---

9. Kurtz, *Sacrificial Worship*.
10. Kurtz, *Alttestamentliche Opfercultus*.

sacrifices as the one Bähr provided in his massive two-volume work. Or rather: he had feared such. For he had read an earlier essay by Bähr, entitled *Die Lehre der Kirche vom Tode Jesu* (*The Teaching of the Church Concerning the Death of Jesus*).[11] From that essay it became evident that Bähr had a certain antipathy toward the "satisfaction theory of the atonement." What Kurtz feared was that Bähr's antipathy toward the church's teaching of Christ's work of substitutionary atonement would play a role in his study of the Law, especially the Law's teaching about sacrifice. Unfortunately his fear was realized. As a result of a particular doctrinal view of the work of Christ, the otherwise so clear and penetrating insight of Bähr did not see what, according to Kurtz, every unbiased reader of the Law had to notice: a *satisfactio vicaria*, or vicarious atonement.[12]

We mention the following points from Kurtz's critique, though we have formulated them for the most part in our own words.

Bähr used Lev 17:11 in a completely mistaken way. It was not a problem that he called this verse "the key to Moses' teaching about sacrifice." But the context in which this verse appears must not be lost from view. That verse does not appear in the chapters specially devoted to the sacrifices, that is, not in Lev 1–7. But it appears in Leviticus 17. And what is Lev 17:10–16 about? What is its main subject? Not sacrifice, though that is certainly mentioned. Even though in that context God is telling the Israelites something about the altar, which is very important, namely, that on the altar he had supplied the Israelites with the blood of atonement for their souls. But even though that is important, it is nevertheless merely a reminder. A reminder brought up in service to a discussion of the main subject of Leviticus 17. Given as motivation for God's command to the Israelites *that they should not eat any blood*. That is what Leviticus 17 is about. That the Israelites had to abstain from using blood. If you read the context, you will see this clearly.

Of course, we must always distinguish properly and take seriously the question whether one or another subject is being intentionally discussed and commented on—Kurtz says: whether a subject is broached *ex professo*, explicitly[13]—or whether a comment is registered incidentally. Even though such an incidental comment can be very important. Especially if it serves as part of an argument. And that is the case in Lev 17:11, with the mention of the significance and function of the blood on Israel's altar. Even though that reminder served to undergird a comment about an entirely different matter, namely, the prohibition to Israel *against using the blood*.

---

11. Bähr, *Die Lehre der Kirche vom Tode Jesu*.
12. Kurtz, *Sacrificial Worship*, 283.
13. Kurtz, *Sacrificial Worship*, 8.

PART 1 | THE SACRIFICIAL TORAH: GENERAL PRINCIPLES

It is a shot in the dark, according to Kurtz, for Bähr to claim about Lev 17:11 that this central verse about sacrifice in the Mosaic system mentions only blood. Nothing else. Not the death of the animal, not the slaughter of the animal. According to Kurtz, that is not surprising, given the subject of that part of Leviticus 17, namely, a prohibition against using the blood. This explains why Bähr's conclusion is mistaken. That conclusion, according to Bähr, would be that with Israel's sacrifice only *the blood* had any significance, but not the death and slaughter of the animal, so that it was impermissible to view the animal's death and slaughter as the principal issues involved in sacrificing, or to view the killing of the animal as an act of punishment. For according to Bähr, it was illegitimate to view the death of the sacrificial animal as a punishment where God is functioning as a punishing judge. Because Lev 17:11 says nothing about death and slaughter. It speaks only about blood. Indeed, says Kurtz, but that proves nothing. Given the context of Lev 17:11, whose main subject is not the sacrificing and slaughtering of animals.

Of course, Kurtz made the very same observation that our readers have already made on their own, namely, that Bähr's entire theory rested on a piece of shrewdness. For you can logically distinguish those two features, the slaying of an animal and the shedding of its blood, but in practice they cannot be separated. When the blood of a person or of an animal is shed, that person or animal is dead. Bähr's appeal to Heb 9:22, where it is established as a rule that there is no forgiveness without the shedding of blood, was an argument that cut no ice. We can readily admit that in connection with slaughtering an animal, the shedding of blood made the deepest impression. Through that shedding the fatal effect was brought about. This explains why Scripture emphasizes that shedding of blood so strongly. But that cannot occur apart from slaughtering and killing the sacrificial victim.

Scripture teaches with equal clarity that without *death* there is no forgiveness. Scripture begins focusing our attention on this indisputable truth when it tells us why death came to us in the world. On account of Adam's transgression (Gen 2:16–17; 3:6). The apostle Paul teaches us to see in that fact the reason for our death (Rom 5:12–14). Our death is retribution for sin (Rom 6:23, and from the parallel that the apostle makes between Adam and Christ, we see clearly to what transgression he credits our death. As through Adam's disobedience, guilt and death have come upon us, so through Christ's obedience justification (acquittal, forgiveness, Rom 8:23) and life have come to us. With this line of argument, did not Paul lead us to view the death of Christ as a substitutionary, vicarious death? He did so with the obvious goal of supplying a proof of his preaching against the Jews who were opposing him, by appealing to the . . . Torah. For from the

Torah alone we know what happened in the Garden. In fact, if Christ is indeed the Lamb of God who came to fulfill the shadows of the Law—which he was, Matt 16:1–29, Jesus of Nazareth appeared as the Passover Lamb of fulfillment!—what then are we to think of the shadows, those symbols? Can the notion of a capital punishment, the substitutionary death, have been completely foreign?

There was something else that Kurtz conceded. Far too often people had lost sight of the fact that the sacrificial animal, strictly speaking, did not represent the one bringing the offering, the person who was sacrificing, but rather was representing Christ. Kurtz repeatedly identified this error, committed by one no less than the Old Testament commentator Carl Friedrich Keil (1807–88). The reason this was mistaken was that the one sacrificing was not atoned for by his own blood. As though this was what was being symbolically portrayed. No, he was atoned for precisely by the blood of someone else. Blood that God had provided upon the altar. That is what Lev 17:11 is saying.

In view of Scripture, it is to the eternal glory of our Lord Jesus Christ that he *was slain* for us (Rev 5:6, 9, 12; 13:8). For that reason it will not do to think that only his *being slain*, and the slaying of the sacrificial animals of the Law who foreshadowed him (Heb 10:1), were something incidental. Our justification (that is, our acquittal, the forgiveness of our guilt) is specifically ascribed to Christ's *being delivered up*. Now then, for what was he delivered up, other than for *death*? This explains why Scripture says that our Savior "was delivered up for our trespasses and raised for our justification" (Rom 4:25).

4. *Our plan for answering the threefold question about Leviticus 17:11*

It is obvious that we are not finished discussing Lev 17:11. We have merely begun our treatment of this very interesting passage. We will continue our discussion. Because Bähr said some very helpful things about this passage, despite his mistaken ideas, we will follow his method in our discussion, as did Kurtz.

In connection with this passage, Bähr dealt with four questions.

1. What was the role of the blood in connection with the one bringing the sacrifice? We have already shown our readers Bähr's answer to this question. His answer was unsatisfactory. For Bähr ascribed such a dominant role to the blood of the sacrificial animal that he retained

PART 1 | THE SACRIFICIAL TORAH: GENERAL PRINCIPLES

no significance at all for the slaying and killing of the animal. But we turn now to his remaining three questions and their answers.

2. What was the function of the blood? Answer: atonement.
3. Who atoned? Answer: God. Who was atoned? Answer: Not God, but the person.
4. How did that happen? Answer: *nefesh* for *nefesh*.

With a view to that last Hebrew word, we would mention that Bähr translated Lev 17:11 this way: *For the soul [nefesh] of the flesh is in the blood, and I have given it to you all for the altar, in order to atone [lekhapper] your souls [naphshothekhem], for the blood atones through the soul [bannefesh].*

5. According to Leviticus 17:11, what did the blood of the sacrifice accomplish?

I have provided two translations of Lev 17:11. The first was the KJV, the second that of Bähr. We saw that Bähr placed several Hebrew words in brackets. The Hebrew word *lekhapper* he translated as *to atone*, as does the KJV. Is that correct?

The question concerning the original meaning of the Hebrew verb *kpr* is answered variously. Some understand the meaning of this word not to have been to *cover*, but to *sweep*, to *sweep away*. Several Hebrew lexica, however, present the development of the word's meaning in precisely the reverse order: first, to sweep, and only later: to cover.

When the etymology of a word provides no solution, the only thing we can do is pay attention to the usage of the word in Holy Scripture. In that connection, the following features are striking.

A. The Hebrew verb *kpr* is used in Jer 18:23 in parallel with *blot out* (Hebrew: *machah*), but that does not yet prove identical meaning.

B. We are told about Noah that he had to cover (*kpr*) the ark inside and out (Gen 6:14). That probably refers to putting pitch on it (as the KJV indicates: "thou shalt pitch it within and without with pitch").

C. We are also struck by the fact that the word *kpr* frequently appears with a preposition (something that unfortunately cannot always be replicated in the translation), one that means *on* or *upon* (*al*, as in Lev 17:11). This usage suggests that the sacrificial blood was *laid upon* in such a way that it *covered*. This would have been the original meaning. This *covering with* blood, this *laying upon* with blood occurred, according to Lev 17:11, on the altar. Therefore, when someone replaces this original meaning of *to cover* or *to lay upon* with *to atone*, that is substantively correct, but thereby one has actually moved one step away from the beautiful, poignant verb *to cover* and the remarkable preposition *upon*.

Fortunately everyone agrees at least regarding the substantive correctness of the translation, *to atone*.

Translated literally, then, we believe Lev 17:11 should read: the blood *covers*. Substantively this may be replaced with: the blood atones.

6. *According to Leviticus 17:11, who atoned and who was atoned?*

We are taking these two questions together, even though it does make a significant difference whether the person is the one who provides the atonement or the person is the one for whom the atonement is effected.

According to Lev 17:11, God was the one from whom the atonement proceeded. Literally: he was the one who provided for the covering with the blood. The one who was covered, or atoned for, was the person. The object of the covering or the atonement was the (souls of the) Israelites. But the Subject of that action was God. The word "I" occupies a position of emphasis in Lev 17:11. "I have given it for you on the altar."

Nevertheless, this did not exclude every use of *means*.

At various times you will read that God provides the covering or atonement, or that the blood atones (here in Lev 17:11), or that the priest atones (Lev 5:6). But then we must recall expressions like "the hammer smashes the rock." Everyone understands very well that it is actually the craftsman doing the smashing with the hammer. So God said to the Israelites that he himself had given them the blood for their covering (or atonement) upon the altar. So it was Yahweh who atoned, although *by means* of the blood. Whereas, when it says another time that the priest atoned, the intention was the same. The priests were but means or instruments, mediators between Yahweh and the Israelites.

It was Yahweh who covered.

He was the one who effected atonement.

The one who benefited thereby was the person. This person was the *object* of the action, and was identified grammatically as the direct object, often with the preposition *on* (*al*; a covering was laid over or on someone), occasionally with the preposition meaning *for the sake of, on behalf of* (*ba'ad*, Lev 9:7; 16:6).

The object of the atonement, then, was the person. Although occasionally it is stated more specifically: *the sin* of the person. Just as we too now and then talk of inanimate things as objects of atonement. In Lev 8:15, Moses performed atonement for the altar. From Lev 16:16 we see that the actual object of covering or atonement was not the inanimate thing, but human sins that had been committed in connection with the Holy Place, whereby it was considered to be unclean. More than once the *sins* of the people are mentioned as object of the atonement (Exod 32:30).

But often the text simply states that *the person* is the object of atonement. That can happen by means of the personal pronoun (as in Lev 1:4, to make atonement "for him" before the face of Yahweh; Lev 10:17, to make atonement "for them" before the face of Yahweh; Lev 12:7, make atonement "for her"). This happens also with the use of the word *soul* (Hebrew, *nefesh*), as we see in Lev 17:11, where we read: to make atonement "for your [plural] souls."

Here, then, we have the answer to the question as to from whom atonement proceeds—from God—and who benefits from the atonement: the person. Yahweh is not covered. Yahweh is not atoned. The person is covered. The person is atoned.

In answering these two closely related questions, the reader will surely have had to think of the New Testament. How clearly we are told there that it is our good heavenly Father from whom atonement for our sins has proceeded. For he was the one who gave us Christ as the Lamb. Christ is called the Lamb . . . of God (John 1:29). Through Christ God has atoned us to himself (2 Cor 5:18). God was in Christ reconciling the world with himself (2 Cor 5:19). The initiative for reconciliation is ascribed in the New Testament entirely to God. Not to the human person. Not even to the Mediator Jesus Christ. For no one should suppose that Christ came to turn God into a gracious God for the first time. Precisely the opposite: we owe Christ as our Savior to our good God. Christ was given. Christ was given by a Father who was already gracious. For God so loved the world that he gave his only Son (John 3:16; Rom 5:8; 8:32; 2 Cor 5:21; 1 John 4:9).

7. *Question: How did the atonement happen? Answer: Soul for soul (Hebrew, nefesh)*

With this we have arrived at the final question. How does atonement work? We have supplied the answer to this question in passing. Atonement occurs by way of soul for soul. In Hebrew the word for *soul* is *nefesh*. We still need to say something more about that word. For we have already made a few comments about it, when we observed that the human person for whom atonement is being made can be identified in Leviticus, both with a personal pronoun (making atonement for *him*, for *them*, for *her*) and by using the word *nefesh*. So then, in the latter usage, how must we translate that Hebrew word *nefesh*? May we simply ignore it? May we view it simply as a broader expression than the personal pronouns?

People who use modern Bible versions or translations will have noticed that, where the older translations were rather literal, they rendered the word *nefesh* with the word *soul*, whereas today that Hebrew word is often rendered with *life* or simply with personal pronouns. Here are some examples.

Hebrew	KJV	NIV
Ps 11:1: say to my *nefesh*	say ye to my soul	say to me
Ps 57:4: my *nefesh* is among lions	my soul is among lions	I am in the midst of lions
Ps 124:5: the stream had gone over our *nefesh*	the stream had gone over our soul	The torrent would have swept over us

You see that in the third column, the word *soul* is entirely absent. The NIV replaces it with personal pronouns (*me, I, us*).

Should we object to that?

Well, Bible translation is such difficult work that we always advise our Bible-studying friends that, if possible, they should use more than one translation *simultaneously*. This works well when reading the Bible in our homes as families. Then we are able to compare translations, and we will often discover that one particular translation tries to provide smooth English (resulting in some aspects of the original language getting lost), while another translation seeks to render the text as accurately as possible (and feels rather wooden as a result, or worse still, is incomprehensible).

As far as the word *nefesh* is concerned, certainly in many cases one can render it into English by means of a personal pronoun, in effect, leaving it untranslated; but someone whose task it is to investigate exactly what was written may never forget that Israel always read that word *nefesh* and always heard it read. We made this general observation earlier. Nevertheless, we would add specifically that there are demonstrable instances when in our English translations we would omit the literal translation of the word *nefesh*, even though this word influences the translation in another way. Occasionally the word *nefesh* is used in Hebrew when someone wanted to say something with emphasis. In Hebrew you can say, "I call," but you can also say, "I call *with my soul*," which then means: "I call aloud." Similarly, you can say in Hebrew, "I long for something," but also, "I long *with my soul*," which means: "I long intensely." In such instances, the word *soul* serves just as well as the word *voice*. Neither would be rendered literally, but neither would be ignored and omitted.

Rather, that word *soul* might indeed disappear from smooth translations, though we should never forget that the Israelites though it was worth the trouble to say and write it repeatedly. In fact, at times when we might sense that it is being used like our personal pronoun, we see it being used in parallel with and as a synonym of *kabod* (the same word we encounter in connection with the tabernacle, but need to translate as *honor, weight, whole being* in Gen 49:6, Ps 7:5, 16:9, and other passages).

For these reasons, it is good that we focus serious attention on the meaning of the word *nefesh* in Lev 17:11, the Scripture passage we are discussing. We must recall that the word *nefesh* appears three times in that verse.

Our attention was drawn in an interesting way to the *context* of Lev 17:11, namely, by the criticism that Kurtz provided of the view of Bähr. That scholarly man had made a serious mistake. For Bähr had completely lost sight of the fact that the main subject in Lev 17:10–16 was not bringing sacrifices, but *the prohibition against eating blood*. That's what was in view. That was the warning in Leviticus 17. Even though that warning was motivated with a reference to Israel's sacrificial ministry. We read immediately in verse 10: "*If any one of the house of Israel or of the strangers who sojourn among them eats any blood, I will set my face against that person who eats blood and will cut him off from among his people.*"

Contemporary Bible translations render the verse this way, or in a similar way. That is, by omitting the word *soul*. But anyone who is familiar with the KJV can see easily that the word *nefesh* appeared here in verse 10. Here is part of that verse in the KJV: "*I will even set my face against that soul that eateth blood.*" That rendering arose from a desire to translate the word *nefesh* literally. If we were to translate the entire verse along this line, this would be the result: "*And whatsoever man there be of the house of Israel, or of the strangers that sojourn among you, that eateth any manner of blood; I will even set my face against that soul* [nefesh] *that eateth blood, and will cut him off from among his people.*" The KJV translates the word *nefesh* as *soul*, and thereafter twice translates the pronouns referring to *soul* as masculine personal pronouns.

Modern English versions, however, no longer prefer the rendering "the soul that," but "the person who," or "the one who." Should we disapprove of this?

Well, our language is a living language. This means that it undergoes change. Words and expressions that were customary at an earlier time sound strange in our time. The language of the King James Version, in which Rom 13:1 reads, "Let *every soul* be subject unto the higher powers," is no longer the way we would say it today, and to ignore this fact is to court the risk of robbing our descendants of an understandable Bible. The ESV correctly renders this, "Let *every person* be subject to the governing authorities."

In this manner as well, the Hebrew word *nefesh* can be translated quite well. Hebrew itself permits this. For occasionally, when people are talking about a soul (*nefesh*), it is spoken of as though it were something feminine, as here in Lev 17:10 (the Hebrew word *nefesh* was feminine), but occasionally if a man was being spoken about, as in Lev 22:11 (if a priest buys a "soul" for money, *he*—namely, the one purchased—may eat of it). Such passages, where one could translate the word *soul* (*nefesh*) with *person* or *one*, are frequent in the Old Testament. So this is a somewhat different use of the word *nefesh* than we discussed above, where *nefesh* was being translated with a personal pronoun (I, me, us). We should recall here that the Israelite eye and ear read and heard the same word *nefesh* in all these instances. Here in Lev 17:10, Scripture speaks explicitly about a soul (*nefesh*) that ate the blood. For people today, that is something strange and weird. An eating and drinking *soul*! How is such a thing possible? But for those familiar with the KJV this is not strange at all. They know that this way of speaking occurred more often in Israel. The KJV of Prov 6:30, for example, reads: "*Men* do not despise a thief, if he steal to satisfy his soul when he is hungry." This way of speaking—about the soul that eats, drinks, etc.—must not have been unusual among other peoples in the ancient world, with whom we are acquainted from the poems of Homer and the writings discovered in the excavations at Ugarit.

This was our introduction to Lev 17:10.

Now we turn to Lev 17:11 itself.

After bringing up in verse 10 the subject about which God wanted to issue a prohibition—don't use the blood!—in verse 11 we learn *the reason why* he prohibited this use of blood. We can surmise this already from the word *for* with which verse 11 begins. One could translate this as *truly* or *verily*.

Verse 11 seems to consist of three parts, which in literal translation read as follows:

1. *For the soul of the flesh—in the blood is it.*
2. *But that have I myself to you all given upon the altar to make atonement over your souls.*

PART 1 | THE SACRIFICIAL TORAH: GENERAL PRINCIPLES

3. *For the blood—that atones through the soul.*

Each time we have translated the word *nefesh* by *soul*. For starters that's always best. If later you want a smoother translation, adapted to modern English, then you can consider what is preferable in each instance.

We will comment on each part of the verse.

In Part 1, we find the word *flesh* The Hebrew word for this can be used in reference to people and animals (Gen 6:17). Here as well we have something like that. In our verse, the subject is not plants. Plants have no blood. Here we are dealing with creatures that have blood. The Hebrew word for *flesh* has been translated as *living being*.

Regarding Part 2, the word *I* is placed emphatically. Not only is the pronoun used, which in Hebrew need not happen, but that pronoun is placed first. Why? Because God wanted to remind Israel emphatically about something that he had done earlier. We are studying Leviticus 17, but before this, in Leviticus 1–7, God had given the sacrificial Torah. Well then, in the sacrificial Torah God had arranged for the blood of the animals to be put on his altar (Lev 3:17; 7:26–27). Part 2 of our verse here is referring back to that (just as we find later in v. 12). To that earlier ordinance, that the blood had to be brought upon God's altar, but may not be used as food. (We will discuss later the purpose for that blood being put on the altar.)

Finally, Part 3 is very important for our purpose of answering the question, how did atonement happen? Even though in the totality of Leviticus 17 this part occupies a somewhat modest place, anyone can see at first glance that Part 3 serves to support the argument expressed in Part 2. That argument insisted that God had intended the blood for the altar for the purpose of atonement. Well then, this is explained further in Part 3 by an explanation about the suitability of blood for that purpose, for the goal of rendering atonement. It atoned through the soul (*nefesh*).

After this initial reading of Lev 17:11, we notice the following two features, First, when we pay attention to the context, namely, a prohibition against using blood, then Part 2 of our text is the most important. For there God gives the reason for this prohibition with particular emphasis. But second, for underscoring that reason, something is said in Part 3 about the blood, something that apparently was thought to be undisputed, namely, that the blood atoned through the soul. So undisputed was this that it could be advanced as an argument. The reader understands that, given the subject under discussion—viz., how atonement was effected—we find Part 3 to be the most important part of our text. More important than Part 2, for it serves as the basis of Part 2.

How, then, shall we translate the Hebrew word *nefesh* in our verse? What is its meaning here?

The word appears three times, once in each part of the verse.

Our eye turns automatically to Part 2, because this part occupies such a prominent place within the entire argument. We read there that God did not want the blood of animals consumed because the blood had been intended for his altar. Upon that altar blood had to perform atonement for the *souls* of the Israelites. We read: "for your souls."

Is it desirable to understand this word *souls* as nothing more than a broader description of the personal pronoun *you* or *you all*? If we do understand and explain it that way, is it desirable to translate it *for you*?

Our modest opinion is that one can advance the same positives and negatives about such an explanation and translation here as with so many other Scripture passages where translators omit the word *soul* (*nefesh*) by using a personal pronoun. In modern English the word *soul* is not used in its broad sense than it was used in the KJV. Modern Bible translators must see to it that the Bible is understood. That is why we said: positives and negatives. For such passages of Holy Scripture do contain not a personal pronoun, at least in the Hebrew, but the word *soul* (*nefesh*). If we want to try to understand as clearly as possible what the Israelites who wrote or read such passages would have thought, then we must remember that he repeatedly wrote or read the complete word *soul* (*nefesh*).

There is something more.

We mentioned already that the word *nefesh* appeared in each of the three parts of the verse. Now we ask: Is it not possible, indeed, probably, that the meanings of the word *nefesh* in each of these three instances would have been very close to each other in the ear of the ordinary Israelite? Let's see once. Let's take the notion of *person* or a personal pronoun (I, you, he, you all), and replace the word *soul* (*nefesh*) with one of those each time in our text. The reader should try this just for fun, in all three parts of the verse:

1. For the soul of the flesh—in the blood is it.

2. But that have I myself to you all given upon the altar to make atonement over your souls.

3. For the blood—that atones through the soul.

You will discover that it won't work. Those pronouns don't fit. You can't talk about an animal like you would talk about a person and still be talking not about persons but about their flesh (Part 1). Even though a farmer might talk about his animal as *he* or *she*, he would not speak seriously to his animals with the address *you all* (Part 2).

Another interpretation seeks to explain the word *soul* (*nefesh*) here as *life*, and prefers to translate it that way: "For the *life* itself of the living being is in the blood; I have given it to you upon the altar in order to perform atonement for *your life*, for the blood effects atonement on behalf of the *life*."

What should we think about this?

This translation flows smoothly. It has the advantage of translating the word *nefesh* with the same word three times. Moreover, it is true that people and animals have this feature in common, that they are living beings, that they possess life. But if we are to be exact, this translation is unsatisfactory, in our modest opinion, for the reason that we would cite from something J. Ridderbos has written:

> Surely the intention is not that the life is restricted to the blood. Hebrew was another word for *life*, and although it is occasionally used synonymously with *soul* (Ps 7:5), it is absolutely not identical. When we read in Genesis 2:7 about "the breath of life," the word *life* cannot be replaced with the word *soul*. Conversely, the intention of our passage [Lev 17:11] is not rendered accurately by translating, "the life of the animal is in the blood.[14]

That difficult word *nefesh* is especially challenging as it appears in the verse we are studying. We believe that translating it with the word *life* comes very close to what the Israelite heard with the word *nefesh*. This is so especially when we recall that the background of our text is slaughter, killing, the elimination of one life on behalf of another life. Nevertheless, we think that J. Ridderbos properly rejected this translation in the words cited above.

That difficult word *nefesh* seems to have given modern Bible translators a few problems. They render it one way here, another way there, in order to produce a smoothly readable and easily understandable text. But if you have Bible readers reading something and thereby believing something that in fact is not there, what have you really achieved? Someone has translated our verse, Lev 17:11, this way: "For the life of the flesh is in the blood, which *I* have given you for the altar in order thereon to perform atonement for your *mistakes*." We have italicized the word *mistakes*. We don't think that this word is substantially incorrect, especially given Lev 16:16, which deals with removal on the great Day of Atonement of Israel's transgression by means of sprinkling blood. Nevertheless, that notion may well have surfaced in Leviticus 16, but not here in Leviticus 17. When people nonetheless incorporate it into the translation, then they are bringing into the Scripture passage something that it does not contain. Despite the best of intentions, this is still incorrect.

---

14. Ridderbos, *Schriftuurlijke Anthropologie?*, 45.

Would not the best solution be to translate the word *nefesh* in Lev 17:11 all three times with the same word? Not one time with this word, another time with a different word? Why not translate the same Hebrew word with the same English word? Would not the word *soul* be the best choice, as we find in the KJV? We would defend this view for the following reasons.

Since the word *nefesh* appears in each of the three parts of the verse, a feature that surely is not without a reason, it seems preferable to us to bring out this fact in the translation.

On account of the multiple meanings with which the word *soul* can be used in English even today, translating *nefesh* as *soul* has this advantage: we are in a position similar to the Israelites, who read and heard the same word *nefesh* in various situations.

The general word *soul* seems to us all the more preferable because it seems not to have been customary in the Semitic world to express ideas as though they were strictly delimited and sharply differentiated from each other. This differs from our custom as Westerners, who are inclined to do that. Rather, the Israelites preferred to work with complexities and words that are more vague in scope and broader in content, such that meanings overlapped. With translation, if you seek a particularly suitable word in our language, then this word will perhaps work well for one time, and another word will work better for another time, but often it will be difficult to make a sharp delineation among our choices, because both words might fit equally well. We need to remember that, based on its context, the Hebrew word *nefesh* can be translated as *breath*, *vital strength*, *life*, *desire*, *courage*, *meaning*, *experience*, *hunger*, *thirst*, *longing*, *inner love* or *hatred* or *great joy* or *sorrow* or *rest* or *fear*, as well as a reflexive form of address ("O my soul"), by *body* or *corpse* (Ps 106:15: "he sent leanness into their soul," KJV), by *corpse* (Num 6:6, a Nazirite was not permitted to come near a dead *nefesh*), by *person* or *human being* (for example, in connection with a census), and by *living being* (Gen 1:20–21, regarding sea animals; Gen 1:24, land animals; Gen 2:19; 9:10, 12, 15, animals in general; Gen 9:16, all living creatures; Gen 2:7, human person). From this array of meanings that we have supplied (and our list was by no means complete), the right choice must surely have been difficult. That is easy enough for a child to understand, so we can surely appreciate it when an expert might say about the word *nefesh*: "not able to translate accurately." No wonder the Israelite continued to preserve, in this single word *nefesh*, the capacity for making various thought associations.

Finally, we consider the translation of *nefesh* in Lev 17:11 with the word *soul* to be the best solution (better than translating the word as *life*) because in this verse there is no talk of plants, but of people and animals. All of these three kinds of creatures share this feature, that they are alive, but only of the latter two do we read that God created them "as living beings." This is not said of plants and trees. Rather, we are told that God created both people and animals as "living souls" (or "living creatures," Gen 1:24).

For these reasons we think that the word *soul* is the best translation of the Hebrew word *nefesh* in Lev 17:11. It says neither too little nor too much.

After all of these considerations, we proceed now to answer our fourth question: How did atonement happen, according to Lev 17:11?

Now that we have been busy together discussing this Scripture verse, we should nonetheless express our surprise that Bähr claimed that Scripture nowhere speaks of an atoning death, of a substitutionary or vicarious death. Not even in Lev 17:11. Especially not there. But if the Bible talks anywhere about such a vicarious death, then surely that place is here.

The entire context talks about killing, putting to death, slaying. Shedding the blood of an animal, indeed, pouring it out, surely that is nothing else than slaying that animal.

Leviticus 17:11 speaks particularly about atonement through death. The one soul is delivered over to death for the other soul. We want to make some comments about both the context and the text.

In Leviticus 17 God prohibited the Israelites to consume the blood of the slaughtered animal. They would even have to carefully bleed out an animal killed in a hunt, and then allow the blood of the dead animal to flow on the ground (Lev 17:13).

The real questions seems to us to be whether we have identified the deepest reason for this prohibition to be the danger of idolatrous drinking of blood among pagans. In Lev 19:26 we read: "You shall not eat any flesh with the blood in it. You shall not interpret omens or tell fortunes." In light of the context, it seems evident that in this passage, as elsewhere in Leviticus, God wanted to keep Israel away from Canaanite superstition. Agreed.

But in Leviticus 17 God went into the subject more deeply. There he returned to his ancient institution. There he connected Israel for the first time with his command that he had given earlier. For he had permitted the first humans to slaughter an animal in order to sacrifice it to him, but not yet with the intention of eating that animal. Apparently God had wanted people to show some hesitation or difference toward the life of an animal, yes, even an animal. For we read that only later, during the time of Noah, did he permit the killing of animals for another purpose than for sacrifice. From then on, killing an animal for eating was permitted, although then as well God certainly desired that respect for a living being would not disappear among people. For that reason, the blood of such an animal that had been slaughtered for eating may not be used for human consumption (Gen 9:4).

Respect for blood!

That requirement was very ancient already by the God who gave the prohibition in Leviticus 17.

In Leviticus 17 that prohibition was simply being renewed. Israel could freely kill an animal, whether from a herd or from the wild, in order to eat it. That was permissible. As long as there was respect for all of its blood that would need to be shed in connection with that slaughter.

But on that ancient basis, something additional was added as something new. Something that we do not read in Scripture before Leviticus. That was God's own remembrance of the high purpose that he was pleased to give to that blood. The sacred purpose for which he wanted it to be used. Namely: as an atonement sacrifice.

It's possible that God had in mind something very ancient. For maybe he was thinking of the time when he instituted (blood) sacrifice in the time of the first human beings. Why would not Cain and Abel have learned about the practice of sacrifice from their parents? Why would not Adam and Eve in turn have learned about sacrifice from God himself?

But *undoubtedly* God had in view at this point in Leviticus everything he had made known to Moses earlier about the sacrifices with which Israel was to serve him in his tabernacle. We are referring to Leviticus 1–7, the sacrificial Torah. From that section people can learn to understand how highly the life of God's creatures is valued by God himself. So highly that he ordained blood to be the chief gift to be laid upon Israel's altar. We will say more about that beautiful subject in a moment. But here we must definitely see very clearly how highly our God esteemed the value of blood with respect to Moses and Israel. So highly that he himself not only used it for his sacred ministry of sacrifices, but apart from that ministry he did not want people to treat blood with indifference. Not because, as is sometimes said, that blood was sacred. No, only the blood that was incorporated into the service of God was sacred. But because such a ministry occurred with blood, God did not want people to do strange things with any and all blood. A deer shot with bow and arrow must be bled out, and its blood drained on the ground. Not just left behind thoughtlessly. Why? For that kind of attitude, God was pleased to make far too high a use of animal blood. For his altar. To serve on that altar for atonement.

So when he was talking about the exalted purpose for which he had placed blood in his service, namely, for atonement, God said something about the manner of that atonement. Something incidentally, but very instructive.

How would blood be able to atone? Answer: because the soul was in it, blood would be able to serve for atonement. Thanks to the soul that was in it (Lev 17:11a).

When it comes down to it, the soul was being sacrificed. For the one soul (the soul of the person) the other soul (the soul of the animal) was being sacrificed. Through this, then, the covering, the atonement occurred. Through giving its blood upon God's altar, the one soul covered and atoned for the other soul. The soul atoned (Lev 17:11c).

But how was that possible?

Actually the answer that our text gives to this question is also very old. For earlier God had said: "But you shall not eat flesh with its life, that is, its blood" (Gen 9:4). Thereby it was evident then already how intimate God saw the connection to be between blood and soul. So intimate that he practically identified the two. The soul... was the blood.

God is talking in the same way in Leviticus 17. For we read in Lev 17:14b: "You shall not eat the blood of any creature, for the life of every creature is its blood." Do you wonder whether blood and soul have anything to do with each other? We could even say that they were identical, one and the same. Soul = blood. But this was then a practical manner of speaking, something that occurs elsewhere (Deut 12:23). But such a manner of speaking is an abbreviated form of speech. For upon closer inspection, *soul* and *blood* are not identical, not the same. Otherwise we would not read in Lev 17:11a: "For the life of the flesh [i.e., of living beings] is in the blood." *In the blood.*

Here, then, is the answer to the last question.

We are not surprised in the least that Kurtz did not pass up the opportunity to point out in response to Bähr that Scripture in general, and here in particular, clearly teaches the idea of substitutionary death.

Others acted the same way, and expressed their view that the Hebrew of Lev 17:11c led one to think of putting up one soul as ransom for the other. The shedding of animal blood served to atone for the one sacrificing. Naturally not on account of the quantity of that blood, but because the fate of the *nefesh* of the animal was most closely linked to the shedding of its blood. For shedding the blood of a living being comes down to the outpouring and killing of the soul. In addition to talking about shedding blood, Scripture talks also about the soul departing, being poured out, ebbing away, as a description of death and dying (Ps 141:8; Isa 53:12; Lam 2:12). That is what Leviticus 17 is about. About dying, and no matter how incidentally, about the dying of the one soul for the atoning of the other soul before God.

It was at least very strange that Bähr wanted to keep those two features so far apart. Those two *cannot* be separated. One can reach that conclusion only through a bias. *Apart from death Lev 17:10–16 loses all meaning!*

In connection with our answering the three questions about Lev 17:11, our readers would surely have thought now and then about our Savior Jesus Christ.

The sacrifices of the Law were shadows that were fulfilled by his coming. Especially through his vicarious death. By Jesus Christ having given his soul in death in order to atone for others.

The latter prophets also predicted that he would be pierced for the transgressions of others, and would ultimately pour out his soul (*nefesh*) in death (Isa 53:12).

Jesus Christ even announced his death as that kind of death. He had come, as he put it, "to give his life [Greek: *psychē*, soul] a ransom for many" (Matt 20:28).

Therefore it is an issue of great importance that the genuineness of Christ's death is established. The genuineness of his human death. Evidently with that in view, the apostle John tells us that he himself saw that a soldier pierced the Lord's side with a spear. The one who saw it bore witness to it and his testimony is true, and he knows that he is telling the truth, so that you also may believe (John 19:35). And when the apostle Paul maintains the genuineness of the resurrection over against some Corinthian Christians, he writes that Christ arose "from the dead" (1 Cor 15:12). He was referring to real death, the kind that he would later call *falling asleep* (1 Cor 15:18).

Just as the Savior really arose from the dead, so really had he died earlier. All the emphasis with which Paul maintained the resurrection from the dead in 1 Corinthians 15 would be in vain if our Savior had not earlier really died (1 Cor 15:13). Apart from real death there is no real resurrection. This rule applies to the Mediator between God and men, the man Jesus Christ. To be sure, he did not lie in the grave for a long time, for years and years, and he experienced "no decay" as other dead people did (Acts 2:31; 13:35), but he was really dead. There is no doubt about that. Otherwise not only the Law and the Prophets, but also the New Testament would lose all its meaning.

Both Old and New Testaments teach the atonement of one soul by the *death* of the other soul.[15]

---

15. Translator Note: At this point, the content of pages 49b–161b has been omitted, which consists of a special section dealing with the issue of the immortality of the soul.

3

The requirements for sacrificial animals

GENERALLY SPEAKING, ALL OF Israel's sacrificial animals had to satisfy four conditions. We will first summarize these conditions and then discuss each one in turn.

    1. Israel was never permitted to appear before God bringing wild animals, but always with nothing other than domesticated animals. For example, not with a deer that one would have captured in the wild. No, only with an animal from one's own flock (Lev 1:2). We sense immediately from this first requirement the great importance of this element of the teaching concerning sacrifices: sacrifices consisted of relinquishing to God something that one owned (2 Sam 24:24), something that one valued highly. Especially someone who loves animals would understand this feature. Animal farmers like the Israelites definitely heard this first commandment differently than we city dwellers do. We don't want to be sentimental. The Israelites were not vegetarians. They ate meat, though not very often. Theirs was an agrarian diet. Slaughtering animals for personal use did occur, but was an exception. Moreover, who would have wanted to kill their own animal? Yet, that was required in cases of sacrificial occasions.

    2. Next, the sacrificial animals were to be only clean animals. We have not yet discussed the distinction between clean and unclean animals. (We mentioned this only incidentally, in connection with the animals gathered into Noah's ark, in our commentary on Genesis.)[1] We discussed this more extensively in connection with Leviticus 11. When he gave the Torah, upon which he based Israelite life at Horeb, God made use of many ancient traditions and supplied them with renewed meaning. Such as with the clean

---

1. Vonk, *Genesis*, 170–71.

animals, seen as animals of life, separated from the unclean animals representing death—the latter included many animals that ate carrion and animals with claws—that is how God had chosen Israel from among the nations that were living under the power of Satan and death (Lev 20:24-26; Acts 10:15; 11:18; 26:18; Eph 2:2; 2 Cor 4:4), in order to be the people of the resurrection and life.

The Israelites were supposed to select their sacrificial animals to bring to God only from the clean domesticated animals and flocks. That meant they could choose them from their cattle and their flocks. The latter term referred to sheep and goats (Lev 1:2). By way of exception birds were sacrificed as well, never anything other than doves.

3. Moreover, an ox, sheep, or goat was not to be sacrificed before it had been with its mother for at least seven days (Lev 22:27). In various cases a sheep or goat had to be at least a year old (Lev 9:3; 12:6), a requirement stipulated several times in regard to a calf (Lev 9:3). The oxen that were sacrificed would not have been all that young, in view of the Hebrew term used for them: not *egel* (calf), but *phar* (young bull) and *phara* (young cow).

4. Finally, the sacrificial animals had to be whole. That is to say: they could not exhibit any defects, such as blindness, for example, or a broken leg (Lev 22:20-22).

In connection with these requirements of the Law concerning sacrificial animals, we would mention the following.

1. Tame animals

Actually the Israelite was supposed to have given himself in death, sacrificed his own person, his soul (*nefesh*). But of course that would not do. That was not permitted. So another *nefesh* replaced his *nefesh*. An animal. Not an animal taken from the wild. No, for his altar God requisitioned animals that were part of people's property, used in service to people, animals that were readily manageable and most innocent. For people were not allowed to sacrifice a human being in the place of another. So God identified among the animals those that resembled human beings most closely. There had to be the closest possible connection between the one bringing the sacrifice and the sacrificial animal itself. When in a later era, due to great distances, the sacrificial animal could be purchased in Jerusalem, this animal was purchased with money that the person rendering the sacrifice had earned by the sweat of his brow, as the fruit of his labor. Notice how Christ satisfied this first requirement of the law pertaining to sacrifices. He had become like us in everything. Thereby he could "give his life (*psychē*) as a ransom for many"

(Matt 20:28). By sharing in the same way in our flesh and blood, through his death he was able to dethrone Satan and liberate us (Heb 2:14–15).

2. Clean animals

The apostle would surely have had in view this requirement of the Law when he wrote about the precious blood of Christ who was "a lamb without blemish or *spot*" (1 Pet 1:19). The word Peter uses here appears also in 1 Tim 6:14 and 2 Pet 3:14. In Jas 1:27, we read: "Religion that is pure and undefiled before God, the Father, is this: to visit orphans and widows in their affliction, and to keep oneself *unstained* [*aspilos*] from the world." With what transgression could people have charged our Savior?

3. Mature animals

A sacrificial animal had to be young and strong. But not too young. Nor aged and decrepit. Mature. Compare this with the requirement that the Levites had to meet. They too had to serve during the prime of life, from twenty-five or thirty years old until fifty. Our Savior also satisfied this requirement of the Law. Several writers in the early centuries of Christianity spread reports claiming that our Savior must have been older than forty when he died, but that must have been based on misunderstanding. The Lord would have given the impression of exhaustion when the Jews said to him: You are not yet fifty years old (John 8:57). People thought that was old. But in general people adopt the view that Christ died at thirty-three years of age. At that age a man is in his prime.

4. Whole animals

We have been comparing the requirements that a sacrificial animal had to meet with those established for ministering Levites. One could compare them, however, with the requirements for fulfilling the office priest as well. Just as someone in a priestly family was prohibited from serving if he were deformed or blind or something like that, so too with an animal. A striking similarity exists, extending to the words used, between the list of physical defects that rendered a person unsuitable for serving in the office of priest, found in Lev 21:16–24, and the list of physical defects that disqualified an animal from being used as a sacrifice, found in Lev 22:17–33. Notice how completely our Savior met this requirement of wholeness. As priest and as the sacrificial Lamb. It was testified about him as lamb that he was without blemish (1 Pet 1:19; *amōmos*, the same word used in Rev 14:5 and elsewhere: in their mouth no lie was found, they are without blemish) and about him as priest, the letter of Hebrews says: We needed such a high priest: holy, without guilt or stain, separated from sinners and exalted above the heavens (7:26). We may summarize both according to Heb 9:14, where we read that Christ offered himself unblemished (*amōmos*) to God through the eternal Spirit.

4

The general procedure for sacrificing an animal

When an animal was sacrificed in Israel, it didn't always happen in the same way. There was variation, according to the kind of sacrifice being brought.

Yet there were some stereotypical actions that occurred regularly in every sacrifice. In this chapter we will review those actions. But first a word about the way we should view them.

We will follow the helpful lead provided by the apostle Paul in 1 Corinthians 10. That passage is dealing with Christians participating in pagan sacrificial events. The Corinthians who were new Christians could not easily avoid those events. The entire life of their day was pervaded with idolatry. For that reason the apostle warns them about such participation. Was not the cup of thanksgiving a fellowship with Christ's blood? With Christ and with his church, which was his body? Could these two things go together: belonging to Christ and his church, and having fellowship with demons? For in the end, that is what idolatrous sacrifices were. So the apostle writes: Look how it went with Israel according to the flesh. Did not those who ate those sacrifices have fellowship with the altar (1 Cor 10:18)?

1. **BY MEANS OF THE SACRIFICES, ISRAEL WAS BEING INSTRUCTED IN THE GOSPEL.**

In Heb 10:4 we read: "It is impossible for the blood of bulls and goats to take away sins."

We know that from memory.

And we all agree with it. For we know that only the blood of Jesus, God's Son, cleanses us from all sin (1 John 1:7), and that only he is the perfect priest that has performed the things we were to do before God, and has sanctified us by the sacrifice of himself once for all (Heb 2:17; 10:10).

But we are not fooling ourselves, are we, that in Israel nothing of that impossible task was understood? To be sure, Israel did not yet know the Christ as we do. So Israel could not yet know that only his blood took away sin. But Israel could know that the blood of bulls and goats did not itself take away sin. Israel saw that impossibility clearly.

This must have likely occurred to anyone who recalled that the above-mentioned declaration of Heb 10:4 (through the blood of bulls and goats no sin is taken away) and other declarations with similar content (no forgiveness apart from Jesus Christ) were made in such a straightforward manner by the apostle, written black on white and sent out to Jewish Christians, without him apparently needing to worry that the recipients of such a letter would have been angered about such a nefarious despising of what was once the hope of their fathers. It was as though these fathers would actually never have received forgiveness due to the animal blood shed by and for them. Because this animal blood took away no sin. Apparently those Hebrews had not believed this earlier, before they had become Christians.

Just as such a thing was not believed by their ancestors when they lived in the age of shadows. For ancient Israel knew far too well that they were dealing with symbols, mere figures. So that the removal of sin had not occurred through the blood itself that flowed alongside the altar, but through God and God alone. The psalmist of Psalm 51, for example, confessed his sinfulness to God and explicitly declared that God "does not delight in sacrifice" (vv. 6, 16). You should be careful not to misunderstand such expressions. They were not intended to turn the Law of Moses upside down. In that Law God had indeed commanded the bringing of sacrifices. It was simply that people should not separate those sacrifices from God's grace, for then people would be turning them into pagan ritual. People were not to view altars and sacrifices as automatic instruments, like machines into which they put a coin and got something out in return. Instrumental worship. We encounter warnings frequently in Scripture against such sacrificial automatism (1 Sam 15;22; Isa 1:11–17; Jer 7:22; Amos 5:25). God wanted to use the sacrifices of the Law as symbolic teaching tools for instructing Israel about sin and grace, about misery, redemption, and gratitude. That is, he wanted to teach Israel the gospel. This is what he placed before Israel's eyes through the ministry of the sacrifices. Would a Near Eastern people like Israel not have understood that, by means of tabernacle worship, a symbolic language was being spoken, just as they were supposed to have understood the symbolism of the tabernacle itself?

2. BY MEANS OF THE SACRIFICES, ISRAEL WAS ALSO BEING ASSURED OF THE GOSPEL.

Israel was strictly forbidden to use the sacrifices of the Law as levers whereby they thought they could put pressure on God. If I paid scrupulous attention to bringing the sacrifice according to all the stipulations, then you can't do anything to me. We cannot reject such a mentality strongly enough. It subjects God to human desires. It turns the Law into a tax code. Pure paganism.

This is not at all to deny, however, that Israel was not permitted to use the sacrifices—properly use them—as means instituted by God for convincing them, for ascertaining, for assuring earnestly, of the veracity of the gospel. We learn this from those declarations in the sacrifice laws that talk of the *priest* making atonement for someone, or of *the blood of the animals* bringing atonement. This does not contradict what we wrote above at all. These ways of speaking find their simple explanation in God's own institutions and in his faithfulness to those institutions. Thereby such institutions of the sacrificial Torah, like priests, altars, and shedding blood, served not only as portraits and figures designed to instruct Israel in the gospel, but served at the same time to assure Israel of God's veracity and good intentions. For the relationship that obtained between these two—on the one hand, priests, altars, and blood; and on the other hand, the gospel—had not been invented and prescribed by a mortal man like Moses at his initiative, but by none other than God himself. This explains why Israel was permitted to view them as pledges of God's love and grace. An Israelite who brought a sacrifice could say, recalling the line of Leviticus 17:11—*nefesh* for *nefesh*—that his sins were covered and atoned by the priest and by the blood of the sacrificial animal. That didn't have to be a brash declaration of someone who had turned God's institution into something automatic, but could be an echo of trust in God's own promise. Just as we today need not exclude God as the only One who accomplishes our redemption when we declare that baptism rescues, delivers, and saves us. That is biblical language (1 Pet 3:21).

THE GENERAL PROCEDURE FOR SACRIFICING AN ANIMAL

3. BY MEANS OF THE SACRIFICES, ISRAEL RECEIVED INSTRUCTION IN, AND ASSURANCE ABOUT, THE SAME GOSPEL CONCERNING THE SAME REDEMPTIVE BENEFITS THAT WE RECEIVE TODAY.

The benefits of salvation that God has bestowed upon us in his promise of the gospel could be identified in various ways. Our readers already know from the preceding that we prefer to summarize them in terms of the following triad: (a) justification, (b) sanctification, and (c) glorification. Ancient Israel also received those threefold benefits in the gospel of the Law and received assurance of that by means of the ministry of the sacrifices. We can observe this best when we review the various actions, one by one, that invariably occurred in connection with the sacrifices.

(a) Justification

The first three actions had to be performed by the one bringing the sacrifice.

He was required first of all to *bring* the sacrificial animal himself. "You must present it at the entrance to the tent of meeting" (Lev 1:3). Why there? Because that is where Yahweh dwelt, before whose face nobody could appear except along the path of atonement. This act of bringing the animal was already a confession. From some passages (Lev 5:5; 16:21) we see that the symbolic act of bringing the sacrificial animal with one's own hands was occasionally accompanied with the explicit declaration of a confession of guilt. The one clarified the other. So here came the one sacrificing with his sacrificial animal, so that something would happen to that animal that he himself had deserved. For the wages of sin is death (Gen 2:17; 3:19; Rom 6:23).

Next the one bringing the sacrifice had to place his hand on the head of the sacrificial animal (Lev 1:4). This was the *laying on of hands* (called *semikah* by the rabbis). This too was a gesture whose meaning is clear. Thereby the one bringing the sacrifice was providing his animal as a means of atonement for his sins. In Scripture the laying on of hands occurs frequently as a symbolic gesture of transference. For example, with this gesture the Israelites transferred to the Levites their obligation that their firstborn sons should serve Yahweh in the sanctuary (Num 8:10). By means of the laying on of hands in connection with the sacrifice, the obligation on the part of the one bringing the sacrifice to provide satisfaction for the guilt of his sin was transferred to his sacrificial animal.

In the third place we have the *slaughter* (the *shechitath*, 2 Chron 30:17). This would have been difficult for many an Israelite. To stab the animal that he had raised and watch it convulse on the ground. This act had to occur always on the north side of the altar. This prescription would certainly have been connected with the idea of night, darkness, and death, which arose in people's hearts at the sound of the phrase, *the North*.

In a later period, the prescription that each one performing a sacrifice had to slaughter his own animal was not maintained rigorously, but this slaughter was performed by the tribe of Levi, and in cases involving sacrifices on behalf of the entire people, by the priests (2 Chron 29:24, 34), and in cases involving sacrifices for individuals, by the Levites (2 Chron 30:16, 17; 35:6, 11; Ezek 44:10–11). This did not involve a change in principle, however. For according to the Torah, the issue of who should slaughter the animal was somewhat incidental, because the Torah stipulated that in cases involving the sacrifice of a dove, the slaughter was performed not by the person bringing the sacrifice, but by the priest. Sacrificing a dove had to occur in this manner, because the quantity of blood would not have been sufficient for having the animal first slaughtered by someone else and then have its blood sprinkled on the altar by the priest. But it appears nonetheless from the sacrificial Torah itself that the command about slaughtering did not have to be followed stringently. Nevertheless, the original symbolic course of events would have been addressed most specifically.

From the beginning, however, the *sprinkling of blood* (*zaraq*) was an act that belonged to the priest alone, and this remained the case. The one bringing the sacrifice was permitted to do only so much to the animal. Leading it to the sanctuary, laying his hand on its head, slaughtering the animal, cutting it up and distributing it. But it was exclusively the priest who caught the blood and sprinkled it on the altar of burnt offering, who occasionally had to apply the blood to the horns of the altar or to the horns of the altar of incense within the sanctuary, and sprinkle the blood on the ground there. The reader knows that the laity were not permitted to set foot in that holy place. To say nothing at all about the work of the high priest in the holy of holies on the great Day of Atonement.

Everything done with the blood—sprinkling it on the altar of burnt offering, "dabbing" the blood on the horns of this altar or on the horns of the altar of incense or sprinkling it on the ground of the holy place or the holy of holies—was purely and only the work of the priests.

This invites us to pay careful attention to such an important moment in the sacrificial process. For that's what it was. By the shedding of blood and by what happened with that blood, atonement occurred. Bringing the animal, laying one's hands on the animal, and slaughtering the animal were significant, but not yet sufficient. The blood had to end up at the required place. This is like experiencing the sense of relief when someone indicates a willingness to pay a huge amount toward reducing our debt, but it is not yet real until that money is deposited in the right account. We must pay attention to this, and always keep in mind our Lord Jesus Christ and everything that he has done for us. Not only did he suffer, not only was he afflicted with great pain, and ultimately died. But he has ultimately brought his blood into the very presence of God (Heb 9:12; 10:19).

We would point to three elements.

First, the sprinkling, dabbing, and smearing of blood could be performed by none other than by a priest given by God. Not just anyone could approach God as a Mediator on behalf of others. Moses himself needed to learn that, when he thought he could render atonement for Israel's sin with the golden calf (Exod 32:30–33). "Blot me out of the book you have written." No, it pleased God to choose only Aaron and his sons for regularly approaching him with Israel's sacrifices (Lev 10:3; 21:17). Only they were the approachers (*qerivim*), and only they were allowed to bring the blood (*yiqrav*) to the place where God wanted it.

Second, the priests were to cover (*kippur*) with that sacrificial blood the one for whom it was sacrificed, the one bringing the sacrifice.

We can see very clearly the intention of the priestly actions with the sacrificial blood—viz., covering, atoning—in connection with the establishment of the covenant at Horeb. At that time the Israelites literally received the drops of the blood of the covenant on their bodies (Exod. 24:8).[1] The symbolism of the covering and atoning (*kippur*) of the Israelites who were present, as souls, as persons, was very obvious.

But later, when the tabernacle ministry was ordained, God instituted the symbolism of applying the blood to certain objects of the sanctuary instead of sprinkling it on persons themselves. These objects functioned from then on as representatives of the Israelite people, in the following way. The layperson, the ordinary Israelite, was represented by the altar of burnt offering in the forecourt, the priesthood by the altar of incense in the holy place, and the people of Israel in its entirety by the atonement covering in the holy of holies. Those were the main lines of symbolism. We have omitted some of the details. When we discuss the atonement sacrifice we will deal more extensively with them.

Third, only when the two preceding prescriptions had been satisfied, would God accept the covering or atonement as valid, and people could believe that their sins were forgiven. So then, only when, first, the blood had been brought to the place required, upon the altar specified for each case (altar of burnt offering or of incense or of atonement; Lev 17:11), and

---

1. See Vonk, *Exodus*, 122–26.

second, only when this blood had been brought to the assigned place by the hand of someone authorized, namely, by the hand of the priest (Lev 1:5, 11; etc.). Let no one argue, therefore, that all blood was simply sacred, let alone, that it had atoning power. This would have been the case only if it had been brought to the right place, and by the priest to the right place, namely, the place that represented either the individual Israelite, the priest, or the people in their entirety.

This was the path of atonement that had to be walked scrupulously in the period of the shadows, if God were to grant forgiveness: (1) Justification; (2) Reconciliation; (3) Atonement. For he was the One who atoned (Lev 17:11).

During this discussion, who would not have had to recall the letter to the Hebrews? With its emphasis on the lawfulness of Christ's priesthood? He did not usurp this, but was called and chosen unto this by God (Heb 5:5). Just as the high priest in the Old Testament entered the holy of holies "not without blood," so too Christ did not enter the heavenly sanctuary without first having given his blood on the cross, "not by means of the blood of goats and calves but by means of his own blood, thus securing an eternal redemption" (Heb 9:7, 12). Such formulations would have been read with intense interest by the original readers of this letter (native Jews, perhaps including converted priests, who were now without employment and income, Acts 6:7; Heb 10:34).

(b) Sanctification

An entirely new stage dawns at this point, the stage of sanctification. The atonement had occurred (symbolically). The sinner was covered. His sins were forgiven. So then, a second benefit was proclaimed and certified to the Israelite by means of the gospel of the sacrifices. Sanctification follows justification. Portrayed and guaranteed by the burning of the slaughtered animal.

That burning did not always occur in the same manner. All the parts of some sacrificial animals were burned and not even the tiniest bit was eaten by anyone. The majority of the parts, not all, of other animals were burned, with only a portion used, and that exclusively by the priests. Finally, there were other sacrifices where the animal was cut into three pieces, with the first piece for Yahweh, which was burned; the second piece was for the priests, as an honorarium; and the last and largest piece, the remainder, was for the one sacrificing, in order to enjoy a meal with his family in the presence of God. We will return to these various kinds of sacrifices in due

THE GENERAL PROCEDURE FOR SACRIFICING AN ANIMAL

course. Here we want to focus attention on several details in order to show that at least *something* from *every* sacrificial animal was burned. The whole was being represented by that *part*, and the entire sacrificial animal was being brought to God and sanctified as representing the one making the sacrifice. For God had given that right to Israel, the right to this symbolic act of burning the sacrificial animal. Thereby he was sealing to his people the promise of sanctification.

Other interpreters have drawn other conclusions about this. For example, the view has been advocated that the burning of the sacrificial animal would have been a symbolic representation of the punishment of hell. By surrendering his animal to burning, the one bringing the sacrifice would have been confessing that actually he himself had deserved the fire of hell. But this view has forgotten to notice that the burning occurred after the atonement. In fact, this view finds no support at all in the entire sacrificial Torah. Nowhere does it speak about the punishment of the condemned. On the contrary, the sacrificial Torah informs us repeatedly that the goal of the burning was delightful, namely, that it brought a pleasant aroma before Yahweh (Gen 8:21; Exod 29:41; Lev 8:21; etc.). This view would also yield the strange result in terms of the grain offering. We will discuss the grain offering separately. Here we will simply make the preliminary comment that a bloody sacrifice was never permitted to be brought except accompanied with a grain offering. Such a grain offering consisted of bread and wine, together with incense and oil. The good works of believers were being symbolized by the bread and the wine, and the incense and oil represented the prayer and the working of the Holy Spirit, respectively. So then, if we would have to accept the view that the burning of the bloody sacrifice represented the punishment in the fires of hell, then in the burning of the ingredients of the grain offering—symbolic of the faith-works, prayer, and working of the Spirit!—we would have to see a representation of the punishment of hell as well. But who would dare claim that such glorious things were referring to condemnation of hell?

We must not go in that direction.

It is better to remember first of all that the burning of a sacrificial animal did not at all intend the destruction of that animal. This appears already from the Hebrew word that was used. In the sacrificial Torah, for example, it was stipulated that the remnants of a peace offering were not allowed to be older than two days, and they had to be burned for sure on the third day (Lev 7:17). But when it talks about burning sacrifices on the altar, then Scripture uses one or another form of the Hebrew verb *qatar*, which was related to the noun *qetoreth*, which meant sacrificial aroma, sacrificial scent (Lev 1:9, 13, 15; etc.). We also find many passages that talk about this latter burning, used virtually as a technical phrase, "unto a pleasing aroma before Yahweh." Next, we must remember that the Hebrew term for that sacrifice, involving a burning that was not connected with any other sacrifice, namely, an entire consuming, where the intention and idea of burning came to clearest expression, was the word *olah*. This means literally "abrogation." From this we may conclude that the burning of the sacrificial animal was not intended to destroy it as though in hell, but on the contrary, to offer it up to God as a tangible and visible proof of thanks for the atonement, forgiveness, and justification that had just been received.

Meanwhile, people in Israel were directed, for this offering of their thankful hearts to God (*in* the offering of the sacrificial animal), just as exclusively to the ministry of the priest and the altar as with the receiving of (symbolic) justification. In that context the *blood* was not to be brought to the altar by anyone other than a priest. We have talked about that. Here, the *meat* of the sacrificial animal was also not to be placed upon the altar by anyone other than a priest. If it was to be burned on that altar so it might rise to heaven in smoke and aroma, then it was to be burned up by God's own fire. By the fire supplied by God himself. For we will read in a moment that when Aaron was ordained as high priest and was about to enter upon his official duties, the fire on the altar was ignited by God himself and consumed the pieces of the sacrifice (Lev 9:24; cf. 2 Chron 7:1). Concerning this altar fire it was prescribed that people might never let it die out (Lev 9:12–13; mt, 6:5–6). Hereby God wanted to teach Israel and us that Israel's sanctification was also his work. Just as much as God's gift of justification was. The sanctification of Israel's heart and life proceeded *from him*. It was through *his* fire that Israel's very best works had to be purified, cleansed, and sanctified, in order to please God. But having been sanctified by such a fire, they certainly were pleasing to God. Israel was being assured of that at the same time. Instructed and assured.

This purification by fire was apparently such an obvious notion among Israel that it could be alluded to without fear of misunderstanding. For example, the work of the Holy Spirit was symbolized by fire (Matt 3:11; Acts 1:5; 2:3). As just as the fire purified the sacrifice and caused it to rise upward, so too through the Spirit of God our Savior sacrificed himself "without blemish to God" (Heb 9:14), and believers "offer spiritual sacrifices acceptable to God through Jesus Christ" (1 Pet 2.5). One day the very best works of believers will have to pass through the purifying fire of Christ's judgment (like salt is purified). Then much will still need to be burned away like wood, hay, and stubble, but we who are saved will enter into the eternal kingdom (Mark 9:49; 1 Cor 3:11).

So, then, the fire on the altar purifies.

THE GENERAL PROCEDURE FOR SACRIFICING AN ANIMAL

And it causes something to rise upward.

Through this, the instruction and assurance were given to God's church that they, out of thanks for the forgiveness from guilt that they received (justification), may respond to God with heart and life, and this would please God. Holy Scripture does not hesitate to call the sacrifices that Israel brought to Yahweh his *food*. You can read this in many passages (Lev 3:11; 21:8, 17). One must resist the temptation to see here the remnants of earlier paganism in Israel's sacrificial worship. There is no talk here of pagan mysticism like we can read, for example, in the story of Bel and the dragon (apocryphal addition to the book of Daniel), just as the same is true about the showbread. God does not permit himself to be served by human hands because he needs this in order to exist (Ps 50:12–13; Acts 17:25). Meat, fat, bread, etc., were called "food for Yahweh" not because of what they really were *for God*, but because of what they figuratively represented, pointed to, taught, and certified *for Israel*. With reference to Israel, God may well have employed a fixed terminology that they had heard pagans using. But for Israel, God supplied such terminology with an entirely unique and different meaning. In this respect as well, he gave Israel the right to believe not only that they repeatedly received from him atonement unto justification, but also that his reconciled people were permitted to repay him for this with the surrender of the whole person unto the service of his God (Deut 6:5; 10:12; Matt 22:37; Luke 10:27). This latter was taught symbolically to Israel and assured to her through the burning of the slaughtered sacrificial animal. God would have been very delighted in this burnt offering, just as we human beings are interested in our daily food. The apostle Paul would have been thinking of this symbolism when, after his precious instruction about our justification through Christ's blood in Romans 3–5, he wrote in Romans 6: "So now present *your members* as slaves to righteousness leading to *sanctification*." And when at the conclusion of that epistle he looked back once more "to the mercies of God," he appealed to that for the admonition that the readers should put their bodies, i.e., themselves, "as a living sacrifice, holy and acceptable to God, which is your spiritual worship" (Rom 12:1). Instead of "your bodies" he could just as well have written "your souls" or "yourselves"; but he apparently wanted to make his allusion to Israel's former ministry at the altar more evident by using the word *body*.

Every kind of sacrifice was a gift, or *corban* (Lev 1:2).

This was the fundamental idea, for example, of that sacrifice that was brought *not at all* for the purpose of atonement, namely, the grain offering, about which we will speak later, but also of that sacrifice that was *no longer* being brought for atonement, namely, the bloody sacrifice after the slaughtering of the animal and the handling of the animal's blood. At that point, surrendering the slaughtered animal *to* the fire, and the purification of it *through* the fire, and the ascending to heaven of its aroma, stood for the surrender to Israel's God of the one bringing the sacrifice. We could better say: all of this guaranteed to the one bringing the sacrifice that God desired to accept him with his whole heart and all his powers to the same degree as if God desired and needed this like a person desires and needs his daily food. For God called this *lechem le Yahweh*, or food for Yahweh.

c. Glorification

The sacrificial ceremony was concluded with a meal.

Of course not every sacrifice ended in this kind of meal. We already mentioned that some sacrifices were entirely burned up. So there was nothing left over to eat. With other sacrifices, something could be eaten, a single portion, but exclusively by the priests. Only when the peace offering was being brought, could the ones bringing the sacrifice, i.e., the one sacrificing and his family and friends, could enjoy a meal with this food. That could occur because, as we indicated, the largest portion of the peace offering was used. You can see that Israel's sacrificial ministry attained a climax in this peace offering meal. At that point (a) the atonement through the shedding of blood, and (b) the sanctification through burning with God's fire had symbolically occurred, and finally, (c) Israel was being taught through the celebration of a sacrificial meal "before the face of Yahweh," and assured of God's promise, that they would one day share in the perfectly restored fellowship with God in Paradise.

Note well that that peace offering meal was not held by the Israelites in their own homes, but at God's home (Lev 3; 7:11–27). We discussed the symbolism of this tabernacle of God in the midst of Israel in our commentary on Exodus. This sanctuary proclaimed that beautiful future, about which we read in Revelation 21 and 22; about the Paradise of God that will descend one day to earth. With the visible down payment of this Paradise promise—for that can be our shorthand description of the tabernacle—the Israelites sat down to enjoy their peace offering meal. As a crowning of God's work, that had occurred symbolically in the earlier justification through the blood and in the sanctification through the fire, Israel received the seal of the promise, the fulfillment for which the forefathers had yearned: the promise of the eternal city, whose maker and finisher is God; the promise of the future paradise-like fellowship with God. Israel received this seal in that sacrificial meal.

The symbolic, and at the same time sealing, function of this meal would have been easier for such Near Eastern people like the Israelites to grasp than for us. Earlier we noted that in the New Testament the future joy of the redeemed on the new earth is portrayed more than once as the celebration of a festive meal (Matt 8:11; 22:1, 10, 11; Luke 14:15; Rev 3:20). And we also noted that when the apostle Paul wrote in 1 Corinthians 10 about the Lord's Supper, he recalled the fellowship with God and his altar—for according to his promise, Yahweh would meet his people at the altar (Exod 20:24)—a joy that ancient Israel tasted as they enjoyed their sacrificial meals (1 Cor 10:18, 21).

It is a disputed matter whether in connection with such sacrificial meals we should view God to be functioning as the host or as a participant along with his people. Scripture itself does not consider this an issue. Our Savior once gave the promise: I will come in with him and eat with him and he with me (Rev 3:20). But so be it; that the first notion—of God functioning as host at the peace offering meal—is not to be dismissed appears to us to follow from the fact that this meal always had to occur "before the face of Yahweh." If we recall as well that by the preceding consuming of particular pieces of the sacrificial animal and by their being burned on the altar, the entire animal—following the principle of part for the whole—was given and brought to God, so that with the meal that followed, the person who had brought the sacrifice was enjoying nothing that still belonged to him but something that belonged to God. He was not enjoying a gift that he had given to God, but a gift God was giving to him. We will discuss something similar later, when we discuss the wave offering and the heave offering. At this point we may point to the position of the tribe of Levi. The Israelites would have understood very well that Levi received its subsistence, its food and drink, not from human hands but from the hand of Yahweh. For this was the situation: Israel was permitted to dwell in Canaan as a land that belonged and continued to belong to Yahweh. Yahweh was Israel's Landlord. Israel's tithes belonged to him. He was free to give those tithes in turn to whomever he wanted. So Yahweh gave his tithes to Levi (Lev 25:23; 27:30; Num 18:21, 24). Yahweh was Levi's portion. Levi did not eat from the hands of people. Moreover, we must also recall at this point the name that Scripture gives those portions of the sin-, guilt-, and peace-offerings that were designated for the priests. They were called "the bread of his God" (Lev 21:17, 22). Therefore, we would not dare to label as unscriptural the view that at the peace offering meal, God functioned both as the donor and as the host. Rather this is very scriptural.

But the main point is that we understand the symbolic instruction that God was giving Israel by means of the sacrificial meal. In the forecourt of his home, which as we have seen, was the shadow and down payment of the promised Paradise, God gave to his people instruction about and a guarantee of the promise of the Paradise fellowship that would be restored one day. The same redemptive benefit to which the apostle Paul pointed in his letter to the Romans, after he had written so extensively about justification and had appealed so powerfully for the manifesting of the second fruit of Christ's redeeming work in daily life, namely, sanctification. For he concluded this way: But now, having been set free from sin, and having entered into the service of God, you have the fruit of your sanctification *and its end, eternal life* (Rom 6:22).

We are going to conclude this section about general principles. With a view to what is coming, we want to tell the reader precisely what we will be discussing.

Not simply "the sacrifices."

Presumably many will think in connection with this phrase exclusively of the *bloody sacrifices* that Israel had to bring before God. We have shown, however, that people often give too narrow a meaning to the term *sacrifices*. The possibility also exists that we ourselves have fed that inclination to this narrowness by dealing almost exclusively with the bloody sacrifice. Even though we added why we did so: because atonement was involved only with *the slain sacrificial animal*. For with God, atonement could occur only through blood, through death.

Therefore we are repeating the classification once more.

To the *corbanim,* or the gifts of Israelites to God, belonged items that were not at all intended to be burned. We mentioned the six wagons and twelve oxen that the heads of the tribes of Israel brought "before the face of Yahweh" on the occasion of the dedication of the tabernacle. These specifically were not to be burned, but used for transporting the tabernacle (Num 7:3). Something similar could be said about those gifts that Israel had to bring later to Yahweh as their Divine Landlord, who was the real Owner of Canaan, gifts in terms of rent or lease. The firstfruits and tithes. These were not intended for the altar. God gave them in turn to the Levites and priests, for their subsistence (Num 18).

By contrast, other *corbanim* (sacrifices, gifts) were indeed intended to be burned, if not entirely, then partially. This explains why they are called *fire offerings* (*ishsheh*, from *esh*, fire), fire offerings for Yahweh. Often this is followed with the standard expression, "with a pleasing aroma to Yahweh" (Lev 1:9). Israel could be convinced that if their fire offerings were brought to the place and in the manner stipulated by God, that he would be pleased with them. According to his promise: there (on the altar) I will come to you and bless you (Exod 20:24). The fire offerings would be "bread for Yahweh."

God would be happy with them. He wanted to receive them on repeated occasions (Num 28:2).

Those fire offerings would then consist either of an animal or of vegetation.

We have already said something about the *animal* fire offerings. For example, that they could consist only of clean animals. And only of tame animals. In the beginning, Israel certainly sacrificed animals to God that they themselves had raised.

When they later entered Canaan, there were also *vegetative* fire offerings, something from the people themselves. They had to smell like them, so to speak, like their work. For the grain offering could not consist of just any fruit plucked from wild nature, but oil and wine, which bore the odor of the spade and the shears in the orchard, and the picking and trampling of the harvesters. And let's not forget the grain, offered while it was still in the ear, as a sheaf, or in the form of a meal or baked as a cake or bread, but in any case smelling of Israel's labor, of which the grain was also a fruit.

As a fire offering, then, that was repeatedly laid on the altar, it was some of the most unique items that the Israelite, together with his wife and children, owned, namely, his own homebred animal and his own harvested fruit from the field.

We are now going to discuss these fire offerings to Yahweh.

There were of two kinds, however. Bloody and non-bloody. Animal and vegetative. But what must we do now?

Must we use this same order as we now discuss the sacrificial Torah? Then we would get something like this:

Fire offerings	
I. Bloody	II. Non-bloody
1. The burnt offering (Lev 1)	5. The grain offering (Lev 2)
2. The peace offering (Lev 3)	
3. The sin offering (Lev 4:1–5:13)	
4. The guilt offering (Lev 5:14–6:7)	

The reader can see from the Scripture passages in parentheses that if we were to follow the above order scrupulously, then we would be departing from the *biblical* order. That would not be blasphemous, for sure. But for those who are looking for a reliable guide for their Bible reading, that would be less desirable. Therefore we have decided to keep to the order of Scripture for the following discussions of each distinct offering.

Part 2

The Sacrificial Torah:
Specific requirements

5

The burnt offering (Lev 1)

TRANSITION

We need not repeat our explanation for thinking that the reason is obvious as to why the book of Leviticus began with the sacrificial Torah.

But why in turn did the sacrificial Torah begin anew with the burnt offering as the first one in the entire series?

The answer: that, too, was obvious. Because in relation to the other offerings, the burnt offering occupied a fundamental position. In the most literal sense of the word. For the other offerings were always brought to the tabernacle on a burnt offering. Literally *on it*. On top of it. On the daily burnt offering for the congregation (Lev 3:5; 4:10; 6:12–13). For this reason it was no surprise that *this* fire offering headed the list.

Only male animals were used for the burnt offering. Only when doves were brought did people not need to pay attention to the gender. That would have been impossible. But otherwise only bulls, rams, and billy goats could be brought as a burnt offering. Masculine animals.

As agreed, we need say no more about the bringing of the animal, the laying on of hands, slaughtering, and cutting up of the animal. But we do need to mention that the *skin* of the animal used for a burnt offering was assigned to the ministering priest (Lev 7:8). This person received at least something of the burnt offering as an honorarium (1 Cor 9:13). For the entire burnt offering was burned up. Everything.

This is how it went.

PART 2 | THE SACRIFICIAL TORAH: SPECIFIC REQUIREMENTS

First the animal was slaughtered and its blood sprinkled by the priest on the altar of burnt offering. Sprinkled. That would have referred to a scattering motion of the hand. The Hebrew verb used for this (*zara'*) referred to the hand gesture of someone who was sowing (Isa 32:30). The priests would have had to sprinkle the blood of the animal brought as a burnt offering against the inside of the four walls of the altar of sacrifice (Lev 1:5).

After the animal had been skinned, it was cut up into pieces. That would make it easier for the fire to penetrate. For these pieces were next laid by the priest on the wood that he had previously arranged on the (constantly smoldering) altar, and laid on the embers. Since it was a burnt offering, everything had to be burned, and to the pieces of meat were added the head, intestines, the fat, and shanks. The *head*, for that had been cut off with the slaughtering and thereby severed from the torso. The *intestines*, for those had to be washed in water to clean them of any remaining food and excrement. The *fat*, referring to the fat surrounding the intestines and that which had fallen out of the stomach cavity with the removal of the intestines. Finally, the *shanks*. Those too had to be washed first before being placed on the altar. These shanks would have referred to both hind legs. Everyone understands why these in particular needed to be washed. Not because they had come into contact with the dust of the earth, for then all four legs of the animal would have had to be washed, whereas only two are mentioned. No, rather because it was precisely the hind legs that are defiled with excrement, which the animals release out of fright when they are slaughtered. Something similar happens when people die. What was sacrificed to God had to be free of stench and death. Clean.

What were the names used for this sacrifice?

One frequent Hebrew term was *olah*, from the verb *alah*, to ascend, cause to ascend, exalt oneself. Another term was *khalil*. In this second term one can hear that with this kind of offering, absolutely everything—*hakkol*, Lev 1:9—had to be burned on the altar. These two terms appear in Deut 33:10, 1 Sam 7:9, and Ps 51:21, where the ESV uses the phrase *burnt offering*, or *whole burnt offering*. The German uses the term *Ganzopfer*, but we don't have such a word in English. The Septuagint (Greek Old Testament) used something like *holocaust*.

Would it be proper to say that the characteristic feature of the burnt offering consisted in the fact that it was an offering that was *burned*?

That would be proper, but not yet sufficient. For the characteristic feature of the burnt offering was not that it was burned, nor that it rose upward, for these things happened with the other fire offerings. But with those other offerings not *to that extent* as with the burnt offering. In its entirety. Therefore the characteristic feature of this offering is expressed most clearly

THE BURNT OFFERING (LEV 1)

by the second term: *khalil*, an offering that was totally consumed. For the animal given in a burnt offering was burned in its entirety and ascended in its entirety with the fumes of the fire and smoke. That total consuming did not occur with any other offering.

We must also pay attention to the *motive* for bringing the burnt offering. The reason why and the purpose were important. Let's compare this with the other offerings.

The reason for bringing a sin offering always lay in one or another event. The reason why a peace offering was brought to God was related to something similar, mostly with thanksgiving for benefits received. But there is absolutely no clue regarding a special reason for the burnt offerings. burnt offerings were brought every day on the altar in the forecourt. Mornings and evenings (Lev 6:8–13). For that purpose, the fire for the burnt offering had to be kept burning on the altar. Because of the morning- and evening-sacrifice, there was a constant column of smoke above the tabernacle forecourt. Stopping the daily sacrifices for the congregation was viewed as a terrible catastrophe in Dan 8:11–13. The cleaning of ashes from the altar every morning was the work of the priest. So that the constant burnt offerings could be brought this could in turn serve in the course of the day as the basis for the other offerings of individual members of the congregation (Lev 3:5; 6:12). Those offerings were literally placed on top.

When we take all of this into consideration, may we not conclude that the burnt offering was brought primarily because, before anything else, Israel had to begin and end each day with the faith that Yahweh alone was God? Was it for that reason that God required this ancient, internationally familiar kind of offering for himself (Gen 8:20; 22:2; Exod 10:25; 18:12)? Just as in the first of the Ten Words he had immediately begun with honoring him as the only God. While automatically connected to the confession of the uniqueness of God (Deut 6:4) was the right of God to Israel's whole heart (Deut 6:5). This explains the command that the burnt offering was to be brought in its entirety, completely, to Yahweh. Perhaps the animals that serves as the burnt offering were cut up into pieces, but that was only to give the fire a chance to consume the material from every side. For everything—everything—including the pieces that had been separated—head, entrails, etc.—had to be burned! The stipulation that only male animals could be used for the burnt offering would be explained by the fact that male animals were usually the prettiest, largest, and strongest. God did not merely want to be the only One who received honor in Israel and who was served with the whole heart and life, but he also wanted this to be done energetically, firmly, strongly, with commitment. This was likely expressed by the requirement that animals brought for the burnt offering had to be male. We recall the

PART 2 | THE SACRIFICIAL TORAH: SPECIFIC REQUIREMENTS

summons: "Be on the alert, stand firm in the faith, act like men, be strong" (1 Cor 16:13). Our heavenly Father surely has the right to our courageous and brave service. Not serving him with a divided heart.

If we may view the special character of the burnt offering to be closely related to *the praise of God*, then we can probably explain in that light the remarkable fact that on specific occasions, definitely nothing more was brought than one sin offering, but more than one burnt offering (Num 7:15–16). That was possible. For if one had asked God one time for the forgiveness of sins, and in the sacrificing of the sin offering had received the assurance of the promise of forgiveness, then naturally it would be inappropriate to do this all once again by bringing another sin offering. That was not authentic. Just as now, in our dispensation, it is not authentic and upright for someone to be sending up to God a petition for forgiveness at every turn. That would be mere routine or self-deception, if not worse. Just as it is not very genuine of someone who has thanked a person for a gift to come back fifteen minutes later to thank him again. That becomes sickly. But when a lad receives from his father a new bicycle and thanks him once, but later he can "praise" him many times by telling him various nice things about his bicycle. In the same way, our *praising* and *exalting* of God need never exceed any limits. Asking God for forgiveness, over and over again, that is a pain in the neck. But talking about God's deeds, praising him for his miracles, for his leading in the life of Israel, of our ancestors, and of ourselves, we won't be soon finished. Therefore the constant repetition of the burnt offerings one after the other had significance, a good purpose.

Perhaps some Bible readers are still privately surprised that Leviticus 1 is a chapter about burnt offerings. Why not about the sin offering? Must we not always and before all else approach God with trembling on account of our sins? And look what happens—the Holy Spirit has me begin in the book of Leviticus, a book in which God's holiness is discussed repeatedly, not with a chapter about the sin offering, but with a chapter about the burnt offering.

If someone were to talk this way, we would point out that every bloody sacrifice began with slaughtering and blood letting unto (the sealing of the promise of) forgiveness of sins. The burnt offering as well, and the peace offering, too. To that extent, in this way the sinner's justification (or forgiveness) was always in the foreground, also when, for example, a burnt offering was slaughtered. But you must not hereby lose sight of the foundation beneath every sacrifice, including the burnt offering. That foundation was the covenant that God had established with Abraham and his seed, plus the covenant that he had additionally established with Israel at Horeb. For that reason, nobody in Israel needed to approach God with his offerings like a foreigner as though he were a foreign God. That would have been strange. The people of Israel were related to God not like a disparate horde of orphans. The people had received the clearest proofs of his love. It had been placed upon the granite floor of God faithfulness, and had received the calling to express their thanks for this unique privilege in a holy walk of life. The first wish that God sounded forth on Horeb was: You shall be to me a kingdom of priests and you shall be a holy nation (Exod 19:6). So then, the first sacrifice with which the sacrificial Torah of Leviticus began was the burnt offering; in other words, that sacrifice whose characteristic feature was God's praise and Israel's sanctification. For every sacrifice involved some kind of burning and a rising to the sky, but no sacrifice had this to the degree that the burnt offering did.

From that offering, no one ate anything. Not even a priest. The burnt offering was completely burned up.

The symbolic language of this burnt offering seems to us not very hard to understand. May the portion of Scripture that treats it speak to us as well, and may it bring us to the daily petition: *Unite* my heart that I may fear your name. I will praise you, Yahweh, my God, with my whole heart (Ps 86:11–12). How the prophets warned, as did our Savior, against a *divided* heart (1 Kgs 11:4; 18:21; Isa 29:13; Matt 15:8). The only difference is the God of Israel, who is now our covenant God, we no longer call Yahweh, but: Our Father who art in heaven. So then, our heavenly Father *is* also unique.

6

The grain offering (Lev 2)

THE SACRIFICIAL TORAH ADDRESSES, in the second place, the grain offering, and for understandable reasons. Grain offerings were always paired with the bloody sacrifice. We will say more about this later.

Notice the remarkable *similarity* between the bloody sacrifice and the grain offering, in spite of the differences.

In the bloody sacrifice, the Israelite bringing the offering was giving his animal to God. The creature that was most like him, almost like himself. The symbolism of this was most clear when a burnt offering was being brought, because nothing would be eaten of that sacrifice, not even by the priests, but everything was burned. Everything for God. But in the non-bloody sacrifice, the worshiper gave something to God that resembled him very closely. For this was the fruit of his labor and diligence from his vineyard and field.

So this was what was going on: he was giving himself (symbolically) in the burnt offering (Lev 1).

And he was giving his labor (symbolically) in the grain offering (Lev 2).

Nevertheless, even though these two kinds of offerings correspond so much, we must not make them identical. As Bähr did,[1] for example, even though only in principle; but he still went too far. We want to take a moment to discuss this, since it can be instructive. Notice how comprehensively Bähr drew the parallels between the bloody sacrifice and the grain offering: the contents of the bloody sacrifice included (1) meat, (2) fat, and (3) blood, while the corresponding elements of the non-bloody sacrifice were (1') bread, (2') oil, and (3') wine.

---

1. Bähr, *Symbolik*, 2:215.

THE GRAIN OFFERING (LEV 2)

At first glance, this view seems persuasive, since in the environs of Palestine, the single Hebrew word *lechem* could refer to meat as well as bread. Another reason was that the second parallel between fat and oil seems to confirm that impression, since oil is also somewhat fatty. In addition, there was apparently wide similarity between (3) wine, and blood, for they were both poured out. Quite a similarity! According to Bähr, this parallelism explains why the blood sacrifice could be replaced occasionally with a grain offering, as in the case of poverty (Lev 5:11).

But Kurtz has shown that this was an ingenious discovery on Bähr's part, just not a correct one. In his view, a more unfortunate appeal to a Scripture text was unimaginable than an appeal to Lev 5:11. If you take the trouble to read this verse, you could see that. For it says: "If, however, they cannot afford two doves or two young pigeons, they are to bring as an offering for their sin a tenth of an ephah of the finest flour for a sin offering. *They must not put oil or incense on it, because it is a sin offering*" (italics added). We recall that with the bloody sin offering, according to explicit prescription, all the fat was supposed to be placed on the altar (about which we will speak later), and we observe that with the non-bloody substitute sacrifice, it was just as explicitly commanded not to add oil to the sacrifice. So this does not at all fit Bähr's supposed parallelism between the animal and the grain sacrifices. Moreover, it was the case that the oil did not constitute the main component of the grain offering. Nor the daily diet of Israel. One might certainly eat bread and drink wine every day, but nobody ever enjoyed a meal simply of oil. Thus with the grain offering, the oil was merely a supplement, and did not have the same status as bread and wine. It was subordinated to these. Finally, the parallel between blood and wine was more apparent than real. For the blood had been given by God to man, as covering for his soul, as an atonement for the sins of his soul (Lev 17:11). But the wine had been given by man to God, and had nothing to do with atonement. In addition, the wine was thought to belong to God's food, but the notion of enjoying blood was nonsense. In that respect, the parallel was not accurate at all.

We thought it would be helpful to set out for our readers this discovery of Bähr and the critique of Kurtz. From it, we can learn that in connection with our interpretation of Holy Scripture, our duty is a solemn one, and we must not be led astray by what may appear at first glance to be an excellent approach.

What seals the argument is that the grain offering was a sacrifice with an entirely unique character.

That becomes evident immediately when we consider the *location* where the offering was brought, or rather, the locations. For whereas the bloody sacrifice was brought exclusively in the forecourt, the non-bloody

PART 2 | THE SACRIFICIAL TORAH: SPECIFIC REQUIREMENTS

sacrifice was brought to God not only in the forecourt, but also in the holy place of the tabernacle. To be sure, occasionally some of the blood from the bloody sacrifice was brought from the forecourt to the holy place, and once per year into the holy of holies, but these were exceptions. In any case, meat was never sacrificed within the holy place and within the holies of holies. This happened exclusively on the altar of burnt offering in the forecourt.

But with the non-bloody or grain offering the matter was entirely different. This was brought not only upon the altar in the forecourt, but also into the holy place, and then the components of the grain offerings in the holy place further specified with a view to the three different "altars" there. We discussed this in our commentary on Exodus, but in order to explain properly the meaning of the grain offering, it may be desirable to repeat a thing or two from that discussion.

On the altar in the forecourt, grain was sacrificed as well as wine, oil, and incense. But in connection with the holy place, a separate action, so to speak, was performed with each of these gifts for the grain offering, in that:

First, loaves were placed and wine was set on the golden table of showbread;

Second, in the lamps of the golden lampstand, oil was offered to God;

Third, incense was offered on the golden altar of incense.

We should observe that everything stipulated for the grain offering that was to be brought into the holy place was more delicate and refined. For...

First, unlike in the forecourt, an offering of ears of grain and of meal (yeast) was never placed on the table of showbread, but exclusively bread that had been completely baked;

Second, in the lampstand nothing but the purest olive oil was to be offered to God;

Third, on the altar of incense was brought not one kind of incense, but a mixture of four kinds of incense.

Finally, whereas the grain offering in the forecourt was probably brought daily, though not throughout the entire day, the loaves of showbread lay *continually* on the table in the holy place, the incense burned *continually* on the altar of incense, and the lamps in the lampstand burned *uninterruptedly* throughout the night in the sanctuary.

The grain offering was regarded highly by God. He did not at all view it as a negligible afterthought. Nor as a disguised inferior sacrifice. Rather, as we will see in a moment, it occupied a beautiful place in the forecourt, and we have seen that it was brought regularly into the holy place, though with more specialization and completeness. To the holy place was brought

THE GRAIN OFFERING (LEV 2)

the atonement sacrifice or the bloody sacrifice only in terms of the blood, and only by way of exception. In any case, never in its entirety.

Let us turn next to the *name* of the grain offering. In Hebrew this was called the *minchah*. Earlier we observed that this term appeared in the story of Cain and Abel, in reference to a bloody sacrifice (for that of Abel, Gen 4:4), but that is the only time. Later, when used in connection with bringing sacrifices, it is the term of a vegetable offering. In Exod 30:9, for example, God prescribes that neither burnt offering nor grain offering (neither *olah* nor *minchah*) may be placed on the golden altar of incense. When it came to specific instances where not only food but also drink was being sacrificed, the word *minchah* itself served especially to indicate the "dry" portion of the non-bloody sacrifice (for example, in Num 6:15 and Joel 1:9).

Leviticus 2 does not discuss the drink offering at all, but deals exclusively with the grain offering, with the *minchah* in the narrowest sense of the term. We read that part of it was "an aroma pleasing to Yahweh"—you will recall that the same phrase was used about the burnt offering in Leviticus 1—and that part of it was for the priests as "a most holy part of the food offering presented to Yahweh" (Lev 2:2–3). Here we have one more proof as to how highly the grain offering was regarded.

Since we mentioned the *drink offering*, we will mention the remaining features of that sacrifice.

We don't have very much information about this drink offering. Its institution did occur at Horeb. In Exod 29:40–41 we read of the command requiring that the morning and evening sacrifices that were to be brought daily in the forecourt had to be paired with a grain offering and a drink offering. In Exod 30:9 we find the command that burnt offering, grain offering, and drink offering were never to be laid upon the altar of incense in the holy place. These commands were given to Moses already before the tabernacle was constructed. But once it was constructed, when God gave Moses his commands concerning the altar sacrifices, apparently he said nothing about the drink offering. At least we find no mention of it in Leviticus 2. Perhaps this can be explained in terms of the circumstances in Israel at that point. Presumably during the time when Israel was in the wilderness, God did not want to press for drink offerings. This assumption is based on Leviticus 23. This chapter deals with Israel's festivals, and we read there that grain offerings and drink offerings had to be brought to God at those feasts (vv. 13, 18, 37). But it is striking that in his introductory comments to Moses about this, God said (note the italicized words): "*When you enter the land* I am going to give you and you reap its harvest . . ." (Lev 23:10). Perhaps this corresponds to what we read in Numbers 15. That is a chapter that discusses grain offerings and drink offerings not in an incidental fashion, but quite intentionally and extensively. There as well we find the following introductory words of God to Moses (again, notice the italicized words): "*After you enter the land* I am giving you as a home" (v. 2).

The drink offering was commanded by God already in the days of "Horeb." What other purpose would God have had for instructing Moses to make those bowls and pitchers for the table of showbread (Exod 25:29; 37:16; Num 4:7)? Perhaps Israel occasionally brought drink offerings to God at Horeb. It was not impossible that Israel could have purchased the required items for that offering from the caravans they saw traveling by. Just as Israel would have had to purchase salt and incense, which would have come from Arabia. Just like some of the construction materials for the tabernacle and its accessories. But it is uncertain whether Israel had constant access to the rather significant quantity of wine required for the drink offering. Perhaps there were periods when Israel lacked sufficient wine, and Israel may have received exemption from observing that command for the drink offering until the time when they arrived in the promised land of Canaan.

Concerning the *time* when the drink offering was instituted and was brought by the Israelites, we cannot speak with certainty.

The same is true concerning the *manner* in which the drink offering was brought. The Hebrew term for drink offering, *nesekh*.

The question arises automatically as to *upon what* this offering was placed. Here as well Scripture provides no clear answer. Some think of pouring wine out on the ground, after first dabbing some on the inside of the altar of burnt offering. This was thought to be the case because the rest of the blood was poured out at the foot of the altar. But others have argued that such a view loses sight of the fact that blood and wine may not be considered as similar things. Blood was used for atonement. But not wine. To understand the meaning of wine as part of the grain offering and drink offering, we must take our starting point in Israel's own eating and drinking. Just as the bread, so too the wine was part of Israel's diet in Canaan. Both were the fruit of Israel's daily labor, and given by God to his people for their subsistence. Just as bread fortifies the human heart, so wine was given to gladden the human heart (Ps 104:15). This explains why both bread and wine could be brought to God as "grain offering" and "drink offering." They were often mentioned in the same breath. This included wine, "that cheers gods and mortals" (Judg 9:13). Together with the bread, the wine was supposed to be placed not beneath the altar but upon the altar. For bread and wine were tied together inseparably.

The wine would have been poured out on the altar, on the burning fat and meat of the atonement sacrifice, as well as on the burning bread; then to

THE GRAIN OFFERING (LEV 2)

the extent that it had not evaporated or been consumed, it would have been absorbed by the earth around the altar.

For the view claiming that the wine was not poured out beneath the altar, not even partially, but was placed upon the altar, we would point to the prohibition found in Exod 30:9. There we read about the golden altar of incense in the holy place. The prohibition reads: "and you shall not pour a drink offering on it." It emphatically says, "on it." When he used this expression in connection with the golden altar of incense (viz., pouring things on it) and gave this prohibition, God was probably thinking of the customary manner of bringing wine as a drink offering and placing it on the copper altar in the forecourt. If that was the case, then according to this verse the wine would have been poured out on, and not beneath, the altar of burnt offering.

All of this pertains to the wine offering that occurred in the forecourt.

But in the holy place wine was also brought to God. What was supposed to happen with that wine? We recall that the priests were not allowed to use alcoholic drink before performing their service (Lev 10:9). This use would then have been completely forbidden during their administering of the sacrifices. Consequently in connection with the drink offering things would not have transpired in the same way as with the grain offering. For part of the latter offering was given to the priests. But we assume that the wine from the drink offering, after having stood for a time in the cups and drink offering pitchers on the table of showbread, would have been poured out completely on the altar. The only altar used for this was the altar of burnt offering in the forecourt.

Regarding the *color* of the wine we find no prescription in Scripture. Some claim it was to be red, but there is no proof for that. Perhaps a mistakenly assumed parallel between the grain offering and the atonement offering may have led to this assumption.

In a moment, we will discuss the *quantities* of wine that had to be brought.

This brings us to the end of our discussion of the drink offering. There was not much that we could say about it, but enough for us to see that this drink offering represented a part of the fruit of Israel's labor before the face of God. Perhaps the drink offering was not in view in Leviticus 2. This would explain why we do not read about the drink offering what we do read concerning the grain offering, viz., that it was "an offering by fire of pleasing odor to Yahweh" (Lev 2:2). But that does not yet prove that this description did not apply to the drink offering. The drink offering may well have come under this classification. There is reason to believe that this in fact is what happened, for in Lev 23:18 we read that the burnt offerings together with the accompanying grain offerings and drink offerings constituted a fire offering that was "a pleasing aroma for Yahweh."

With regard to the grain offering we have discussed that part called the drink offering. If we set that aside, then we are left with the "dry" part of the grain offering, the grain offering in the narrow sense.

As we turn to discuss that now, we will employ a distinction between (1) the main component of the grain offering, and (2) the elements added to the grain offering.

(1) THE MAIN COMPONENT OF ISRAEL'S GRAIN OFFERING

This consisted of Israel's grain. Israel was an agrarian people. The main dish in their diet was surely not eating meat every day. Some Bible readers might be inclined to think that meat was central to Israel's diet, because they read so often in Scripture about the slaughtering and sacrificing of animals. But that was related to the ministry of the sanctuary. But Israel herself did not eat meat every day. As a result, Israel's grain offering consisted mainly of grain. Sometimes this is also called the food offering.

After virtually every bloody sacrifice, that is, the sacrifice of animals, there was a grain offering, except after a sin offering and a guilt offering. That was not surprising, because with these kinds of offerings the notion of atonement was prominent, so much so that it drew all the attention. I hope to comment on that in due time. Less explicit was the atoning character of the burnt offering and the peace offering. This feature was entirely absent from the grain offering and drink offering. With these latter two Israel was permitted to acknowledge gratitude to her God for the covenant and repeatedly receive atonement.

At Horeb and in the wilderness, it is likely that not very much occurred with regard to observing the commands for the grain offering. Israel had animals in its possession, for which they could find pasture from time to time in various oases. But Israel had no access to grain and flour, which explains the fact that God sustained his people by means of manna.

Nevertheless, at Horeb God did institute the grain offering, with which he was confirming again the promise that Israel would one day inherit the land of Canaan. Soon, within months, Israel would see acreage that was famous, among other things, for its grain harvests. For Canaan was a part of Syria, and Syria was one of the granaries of the ancient world. Unfortunately the trip from Horeb to Canaan took not months, but years. Those were years when faithful observance of the ministry that God had established at Horeb was not to be seen (Amos 5:25–27; Acts 7:42–43).

Israel was allowed to bring her grain offering to God in three ways. You can read extensively about this in Leviticus 2.

Dough was made from choice flour and oil, and this dough was baked, either as loaves in an oven or on a baking surface, or as one pastry, like a tart, in a pan. Next, either one loaf (Exod 29:23) or one of the parts that had been cut from it earlier was placed on the altar, after which all the rest was given to the priests (Lev 2:5–10).

The third possibility was that one brought ears of grain as an offering. They would take fresh ears of grain, roast them, peel them, and mix the resulting grain with oil. After offering a portion of this, the remainder was given to the priests (Lev 2:14–16).

What, then, was the significance of this grain offering?

By now the reader will have understood that the meaning did not lie in the atonement. No flour was needed for atonement, but blood was. By means of the grain offering what was being symbolized was not something that God gave to people but something that people gave to God, namely, a thankful and obedient heart and life. The grain offering symbolized the good works of faith. This will become clearer in what follows.

(2) THE ELEMENTS ADDED TO ISRAEL'S GRAIN OFFERING

a. In the first place we would mention the oil. We have discussed this before. Oil always referred to olive oil. The place that this olive oil enjoyed in ancient Near Eastern life is hard to overestimate.

It was used, for example, for anointing the body, such as the feet (Gen 28:18), or for tending to and healing wounds (Isa 1:6; Mark 6:13; Luke 10:34; Jas 5:14), and even mixed with aromatic spices to serve as a rejuvenating cream or as a scent with which guests would be welcomed (Ps 23:5; Luke 7:46), or also, a person would be identified as being called to an important task (1 Sam 10:1; 16:13; 1 Kgs 19:16).

But oil was used especially for preparing food (1 Kgs 17:12). Cakes prepared with oil were actually called "anointed" cakes (Lev 2:5; 7:12).

Oil served also as fuel for lamps (Matt 25:3). The wick of such a lamp was, so to speak, anointed with oil.

So we see a threefold use of oil, which we see in the ministry of Israel connected with God's tabernacle. Here indeed we may speak of a genuine parallel.

For first of all, not only the bodies of the priests, but also the tabernacle with the associated furnishings, was anointed with oil (Exod 29:22; Lev 8:10).

Next, in the forecourt the grain offerings (whether of dough or baked or ears of grain) were prepared with oil to be a pleasingly aromatic sacrifice (Lev 2:2).

Third, the most glorious oil sacrifice occurred with the lamps of the golden lampstand that stood in the holy place (Exod 27:20–21; 30:17).

We need not add very much to what we wrote in our commentary on Exodus about the significance of the oil.[2] The oil served to symbolize the Holy Spirit.

b. Incense was always added to the grain offering. The reason for that was obvious. Burning incense causes a penetrating odor that we recognize from burning resins. God had a high regard for this burning of incense. A relatively small portion of the grain offering was burned on the altar (the rest was for the priests, and the loaves of showbread were entirely for the priests), but all the incense of the grain offerings, including that which was laid on the table of showbread, had to be burned (Lev 24:7). The reason for this would have been that incense could not be consumed as food, but especially that worship belonged exclusively to God.

For incense symbolized prayer, the highest expression of worshiping God. In Ps 141:2 prayer itself is described this way: "Let my prayer be counted as incense before you." When Zechariah carried the incense sacrifice into the temple, we read: "And the whole multitude of the people were praying outside at the hour of incense" (Luke 1:20). The four living creatures and the twenty-four elders of Revelation 5 fell down before the Lamb, "each holding a harp, and golden bowls full of incense, which are the prayers of the saints" (Rev 5:8). The prayers of the saints, according to Rev 8:3, rise to heaven like a cloud of incense (cf. Isa 6:3–4).

So the grain offering symbolized the good works of believers.

Incense symbolized believing prayer.

A grain offering may never omit incense.

Only through our believing prayer, our good works become acceptable before God, because in that praying we appeal to Jesus Christ, our High Priest, who mediates for us with the Father.

c. The last ingredient that must accompany every grain offering was salt. Undoubtedly God was again making use of an internationally understood concept, when at Horeb he provided his people Israel a special covenant foundation in the Torah, and prescribed *salt for the grain offering.*

---

2. See Vonk, *Exodus*, 237.

THE GRAIN OFFERING (LEV 2)

Along the same ancient route, from times long ago, both incense and salt were exported by Arabia (Isa 60:6; Jer 6:20). Israel was familiar with salt mining near the Dead Sea (Zeph 2:9). A location in that region was called Ir-Hammelach (*'ir-hammelach*), or Salt City (Josh 15:62). There was always salt in Assyrian temples. Persian officials who tried to reproach Ezra before king Artaxerxes, demonstrated their loyalty by saying, "we eat the salt of the palace" (Ezra 4:14). The Greeks were familiar with the ceremony of eating bread with salt when making a covenant. The salt payment of Roman soldiers was called *salarium* (from *sal*, which means *salt*, which later was used for money, which explains the meaning of *soldij*, the Dutch word for *payment*). Scripture also speaks of a covenant of salt (Num 18:19; 2 Chron 13:5), and we read in Leviticus 2 itself: "You shall season all your grain offerings with salt. You shall not let the salt of the covenant with your God be missing from your grain offering; with all your offerings you shall offer salt" (v. 13). For the Israelites, the symbolism would have resided here, seeing the common use of salt in the life of ancient peoples, especially in making covenants, treaties, and contracts. Salt would have represented fidelity. Salt would have symbolized the promise that one would refrain from infidelity and breaking one's word. This explains why our Savior said, when speaking to his disciples about their duty in the future of denying themselves ("cutting off" hands, "plucking out" eyes, when it came to facing temptations to sin and unchastity): "For everyone will be salted with fire" (Mark 9:49). With these words he would have been alluding to the altar fire and altar salt of the Torah, both of which gave visual symbolic expression to the one bringing the offering of God's requirement of fidelity and purity of heart. This would have made people think all the more of Leviticus 2, because in this chapter immediately preceding the command regarding salt we find the prohibition against leaven and honey (Lev 2:11–12). We'll say more about this in a moment.

Even though this leads us to think of the direct connection in Leviticus 2 to the required uprightness and faithfulness among Israel as God's covenant people, we would not wish to exclude the possibility that at the same time God was thinking of other properties of salt when he commanded its use with every grain offering. Perhaps the feature of the salt's tastiness was also in view, the flavor that salt gave to the food being offered. As a result, we find in Scripture comments about empty talk being "tasteless talk" (Job 6:6; Col 4:6). Perhaps we might recall the occasion when Elisha said: "Bring me a bowl, and put salt in it." The servants did so, and Elisha took it to the well, threw the salt into the water, and said: "Thus says the Lord, I have healed this water; from now on neither death nor miscarriage shall come from it" (2 Kgs 2:20–22). Surely with this symbolic action that he performed

PART 2 | THE SACRIFICIAL TORAH: SPECIFIC REQUIREMENTS

with the salt, Elisha would have been alluding to the purifying work of salt. Thereby it could be used to symbolize resisting impurity and decay. Little wonder, then, that God viewed this ingredient of the grain offering as referring to Israel's calling to keep the covenant uprightly in all of life—the grain offering represented Israel's labor and daily bread—a covenant with which God had honored Israel in such a regal manner at Horeb.

While every grain offering had to include salt, the elements of leaven and honey were definitely forbidden. Just before the command about the salt, we read the prohibition about leaven and honey. That sequence would not have been accidental. According to Israelite understanding, leaven and honey would have stood approximately in the same opposition to oil, incense, and salt, as flesh and Spirit are opposed in the New Testament, or the old man against the new man.

For the Israelites, the prohibition against using leaven with the grain offering would have been something automatic. They would have understood the purpose of that prohibition immediately. For them, the use of leaven had been forbidden with the exodus from Egypt. At that time they had to eat unleavened bread (Exod 12:8; 13:7). The biblical leaven or yeast is not to be confused with the yeast that required a day or more for baking bread. When we think about how quickly in our own part of the world, during the warm summer months, food can spoil, we can readily understand how badly a portion of dough would stink in hot regions like Egypt and Palestine. And yet, such an old portion of dough that had become thoroughly sour could be useful. When it was put in with new dough, for example, the new would begin to ferment and to rise, and one could get a pastry that was far lighter and more digestible than if it had been baked without that "old" dough or leaven. So in Scripture, the term *leaven* did not always have an unfavorable meaning. Understandably so. For it could also serve as an image for the powerful working of good as well as evil. Recall the Lord's parable of the woman who with a small amount of yeast was able to get a large quantity of dough to rise. She took three measures of meal, the Savior said, which was a ratio of 40 to 1. But in the same way, the Lord Jesus was saying, the world would soon be turned upside down by the simple preaching of the apostles (Matt 13:33). This was something good.

Nevertheless, the image of leaven appears most often in Scripture with a negative connotation. In 1 Corinthians 5, for example. There the apostle alludes to the duty of the Israelites to see to it that from the 15th to the 22nd of the first month, their bread was unleavened. Leviticus 23:6–8 discusses this (the feast of unleavened bread). When there was a man in Corinth who belonged to the church of the Lord there and who had married a woman who had been the wife (or one of them?) of his own (deceased?) father, and

THE GRAIN OFFERING (LEV 2)

Paul learned about this, he was so upset that he wrote: "Do you not know that a little leaven leavens the whole lump?" (1 Cor 5:6). This passage is almost identical to Gal 5:9. When writing such words, the apostle Paul must surely have recalled the Law with its prohibition against leaven being used with the grain offering. Just like our Savior, when he warned his disciples for "the leaven of the Pharisees and Sadducees." He used the word "leaven" with reference to their wicked teaching and their wicked living, as well as their dangerous influence often exercised through doctrine and life by respectable religious people.

We can say the following about the honey.

As an ingredient, God would have kept honey far away from his grain offering for the same reason as leaven. For later the Israelites would have been allowed to bring the first fruits of their honey harvest to the sanctuary (though it would not be placed on the altar, but enjoyed by the priests, 2 Chr 31:5). That was fine. Just like the first loaves coming from the grain harvest were brought at the feast of Pentecost (which were leavened, also to be enjoyed by the priests, Lev 23:17). That was something different (Lev 2:12). But honey was disallowed as an ingredient of any grain offering, and as something to be placed on the altar.

In this respect, in the Torah God was pointing Israel in a direction that was entirely different than that of pagan worship practices. For Egyptians, Assyrians, and Canaanites did offer honey to their gods. So Israel would surely have understood clearly what God was intending with these measures that we find in Lev 2:12. Notice the command in the next verse about using salt (2:13), and notice the fact that in the preceding verse (2:11) leaven was forbidden. This was because the date-palm resin that was in view caused rapid fermentation and thus spoilage. We too would properly understand God's intention with his prohibition of honey if we were to see in it God's disapproval of everything that swarmed around death and decay. Honey and leaven would for that same reason have been just as unpleasant to God in the grain offering as physical defects and any remaining excrement of the animals that were offered to him as sacrifices. Because he had and has no delight in rottenness and stench, but in purity and life.

For believers in our own day, the teaching about Israel's grain offering contains more than one lesson. These instructions teach us to know God. To know what pleases him and what he hates. And what is fitting for us with respect to him. Notice especially the contrast between the prohibition of leaven and honey, and the command for oil, incense, and salt. Israel's grain offering—symbol of the fruit of their labor—had to be pure, the demonstration of a heart that was upright and faithful toward their God of the covenant. But this good God was also just as holy, so that even the grain offerings of the most holy were not allowed to be brought to God without oil, incense, and salt. So too in our day. For when our best works are always accompanied by faithfulness to God's covenant, this happens because they are inseparably joined to the oil of the Spirit of Christ, who has been given to us from the Father, and with the incense of our prayer that God would look upon our very best works not as though coming directly from us, but as made sweet smelling by the perfect obedience of our Savior demonstrated long ago upon earth, and with the constant prayer with which he intercedes for us above, with the Father. For then these good works are similar to Israel's grain offering, "an offering with a pleasing aroma to Yahweh."

Having reached this point in our discussion of the grain offering, the time has come for us to keep our promise that we would discuss the *quantities of wine* that were offered to God in the drink offering. The quantity of flour, oil, and wine used in the grain offering and the drink offering are discussed in Numbers 15, but we wish to review them here, for the following reasons.

By whom were these quantities, the amounts of the ingredients of the grain offering and the drink offering specified?

By the one bringing the offering? In terms of his economic ability, for example? Or by his inner sense of gratitude toward God? Or by his great love toward him? Or were one or another quantity determined by the immensity of his sin? Or the depth of his penitence?

If any of these questions were to be answered affirmatively, the quantities of the ingredients of the drink offering and the grain offering would have depended on something human. On a subjective consideration.

So the answer must not be affirmative, but rather negative. Those quantities depended only on the kind of sacrificial animal that was slaughtered and sacrificed in connection with the grain offering. For that is how it usually went. The grain offering usually followed the bloody sacrifice.

By means of this sequence, the influence of the human factor was minimized.

Should someone ask how the kind and size of the sacrificial animal was to be determined, we would quickly answer that in this respect as well, little or nothing was left to human arbitrariness. Not even in connection with the sin offering. We will come back to that, of course. But now we wish to direct the attention of Bible readers to the fact that in the sacrificial Torah, all subjectivity was excluded *at least in terms of the relationship between the ingredients of the animal offerings, the grain offerings, and the drink offerings.* Those relationships were specified not by people, but by God. In this way:

THE GRAIN OFFERING (LEV 2)

Cattle	3/10 ephah of flour	1/10 hin of oil	1/10 hin of wine
Ram	2/10 ephah of flour	1/3 hin of oil	1/3 hin of wine
Sheep or goat	1/10 ephah of flour	1/4 hin of oil	1/4 hin of wine

Scholars are not entirely agreed about the size of the measurements mentioned in the list above. Presumably the content of an ephah was 22.9 liters (about 6 gallons), and of a hin, 3.83 liters (about 1 gallon).

But everyone can see one thing clearly from this list: the quantities of flour, oil, and wine increase or decrease according to the size of the animal. Everything was regulated. Even to the point of requiring that a bit more flour, oil, and wine be used with the sacrifice of the male sheep, than with a female sheep.

You will likely have noticed that our list does not include the quantities of incense and salt. We could not include those, because we read about them nowhere in the Law. We do read that they were to be added and when they were to be added, but not how much was to be added. Did the absence of any information about this tell Israel something? For example, that the Israelites were permitted to offer to God as much salt (symbol of faithfulness) and as much incense (symbol of prayer) as they wanted? We simply don't know.

When someone in Israel went to the tabernacle and brought a grain offering to God there, he was not to imagine that his grain offering was placed on the altar in its entirety. Or virtually in its entirety. Not at all. Rather, the opposite was the case. The largest portion was not burned but went to the priests.

All of the incense, however, did end up on the altar. That was entirely burned up. Earlier we explained why this presumably occurred. Because all worship belonged to God alone. We have also indicated the assumption that the same thing happened with the wine. Finally, it could have happened that the grain offering was not brought by an ordinary member of the congregation, but by one of the priests himself. It was obvious that from such a grain offering made by a priest, no portion, let alone the largest portion, would have gone to the priests.

Otherwise, the grain offering in the narrower sense, that is, without the incense and wine, was largely for the priests. That was their honorarium. That is reported to us in the New Testament by none other than the apostle Paul. In 1 Corinthians 9 he is discussing his authority, as a preacher of the gospel, to be cared for by the church of Corinth. He writes: Don't you know that they who perform ministry in the sanctuary, eat from the sanctuary, and they who serve at the altar receive their portion from the altar? The

PART 2 | THE SACRIFICIAL TORAH: SPECIFIC REQUIREMENTS

Lord also established the rule for those who proclaim the gospel that they were to live from the gospel (1 Cor 9:13–14). We know that this rule was indeed given by our Lord Jesus Christ, in such declarations as Matt 10:10: "for the laborer deserves his food." But the apostle Paul clothed his recollection of that teaching in a garment with a strikingly Old Testament color.

How large, then, was the grain offering that was placed on the altar?

It was never all that large. In the case of an offering of dough, for example, only a handful of dough was put on the altar, and when the grain offering consisted of cakes, then only one cake was placed on the altar. The rest was for the priests. When we review the list above, we will see that rather significant quantities of food were given to the priests.

Nevertheless, the priests were not free, on account of this abundance, to use their income from the grain offerings carelessly. They were always to remember that these were "most holy" wages. The same was true of the entire tabernacle and its furnishings (the ark, the table of showbread, etc.). That portion that the priests received from the grain offering of the members of the congregation was also called "most holy." So they were to eat it only "in a holy place," viz., not outside the tabernacle perimeter (Lev 6:16).

What explains that especially exalted holiness?

The fact that earlier, a *portion* of this grain offering had been sacrificed to Yahweh. In this manner the *entire* grain offering had been devoted to him. Once again we have a rule to which the apostle Paul referred. For in Rom 11:16 he wrote: If the dough offered as firstfruits is holy, so is the whole lump."

When someone in Israel went to the tabernacle and brought a grain offering there, he saw a very small portion of his sacrifice, at least as a grain offering in the narrow sense, end up on the altar of God. But that need not have grieved him. For not only was his entire grain offering elevated to something holy by the sacrifice of that small portion. But his grain offering was not to leave the holy place, by being taken, for example, to the home and family of the priest. Moreover, the small portion that had been sacrificed earlier on his behalf by the priest as an *azkarah*, that is, as a "memorial offering" (Lev 2:2, 9, 16). The verb *zakar* ("to remember") that belongs to the noun *azkarah* appears in Exodus 28 as well, where we read that the high priest had to carry on his shoulders the two stones on which were written the names of the twelve sons of Jacob (v. 12), and similarly, he had to wear on his breastplate twelve stones with these same names, when he entered the sanctuary, "before the Lord on his two shoulders for remembrance" (v. 29). Nehemiah also used this verb when he asked if God was willing *to remember* the good that he had done for Israel, for the house of his God, and for his precepts (Neh 5:19; 13;14, 22, 31). People in Israel would pray

THE GRAIN OFFERING (LEV 2)

for one another that God "would *remember* all your offerings" (Ps 20:3). And we might mention from the New Testament that the angel assured Cornelius: your prayers and alms have come to God's *remembrance* (Acts 10:4). We also recall that the dejected Israelites must not suppose that their good works did not continue in God's memory. "For God is not unjust so as to overlook your work and the love that you have shown for his name in serving the saints, as you still do" (Heb 6:10).

By means of the grain offering and drink offering, God wanted to assure and instruct his people Israel that he took great pleasure in their keeping his covenant in their daily living and in their remembering to keep his commandments. Thinking of this, the apostle Peter urged his readers who had recently become Christians, "to be a holy priesthood, to offer spiritual sacrifices acceptable to God through Jesus Christ" (1 Pet 2:5; the term *spiritual* is equivalent to *Christian*).

7

The peace offering (Lev 3)

Our older readers will not recall from older Bible versions the name of this sacrifice that appears above as the title of this chapter. It does not appear in those versions. The kind of offering that we are now going to discuss were identified in older Bible versions as "thank offerings." But the new translations used the phrase "peace offering." We have also chosen this latter rendering.

People came up with the older phrase ("thank offering") on account of such Scripture passages as Ps 50:14: "Offer to God a sacrifice of thanksgiving, and perform [*shallem*] your vows to the Most High." The Hebrew word for these sacrifices was *zavach shelamim*, occasionally shortened to *shelamim* (Num 15:8; Deut 27:7), appearing once as *shelem* (Amos 5:22), and elsewhere simply called *zevach* (Deut 12:27; 18:3).

The word *zevach* meant sacrifice, and in the word *shelamim* we have the verb to *shelem*, which meant to be whole, to be complete; the verb *shallem* meant to make whole, to make complete, to pay. In view of these meanings, earlier translations and commentators rendered these as "thank offering."

But another view is the translation of "peace offering" better expresses the meaning. It is more suitable for all the passages, including those where the rendering of "thank offering" would not fit well. For example, when we read that Israel prayed for deliverance while in distress, and in that context brought "burnt offerings and *shelamim*" (Judg 20:26; 21:24; 1 Sam 13:9), one can hardly translate that latter word (*shelamim*) as "thank offering." The phrase "peace offering" fits much better. For that fit the situation better. For that had been a need, even though there was nothing deficient about the

THE PEACE OFFERING (LEV 3)

good relationship between God and those who were bringing the sacrifice. Therefore the phrase "peace offerings" fits better at this point.

Moreover, everyone has heard that there the Hebrew words *shelem* and *shalom* are related. The former was the term for a kind of sacrifice, which we are discussing here, and the latter meant "peace." But we must remember that the word for peace (*shalom*) had a much wider meaning in Israel than among us. With the word "peace" we all too often think of the situation where there is no war, but the Hebrew word *shalom* meant much more, namely, that everything was good. There life was lovely. That there was happiness and prosperity. That relationships were whole. Apparently the meaning of the term for the kind of sacrifice we are discussing lay in this direction as well. It communicated that things were good between Yahweh and the person bringing the sacrifice. There was a relationship of *shalom*. This word leads us and Bible scholars to recall the name of Solomon, the prince of peace.

The phrase "peace offering" was actually a composite term. This term referred to an entire group of sacrifices. At least three sacrifices. We must investigate this further.

In the first place, such a peace offering could be more specifically a *praise offering* (Lev 7:13, 15). When you read the Bible, you will encounter these kinds of peace offerings often. They were frequently brought out of gratitude for blessings enjoyed. Recall Psalm 116: What shall I render to Yahweh for all his benefits to me? I will pay my vows to Yahweh in the presence of all his people (vv. 12, 14).

Next, a peace offering could be more of a *votive offering*. Such a vow was absent with the former, the praise offering. Praise offerings were brought out of gratitude for a good harvest and at feasts (Lev 9:18; 23:19, 37–38; Num 29:39; Deut 12:6; Josh 8:31; 1 Kgs 8:63). But when someone was paying a vow to God that after receiving from him this or that benefit he would render a sacrifice to him, that was a votive offering. People were not permitted to make such vows and then not honor them (Num 30:3; Deut 23:22). We recall Ps 50:14: "Offer to God a sacrifice of thanksgiving [*todah*], and perform your vows [*nedareikha*] to the Most High." Here both of them are mentioned, the praise offering and the votive offering. At the same time, we see here that we should not separate the praise offerings and votive offerings like an accountant. We saw this a moment ago in Psalm 116, where they were also mentioned together.

In the third place, there was also the *freewill* offering, (You can find all three mentioned in Lev 7:11–12.) The addition of "freewill" did not mean that the first sacrifice, the praise offering, was involuntary, for no praise offering was involuntary, but the addition was related to the second offering mentioned, the votive offering. The last two offerings, the votive offering and the freewill offering (*neder* and *nedabah*) corresponded with each other. In Lev 7:16 they are mentioned in the same breath, and in distinction from the praise offering that precedes them. But there was a difference. Someone who earlier had made a vow—and he had done so voluntarily, of course—was automatically obligated to pay it later. As a result, there was nothing involuntary about the votive offering. That was not the case with the third offering, however. This explains why *this* offering, in contrast to the votive offering, received the special name of *freewill offering*. Consequently, the difference between the last two sacrifices was this, that in the case of the votive offering, one brought that sacrifice only after receiving the benefit envisioned, but in the case of a freewill offering, one brought that beforehand. Perhaps someone had asked in his prayer that God would grant this or that benefit, but instead of waiting to bring his offering when the prayer was answered, he instead brought his sacrifice right away. As if he were reinforcing his prayer.

What was the uniqueness, the special character, of all of the peace offerings? What received the emphasis in connection with the peace offerings?

Was that perhaps the atonement?

Absolutely not. To be sure, the same actions preceded the peace offering that would have occurred with the slaughter of every sacrificial animal: leading the animal to the priest, placing the hand on its head, slaughtering the animal and retrieving its blood. As we saw earlier, all of that proclaimed the justification of the sinner. Consequently, the peace offering also spoke of atonement, to the extent that it had in common those initial actions connected with every bloody sacrifice. But the burnt offering was the same. So that did not constitute the uniqueness of the peace offering.

So too with *sanctification*. Later we will see that part of the peace offering was burned up, even quite a bit of it, so that according to the rule, part for the whole, the animal brought for peace offering was offered to God, namely, on the wings of the fire. But this happened with the sin offering as well (as we will see later), and happened 100 percent with the burnt offering (as we have already seen). So the uniqueness of the peace offering did not consist of that.

So there remains the third benefit of redemption: *glorification*.

The uniqueness of the peace offering was the Paradisal element that it contained. By means of the peace offering, Israel was being taught and assured regarding the promise of that beautiful future when there would be perfect peace between God and his people. The absolutely unique character of the peace offering surfaced in the meal that was always connected with it. A meal that was offered by God as the Host to the Israelite as his guest. That did not happen with any other sacrifice. So we must pay attention especially to that feature.

When a peace offering was brought, a complete *distribution* of the sacrificial animal occurred. By whom? By God. The Israelite bringing the sacrifice gave the sacrificial animal to him. The one bringing the offering had to approach him (Lev 3:1). So the distribution was guided by God. He divided the peace offering animal into three portions, this way: one portion was for himself, a second portion was for the priesthood, and the rest was given to the one bringing the offering, the Israelite himself. We will say something about each of those three portions.

1. THE PORTION DESIGNATED FOR YAHWEH

All of the fat was for God. We understand what this meant immediately when we recall a familiar expression in Scripture like "the fat of the land," which refers to the best products (Gen 45:18), "the finest of wheat," referring to the best wheat (Deut 32:14; Ps 81:16), and "the best of the oil and the best of the wine" (Num 18:12). "The fat of the mighty" were the warriors of the first rank (2 Sam 1:22; cf. Judg 3:29; Ps 78:31; Isa 10:6), and "the fat of the land" were the preeminent and noble (Ps 22:29; cf. 65:12–13).

Four was the number of the pieces of fat that were burned on the altar, namely, first, the fat around the entrails; second, the fat around the heart; third, the fat around the kidney—items that every butcher is familiar with—and fourth, the fat surrounding the liver, called "the long lobe of the liver," which was to be removed along with the kidneys (Lev 3:3–4).

If this is accurate, perhaps with this regulation God wanted to protect his people Israel from the familiar pagan practices associated with the liver of sacrificial animals. From remote India to Rome, the liver of a sacrificial animal was used in connection with divination. In Mesopotamia this form of divination had developed into a full-blown technology, adopted by Etruscans, Greeks, and Romans. To make interpreting the liver easier, models were made out of clay or bronze. A large number of those models were discovered at the excavations in Mari. The prophet Ezekiel describes for us the king of Babylon standing before a decision. Should he embark against Rabbah of the Ammonites, and destroy him, or should he march against Jerusalem? "He looks at the liver," we read (Ezek 21:21).

Similar to what God had done in many respects at Horeb, by enlisting a number of the religious customs of the pagans, in what God was prescribing about the liver, or at least part of it, perhaps he was calling a stop to the inclination for divination that was very real among Eastern peoples and

PART 2 | THE SACRIFICIAL TORAH: SPECIFIC REQUIREMENTS

possibly among Israel, one that was far more relevant than we today could imagine. The best part of the entire animal, indeed, the best part of the liver, had to be burned.

Whatever the case may be, the fat belonged to God and had to be burned. We said earlier that this had to occur on, on top of, the altar (Lev 3:5).

The emphasis that God placed on the offering that all the fat be given to him has led in this chapter of Leviticus 3 to an interesting digression. It involves the case of someone who would want to bring a *sheep* as a peace offering animal. With the choice of animals for their peace offerings, the Israelites enjoyed far more freedom than with their burnt offerings, for example, their choice was always limited, of course, to clean animals, such as animals from a flock. But then it could be large livestock, like cattle, but also small livestock, like sheep and goats. For the peace offering they did not need to use only male animals as sacrificial animals, as was the case by contrast for the burnt offering, but offering female animals was permitted for the peace offering. Not only bulls, but also cows, not only bucks, but also a doe. For the peace offering it was required that the animals used had no defects (Lev 22:22, 24), but even this requirement had an exception. At least for one kind of peace offering, the so-called freewill offering. For freewill offerings, we read this permission: "You may present a bull or a lamb that has a part too long or too short for a freewill offering" (Lev 22:23). As we can see, in various ways, things were made easy for someone who wanted to come into the presence of Yahweh in the tabernacle to celebrate a peace offering meal. Except we do not read that people were allowed to use doves for the peace offering. But that was logical, because a dove provided far too little to eat. You couldn't make a festive meal with doves.

And now the interesting digression about the sheep.

Entirely differently than our European and North American sheep, a sheep in Palestine had to have an incredibly fat tail. That could weigh as much as seven kilograms (more than fifteen pounds). Even today, such a fatty tail is still today a delicacy among the farming populace. However, that a sheep in Palestine back in those days would have had such a remarkably fat tail can be seen from the terracotta figurines of sheep from ancient times. The sculptors of those appeared to have enjoyed replicating especially the sheep's fat tail.

This explains why, in Leviticus 3, an entirely distinct section is devoted to the case where a sheep was brought as a peace offering. Three sets of instructions are given. The first involves the offering of an *ox* (vv. 1–5), the second, a *sheep* (vv. 6–11), and the third, a *goat* (vv. 12–15). The latter two sets would have corresponded to the extent that a sheep and a goat resemble one another anatomically. But on account of the sheep's fatty tail, a separate set of instructions had to be given for the offering of *this* animal. For the fatty tail would have to be cut off rather close to the spine! So that all the fat could be sacrificed to Yahweh.

(For the same reason, when we come to the sin offering in Leviticus 4, we will find a separate section regulating the case of bringing not a goat [vv. 27–31] but a sheep [vv. 32–35].)

Always the very best was for God.

2. THE PORTION DESIGNATED FOR THE PRIESTS

After the fat had been offered to God, the priests of Yahweh were the next to receive their share. For they stood alongside him. That became evident in the two pieces of the sacrificial animal that were theirs. For there were two pieces, first, the breast, for the entire priesthood; and second, the shank, for the officiating priest.

The breast belonged to the tastier parts of the ox, sheep, or goat. This was rather fatty. It was surely for this reason that precisely this piece of the peace offering animal was assigned to the priest. For the four premier fatty pieces had been sacrificed to Yahweh as the best of everything. But the next in quality had to be given to those who were allowed to approach Yahweh most intimately. And that would be the priests (Lev 7:31).

But the shank that we mentioned was especially for the officiating priest. As a personal honorarium for his ministry at the altar, which included sprinkling the blood, for example. This shank was the hind quarter, just as with the burnt offering, the right hind quarter (Lev 7:32). For an understandable reason, because the right side was considered the more honorable (Gen 48:14).

The question could be raised here whether in these regulations consideration was given perhaps to what was customary in the pagan temples all around in that day. Some scholars claim that the pagan priests always received the right hind leg. If so, then here again we have a remarkable difference between the *cultus* of Yahweh and that of the pagans. Perhaps with these instructions, without much change but in a manner that could be easily understood by those acquainted with such practices, because Yahweh wanted to have people sense his sovereignty in the worship he had prescribed at Horeb, he adapted much that was customary among the pagans while in some respects distancing himself in very striking ways.

We just mentioned as the two portions of the peace offering animal that were designated for the priests, first, the breast, and second, the shank (Lev 7:30, 32).

Presumably many a Bible reader has often wondered what was being signified by this. We will try to answer that question, though we must say at the outset that on account of the absence of adequate data in Scripture, we cannot speak with complete certainty. But the following strikes us as acceptable.

The word "wave" was used as an adjective of the noun "breast," to suggest a certain movement performed by the priest, in the direction of the tabernacle and back. This was the "wave offering" (*tenuphah*), or a kind of weaving, whereby the hands were moved back and forth. By means of this back-and-forth movement of the breast in the direction of the tabernacle—for we read: "before Yahweh" (Lev 7:30)—was the recognition by the priesthood that they were not involved in a reciprocal exchange, but in receiving their rightful share from what lawfully belonged to Yahweh. They were acknowledging that they lived from the hand of God and not the hand of people. Yahweh was Levi's inheritance. The priests received their share of the peace offering not directly from the hand of the Israelites, their brothers, but along a kind of detour. Along God's detour. The entire animal was surrendered and carried first to God. And only then did Yahweh grant to each party their portion. To his priests first.

The "waving" was part of that detour.

Presumably the word "heave" (as in the older expression, "heave offering") was as well.

The Hebrew word of "heave" was used as well for the priests bringing the memorial offering (Lev 2:8). This, however, was laid on the altar. But occasionally the word "heave" (*terumah*) was used for gifts that people gave to God without those being placed on the altar, and such a "heaving" (*terumah*) was also called a "waving" (*tenuphah*) (Exod 25:2; 35:22), from which it follows that there was no difference between the two. The intention would have been the same. Nevertheless, when the breast was involved, there was always talk of "waving," and when the shank was involved, of "heaving." The small difference would have consisted in this, that the moving of the *wave breast* occurred in the direction of the tabernacle and back, while the heaving of the *thigh* occurred in the direction of heaven and back. Tabernacle and heaven would both have been viewed as God's dwelling places.

That God, then, granted from his own possession not merely something for the priesthood in general, namely, the wave breast, but granted a special gift to that priest who had performed this specific sacrificial ministry, namely, the shank, designated for the officiating priest (Lev 7:33).

By means of the *first* gift, that of the breast, to all the priests, the priestly privilege was being honored in general. The breast was a precious piece of meat. Therefore it was for those who stood next to God. For the priests.

THE PEACE OFFERING (LEV 3)

But by means of the *second* gift, that of the thigh, for the priest who had performed the sacrificial ministry, God wanted to honor in a special way the priestly work and effort.

3. THE REMAINDER FOR THE ONE BRINGING THE OFFERING

The peace offering was in every respect a joyous sacrifice. It provided joy to everyone involved. To Yahweh, for whom the best was given. To his priests, for whom the next best was given. And to his people, that had enough left over for celebrating a joyous feast. A feast under the gaze of Israel's God. In the shadow of his palace on earth. That visible proof of his favor in dwelling among Israel. And of his grand plan that one day he would bring back the joy of Paradise and enjoy it together with his redeemed humanity.

With the peace offering, heavy emphasis fell on the meal.

We mentioned earlier that the occasion for eating well was arranged as openly as possible. For example, with the choosing of the sacrificial animal for the peace offering, the details were not as specific as with other offerings.

But there was still more that was done especially to advance the success of a peace offering meal.

As you will recall, there were three kinds of peace offerings. The praise offering was the most important. For that reason, God had stipulated that the associate meal was to be eaten exclusively on the first day. That is, on the day the animal was slaughtered. Not later (Lev 7:15; 22:29–30). But with the other two peace offerings, the votive offering and the freewill offering, the situation was different. The associated meals could be eaten on the day after the day of slaughter, a period of two days (Lev 7:16). But not thereafter. The meat that was left over on the third day would have to be burned. Understandably so. Israel lived, both in the wilderness and in Canaan, in a warm climate, whereby the meat of slaughtered animals spoiled quickly. That was not only dangerous for those consuming it, but also detestable for God, who has an aversion to sin and all its consequences, including decay and death (Lev 7:18). For the same reason, the meat of the peace offering meal was not to be eaten by someone who was "unclean." Nor was this meat itself to be unclean (Lev 7:19–20). (We will discuss this defilement in connection with Leviticus 11–15.) But further, the possibility of participating in the peace offering meal was arranged as openly as possible, in order to heighten the festive joy.

That could be seen clearly in the loaves.

At other times, every grain offering that was coupled with a bloody sacrifice had to be prepared *without leaven*. The reader will recall this.

Nevertheless God had made one exception to that strict rule. For celebrating the peace offering meal. There the loaves could be leavened. So then, not the loaves that were placed on the altar. On Israel's altar no leaven was ever to be sacrificed. At all. But we have also seen how small a portion of the grain offering was placed on the altar (the memorial offering). So then, one loaf of each kind of pastry that was offered to Yahweh in the peace-grain offering had to be unleavened (Lev 7:12, 14). But all the other loaves that people prepared for the sacrificial meals could be leavened and thus the dough could rise and become tastier. This was permitted with a view to enhancing their enjoyment of the peace offering meal.

Everything pointed to the special character of the peace offering, which would become visible in the meal that was connected to it. That would surely have impacted Eastern people like the Israelites far more than us. With the grain offering we saw that whenever you had salt fellowship with someone, this signified that you stood in a covenant relationship with that person. The same was true if you had table fellowship with someone. The Egyptians did not eat meals "with the Hebrews" (Gen 43:32). The Jews did not eat meals with the Gentiles (Gal 2:12). The suggestion has been made that the familiar Hebrew word for "covenant," namely, *bĕrît*, would have been a cognate of the Hebrew word for "eat," namely, *barah*. Then *berith* would mean a fellowship meal. But it is also clear that *berith* means something close to "bond of fellowship," because the establishing of a covenant formed a circle that included both parties. The Hebrew word for "covenant" would then be related to the Assyrian word *biritu*, which means "fetter."

When celebrating a peace offering meal, Israel did so based on the premise that God had made her his covenant people at Horeb. Rather: it was God himself who had placed Israel on a special foundation at Horeb, the One who had instituted in the sacrificial Torah the celebration of such a sacrificial meal, thereby obligating his people to keep his covenant. From everything taught here, we can see that the meal at which that celebrating of the covenant occurred must have been an especially joyful meal.

Not that the notion of atonement was completely foreign to the peace offering. That notion was certainly part of every bloody sacrifice. Then as now. Without the atoning blood of Christ we could not exist for one day before God. From the animal connected with the peace offering, some blood was always sprinkled on the altar in the forecourt. But nevertheless the idea of atonement was certainly not in the foreground with the peace offering (completely different than with the sin offering and the grain offering, which we will discuss later).

No, the peace offering was brought when things were good between God and his own people. When nothing was wrong. At least nothing bad.

THE PEACE OFFERING (LEV 3)

But the peace offering was brought by the Israelite when he could appear before Yahweh with a clear conscience, and say to him: I walk in my uprightness, I wash my hands in innocence, I do not consort with people who commit this or that evil. I have no delight in that. But I do delight in your service, O Yahweh. Therefore I appear at your altar. For this confession of faith, see Psalms 26, 44:17–18, and 119:176.

We can learn from that.

On account of their struggle with the Roman Catholic Church, our ancestors saw themselves compelled to place a very heavy emphasis on the truth that absolutely nothing of ourselves can contribute to our salvation. Notice how emphatically they do this, for example, in the first section of the Heidelberg Catechism (concerning human misery). But the intention of that first section was not, of course, that in every situation, in season and out of season, we would have to lament about our sins. There must be concrete reasons for doing so, which we set before God reverently. Otherwise such lamenting becomes simply a pose, affectation, and we don't know what to do with Psalms 26, 44, and the like. No, our confession in Section 1 of the Heidelberg Catechism (that our salvation cannot proceed from us in even the tiniest way) has the purpose to prepare us immediately for Section 2, where we confess that our Savior Jesus Christ is not a partial savior, but *a complete Savior*. That last claim was challenged fiercely by the opponents of our forefathers!

It is appropriate now as well that we always approach God first of all with thanksgiving in our hearts for the historical fact that we are heirs of the kingdom of God and of his covenant. Christ commanded us to address God this way: "*Our Father* who art in heaven." We may never bring this address into discredit in our subsequent prayer, and of course, also not in our conversations, our preaching, etc. We may never render this approach dubious or questionable, for that doubt is like a wave of the sea (Jas 1:6).

Standing and proceeding on that foundation (placed by God himself under our feet, when as yet we did not know him; just like God in fact took Abraham into his covenant, Gen 15:12, 18), we approach God, no, not always to confess this or that sin. Israel did not do that either. Israel did not always bring only sin offerings, but once in awhile brought peace offerings. Why? If there is nothing wrong between God and us, at least, nothing sinful, then something entirely different can be going on.

For example, in Israel someone was very sick. He thought he would die any moment. Therefore he prayed: O, Yahweh, deliver my *nefesh* (Ps 116:4). In our modern prayer language, that means: O, heavenly Father, let me live awhile longer, please.

Now, God had heard that Israelite's prayer, and permitted him to walk awhile longer "in the land of the living" (Ps 116:9). The psalmist added: "before the Lord." Would our heavenly Father not do well if he were to have us rise from our sickbed to enjoy life again? "For he does not afflict from his heart or grieve the children of men" (Lam 3:33). So good is our Father. After your illness is past, do not praise only your doctor—to "praise" is to say many good things about your doctor: skilled, personable, etc.—but praise especially your Father above.

At that point, the Israelite who was raised from his sickbed went to the sanctuary, and there he showed his inner gratitude for the healing given him by bringing a praise offering.

The superscription above Psalm 100 reads: "A psalm for giving thanks."

From the Psalter we see that there were many praise songs or psalms of thanksgiving, and later these would have been sung along with the praise offerings, but also with the votive offerings and the freewill offerings. Think of Ps 56:12–13: "I must perform my vows to you, O God; I will render thank offerings to you. For you have delivered my soul from death, yes, my feet from falling, that I may walk before God in the light of life."

Today much has changed.

Our heavenly Father no longer desires bloody sacrifices from us. Nor any meat portions accompanied with loaves of bread. Nor does he stipulate any longer the condition of "Levitical purity," about which we must yet speak in connection with Leviticus 11–15. All of that belonged to the past, now that the Law has been fulfilled by Christ. But of course we must still call upon God in our need. Why should we not make vows to him, and "pay" them when he has helped us? In fact, even when there is no special reason for gratitude, we may regularly recall that God has in pure mercy called us out of paganism and engrafted us into ancient Israel (Rom 11:13–24; 1 Pet 2:10). It is fitting that we thank God for the very same redemptive benefits that Israel received in her day. We too are justified (that is, we receive the forgiveness of sins through faith in the Lamb of God, Jesus Christ), and we too have peace with God through our Lord Jesus Christ, and we too may face the future with good confidence and "rejoice in hope of the glory of God," that will be granted to us on the new earth, in Paradise (Rom 5:2). Concerning this peace with God, now and later, the peace offering spoke to ancient Israel through the gospel of God's tabernacle and sacrifices, especially through the constantly accompanying covenant meal. Just as with the Lord's Supper, we today are not only assured of our having peace with God through the blood of Christ, but at the same time we look forward to the glory of the kingdom that will descend from heaven, in which pagans, such as we once were, will sit with Abraham, Isaac, and Jacob at the wedding of the Lamb.

THE PEACE OFFERING (LEV 3)

The apostle called the Hebrews who had become Christians to no longer bring to God a bloody sacrifice. Their Jewish brothers were still doing that, at the Jerusalem temple. Slavishly following the Law. For they did not understand that the Law was fulfilled by Christ, who had "suffered outside the gate" (Heb 13:18). This explains the appeal to the Hebrews: "Through him [Christ] then let us continually offer up a sacrifice of praise to God, that is, the fruit of lips that acknowledge his name" (Heb 13:15). This is referring to our conversations and our songs. May the hope of Christians ring in those conversations. For Christians are not simply people of faith, but especially people of hope, the firm hope in the Paradisal future when one day we will open our eyes. That is where we are headed. And as a model for our singing today, the ancient psalms that Israel sang as songs of the covenant can still serve us well. But so too the beautiful poetry of Isaiah 35, together with Isa 9:6, Joel 4:17, and Amos 9:13, concerning the peaceable kingdom of Prince Messiah.

In this way, the divine teaching of the peace offering remains valid for us. Some people can get very excited about the continuing validity of "the Ten Commandments." We agree. As long as—for honesty is best at this point—people do not isolate them and instead explain and apply them in principle no differently than the entire corpus of the Torah or Law of Horeb, which in its entirety remains for us the Word of God given to make us wise (2 Tim 3:15–16). We will return to this matter when we discuss legalism.

8

The sin offering (Lev 4:1–5:13)

The sin offering is discussed in other passages. But the passage in this chapter's title is the primary source of our knowledge about this offering. In order that we can obtain a comprehensive understanding, we will divide it into two parts. It does consist of an indivisible unity. So we regret that in ancient times, people divided this into two chapters. The first part was Leviticus 4, the second was part of Leviticus 5. That has always been regrettable. In the Hebrew Bible it is not arranged that way. But even though we may not separate the two parts, we do have to distinguish them.

4. Leviticus 4
5. Leviticus 5:1–13

1. LEVITICUS 4

Before we proceed to read this chapter, we will advise our readers to underline a couple of words in that chapter. We are referring to the following:
In 4:3: *the anointed priest*
In 4:13: *the whole congregation*
In 4:22: *a leader*
In 4:27: *anyone of the common people*
This helps clarify what is being taught.

In this way we can obtain something of an overview of this rather large chapter. We learn to recognize the differing "situations" in which a sin offering was supposed to be brought. We see the contents, in terms of what kind of animal, had to be brought in the various cases of the sin offering.

THE SIN OFFERING (LEV 4:1–5:13)

For our readers should keep in mind at this early point in the discussion that the sin offering was a bloody offering. Like none other. For example, it was evident from the fact that a sin offering was never coupled with a guilt offering. Burnt offerings and peace offerings, yes, but never sin offerings. Because with that offering, all attention was required for the blood.

For ease of reference, we have arranged in the table below all the information regarding the sin offering that Leviticus 4 provides. (We took the liberty of including a few details from the following chapter, Lev 5:1–13.)

For whom	*What*	*Where blood was placed with the finger*	*Where blood was sprinkled*
(High) Priest	Bull	Horns of the altar of incense	In front of the veil 7x
Whole congregation	Bull	Horns of the altar of incense	In front of the veil 7x
Tribal leader	Male goat	Horns of the altar of incense	
Member of the congregation	Sheep or goat	Horns of the altar	
A poor person	A pair of doves		
An indigent person	1/10 ephah of flour		

In this brief overview, we are struck by the fact that actions were performed with the blood of the sin offering animal that did not occur with the other sacrifices—the burnt offerings and the peace offerings. The third column indicates that the blood was to be placed on the *horns* of the altar and *of the altar of incense*. Thereby our attention is drawn to the blood. With the sin offering, the blood played a role that was even more important than with the other bloody sacrifices.

We see that same emphasis on the blood of the sin offering in what we are about to narrate, which could not be included in the table above. When someone was too poor to offer for himself a sheep or a goat as his sin offering, he was allowed to offer two doves. But then the first dove in particular was being offered as a sin offering. That signified that this dove was not to be cut into pieces. That did have to occur with the second dove. That one was offered as a burnt offering, and therefore sacrificed in several pieces. But the first dove had to remain whole. For what was most important was the *blood*. That blood had to be sprinkled on the side of the altar. Why. "It is a sin offering" (Lev 5:9).

If someone was extremely poor, so that he could offer only some flour, then no incense or oil was to be added to that flour. Why? Again, so that people would not forget that it was a sin offering—which could happen, for example, by thinking that it was a guilt offering. No, "for it is a sin offering" (Lev 5:11). In fact, the stipulation that a little bit of flour was permitted only by way of rare exception helped to direct attention to the rule that sin offerings otherwise had an extremely bloody character. For exceptions prove the rule.

Let us consider the *name* of the offering. In Hebrew the sin offering was called *ḥaṭṭā' t*. This word meant in the first place, "sin." But then also "sacrifice for sin," "sin offering."

The reader will recall that the shedding of blood with other sacrifices served as a covering of sins, for atonement. But given the name of *this* sacrifice—it was called for short: "sin"—we can understand that the covering of and atonement for sins played a very special role with *this* sacrifice.

So we will discuss first the sins that were especially covered by this bloody sacrifice. What special character did these sins have?

Those sins are mentioned immediately in Leviticus 4, already in verse 2. There a general rule is instituted, that is repeated in verses 13, 22, and 27. It goes like this: "*If someone sins unintentionally and do any one of the things that by the Lord's commandments ought not to be done, and they realize their guilt . . . .*"

What does the expression "sin unintentionally" mean?

Sometimes the Hebrew is translated as "sin through ignorance" (KJV). Moses declared concerning the unintentional manslayer, of whom Num 35:11 said that he committed his deed "without intent, that such a person had acted 'unintentionally'" (Deut 19:4).

Let us pause at this point.

We are taking the liberty of saying something first about the subject of *the capacity for the atonement of sins according to the Law.*

Sins could be committed in Israel for which there was, to put it bluntly, no atonement. For example, the man who had been involved with the wife of another man was to be put to death immediately on account of his adultery. So too, a murderer, someone who had killed another person with malicious intent, was sentenced to death. But the unintentional manslayer did not need to be put to death. The Law had instituted this rule: unintentional sins can be atoned, but intentional sins cannot. You can read about this in Number 15:22–31. The intentional sin is there called a sin "with a high hand" (v. 30).

That was the rule.

THE SIN OFFERING (LEV 4:1–5:13)

We must always read Scripture with respect, however, and therefore also with care. For example, one should not suppose that this rule (unintentional sins can be atoned, intentional sins cannot) was applied within Israel in the foolish manner employed by fanatical folk who through their extreme insistence on this or that rule, give the appearance of wanting to prove that *they* are still principled people. No, among Israel, people never inferred from that rule in Numbers 15 (about unintentional and intentional sins) that Israelite authorities were obligated to put to death every *thief*. Even though a thief would surely have committed his sin intentionally. If someone would have told the judge that he had broken in somewhere at night accidentally, or if a pickpocket would have said he had unintentionally lifted someone's gold watch, the judge would certainly not have been satisfied with such excuses. People who steal always do so intentionally. The same is true about lying. Nevertheless, God never commanded that all *liars* among Israel had to be put to death immediately.

Perhaps a hotheaded Christian might find this troublesome. Was God being consistent? Was he himself not actually contradicting his own rule in Numbers 15 (unintentional sins can be atoned, but intentional sins cannot)?

God is wise.

And God is merciful.

He never wanted that rule to be applied in the hardhearted and pitiless manner of such fanatics that occasionally surface in God's church and temporarily sweep people along with their appearance of sincerity. God wants that rule to be applied with thoughtfulness. Something that often requires a lot of wisdom. Cutting through knots is easier than untangling them. The first looks much more firm. But the one who wins souls—and thereby saves lives—is wise (Prov 11:30).

The following cases could occur.

1. In Israel, sins could be committed for which there was absolutely no pardon. An example of this kind of sin could be found in Numbers 15. Our attention is drawn to the fact that in Numbers 15, right before the rule in question—intentional sins are worthy of death—follows the story of a man who had gathered wood on the Sabbath. Gathered. As in: picked up. In other words, he had not simply picked up a twig like someone might do when taking a walk, but he had acted as though it was a workday. And this, when God had laid claim to the seventh day when he had established the Horeb covenant, and did so already when he had regulated the manna-gathering. God had elevated that day to the position of a seal of the covenant (Exod 16:22–30; 20:8–11; 31:13–17; 35:1–3). Nevertheless, that man had lugged wood on the Sabbath. As a result, that Sabbath violator was stoned at Yahweh's own command (Num 15:32–36). A characteristic passage. After

PART 2 | THE SACRIFICIAL TORAH: SPECIFIC REQUIREMENTS

giving the rule, providing the application of it in practice. This then was the kind of sin that warranted the capital punishment. There were more such sins. Earlier we mentioned murder. In Deut 17:2–7 Moses identified idolatry as such a sin. Anyone guilty of that sin was not to be excused, even if it was one's own husband or wife.

But people were not supposed to use the same measure of strictness in response to every other sin, even if it had been committed intentionally. We would mention again the example of stealing. Two possible situations could occur.

2. The first possibility was that such a thief had voluntarily surrendered, out of penitence, but that contrary to his plan, his sin came into the open, whether later or right away. But suppose that people had trapped such a person in his crime, even then, they were not allowed to do everything to him that they may have wanted. Indeed, if the robbery had occurred during the day and in catching him someone had hit him so hard that they killed him, then guilt would come upon the one who killed him (Exod 22:2–3). In this way, we see that God wanted to see the life of the thief protected. Even though a thief really had been guilty of an intentional sin. He would, of course, need to pay restitution for his sin, but people were not allowed to put him to death.

3. There was yet a second possibility, namely, that the thief would be filled with remorse and bring his own sin to light. In such a case, the sin of such a person would definitely not result in capital punishment. Even though it had been committed "with upraised hand." Intentionally, with premeditation, like it always happens with stealing. Nevertheless, in Israel such a thief was definitely not to be put to death. A thief who repented and turned himself in would be required to pay less restitution. In this respect, the Law of Yahweh breathed a spirit of mercy. We will discuss this more when we come to the guilt offering.

In this digression we have wanted simply to point out that the rule of Num 15:30 (one who commits evil with premeditation shall be put away from the people) was not to be applied among Israel in a fanatical manner. On the contrary, with wisdom and discernment people were supposed to make careful distinctions between one case or another.

After this intermezzo, we can actually explain the reason why we have preferred to divide into two parts the large Scripture passage that deals with the sin offering, Lev 4:1–5:13.

We did this because the first part, Leviticus 4, deals with intentional sin that was atoned. And because the second part, Lev 5:1–13, deals with intentional sins that were also atoned.

THE SIN OFFERING (LEV 4:1–5:13)

Everyone will admit that we need to discuss them separately. No matter how much we keep in view their inner unity. For one and the same sacrifice applied to both kinds of sins (unintentional and intentional). That was the sin offering.

So now we will first discuss the sin offering for unintentional sins.

A sin offering for an unintentional sin?

Perhaps the amazement of some readers is even greater than it already was. For they first learned that God had established the rule that intentional sins were worthy of death. Then immediately thereafter they learned that he softened that rule considerably by not requiring capital punishment for every intentional sin, but opened the way of atonement for some of them. God's *lenience* thereby become evident!

But now we must observe that this same lenient God has given an entire chapter (Lev 4) prescribing painstaking regulations about how things should go if someone had become guilty of an *unintentional* sin. Was that sin taken with such seriousness? Can that sin fit in with such lenience?

Yes, it can.

As long as we keep the following in mind.

We must recall, first, that Yahweh had covenanted himself to Israel with condescending grace, but he was and remained the Holy One. God dwells in unapproachable light (1 Tim 6:16). His eyes are too pure to look on evil, and he cannot tolerate wrongdoing (Hab 1:13). God is light and in him is no darkness at all (1 John 1:5). Just how averse to darkness (i.e., to sin) he is became evident in Paradise, when he warned our first parents about death. But in vain, with the well-known result.

Nevertheless, that holy God has continued to harbor the desire to enjoy concourse again in peace with human beings. You can see down through the ages his repeated attempts to draw near to people. Notice the friendly manner in which he spoke to Adam and Eve immediately after their rebellion. And later to their wicked son, Cain, who had been guilty of a sin that had deeply grieved God, murder. Behold God's patience toward the pre-Flood world, with its unchastity and violence. After the Flood he graciously established a covenant with Noah as the prince over a new humanity and world. When the post-Flood world had disappointed him once again, he made a new and immense beginning with Abraham, even though he had descended from an idolater. But at that point, centuries before Horeb, God already intended to bless all the nations of the world in Abraham, and one day to enjoy in their midst a renewed Paradise fellowship.

Along God's route to fulfilling that intention, Horeb was a beautiful staging place. With a view to the *old* realities that were confirmed there, and with a view to the *new* realities that were bestowed there.

PART 2 | THE SACRIFICIAL TORAH: SPECIFIC REQUIREMENTS

By means of the history of Horeb, the covenant with Abraham was confirmed. Because God was remembering his covenant with Abraham, God had led the Israelites out of Egypt and had brought them to Horeb.

But there God had laid a new foundation under the (Israelite) world. But this was also granted to Israel out of divine love. This explains why later the prophets compared his relationship to Israel with betrothal and marriage. But love watches intently. Trespasses that damage that covenant basis may not be tolerated, like idolatry and worship of images (Deut 6:14; 15:13; 16:18–17). Like abusing Yahweh's name, which was the sin committed by the son of an Egyptian father and an Israelite mother (Lev 24:10–23). Like violating the Sabbath day, which day was a seal upon Yahweh's covenant at Horeb; this was the sin of the wood-gatherer (Num 15). Like a son's coarse disobedience to father and mother (Deut 20), or murdering one's neighbor, or adultery—three sins of a covenant breaking nature, sins against Yahweh's fellow covenant members, again fellow vassals!

To this new covenant foundation, on which God had placed the Israelite nation at Horeb, the tabernacle belonged with everything that was related to it.

In that tabernacle, the holy God lived in the midst of sinful people. This explains why the tribe of Levi was provided to function like an isolation boundary zone between Yahweh and his people. This also explains why God's commands regarding the *cultus*, relating to the tabernacle, served as a protective fence for Israel.

In this way, Israel received an honor from God that had been given to no other nation at that time. One single ray of light in a sea of darkness, arranged around the tent of the God of life, Israel found herself surrounded by nations that, despite all appearances to the contrary, lived in the stranglehold of Satan and in the power of sin and death.

This explains why at Horeb, Israel was forbidden to show any hint of behavior or attitude that intimated an abandonment of Yahweh's covenant domain and a return to the pagan terrain with its uncleanness and darkness, and with its night of death. This explains the prohibition against taking even one step across the threshold of the Law that God had put as a fence around his people. Indeed, even to touch that holy fence was prohibited for Israel. Just as for us, it is fatally dangerous to touch a high-tension electric cable.

Two things were possible.

Israel could nonetheless possibly touch that fence, even go beyond it, and do so either intentionally or unintentionally.

Of course no one would be surprised if God would have refused to tolerate a person's intentional violation of his sacred line, the Torah. Everyone would see it as fair that God condemned the Sabbath violator to death. Or if

THE SIN OFFERING (LEV 4:1–5:13)

someone in Israel intentionally withheld his tithe from God, that too would be blasphemous and just as worthy of capital punishment as the brutality that the men of Beth Shemesh demonstrated toward the ark (1 Sam 6:20), and as the deed of Achan who stole from the loot of Jericho that belonged to Yahweh (Josh 7:1). Anyone practicing idolatry would also have crossed the line. A person did not do such a thing except intentionally. In so doing, a person stepped across the holy command of Horeb, and placed his feet in enemy territory, in the territory of paganism and death.

For such sins, no means of atonement had been provided.

But now the other possibility.

It could also happen that an Israelite unsuspectingly and unintentionally landed on the wrong side of the life-boundary established by God at Horeb. Through thoughtlessness he had crossed over into the territory of death. That was *chata*, sin. In the Septuagint, this word is often translated as *hamartia*, from the verb *hamartano*, miss the mark, miss the target. According to the Torah of Horeb, one would have sinned, but would not need to have been put to death. That is why the sin offering was prescribed. That is what Leviticus 4 is about. About such unintentional sins.

It is very possible that this may strike some as strange. They might even wish to speak of unfairness, if they dared. But what would be the reason for doing that? Without having given much consideration to the matter, would they perhaps have adopted the view that a sin that was not willed, an unintentional sin, is actually not a sin at all? But is that (Roman Catholic) view scriptural? The apostle Paul surely did not hold such a view. Although to his embarrassment he had to admit that he had acted in ignorance when he persecuted the church of God, he continued even in his last letter to identify those former sins as sins. Using words like "blasphemer, persecutor, and insolent opponent" (1 Tim 1:12–16). Consider as well Acts 3:17 and 1 Cor 2:8, about Israel's crucifying their own Messiah "in ignorance." In those instances, Paul and all of Israel did not commit the sin against the Holy Spirit in the sense of Matthew 12:32b. They did not engage in coarse resistance against the testimony of the Spirit that had come to them in the words and deeds of our Lord Jesus Christ, in full agreement with the testimony of the Spirit through "Moses and the Prophets." Certainly, some have observed that agreement and acknowledged it in their hearts, but despite that, did not stand on the side of Christ (John 12:42). That moved in the direction of blaspheming the Holy Spirit. A sin that would not be forgiven, the Savior said (Matt 12:31). Of this sin, however, Paul and the many Jews to whom Peter had to direct the accusation that they had nailed Jesus the Nazarene to the cross and killed him (Acts 2:23) were not guilty. Therefore there was forgiveness for them. But it was sin nonetheless. Peter said: Repent and be converted, so that your *sins* may be blotted out (Acts 2:38; 3:19). Later, Ananias said to Paul in Damascus: Let your *sins* be washed away (Acts 22:16). Sins, committed in ignorance, to be sure, but sins nonetheless.

According to Scripture, a person can become guilty of sin without knowing it or wanting to, so that he requires atonement.

We should keep this in mind as we read Leviticus 4, concerning the sin offerings for sins committed unintentionally.

Finally, we will mention a few examples of such unintentional sins for which a sin offering had to be brought.

1. In a moment, we will read Leviticus 8–10, where we read about the two sons of Aaron, called Nadab and Abihu, who had hardly been consecrated as priests and they were suddenly killed. Just imagine that their father Aaron and their brothers, Eleazar and Ithamar, would have burst out in response with loud complaining. We read that Moses joined them immediately in order to restrain them from doing that. But imagine that they had ripped their turbans and hats (symbols of life!) from their heads. That would have been a sign of grief to let their hair hang down loosely and to tear their high priestly clothes and priestly garments. As we know, this was not permitted for the priests. But what do people do when they are suddenly overcome with deep sorrow? If that response would have occurred, a sin offering would definitely have been required for them (Lev 10:6–7).

2. When a leper was healed, he had to bring a sin offering in connection with his purification (Lev 14:19).

3. When a Nazirite had come into contact with a corpse during the time of his vow, he had to bring a sin offering in connection with concluding his time of consecration (Num 6:14).

4. When a woman gave birth to a child, a sin offering had to be brought in connection with her purification (Lev 12:6).

5. When a man or woman experienced a discharge, a sin offering had to be brought in connection with their purification (Lev 15:15, 30).

More examples could be mentioned.

But these are sufficient. Anyone who concludes, on the basis of these human examples, that "An action that I did not intend is not a sin," will run stuck. Such a person, if he dared, would be criticizing God, who in his Law, note well, demanded a sin offering for a woman who had just given birth. Such a person would indignantly exclaim: "What in heaven's name did that woman do wrong?" Or if such a person discovered for this "case"

THE SIN OFFERING (LEV 4:1–5:13)

an "explanation" in the view that such a woman who had just delivered a baby was obligated to bring a sin offering on account of her "original sin" inherited from Adam, he would still run stuck in the case of a sin offering required from a leper who had been healed. Or in the case of a sin offering required from a Nazirite who had accidentally touched a corpse.

That is what happens when people elevate their thoughts above God's thoughts. Also when the question involves what is sinful.

God watched over Israel like a diligent Father. He gave his Torah to be a *paidagōgos*, a guardian, a babysitter, to protect Israel en route to the coming Christ (Gal 3:24). Just as we would never allow our own children near an electric power line, God does not allow his people Israel to set one foot off the covenant foundation on which he had placed them at Horeb. He refused to permit them to slide away from the territory where the powers of the coming age were at work. Where Israel enjoyed his fellowship in happiness and life. The Bible reader must never forget this. For example, don't forget this when we come later in Leviticus to chapters dealing with the purification of women who have just given birth, those with a bodily discharge, etc. Let this help you already now, as you read Leviticus 4. In fact, you will be able to pray the psalmist's prayer: "Who can know his sins? Forgive me those sins about which I am not even aware" (Ps 19:12). Is this petition antiquated for us? We too have been delivered by God from the power of Satan and paganism, and transferred into the kingdom of his beloved Son (Acts 26:16; Col 1:13). But we too can "come into contact," unintentionally and unsuspectingly, with the power of the demons and of paganism, and thereby bring reproach upon God's name, and put ourselves and our descendants at great risk. In way too numerous to mention, we can allow paganism and corruption to slip in among us once again. With serious consequences. Just as it can happen by mistake that when someone digs a grave, for example, he might be injured by an electrical cable, an instrument that supplies our home with light, warmth, and energy. Of course it would have been a mistake. But we can be fooled. When a landscaper digs around a plant with his shovel, and severs its roots, that will result in the plant's death even though he did that ignorantly. The plant's contact with its source of life has been broken. It has been severed from its foundation.

So too, God did not want even one finger lifted toward, let alone touch, the fence that he had placed around Israel with his Torah, or that even one foot would slip away from the force field of the gospel within which he had placed Israel during all those wondrous events that later were summarized with the shorthand expression "the foundation of the world."

This, then, is our initial commentary on Leviticus 4, especially on the words of verse 2 that reappear time and again in that chapter: *If anyone sins unintentionally in any of the Lord's commandments* . . . .

2. LEVITICUS 5:1–13

We can be brief here.

This Scripture passage consists of three parts, the last two of which we have already discussed. That included verses 7–10, about the case where a *dove* could be used for a sin offering, and verses 11–13, about the case where a little bit of *flour* could be given as a sin offering. So we need to deal with verses 1–6 now.

You will recall that we were just discussing those sins that were committed intentionally but for which atonement was possible. This kind of sin is the subject of this part.

Three examples of this kind of intentional sin are mentioned here.

The first is in Lev 5:1.

Suppose that a crime has been committed in Israel. Let's say it was stealing. The robbery was detected, but the thief is nowhere to be found. Even though a curse was pronounced on the (as yet unknown) thief, whether by the one robbed or by the judge (Judg 17:2; Prov 29:24). Suppose that there is one man, however, who knows about the robbery. He knows who committed the robbery. He also knows what curse has been pronounced on the guilty party. But for some reason, perhaps out of fear of revenge, he does not bring the crime to light. Naturally that person is also guilty.

The second is Leviticus 5:2–3.

Someone has become unclean by touching a human corpse or an animal corpse. Such a thing could happen without knowing it. Later the person comes to the realization that he had become unclean. Then according to the pertinent regulation, he was supposed to purify himself and in the evening of that day everything would be fine again (more about that in Lev 11). But suppose that someone, after discovering his uncleanness, intentionally omitted the purification. For whatever reason, let's say it was laziness. Then too, such a person would incur guilt.

The third is Lev 5:4.

Someone has sworn a rash oath. Of course no one does something like this mechanically. But it could happen more or less involuntarily, like when a person lacks self-control due to his temper, for example. This happened to David when he was injured very rudely by Nabal (1 Sam 25). At a moment like this, a person does not consider the import of his words.

THE SIN OFFERING (LEV 4:1–5:13)

Suppose now that a person in one of these three situations, or in one similar, later was penitent and voluntarily confessed his sin. Then for such a person, there was forgiveness to be obtained along the path of the sin offering. It's possible that he had incurred guilt for a sin of which he became aware only later when someone pointed it out to him. That is what the previous chapter, Lev 4:28, dealt with. Here, by contrast, the Law is speaking about intentionality. But through penitence and confession, the issue stands in a more favorable light.

With this we conclude our discussion of Lev 5:1–13. Let's review for a moment.

We get the impression that with all three sins that were posited as examples, we encountered the same contrast as in Leviticus 4, namely, between death and life. For when the person in the first instance heard that curse in Israel, the name of Yahweh must surely have echoed in his ears. So too the name of Yahweh was involved in the third instance, with the swearing of a (rash) oath. In other words, the name of him who had rescued Israel from the Egyptian grave had promised always to be with Israel, had placed Israel on his side, had set Israel on the foundation of life in his fellowship, and therefore had commanded Israel to abstain from coming into contact with death, whether dead people or dead animals, and from pagan mourning customs. "For you are the sons of Yahweh your God" (Deut 14:1). This background was very clearly evident in the second instance.

With great deeds and illustrious miracles, God had exalted his people at Horeb to a pedestal of living with him. Therefore he did not want anyone in Israel to violate the Torah, that sacred garden that he had placed around his people.

Not even unintentionally.

And not at all intentionally. Although when there was penitence and confession, there did remain a place for the sin offering. So that even such a person could still be restored in the exalted position of the Horeb covenant that he had despised. Even with a certain degree of intentionality.

The preceding provided us more than one opportunity to give our readers the impression of the special nature of the sins for which the sin offering was instituted in Israel. Time and again we encounter the demand of God that his people remain close to him and his Torah, and stay far away from corruption and death. For that was not suited to the covenant people of Yahweh. We will now learn still more about this as we proceed to discuss:

3. the various *kinds of animals* used for the sin offering; and
4. the actions relating to the *blood* of the sin offering.

PART 2 | THE SACRIFICIAL TORAH: SPECIFIC REQUIREMENTS

3. THE VARIOUS KINDS OF ANIMALS USED FOR THE SIN OFFERING

If you review our earlier table, you will find three kinds of animals mentioned in the second column. We need to pay extra attention to these.

The three are bull, ram, and sheep/goat.

Perhaps you are thinking that we've made a double mistake. First, because the dove is mentioned there as well. Indeed. But the sacrificial dove designated for a poor person, together with the sacrificial flour for the extremely poor, was not the usual sin offering and was thus not normative for our quest to learn the nature and character of the particular sins for which the sin offering was needed.

Even so, a few readers might still be thinking that we made another mistake, since bull, ram, and sheep + goat equal four, not three, animals. That is true as well. But no distinction should be made between the latter two animals. They were equal. If we were to classify them, both would belong to the category of small livestock. This included sheep and goats. So we end up with three kinds of animals: first, the bull; second, the ram; and third, the sheep or goat.

Those three animals are closely related to three possibilities that could occur and that we need to review. For ease of discussion, we will take them in reverse order.

The first possibility.

Let's say some member of the congregation sinned. Not a priest or a ruler, but an ordinary member of the congregation. What kind of sin offering had to be brought for such a member of the "laity"?

Ten to one, we would answer: "That would surely have depended on the seriousness of the sin that person had committed. For a little sin, a smaller animal would have been sacrificed, and for a greater sin, a larger animal."

Wrong. The kind of animal that was to be brought for a sin offering was not determined by the seriousness of the trespass, but *by the place of the person in question among Yahweh's covenant people.* This explains why for an ordinary member of the congregation the most simple normal sin offering animal was sufficient. It could be a sheep. It could also be a goat. Just as long as it was not a male sheep (a ram) and not a male goat. For the sin offering, the animal for an ordinary member of the covenant congregation had to be a female member of the herd. Everyone understood why. Because the female animal was not esteemed as highly as the male. It was only for an ordinary member of the congregation.

The second possibility.

THE SIN OFFERING (LEV 4:1–5:13)

Let's say that a ruler had committed a sin. In view here is a tribal head. What kind of sacrificial animal had to be sacrificed for such a ruler?

For that, a male goat was to be sacrificed. A much more respectable animal. Apparently on account of the respectable position of a tribal head in the midst of God's covenant congregation. This explains why a male goat had to be used in this instance. We must point out that the word for "buck" or "male goat" does not have in Scripture that rather negative ring that it has for us. On the contrary, certain rulers and regents occasionally received the title "buck." Completely different than with us. We would be insulting someone if we called him a "buck."

There were two kinds of male goats. One had short hair, the other had long hair. The Law stipulated that male goats of the latter kind were to be used in the sin offering for the rulers. The assumption was stated that this animal with its long hair was the most suitable for that purpose. On account of its somber and miserable exterior, it was a symbolic portrait of sin and death. At the same time it was a symbol of fertility and life.

The third possibility.

As we said, we have reversed the sequence. First a sheep or goat, then the male goat, and finally the bull. So we come to the animal with which the discussion in Leviticus 4 began. (We have seen more often that the Torah has the custom of identifying the most preeminent as the first.)

Here a sin has been committed by the (high) priest or by the entire congregation. (Note carefully, we are not dealing here with the sin offering brought on the feast days—that was always a male goat—but with special cases of sin in the congregation or by the priest.) That came down to the same thing. In both instances, guilt had been brought upon the entire people, and in both instances, a bull had to be sacrificed. The most expensive animal. A bull. The symbolic portrait of life.

(Just this brief comment. We placed the word "high" between parentheses next to the word "priest." In Lev 4:3 the phrase "the anointed priest" would have referred primarily to the high priest. But in the case of a sin offering for an ordinary priest, a bull had to be brought as well. This explains our use of parentheses.)

So much, then, for the various animals that were slaughtered for the sin offering. What a striking resemblance between our result here and that which we reached after (1) and (2) above. Here too our attention is drawn to the foundation on which God placed his people at Horeb on the day of "the foundation of the world." With those sins for which the sin offering was instituted, God apparently considered that his covenant that had just been entered at Horeb was being affected in a very special way. For the question about which animal was to be brought in each distinct situation as a sin offering, was answered exclusively in terms of the place on the covenant foundation of holiness and life upon which God had set the person—or persons—in question next to him at Horeb. The standard was not the person. Nor the transgression he had committed. Nor what had befallen him. The main issue was the place that God had assigned to each person in the covenant zone. The spot he had assigned in the midst of the Israelite "world" or society for each person to stand. That of the (high) priest. That of the ruler. Or that of the member of the congregation.

The teaching of the sin offering signified the deathblow for all subjectivistic piety, for all religion that put the human person at the center.

4. THE ACTIONS RELATING TO THE BLOOD OF THE SIN OFFERING

Our thoughts are led in the same direction by what Scripture tells us about the blood of the sin offering.

Once again we draw the reader's attention to the earlier table, this time, to the third and fourth columns. Consider the following comments in that connection.

1. Three kinds of actions could be performed with the sacrificial blood. It could be thrown, dabbed, or sprinkled.

With all the bloody sacrifices other than the sin offering, some of the blood was *thrown* (Lev 1:5; 3:2; 7:2). In the preceding, we have stated more than once that we should understand this throwing to resemble sowing. That is what the priest did with the blood of the burnt offering, peace offering, and guilt offering. Some of the blood was *thrown* against the sides of the altar in the forecourt.

But with the sin offering the priest dipped his finger—likely his right index finger (Lev 14:16)—in the blood that had been collected and immediately brought some of it on the horns of either the altar of burnt offering or the altar of incense offering. It could occur with the sin offering as well, that the priest would sprinkle the blood seven times with his finger (*hizzah*, which some translate as *splash*) in the sanctuary on the floor in front of the curtain hanging in front of the Holy of Holies. Indeed, simply to complete our description, once per year, on the great Day of Atonement, the high priest sprinkled the blood of the sin offering on and in front of the atonement covering in that Holy of Holies.

The reader will have noticed that the actions done with the blood of the sin offering were entirely different than those with the blood of other sacrifices.

THE SIN OFFERING (LEV 4:1–5:13)

2. You will also have noticed that the blood of the sin offering did not always end up in the same place. On what did this depend?

That depended on the position occupied by the person or persons for whom the sin offering was being brought, within the covenant congregation.

If the sin offering was brought for *an ordinary member of the congregation or for a tribal leader*, the blood of that offering came no further than the forecourt. At that point, some of the blood was dabbed by the priest, brought (*natan*) on the horns of the altar of burnt offering in that forecourt.

But if a sin offering was brought *for the (high) priest or for the entire people*, the priest went with that blood into the holy place; he first sprinkled some of that blood seven times on the floor "before the face of Yahweh in front of the veil" (Lev 4:16–17), and second, he put some of the blood on the horns of the altar of incense in that holy place.

We mentioned what happened on the great Day of Atonement with the blood of the sin offering. That blood was then sprinkled on and in front of the ark in the Holy of Holies.

3. Next we want to say something about putting blood on the *horns* of the two altars, the altar of burnt offering and the altar of incense.

To understand the purpose of these actions, we must begin by looking at these altars, then we can look at the horns on these altars.

We must always recall that God gave Israel the promise that he would come to Israel via *altars*. At least via the kind of altars that *he himself* commanded to be built unto the remembrance of his name (Exod 20:24–26). There would be the meeting places between him and his people. There he would come to Israel and bless her. Such an altar would represent not only God, but also his people, and thus the covering of Israel's sins could occur by means of bringing blood upon that altar. Because they represented the presence of the people involved before the face of God, bringing the blood on the altar represented the covering and atoning of their sins before the face of God. For the first party involved with such an altar was Israel's God. He had promised that they would find him there and he had instituted that there the blood would cover the *nefesh* of the one bringing the offering (Lev 17:11; Heb 10:22).

In this way, the fact that blood was put on the altar of burnt offering, the blood of burnt offerings, peace offerings, and guilt offerings, already constituted the preaching of the forgiveness of sins. Constantly.

But when blood was put on the altar of burnt offering that had come from a sin offering, that preaching was strengthened even more. How? In that the blood brought at that time was put on the horns of the altar.

PART 2 | THE SACRIFICIAL TORAH: SPECIFIC REQUIREMENTS

We have discussed in our commentary on Exodus the significance of the horns on Israel's altars.[1] It was possible that such altar horns were an international phenomenon. But wanted to annex these horns from the religious property of the nations around Israel in service to his gospel. Just as at Horeb, at the foundation of the (Israelite) "world," he had provided an entirely new meaning to so many other religious items, namely, the meaning of his royal covenant with Israel and of his nearness to this nation of his love, so too with having blood put on the *horns* of Israel's altars he was again emphasizing and underscoring the promise of his presence and forgiveness. For the symbolic significance of blood on the horns of the altar would surely have meant something more for Israel's ancient Near Eastern thinking than for ours. Perhaps the horns were part of the altar, so that the covering of those horns with blood symbolized the covering of people and their sins. God was not being covered, of course, and God was not being atoned for, but the one bringing the offering, the human being. But although the altar represented that person bringing the offering, it was still a (promised) place of meeting with God. And although as part of the altar, the horn represented the person, the one bringing the offering, it accentuated the promise of God's presence, so that by bringing the blood specifically on such a horn, God's promise of covering and atoning Israel's sins was being sealed and sworn with extra force.

4. This juncture seems to afford us a suitable opportunity, as we conclude this discussion, to draw the attention of our readers to the unique and special character of the sin offering. By now, this will have become all the more clear, as we repeat the familiar triad.

The emphases was as follows:

The *sin offering* emphasized *justification*;

The *burnt offering* emphasized *sanctification*; and

The *peace offering* emphasized *glorification*.

With no other kind of sacrifice were such obvious actions performed with the blood, and through no other single sacrifice was the declaration of the gospel of the forgiveness of sins (or justification) made as powerfully and as loudly as through the sin offering.

5. But finally, the question remains as to the meaning behind bringing the blood of the sin offering to three different locations.

Consider the following.

The reader will recall that there were three locations.

(a) First, there was the altar of burnt offering. This stood in the forecourt. Upon this altar was placed the blood of the sin offering for a member

---

1. Vonk, Exodus, 166.

THE SIN OFFERING (LEV 4:1–5:13)

of the congregation or a leader. The blood designated for this purpose went no further. For neither of the parties bringing the sacrifice of this blood was a priest. To be sure, a priestly task was assigned to all Israel, but the people themselves had declared their own inability to fulfill that task. This explains why they had received from God the "mediators" to serve them before God. So God maintained that practice.

(b) Second, there was the altar of incense. This stood in the holy place. Upon this altar was placed the blood of the sin offering for the (high) priest and the entire congregation. After what was explained in (a), this is rather obvious. The holy place was the place for the priests. There they were allowed to appear, in that characteristic location their sin had to be covered. Not at the people's altar, but at the priest's altar. The altars symbolized and guaranteed the place of each respective party bringing the offering before God.

But the people as a whole, when they had sinned and had to receive covering for that sin, were represented by the altar of incense. For although each individual member of the congregation and each "lay person" among Israel did not possess the priestly privilege, as a people Israel did bear a priestly character. You could contrast this with the situation among the pagans, in contrast to by far most pagans, Israel as a unit lived close to Yahweh. As his priesthood. It is possible that this was why God wanted the atonement relating to the sin of the entire people to occur in the holy place, because he looked upon the entire people in terms of its most exalted part, namely, the Aaronic priesthood. According to the rule of the Torah, that the best was first.

And then in the situation now under discussion, namely, that of a sin offering for the (high) priest or entire nation, the blood was sprinkled seven times before the veil in the holy place. On what? That was not stated explicitly, but the place must surely have been the floor or the ground. Picture it this way: by means of the sevenfold sprinkling, a red line or corridor emerged on the ground in the holy place of the tabernacle, which pointed in the direction of the Holy of Holies that lay behind the veil. It did so with clear intention, indicated by something that was added. For this was to occur "before the face of Yahweh" (Lev 4:6–7). Those words point especially to the ark of Yahweh. In fact, to that place the bringing of blood to the horns of the altar of incense also pointed. Then as well, it was added that the altar of incense stood "before the face of Yahweh" (Lev 4:17–18). This was referring to the ark, which further clarifies the purpose. For actually, the blood of the sin offering in all these cases that we are now discussing—cases where sin guilt had fallen on the entire covenant people (Lev 4:3)—had to be repeatedly sprinkled on Israel's preeminent altar, the ark. But that did not happen every time. It happened only on the great Day of Atonement, once per year, and then actually when a sinful man approached God, functioning as a priest on behalf of others. Fine, that was allowed. As long as he had offered the required sacrifice for himself first (Heb 7:27). Once per year. But no more than that. Otherwise Israel might have thought that the grand purpose—the restoration of Paradise fellowship between God and men—had already been achieved. But for that, another sacrifice was needed first.

This explains that strip or band of blood. It functioned like a traffic sign: Go that way! To the place of complete atonement for the people of the covenant.

For the reader will have paid close attention to the number seven, right? The blood had to be sprinkled seven times. The number seven was the number that recalled the establishing of the covenant with sacred oaths. The covenant was involved in the sin offering!

(c) Thirdly, there was the ark that stood in the Holy of Holies. On that altar the blood of a sin offering was placed at no other time than on the great Day of Atonement. We read about this in Leviticus 16. But the sprinklings that we discussed in (b) pointed fundamentally in the direction of the ark in the Holy of Holies. On the great Day of Atonement, however, that blood was sprinkled right next to the ark, even on the ark itself.

The actions performed with the blood of the sin offering have shown us again Israel's unique privilege of being Yahweh's covenant people. That was a great privilege, but it entailed for its possessors no lazy and sloppy living. Israel had to remember well that Yahweh could not tolerate it even when the feet of his people accidentally slipped toward the realm of paganism and death. Not to mention when this did not happen accidentally at all. Even though there was forgiveness with Israel's good God. Not, of course, when a member of the covenant people committed the vulgarity of intentionally and knowingly walking beyond the holy parapet of the Torah with which God wanted to ensure the safety of his people, to the point of kicking against it.

We have also seen the special nature of the *sins* for which the sin offering was instituted. Not that we find in Scripture a complete catalogue of those sins. As far as we know, Israel never received such a catalogue. Their understanding of these particular sins was granted to Israel by God with the use of a symbolism that spoke powerfully. It was just as with marriage. Of course, no man or woman entering marriage would present each other on their wedding day with a list of sins that would destroy their marriage. That's not how people get married. In fact, a married man can hardly countenance the notion that his wife would slide away from the realm of their marriage covenant. Not to mention that this would happen not accidentally,

THE SIN OFFERING (LEV 4:1–5:13)

but by culpable carelessness. Although forgiveness for this is certainly possible, and the concourse of the marital covenant can be continued normally. But when a wife would act as though she were not married, such misconduct would erode the foundation beneath her marriage. In the situations mentioned earlier, people were simply being directed to that foundation.

In this way, within Israel, people could sin against God to such a vulgar extent that the pedestal to which Yahweh had elevated his people Israel with the foundation of the world at Horeb would thereby be destroyed. At that point those who did that would have placed themselves outside the sphere of the covenant with Yahweh, into the sphere of paganism. Such a person would be acting as if the theocratic Torah did not apply to him. He would be acting like a pagan, identifying with paganism, behaving as though he was not consecrated to Yahweh, not Yahweh's possession and beloved, but autonomous. Such abandonment of Yahweh and his fellowship of life rendered as guilty the idolater, the Sabbath breaker, and the murderer. The feet of such covenant members would not merely have slipped, but had actually been set on the path to the realm of death, far away from Yahweh. He would not have slid down accidentally, but would actually have walked away.

But in order that Israel would know very well that God could not tolerate this at all if their actions would merely nod in the direction of the realm of death and corruption, he surrounded Israel with a Torah filled with warnings, which we must still explain in due time. For example, when we discuss leprosy, uncleanness through death, etc. When the church of God was still a toddler, she was surrounded with loving care, but at the same time treated somewhat strictly. That is what the period of shadows was about. Christ had not yet appeared. A public display of Satan had not yet occurred, nor had he yet been pushed into retreat from pagan lands by the power of the apostolic preaching.

We now live in a time when this has happened. This explains why we now belong to that one church that has existed throughout all the centuries. The force field of the coming age had reached us, we who are former pagans. Indeed, the clock of church history is showing the lateness of the hour, such that the force field of the Spirit is again visibly shrinking. In our day the apostasy is great. And that gives us reason to fear. For even though the sacrificial Torah, and with it, the teaching of the sin offering, has been fulfilled, nevertheless it continues to preach to us as to who God is and in what ways he deals with us people. The doctrine of the gospel according to the New Testament is in a certain sense even more strict. For during this time of fulfillment, the church knows God not only as *Yahweh, the One who is near*, who once dwelt in the midst of Israel in a tent and who according to promise met Israel at the altars, but also as *our heavenly Father*, who has given us One who is no less than his own Son, and who has given us the Spirit of Christ to dwell among us and to work in our hearts and lives. This explains why the apostle writes: "Or do you not know that we all who are baptized into Christ have been baptized into his death?" This explains why we stand not only under the sealed assurance of the fact of living with Christ, but also under the strengthened demand of being obligated to live with him (Rom 6:3-4). This explains why the letter to the Hebrews says:

> For if we go on sinning deliberately after receiving the knowledge of the truth, *there no longer remains a sacrifice for sins*, but a fearful expectation of judgment, and a fury of fire that will consume the adversaries. Anyone who has set aside the law of Moses dies without mercy on the evidence of two or three witnesses. How much worse punishment, do you think, will be deserved by the one who has trampled underfoot the Son of God, and has profaned the blood of the covenant by which he was sanctified, and has outraged the Spirit of grace? For we know him who said, "Vengeance is mine; I will repay." And again, "The Lord will judge his people." It is a fearful thing to fall into the hands of the living God (Heb 10:26-31).

Has the Christian church devoted appropriate attention to the teaching of the sin offering?

Have Christians sufficiently considered that not only does God get angry about the insolent abandoning of the terrain of life itself, in which terrain he has placed us, but he disapproves of the smallest stumbling movement whereby we could slip away from that terrain?

What John writes about this is instructive. This apostle not only cursed the (Gnostic) members of the church who had broken outright the fellowship with the Father and his Son Jesus Christ (1 John 1:3), and had hated the brothers and departed from them (1 John 2:11, 19). These folk had sinned unto death (1 John 5:16). But John also went on, against the background of this culpably fatal desertion of Christ and his people by the Gnostics, to issue a very serious warning directed to the Christians who had remained faithful, that they themselves *not go in the direction of those Gnostics*. He wrote: "Little children, abide in him" (1 John 2:28); "everyone who hates his brother is a murderer" (1 John 3:15); and "let us love one another . . . whoever abides in love abides in God, and God abides in him" (1 John 4:7, 16). And for Christians among whom such sinning, such backsliding, such stumbling nonetheless did occur, he gave the comfort that if someone may have sinned once (this verb is in the aorist tense, meaning that the sinning had occurred one time, it was a slip up), for such a sin that was not unto death, forgiveness was available with the Father, thanks to the atonement and advocacy of Christ (1 John 2:1; 5:16).

It is of concern that as the church that came from paganism, we have devoted inadequate attention to the new covenant, to the firm basis of the promise of life in Christ that God has placed under our feet along the pathway of historical acts of redemption. In saving our ancestors he also saved us from the power of paganism, darkness, and death, and transferred us into the kingdom of his beloved Son (Acts 26:18; Col 1:13; 2 Pet 1:11; 2:1). It would have been appropriate for us to compare these great works of God with what he did with Israel at Horeb, the more so since the New Testament often speaks using formulations borrowed from the Old Testament. Not in order to place us under the Law once again—far from it!—but to teach us God's pedagogy. But sadly, to do that, the Old Testament, and certainly the gospel of the Law with its teaching about the name of Yahweh, the covenant of Horeb, the new foundation for Israel, consisting of commands regarding tabernacle, sacrifices, cleansings, feasts, etc., in short: the foundation of the world, was unfortunately all too unfamiliar (the phrase "foundation of the world" was regrettably identified with creation.) The teaching about the sin offering remained a closed book for many people. While in fact it is so extremely important. For with the sins related to the sin offering, what was involved was the question whether it was dealing with unforgiveable or a forgivable lack of respect for the sacred cable that God himself had tied around himself and his people Israel. No one was permitted to damage that cable. Better not even to come near to it. Better not to risk slipping off the life-foundation of Horeb.

5. THE REMAINING ACTIONS CONNECTED WITH THE SIN OFFERING

We need not say anything more about the actions preceding the sin offering, in connection with the animal (leading the animal, etc.), since we discussed this under "General Principles." Nor do we need to say anything about the pouring out of the remaining blood from the sin offering "at the foot of the altar."

We conclude with the following discussion of *the fat and the meat* of the sin offering.

All the *fat* of the sacrificial animals was designated for Yahweh. This included the fat of the animals used for the sin offering. In Lev 4:35 we are told very poignantly that if the animal used for the sin offering were a sheep, then the fatty tail of this animal was to be treated in the same manner as with that of the sheep used for the peace offering. Notice how scrupulously everything was regulated! The best was always set aside for Yahweh!

But what about the *meat* of the animal used for the sin offering?

As we've said more than once, there were two possibilities: (a) the sin offering could be brought for an ordinary member of the congregation or for a tribal leader, and (b) the sin offering could be brought for a (high) priest or for the entire congregation.

(a) In the first situation, the meat of the sin offering was eaten. Perhaps not by the one bringing the offering. Why not? Because though atonement for him had occurred, he was not supposed to think that this was connected to a festive meal. Are we to recall here that a sin offering was never joined with a peace offering? No bread and no cakes.

In fact, the distinction had to be kept in mind between a sin offering and the burnt offering. A burnt offering was entirely burned up on the altar. Everything except the skin, which was for the priest.

So even though the meat of the sin offering was not to be eaten by the one bringing the sacrifice, the priests were allowed to enjoy it. At least if this was a sin offering for the laity. Then the priests were allowed to eat the meat of that sacrifice. This came their way as part of the honorarium for their ministry in the sanctuary. But they were not permitted to eat this meat from the sin offering anywhere else other than in a sacred location, that is, not outside the forecourt. So they were not allowed to take it home, unlike the breast and shank of the peace offering. The latter they were allowed to take home for their wife and daughters to eat (Lev 6:26, 29). But not any of the meat from the sin offering. That was not allowed to leave the forecourt. Moreover, in other respects they had to be careful with this meat of the sin offering, for everyone who came into contact with it would be holy. Perhaps this was referring to such a person as one who had become indentured as a servant in the sanctuary and could be redeemed only at a price. The same concern that sought to prevent any part of the most holy meat from the sin offering ending up outside the area of the sanctuary was manifested in the following stipulations about the cookware in which this meat of the sin offering was cooked. If this was earthenware, it had to be broken afterwards. (You should recall that unglazed earthen cookware retained moisture.) If it was metal, it had to be cleaned carefully. If any of the blood of the sin offering splattered on someone's clothing, the priest had to wash it out well before the person with that garment could leave the forecourt (Lev 6:24–30).

(b) In the second situation as well, *when the animal of the sin offering was slaughtered for the (high) priest or the entire people,* the priests were not allowed to eat its meat. The reason is clear. It was the same reason that the ordinary member of the congregation and the leader were not permitted to

THE SIN OFFERING (LEV 4:1–5:13)

eat the meat from the sin offering. These people were not supposed to think that they had brought a peace offering. The same applied to the priests. Even though their guilt and that of the people (for whom they functioned as substitutes) was atoned by the blood of the animal sacrifice in the sin offering, they were not supposed to think that they had brought a peace offering, to which a joyous meal was always connected. The rule was obvious: the person for whom a sin offering was brought may not eat of its meat. Consequently, all the meat of the sin offering in this second situation was *burned*. Not on the altar of burnt offering in the forecourt. The reason for that is clear as well: because people were not to suppose that they were involved in a peace offering. Therefore the entire animal of a sin offering—skin, head, legs, intestines, and manure—had to be burned, but not in the forecourt, but in a clean place outside the camp, the same place where the ashes of the sacrifices were deposited (Exod 29:14; Lev 4:11–12; 16:27). We should not look for anything more behind this practice. We do see here that extreme care was taken to avoid any and every profaning of the sin offering. For in the case of a sin offering for a priest or for the entire people, this was most holy (*qōdeš qādāšîm*), forbidden for any consumption (Lev 6:25, 30).

It is so very desirable that people be thoroughly acquainted with this teaching of the sin offering, when they come to Heb 13:9–14. There we encounter the familiar words about Jesus, who "suffered outside the gate in order to sanctify the people through his own blood." Everyone will also recall the admonition: "Therefore let us go to him outside the camp and bear the reproach he endured." This Scripture passage is not always properly understood.

Perhaps the misunderstanding arises in connection with the words we just quoted, about Christ's reproach, as if the meat of (some) of the animals used for the sin offering were burned outside the camp *on account of its uncleanness*. Jesus would then supposedly have been cast outside Jerusalem like *an unclean sacrificial animal*. Some make this argument. O how much has been made with this argument! From the preceding, however, we have seen how completely mistaken this notion is. The blood and the meat of the sin offering were very holy. So we must not go in that direction.

The original readers of the letter to the Hebrews, native Jews, would have understood better than we the author's allusion to the teaching of the sin offering in these verses. For a twofold reason, if the assumption is correct that they, or at least some of them, were converted priests. Those people would have been thoroughly familiar with the sacrificial Torah. They would also have been thinking especially and frequently about what a good salary they had earned in the temple in former times. So let's walk through the Scripture passage.

PART 2 | THE SACRIFICIAL TORAH: SPECIFIC REQUIREMENTS

Hebrews 13:9a: Do not be led away by diverse and strange teachings. It was not impossible that some of the Hebrews were so exhausted from being persecuted that they were considering going back to the synagogue, the Jewish church. There you could earn a living. There were the familiar secure practices of ancient times, they were thinking. But the author showed them that the Jewish worship had become something altogether new and foreign. The Torah, stripped of the grace of God that was given in the suffering Messiah Jesus, became a book filled with "strange teachings." The Law of Moses emptied of God's grace is a pagan book.

Hebrews 13:9b: For it is good for the heart to be strengthened by grace, not by foods. It is certainly not unbiblical to say that a person's heart is strengthened by bread (Ps 104:14–15), but it is unbiblical to think that such a thing happens exclusively by bread, by food alone (Deut 8:3).

Hebrews 13:9c: Which have not benefited those devoted to them. When during and after the appearance of Christ in Jerusalem, people had to choose between the worship in the temple and believing in him, many unfortunately stayed with the "foods," thinking surely that they were continuing with the ancient ways, whereas this was being fulfilled, however, and rendered obsolete and antiquated (Heb 8:13). Continuing that worship thus had no meaning any longer and brought no benefit, unlike formerly, under the Law.

Hebrews 13:10: We have an altar from which those who serve the tent have no right to eat. The writer is now making use of a masterful allusion to the Law, to which the Jerusalem priests even today are said to observe. They stuck with the temple and wanted no part of Jesus. Now then, says the writer to the Hebrews, ironically that is what should have been the case. That fit. For the Law prescribed that priests were not permitted to eat of the sin offering that had been slaughtered *for the people as such,* and the blood of which was brought into the holy place and put on the horns of the altar of incense. The writer is counting on his readers being well informed of the teaching of the sin offering. Down to the details. This explains the subsequent "refined" argumentation.

Hebrews 13:11: For the bodies of those animals whose blood is brought into the holy places by the high priest as a sacrifice for sin are burned outside the camp. The priests were not allowed to enjoy the sin offerings that were slaughtered for the people as such and whose blood was brought by the priests into the holy place, and on the great Day of Atonement by the high priest into the Holy of Holies. For such sin offering had to be completely burned outside the camp. So then, Jesus was just such a sin offering for the people. No wonder, then, that the Jerusalem priests today have no part in him. They do not "eat" him. Can you savor the irony?

THE SIN OFFERING (LEV 4:1–5:13)

Hebrews 13:12: So Jesus also suffered outside the gate in order to sanctify the people through his own blood. O how he was a genuine sin offering! He died on the cross outside the gate of Jerusalem—which had come in the place of the ancient tent camp from the wilderness period. He gave his blood—his *own* blood—for the people! He was a genuine "animal" sacrificed as a sin offering for the people.

Hebrews 13:13–14: Therefore let us go to him outside the camp and bear the reproach he endured. For here we have no lasting city, but we seek the city that is to come. The allusions to the circumstances under the Law are tangible once again. To have fellowship with the Jewish worship as that was continuing to be practiced in Jerusalem could hardly go together with fellowship in Christ's crucifixion and death, even though such would bring you reproach and persecution for the sake of Christ (Heb 10:33; 11:26). (The reproach of Christ here is our reproach for Christ's sake.) Be warned, however, you Hebrews! In the long run, you will increasingly find yourselves excluded from the synagogue, the Jewish church, with its economic and social benefits. But it does not have the last word. It is disappearing. Just like what happens with unstable tents. They are suddenly flattened. But soon Paradise will descend to earth, for which Abraham and the other patriarchs were already looking. The city with firm foundations. That reward is being preserved for you in heaven. The eternal inheritance (Heb 11:10, 14).

It is understandable that some came to think that our Lord Jesus Christ was presented in Heb 13:12–13 as an "unclean" sin offering. They would have thought of such Scripture passages as 1 Pet 2:24 ("He himself bore our sins in his body on the tree"). Nevertheless, that view was thoroughly mistaken. It opposed the teaching of the sin offering in the Law, and as we have seen, it violated the context of Heb 13:9–14 itself. Sin offerings were not unclean at all. They were holy to the highest degree. Including those sin offerings that were burned up outside the camp (because they had been brought *for the people* and its blood was *therefore* brought into the sanctuary, so that their meat was not allowed to be eaten by the priests, but had to be burned outside the camp in a clean place). Even the various concluding actions in connection with the sin offering had to serve to convince the Israelites of the utmost holiness of this kind of sacrifice.

Why did the Israelites have to be directed repeatedly to that special holiness of the sin offering? So that they would be constantly reminded of the covenant that God had established with them at Horeb. Reminded of the exalted pedestal on which they had been placed with the "foundation of the world" that occurred there. So that they would be reminded of the sphere of holiness and the climate of life in which they were allowed to enjoy fellowship with Yahweh, and so that they would be warned never to

PART 2 | THE SACRIFICIAL TORAH: SPECIFIC REQUIREMENTS

forsake this foundation, because beyond it lay the uncleanness of paganism and the corruption of death.

When we later encounter various situations that required sin offerings, this scope of the teaching of the sin offering will become still more clear.

9

The guilt offering (Lev 5:14–6:7)

THERE IS BOTH SIMILARITY and dissimilarity between the sin offering and the guilt offering.

Regarding the *similarity*, this will become clear to our readers in a moment. The guilt offering was not of the same kind as the burnt offering and peace offering. These were atonement sacrifices in general—every shedding of blood spoke of atonement—but not in particular. By contrast, the sin offering and the guilt offering was such. They were atonement sacrifices. That constituted the nature of both. Therefore our initial characterization can include them together, to say that the uniqueness of these two sacrifices came out in the fact that they emphasized the gospel of justification (or forgiveness). We will return to this below.

But first something about the *dissimilarity* between those latter two, the sin offering and the guilt offering. This difference was caused by the difference between the sins for which these two atonement sacrifices were brought.

We have discussed the sins for which the sin offering was brought. And we will get better acquainted with them as we read further in Leviticus (for example, about the "sins" of a woman who has just given birth, and of lepers). These were always sins involving, at least in principle, the forsaking of the life-sphere of God's covenant with Israel.

But now something regarding the sins for which the guilt offering was brought. To clearly illuminate the difference between the sins behind the sin offering and those behind the guilt offering, we will use the following analogy borrowed from marriage.

A wife who is unfaithful to her husband and forsakes him to be involved with other men, has of course become to her husband like someone dead. That is obvious. But if a wife does something out of carelessness, something that appears to move in that direction in some sense—and only in some sense—when seen from a distance, that is far from acceptable to her husband and must of course be remedied along the route of atonement, but the foundation beneath the marriage was not destroyed. The marital relationship continues and marital life goes on.

This is analogous to the sin offering.

But in a good marriage, where such fundamental conflicts or such conflicts that could eventually lead to a fundamental separation never arise, nonetheless other things could arise that are not nearly as serious but still far from acceptable. A wife who otherwise demonstrates exemplary fidelity in keeping the marriage bond, could occasionally, without intending any wrong, without even realizing it, injure her husband's position and usurp his rights. In such a situation, the wife would be doing her husband an injustice. It could also happen that a homemaker who in everything is faithful to her husband can conduct herself toward others with dishonor by incurring debts that she fails to pay. Such conduct injures her husband's honor, and she is doing her husband an injustice.

This is analogous to the guilt offering.

So you can see the significant difference between the sins involved in the first situation, and those involved in the second. You can also understand that the reconciliation needed was correspondingly different.

The wrongdoing for which God instituted the guilt offering resembles the wrongdoing of the second wife. The wife who injured the covenant between her husband and herself, but who did him an injustice. Whether directly, by wounding him, or indirectly, through her conduct toward others.

Our current Scripture passage is Lev 5:14–6:7. Other Scripture passages speak of the guilt offering, but nowhere as broadly as here. So this Scripture portion is our primary source for the Bible's teaching about the guilt offering.

For the purpose of a bird's eye view, we will need to divide this passage into two parts. Clearly it constitutes a unit. We find it very regrettable that on account of the chapter and verse divisions in our English Bibles, this is no longer evident. Originally it was, something you can still see from the text of the Hebrew Bible. There, Leviticus 5 ends not with verse 19, but the following seven verses belong to Leviticus 5 as well, so that this chapter has twenty-six verses in the Hebrew Bible, and the teaching of the guilt offering can be found in Lev 5:14–26. In the Septuagint translation in common use (Ralphs) the same is true. The reader may be asking: But how did we get that obnoxious division in this single Scripture passage, where the teaching about the guilt offering is now spread over the two chapters of Leviticus 4

THE GUILT OFFERING (LEV 5:14–6:7)

and 5? The Vulgate is responsible for that, which is the official Bible of the Roman Catholic Church. That explains the strange division that we now have in our English translations. Nevertheless, we will be following this arrangement, since it makes things easier for our readers. But you may wish, depending on the English version of the Bible that you are using, to draw a thick line above Lev 5:14, or use another technique to indicate that with the words, "Yahweh spoke to Moses, saying," a new Scripture section is beginning, one that turns to the guilt offering. Some of our English Bibles will indicate that with editorial headings.

So Lev 5:14–6:7 is a unit. This entire section deals with *offense*. In fact, this entire passage is dealing with *committing offense against Yahweh*.

But within this single unit we must distinguish between a first and a second section, where the first consists of Lev 5:14–19, which deals with unintentional offense against Yahweh, and the second consists of Lev 6:1–7, which deals with non-unintentional offense against Yahweh.

1. LEVITICUS 5:14–19: UNINTENTIONAL OFFENSE AGAINST YAHWEH

To our regret, we must begin our discussion of this passage with a criticism. This concerns the way in which contemporary English translations render the opening verses. Leviticus 5:14–15 read this way in the NASB and the TNIV: "Then the Lord spoke to Moses, saying, 'If a person acts unfaithfully and sins unintentionally against the Lord's holy things....'"

These Bible translations confront the reader with an unnecessary dilemma. It involves the question: How is it possible to be unintentionally unfaithful? Is that possible?

No, of course not. Every Bible reader who reads this first part about the guilt offering and surmises that unfaithfulness is never unintentional but always intentional, is correct. To speak of being "unintentionally unfaithful" is just as strange as speaking of dry water.

In Hebrew we find the word *ma'al*. This word can indeed mean unfaithfulness, infidelity. For example, it is used by Daniel, when he spoke about the sin of his forefathers, which had angered Yahweh so much that the Babylonian captivity resulted. "Because of the treachery [*ma'al*] that they have committed against you" (Dan 9:7). But although this Hebrew word can occasionally be rendered quite suitably as "unfaithfulness," this doesn't work in Lev 5:15, because something comes after the word *ma'al* that further restricts this evil to evil that is committed *unintentionally*. Therefore in this instance, translators should have chosen a different word

PART 2 | THE SACRIFICIAL TORAH: SPECIFIC REQUIREMENTS

than "unfaithfulness" for *ma'al*. As it is, translators have confronted most of their readers with an unnecessary difficulty as they enter this rather challenging passage.

There is something else that makes it necessary, if readers are not to be confused, to clarify what we are accustomed to calling unfaithfulness. You may recall what we said earlier about the rule: There is no forgiveness for intentional sins. That rule applied as well to the evil mentioned here, to *ma'al*. For example, this was intentionally committed by king Zedekiah. This man had pledged loyalty and fidelity to Nebuchadnezzar, who had occupied his country. He had done so with an oath. He had sworn that oath before Yahweh. Nevertheless, he broke his word. God called that: unfaithfulness (*ma'al*), which he committed against me (Ezek 17:20). For intentional *ma'al*, including breaking an oath sworn before Yahweh, there was as a rule no pardon. We see this as one more reason why translators should not have used the word "unfaithfulness" in Lev 5:15, because everyone would immediately relate that to intentionality, which the subsequent verses clearly exclude. In this section, we are not at all dealing with sin like that committed by king Zedekiah.

So a different translation is preferred.

We would prefer to translate the word *ma'al* in Lev 5:15 as "injure." Sometimes this happens unintentionally. Mother can unintentionally overlook a child who is sitting at the table, and thereby "injure" the child. And as we will see, people can injure Yahweh unintentionally. That was, to be sure, a serious injury.

So we propose the following translation: "Yahweh spoke to Moses: If any commits a serious injury by sinning unintentionally against the holy things of Yahweh . . . ."

Before going further, we must say something about the expression "the holy things of Yahweh."

This phrase is not referring to the so-called *most holy* things. We saw earlier that this latter phrase referred to the tabernacle and its furnishings—ark, table of showbread, etc.—but also the share of the food offering that was left over for the priests. We have also met the phrase when we were discussing the meat of the sin offering. The food offering and the meat of the sin offering were most holy, which explains why they were assigned exclusively to the priests. Ordinary members of the congregation had no rights with respect to these. But also no obligations that they could possibly fail to perform.

But there were also *holy things*, things that were not the *most* holy, but simply holy. We encountered an example of this. For the so-called wave

THE GUILT OFFERING (LEV 5:14–6:7)

breast and the shank of the peace offering were devoted to Yahweh. Those were a "holy portion for the priest" (Num 6:20). But the priests did not need to eat them exclusively in the holy place. They could enjoy them at home, with the members of their families.

Among *the holy things for Yahweh* were also all the firstborn clean animals, and all first fruits and tithes of the land. You can read more about this in Numbers 18. It was obvious that God has assigned special rights to these. Regarding the firstborn, we recall the history of Israel's deliverance from Egypt, when the firstborn children of Egypt were killed, but those of Israel were spared. Regarding the gathering of tithes and first fruits in the land of Canaan, these would belong to Yahweh as the Landlord. Because *he* it was who would conquer the land. Therefore Israel would receive the use of the land, but Yahweh remained the Owner. "For the land is mine," he said (Lev 25:23). Because God had a right to all the income that was his as Israel's Landlord, and could use it as he wished, he could also give it to whomever he wanted. At Horeb already, he had assigned this to the tribe of Levi (Lev 27:30). To the priests and Levites. So you can easily understand that withholding any of this from the priests and Levites was basically to injure the rights of Yahweh. For Israel was supposed to leave "the holy things" for Levi, though she actually brought them to Yahweh, who in turn assigned them to the servants in his sanctuary. Recall what we said earlier in connection with the wave breast and the shank of the peace offering, about the "detour."

There you have an explanation of *the holy things of Yahweh*.

With this, the character of the evil for which the guilt offering was instituted will have become clearer. This evil consisted in an assault against rights, in particular, property rights. That is what we are discussing here. According to the customary manner of the Torah of always placing the preeminent first, it speaks first of all about injuring the property rights *of Yahweh*.

Here is an example. Let's suppose that by accident the tenth portion of the harvest from a field was not brought to the sanctuary. Pure oversight. What had to happen?

Three things.

First, what was held back had to be given. Today, we would call that the restitution of what had been stolen.

Second, 1/5 of the stolen material was added as extra payment. Today, we would call that compensation.

So the total of restitution + compensation = 6/5 of what was stolen.

Third, a ram had to be brought as a guilt offering. Of course, this would have to be a whole or healthy ram, without any defects. But what was special is that this was an expensive animal. The priests had to pay close attention to this. Naturally the estimate about whether the ram was expensive enough was assigned to Moses. We read literally: "with the estimation by shekels of silver" (KJV). Though this estimate was originally made by Moses, later this task was given to the priests, so that "according to your estimate" became a technical phrase that meant according the estimate of the priest (Lev 27:2–3). For what purpose was this estimate necessary? Surely to prevent the Israelites from finishing off too easily the payment of their debt. In fact, even with enlisting the priests and their estimate, the danger of corruption remained close at hand. According to 2 Kgs 12:16, it had become common practice that the guilty party paid the priest the value of a choice ram and the priest was supposed to take care of the remainder. That payment had to be given in silver, in silver shekels, and holy shekels, shekels of the sanctuary (Lev 5:15). In this connection we must recall that the shekel was not a coin like we use every day, no piece of currency, but a weight. People used pieces of gold and silver of a certain size, but those pieces still had to be weighed. People carried in their belts a scale with stones. Silver was the usual means of payment, which explains that the word for "silver" can also mean simply "money." What was involved here was undoubtedly the officially established weight for the payments and sacrifices given for the temple, in contrast to the weights used in the market, which depended on various factors like local values, weights for buying or selling, or simple contractual agreement. It seems that we should value the holy shekel to have weighed about ten grams.

With this we are not yet finished discussing the first part of Lev 5:14–19, regarding the guilt offering. For it could be possible that an Israelite had not aggrieved Yahweh in an unintentional manner, but rather had aggrieved one of his neighbors. So the injured party was not Yahweh himself. That latter possibility was what the Torah began with before turning to the former possibility.

Someone in Israel could well have thought that aggrieving the neighbor simply wasn't in view. That the only thing that mattered was that Yahweh was not aggrieved. Which practically speaking simply meant: just so the priests and Levites got their portion—the tithes, etc.—then everything was fine. But aggrieving other people, ordinary people, so what? Was not a human being far less than God?

That is exactly the kind of thinking that our passage warns of in the second half, namely, Lev 5:17–19: "If anyone sins, doing any of the things that by the Lord's commandments ought not to be done, though he did not know it, then realizes his guilt, he shall bear his iniquity. He shall bring to the priest a ram without blemish out of the flock, or its equivalent for a guilt offering, and the priest shall make atonement for him for the mistake that

THE GUILT OFFERING (LEV 5:14–6:7)

he made unintentionally, and he shall be forgiven. It is a guilt offering; he has indeed incurred guilt before the Lord."

The key element in these verses is that no matter how unintentional the harm, and no matter that it was not committed against Yahweh, one was still guilty. Guilty before Yahweh.

The reader should observe well the difference between the first and second halves of our passage. The most important One was first. It began with unintentional harm to Yahweh, in verses 14–16. Then the passage continued with a more general section that treats committing harm in general, in verses 17–19. But even the latter form of committing harm was seen as an evil that rendered a person guilty toward God. In our humble opinion, verse 19b expresses that emphatically.

So a person was already guilty toward Yahweh if he unintentionally aggrieved his neighbor. Now then, how guilty would a person be if he did not act unintentionally, or in other words: had acted intentionally?

To that we now turn.

2. LEVITICUS 6:1–7: INTENTIONAL OFFENSE AGAINST YAHWEH

Both of these sections begin with the same introductory formula: "Yahweh spoke to Moses" (Lev 5:14; 6:1).

From those two introductions, you can see immediately that the one Scripture unit that deals with the guilt offering (Lev 5:14–6:7) consists of two sections. The fact that the second section begins with the same words as the first shows that in this section we are beginning an entirely new subject.

What is the content of this new section?

Is it perhaps the case that whereas the first section began with the sin of unintentional offense against Yahweh, the second section will now deal with the intentional offenses against Yahweh?

No, the second section will not deal with that. In fact, it cannot, for we learn what God thinks about members of his covenant people who committed intentional offenses against him from the story of Achan in Joshua 7. That man committed an offense against Yahweh "with a high hand," as it says in Num 15:30. That man committed the sin unto death, the sin for which there is no pardon.

No, we need not expect that this second section will deal with intentional offenses against Yahweh.

What then remains? Intentional offenses against the neighbor.

Two comments before going further.

An offense against the neighbor in Israel was viewed as an offense against Yahweh, which explains why Lev 6:2 begins this way: "If *anyone* sins and commits a breach of faith *against Yahweh by deceiving his neighbor* . . ." This shows that this sin against the neighbor was viewed as committed indirectly against Yahweh.

Second, you will recall what we said earlier about intentional sins. It simply was not the case that in Israel, for example, every thief was simply put to death, even though stealing is certainly a crime that is always committed intentionally. This was so, despite the rule: whoever sins intentionally must be put to death, a rule that was enforced only in the case of intentional sin committed directly against Yahweh (think of Achan). But it was also the case that when a robbery became known, whether immediately or later, the judges did not have the death penalty enforced against the guilty person, though they did enforce another rather severe punishment. Stolen money had to be repaid double (Exod 22:7), stolen small livestock fourfold, and stolen cattle fivefold (Exod 22:1). But if a thief turned himself in, a far more mild punishment was given. That is what this second section is talking about (Lev 6:1–7).

To assist in clarity, we offer the following overview of the entire subject.

	ma'al against Yahweh		
direct		indirect (via the neighbor)	
intentional	unintentional	unintentional	intentional
(Achan)	(Lev 5:14–16)	(Lev 5:17–19)	(Lev 6:1–7)

Our section provides us an interesting look at the life of the Israelites together. For that is what is in view. Intentional offenses that violate the neighbor's rights. Actually, the word *neighbor* is never mentioned, but rather *fellow citizen*. That did not mean, of course, that people in Israel were permitted to do anything they wished to the sojourner. They were not permitted to oppress and harass the sojourner (Exod 23:9; Lev 19:34). But committing an offense against one's fellow citizen was for that reason so serious, of course, because he too was a covenant partner of Yahweh. Just imagine that a powerful prince like one or another Hittite or Assyrian king was favorably disposed to establishing a covenant with two of his vassals (subordinate rulers), and that those two vassals later waged war against each other. Such a mutual conflict was not tolerated by the treaty into which the king of kings had invited his (subordinate) covenant partners.

Committing an offense against one's own fellow citizen, the brother and fellow covenant member, was the most serious. Here again we see the

THE GUILT OFFERING (LEV 5:14–6:7)

custom followed in the Law of putting at the beginning what was the preeminent part. This example of committing an offense against an Israelite fellow citizen was the most poignant.

How could people commit offenses against each other?

It could happen, for example, that one Israelite gave something of his own to another Israelite as security. Imagine the nomadic, constantly mobile life of shepherds. How often and how long were they required to travel with their flocks away from home? On such trips, they couldn't take everything with them, even for an animal that might become sick. Using security deposits must have been widespread among Israel, especially in regions where they walked around for months bring their flocks to pasture. All kinds of objects, including money, would have been left behind with others, including those who were guarding a village.

For example, one Israelite would give another a sheep as security. Or a sum of money. But when he returned to retrieve his sheep or his money, he was told: "I don't know anything about it. What are you talking about?"

It could also happen that one Israelite simply stole outright from another. Or that one Israelite swindled another, without the other noticing it or being able to prove it. Or someone found an object that another had lost, which he failed to return but kept for himself. When the lawful owner later spotted his lost object and said, "That's mine," the fellow would deny emphatically that he had found it, perhaps with an oath, insisting with all his energy that it had always belonged to him.

Such difficulties can occur among people. If one says "yes" and the other says "no," and there are not witnesses, then a resolution to a potential drawn-out conflict can occur only when the guilty party repents, when his conscience speaks up.

When something like this happened in Israel, there would be forgiveness for the (intentional) transgressor of God's commandment. Of course he must return to his brother what he had taken. In addition, he had to pay one-fifth of the value of what he had taken as a fine. But finally he would have to bring a ram as a guilt offering to Yahweh. For although he had *directly* injured his brother, he had *indirectly* offended Yahweh, whose covenant partners both individuals were. The priest should make atonement for him in the presence of Yahweh, and forgiveness would be granted to him.

Notice how clearly we see here the *evangelical (gospel-filled) character* of the Torah. Naturally, it shows clear traces of correspondence with legislative collections that were enforced among the nations around ancient Israel. But what we saw in connection with the tabernacle, we see here again. The Tabernacle also showed unmistakable traces of similarity with pagan sanctuaries that existed before and during its construction. But thanks to the gospel of God that was exhibited in that tabernacle—the gospel of justification (or forgiveness), sanctification (or conversion or regeneration or the daily renewing of our lives), and glorification (or the Paradisal concourse restored between God and humanity)—this tent became something entirely different from every other contemporary or subsequent sanctuary among the pagans.

Here as well, the laws of sacrifice in the Torah were saturated with God's compassion and patience with his ancient covenant people. We want to alert all Bible readers that they need to pay constant attention to this feature. Otherwise we turn the lovely Law of God into a gruesome pagan document. Recall how earnestly Paul warned (Gal 4:3, 9; Col 2:8, 20) against such a return to the legalistic Jewish and pagan attitude in connection with reading the Law.

Unfortunately in those passages in Galatians and Colossians, our Bible versions leave much to be desired with regard to clarity. For the apostle uses the Greek work *stoicheia*, which referred to heavenly bodies. The primary referent was Israelite worship, in which days, weeks, and months that were regulated by the orbiting times associated with sun and moon, played an important role. We will discuss this further in connection with Israel's feasts. When God's grace was removed from that Israelite worship, what remained was just as empty as the idolatrous worship of sun, moon, and stars, which belonged to the pagan calendar religion. In those four passages mentioned above, you could read the word "calendar" in place of "elementary principles" or "elemental spirits." You need to be very careful not to turn the Torah into a hard-fisted rule-book. For even Paul called the Law "holy, righteous, and good" (Rom 7:12). The Law was lovely. By means of the Law, God wanted to lead his people Israel, with his fatherly hand that was at the same time disciplinary yet friendly, to meet the day of Christ. For this reason, the Law was lovely, because it was to be fulfilled by Israel in love (Rom 13:10).

A wise and loving father does not punish all the sins of his children with equal strictness and severity. Therefore a guilt offering was not the same as a sin offering. The actions that occurred with the former were not all that remarkable. Even though it was an atonement sacrifice, the blood of the guilt offering, unlike with the sin offering, was not dabbed on the horns of the altar, either the altar of burnt offering or the altar of incense offering, but simply sprinkled (*zaraq*) on the (inner) sides of the altar of burnt offering in the forecourt (Lev 7:2). The other actions were identical to those that occurred with the peace offering (laying on of hands, burning the fat). The meat of the guilt offering was not allowed to be eaten by anyone other than the priests, and then only in the holy place, which is to say: not outside

THE GUILT OFFERING (LEV 5:14–6:7)

the forecourt. In this respect, the similarity with the sin offering was undeniable. The intention of this stipulation would have been correspondingly similar, namely, that Israel was not to think lightly of the sins for which the sin offering had been instituted.

The question is asked why for this sacrifice a ram was always to be slaughtered? The correct answer to that question is likely this: because in the ancient world, the sheep was preeminently used for making payment. Especially in the case of bringing tribute to kings. Similarly, the guilt offering was required when the royal legal order that God had instituted in Israel, when he exalted the people of Israel to be his covenant partner, had been violated.

Why did this usually have to be a male sheep, a ram? Probably thereby to underscore the serious character of the evil that had been committed. This was comparable to the sin offering for a leader, that could not be a female specimen of the flock, but always had to be a male.

3. EXAMPLES OF INTENTIONAL INDIRECT OFFENSES (MA 'AL) AGAINST YAHWEH

As we said earlier, the unit of Leviticus that we are discussing here (Lev 5:14–6:7) is the preeminent Scripture passage that deals with the guilt offering, but not the only one. There are more, and we would identify a couple of them, since they shed light on the section of Leviticus dealing with the guilt offering.

First, Num 5:5–10.

The situation was this: someone had treated another person indecently, had hurt them. After some time had passed, he repented of his unlawful conduct. He confessed it and wanted to make it right. But he could not, for the one he injured had died. What was supposed to happen in such a situation?

The guilty party must repay the value of the item stolen, plus one-fifth of the value, and pay it to the next of kin (*go'el*) of the one who had died, whose task was to secure the claims of the deceased.

But what if there was no next of kin? Then the debt could be paid to Yahweh, and Yahweh in turn paid it to the priest—here is that familiar "detour"—to whom the person in question confessed his guilt and who would then perform a guilt offering for that person.

This small piece about the guilt offering in Numbers 5 clearly shows evidence of being a later addition, added to Lev 6:1–7, to what we discussed in (2) above. The purpose of this is clear. God wanted to provide a way for a penitent sinner who faced a situation where the person he swindled was no longer accessible, to nonetheless be able to live with a clean and quiet conscience among Israel, a people who since Horeb was a nation of covenant partners under the Great King Yahweh.

Another situation is different. It is described in Lev 19:20–22. Someone had sexual relations with a female slave belonging to someone else. Such a thing never happened, of course, without forethought, but always intentionally. The temptation to *this* evil would have occurred more easily than the sin of adultery with someone's wife, given the lower position of female slaves.

Should such a man who had sexual relations with the female slave, who belonged to another, be put to death?

Perhaps according to some fanatics, that should have happened. They would probably point to the Seventh Commandment: "You shall not commit adultery." But God's Word does not point us in that direction at all. According to the Torah, that man had not committed adultery. He had not been involved with the wife of his neighbor; for that, to be sure, the death penalty was required (Lev 20:10). Rather, the evil he had committed was viewed as a violation of his neighbor's property rights. The female slave was his property. Therefore the one who committed this evil was first given a punishment. We do not know what that punishment consisted of, though some think it may have been some kind of corporal punishment, like a beating. But that strikes us as somewhat romanticized. We could better suppose that the punishment was monetary. This would have been stipulated by the priest, and the amount would have been paid to the owner of the female slave as compensation for damage. Then the man who had committed the crime would have been required to have the priest sacrifice a ram as a guilt offering for himself. Then the man would have received forgiveness, and would have been able to live again with a good conscience among the people of the covenant made with Yahweh. The violation of the law was covered (symbolically) before God's face by the atoning blood of the ram.

4. EXAMPLES OF UNINTENTIONAL DIRECT OFFENSES (MA'AL) AGAINST YAHWEH

The last situation that we just discussed fit clearly with Lev 6:1–7 (an intentional indirect offense against Yahweh).

We wish to mention two other situations that display the nature of Lev 5:14–19, especially verses 14–16 (unintentional direct offense against Yahweh).

THE GUILT OFFERING (LEV 5:14–6:7)

An Israelite has come down with leprosy. But the sickness has gone away; he is healed. Later we will see, with Leviticus 13–14, all that had to be done in such a situation. Here we would observe initially nothing more than that a sheep had to be brought as a guilt offering for him (Lev 14:12). The reason for that is not mentioned explicitly. At the same time, a sin offering had to be brought, and that would have been required with a view to his having left Israel's life-foundation (more about this later). But because during the time of his impurity the leper had to dwell outside the camp, and at that point did not participate in the *cultus* in the forecourt (a service, *avodah*, Exod 3:12; 12:25–26; 13:5), so that Yahweh was shortchanged by him, this guilt offering for the leper would have been brought with a view to his offense or evil (*ma'al*) committed directly against Yahweh, no matter how unintentional, and for this wrong, such an atonement sacrifice, namely, this guilt offering, was required.

But because this evil had been committed against Yahweh without intention, this time it was prescribed that not a ram, but a sheep, was to be brought as a guilt offering. The leper did incur guilt. For the fact that sin, and thus also leprosy, had entered the world was surely not God's fault. But one could hardly speak of a personal, angry intention at work in this situation. Presumably in this situation, therefore, the person could suffice with a sheep as a guilt offering, rather than a ram.

As the last example we would mention that of the Nazirite, who during the time of his vow had become unclean due to some contact with death in his surroundings. Thereby the entire preceding time of his vow had been rendered void, and he had to start all over again. Moreover, a sheep had to be brought for him as a guilt offering (Num 6:12). The reason for that was that vows made to Yahweh had to be kept. A wrong had occurred against Yahweh. For at bottom, the cause of the interruption of the votive period, namely, death, was not to be blamed on God. Nevertheless, the factor of unintentionality was also in play. With that in view, the Nazirite was required to bring not a ram, but a sheep, as a guilt offering.

In such small details, we must observe God's gentleness. We can see this throughout the Torah. No wonder, since it is a book filled with gospel. That is its pervasive nature. Anyone who does not see the evangelical (gospel-filled) character of the Torah, is left with a pagan document, full of annoying regulations. With the lovely Law of Moses in his hands, such a person has fallen back into our pagan past, with its honoring of "the elemental spirits."

10

The second section of the sacrificial Torah (Lev 6:8–7:38)

WE CAN BE BRIEFER here. In our preceding discussion about the different sacrifices and their distinct regulations, we have mentioned various things.

Nevertheless, you should not think that what follows next will contain nothing new. This conclusion of the sacrificial Torah is itself a distinct entity with its own character.

Actually it was the case that the entire sacrificial Torah consisted of two parts that differed in this way.

Part 1 was commanded to Moses by God with an eye to the *laity*. "Speak to the Israelites and say to them . . ." (Lev 1:2).

Part 2 was given with an eye to the *priests*. "This is the portion of Aaron and of his sons from the Lord's grain offerings, from the day they were presented to serve as priests of the Lord. The Lord commanded this to be given them by the people of Israel, from the day that he anointed them. It is a perpetual due throughout their generations" (Lev 7:35–36).

In order to show a bit more fully the *priestly* character of this conclusion of the sacrificial Torah, we will take our readers on a brief stroll through this passage. We will use italics to indicate each distinct part of this passage.

COMMANDS FOR THE PRIESTS INVOLVING THE DAILY MORNING AND EVENING SACRIFICES (LEV 6:8–13)

In the sacrificial Torah, the burnt offering is discussed twice, first in Leviticus 1 and the second time in this passage.

THE SECOND SECTION OF THE SACRIFICIAL TORAH (LEV 6:8–7:38)

The difference was this. Leviticus 1 talked about the burnt offering that was brought voluntarily *by a member of the laity*, but here it speaks about the two burnt offerings that were to be brought daily for all of Israel, one in the morning and one in the evening, *by the priests*. For that reason, this burnt offering for the congregation was called the continual burnt offering (*tāmîd*). The institution of this sacrifice—a lamb that was always to be accompanied with a grain offering—was described back in Exodus (29:38–46), and again in Numbers (28:1–8).

This continual sacrifice was not voluntary, but a daily obligation. Interrupting or stopping it was something terrible (Dan 11:31; 12:11).

You can imagine that a constant column of smoke went up from Israel's forecourt, ascending in the form of a tower. Pointing to the blood of the lamb that atoned daily, and to the grain offering in which Israel continually offered their heart and life to Yahweh. This symbolism would speak to a Christian today. What does God require of us, now that we have received a new and better covenant, of which Jesus has become its Surety?

Daily provision for this continual burnt offering had to be the first task and the last task. The other sacrifices were permitted, in the course of the day, to be brought *on*, literally, *above* this altar of burnt offering. So this sacrifice has a fundamental place, comparable with the first of the Ten Words: "You shall have no other gods before me." This, too, God had placed first when he gave the Ten Words at Horeb. So, too, the burnt offering had priority. Every morning it was the first sacrifice, and every evening it was the last. Hear, Israel, Yahweh is our God, Yahweh alone. You shall love Yahweh, your God, with all your heart and with all your soul and with all your strength (Deut 6:4–5).

We Christians have all the more reason to open and close each day with such a prayer of praise and thanks, given the unshakeable foundation of the new covenant, upon which the God and Father of our Lord Jesus Christ has now placed us.

Each day, this prayer must be our first and last priestly work (1 Pet 2:9–10), continually (*tamid*), which, if it were to stop, would be terrible.

COMMANDS FOR THE PRIESTS CONCERNING THE GRAIN OFFERING (LEV 6:14–18)

As we just observed, the daily burnt offering was always accompanied with a grain offering. A couple of times it was even *called* "the evening sacrifice" (*leminchath ha'arev*, Ezra 9:4–5).

PART 2 | THE SACRIFICIAL TORAH: SPECIFIC REQUIREMENTS

We wrote earlier about the ingredients required for the grain offering, the quantities used and the most holy character of this sacrifice. Naturally, the hint God was giving Israel in this sacrifice is all the more powerful for us, because God has granted to us the knowledge of the gospel of his Son. So we do not labor in the first place to please ourselves with this, do we? It is true, isn't it, that Christians do not work in the first place in order to eat? But in order, with the fruit of their labor, to serve the God and Father of their Savior.

COMMANDS CONCERNING THE DAILY HIGH PRIESTLY GRAIN OFFERING (LEV 6:19–23)

In addition to the already mentioned grain offering of the priests—of which nothing was eaten—each morning and evening yet another grain offering was to be brought, this one by the high priest. Thus, first by Aaron and later by his successors, from the day of their inauguration into office. This is what the apocryphal book Sirach would have had in view when it says: "Their sacrifices shall be wholly consumed every day twice continually" (45:14). This high priestly grain offering was remarkable.

Everything was perfectly regulated. Each morning and evening, the priests brought a burnt offering and a grain offering. And still it wasn't enough. The grain offering of the high priest had to be added. For he was ultimately the only priest who represented the entire nation. The priest did as well. Their work was also not perfect.

The New Testament teaches us that the ministry of Aaron in turn found it fulfillment in the ministry of our High Priest, Jesus Christ, with his sacrifice rendered once on the cross, and with his daily intercession in heaven for us.

COMMANDS FOR THE PRIESTS CONCERNING THE SIN OFFERINGS (LEV 6:24–30)

We drew a lot from these verses earlier when we discussed the sin offering, so we need not comment any further, except for this one item. This sacrifice was like regulated in such a way that with the eating of the meat of the sin offering, the *officiating* priest had precedence (v. 26). Only if there was enough left over could the other priests who had not officiated eat it. But no one else, for the meat of the sin offering was most holy (v. 29).

THE SECOND SECTION OF THE SACRIFICIAL TORAH (LEV 6:8–7:38)

COMMANDS FOR THE PRIESTS CONCERNING THE GUILT OFFERINGS (LEV 7:1–10)

In connection with this section, we will make only two comments.

1. Here again we see very clearly that we must always read sacred Scripture appropriately. For in verse 7 we read: "The guilt offering is like the sin offering; there is the same ritual for them." A person given to fanaticism would easily infer too much here, as though no difference existed between the guilt offering and the sin offering. But if you reflect on this, you will understand that this stipulation was related merely to the final destination of the meat of the guilt offering and the meat of the sin offering. Both of these kinds of sacrificial meat belonged exclusively to the priests. The meat of the guilt offering was specifically for the officiating priest first of all. God is not served without compensation for his servants.

For that reason, verse 8 immediately adds the stipulation that *the skin of the burnt offering* (which, as you recall, was completely burned up) was also for the priest who had performed the service.

Parenthetically, we never read about the skins of the animals that were slaughtered in connection with the other sacrifices—peace offering, sin offering, and guilt offering. Presumably with few exceptions those skins always went to the officiating priest. But the fact that in this instance alone, something is said about the skin of the animal used for the burnt offering, is to be explained from the reality that the burnt offerings had to be burned up entirely, and no one, absolutely no one, received anything to eat from it. So absolute was the rule that God was not served without compensation for the officiant, so that at least the *skin* of the animal used for the burnt offering had to be given to the priest. It was understood that this went to the officiating priest. For we would bring great sadness to our good God if we were to suppose that he was stingy and tight-fisted. God never permitted people to serve him without compensation. Proof? His command in connection with the skin of the animals used for the burnt offering.

2. Next, we can also see here that already in the days of the Israelite church, the Holy Spirit did not enjoy tiring people out with a monotone system. One might better describe this section of instructions as rambling from one subject to another. For in verse 7, the designation of the meat from the guilt offerings and the sin offerings is discussed. Next, in verse 8, God immediately added the stipulation about the skin of the burnt offering animals. To this, in verse 9, yet another regulation was added regarding the grain offering. Actually, this was a twofold regulation. First, that every grain offering that was baked (regardless of how they were baked) would be

PART 2 | THE SACRIFICIAL TORAH: SPECIFIC REQUIREMENTS

designated for the officiating priest (v. 9); and second, that every other grain offering could be used by the rest of the priests (v. 10).

There you see that even though this passage began by talking about the guilt offering, several regulations about the sin offering, burnt offering, and grain offering were simply joined to it.

Those who suffer from the disease of systematitis will shudder at this. Or allow themselves to be healed and become somewhat more moderate.

COMMANDS FOR THE PRIESTS CONCERNING THE PEACE OFFERINGS (LEV 7:11–21)

We will tell the reader in advance that in the conclusion of the sacrificial Torah, the peace offering is discussed twice. The first time here, and the second time in Lev 7:28–34. What is the difference between these discussions?

The first one is directed to the priesthood and says: "Care for my people." The second one is directed to the people and says: "Care for my priests."

So here we have the first passage, dealing especially with the priests. Those servants had to pay special attention to issues like this: what kind of peace offering was being brought (praise offering, etc.); the age of the meat used in this or that kind of peace offering; and the like. The priests were supposed to pay very scrupulous attention to this technical side of the peace offerings. For even though the meal associated with the peace offering was allowed to be ever so joyful for Israel, eaten right under Yahweh's eyes, it had to be done in a sacred manner, so that, for example, no rotting meat was consumed. For stench and decay were incompatible with God, and with the people of life. (Later we will be discussing how, on account of uncleanness, people could be prevented from participating in such a meal connected with the peace offering [Lev 7:19–20].)

COMMANDS (FOR THE PRIESTS TO SEE TO IT) THAT THE ISRAELITES WOULD NOT USE ANY FAT OR BLOOD (LEV 7:22–27)

Suddenly this passage includes a word that Yahweh spoke to Moses with a view to *the Israelites* (vv. 22–23). Nevertheless, it was obvious that this received a place here in the "priestly" conclusion of the sacrificial Torah because the priests were the individuals appointed to oversee the proper course of events in connection with the sacrifices. That this was inserted specifically at this point would be related to the fact that the peace offerings

THE SECOND SECTION OF THE SACRIFICIAL TORAH (LEV 6:8–7:38)

had just been discussed. These were the only sacrifices of which a portion was used by non-priests.

We may point Bible readers to the fact that this passage must be understood in connection with the time to which it applied. Otherwise they might infer from the words: "You shall eat no fat of ox or sheep or goat," that Israel was never or rarely permitted to enjoy the fat of these animals. But in addition to the fact that there were other clean animals (deer, gazelle), this prohibition given with respect to the animals mentioned was an absolute prohibition only for a time, namely, during the wilderness travels. In connection with Leviticus 17, we will see what God wanted to prevent by means of this prohibition, namely, that here or there among the people an animal (suitable for sacrificing) would be slaughtered and used in connection with pagan sexual abominations. Therefore at Horeb God stipulated that all slaughtering of animals was to occur in the forecourt of the tabernacle, under the watchful eye of his priests, as peace offerings, from which, as you know, the fat was to be brought before God on the altar.

As will become clear in due course from Leviticus 17, this drastic measure was adopted with a view to the special circumstances in the days of Israel's stay at Horeb and in the wilderness. The intention was, as we indicated, to clamp down radically on any and every impulse toward (idolatrous) abominations. Remember where Israel came fRom From Egypt! And where Israel was headed. To Canaan! With a view to that danger, God was now speaking so absolutely. Absolutely no fat (Lev 7:23, 25). But later a change was made to this regulation by Moses (Deut 12). At that point it was the night before Israel would receive her joyful inheritance, when Israel would settle in the land of promise and spread out therein. Then Israel would not be dwelling so close to the tabernacle as during her wilderness travels. So the regulation given here, and the one given in Lev 17:1–7, were suspended at that point. Not, of course, the prohibition against pagan sexual abominations, which continued in force, but the command that people would perform every slaughter for consumption in the forecourt of the tabernacle. Later that was impossible to implement. Naturally, people were then allowed to keep the fat of such an (ordinary) slaughtered animal for themselves, and enjoy it themselves.

Meanwhile at Horeb two other prohibitions were given that later were not suspended by Moses. That is what we'll be discussing in the remainder of our passage.

1. Verse 24. The fat of animals that died on their own, or were killed by other animals, Israel was not permitted to eat either now or in the future. This was stated throughout, in the interests of clarity. For the Israelites knew from many different regulations that her God had an aversion against his

people coming into any contact with death. We will come back to this in connection with Leviticus 11–15 (regarding contact with uncleanness and death).

2. Verses 26–27. Any and all use of blood was and continued to be forbidden. After everything we have said about Lev 17:11, and in view of what we will be saying about Leviticus 17, we need to go into great detail here. Behind this prohibition lay Yahweh's intention to remind his people of their noble position as a holy nation, a people of life. For blood signified death. And death was incompatible with a people who possess such rich promises.

By means of this prohibition, God perhaps wanted simultaneously to keep his people from the superstitious drinking of blood that occurred among the pagans. They seemed to think that through this practice, they came into closer fellowship with their gods. With the Dionysian orgies it happened that those who believed in ecstasy would take an animal that supposedly incarnated the deity and tear it open and eat it raw. The devil surely knows how to deceive our human race with the most ridiculous follies. Those practices seemed to have swirled around Israel. In Leviticus 19, where God warned Israel against other Canaanite abominations, he gave this prohibition: "You shall not eat anything with its blood. You shall not practice augury or witchcraft" (v. 26; notice the sequence of blood and pagan superstition).

Nevertheless, the history of these two remaining prohibitions in our passage continued into the New Testament time.

By means of the shedding of the blood of our Lord Jesus Christ, the shadows of the Law were fulfilled. The animal blood had fulfilled its instructional, symbolic task. The dominion of the commands concerning unclean animals, etc., had also ended. God said: Rise, Peter, kill and eat (Acts 10:13). Gradually the light broke through, and Christians realized that the Law possessed only a shadow of the future benefits. Gradually. (We will return to the epistle to the Hebrews.) Among some of them, this insight was never achieved. These were the so-called Judaists (Judaizers), intense Christians from among the Jews, who continued holding to the letter of the Law with a semblance of legitimacy. But in reality, Paul says, they were instruments of Satan (Eph 6:12; 1 Thess 2:18), in terms of their attempt to turn the Christian church into a Jewish church and to bring Christians who came from the Gentiles under the yoke of the Law of Moses (read in a Pharisaic, i.e., pagan manner). Fortunately, the apostles did not yield an inch to these ruthless quasi-brothers, so that we who are Christians of pagan origin may now stand in the freedom of the cross of the Lord.

But the apostles gathered together for the purpose of deliberating the issue of the place of converted Gentiles in the church of Christ (Acts

THE SECOND SECTION OF THE SACRIFICIAL TORAH (LEV 6:8–7:38)

15:1; Gal 2:12), and at the recommendation of James, who was the leader in Jerusalem and was deeply involved with that ostensible seriousness of the Judaistic fanatics, they decided that these Gentile Christians should abstain from four things: (1) from things polluted by idols; (2) from fornication; (3) *from whatever has been strangled*; and (4) *from blood* (Acts 15:20). Of course, these four points were not related to such wicked sins as idolatry and sexual immorality in general. The Gentiles would have understood immediately what was wrong with these. But these four points involved special difficulties in the transition period of that time. Perhaps we could speak of boundary situations. By this is meant that Gentile Christians would have related to their fellow Christians of Jewish blood, first, by not offending them through the use of meat that came from pagan temple festival halls; second, by entering marriages involving the degrees of kinship forbidden in Leviticus 19; third, by *using animals that had not been suitably bled out at the time of slaughter, but who died on their own or were strangled in a snare or drowned*; and fourth, by *using the blood of an animal in ways similar to what we see today in certain dishes that are widely prepared and enjoyed, for example, blood sausage*. Today there is nothing wrong with that. But in the early days of the New Testament church, a time of transition, it was wise for the apostles to facilitate fellowship between Gentile and Jewish Christians, by earnestly imploring the former group of Christians to abstain from things that were very offensive to the latter group of Christians. This gentle wisdom aimed at facilitating the living together of two so entirely different groups, as Christians in one place, the apostles confessed to having received from the Holy Spirit (Acts 15:28). For he is a Spirit of peace (Rom 15:17).

We know that the Gentile Christians honored these friendly requests coming from Jerusalem. When, for example, people sought to extract from the woman martyr, Biblias of Lyon, a confession about certain shameful acts committed by Christians amongst one another—incest and eating children—she cried out: "How could such people eat children, since they are not even permitted to taste the blood even of irrational animals? (Eusebius, *Church History*, V.1.25–26). (You should also read, however, the appeal of Guido de Bres in his "Baston" to *the provisional character* of these Jerusalem decisions, in order thereby to oppose the legitimacy of subsequent ecclesiastical regulations under which believers in his day were groaning.)

PART 2 | THE SACRIFICIAL TORAH: SPECIFIC REQUIREMENTS

COMMANDS FOR ALL ISRAEL CONCERNING THE PORTION OF THE PEACE OFFERINGS ASSIGNED TO THE PRIESTS (LEV 7:23–34)

In this passage, the Israelites heard the drumbeat of: Care for my priests!

The reader knows what we have said about the three "portions" of the peace offering. The first was for Yahweh. The second was for the priests. The third was for the people. That last one is not discussed in this passage. The first one is, which involved the fat that belonged to Yahweh alone. And the second portion, which actually was also designated for Yahweh, but was given by him—along the familiar "detour"—to the priests. This passage is talking most extensively about that portion. Care for my priests!

Paul appealed to this divine care for Israel's priests, in terms of the right for those proclaiming the gospel "should get their living by the gospel" (1 Cor 9:13–14). Here again we see that the offerings preached the gospel! Unfortunately, Israel did not always faithfully observe God's command in this passage (Judg 17:7; 1 Sam 2:36).

Nor did the later Christian church. Witness, for example, the struggle of many a minister to "keep his head above water," although that could have involved significant personal culpability as well.

CONCLUSION OF THE SECOND SECTION OF THE SACRIFICIAL TORAH (LEV 7:35–36)

We read this: "This is the portion of Aaron and of his sons from the Lord's food offerings, from the day they were presented to serve as priests of the Lord. The Lord commanded this to be given them by the people of Israel, from the day that he anointed them. It is a perpetual due throughout their generations."

As you can see, these verses relate to the immediately preceding, to what in the last large section of the sacrificial Torah, the second main section, was laid especially upon the hearts of the priests.

POSTSCRIPT IN CONNECTION WITH THE ENTIRE SACRIFICIAL TORAH (LEV 7:37–38)

The concluding postscript, however, places one more finishing touch to the entire sacrificial Torah. It consists of a summary of all the kinds of sacrifices that we have been discussing. Burnt offering, grain offering, etc. Therefore

THE SECOND SECTION OF THE SACRIFICIAL TORAH (LEV 6:8–7:38)

you might suppose you could easily skip over these verses. But when you read them carefully, you are struck by the appearance of the name of one kind of sacrifice that we've not yet encountered in Leviticus, namely, the name "ordination offering." The KJV renders this as "the consecrations," and referred to installing someone as priest. We will return to this in the next chapter. Among the Israelites this name was apparently so common that people talked of consecrating the altar (Ezek 43:26). Such a consecration offering had not yet been mentioned in the sacrificial Torah, though it had been mentioned in Exodus 28–29, when it spoke of the future installation of Aaron and his sons. But here in Leviticus, that is still coming, in Leviticus 8–10. Nonetheless, the person who collected and arranged the various components of the sacrificial Torah wanted, in this final postscript that he appended, to point all Israel to the right of the priests to their share of the sacrifices that they had coming to them from the day of their installation.

This, then, is how the beautiful sacrificial Torah ends. The first main section of Leviticus, an important component of the foundation on which God had established the Israelite "world" at Horeb, permeated with his grace and love. Therefore, it is fulfilled properly by reciprocal love, that is to gives one's heart, indeed, one's very self. The godly in Israel confessed this, as we see in Psalm 40: "Sacrifice [= peace offering] and offering you do not desire [rather stout faith-language, meaning: you are not satisfied with that], but you have given me an open ear [LXX: you have prepared my *body*, i.e., every part of me]. Burnt offering and sin offering you have not required. Then I said, "Here I am; in the scroll of the book [of the Torah] it is written of me." Not only imposing figures like David understood that the sacrificial Torah demanded their heart, but simple church members knew this as well, evidenced from their singing this worship song of Ps 40:1–10. "I delight to do your will, O my God; your Law [Hebrew, *torah*] is in my heart (v. 8). No wonder, however, that when the author of the letter to the Hebrews was describing how Christ had come to fulfill the Law, put these words, according to the above-mentioned Septuagint translation, specifically on the lips of our Savior. For people did not, and do not, understand the Torah, including the sacrificial Torah, unless they are led by one and the same Holy Spirit who had directed Christ entirely, and in every detail, who is now called the Spirit of Christ (1 Pet 1:11).

Part 3

The Priesthood

11

The "installation" of Aaron and his four sons (Lev 8)

IN THE CHAPTERS OF Leviticus now up for discussion, Leviticus 8–10, we have the report of the installation of Aaron as high priest and of his four sons as priests. *They* would be permitted to be the "approachers" to God on behalf of Israel.

Their installation would have occurred not long after the construction and dedication of the tabernacle. At the close of Exodus, we read that Yahweh entered into his sanctuary. But he had not yet prescribed the ministry of sacrifices in and around that sanctuary. He probably set that out for the first time to Moses when in that tabernacle. Leviticus 1–7 is the report of that, the sacrificial Torah. Our book opens with that. If you have read that section, you will be able to follow more easily the course of events in connection with the installation of Aaron and his sons.

But now those two components, this sanctuary and the "personnel" that would be performing the *cultus* in connection with this sanctuary had to be publicly connected together.

We read about that in Leviticus 8–10, the second large section of our book.

At the same time, along with the consecration of the tabernacle and its accessories, Aaron and his sons are also consecrated.

In a manner that is clearly a symbolic form of speaking, the sanctuary and cultic personnel are publicly connected to each other. Everything according to God's detailed prescription that we can find in Exodus 29. In Exod 30:22–23 we find the recipe for the anointing oil of consecration that was to be used for this occasion. It had to consist of olive oil mixed

PART 3 | THE PRIESTHOOD

with myrrh, cinnamon, cane, and cassia. These four ingredients probably pointed to the ministry of the priests in connection with the sanctuary of Yahweh on behalf of the twelve (3 x 4) tribes. The *oil* would have "spoken" of the promise to equip, and the *incense* would have pointed to the blessing that the worship conducted by this consecrated cultic personnel in this anointed sanctuary would be pleasing to God. What a place! Later, Heb 7:11 says that the Torah or Teaching of Israel *rested* upon this priesthood. And recall how Aaron and Christ are repeatedly compared in Hebrews 5 and 7:1–10:18. For this is what we need to state at the outset: in Leviticus 8–10, Aaron is the main figure. Pay close attention to him. Then you will sense the growing tension in these three chapters.

The main themes in this section of Scripture could be identified with the following familiar words:

1. Leviticus 8: *Installation* (our chapter 12)
2. Leviticus 9: *Inauguration* (our chapter 13)
3. Leviticus 10: *Deposition* (our chapter 14)

We turn first, then, to the "installation" of Aaron and his four sons (Lev 8).

We can read in Exodus about the *mandate* to install Aaron and his four sons as priests. It was given to *Moses*. "Then bring near to you [singular] your brother Aaron, and his sons with him, from among the Israelites, to serve me as priests—Aaron and Aaron's sons, Nadab and Abihu, Eleazar and Ithamar" (Exod 28:1). Well, with a palpable throw-back to that mandate, the narrative in Leviticus begins describing the fulfillment of this mandate: "Yahweh spoke to Moses, saying, 'Take Aaron and his sons with him, the vestments, the anointing oil, the bull of sin offering, the two rams, and the basket of unleavened bread; and assemble the whole congregation at the entrance of the tent of meeting'" (Lev 8:1–3).

How scrupulously that mandate was fulfilled!

Moses functioned temporarily as priest. This explains why he later receives the honorarium belonging to him for that service, namely, the wave breast of the ram of consecration (Exod 29:26; Lev 8:29). The rule, "God is never served without compensating his servants," is implemented even here.

Moreover, the "installation" did not occur secretly. Every appearance of the priesthood being a family club is completely avoided. Moses had to call together "the entire assembly" in the forecourt (Lev 8:3). Please do not interpret this "democratically." Just as with other occasions, only Israel's elders would have been summoned (Lev 9:1), but to an official meeting all were summoned so that all Israel would know that Aaron and his sons had not appointed themselves as high priest and priests. They had been chosen

THE "INSTALLATION" OF AARON AND HIS FOUR SONS (LEV 8)

by God for this. So later everyone would need to be silent. But we know that unfortunately, this did not happen. These who were God's anointed very soon encountered opposition from a quarter where nobody would have expected it. From his own sons.

At this point, we will draw the attention of Bible readers to the following five-step process leading up to the installation.

STEP 1: WASHING WITH WATER (LEV 8:5–6)

This washing naturally possessed a symbolic character. For washing occurs in daily life to remove the dirt from the body. But this washing of Aaron and his sons, seen in the light of so many washings that the book of Leviticus will be mentioning, would have proclaimed very loudly the demand of complete forsaking of everything that tended toward uncleanness, decay, and death, since they could not for one moment be combined with the service of Yahweh in his sanctuary. We'll say more about these washings later.

STEP 2: ROBING AARON (LEV 8:7–9)

Aaron was first robed with that beautiful and significant high priestly ornamentation we discussed extensively in our commentary on Exodus.[1]

The Bible reader should pay close attention to the fact that not all five men received their priestly garments *at the same time*. Consequently, we must assume that Aaron's sons were also washed later—we can hardly assume that they would have had to stand all that time naked—even though the reports of the washing of all five were combined into one report in verse 6. That was substantially correct. But with emphasis we are told *first* of the robing of Aaron. In verses 7–9 we read about him (singular), not them.

God's intention with this robing was obvious. Hereby Aaron received from the outset the visible and tangible assurance, both with respect to himself and to his surroundings, of his calling and election to the high priesthood. This was unique.

---

1. Vonk, *Exodus*, 265–98.

PART 3 | THE PRIESTHOOD

STEP 3: ANOINTING THE TABERNACLE AND AARON (LEV 8:10–12)

This was the sequence. First the tabernacle was anointed, then Aaron was anointed. Yes, Aaron, that man who was so gifted, was but a servant. Christ himself is called God's Servant.

But both tabernacle and high priest were anointed with the same oil. Thereby those two entities were being publicly connected. In contrast to Israel's elders. Identified and connected as worker and workplace that would henceforth belong together.

You must not ascribe *any magical significance* to this anointing and consecrating of the tabernacle and of Aaron. The oil was no tool of magic. It was not needed in order for *the tabernacle* to become a divine sanctuary, for it had been accepted by God as such already (Exod 40). Nor was it necessary for Aaron to be anointed as a way of elevating him to some kind of supra-earthly, semi-divine status. No, the anointing served merely to help make observable to the senses, to make visible and understandable God's requisition. This man would have to serve God in this tent. Pay attention to the sprinkling of the anointing oil seven times on the altar. Seven was the number of the covenant. This man would be permitted to approach God here as a representative of the covenant people of Israel. You could see that on this day. And smell it!

This anointing of Aaron occurred at an entirely different time and in an entirely different manner than that of his sons, something we'll discuss in a moment. First, it occurs *immediately after* his robing with the high priestly garment. That of his sons occurred some time later, after they had received their priestly garments. Second, the oil of anointing was suffused on Aaron's *head*, one of our most preeminent body parts. *Suffused*. Not simply covered or sprinkled, but suffused. Hereby, not only is the promise given to Aaron, together with assurance of his being equipped in a special way for his task by God's Spirit, but with respect to his surroundings he is also being guaranteed the highest place among God's priests. Are not the readers here being prepared already, for when the oldest two sons of Aaron did not respect this special privilege of their father, and were punished severely for that? Aaron was *the* priest. The high priest.

STEP 4: ROBING AARON'S SONS (LEV 8:13)

In our commentary on Exodus we discussed the manufacture and meaning of the garments of the priests.[2] We would point out once more that you need not assume that the four sons of Aaron had to stand in the forecourt naked during the rather lengthy time after their washing until they received the priestly garments. Apparently they were washed later, though this was reported to us in verse 6 at the same time we are told of their father's washing. Next, their robing occurred after that of their father, and their anointing followed much later. All of this had the wise intention of drawing the attention of both Israel's elders as witnesses and the four ordinary priests themselves to the entirely unique character of Aaron's office. Only *he* was called to the high priesthood. The four ordinary priests received in their elegant official garments a divine certificate of their calling. But no matter how exalted it was, it was not as exalted as the election of Aaron. As though to underscore this great difference one more time, they were not anointed at this time. Something altogether different came next.

STEP 5: COVENANT MAKING (LEV 8:14–36)

Once again we are using the word *covenant*. But now we do not have in mind with that word the covenant that God established with Abraham, nor the covenant of Horeb made with all Israel. The covenant we are now talking about was established by God with Aaron and his sons.

It is true that the *word* covenant does not appear in these three chapters of Leviticus that we are now discussing. But it does occur in Num 18:19, Deut 33:9, Neh 13:29, Jer 33:21, Mal 2:4, and the apocryphal book, Sir 45:15. Even though from the course of events described here, we can clearly see that God entered a covenant with Aaron and his sons. This will become plain when we pay attention to the following five moments.

Moment 1 of the covenant making (Lev 8:14–17)

The first three moments of covenant establishment are very closely connected with the slaughtering of one of the three animals that were just mentioned, namely, a bull and two rams.

First the bull was slaughtered. For it was a sin offering for the priests. Aaron and his sons were not yet priests, but they would soon become priests.

---

2. Vonk, *Exodus*, 256–64.

First they placed their hands on the head of the bull, after which "someone" slaughtered the animal. That term "someone" probably refers to those bringing the sacrifice, namely, Aaron and his sons.

But then Moses became involved as priest, whose name is explicitly mentioned. With his finger he dabbed some of the blood of the sin offering on the horns of the altar. Of which altar? Certainly not the altar of incense, since the Sacrifice Torah prescribed this to be used in the situation of a sin offering for the (high) priest, but rather the altar of burnt offering in the forecourt, as was supposed to occur when a sin offering was brought for ordinary members of the congregation. Aaron and his sons were not yet priests with full rights and with full duties. We read only later that Moses entered the holy place. Not yet at this point. And not with this blood.

Why was that blood of the sin offering placed *on the altar*? Because the altar was the meeting place for God with his people that he had promised, and the altar represented his people before his face. The purifying of the altar symbolized and guaranteed the atonement, the covering, of the sins of Aaron and his sons. Why was the blood of the sin offering placed on the horns of the altar? To ratify God's promise to cover the sins of the soon-to-be-installed priests.

Next the rest of the blood was poured out alongside the altar, and the fat of the animal sacrificed as a sin offering was burned on the altar. Everything was to go according to the rules in the sacrificial Torah that are by now sufficiently familiar to us.

Nothing of the meat of this sin offering animal was eaten by anyone. Perhaps because Aaron and his sons were viewed as priests in some sense. We recall that in the situation of a sin offering for priests, nothing of the sacrificial meat was permitted to be eaten. Or perhaps because Aaron and his sons were viewed in some sense as "laity," as members of the congregation, whereas Moses, who only on this occasion functioned as priest *in loco*, was not viewed by God as eligible to eat the meat of the sin offering. Perhaps that's going too far.

In any case, everything pertaining to the sin offering, except the blood and the fat, was burned outside the cap.

Moment 2 of the covenant making (Lev 8:18–21)

Next, one of two rams was slaughtered to serve as a burnt offering. Once again, according to the rule that applied to this kind of sacrifice. Earlier we became acquainted with the unique preaching of the burnt offering. The sin offering spoke of the promise of the forgiveness of sins, whereas the burnt

THE "INSTALLATION" OF AARON AND HIS FOUR SONS (LEV 8)

offering spoke of the promise of sanctification and complete surrender *to* God and acceptance *by* God.

Moment 3 of the covenant making (Lev 8:22–29)

The other ram was then sacrificed, as a "ram of ordination" or "ram of consecration." (The nasb has a footnote indicating the literal meaning of the word as "ram of *filling*"; to "fill someone's hands" meant to appoint someone as priest.)

What was the nature of this third sacrifice?

With a view to the special occasion (installing a priest), it was called a sacrifice of filling or of consecration, but in terms of its *nature*, it was really a peace offering. You will recall that only a peace offering was followed by a related meal. That is what happened with this sacrifice. We will return to this in a moment. First we need to point to two facts.

1. After the usual actions had been performed with this ram (laying on of hands, etc.), Moses took some of its blood and placed it on the lobe of Aaron's right ear, on his right thumb, and on the big toes of his right foot. He then did the same with Aaron's sons.

The significance of this was obvious.

The *right side* would have been seen as a person's most important side. By placing blood on the *ear*, the assurance is being given that God would use the priest's ear for knowing his Torah and teaching it to his people. By dabbing the *right thumb* and the *big toe of the right foot*, the calling is being emphasized of occupying the appointed position with conduct and behavior that would be exemplary to the flock. For in all covenants there are contained two parts. A promise and a demand.

God did not think it necessary that Aaron and his sons be covered entirely with the sacrificial blood. They were not sprinkled with this blood, nor was it poured out over them, as reportedly happened with the Greek mystery religions. Just as Christians of a later time, who lived in northern climates, understood that because of unfavorable climate conditions, baptism did not have to be administered by means of immersion, but they could suffice with sprinkling water on a person's head. We need to pay attention, however, to the fact that stipulating those particular body parts of Aaron and his sons—ear lobe, thumb, big toe—would have had special significance. The *ear* was needed to learn to know God's will, while *hand* and *feet* were needed for doing God's will.

2. Next, the hands of Aaron and his sons were literally "filled." By whom? You might reply, "By Moses." But Moses would have been acting only by divine mandate.

With what did God fill their hands? With portions of the "sacrifice of filling"—as this particular peace offering was called—and with portions of the grain offering that went along with it, which otherwise no mortal human was permitted to touch with so much as his finger, and which otherwise was always supposed to be placed directly on the altar and burned. With these portions of the sacrifice, which otherwise had to be reserved for God alone, *they* were permitted to hold in their hands. Note well. Not the familiar portions of the peace offering that were given to the priests as gifts (wave breast and hind quarter). Nor with the remainder that was allowed to be used by the person himself who had brought the sacrifice, enjoyed in the company of his family as the joyful sacrificial meal. No, rather, those five men were permitted to hold in their hands God's private portion. After which, naturally, this was burned up. But this was nonetheless a highly important moment. At that point, those men were being publicly identified in a very explicit way as priests of God. They, and only they, were deemed worthy to stand before God's face with filled hands—and note with what they were filled!—and to be active before the face of God with *the unique portion belonging to God*. That fact proclaimed the very close connection of these men to the ministry of Yahweh. And clearly it was being portrayed clearly to these men themselves how this exalted privilege obligated them to an impeccable obedience to their divine Sovereign!

Moment 4 of the covenant making (Lev 8:30)

Now follows, however, the actual inclusion of Aaron and his sons in the special covenant we mentioned.

To understand properly the various details, you need to recall what happened with the establishment of the Horeb covenant (Exod 24). Not that we want to identify the Aaronic covenant and the Sinai covenant. But they are similar. So then, when God established a covenant at Horeb with all Israel, first the altar was sprinkled with one half of the blood. This represented the atonement of the twelve tribes with God. The altar with its twelve stones represented the twelve tribes. The nation. For no one can approach God unless his sins had first been covered. But then the other half of the blood was sprinkled upon the people. For what purpose? This time not for the purpose of atonement, for that had already occurred on the altar, but for the purpose of *consecrating* the nation. At that point the nation was acceptable before

THE "INSTALLATION" OF AARON AND HIS FOUR SONS (LEV 8)

God as a covenant partner. Moses said at that point: Behold the blood of the *covenant* that Yahweh is making with you (Exod 24:8).

We should recall this now in connection with the covenant God is making with Aaron and his sons.

In this context, what is sprinkled is not just blood, but blood together with oil. Both of these ingredients would have been mixed together beforehand.

Earlier in connection with the making of the Horeb covenant with all Israel, sprinkling with *oil* did not occur. The nation had been consecrated as covenant partner. This explains the sprinkling with blood (Exod 24:8). But Israel was not being called to a special office. This explains why there was no sprinkling with oil. But Aaron and his sons were sprinkled with *both* blood and oil. First, with *blood*, about which it is stated explicitly: "the blood that was on the altar" (namely, that had been thrown against on the sides of the altar [Lev 8:24]). That blood had been put there beforehand for atonement. Now it was being applied for consecration. Second, with *oil*, whereby assurance is given of equipping these men for their priestly covenantal task.

With this mixture of blood and oil the clothes of the five men, and in them, all subsequent office-bearers, was sprinkled. So that in this way, the sons of Aaron received the anointing that God's commandments extended to them as well (Exod 40:15). To them as well. But the first anointing that we discussed—see the third moment—they did not receive. They had been included by God in the covenant of the priests, but not as high priest.

Moment 5 of the covenant making (Lev 8:31–32)

We have already directed attention to the fact that the third sacrifice brought on this occasion was called a sacrifice of consecration or of "filling," but that its nature and kind was that of a genuine peace offering. We see this now from the three familiar "portions." The first was for Yahweh, the fat (v. 28). The second portion consisted, as the reader knows, of the wave breast—designated for the officiating priest, on this occasion, Moses (v. 29)—and the hind quarter. The latter part was actually designated for the priesthood, but because this did not yet exist, this time the hind quarter was burned, together with the fat and the cakes, which together with the meat, were waved (vv. 25–28).

At that point, there was yet a third portion of the peace offering, consisting of all the remainder designated for the one(s) bringing the sacrifice. In this case, for Aaron and his sons. Indeed, these men ate the remaining meat of the peace offering. Entirely according to the rule that would soon become quite customary.

Nevertheless, there was something very special connected with this peace offering meal. Otherwise it would have been permissible that besides the one bringing the offering, others could share the meal. But on this occasion that was not allowed (Exod 29:32–33). This time as well, for increasing the joy of the peace offering, the cakes used with the meat were unleavened (that is, without yeast, unraised). Nothing was permitted to be left over for the next day, but all the excess meat and bread had to be burned. But otherwise it was through and through a peace offering, just like the one offered at the establishment of the Sinai covenant with all Israel (see our commentary on Exodus).[3]

At the close of Leviticus 8 (vv. 33–36) we are told that the above-mentioned ceremonies lasted for seven days. Each day all over again. Thereby strong emphasis was being placed on the covenantal character (seven times) and the difficult nature of the task of Aaron and his sons, namely, of approaching God on behalf of others. They couldn't do that even for themselves. Therefore, in connection with this chapter dealing with the installation of the Old Testament priesthood, we automatically think of our Savior. He was able to remove with his suffering and bloodshed the great chasm that lay behind all the washings, purifications, etc., because he was a high priest: holy, without guilt or stain, separated from sinners and exalted above the heavens (Heb 7:26). But for that reason Hebrews also says that as Surety, High Priest, and Mediator, Jesus has become a *better* covenant (Heb 7:22; 8:15).

---

3. Vonk, *Exodus*, 123–25.

12

The "inauguration" of Aaron and his four sons (Lev 9)

IN THIS CHAPTER, WE are told that not only the high priest Aaron entered his office, but his sons had also begun to perform some priestly work already. But far and away the heaviest emphasis falls on the former, Aaron's entrance into his office. In this chapter you see Aaron becoming more prominent, until he is entirely the main person functioning in the sanctuary.

Initially Moses was that person. For example, it was Moses who communicated the commands found in Exodus 29, commands given to him on the mountain by Yahweh, regarding Aaron's anointing and entrance into office. Already during that conversation with Moses, God had given the mandate that when he entered into his office, Aaron would later need to bring sacrifices for himself and his sons (Lev 9:1, 2, 7), and only then for the nation (9:3–4, 7). Moses was permitted to pass along the promise that after the required sacrifices had been brought by Aaron (with the cooperation of his sons), a revelation of God's glory would occur (Lev 9:4, 6). Of course that would then signify a public approval of God on Aaron's entrance into office. For Aaron's "inauguration" did not happen in secret, but in a public assembly of the church, understood as being represented by her elders (Lev 9:1, 5).

The sequence would be this.

Aaron would render a sacrifice first for himself and then for the people (v. 7), as we read in most of our English translations. First there he "made atonement for you and for the people," and then: "bring the offering of the people." So in our English versions, the *people* appear in both actions, in both parts of verse 7.

But the Septuagint puts it differently. In verse 7a, it reads: "make atonement for you and *for your house,*" and only in verse 7b: "then you shall perform the sacrifices *for the people* and make atonement for them."

This fits much better.

It is possible that the Septuagint was following an ancient Hebrew manuscript that provided its reading. First: "for you and *for your house.*" And only then: "*for the people.*" Perhaps this was the original Hebrew reading, but a later copyist inserted the word "people" from verse 7b into verse 7a. That was written too soon. Much too soon.

If this is accurate, then the Septuagint has preserved the oldest and best reading of verse 7, indicating that Aaron sacrificed first for himself *and his house*, and only then *for the people.*

In any case, this is the substantive sequence in the verses now under consideration.

1. The sacrifices of Aaron for himself (vv. 8–14);

2. The sacrifices of Aaron for the people (vv. 15–21).

1. AARON'S SACRIFICES FOR HIMSELF (LEV 9:8–14)

That's what it says. These were Aaron's sacrifices.

The sons of Aaron were certainly allowed to assist their father. They were certainly allowed to handle the sacrificial blood. But the leadership remained with Aaron and we read explicitly that the sin offering was a sacrifice for him (v. 8). Surely we think here of the writer of the letter to the Hebrews, who did not tire of reminding his (Jewish) readers: first the high priest in Jerusalem had to render sacrifice "for himself" (Heb 5:3; 7:27; 9:7). For the Law appointed as high priests men who were filled with weakness (Heb 7:28). Nevertheless the relationship between Aaron's work and that of his sons does not escape us. *He* was the leader. *He* rendered the sacrifice.

These sacrifices that Aaron had to bring for himself were two in number. First, a sin offering, and second, a burnt offering. We know the significance of these. The sin offering preached atonement with God, and the burnt offering gave assurance that the complete surrender to God of the person who was rendering the sacrifice was accepted.

It is striking that with Aaron's entrance into office, God did not require a bull, although this was the animal designated for the high priestly sin offering, but only a calf. This reduced requirement was perhaps related to the rule of a male goat, rather than a bull, as a sin offering in connection with festival occasions (Lev 16:5; 23:19; Num 28:15, 22; etc.), but could also be explained on the basis of God's gentleness and accommodation (cf. the meager guilt offerings in the case of leprosy and the like). For Aaron was not yet high priest in full service. Nor did he yet have a full year of official ministry behind him, as he did later on the great Day of Atonement. For that occasion, a larger animal was required. A bull. Now only a calf.

That Aaron was not yet fully functioning as high priest can be seen as well from the fact that some of the blood of this first sin offering that Aaron himself sacrificed was not dabbed on the horns of the altar of incense, in the holy place, but on the horns of the altar of burnt offering in the forecourt. Later Aaron would enter the sanctuary for the first time (Lev 9:23).

2. AARON'S SACRIFICES FOR THE PEOPLE (LEV 9:15-21)

Here we are dealing with those people rendering sacrifices concerning which all of Scripture, all the way to Heb 7:27, speaks in the second place: "First for his own sins and *then for those of the people.*" Naturally these last words refer especially to the sin offering that Aaron brought.

He brought four sacrifices altogether for the people, namely, the sin offering, the burnt offering, the grain offerings, and the peace offering. We have discussed the significance of these sacrifices sufficiently enough that here we may limit ourselves to a few comments about the first and the fourth, the sin offering and the peace offering.

1. On this day, no bull was slaughtered as *sin offering for the congregation*, but only a male goat. Here again we may see God's accommodation. On this occasion there was no sin offering being sacrificed for the people with a view to a concretely identifiable sin. Therefore God was satisfied with a smaller sacrifice. Perhaps we may learn from this that God does not take pleasure in creating within us human beings a greater sense of guilt than is real, and in any case, that when we confess our sins we must not be guilty of putting on a banal parade of generalities.

2. Concerning the twofold *peace offering*, a cow and a ram, naturally the first "portion" of the animal, namely, all of the pieces of fat, were to be burned on the altar. Next the second part was waved, and the portion went to the priesthood. The wave breast and the hind quarter. The third portion, the remainder, would have been given to the elders, as representatives of the people, for celebrating the peace offering meal. We don't read of that explicitly. But what else would have been done with this third portion? This was, after all, a peace offering for the people. This is also about how things went with the making of the Sinai covenant (see Exod 24:11). But the narrator paid no attention to this detail, something we can explain from

the familiarity with the rules for the peace offering that he assumed were known by his hearers and readers, together with the fact that he was in a bit of a hurry. For now we encounter the high point of the day. His narrative now becomes very exciting.

3. AARON'S FIRST BLESSING OF THE PEOPLE (LEV 9:22)

Verse 22a reads: "Then Aaron lifted up his hands toward the people and blessed them." The Hebrew does not emphasize the word "then": in fact, it's not in the Hebrew text. We read simply: "And Aaron lifted up his hands." So you should not overestimate the significance of this moment, since there was absolutely no magical power that streamed out over the people from his uplifted priestly hands. The hands uplifted to bestow blessing would from that time on be an integral part of the priestly task (Num 6:22, 27; Deut 10:8). But it was only a symbolic gesture, though a very meaningful one. For the first time, at least, it occurred in the region of the altar of burnt offering, after the sacrifice. Hereby God would have wanted to provide the people once again the assurance that Israel's sacrifices would be acceptable to him (Lev 1:9, 13, 17; etc.), and as the people walked the path of sacrificing, they could count on enjoying a good life with God. We infer this latter idea from the *words* that comprise the high priestly blessing, found in Num 6:24–26: "The Lord bless you and keep you [i.e., protect you, O Israel, singular]; the Lord make his face to shine upon you [a petitioner at the feet of a lord could be happy if he saw friendly eyes looking his way] and be gracious to you; the Lord lift up his countenance upon you [the opposite of turning his face away in anger] and give you peace." For the rich significance of the Hebrew word for "peace" (*shalom*) see our earlier discussion. To know what the words had in view in asking God to visit his people with blessing and not with curse, you could read chapters like Leviticus 26 and Deuteronomy 28–29, and in the light of these chapters, the books of Joshua, Judges, Samuel, and Kings. Later Israel often suffered various catastrophes on account of forsaking the covenant. Then she was clearly not enjoying *shalom*, or peace.

On this day Aaron was allowed to "place" upon Israel "the name" of Yahweh. From now on that would be priestly work (Num 6:27). With this expression we should not think primarily of a magical action. Nor should we suppose that on the day when Aaron and his sons accepted the priesthood, Israel for the first time was embraced in the protective fellowship of Yahweh.[1] Israel had already been embraced in that fellowship. This priestly

---

1. Concerning the significance of the word "name," see Vonk, *Exodus*, 46–47.

blessing could serve to confirm and to certify for the Israelite church God's promises, particularly for fellowship and mighty protection.

If we may not overestimate the blessing of Israel by Aaron and his sons which was assigned to them by God, we today have even less reason to do so with respect to the custom that had arisen in the church after Christ and his apostles, with ordained leaders lifting their hands and declaring words of blessing upon a group of gathered Christians on various occasions. There exists absolutely no mandate from God for doing this. The only obligatory symbolic actions that remain for us as an apostolic church in the New Testament era are those of baptizing and celebrating the Lord's Supper. There is no other. Lifting up the hands at the beginning and at the end of our congregational worship services by ordained leaders is a humanly invented symbolic action with an Old Testament aftertaste.

4. AARON'S FIRST ENTRANCE INTO THE HOLY PLACE (LEV 9:23A)

"And Moses and Aaron went into the tent of meeting, and when they came out they blessed the people."

Although entering the holy place was later permitted for the ordinary priests, on this day Moses took along with him into the holy place no one but Aaron. For both of these men would not have gone any further than the holy place. Entering the most holy place was permitted only on the great Day of Atonement. In fact, the holy place was far enough. If an ordinary Israelite or a Levite would have entered there, he would probably not have been carried out alive. But after a period of time, Moses and Aaron came out of the tabernacle unharmed. "When they came out they blessed the people."

With the word *bless*, which can have a variety of meanings, something else is being identified here than in the immediately preceding, referring to Aaron's first official blessing. Aaron performed that blessing at that time in his capacity as high priest. But this time he did not, for we read that both men ("they") blessed the people, and Moses was not a high priest. Not even a priest, actually. Therefore with *this* blessing we should probably think of a joyful greeting of the people. Was that not to be expected? For the high priest of Israel had just accepted his office in the forecourt. But would God now accept this man in his sanctuary? The answer to that question Moses was, as it were, going to retrieve by taking Aaron along with him as he entered the holy place.

Did the men stay there long? Did they pray to Yahweh there? Did they fall down before the inner curtain? We do not know. We do know that Moses and Aaron came back out and joyfully greeted the people. Now visible proof was being given to one and all of the fact that Aaron's ministry was accepted by God and that thanks to this ministry, the Israelites were safe and would be able to dwell in their camp, even though such a holy God as Yahweh had built for himself a dwelling in their midst. And if before this, some anxiety existed in the hearts of Israelites on the basis of Aaron's hardly unimpeachable past (golden calf), then such anxiety was here being graciously removed. He came out unharmed with his brother Moses. For Aaron did not become a high priest because there was something in or about him that made him more acceptable before God than another person. It was not for that reason that he was acceptable, now and later, in the ministry of atonement with God on Israel's behalf. It was Yahweh who had sovereignly called and chosen him to stand before him as Israel's high priest.

5. THE APPEARANCE OF GOD'S GLORY (LEV 9:23B–24A)

Next we read: "And the glory of the Lord appeared to all the people. And fire came out from before the Lord and consumed the burnt offering and the pieces of fat on the altar" (v. 23b-24a).

Here we see happening what Moses had promised from the outset. Yahweh would make his *kavod* (glory) visible.

We discussed this *kavod* of Yahweh in our commentary on Exodus.[2] Readers will recall that when Yahweh had accepted the tabernacle as a gift from the hands of Israel, his *kavod* filled it (Exod 40:35). So powerfully that Moses could not initially enter the sanctuary. Later he could (Lev 1:1). Had the *kavod* of Yahweh meanwhile retreated to the most holy place? You could infer this from the instructions for Aaron on the great Day of Atonement: "The Lord said to Moses, 'Tell Aaron your brother not to come at any time into the Holy Place inside the veil, before the mercy seat that is on the ark, so that he may not die. For I will appear in the cloud over the mercy seat.'" (Lev 16:2).

What happened there?

Did a universally visible appearance of God's glory occur on the day of Aaron's entrance into office, like we read, for example, in Exod 16:10, consisting in a special light phenomenon? Did a second phenomenon occurred as well, with fire proceeding "from before Yahweh" (i.e., from the most holy place), whereby what lay on the altar was consumed? Or were these not two distinct phenomena, but one single event, so that we could better translate

---

2. Vonk, *Exodus*, 184–85, 306.

THE "INAUGURATION" OF AARON AND HIS FOUR SONS (LEV 9)

verse 23b: "And the glory of Yahweh appeared to all the people; *namely*, fire from before Yahweh and this consumed the burnt offering and the pieces of fat on the altar"?

The latter explanation seems to us to be the simplest.

Literally we read that fire "ate up" what was on the altar. Clear proof of God's acceptance. The parts of the sacrifice had already been burned. But with the sudden accompanying fire, they were consumed far more quickly than normal.

The assembly of elders (representing the entire people) leaves us with no doubt as to whether the divine language being spoke to everyone in what happened was understood. With joy, they fell down to the ground, in the most respectful manner, prone, with foreheads pressing the ground. As though before a king. Now the Israelites had a high priest who could intervene for them in the things that involved their relationship with God.

In this way the promise was now fulfilled that God had given earlier to Moses on the mountain during the very first conversation about the sanctuary he was to build, from which he would sanctify Israel through his glory. "I will consecrate the tent of meeting and the altar. Aaron also and his sons I will consecrate to serve me as priests. I will dwell among the people of Israel and will be their God. And they shall know that I am the Lord their God, who brought them out of the land of Egypt that I might dwell among them. I am the Lord their God" (Exod 29:44–46).

That was what God was busy doing.

That was the goal of God's establishing a covenant at Horeb, first with Israel in its entirely, and now with the house of Aaron in particular. Taking an important step in the direction of the goal he had set ever since the Garden of Eden: restored concourse between God and people in the Paradise of the new earth![3]

---

3. See Vonk, *Exodus*, 181–82.

13

The "deposition" of Nadab and Abihu (Lev 10)

IN THE TWO CHAPTERS dealing with the installation and inauguration of Aaron and his sons, we have read that Moses was constantly functioning according to the instruction that God had given him earlier on the mountain. During this conversation God had also told Moses something that he had not mentioned earlier, but only later, as a result of a sudden terrible event.

Parenthetically, something like this happened more frequently. For example, only later did Moses narrate, shortly before his death, that God had received with immediate approval the request of the Israelites at Horeb, on the day of the proclamation of the Ten Words, that if possible God would no longer speak directly to them but through Moses (Deut 5:28).

In this way, during his conversation with Moses about the future sanctuary, with its ministry of atonement and its priesthood, God had also made the comment at one point about these priests, that he desired exemplary conduct from them. God had said at that time:

> Among those who are near me I will be sanctified,
> and before all the people I will be glorified.

As you can see, we have placed the verse (Lev 10:3) in two lines. But in both lines we have something that happens more often in Hebrew poetry, namely, a repetition of an idea. That idea is this: at Horeb God had made a covenant with Israel. But it would be good to have to recall the exalted glory with which it was connected. Israel would have to learn that from her priests. Those men were to give Israel Torah, instruction (Lev 10:11). But then the conduct of those men—who in addition had been designated

THE "DEPOSITION" OF NADAB AND ABIHU (LEV 10)

through a special covenant to approach God on Israel's behalf—would naturally have to be consistent with that instruction. That is the first rule of every sound pedagogy. Children retain what their parents do far better than what they say.

On this day, together with the events that conclude the time when Aaron and his sons entered in office, Moses brought forth the divine declaration of Lev 10:3. In connection with the sin and punishment of Nadab and Abihu. These had barely occurred when Moses said: "This is what Yahweh told me." And then Moses supplied God's declaration, surely on account of its deeply impressive content, formulated in poetic form:

> Especially from my priests I demand respect for my holiness,
> So that my people may bow down before my exalted majesty.

Leviticus 10 consists of three parts. We will explain the middle part first, and then discuss the first and third parts.

1. REGARDING PART 2 OF LEVITICUS 10 (VV. 8–11)

Anyone reading Leviticus 10 will notice immediately that this middle segment looks like it was added later. In that practical manner that we find more often in the Torah, entirely differently than our lawbooks. Sometimes a stipulation is explicitly connected to one or another event, and other times it seems only implicitly related.

In this part it was prohibited for the priests to use wine or strong drink while they were working. The reason was appended to the stipulation. Through the use of alcohol they could lose control of their capacities momentarily, and the people might think that tabernacle worship need not be taken all that seriously. Whereas it belonged to their task to imprint upon Israel that Yahweh would tolerate no confusion in connection with the sacred and the profane, the clean and the unclean.

Why is room given to this material at this point? Probably because the last-mentioned subject (the distinction between clean and unclean) would immediately follow this section (in Lev 11). So this functions as a kind of introduction to that chapter.

But was it done perhaps also because people supposed that the sin of Nadab and Abihu consisted in entering God's sanctuary under the influence of strong drink? But nothing is reported about that.

In fact, we must point out that in addition to the first part (vv. 1–7), which does indeed report the sin and punishment of Nadab and Abihu, our chapter also contains a third part (vv. 12–20), which says nothing at all about any assault against the sanctuary by Aaron and his surviving sons, Eleazar and Ithamar. On the contrary.

If we removed for a moment the inserted portion of verses 8–11, we would have left a story consisting of two parts, each with the same subject. Both issue a warning: priests, be careful in the presence of a holy God!

With this, the theme of the middle part corresponds entirely, and as a result it seems obvious that we keep it in this spot, after the story about the sin of Nadab and Abihu.

2. REGARDING PART 1 OF LEVITICUS 10 (VV. 1–7)

So we do not believe that Nadab and Abihu were punished so severely by God because they were guilty of misusing alcohol. But one can be overcome with other things beside drink. Would not Nadab and Abihu have become drunk with *ambition*?

For into what sin had they allowed themselves to be tempted? We read that they brought "strange fire" before Yahweh (Lev 10:1; Num 3:4). Each of them took a censor, scooped up fire in it, put incense on it, and with this they had entered the sanctuary.

Where did they get that fire? Perhaps from the place in the forecourt where the sacrificial meat was cooked? In that case the expression "strange fire" could be explained easily. For then what was involved was simply a mistaken ritual. Nevertheless, this assumption seems to us rather unlikely. With the self-directed activity of Nadab and Abihu, something that was definitely in play here, it seems far more likely that they took the fire from the altar of burnt offering. This had been designated for the high priest, as we see from Lev 16:12, the chapter dealing with the great Day of Atonement. They took holy fire, but this became "strange fire" because such taking of that fire was "unauthorized fire before the Lord, which he had not commanded them" (Lev 10:1). First of all, it was not a great Day of Atonement. That appeared clearly from the less stringent requirement for the sin offering for Aaron and the people (Lev 9, a calf and a male goat for each). And in the second place, *they* were not high priests, but ordinary priests whose task on this day was merely to assist their father. Not to replace him. And in the third place, why would God have punished a ritual impropriety so severely? Later another ritual impropriety would occur, with Eleazar and Thamar, that was not punished so severely.

You will recall how, with Leviticus 8–9, we repeatedly pointed out that with the "installation" and "inauguration" the role of leader was explicitly assigned to Aaron. Yahweh was showing clearly that the high priestly office was given to Aaron. Nevertheless, for this unique distinction given to their father, Nadab and Abihu presumably lacked sufficient respect. Were they also not experienced men? Were they presumably men approximately fifty years in age? On the day when the Horeb covenant was established, were they not deemed worthy, together with their uncle, Moses, and their father, Aaron, and the seventy *elders* of Israel, to see a glorious theophany of Israel's God and to share in the sacrificial meal? Had they not emerged from there unharmed (Exod 24:9–11)?

The phrase "strange fire" would not mean a fire different than the fire of the altar of burnt offering, but fire to which on this particular day they should not have extended *their* hands. Not yet. For this reason alone, their activity did not please God.

Moreover, the expression "before Yahweh" in verse 1 indicates that the brothers went into the tabernacle intentionally. Think about it. The sanctuary. Into which their father, Aaron, had just been allowed by Moses as God's substitute, to go in and come out, to which event God had attached his intense approval by sending fire out of this very sanctuary, fire that "ate up" the sacrificial portions on the altar. Hereby a very exceptional position was very obviously being given to Aaron. Every humble heart would have recognized this immediately. But the eyes of Nadab and Abihu were apparently clouded with arrogance and could not see clearly. With a familiar result, they had sinned with fire, so they were killed with fire. In this context, let's remember that a priest's daughter in Israel, who had profaned her father by committing immorality, also had to be burned with fire (Lev 21:9). And in the instance of yet another serious offense—when someone took a woman and her daughter—the punishment was also death by fire (Lev 20:14).

Did Nadab and Abihu actually reach the holy place with their incense, and were they killed there? We doubt it. In verse 2, we do read that they died "before Yahweh," but this phrase could also be referring to the forecourt. Later, when both brothers were slain through fire that proceeded from "before Yahweh" (literally the same expression as in 9:24), which in this case means from the most holy place, they were dragged away by two men who were not priests and thus were not authorized to enter the *holy place*. They were Mishael and Elzaphan, nephews of Aaron, who also belonged to the tribe of Levi, but were not priests. In fact, the Levites had yet to receive their special position in connection with the sanctuary.

Next, Nadab and Abihu, clothed in their beautiful priestly robes, were dragged out of the forecourt to a place outside the camp. Apparently to be buried there.

Pay close attention to the next part of the story.

Moses anxiously saw to it that nothing performed in connection with the required burial and grieving was performed by Aaron and his two surviving sons, Eleazar and Ithamar. This father with his two sons were not allowed to demonstrate any signs of bereavement, for example, by uncovering their heads. Not only was it prohibited for Israel's high priest ever to engage in grieving (Lev 21), but it was naturally obvious that his sons as well, the priests, surely might not defile the tabernacle through improper grieving. For they functioned as mediators between God and Israel. From now on, that would be their position. So what would become of the people on this day if the holiness of Yahweh, who had already been offended so seriously by Nadab and Abihu, would have been assaulted once more by sounds of mourning and tearing of clothes in his own sanctuary? In that case, the full wrath of God could have burst forth upon everyone, Moses said. And he knew all too well, every since the incident with the golden calf, how scrupulously Yahweh was to be feared. Moreover, God had told him earlier that one day he would expect exemplary conduct from his priests, with a view to all the people. This explains why on this occasion, Moses recited that divine warning in poetic form, as we mentioned earlier. Something like this:

> Especially from my priests I demand respect for my holiness,
> So that my people may bow down before my exalted majesty.

Pay close attention to the fact that Nadab and Abihu immediately on the same day when for the first time they might function as priests they were fired from their ministry (Lev 10:19; cf. "today"). This was something that we can still experience today. "Inauguration" and "deposition" on the same day. From this we learn to know Yahweh as our heavenly Father as well, to know him as a God toward whom not everything is simply permitted. What a deep respect for our Savior that we obtain through an episode like this, our Savior who has perfectly fulfilled "the righteous requirement of Torah" (Rom 8:4), so that we may approach the throne of grace with confidence (Heb 4:16). For him the rule was also intensely operative: In those who draw near to me I will be sanctified.

"And Aaron held his peace."

You should not ask what must have been going through the heart of the old man. How beautifully the day had begun! But how foolish did his two sons behave! As though they had not received enough honor, they grasped for more. Nevertheless those two men were Aaron's own flesh and blood. Who would not have wept at losing such precious security?

"And Aaron held his peace."

In fact, he would have had to acknowledge the guilt of his sons on this account, because as we might appropriately suppose, Moses would

THE "DEPOSITION" OF NADAB AND ABIHU (LEV 10)

have spoken with his brother Aaron and his sons often enough, during the months preceding the construction of the tabernacle, about everything that God had revealed to him on the mountain with respect to the tabernacle and the ministry of the sacrifices and priests. So Aaron would have understood very well what kind of impertinence his two oldest sons had become liable for committing. Just as they themselves must have understood this as well. Just as Aaron had earlier discerned from Moses that an Israelite high priest was never allowed to grieve. Although Moses nonetheless immediately reminded him of that, just to be sure. For these reasons we believe that Aaron's silence here is mentioned as a glimpse of his obedience. He had placed God's calling above the appeal of his own flesh and blood.

3. REGARDING PART 3 OF LEVITICUS 10 (VV. 12–20)

The middle part, however, applies very well not only with the first part, but also with the last part of our chapter. There we are told about what happened after the inauguration. It constitutes a beautiful page in the life-book of the severely tested, but humbly obedient, high priest, Aaron.

For a brief moment, our attention is drawn to Moses.

Was it perhaps the case, as a result of the general dismay occasioned by the sudden death of Nadab and Abihu, that Moses sensed more strongly still his responsibility for the proper course of events during the rest of the day? In particular, no *second* transgression of God's command must occur on the part of the priesthood. Therefore it would have been the case that Moses would have exercised very scrupulous control over everything. And what did he suddenly discover? That there was already something wrong.

As the reader knows, on the day of Aaron's inauguration into office, four animals had been sacrificed for the people. We discussed this briefly, and we need to add to that the following:

With those four sacrifices, Aaron and both of his surviving sons, Eleazar and Ithamar, were not yet finished with everything. Let's follow their steps

1. They were finished with the *burnt offering*. For that was always "entirely burned up."

2. But not with the *grain offering*, that this time as well was coupled with the burnt offering. The required portion of that sacrifice, the *askarah*, was also burned on the altar of burnt offering. But the remainder had yet to reach its appointed destination. They were to be eaten by the priests and that "in a holy place," that is, not outside the forecourt. For the grain offering was "most holy," as we have seen.

3. The matter of the *peace offering* was also not yet fully completed. The priestly portion of that offering, the wave breast and hind quarter, still needed to be used. As the reader knows, this priestly portion of the peace offering was holy, so that it had to be eaten in a holy place, but it was not most holy, so at least in ordinary circumstances the forecourt could be left and this portion could be used by all the members of the priestly families.

All of this still had to happen. And it could happen as well. But now in connection with the fourth sacrifice, Moses thought he discovered that a culpable omission had occurred.

4. According to him, something had gone wrong with the *sin offering*. This was in reference to the sin offering that was brought for the congregation, not for the priests themselves. The priests were never allowed to eat the meat of such sin offerings, because the blood of such a sin offering was always brought beforehand into the holy place (to the horns of the altar of incense). But in this case, this had not (yet) happened with the blood of this sin offering for the congregation.

At the conclusion of everything, Aaron had just set foot in the holy place, led there by Moses, and thus the meat of *this* sin offering might indeed be eaten by the priests. With respect to God, this "may" naturally turned into "must." Otherwise people would through ingratitude have offended that good God, who dealt with his servants so gently.

As a result, this was the last point, in terms of which Moses launched an investigation. He look around, he searched and searched, but nowhere was the meat of the animal used for the sin offering to be found. The reader will recall that this time the animal was a male goat. Nowhere was the meat of the male goat used for the sin offering to be found. Until Moses learned upon investigation that people had burned the animal. But according to Moses, that was in complete contradiction of the rule instituted by God. For the meat of those animals used for the sin offering, no blood from which could be brought in the holy place and dabbed on the horns of the altar of incense, was not supposed to be burned, but might (= must) be eaten by the priests.

Moses became angry about that. Something that we should not blame this gentle but certainly passionate man all too severely for doing. He would have been afraid of a new catastrophe. For this reason he talked intensely with his nephews, Eleazar and Ithamar, about this. But these men had not acted without the knowledge of their father. Therefore it was Aaron who provided the answer to his angry brother Moses. Did Moses himself perhaps understand that Eleazar and Ithamar had burned the goat of the sin offering *in consultation with their father*, but had he wanted to spare his brother any more intense pain on this particular day?

THE "DEPOSITION" OF NADAB AND ABIHU (LEV 10)

What did Aaron answer?

The man who in connection with the sudden death of his two sons had obediently *held his peace*, because he was aware that with the high priest of such holy God as Yahweh, and certainly in his own sanctuary, no grief and lament for the dead was appropriate, this very same man now spoke. And that for the same reason for his earlier silence, with a view to the holiness of Yahweh.

This is what he said. Surely today a sin offering (with a burnt offering) was first brought for Eleazar and Ithamar themselves. For this reason they would have been allowed to eat the meat of the sin offering. But what then overcame me and my house on account of such a great disobedience in my family? In a certain sense, did not that sin and that punishment touch upon us as well? Was Israel's priesthood consequently on this day of sin and death within her own midst worthy to eat of this meat, that was most holy and spoke of atonement and life for Israel with Yahweh? Would we have been truly pleasing to God if we had held strictly and scrupulously to the letter of the prescribed rule and, despite what God had testified today, nonetheless had eaten of this meat from the sin offering?

When Moses heard his brother Aaron talking in this respectful manner about Yahweh and about what his eyes beheld, it was his turn to keep his peace. This time it had been *his* eye that was somewhat clouded. Through great zeal for the *letter* of the Law, he had for one moment had a less clear view of the intention of the Spirit of the Law than his bereaved brother. For the facts show us that God did not disapprove, but approved the conduct of Aaron and his sons, something that, viewed by fanatics on closer inspection as a (self-conscious) violation of God's own prescription, would be strongly condemned. For there they were standing, Aaron and his two surviving sons, alive and all.

Even in the Old Testament, God did not want rote obedience from his servants. Legalism, slavish service was displeasing to him at Horeb already. There, in fact, his Torah testified to that. For that Torah was by its nature not a burdensome straightjacket, but spiritual, lovely, and mild. Nothing less than the gospel as given to us today. Behind both of those stands the same Spirit of Christ. This Spirit teaches us as well: Do not be overly righteous (Eccl 7:16). Already at Horeb, God showed that his sacrificial Torah was nothing like a code book, nothing like a program schedule.

The episode of Nadab and Abihu made a deep impression among Israel, dying as they did "before the face of God," and "they had no children" (Num 3:4; 26:61; 1 Chron 24:2). We could use the heading, "I will be sanctified in those who draw near to me." Recall the destruction of Shiloh and

Jerusalem itself, and remember through what perfect obedience our Savior himself had to be sanctified toward God on our behalf (John 17:19).

We used to hear a lot about persons in the Old Testament being "types" of Christ, and we used to employ that language ourselves, but at present we no longer prefer that language. For where is the limit? Why, for example, could such ancestors of the Lord like David and Solomon be types of Christ, but not someone like Jonathan, who thought so much more highly of his neighbor David than of himself, that he gave David his robe, armor, sword, bow, and belt, and bowed humbly beneath God's sovereign decision that David would be king instead of his father Saul and Jonathan himself (1 Sam 18:4; 20:13)? If ever a person resembled Christ, it was Jonathan (Phil 2:3, 5). Why could only men be types of Christ, but not women like Deborah, Hannah, and Mary? For that reason, we could better say with Peter, that such believers spoke and acted as they did because they were being led by the Spirit of Christ (1 Pet 1:11). For no one has had that eternal Spirit work in him as did our Savior, who presented himself to God as an unblemished sacrifice (Heb 9:14).

To that Spirit, however, whose will was sufficiently know to them from Moses' instruction, Nadab and Abihu were not submissive. Perhaps they supposed that God would be very appreciative if they, with who knows what kind of exalted display, went into the holy place to bring him incense. After all, they too were priests and soon they would be allowed, indeed, required to enter that holy place repeatedly. And after all, Nadab was Aaron's oldest son, the one who would succeed his father one day. But their religiosity was disobedience, fleshly rather than spiritual. For there is also fleshly piety, with which God is not at all pleased (Prov 28:9, prayers; Isa 1:13, sacrifices; Col 2:23, fasts "for the indulgence of the flesh").

But on this day, *father Aaron*, the one they all too confidently bypassed, was living from the Spirit of Christ, as we see from his obedient silence, and his humble bowing under the blows of God that descended upon his "house" on this day, and especially from his deep respect for the holiness of God, whereby he understood better than Moses did that situations could arise with respect to a command of God where one must not be all too righteous.

We must distinguish sharply.

The conduct of Nadab and Abihu, viewed on the surface, showed some similarity to that of their father Aaron and their brothers Eleazar and Ithamar. In both instances, people were holding scrupulously to the letter of the Law. But on further inspection, the *first* was condemned by God and punished as self-made piety. But ultimately God could not withhold his approval from the *second*. For the letter kills (makes dead), but the Spirit makes alive (2 Cor 3:6).

THE "DEPOSITION" OF NADAB AND ABIHU (LEV 10)

It is so highly desirable that we as Bible readers are well informed about the task and place of the priests in the Old Testament. This will assist us in reading the New Testament, books, for example, like the Gospels and the epistle to the Hebrews. Not to mention the book of Revelation. One Reformed exegete (Dr. Cornelis van der Waal) entitled his dissertation on this last book of the Bible, "Old Testament Priestly Motifs in the Apocalypse." Later we ourselves will need to say something about the significance of the Horeb covenant and the Aaronic priesthood for the context of Hebrews and our own day.

Part 4

The people of Yahweh

14

General observations

THE NEXT UNIT THAT we will be examining is Leviticus 11–15.

These chapters have likely scared away many a Bible reader because of their formidable length. We have in mind, for example, Leviticus 13–14, concerning leprosy afflicting people and infecting houses.

Leviticus 12 is rather brief, only eight verses. But this little chapter, concerning the uncleanness of a birth mother, strikes us as strange today. In fact, Leviticus 15, concerning bodily emissions of males and females, also strikes us as a bit strange.

Indeed, this unit's first chapter already, with its talk about clean and unclean animals (Lev 11)—what are we supposed to do with this? We don't really understand very well what all of this meant at the time for Israel, not to mention what it means for us today.

Come along, dear reader. Let us comfort you.

A person need not know everything. There are even today particular books that you and I may never get around to reading. For example, literature in various professional fields. Well, here we are dealing with something like that.

1. A MANUAL FOR PRIESTS AS THEY INSTRUCT ISRAEL

We hardly need to be ashamed by the fact that these five chapters hit us somewhat strangely. In ancient times that was certainly the case as well for many a proselyte, someone from among the Gentiles who became a Jew. Although such a person had become quite familiar in his own context that resembled in some sense the life patterns explained in these chapters. For here again we encounter that remarkable phenomenon that we identified in our commentary on Exodus as "The Great Annexation."[1] Israel had many things in common with the Gentiles, although at Horeb God supplied those things with an entirely different meaning, at the foundation of the (Israelite) world.

Well then, this "differentness," this new feature of the divine patterns, the priests had to teach Israel on behalf of Yahweh. We find a summary of a large part of that instruction here.

In the preceding section of Leviticus, we have been somewhat prepared for this. In the chapter about the sudden death of Nadab and Abihu (Lev 10), we find the regulation that during their exercise of official duties, priests were not permitted to use alcohol. Why not? "You are to distinguish between the holy and the common, and between the unclean and the clean, and you are to *teach* the people of Israel all the statutes that the Lord has spoken to them by Moses" (Lev 10:10–11).

The italicized word, *teach*, is the same Hebrew word that we find here in this section of Leviticus, in 14:57. After first speaking about various thing in connection with leprosy, the postscript reads: "This is the law [*torah*, instruction, teaching, lesson] for any case of leprous disease . . . to *show* when it is unclean and when it is clean. This is the law [*torah*, instruction] for leprous disease" (Lev 14:54–57).

Twice we meet that phrase *to instruct*.

Israel's priests were especially supposed to function in an *instructional* capacity (Deut 27:14; 33:10; 2 Chron 15:3; Mal. 2:6–7). Permit us to point out at the same time, that in these chapters the name of Aaron appears in the inscriptions. Otherwise we read merely: "Yahweh said to Moses." But here more than once we find: "Yahweh said to Moses and *Aaron*" (Lev 11:1; 13:1; 14:33; 15:1). Why? Apparently because in his capacity as head of the priests, Aaron would get to deal especially with the issues mentioned here.

Indeed, when this part of Leviticus is concluded, God directs his words to all the priests. "Thus you [plural, you priests, whose ordinary priests was discussed in the preceding] shall keep the people of Israel separate from their uncleanness, lest they die in their uncleanness by defiling my tabernacle that is in their midst" (Lev 15:31). For an unclean person was not permitted to approach the sanctuary. He was not permitted to participate in a meal associated with the p/o (Lev 7:20–21; cf. 1 Sam 20:26). In some cases of uncleanness it was not even permitted to remain within the camp (Lev 13:46; 14:3; Num 5:1–4).

---

1. See Vonk, *Exodus*, 299–304.

Everyone understands: such things had to be taught. Everyone also understands that such rules could yield some problems in complicated situations. In those instances, the priests had to be able to point the way. Israel did not find these things as strange as we do. The distinction between clean and unclean animals, for example, did not sound altogether new in the days of Horeb. The nations around Israel knew something like this as well. Recall what we wrote in this connection in our commentary on Genesis about the time of Noah.[2]

2. THE SEPARATED ONES

In these chapters, when we encounter the words "clean" and "unclean," people should not automatically give these words an all-too-modern content. For example, here the word "clean" does not mean the same thing as our modern medical term "sterile." It doesn't even mean what is particularly important to our Dutch homemakers: proper, tidy, neat. Nor when reading Leviticus 11–15 should we understand the word "unclean" as a synonym of dirty or messy or unhygienic.

In addition, we need to be careful of the notion instinctively associated with God being not at all attracted by the messiness of Israel's military camp. That would not fit with the prescription of Moses: "You shall have a place outside the camp, and you shall go out to it. And you shall have a trowel with your tools, and when you sit down outside, you shall dig a hole with it and turn back and cover up your excrement. Because the Lord your God walks in the midst of your camp, to deliver you and to give up your enemies before you, therefore your camp must be holy, so that he may not see anything indecent among you and turn away from you" (Deut 23:12–14).

Israel's health did indeed play a role in the Law. For example, God sternly threatened Israel with the removal of health as a curse! But when he granted Israel "shalom," peace, then they would not be visited with those terrible epidemics for which tropical lands are famous (see our commentary on Exod 15:26, "I am Yahweh, your Healer").[3]

To that degree, observing God's Torah, including Leviticus 11–15, was surely connected to Israel's health. Indirectly.

But not directly.

In our time, this viewpoint is being advanced in response to our writing. Regarding the laws of Leviticus 11–15, some insist that these laws were given for the advancement of health. We believe, however, that this does not

---

2. See Vonk, *Genesis*, 156–72.
3. Vonk, *Exodus*, 79–80.

correctly characterize God's intention with Leviticus 11–15. We definitely do not agree that with such regulations—for example, that Israel was not to eat any unclean animals like pigs, and that no leper was permitted to approach the tabernacle—we are dealing with measures whose principal purpose was Israel's health. First, because in those chapters we read nothing directly reported about such a purpose. But in addition, because then we would face the question why God no longer forbids eating pork now? Was he more careful with the Israelites than with Christians? But what then about Gal 3:28 and Col 3:11 (which reminds us that in Christ, Greeks and Jews, barbarians and Scythians, are equal before God)? And why didn't God provide more care for the health of the Israelites by supplying, in addition to a list of animals, also a list of plants and fruits whose use would have been prohibited because they were equally harmful to health? For how many poisonous plants and fruits were there? As far as leprosy was concerned, why was it only the leper who was not allowed to approach God's sanctuary, and why not someone suffering from one or another disease? Why was a person considered unclean who had an emission from his or her sexual organ, but not a person who had just urinated or defecated, nor even someone with a festering wound or with tuberculosis, whose saliva would have been just as dangerous for his surroundings? Why were not everyone with an infectious disease banned from the camp, but only lepers?

We hold a different view.

We believe that the commandments of Leviticus 11–15 form a part of that entire complex of symbols with which God wanted to instruct the Israelite church and firmly assure her of covenant fellowship with him, within which she had been incorporated. A fellowship with him, Yahweh, that abhorred paganism and death.

For that purpose God employed, for example, the custom found among other nations, of making a distinction between clean and unclean animals. Perhaps this custom went back to the days of Noah (Gen 7:2). What God had intended back then, in Noah's day, with that distinction, we no longer know with certainty. But the significance that he gave to this distinction in Moses' day we do know. For he himself said to the Israelites, at Horeb, albeit through Moses: I am Yahweh, your God, who has separated you from the other nations. Therefore make a distinction between clean and unclean beast, and between clean and unclean birds, so that you do not make yourselves detestable by beasts and birds and everything that creeps on the earth, that I have forbidden to you by declaring it unclean. Be holy unto me, for I, Yahweh, am holy, and I have set you apart from the nations, so that you would belong to me (Lev 20:24–26).

Did not God hereby declare his intention when he mandated Israel to pay attention to the difference between clean and unclean animals? Did he himself not hereby testify that he was doing that in order thereby to remind them of the covenant that he had established with them at Horeb? With them and with no other nation?

Was a special reminder (of the covenant) like this something that was so strange? Had not God already given Abraham such a reminder with circumcision? Had not the Israelites, as Abraham's descendants, received a covenant sign in that very circumcision? Woe to those who neglected that sign, for example, by participating in the Passover meal without having been circumcised (Exod 12:43-49). Already through circumcision, God had assured Abraham and his descendants: You are my separated ones.

In addition to that covenant of God with Abraham there came next the covenant of Horeb. God wanted once again to remind Israel of *this* covenant by means of signs. Quite a number of signs, including the Sabbath (Exod 31:17), about which we'll say more later.

But also by means of *clothing* and *food*.

By means of *clothing*. The Israelites were supposed to guard against intermingling with pagans. Therefore they were not to wear clothes made out of two kinds of material, for example, wool and cotton (Lev 19:19; Deut 22:8). Rather, on the corners of their garments they were to wear a tassel (or knob or button) in which a dark blue thread had been woven, in order thereby to think about the commandments of Yahweh who had adopted them as his people (Num 15:37-41; Deut 22:9-12; see our commentary on Exodus[4]).

So then, Israel was reminded of the Horeb covenant by means of some of her *food* as well. God made use of her food to remind Israel of her apartheid, *of her being set apart from the pagans*. He said that himself (Lev 20:24-26).

The laws concerning the leprosy of persons and houses had a similar significance, as we will see.

At this juncture, we need to point out clearly that the Horeb covenant is antiquated. Obsolete (Heb 8:13). Today we enjoy eating pork, at least if the doctor does not prescribe against it for health reasons. We would not be fazed at all by people who want to continue to depend on the religion of food laws ("whose god is their belly," Paul would say, Rom 16:18; Phil 3:19). Today we also wear with confidence a shirt made of mixed materials. Without a tassel containing a dark blue thread. For we no longer stand under the Law. Therefore we have mentioned elsewhere[5] and repeat here our regret

---

4. Vonk, *Exodus*, 213-15, 254-56.
5. See Vonk, *Exodus*, 93-94.

that some Christians have adopted the custom of reading the Ten Words of the Sinai covenant in their Sunday worship gatherings. (Such a custom easily carries with it the apparent authority of a divine prescription.) For in this way the notion is automatically fueled that the church of Christ continues even now to live under the Horeb covenant. But according to the New Testament, that definitely may not happen! That would be to "remember earthly things" (John 3:12; Phil 3:19–20; Col 3:1–2; Gal 4:24–26).

The spirit of Judaizing, rabbinism, casuistry, and lawyerism is certainly not at all related to the Old Testament. Paul despised that spirit as a satanic impulse that lay behind his jealous Jewish family, his "flesh and blood" (Eph 6:12; 1 Thess 2:14–15, 18). That spirit wanted to turn the Christian church into a Jewish church, and presumably contributed to the martyrdom of both Paul and Peter. That spirit has slain the gospel in the Law. We must speak more extensively about this later.

3. A KINGDOM OF PRIESTS AND A HOLY NATION

God's intention with the laws of Leviticus 11–15 was definitely not merely negative. Just as today it is not enough when Christians are simply against this and against that. The sexually immoral person mentioned in 1 Corinthians 5 had to be banned from the church, but the apostle was not forbidding every contact with people who were guilty of sexual immorality. A Christian who happened to be a baker would not have hesitated to bring bread to a brothel owner. Otherwise "you would need to go out of the world" (1 Cor 5:10). But Christians must always deal with one another and with unbelievers in such a way that the love of Christ for sinners becomes visible, as it were. By means of solicitude toward those in distress, by means of doing good to the poor, caring for the sick, comforting the bereaved, Christians in the early centuries probably achieved more than by means of direct gospel preaching. "Go to the Christians. They will help you!" That has won many a heart for Christ, and sanctified many a life.

Israel also had not only the duty of abstaining from pagan abominations and impurities, but was supposed to be a particularly holy people. Israel had barely arrived at Horeb, when God expressed the desire that they would be "a kingdom of priests and a holy nation" (Exod 19:6). So then, God reminded them of that positive calling in various ways, including through the laws about clean and unclean. To mention but one thing, it is striking that what was supposed to happen with the re-inclusion into the community of Israel of a leper who had been healed showed so many similarities to the ceremonies accompanying the consecration of the priests.

For with a healed leper as well, the right ear lobe, the right hand, and the right big toe were dabbed with blood and oil (Lev 14:14, 17).

By means of the laws of Leviticus 11–15, Israel was continually taught about and reminded of the foundation on which Yahweh had placed his people at Horeb, and of the path she was to walk. Beneath the entire Israelite world, God had laid the covenant with him, Yahweh, the God of redemption, and he had set her feet on the path of life leading to the future Paradise, toward which not only the hope of the fathers looked (Heb 11:15), but also the tabernacle and its sacrificial ministry with their symbolic preaching powerfully pointed.

A holy people. A people made up of those who carried along the promise of eternal life.

4. EXODUS 19:6 IS VIRTUALLY IDENTICAL TO 1 PETER 2:9

When at their wedding, two lovers exchange rings, that does not create a new relationship, but serves as a visible and tangible pledge to remind each other continually of an already existing covenant.

This is also why God gave his Israelite church the laws of Leviticus 11–15, with the intention of reminding her of the foundation on which he had placed her in connection with the establishment of the covenant that is narrated for us in Exodus 19–24. To be sure, this Sinai covenant is now fulfilled and obsolete, but the reminders of it in the Law and the description of it in the historical narratives of the Prophets are nonetheless still instructive for us. Because through them, we come to know God better, he who was known to Israel as Yahweh and is known now to us as our God and Father in Christ. From these, we learn how God wanted to protect his little child, Israel, with his Law, against the deadly dangers of the surrounding paganism. We should see in this Law especially not an irritating anchor, but a paternal embrace of his people, though with a rather firm hand, an embrace of a people who were en route to the day of Christ's coming. By these means he reminded Israel, in various ways, of her calling to be a holy nation of priests.

Basically God deals with us today similarly, even though with a view to our instruction regarding the new covenant, of which Jesus has become the Surety, he now uses the preaching of the apostles (preserved in the New Testament) and he assures us today of that better covenant only through our baptism and our Lord's Supper (Matt 26:28; Mark 14:24; Luke 22:20; 1 Cor 11:25; 2 Cor 3:6; Col 2:11; Heb 7:22; 8:6; 9:15; 10:29; 13:20). For today we may belong to adult Israel (Gal 4), with whom God no longer has the covenant of Horeb, but nonetheless the same covenant that he established with Abraham (Gal 3:8, 14, 29). The Sinai covenant is obsolete (Heb 8:13).

Nevertheless, all who are called to provide nurture and instruction can still learn about God, who nurtured Israel as well. For example, that we must be reminded daily of that covenant of God with Abraham that is now also for us. Hold on to it! Every day in our families God must be thanked for saving us by means of the historically verifiable leading of his Holy Spirit out of the power of Satan. This happened in connection with our pagan ancestors (Acts 26:18; Col 1:13-14). We are liberated pagans. This explains why the devil always wants to rob us of our freedom, as he did the Romans, Galatians, Ephesians, Philippians, and others who became Christians. In Paul's day he made use not only of the absolutely inveterate Jews, but also some jealous Jews who had become Christians, who could not tolerate Paul (so they thought) simply setting aside the Law. But the apostle saw through them. He did not stare himself blind at his envious kinfolk, his "flesh and blood" (Eph 6:12), but understood that Satan was at work behind them, who wanted his prey back, in order to put them in bondage again. For Satan's tactic is to keep people stupid. Keep them in the dark. But our tactic must be: Daily thanking God in our homes for our liberation, and calling on him for help against Satan, who is constantly busy seeking to rob Christians of the true light and knowledge. Behind people *he* is active (2 Cor 2:11; Eph 6:12; 1 Thess 2:15, 18). In order to rob us of our freedom in Christ. Of our liberation. Of our redemption. Of our life one day on the new earth.

For we are a liberated people. Just as much as Israel was liberated from Egypt, so we have been freed from the power of the demons and of paganism. That is so absolutely true, that the apostle Peter came close one time to writing almost the same words that God had spoken to the Israelites when they arrived at Horeb, words that Peter wrote to Christians in Asia Minor, people who formerly had been pagans. He wrote to them: "But you are a chosen race, a royal priesthood, a holy nation, a people for his own possession" (1 Pet 2:9). Compare this with Exod 19:5-6: "Now therefore, if you will indeed obey my voice and keep my covenant, you shall be my treasured possession among all peoples, for all the earth is mine; and you shall be to me a kingdom of priests and a holy nation."

We Christians are a liberated people.

But Satan has succeeded far too often in making us forget this so easily. So much so that someone who reminded us of this redemption was criticized as a superficial person, like Paul was among the Judaizing Christians. We Christians have often preferred to surrender to the folly of that married woman who hoped and hoped that she might one day find grace in the eyes of her husband, so that he would then ... go ahead and marry her.[6] The poor soul!

If only we had listened to the Law.

Not in order to place ourselves under the Law once again. Not that. But to learn from the Law the good method of nurture and instruction.

In a myriad of ways God impressed upon his people that they were a redeemed people. Not that they would become a redeemed people, but that they were a redeemed people. And had to remain redeemed. By means of things like those discussed in Leviticus 11–15 (certain foods, leprosy, etc.).

Practically speaking, that means: daily.

Just as we must pray daily for protection against the Evil One, so that we do not neglect our salvation that God has bestowed upon us in his well-meant promises of the gospel. For Christians who would neglect their salvation would be sinning even worse than Israelites who "set aside the Law of Moses," because we would be despising the blood of the covenant of Christ through which we have been sanctified, and would be angering the Spirit of grace (Heb 10:28–29).

We too must constantly stir up each other especially to *continue* in God's grace (Acts 13:43). We need not make a big show of coming to God, as various revival preachers would want us to do, for God has come to us long ago when his Spirit immersed our pagan ancestors, by means of the messengers of the gospel, in the water of the Word (Eph 5:26). At that time we too were adopted into God's fellowship, a fellowship of promises of justification, sanctification, and glorification. But just as God used various rather strict measures like Sabbath, clothing, food, etc., to remind his Israelite church daily, since she was still a child (Hos 11:1), of his historic acts of redemption, in order to keep Israel close to him and to preserve Israel's life in Canaan, preserving her for eternal life with Christ in the promised Paradise, so we Christians, too, even though the strict measures suitable to the church's childhood have now become obsolete (together with the Sinaitic covenant), must not overestimate ourselves, but continually remind one another of our ancestry, and in so doing, of the historic acts of redemption performed by him who has called us out of darkness (of Satan and of paganism) to his marvelous light (Eph 5:8; 6:12; Col 1:12–13; 1 Pet 2:9–10). "And let us consider how to stir up one another to love and good works" (Heb 10:24), maintaining the way of life unto the praise of Christ, "who loves us and has freed us from our sins by his blood and made us a kingdom, priests to his God and Father" (Rev 1:5–6). Otherwise on the day of judgment, it will be more tolerable for pagans like those of Tyre and Sidon than for apostate Christians who "no longer did their duty."

---

6. See Vonk, *Exodus*, 11.

15

Torah instruction with regard to eating clean and unclean animals (Lev 11)

PALESTINE HAS ALSO BEEN discovered by modern tourists. No wonder. It has a pleasant climate, though there is variety. In general it is sunny. Hardly any rain falls from May through September. December, January, and February are known as rainy months there. Nevertheless in the Negeb (the "South" of Ps 126:4) it is wonderful, and there is rainfall at Eilat (the biblical Elath, on the gulf of Elath or Aqabah, a tributary of the Red Sea, where Ezion-Geber was situated, the harbor for the fleet of king Solomon). The region with the greatest rainfall is Upper Galilee, while the Negeb has the least rainfall. In Jerusalem and environs, the annual rainfall is higher even than in London or Paris.

This information is readily available from any tourist service. Such information packets will tell you as well about the flora and fauna of Palestine. Let's review some of this contemporary material by way of introducing Leviticus 11.

(A) MAMMALS

Of the mammals, the predatory animals are the most numerous. Jackals are very common, especially in cultivated regions; the hyena is found mostly in the Negeb. Less numerous are the wild cats, lynx, foxes, spotted weasels, and mongooses (something like our polecats). Especially rare are the otter, the leopard, and the wolf (only in winter in Galilee). Mountain goats live in the region of the Dead Sea (in the wilderness of Judah). Porcupines are numerous, especially on Mount Carmel. In the Wadi Aravah you will find gazelles and wild camels. There are also eagles, rabbits, wild boars and beavers (in the Jordan region), gerbils, and the smallest known mammal: water shrews.

(B) BIRDS

Thanks to reforestation many birds have returned that, for centuries, had not appeared in this region. In this regard, among the countries of the Near East, Israel is the richest in bird species (about four hundred). It lies on the route of migratory birds. In addition to many kinds of predatory birds (especially vultures), there are storks, doves, partridges, quail, swallows, and other songbirds. Waterfowl like wild ducks, geese, and swans are found chiefly in the sea of Tiberias and Lake Hula, the non-dredged portion of which has been declared a nature preserve. Pelicans and cranes are also found here.

With respect to birds, we think it would be natural to mention trees in this context. For many centuries, Palestine has undergone terrible deforestation. But in 1948 people began a program of systematic planting of trees. In biblical times, the most prevalent trees were the cedars and oak forests, which have disappeared, with a few remaining stands preserved in the mountains of Lebanon. Inland, however, you will find various kinds of palm trees and pine trees, the maple, the cypress, the carob, the tamarisk, and the acacia, which appears everywhere in the wadis of the Negeb.

(C) REPTILES

Reptiles are prevalent especially in desert regions, including about three dozen kinds of snakes, some of which are poisonous, like the adder; in addition, there are lizards, geckos, chameleons, and turtles. Amphibians, like frogs, toads, and salamanders are also present, wherever there is fresh water. You can find them even in the barren desert region at the oasis of En Gedi along the Dead Sea.

(D) INSECTS

In Palestine, insects are innumerable. Scorpions often lodge beneath stones.

PART 4 | THE PEOPLE OF YAHWEH

(E) FISH

The freshwater lakes in the Jordan River region have a thriving fish population, and among the many kinds, you will find several that are unique to the region. In the lake of Tiberias you find the St. Peter's fish (Galilean Tilapia) and the catfish (Clarias Lazera). The Mediterranean Sea is rich with fish, as is the Gulf of Aqabah Although this gulf lies almost too far north for growing coral, it nonetheless has beautiful coral reefs. The assortment of colorful fish and other underwater creatures (like turtles) belong to the tropical marine fauna and are similar to the varieties found in the Indian Ocean. Because of its high salt content, the Dead Sea contains very few forms of life.

After this introductory section for Leviticus 11, we need to make a confession regarding our title for this chapter, namely, that on closer inspection, it was correct. Many modern English versions use this heading, but it is incomplete. Leviticus 11 deals not only with clean and unclean animals. Moreover, it does not deal exclusively with what is or is not permissible to eat. We could almost say: "Fortunately not." This delight with a mistake will come in handy for us in terms of the scope of this chapter. When we read through it, we see that it consists of six or seven sections.

1. Leviticus 11:1–8. This section deals with the clean four-footed animals. They are not listed, at least not here. Later Moses did list them (see Deut 14:4–5). He listed Israel's domestic animals first—ox, sheep, goat—and went on to mention deer, gazelles, etc., animals that lived in the wild. But here in Lev 11:1–3 such a list is not found, but only the general rule that the Israelites were permitted to eat only those animals that had cloven hooves and also chewed their cud. Those two characteristics had to appear simultaneously and obviously. That is explained further in verses 4–8.

There was, for example, the *camel*, which did chew the cud and had cloven hooves, but only partially cloven, namely, on the top, but not on the bottom. The camel walked on the calloused soles of both of its toes, on a kind of ball or pad. For that reason, Israel was not permitted to eat the meat of camels. For similar reasons, the *dassie* and the *hare* were unclean animals for Israel. For *they* did chew their cud, at least in appearance. They made a movement with their mouth that closely resembled the movement of cud-chewing cows and sheep, which explains why in everyday language—the language used in Scripture, rather than the language of scientific zoology—people called them ruminants. Nevertheless, they were not permitted as food because they were not real ruminants. Just as the camel did not have a real cloven hoof. The characteristics had to be *obvious*.

That *the pig* did not meet the established rule is immediately understandable. For this animal did have cloven hooves, obviously enough, but it

EATING CLEAN AND UNCLEAN ANIMALS

was not a ruminant. The two characteristics had to appear *simultaneously*. Obviously and simultaneously.

2. Leviticus 11:9–12. Next, the fish are mentioned. Water creatures that had both fins and scales, would be clean, but all the rest would be unclean and were not to be eaten. In the Old Testament we rarely read about catching fish (Hab 1). But in the New Testament we read often about that. The practice could well have occurred among the Israelites, from ancient times. In any case, the Israelites in Egypt loved to eat fish (Num 11:5).

3. Leviticus 11:13–19. This section deals with birds, or rather, unclean birds, which are the only ones mentioned. But of course the intention was thereby to declare the other birds clean and permissible for eating by the Israelites. When Moses talked about this later, he began this way: you may eat every clean bird (Deut 14:11). But he did not supply any specifications for the clean birds as he had for the four-legged animals. From the rest of Scripture we know very little about the birds that Israel was accustomed to eating. For example, we do not know in which century the Israelites living in Canaan began to hunt grouse. Perhaps they became familiar with these birds in Egypt. Everyone will recall the rooster crowing in the night when Peter denied our Savior. But in the Old Testament, chickens and hens are not ever mentioned. This does not prove, of course, that Israel was unfamiliar with them. A seal has been discovered in Palestine, showing the fanciful image of a hen in an attack posture, dating probably from around 600 BC, the time just before the Babylonian captivity. Among the domestic animals that the Israelites had from early on was the dove. This bird was mentioned frequently in the Sacrifice Torah. This was the only bird that was allowed to be sacrificed. Later people could buy them at the temple. The fatted birds eaten at Solomon's table, and therefore grown in Israel, were fattened geese, according to one interpreter, or fowl, according to another, or cuckoos, according to someone else. The latter is hardly credible.

4. Leviticus 11:20–23. These verses speak about smaller animals, the kind we often call *vermin* or *insects*. For this the Israelites used the word *sherets*, referring in general to small insects that swarmed and crawled. But three kinds of insects are described.

First, insects in the water; second, insects on land, which flew; and third, insects on land that did not fly, but crept.

Naturally, the category of animals now in view did not belong to the first kind, which swarmed in the water. Those were mentioned earlier, in connection with the water creatures. But it was obvious that here the second kind would be mentioned, the insects that fly, since the birds had just been mentioned. So the connection was obvious. (We would conclude that the *swimming* insects of v. 10 and the *flying* insects of v. 20 are completed with the *creeping* insects of v. 41.)

So Lev 11:20–23 is dealing with the flying insects. Concerning this creature we are told, almost repetitiously, that it "goes on all fours," an expression that should be taken at face value and not be forced. Because there are no insects that walk on four legs. True enough, but this is a rather popular way of describing everything that moves horizontally. In view here are all winged insects, like flies, mosquitoes, and beetles. They were not to be eaten by Israelites. An exception to this were four kinds of the specifically identified locusts. In this connection one would think automatically of John the Baptist, whose food consisted of locusts and wild honey (Matt 3:4). Still today, grasshoppers that are roasted or boiled or dried belong to the diet of poor people. People pluck off from the dried locust its head, wings, and legs, and grind the body with a stone or hand mill. This "flour" is mixed with ordinary flour and used for baking bread. The bread would have had a somewhat bitter taste. For that reason people either added honey to it or ate honey along with it.

5. Leviticus 11:24–40. Which animals are in view here?

Well, be careful, this passage is not just about animals. It deals with objects as well. And people.

Therefore we need to distinguish various smaller units in the rather large section. But those units are dealing with *this single subject: defilement through death.* Let's keep that in mind. (We had this section of Leviticus 11 in view when we wrote earlier that our chapter title—about eating clean and unclean animals—strictly speaking was not accurate.)

Leviticus 11:24–40 consists of Units A, B, and C.

Unit A. *Leviticus 11:24–28: defilement through unclean large animals that have died*

1. *Leviticus 11:24–25: Introduction*

    A. V. 24. And by these (i.e., the following) dead animals you shall become unclean. Whoever touches their carcass shall be unclean until the evening.

    B. V. 25. But whoever carries any part of their carcass, for example, to move it out of the way, shall wash his clothes and be unclean until the evening.

2. *Leviticus 11:26–28: which unclean dead animals defile a person*

EATING CLEAN AND UNCLEAN ANIMALS

- A. V. 26. Animals that do not both clearly and simultaneously possess the two features of clean animals (see vv. 4–8, camels and pigs).
- B. V. 27. Dead animals that walked on feet, like a cat and a dog, would automatically defile a person.

Unit B. *Leviticus 11:29–38: defilement through unclean small animals that have died*

1. *Leviticus 11:29–31: which animals*

   A list of various animals that often hide in or around houses or sheds: mole, mouse, toad, lizard, hedgehog, snail, and chameleon. A stern warning not to become defiled with any of these—implied: if they are dead.

2. *Leviticus 11:32–38: cases that can occur*

   - A. V. 32. Such a dead animal could fall into one or another wooden piece of equipment (bowl or bucket), or onto a garment or skin or sack. Or any implement used for work. Then that thing must be washed and would be unclean until evening.
   - B. V. 33. If a dead animal fell in an earthen vessel, like a pot, then that pot had to be destroyed.
   - C. V. 34. If a dead animal came into contact with any food or drink, that would be unclean. At least if that food was not dry, but wet. By means of water, uncleanness can penetrate inside everywhere.
   - D. V. 35. If a carcass fell against an oven or stove, usually made of clay, it should thus easily be broken up. Perhaps we should think of a small hearth with two round holes on top, over which two pots could be placed. This hearth would have been made of clay, and could be broken up easily.
   - E. V. 36. If the dead animal fell into a spring or cistern, a receptacle for water, then that spring and cistern did not have to be considered perpetually unclean. A spring always had flowing water, and a cistern could be refilled with rain again. The one who had fetched the dead animal from the water would be unclean (and would have to follow the regulations in v. 24).
   - F. V. 37. When a dead animal fell or lay in seed grain that was to be sown, which was dry, the seed remained clean. As long as such seed had not been moistened with water, the uncleanness cannot penetrate it. As seed for sowing, it is not food for human consumption. The ground in which it is sown absorbed the uncleanness.

G. V. 38. But when the carcass came into contact with seed that had been moistened (in order to use it), this seed would be unclean

Unit C. *Leviticus 11:39–40: defilement through clean livestock that died on its own*

1. V. 39. When a clean animal, such as a sheep or deer, died on its own, one became unclean through touching that carcass.
2. V. 40. Anyone who ate from such a carcass or who moved it aside, would have to wash his clothes.

That a person would become defiled simply by touching the carcass of a clean or unclean animal is taught in Leviticus 11. But not that in such cases a person needed to wash. Nevertheless, on the basis of comparison with Lev 15:7 and 17:15, such an act was likely.

6. Leviticus 11:41–43. In this last section, we read for the third time about insects. Earlier we observed that there were three kinds: swimming, flying, and creeping insects. The last kind are in view here. Insects that live in and on the ground. It could be that they moved on their belly (worms and snakes) or walked on four legs (beetles, ticks, etc.) or that they crept along on more legs (centipedes). This kind of creature was also supposed to be detestable among Israel. The term "insect" was almost synonymous with "detestable," perhaps because of similar sounding Hebrew words.

7. Leviticus 11:44–47
We have here a double conclusion.

A. Leviticus 11:44–45. The first conclusion is directly connected with the preceding verses, where we read about various insects that creep on or in the ground (like worms and such). With this in view, God commanded Israel to remember always that she was his people, the people of Yahweh, who was holy and who had taken Israel out of Egypt. Was God perhaps alluding to a certain correspondence between the Egyptian house of bondage, indeed, the Egyptian grave, and these eerie (creepy) insects?

B. Leviticus 11:46–47. The second conclusion is related to the entire chapter, to all preceding six sections. In each of them there was mention of eating. These concluding verses contain the command that Israel was to distinguish between clean and unclean animals, and in so doing, between animals that may and may not be eaten. Naturally, this postscript provides a very abbreviated overview. It does not intend to be complete. For example, it says nothing regarding defilement through contact with this or that. Nor about defilement through defiled objects. We would have liked to have read about this here. But apparently Israel did need that. What explains the sizeable difference?

Earlier we indicated that the ancient Eastern peoples had more feeling for symbolism than we do, and that with various commandments of the Law, God could make use of shared Eastern institutions. We have also mentioned that the distinction between clean and unclean animals given at Horeb would not have given Israel the impression of being an unheard of novelty. The religions of the surrounding nations were also familiar with something like this, Israel would likely have inherited knowledge of this along with the story of the Flood that came down from earlier generations (Gen 7:2). Even though we don't know exactly which animals were clean and unclean for Noah. But we do know that the Noahic distinction between clean and unclean that functioned in the time before the Flood did not yet have any significance with regard to eating. For using meat was permitted for the first time after the Flood (Gen 9:3). The distinction indicated there was probably related to the suitability of various animals for sacrifice.

At that time the situation resembled the situation with circumcision. This too was not a complete novelty in Abraham's time, but was annexed by God and used with a completely new and unique meaning. In this way, God apparently gave a new significance and a new mandate to the ancient distinction between clean and unclean animals, namely, to function for Israel as a means of visual instruction. To warn Israel about everything out there, beyond the intimate presence of Yahweh. Out there was the darkness of paganism. Out there was death.

That is what Leviticus 11 preaches.

Beware of death!

And if we may look ahead for a moment to our discussion of the following chapters, that is in fact the sermon of all of Leviticus 11–15.

This can easily be shown from Leviticus 11. If we have understood this chapter properly, then we observe that God prohibited Israel from eating precisely all those animals whose existence and manner of living were closely connected with decay, dissolution, rottenness—in short, animals who were at home in the realm of death. But with every other group of animals, even when not eating them but simply touching them was forbidden, it was clear that God's warning was constantly being sounded against death. Just look at this.

1. The meat of animals that clearly and simultaneously chewed the cud and had cloven hooves was not forbidden. For these animals were not

carnivores. They didn't eat carrion. They didn't tear apart their prey, but ate vegetation. Their hooves were not like the claws of predatory animals that used those as terrible instruments of killing. These were forbidden. Along with every animal that might not have been a predator, but nonetheless displayed something—like not chewing the cud, or not clearly cloven hooves—that moved in that direction.

2. For that reason, Israel could continue eating fish, as they had done to their heart's content in Egypt. But water creatures that were not real fish would have been prohibited. Like insects, swimming insects, without fins and scales. Like paling.

3. Therefore Israel was also prohibited from eating the meat of predatory birds and birds that ate carrion. But birds that did not eat other living and dead animals, or carcasses, could be clean and were allowed to be eaten.

4. Therefore Israel was also not permitted to eat various flying insects. Except certain locusts, which ate vegetation. But we know that wherever meat lies rotting and stinking, insects are swarming around the stench. Those would be prohibited for Israel.

5. For the same reasons, Israel was forbidden to eat not only (a) the meat of unclean large animals, but if they were dead, touching them would have brought defilement. And (b) Israel was explicitly warned about unclean animals that were dead, because people could easily be defiled by the carcasses of moles, mice, lizards, etc., in a shed, workshop, and garden. Indeed (c) Israel was supposed to remember that defilement accompanied clean livestock that had died on its own.

6. Therefore Israel certainly had to watch out for contact with various insects, vermin, that lived in garbage and in manure and in places where carcasses could be found. For even though these animals were alive, the grave was their home. So even though these lived, they were unclean insects!

7. Finally, with this *last* category, God was recalling Israel's deliverance from Egypt. Even though they were at the same time referring back to other prohibitions. Watch out for death. That does not fit your identity. Because it does not fit mine. I am Yahweh, who brought you out of the land of Egypt, to be a God unto you. Be holy, for I am holy.

Is this the proper interpretation of Leviticus 11?

Yes, it is, as we learn from a man no less than Moses, from what he said about these things when he spoke about the name of Yahweh (in connection with the Third of the Ten Words), found in Deut 14:1–21a. When you read this part of Moses' preaching in Deuteronomy, remember that the name *Yahweh* formed the brief compendium for Israel of the story of her deliverance from Egypt, and that God was at the same time guaranteeing his future assistance to Israel. The name Yahweh signified, in view of the past, "Savior of life," and at the same time, in view of the future, "The One Nearby."

In Deuteronomy 14, Moses was pressing upon the hearts of the Israelites two particular realities in connection with the name of Yahweh. He was making a connection, first, with what Yahweh had done in the past, and second, with what Yahweh wanted to be for Israel in the future.

In the first place, Moses reminded the Israelites that they were children of Yahweh. God had made them such. By means of his redemptive deeds. Thereby God had shown that he was seeking Israel's life and happiness. So then, such a privileged people were now supposed to grieve like the pagans. At the death of a loved one, they were permitted to sorrow, but theirs was not to be *pagan* sorrow. Not like those who had no hope. For originally the expectation that all the dead would rise again was shared by everybody. All of Adam's children naturally knew about God's good intentions with our human race. Intentions that extended beyond death and the grave. But over the course of time, this inheritance was sadly mutilated. Into something unrecognizable. The fantasies of the Egyptian ka—something like an invisible twin of a human being—of the Brahman reincarnation of souls, the Buddhist nirvana, and the late-Greek immortal soul, are proof both of the original richness (of tradition handed down from the Paradise gospel) and of the later poverty (due to pervasive, often erudite, ignorance). This explains that terrible despair among pagans when the dead came to be separated from them. As though that death had the final word. But Israel could know better, not only from time immemorial, but now for sure after "Egypt." Otherwise God could have allowed them to perish in Egypt. But for this reason, since he had brought them from death to life, brought them out of Egypt, God definitely did not want to see any pagan grieving rituals among Israel. Like a wealthy man who married a poor woman would not wish to see his wife going about clothed like a slutty beggar. In the same way, God would not tolerate his people of life wearing a garment of pagan despair in the face of death.

But what Moses went on to say to Israel in Deuteronomy 14 in connection with the name of Yahweh was related more to God's promise that he as the Nearby One would live among Israel in a sanctuary. That is why he had delivered them (Exod 29:46; for God was "en route" to Paradise). But then Israel would need to conduct herself in a way suited to her exalted companion. So they had to learn to bring to mind God's ancient mandate to engage in the life and death battle against Satan and his party.[1] Perhaps that ancient mandate had been virtually forgotten among the human race, possible even among Israel, after their long stay in that pagan environment, but God wanted to accustom Israel gradually to that fight once again. He wanted to see Israel one day living in constant opposition against Satan's entire realm.

May this goal become far more familiar and well-known to us today, we who live after Christ's duel with the devil.

By means of his constant warnings about death in the book of Leviticus, God portrayed that fight for ancient Israel. For the true nature of that death was no longer seen within paganism, namely, death as Satan's companion (Heb 2:14), under which paganism has always crept around in fright. Death was Satan's domain, for pagans (Acts 26:18). But Israel, who had been placed afresh and powerfully on the side of Yahweh, the God of life, would need to learn to view and perceive death as something unsuited to Israel.

To give but one example. Even when a clean animal had died in Israel—not slaughtered, but died on its own—the carcass of such an (originally clean) animal was supposed to be extremely unclean for Israel, and people were never allowed to eat its meat. People could give it to the dogs, as they were traveling through the wilderness (Exod 22:30), and later in Canaan, people could give such meat as a gift to the *ger*, the "sojourner," i.e., the foreigner who had come to live in Israel, or they could sell it to the *nokri*, the foreigner who was staying temporarily, perhaps for business reasons, among the Israelites (Deut 14:21). For such pagans were aligned with the devil and with death. But Israel was the people of Yahweh, who despised sin, death, and the demons. Today we may know that it was God's intention back then already to put an end once and for all to the dominion over pagans—including our own ancestors—on the part of the great murder-from-the-beginning, by means of the coming and the sacrifice of his beloved Son (Eph 1:4; 3:10; 2 Tim 1:9).

That is how we may understand the Law today.

Just as the intention of an architect regarding the placement of the foundation for a building is able to be known only when this building has been constructed on that foundation and is visible to everyone, so too God's intention with the Law of Moses is fully evident only now, thanks to its fulfillment through the sacrifice, death, and resurrection of our Lord Jesus Christ.

---

1. See Vonk, *Genesis*, 123.

When we read Leviticus 11, or when we come later to Deut 14:3–21a, then we must pay attention to the unique place that "Horeb" occupies in the history of redemption.

We have seen God at work earlier on earth combatting death. Already in Paradise. And when he took pity on Noah. And when he saved Abraham. And also when he led Israel out of Egypt.

But at Horeb he gave to Moses for Israel his Torah (Instruction, Knowledge, Law) as teaching regarding the redemption of life that would come like never before.

So expansive. Laying such a wide-reaching claim on various things in the life of the Israelites. For example, on animals with which they would come into contact, whether as part of their diet, or not. For they already had to avoid some animals that were not dead but were as alive as ever. Not because they despised creation, such "pests" as worms and rats had also received from God their particular place and task in the creation. The Israelites would have seen and understood that. But God gave to those beasts the function of letters in the Law, whereby Israel had to learn not only who she was, namely, a people whom God had claimed for himself and to whom he had given a priestly calling (Exod 19:6; Lev 20:25–26)—which explains why the duty of purity applied even more strictly to the priests and the high priest (Lev 21 and 22)—but also who God was. God hated the world of death, sin, Satan, paganism. God, who planned one day to open up for all nations a path to life. Just as we may know today, because the gospel of Christ's resurrection has been shared with pagans.

This explains why the church of the New Testament was protected so fiercely by all the apostles, but especially by the apostle to the Gentiles. Paul protected against Judaizing Christianity. "Therefore let no one pass judgment on you in questions of food and drink, or with regard to a festival or a new moon or a Sabbath. These are a shadow of the things to come, but the substance [literally: the body] belongs to Christ" (Col 2:16–17). Compared to the instruction that God gives us today by means of the gospel of Christ's incarnation, death, and resurrection, the instruction about God's hatred of sin, the devil, and death by means of the Law virtually disappears into nothing, just like the light of a candle, no matter how highly we value such light in the night's darkness, nevertheless pales to nothing when we throw open the curtains of our bedroom and the full light of day streams in.

The Law of Leviticus 11 also belongs to the past.

By removing its applicability to us, however, God did not subordinate us to Israel. As though he would hand us over to unclean animals, or even to death.

It is not God's fault that in the Middle Ages, our ancestors were repeatedly afflicted with epidemics because they raised pigs in such an unhygienic manner that the rats could thrive so well among them, and in the cities as well. In the late Middle Ages, in Rhenen the pigs of the residents walked freely through the city, as was customary. If the Jews of that time suffered less from epidemics because they did not raise pigs, then this does prove that our ancestors lived unhygienically, but not that in Leviticus 11 God was providing teaching about diet and health, not even that the dominating idea was the advancement of health, even though there were underlying motives that affected other dimensions of life. Without wanting to argue the opposite position, namely, that Israel's health was not important to God, we believe that the Law of Leviticus 11 was not first of all a sanitary or medicinal or dietary regulation, but bore a gospel symbolizing character, because it had the focus of instructing and assuring the Israelites that their God was Yahweh, who despised sin and death among his people and was en route to giving to the world eternal life in his Son, Jesus Christ. The primary part of that great work has been accomplished today. For God performed this work in stages. But when that Christ returns one day, then that work will have reached the point when "shall come to pass the saying that is written: 'Death is swallowed up in victory'" (1 Cor 15:54).

Truly, Leviticus 11 is a very beautiful resurrection chapter!

Having heard the preaching of later prophets—back to the Law and the Testimony!—we need have no illusions about Israel's observance of the Law of Leviticus 11, though there were some who remained faithful (Ezek 4:14). As punishment, Ephraim would have to "eat unclean food in Assyria" (Hos 9:3; cf. Amos 7:17b). This was a fate that Daniel escaped through his humble request (Dan 1:8–9).

In a later time, however, the remarkable phenomenon occurred that the Jews observed the regulations of Leviticus 11 with a kind of fanaticism. We have in view not only the days of the Maccabees, when many chose martyrdom rather than to defile themselves by eating pork. Hereby they were simply demonstrating obedience to the divine commandment still applicable at that time. Even though the story about these events that we read in 2 Maccabees 6 and 7 (about the refusal of an old man and seven brothers to eat pork) makes a somewhat strange impression. Nevertheless, when our Savior came to earth, he was surrounded by a people who no longer understood God's wonderful gospel intention with the Law, but who instead were sighing under the Law as under a yoke that was hard, and under a burden that was heavy (Matt 11:30). Whereas in reality God's commandments are never heavy (1 John 5:3). And whereas the teachers of those people were not even observing the a-b-c's of that Law. Read the angry words of our Savior spoken to the scribes and Pharisees (Matt 9:13; 12:7; Mark 7:8; Luke 11:46). And these people from their side were no less raging against Christ, who dared to assault their ancestral doctrine (Mark 7:5, 9; Acts 6:13; 7:53–54). They were so blinded that they had identified their doctrine with God's teaching. Paul had also been such a "heartfelt zealot" (Gal 1:14), even a persecutor of the church (1 Tim 1:13). The Pharisees understood nothing more of the evangelical meaning of the ceremonial law. That had been given as the gospel of shadows, which looked forward to being fulfilled; thus, it was the preaching of grace; they, however, had turned it into an eternal precept and thereby had destroyed not only its provisional character, but also its grace-content; their notion was that this law no longer pointed to the deliverances that God would accomplish, but to the works that they themselves had accomplished.

We have discussed this before, namely, that this un-evangelical commitment to the Law slipped into the Christian church as well. Some Christian Jews, when they accepted Jesus as the promised Messiah, did not lay aside their garments of Jewish pride and conceit, but demanded that converted Gentiles should still observe the entire Law of Moses. They do not say that the shadows of the Horeb covenant and the Law were fulfilled by Christ, and the time was past when the gospel of the forgiveness of sins and eternal life was given only to Israel and beyond, among the Gentiles, darkness and death dominated. It was indeed a massive change. The Law was, after all, God's own Word. Were people allowed to set it aside just like that? Even Peter had difficulty seeing this, and when he did see it, to keep on seeing it. Regarding the former, we read in the story of Peter's vision of the sheets that held—note well!—*creeping animals*! The insects about which the Law spoke. And regarding the difficulty that Peter apparently had sometime later in *continuing to see* the fulfillment of the Law and the completely altered relationship between Israel and the Gentiles, you can read in Gal 2:11–21. From there we can learn that we must not yield to the spirit of a certain kind of Christianity that wants to bind us still today to a requirement of the Horeb covenant like the Sabbath and various other religious days. No more than Paul yielded to his brothers Peter and Barnabas. For even in Antioch, these highly gifted men acted for a moment, out of fear of men, as though the Law of Leviticus 11—separation between Israel, the people of life, and the Gentiles, children of death—had remained valid. But Paul rebuked them openly and honestly. He had to. For otherwise "Christ would have died in vain" (Gal 2:21).

16

Torah instruction with regard to the uncleanness after childbirth (Lev 12)

When we read Leviticus 12, let us remember that by means of many symbols, God wanted to instruct and assure his ancient covenant people of *the gospel of the old covenant*. If we don't keep this in mind, this short chapter will present us with a very difficult riddle.

For here we encounter regulations pertaining to childbirth in Israel, to a woman who had given birth to a baby, just like our mothers gave birth to us. Was this a crime in those days? A crime so serious that in Israel they had to be punished for this with seven days of total isolation and thirty-three days of partial isolation? (And twice these amounts if they gave birth to a girl: fourteen days of total isolation, and sixty-six days of partial isolation.) Was this a crime so serious that a sin offering had to be brought for it?

Who would believe such a thing?

That would not fit very well with the high esteem that God commanded us to have for marriage. Or if people sometimes suppose that it was the sexual intercourse of husband and wife that was being punished, then it must be stated that according to God's Word, sexual intercourse is not at all sinful, otherwise God would not have commanded it in particular situations (Exod 21:10), but if it was legitimate, then it would have been egregiously unfair to punish the wife for such a sin and not the initiator, the one who begat the child, the husband.

We should not go in that direction with Leviticus 12. Moreover, let us be reminded once more that we may not deduce from a person's obligation to bring a sin offering that he or she had become guilty of one or another misdeed. We learned differently in connection with the teaching about the sin offering.

In order to understand Leviticus 12 correctly, we need to pay careful attention to two things. First, to the *location* of this chapter, and second, the special *content* of this chapter.

Regarding the *location* of Leviticus 12, it is preceded by Leviticus 11 and followed by Leviticus 13–14.

We have not yet discussed Leviticus 13–14, but at this point we can say that both of these chapters deal with leprosy, and that God held up leprosy to Israel as a symbolic death. Let us mention only one thing by way of preliminary comment. When Mariam and Aaron rebelled against Moses, and Miriam was punished with leprosy, Aaron said to Moses: "Oh, my lord, do not punish us because we have done foolishly and have sinned. Let her not be as one dead, whose flesh is half eaten away when he comes out of his mother's womb" (Num 12:12). Later we will see that for this reason lepers had to be excluded from Israel's military camp, because Israel had received the promise of being the people of life, whereas leprosy was a mirror of death.

So this is what the next chapters will be discussing.

Regarding Leviticus 11, immediately preceding our present chapter, we can be very brief. In Leviticus 11 we read not only about the difference between clean and unclean animals, but also specifically about dead animals. By means of the Torah or instruction of Leviticus 11, God reminded the Israelites that they had received from him the privilege of his living among them in the tabernacle. For that reason they had to beware of any contact with the kind of animals that had anything to do with death. Not only if such animals were dead, but also if it was the kind of animal for whose nature death and decay were its element. Leviticus 11 preached the message: Beware of death!

So then, is it not likely that here, in a chapter located within this context, we would find teaching about the gospel of life and a warning about death?

This assumption is confirmed by the *content* of Leviticus 12. That content involves two matters: 1. The uncleanness of a woman following childbirth; and 2. The sacrifices required for a woman following childbirth.

1. THE UNCLEANNESS OF A WOMAN FOLLOWING CHILDBIRTH

If the baby was a boy, this uncleanness lasted forty days. But during that time, the degree of uncleanness was not always the same. This time was divided into two parts.

(a) The first period of uncleanness lasted seven days. "As at the time of her menstruation, she shall be unclean," says verse 2. It was assumed that Israelite readers would know the purpose behind this. We have not yet discussed this. This was referring to the flow of blood experienced by a menstruating woman or girl. This is discussed further in Lev 15:19–24. There we learn that the uncleanness resulting from the monthly blood flow lasted seven days, and that anyone who came into contact with such a menstruating woman or girl was also unclean, though for only one day. Moreover, in due course we will see that Leviticus 15 is dealing with no other matters than what is more or less related to the procreation of the human race. Matters, thus, that involve preeminently life and death.

(b) The second period of uncleanness lasted thirty-three days. During this time, the uncleanness no longer as severe as during the preceding time, but it was still forbidden for the new mother to be involved with anything holy, such as appearing in the sanctuary and participating in a sacrifice meal. That was permitted only when the forty days were ended. When she had given birth to a girl, that was permitted only after a total of eighty days.

These numbers—forty days for a boy, and eighty days for a girl—will perhaps appear rather puzzling to our Bible readers. In reality, however, those numbers supply us with precisely the help we want for explaining Leviticus 12.

Let's take first the number seven. We must take note how often this number appears in the purity laws. In Leviticus 12 as well, we encounter this covenant number. Here as well, it has obvious symbolic—i.e., metaphorical, instructional, homiletical—significance. Witness the reference in verse 2 to Lev 15:19, concerning menstruation. For in connection with menstruation, the number seven has no medical relevance, as everyone understands. For one can hardly claim that menstruation lasts seven days every time. Usually it lasts only three or four days at most.

This symbolic import of the number seven seems clear to us from the doubling of the two periods of uncleanness (first seven, then thirty-three, a total of forty days) when the mother had given birth to a girl.

We'll comment first on that doubling.

This feature as well had no other purpose than a symbolic one. Naturally, it had no medical purpose. Nobody today would argue what people used to claim, that a mother who had just given birth to a girl would have had a bloody flow that lasted longer than that following the birth of a boy. That is pure fantasy. The extending of the time of uncleanness in connection with the birth of a girl can be explained simply from the fact that the female gender is weaker (1 Pet 3:7). And that is very important in Leviticus, where we are repeatedly placed before the contrast between death and life. Because

UNCLEANNESS AFTER CHILDBIRTH

the weak one must be seen as more vulnerable to death. And because even the newborn baby girl can already be viewed as a human being who later would be subjected to the regularity of the female flowing of blood and its uncleanness. This is expressed here by raising the numbers seven and thirty-three, in fact, by doubling both of them.

Why was the number seven doubled?

For similar reasons.

Because it was apparently God's intention to increase the days of the second period of uncleanness in such a way that the number forty would not be lost but be preserved.

For according to Holy Scripture, the number forty also has a unique significance. We find it frequently in the Torah in places that have somewhat of a somber tone, a serious, oppressive tone. See, for example, Gen 7:4 (forty days and forty nights of rain on the earth), Exod 24:18 and 34:28 (Moses on the mountain for forty days and forty nights, when "he neither ate bread nor drank water"), Num 14:33 (Israel's forty-year wandering in the wilderness), and Deut 25:3 (forty blows before the judge).

Now in order to reach the number forty as the sum of both periods of uncleanness for a mother who gave birth to a boy, the first period lasted seven days and the second period lasted thirty-three days. What then happened with the birth of a girl? God wanted to express this by increasing the number. But in such a way that both the symbolic meaning of the number seven and that of the number forty would be preserved.

So then, he simply commanded the doubling of both periods.

The first period of uncleanness totaled 2 x 7 days, or 14 days.

The second period of uncleanness totaled 2 x 33 days, or 66 days.

14 + 66 = 80 days

In this way, both the number seven and the number forty were preserved. For 80 = 2 x 40.

In this way, attention remained focused on the weakness of the female gender and on the strengthened contrast between life and death.

Comment: Another explanation prefers the understanding that the periods of uncleanness in the case of the birth of a boy were shorter because after seven days the baby boy was to be circumcised. But we read nowhere in Scripture that circumcision possessed atoning power, not for the child or his mother.[1]

---

1. See Vonk, *Genesis*, 230–33.

2. THE SACRIFICES FOR A WOMAN FOLLOWING CHILDBIRTH

That atoning power God tied (symbolically) to the two sacrifices that had to be brought by the mother who had given birth to the sanctuary after the entire period of her uncleanness had ended, thus, after forty or eighty days. The required sacrifices were "a [male] lamb a year old for a burnt offering, and a pigeon or a turtledove for a sin offering" (v. 6). The priest would sacrifice these in the presence of Yahweh and make atonement for her. Then she would be purified from her flow of blood (v. 7).

We believe that we have said enough about the two kinds of sacrifices mentioned here: the burnt offering and the sin offering, as well as about the sequence in the case of a woman who has given birth. The main focus here is on the sin offering given for the woman who has given birth. For that sacrifice, more than any other, spoke of atonement.

Atonement. For some evil that this woman had committed?

Anyone who has read our discussion about the teaching connected with the sin offering knows that it was not always legitimate to conclude from a persons' bringing a sin offering that the person on whose behalf this occurred must have committed a crime. For example, take a leper who had been healed. Such a person was definitely not permitted to return to Israelite society unless he had brought a sin offering. But it was nevertheless clear that such a person did not bring that sin offering on account of committing a crime. Sickness is not the same as sin, after all. So it was also not the case that after childbirth, a woman was obligated to bring a sin offering because she had done something evil. Some kind of "sin of commission."

But then for what purpose was atonement necessary?

Some who understand very well that such atonement was not needed for a "sin of commission" on the part of the woman who had given birth, reply that this was required in terms of "inborn sin" or "original sin."

One Reformed commentator wrote about Leviticus 12 that the sin offering spoke of the covering of sin, something of which became public in connection with the birth and its outcome. (In this connection, some refer to Psalm 51:5: "Behold, I was brought forth in iniquity, and in sin did my mother conceive me." This Bible verse is used as proof of the depravity of human nature, which, according to Belgic Confession, article 15, is original sin.)

The German commentator Bähr also seems to go in this direction, for he writes that the sin offerings and the guilt offerings in connection with the purifications point in the direction of sin and guilt, not specifically, however, to an independently identifiable transgression, but to the general corruption by "sin."[2]

But, with all due respect, we cannot agree with this.

Please understand.

We do believe that the first disobedience of Adam was also committed by all his descendants, so that they are all born as being worthy of death, doomed to commit sin. (Something that indeed happens, unless God's Spirit teaches us through his Word to believe, so that through this faith we are regenerated, as we learn from Heidelberg Catechism, Lord's Day 3, and Belgic Confession, articles 22–24.) The apostle teaches us this in Romans 5, and we see it with our own eyes. For some babies die a few days or hours after birth. Indeed, some enter the world stillborn. Nevertheless, because it must remain fixed for us that God never, ever commits injustice, and because we also know that babies commit no personal sin while in their mother's wombs (Rom 9:11), we must see the cause of the death of these little ones in their participation in Adam's first transgression.

So we do believe that all people are born as children of wrath. This is something we see confirmed in those who do not die in infancy but reach the "years of discretion." When these children, who have been born already as heirs of the kingdom of God and of his covenant, do not accept the preaching of our Lord Jesus Christ, and this faith then does not regenerate them to live a God-pleasing life, the wrath of God abides on them and they continue to dwell in "original sin," inclined toward all evil and incapable of any good.

All of this is true.

But should this be applied to Leviticus 12?

We do not think so.

We must not speak here about the little babies and the capacities with which they are born, for Leviticus 12 is not talking about them. We are dealing here not with the uncleanness of our human race in general, nor with that of babies in particular, but with the (symbolic) uncleanness of mothers who give birth.

Let's pause for a moment.

We can hear someone saying: "But what about the story of the presentation of our Savior in the temple, then, in Luke 2:22–29? Does it not begin with the words: 'And when the time came for their purification according to the Law of Moses'? The word *their* is plural, isn't it? Well then, that word must have had in view both mother and child."

Let's see.

---

2. Bähr, *Symbolik*, 2:483; cf. 2:492.

Indeed, a literalist could claim that a purification sacrifice was brought for our Savior when he was forty days old. For it does say "their" purification. But anyone who reads Holy Scripture in terms of its entire context will not say such a strange thing about our Savior. And by comparing one passage with another, such a person will discover the proper explanation.

First, as far as we know, nowhere in the Law or in the Prophets do we find that a newborn baby was unclean in the sense of all contact between the child and something holy would have been completely impermissible. The baby was not unclean in a cultic sense. The mother who had just given birth was unclean in a cultic sense (Lev 12:4).

In addition, in Leviticus 12 we read explicitly that the purification sacrifice was for the mother. Not for the child. "He [viz., the priest] shall offer it [viz., the sin offering] before the Lord and make atonement *for her*. Then she shall be clean from *the flow of her blood*" (v. 7).

We would place Luke 2 alongside this. What is being told us there? First: the release of Baby Jesus (vv. 22b-23). For the Lord was Mary's firstborn son. Such a boy had to be "ransomed" (Exod 13:2; Num 18:15). Second: the purification of Mary (V. 24). Luke wanted to tell us about those two things in verses 22b-24.

But how does Luke introduce the story about those two things (regarding Baby Jesus and his mother Mary) for us? By means of the following sentence in verse 22a: "And when the time came for their purification according to the Law of Moses."

Does not everyone see that in that introductory sentence, Luke was giving us a *summary*? That at this point, with the word *purification* he was including what he would go on to report about both the mother and the Baby? That is obvious. For obligations lay upon both the Lord Jesus and his mother, with respect to one and the same *Law of Moses*.

The First One had to be redeemed as the firstborn, the second person had to be purified as the mother who had given birth. So then, at that point Luke was summarizing those two things in the introductory clause, using the single word *purification*. Apparently he thought that this word could be used with a wide range of meaning. But according to the preference of people who suffer from the disease of literalism, he should of course have written expansively: And when the time came when according to the Law of Moses, Baby Jesus was to be redeemed and Mary was to be purified." But Luke abbreviated this by using the single word *purification* to indicate two very different obligations, both of which flowed forth from the one Law. He preferred to leave it to the goodwill of the Bible reader. Like he does later, when without much commentary he writes that for Mary, not *a lamb* plus a dove were slaughtered, but *two* doves. He figured on people having

UNCLEANNESS AFTER CHILDBIRTH

the goodwill to recall the exception granted in Lev 12:8: "And if she cannot afford a lamb, then she shall take two turtledoves or two pigeons, one for a burnt offering and the other for a sin offering. And the priest shall make atonement for her, and she shall be clean." We are being told in a delicate way that the male lamb required for the burnt offering was replaced for Mary with a dove *on account of her poverty*. That makes for a sacrifice of *two* doves.

So Leviticus 12 is dealing with the uncleanness of the mother, the woman who has given birth. Granted that it is not dealing with her medical impurity, but with her (symbolic) impurity according to the Law.

Why did such a woman who had given birth have to be considered unclean, according to the Law? For what reason?

Answer: her flow of blood.

We read that when the priest had performed the sacrifice for her and made atonement for her, she would be clean "from the flow of her blood" (v. 7).

That *flow of blood* was the "sin" that had to be atoned. For that, the priest had to bring the sacrifice and that was what he had to atone (cover).

Meanwhile we must of course keep in mind here that this "flow of blood" was of a particular nature. Not the kind of blood flowing that happens when someone injures himself seriously with a knife or some other object and lost so much blood that he was in danger of dying. That kind of flow of blood prevented no one from entering the sanctuary.

But rather the kind of flow that we will discuss in connection with Leviticus 15, connected more or less with sexual relations. Our present chapter points us to that. In verse 2. With those words: "as at the time of her menstruation." That was referring, as we've already said, to the uncleanness of menstruation mentioned in Lev 15:19–24. We will see later that the stipulations found in all of Leviticus 15 involve human procreation. Such an occasion involved human life in a preeminent way.

Let us look, finally, at the sacrifice of atonement that had to be brought for the woman following childbirth. We recall in that connection what was said earlier about the teaching of the sin offering. By means of the sin offering, God was urgently appealing to his people Israel: Know where you stand. On the foundation of redemption and life. Don't move one hair's breadth from that foundation, in the direction of death.

Is not the lesson of Leviticus 12 obvious for us?

The lesson for us Christians, still?

No, when it comes to Leviticus 12, we must not start talking about "original sin." In connection with Leviticus 12 we must talk about the covenant. Something that God has today as well with us and our children, though it is no longer the Sinai covenant. With us things are far better, but thereby also far more serious. God's Spirit has flooded us with the great historical Word-bath of the gospel of Jesus Christ, and in that flood of promises he has sanctified us with the blood of his Son and placed us on his foundation, where the power of the coming age are at work (Eph 5:26; Heb 6:5; 10:29).

Today the church of the new dispensation are being warned seriously by means of chapters like Leviticus 11 and 12 not to trample upon the blood of Christ and not to despise the Spirit of Christ by falling back into self-righteous religion, paganism, and service to the devil. It will be that much worse for the church than for someone who in ancient times set aside the Law of Moses, says Hebrews 10:28–31. Just as genuine love cannot bear for one moment if one's beloved shows any inclination of taking one step in the direction of a fatal danger, so too chapters 11–15 teach us today, as we read them in the light of the New Testament, that we must oversee ourselves and each other, so that no one departs from the living God, nor even move toward the outer edge of the life-world in which the Spirit of Christ has placed us. For on the other side of that boundary lies death and eternal destruction.

And to see before our very eyes today how many fall away, people who bear on their foreheads the sign of God's (new) covenant. To see that they are not turning their backs any longer on a tent, a tabernacle, or a wilderness camp, symbols of life, but are turning their backs on Christ, who became Life in his own person and who is the Fountain of Life, acknowledged by God and crowned as King over the citadel of Zion, his church.

To such Christians, who were redeemed in their ancestors from paganism but have returned again to that paganism and to death, indeed, to hell and to the devil himself, to such Christians the statement of the apostle Peter applies: "What the true proverb says has happened to them: 'The dog returns to its own vomit, and the sow, after washing herself, returns to wallow in the mire'" (2 Pet 2:22).

Let us oversee each other and warn each other, when someone is running the risk of forgetting his nobility. Just as God warned Israel about that through the Law about the woman after childbirth. But through many other means as well! Read what follows.

17

Torah instruction with regard to the uncleanness of leprosy (Lev 13–14)

Now come those two chapters that have probably frightened many people because of their length. And perhaps also because of their content, that struck some as totally incomprehensible. Or at least of very little use to God's church today. Whereas in reality these are genuinely evangelical, gospel-filled chapters. Full of instruction for Israel, and thus also for us, regarding this truth: that God's greatest desire and love is for our life. Something he revealed most clearly when he sent his beloved Son who became Life for us in his very person (John 1:4). But anyone who is outside of God and his Christ is with the devil and with his assistant, namely, the prince of this world, death (John 12:31; 14:30–31; 16:11; Heb 2:14).

We will address the following questions:

1. What must we understand by leprosy in the Bible?

2. What are the subjects discussed in Leviticus 13–14?

3. What is the outline of Lev 13:1–46?

4. What happened in connection with the purification of lepers, according to Lev 14:1–32?

1. WHAT MUST WE UNDERSTAND BY LEPROSY IN THE BIBLE?

Leprosy!

PART 4 | THE PEOPLE OF YAHWEH

From the time we were young, we learned to shudder at the sound of that word. For leprosy was—so we thought—the name of a terrible disease. Pictures of people suffering from this repulsive disease showed that. These poor wretches came down with growths on their foreheads, deformed nose and ears. It also happened that during the patient's lifetime, one or another body part would die and fall off. On account of the infectiousness of their disease, such people were strictly isolated. Taken away from parents, from spouse and children. We sympathized with these "lepers" and thought of such sick people when we heard the Bible stories about Miriam, Naaman, and king Uzziah, and all those other times when we encountered the word *leprosy* in Scripture.

Until on a given day we read about a physician, K. P. C. A. Gramberg, who argued that with this understanding of leprosy, our interpretation of the biblical stories involving this disease were completely wrong. This physician could be called an expert. For years he was involved with the "leper colony" that was established in 1907 on the northern coast of Java, and more than any other health worker, he became acquainted with the pain of those suffering leprosy. But what was the primary nature of that pain, according to him? It consisted of their terrible loneliness. In the aversion and disgust they encountered everywhere. Remarkably they encountered this precisely where people would have expected the opposite, namely, where *Christianity* had taken root. For along with Christianity came the idea that lepers had to be avoided and excluded. Isolated from society. How did people reach that conclusion? Apparently that was the continuing result of the laws about leprosy found in Leviticus 13-14. Whereas, according to the physician we mentioned, that infectiousness of the leper was not that serious. According to him, that infectiousness was no greater than that of the diseases suffered by others who were not at all forcibly banned from society.

That was news to us. And as usually happens when someone surrenders his commitment to an age-old misunderstanding, so here as well, when that physician Gramberg was contradicted by another doctor, A. C. Drogendijk. The bottom line is that the Jews used the term *leprosy* in a broad sense to include other skin diseases as well.

According to a number of medical experts, throughout the course of time a tremendous confusion had arisen concerning various diseases, and nowadays those poor folk suffering from leprosy have become the victims of a ghastly misunderstanding. This has led to everyone thinking that they need to avoid and shun such patients, as they used to do in Israel with the so-called "lepers." But in fact, there is no basis for this, not only from a medical viewpoint. As one physician has stated, people talk far too much about the infectiousness of the leper. We do not know the manner of contracting the disease and the chances of infection are very slim for most people. But there is also no basis from a historical viewpoint, and we can identify the historical route of this misunderstanding as follows.

1. The biblical term is *tsara'ath*. It appears elsewhere in Scripture, but nowhere are the phenomena of *tsara'ath* discussed as extensively as in Leviticus 13–14. It is clear that in these chapters, *tsara'ath* refers to a skin disease manifesting itself in tumors or spots on the skin that are often white and occasionally reddish-white in color, the essential feature of which is that they lie beneath the surface of the skin, and the hair above the infected spot is white. The spots have the tendency to expand quickly or to shrink quickly. In earlier cases, something appeared on the skin that people used to describe as "wild flesh." These ulcerations could heal, after which the whiteness could spread over the entire body, so that the priest found that the *tsara'ath* had covered the entire body, but then the person afflicted with *tsara'ath* is clean.

2. In terms of medical thought and knowledge today, the entire description of the disease in Leviticus 13 is somewhat unclear, but there is certainly no single point of agreement other than perhaps the white coloring of the skin. One scholar has argued that *tsara'ath* should be seen as identical to what is called *vitiligo* (a condition in which pigment is lost from areas of the skin, causing whitish patches). The white color in particular is an argument for his position, especially the hair turning white, the quick spread, and especially the fact that from the description of *tsara'ath* you get the impression that it was not the kind of disease that led to death or deformity, but a sickness or plague that, due to its characteristic alterations of the skin, must have been very shocking, especially to the non-expert. And in agreement with the rabbis of the Mishnah, some prefer to translate Lev 13:10 not as "raw flesh," but "healthy skin." The healthy skin that according to Leviticus developed into the whitened leprous spot, are those islands of pigmented skin that we see, in connection with the spreading vitiligo spots, that arise when the spots multiply and the healthy skin shows up in smaller spots among the larger white blotches. The translation of the words that are rendered as *swelling*, *rash*, and *light spot*, is doubtful.

If the disease referred to in Leviticus, which today is named after the one who discovered the bacterium causing it, and called Hansen's disease, it would be puzzling why nothing is mentioned about the insensitivity of the spots and of the extremities, which is one of the characteristics of leprosy, to say nothing about the serious swelling of the face, the hoarse voice, deformities—all of these symptoms that immediately catch the eye of someone less accustomed or expert. When people respond by arguing that Leviticus is dealing only with the beginning symptoms, then it needs to be pointed out that in verses 9–17 it does speak about chronic leprosy.

3. When the men who translated the Septuagint faced the task of translating the Hebrew word *tsara'ath*, they simply used the word *lepra*. That word was sufficiently neutral. In those times, the word *lepra* did not refer to Hansen's disease, but Hippocrates used it to refer to a scaly condition that was quite curable. Hansen's disease would have existed back then (though people have never found anything like *lepra* in the ancient mummies), but it was not called *lepra*, but *elephantiasis Graecorum*. The *lepra* of that time belonged to that large group of skin conditions that included scabies, impetigo, psoriasis, and the like (terms for scabs and rashes).

4. The Vulgate, which was the Bible of the West, adopted the word *lepra*. That occurred around AD 400. Only later, around 700 and the time of the crusades, did leper homes come into existence. Anyone who was accepted into one of these homes was thought to be privileged. For he had the same disease, so people thought generally, as Lazarus, who was featured in one of Jesus' parables; such a person was thought to be already cleansed by God, so that later his soul would have an easier time in the hereafter. This explains why these patients were called "God's beloved sick ones," and also "lepers," terms that arose as corruptions of the French *mal de Ladre*, i.e., disease or sickness of Lazarus. Because many people wanted such a privilege and eventually far too many candidates sought entrance into the leper houses, the government issued certificates that people had to carry on their persons if they wanted to be given the full rights of a leper. What is remarkable is that in the era of the Reformation, the ambition for obtaining a proper and holy place in a leper house quickly disappeared.

5. In the previous century people learned to distinguish more accurately among the different diseases that formerly had been classified as *lepra*, or leprous-like and similar sicknesses with lacerations, like syphilis, scorbut, and psoriasis. Finally, Hansen's disease was discovered, and received its proper classification. Today it is also called *lepra*, but it is now clear that medically speaking, it won't do to identify that disease with the leprosy discussed in the Bible and with the Lazarus-disease of the Middle Ages. Otherwise those who suffered such diseases, the lepers, would remain victims of a silly misunderstanding. Because then they are "shunned like a leper." When in reality, biblical leprosy was not the same as what is meant by *lepra* or Hansen's disease, not even belonging to a complex category that included this disease.

Support for this conclusion comes not only from medical authorities, but also from linguistic experts. The recognized Hebrew expert, the Zürich professor L. Köhler, provides his understanding in his well-known Hebrew lexicon, where he explains the Hebrew word *tsara'ath* to mean "skin disease" (Hautkrankheit), and notes parenthetically: "not leprosy, which was curable, Lev 13."[1] That is clear language. But in one of his other works, Koehler discussed more extensively what we should understand the biblical term *tsara'ath* to mean. After observing that the Hebrew word *tsara'ath* means "blow," he writes: "The meaning of this description is clearly that God has stricken the sick man and has punished him thereby for sin."[2] Next Koehler pointed to the various lepers healed by our Lord Jesus in the New Testament. He translated this Greek word as "leprous" (*Aussätzige*), and continues:

> Now the disease described in Lev. 13 is certainly not the one which we call leprosy but a skin disease (vitiligo) and one which, as it is known, can be healed in a moment by a violent inner shock in this case that experienced when the men, oppressed by their illness and their consequent separation from the community, are brought face to face with the holiness of Jesus. We should not therefore speak in the New Testament at all of leprosy and lepers but of skin complaints and diseases. The same is true of the Old Testament, in Lev. 13 and in the case of Naaman the Syrian (II Kings 5).
>
> What we today call leprosy is quite different. This leprosy was once very prevalent in western Europe but has now almost died out apart from a small number of cases, for example, in Norway and France; whereas in the East and in Africa thousands still suffer from it. For even now leprosy except in its very earliest stages is quite incurable. The sick man can only be avoided which is unchristian or cared for; he cannot be cured.[3]

If there is one result from becoming acquainted with the literature we have mentioned that deals with leprosy as the Bible discusses it, then that result is this, that we no longer believe as we once did that the word *tsara'ath* refers to those poor people, portrayed in all kinds of creepy pictures, who suffered from Hansen's disease. Rather, it refers simply to "vitiligo and related diseases." This means that the urgent plea from medical experts that the term *leprosy* not be applied to Hansen's disease, strikes us as eminently worthwhile and able to be followed without much difficulty. For them, it is first of all a matter of terminology. They have done their best to retire the word *leprosy* from usage in connection with hospitals, institutions, colonies,

---

1. Köhler, *Lexicon*, 52.
2. Köhler, *Hebrew Man*, 48.
3. Köhler, *Hebrew Man*, 49-50.

etc. And medical terminology will gradually seep down into common usage, with the result that the word *leprosy*, that is so familiar to Bible translators and Bible readers, will come to mean nothing other than "vitiligo and related diseases." In point of fact, the biblical leprosy was nothing other than that.

We would observe the following.

From more than one account it appears that the Scriptural leprosy can come and go. That is probably what both terms are referring to that we read in Lev 13:2 and 47: *negaʿ tsaraʿath*, or "case of leprosy." The phrase literally means "blow" in both instances. One commentator notes that the meaning of each word in that phrase is not in the first place *lepra*, or leprosy, but points to the circumstance of being struck, in this instance, by Yahweh. Notice how suddenly various people in the Bible come down with leprosy: Moses (Exod 4:6), Miriam (Num 12:10), Gehazi (2 Kgs 5:27). Notice the relatively brief time (either seven or fourteen days) during which the priest had to render a decision about whether or not leprosy had been removed. The tempo of Hansen's disease, by contrast, is gradual and slow, something required a far longer period of observation.

In addition, concerning biblical leprosy we read not only that some are healed from it in a miraculous way, but also that *by its nature this sickness was not incurable*. The entire ceremony for declaring someone clean, which we read about in Leviticus 14, proceeded on the assumption that healing occurred and the one healed would return to society after the purification was verified. Perhaps we have an example of such an ordinary, non-miraculous cure in the following two reports. First, the mother of Jeroboam, who was called Zeruah, which means Leper. Perhaps that woman was healed of *tsaraʿath* and owed her nickname to that (1 Kgs 11:26; according to Koehler, this was a name in which this disease was "wished away" for a child). Perhaps a second example of such healing and such a nickname was Simon the Leper, in whose home our Savior was anointed by Mary shortly before his death (Matt 26:6; John 12:3), although we naturally admit the possibility that the man was healed miraculously by the Savior. But we should think, in connection with the *leproi*, or lepers in the New Testament, of the same disease that in the Old Testament was called *tsaraʿath*, appears from the command of our Savior to such a healed *lepros*: "Go, show yourself to the priest and offer for your cleansing what Moses commanded, for a proof to them" (Mark 1:44; cf. Luke 4:27).

In addition, we are struck by the fact that in connection with leprosy, Scripture talks so often about the color white. Now according to medical experts, white hair and white skin are definitely not characteristics of Hansen's disease, though they are just as definitely characteristics of biblical leprosy, as we can see from Leviticus 13. It is also noteworthy that of all three persons who were suddenly afflicted with *tsara 'ath*—Moses, Miriam, and Gehazi—we are told that they were "as leprous as snow" (*kassaleg*, Exod 4:6), which of course here cannot refer to the color of purity, as in Psalm 51:7 and Isa 1:18, but the color of impurity, namely, the color of death. This is thoroughly confirmed by the exclamation of Aaron when his sister Miriam was suddenly struck with *tsara 'ath*. He compared her to a stillborn child. You know how colorless such a stillborn child can be.

Moreover, we recall that the lepers in Israel were obligated to appear in public just like people were in deep sorrow, first, with torn clothing, second, with bare head, and thus with loosely hanging hair—in Israel all the men had long hair—and third, with the face covered to the mustache or the upper lip. All three of those were grieving customs that were very familiar (Gen 37:34; Lev 10:6; Ezek 24:17, 22).

Lepers were not allowed to mourn for the death of someone else, but over their own death. They were supposed to declare their own death publicly. For it was not enough that their fellow human beings were repulsed from them on account of their creepy white corpse-like color, but they were also supposed to be warned by means of the loud cry: "Unclean! Unclean!" (Lev 13:45).

Finally, lepers were obligated to live outside the camp and to remain there until they were cured and declared clean by the priest. We can read about this isolation of lepers from the camp in Numbers 5. We will study this later. First, in Numbers 1–4, the army of the Israelites is characterized as an "army of life." Then comes Numbers 5, telling us of the command that outside this "army of life" would have to dwell "everyone who is leprous or has a discharge and everyone who is unclean through contact with the dead" (Num 5:2). Hereby lepers were being identified as those who were symbolically dead.

On the basis of these facts, we believe that in the Bible, leprosy referred to a skin disease of the kind that gave its victim a nasty necrotic color.

What we read further on in Leviticus 13–14, about leprosy on *clothing*, on *leather* or on something made of leather, and on *houses*, comports very well with this view.

For these chapters discuss, in addition to leprosy on *people*, also leprosy on *things*, on *objects*. Two kinds of leprosy. But both of them were related, of course, as we might expect. The Hebrew words that identify them are literally the same. And the location of the passages where each is discussed also tells us something. These are being discussed in Leviticus, specifically, in the section about clean and unclean (Lev 11–15), and right next to each other (Lev 13–14).

So that *leprosy in houses*, to begin with that, appears to have been nothing else than so-called dry rot. This appeared especially in old houses that had been restored in an amateurish fashion. In damp air, mycelium flakes would form on the wood (mycelium is the term for what arises with and develops from rot, based on the Latin word *mucere*, to be musty or moldy, starting out as white, later gray, eventually with yellow and violet flakes). In addition to ruining houses, such mold can destroy books, carpet, straw plaiting, etc. When new spores emerge, these are yellow or yellowish red, rust colored. The term sometimes used, wall fungus, is a bit misleading, since the wall is not growing food. Removing house mold is particularly difficult. Its "strands" can be very long and its "spores" widespread. People knew early on in the construction world that the wagons with which the materials were infected with mold were taken away, along with the tools and the clothing of the workers in order to be cleaned carefully, to prevent the spread of the mold spores. Modern means of removing mold include using creosote.

We are given the impression that just as *tsara'ath* or leprosy in people left those who were afflicted with it with a gruesome necrotic color, so too its appearance in houses infected with *tsara'ath*, as mentioned in Lev 14:32–53, due to their being covered with the white, or grayish white, and rust colors of the mold, would have left a gloomy impression on those who saw it.

The same impression would arise at the sight of *clothing* and *leather* infected with *tsara'ath*. Notice carefully that the Law was not at all referring to the clothing or leather objects that were infected by people or patients suffering from *tsara'ath*. Scripture nowhere mentions that. Rather, when Lev 13:47–59 talks about leprosy in clothing or leather or leather objects, what is apparently being referred to are particular kinds of mildew known in Palestine. This would spread to objects and penetrate skin so deeply that it could not be removed simply by a few washings. In the ancient East, that phenomenon would have been a real burden, in a society where people enjoyed wealth, not only in terms of fields and livestock, but also in terms of clothing and garments.

2. WHAT ARE THE SUBJECTS DISCUSSED IN LEVITICUS 13–14?

From the preceding, our readers will have surmised that the one subject being discussed in both of these chapters is *tsara'ath*, or leprosy. But that discussion is conducted in a way that we might outline as follows:

A. Leviticus 13:1-46: leprosy in people
B. Leviticus 13:47-59: leprosy in clothing and leather (animal skin)
C. Leviticus 14:1-32: the cleansing of a leper
D. Leviticus 14:33-53: leprosy in houses
E. Leviticus 14:54-57: summarizing postscript

If readers would like a piece of advice, they might consider distinguishing these five sections in their Bibles with a pencil. That will give them an immediate overview of these interesting, but somewhat long chapters. Perhaps you would like to write the subject in the margin.

Obviously we cannot discuss these sections of Scripture individually. We will limit our attention to the first and third.

3. WHAT IS THE OUTLINE OF LEVITICUS 13:1-46?

This Scripture passage deals with leprosy in people. We have already discussed several features of this phenomenon. Nevertheless, perhaps Bible readers would appreciate it if we took a moment to display the parts that make up this passage. There are eight of them.

1. Leviticus 13:2-8: introduction, describing the course of events in a case of leprosy.

v. 2
A spot appears

v. 3	vv. 4-5	v. 6	vv. 7-8
Obvious leprosy	No leprosy observed.	No leprosy evident	Leprosy has appeared
Observed. Unclean	Isolation for seven days	The spot is non-leprous	Unclean
		Clean	

Leviticus 13:9–17. Now follow the special cases. First, the case of long-term leprosy.

| | v. 9 | | |
| | To the priest | | |
vv. 10–11	vv. 12–13	vv. 14–15	vv. 16–17
Leprosy verified.	Leprosy observed	"Healthy skin"	The spots of "healthy
Unclean.	over the entire body	observed throughout	skin" disappear, patient
	Leucoderma (vitiligo)	No leucoderma.	is entirely white.
	Clean	Unclean	Leucoderma. Clean.

As you can see, we have translated the phrase in verses 14–16 that the ESV renders as "raw flesh" with the phrase "healthy skin" (see our earlier discussion). The order here is not the same as with the first part, though it is the same in the following parts. Regularly an examination was made according to the same rule, and then the diagnosis is made as to whether or not leprosy was present.

2. Leviticus 13:18–23: the case of a healed ulcer.
3. Leviticus 13:24–28: the case of a burn injury.
4. Leviticus 13:29–37: the case of impetigo or scalding, clearly involving what is called *favus* or *tinea capitis*.
5. Leviticus 13:38–39: the case of an innocent spots.
6. Leviticus 13:40–44: the case of baldness.
7. Leviticus 13:45–46: finally, here we find a prescription about how the leper must be clothed, what he must cry out when he sees someone approaching, and where he must live by himself.

When in this way we provide an outline overview of this Scripture passage, then it won't be difficult to understand what we are reading.

4. WHAT HAPPENED IN CONNECTION WITH THE PURIFICATION OF LEPERS (LEV 14:1–32)?

We used the word *diagnosis* just now. That is a genuinely medical term, and we may have generated the misunderstanding that Israel's priests had received a hygienic or medical task from God. As though perhaps God had given Israel these priests to be their *doctors*.

If that were true, then we want to remove that misunderstanding quickly. Israel's priests definitely had no medical mandate. They were not commissioned to care for the sick. Not even particularly for lepers. We read nowhere in these chapters about any medicine or curative applications. No, Israel's priests were far rather called to be teachers, they gave Torah, instruction, and the disease of leprosy—to be understood as biblical leprosy, whitish skin—was chosen by God to serve as a pedagogical tool, namely, hereby to remind the Israelites about the foundation beneath their feet ever since "Horeb." God had made them a people of life, in contrast to the pagans, over whom the devil and death reigned. In various ways, he wanted to remind them of that, including by means of leprosy. Even though at that time, there were other diseases, though some of them have disappeared today. But none of them was seen by God as suited to be a symbol of death. No other disease was mentioned in the same breath as death (Num 12:12; cf. 2 Kgs 5:7). Notice as well the prescribed mourning clothing to be worn by lepers, clothing that testified of their own death even though they were not really dead. Notice also the widespread agreement between the means of cleansing in connection with a leper being declared clean, and those means required when someone had become unclean through contact with a corpse (Lev 14:6; Num 19:6; cedarwood, hyssop, and scarlet yarn). Notice as well the number seven, which would later reappear more than once, a number with symbolic significance. Notice as well that among the sacrifices that were brought in connection with the cleansing of a leper, there was no thank offering, no thank offering for healing received (for this, see the teaching connected with the thank offering). Not one word is said about healing. Certainly about the leper's cleansing—from his symbolic death—and his readmission into the community of fellow Israelites and the sanctuary of Yahweh. Later in the New Testament, we are almost always told, with regard to the lepers whom our Savior encountered, that they were *cleansed*. Not *healed*, but *cleansed*. (In Luke 17:15 we read that a leper was *healed*, but . . . that involved a Samaritan!).

You may recall that when we discussed Leviticus 12, we were not satisfied with the claim that the Israelite mother who had just given birth was to be viewed as a figure and demonstration of so-called original sin, the depravity of our entire human race, but that in the ceremonies prescribed in that chapter, we heard the repeated preaching of God whereby Israel was reminded of his Horeb covenant, his life-foundation, and life-domain, and was warned never to forsake this arena of life, because beyond it, death and paganism reigned.

So too here, let no one say that by means of leprosy, God wanted to make Israel understand that because of sin all people are unclean before him. Such that leprosy functioned as a metaphor of the consequences, the blemish, of sin. Or that by nature all of us are lepers from head to toe, as we once heard from the pulpit when we were young. That last claim is mistaken on two counts, for someone who was a leper from head to toe was declared clean (Lev 13:13). Rather, Leviticus 13–14 contain (as does Lev 11–12) a warning against *death*. In addition, leprosy was not simply a metaphor of "human misery," particularly of his depravity and original sin. But by means of his Torah regarding leprosy, God wanted to preach to Israel that there was life in the covenant with him, but outside that covenant there was paganism and death. Thanks to the light of the New Testament, which calls death "the prince of this world" (John 12:31; 14:30; 16:11), and a powerful instrument of the devil (Heb 2:14), in whose bonds the Gentiles lie ensnared (Acts 26:18; Eph 2:2), we now know that with the Torah of Leviticus 11–15, God wanted to preserve his people Israel from Satan and his corruption.

The cleansing of a leper occurred in two stages.

As stated, a leper was not only excluded from the fellowship of household, family, and nation, but also from Yahweh's sanctuary. For that reason, the ceremony of his readmission occurred in two stages.

- A. Leviticus 14:2–9 deals with the readmission of the (former) leper into the fellowship of God's people.
- B. Leviticus 14:10–31 deals with the readmission of the (former) leper into the fellowship of God's sanctuary.

(a) Readmission into fellowship with God's people (Lev 14:2–9)

We get the impression that biblical leprosy occurred rather frequently. "There were many lepers in Israel in the time of the prophet Elisha" (Luke 4:27). In Num 5:2, lepers are grouped together with "everyone who has a discharge and everyone who is unclean through contact with the dead." Notice how ordinary and everyday such occurrences were. But we also get the impression that biblical leprosy was cured more often than people suppose. If these healings had occurred only by way of rare exception, such general Torah instruction would not have been provided.

But returning once more to live among the people was something that did not happen automatically.

The ceremony of being declared clean was apparently conducted outside the camp, for the priest had to go to the one who was cured, "go out of the camp."

Next, the declaration of cleansing—we almost wrote: "his declaration of life"—occurred in a way that was symbolic from start to finish. The Bible reader must beware of thinking that the slaughtering of one of the two birds that we see playing a role in the cleansing ceremony was part of a sacrifice ceremony. The notion has been defended that the ceremony involving the birds, recorded in Leviticus 14 (about the leper) belonged on the same level as that of the two male animals in Leviticus 16 (about the great Day of Atonement). But that is entirely mistaken. For the ceremony involving the two birds that were slaughtered (Lev 14) did not involve the slaughter of the birds for sacrifice. For then it would have been prescribed that this bird was to be a dove, since the dove was the only bird that we see identified in the Torah as a sacrificial bird. Moreover, the blood of that (one, slaughtered) bird was not splashed on the side of the altar. The blood of this animal was mixed with water, something that never ever occurred with the blood of any sacrifice.

No, in this first stage we read nothing at all about sacrificing. That happens only later, in the second stage.

But if someone should ask: why then was that bird slaughtered?, the answer must be: only because blood was needed to serve as a symbol of life.

For all the elements that comprised the ceremony of declaring a leper to be clean spoke of *life*, and only of *life*. As we see from the following.

In the first place, the prescription said that the birds had to be "living" birds. Of course that did not mean only that they could not be dead birds, but the intention was that they needed to be alert, energetic, lively.

Next, one of the two birds was slaughtered above an earthen pot containing living water. Presumably it therefore had to be an earthen pot because after using it, the pot would be smashed. But what living water referred to, everyone knows. Not dead water. Not standing water. But streaming and flowing water, scooped from the stream or fountain. In that "living" water therefore was dripping the blood of the "living"—that is: lively—bird.

Now, the ingredients that had to be added to this mixture of water and blood. There were three: (1) cedarwood, (2) scarlet yarn, and (3) hyssop.

(1) Even someone who has never seen a cedar tree would surely recognize the scent of cedar wood. In our modern day, cigar factories often use the penetrating cedar smell for aromatizing their cigar boxes and cupboards. But in antiquity, the cedar was no less well-known because of the durability of its wood. People would rub corpses with cedar oil to prevent decay. The Israelites would therefore not have been surprised that in connection with

the ceremony for declaring a healed leper clean, God would have wanted to see them use cedar wood as a symbol of life.

What kind of cedar wood would have been used by Israel during their travel through the wilderness?

In a very interesting book about plants in the Bible, we read that, as we come across mention in Leviticus 14 of cedar trees, we are supposed to think of the well-known cedars of Lebanon, one needs to remember that this kind of cedar was a perpetual evergreen, held in high esteem in antiquity not only because it was so beautiful and lived so long, but also because of its many uses and aromatic smell. But because the cedarwood mentioned in Lev 14:4 and Num 19:6 are mentioned in a particular context, namely, ceremonies of cleansing, and are referring to events in the time of the wandering in the wilderness, we are not to think of the cedars of Lebanon. Rather, it is probably referring to the small desert shrub *sabina phoenicia*, the Phoenician juniper that grows in the Sinai peninsula. The wood of that shrub is also aromatic, and when people burned this wood along with dead animals, the incense smell would drive out the distasteful smell of carcasses. This last observation is something worth noting!

(2) Next we mentioned scarlet yarn.

In Scripture the phrase is *sheni thola ʿath*. The color here was probably light red or rose, the color of blood. But since one could not suffice simply with a color, but needed something, an object, of such color, what is meant here is that in the mixture of water and bird blood, to a piece or pieces of cedarwood, some wool or woolen yarn of light red color would be added. But we do not read here of any cloth, whether of wool or of another substance. Therefore it seems best to us to follow the lead of W. H. Gispen to translate *sheni thola ʿath* as crimson. This is the color of deep red or purple. The literal meaning of *sheni thola ʿath* is red paint (*sheni*) from the worm or louse (*thola ʿath*). Thus, people added to the mixture of blood and water first some aromatic cedarwood, and then a bright red colored material. Clearly this latter ingredient spoke the language symbolic of life.

(3) And then the hyssop. We read in the literature that nowadays people generally agree that the plant in question must have been Syrian oregano (*origanum maru*), of the species *Labiaten*. Both the oregano flowers and plants are covered with woolly bristles; thereby they retain moisture and can be used as kind of brush or broom, which fits with Exod 12:22 ("take a bunch of hyssop"), Ps 51:7, and Heb 9:19. Oregano grows in every country around the Mediterranean Sea. It is aromatic and since antiquity has been used for seasoning food and for medicinal purposes.

There you have the mixture.

With this mixture, the leper being cleansed was sprinkled seven times. In our commentary on Exodus we discussed the symbolic significance of the number seven, and the action of sprinkling (not splashing).[4]

But there was one bird left. This was not killed, but after the sprinkling of the cured leper, the live bird was dipped into the mixture of water, blood, cedarwood, and scarlet, and then released. The bird flew away happily back to its nest. In the same way, the leper now declared clean could return to his family and to the holy people of God.

But not all at once.

Before returning to the camp, he had to wash his clothes and take a bath. All of his hair had to be shaved, something that reminds us somewhat of what the Levites had to undergo with their consecration to the ministry of the sanctuary (Num 8:7), but reminds us more of the fact that it was with the hair that the leprosy was initially detected (Lev 13:3, 20). Then the person who was declared clean was allowed to go back into the camp, but he was not to enter his own tent. That lasted seven days. Why could he not enter his own tent? Probably because in connection with returning to his own tent, he would face all kinds of possibilities for defilement (for example, through intercourse, Lev 15:18), whereby one became unclean until evening, so that the period of seven days would have lost is symbolic length. For someone who was unclean was not allowed to go near the sanctuary. And that is precisely where the person cured of leprosy was to appear at the end of those seven days.

(b) Readmission into the fellowship of God's sanctuary (Lev 14:10–31)

Now began the stage of sacrifice.

After the end of the seven days, all the hair was once again shaved from the leper, including his head, his beard, his eyebrows, and after he had once again washed his clothes and bathed, on the eighth day he had to appear at the tabernacle with the following sacrifices.

1. First, a one-year old female sheep had to be brought as a guilt offering, together with a log of oil. We discussed this earlier, in connection with the guilt offering. At that time, we stated our assumption that in this case, a person could suffice with a sheep as a guilt offering, because during his absence, the leper was deficient in regard to the services of Yahweh at the sanctuary, but he had nonetheless remained obligated to perform them. This explains why a female sheep was to be offered. A log of oil was one of the smallest quantities. Some people think that it was one-twelfth of a hin

---

4. Vonk, *Exodus*, 198–99.

and thus about ½ of a liter. Others think it was no more than 1/3 of a liter. Some of this oil was later placed in the empty hand of the priest.

Both of these, the sheep and the oil, were "waved before Yahweh as a wave offering." This was the so-called *tenuphah*, which we discussed earlier. Due to this *tenuphah*, both the blood and the oil could now be used for the following purposes. First, the priest had to dab some of the blood on the right ear lobe, the right thumb, and the right big toe of the person being declared clean. Next he had to pour some of the oil on his left hand, dip his right index finger into it, and sprinkle it seven times "before Yahweh," i.e., in the tabernacle, after which the three body parts of the healed leper were to be dabbed with some of the remaining oil. The oil left over after that was poured out on the head of the one being declared clean.

What is remarkable are the line of correspondence between this ceremony and the one accompanying the "installation" of Aaron and his sons, whereby these men were assured that God had accepted them in the priestly covenant and would equip them by his Spirit for the work in that office. Nevertheless there was also a difference. Whereas with the installation of the priest the sprinkling occurred as a single act, apparently with a mixture of blood and oil, with the leper being declared clean, people worked in stages. First, blood was applied to him. Hereby he was being once again lifted up from the status of sojourner and outsider, indeed, from death, to member of the people of Yahweh, the people of life. Then oil was sprinkled on him, for actually every member of the Israelite covenant community was called to the priesthood (Exod 19:6). Therefore God was guaranteeing him as well, by means of the symbolic action with the oil (which represented the work of the Spirit[5]), that he would equip him through his Spirit, with his ear to listen to God's command, with hand and foot to follow him willingly. But that was all. The garment of the person declared clean was not sprinkled with blood and oil, as happened with the official garments of Aaron and his sons. *They* too were specially called to that office. But the ordinary person in Israel did not wear any garments of office. Not even the Levites.

2. The other sacrifices for the cleansed leper were a sin offering and a burnt offering, together with the accompanying food offering.

These two—the sin- and burnt-offering—consisted of sheep. The food offering consisted of 3/10 of an ephah of fine flour. Enough has been said concerning the significance of the sin offering, burnt offering, and food offering.

Atonement had now occurred. The "sin" of the one who had been forsaken by the God and the people of life, and the going over to paganism,

---

5. See Vonk, *Exodus*, 238.

death, and the devil, was now covered. And the assurance had now been given that God wanted to enable this Israelite to dwell henceforth on the foundation on which he had placed Israel at Horeb, in the midst of the people of Yahweh.

Because it always remained a possibility that the sacrificing of *three sheep* was somewhat problematic for a person, it was stipulated that the sheep for the sin offering and the burnt offering could be replaced by two doves. Correspondingly, the quantity of fine flour had to be reduced from 3/10 to 1/10 of an ephah. But any changes beyond those were not possible. The lamb for the guilt offering and the log of oil were perpetually required, even in cases of extreme poverty. From this we learn to understand all the more deeply God's purpose behind the symbolism surrounding biblical leprosy. He wanted to remind his people powerfully that Israel had to abide with him constantly on the basis of Horeb. Anyone who forsook that sinned against him! Beyond that foundation were darkness, paganism, and death. And anyone who had departed from that foundation, *even symbolically*, could be readmitted to Israel, the people of life, in no other way than the way of bloodshed, whereas by means of the symbolism of sprinkling the oil, God was simultaneously preaching that being led by the Torah, i.e., by the instruction of God's Spirit, was indispensable, if one wanted to please God with a holy walk and holy conduct.

Having read this discussion of the Law for the cleansing of a leprous person (Lev 14:1–32), our reader will have no difficulty understanding God's parallel intention with his Law for cleansing leprous *houses* (Lev 14:33–53). Notice how here, more than once, we find the symbolic number seven. Note as well the fact that here we read only of symbolic actions that we discussed earlier under (a). But no sin offerings and no sprinkling with oil, because these naturally were not suited for leprous houses.

18

Torah instruction with regard to uncleanness through discharges of males and females (Lev 15)

LOVE IS RESOURCEFUL

God availed himself of every possible means for reminding the Israelite society ("world") of the foundation on which he had placed her with the covenant at Horeb.

This appears again from Leviticus 15.

Here we have a chapter, the understanding of which must not be complicated by otherwise well-intentioned notions about God's fatherly care for Israel's well-being and health, a care that would be imported here in terms of various hygienic prescriptions, as though Israel's priests would have been doctors.

They were not.

Leviticus 11–15 is not discussing various infectious diseases, but even if it were dealing with diseases (something not at all the case), it would have in view only a few very specific diseases. Leviticus 15 is not dealing with various discharges, like the secretion of mucus, pus, or saliva from the mouth or nose, wounds and ulcers. Nor is it discussing diarrhea or dysentery, sicknesses that have been a concern of military commanders since antiquity, from Caesar to Rommel. We prefer to believe that the command of Moses, that everyone must take care of his need outside the camp, using a shovel to cover his excreta, preserved the Israelites from serious disasters

UNCLEANNESS THROUGH DISCHARGES OF MALES AND FEMALES

(Deut 23:12-14). But in Leviticus 15 we read about very specific discharges, namely, discharges from male and female genitalia.

Nor should we think, however, that Leviticus 15 is a chapter dealing with sin, specifically original sin. As though God wanted to teach the church of all ages, Israel and us, about the judgment that has come upon all humanity on account of Adam, falling especially on human sexual activity as being the most defiled and corrupted. Is that really the case? Is the appeal underlying that claim, to Gen 3:16, the punishment of Eve, valid? Did not that punishment pertain especially to Eve's role in tempting Adam? Such words were not spoken to Adam and in that way to all people. Did not God always highly esteem marriage, before and after human rebellion in the garden (Gen 2:22; Eph 5:22-33)? How could he otherwise have commanded the performance of sexual responsibilities (Exod 21:10)?

Rather, Leviticus 15 is giving us covenant instruction, teaching about Yahweh (how holy he was), about Israel (that she was his covenant people), and about the relationship between them (that Yahweh wanted to dwell among them in the tabernacle, v. 31).

Leviticus 11-14 discussed these matters as well.

And now it happened again.

This time using such contingencies in the human experience of all of us as ejaculation (with men and boys) and menstruation (with women and girls).

Perhaps at the same time God had in view certain superstitious practices among the pagans. These would have been stopped immediately. But we dare not say a lot about that, since Scripture does not proceed in this direction. But when we view Leviticus 15 as part of the large Scripture book of Leviticus, and specifically of Leviticus 11-15, then we perceive once again God's raised finger of warning against *death*! Death was the irrevocable lot of those who find themselves and who move outside God's communion of promise and life. In Leviticus 11 God used clean and unclean animals to provide that warning. In Leviticus 13 and 14, it was leprosy. In Leviticus 15 he is referring to such sexual phenomena and ejaculation, in terms of which our thoughts are immediately directed to the source and boundary of life. After all, marriage is very wonderful, but it can present significant challenges as well. Sexual matters occupy a place very near the boundary between death and life.

God used this to remind Israel of the exalted level on which he had placed Israel at Horeb. Whoever forsakes that, lowers himself to the level of paganism. And there he would encounter death.

A number of things will become clearer with the discussion of Leviticus 15.

That context can be divided into two parts. The first part deals with men (vv. 2–18), and the second with women (vv. 19–30). At the end, we find two postscripts. In the first one, God says: unclean Israelites who come near to my sanctuary would have to pay for that with death (v. 31). The second postscript provides a summary of the preceding (vv. 32–33).

In addition, each main part consists of a section dealing with a normal discharge, and a section dealing with an abnormal discharge. In this order:

I. A. Abnormal discharge with men (Lev 15:2–15)

I. B. Normal discharge with men (Lev 15:16–18)

II. A. Normal discharge with women (Lev 15:19–24)

II. B. Abnormal discharge with women (Lev 15:25–30)

I. A. ABNORMAL DISCHARGE WITH MEN (LEV 15:2–15)

Two things stand out right away.

First, the men are discussed before the women, which does not surprise us. This happens more frequently in the Torah, the leader is first.

But the second thing is that, in Part I, dealing with the men, not the normal but the abnormal is treated first. This fact finds its general explanation in the custom that we mentioned and have observed often in the Torah.[1] The most prominent, the most notable, etc., is always mentioned first. This surely explains why the "most serious" defilement of the man is discussed first. But in addition, there would also have been a particular reason, namely, because male ejaculation could occur in relation to the woman, that could better be mentioned in the second place. As a result, verse 18 functions here as a transition, a hinge. It joins together the discussion of both the man and the woman. Moreover, the man himself would be mentioned in the section dealing with the woman's menstruation (v. 24). The best transition between the various subjects is obtained by arranging the chapter as we now have it.

This section of Leviticus 15, dealing with the abnormal discharge of men, can be outlined this way:

I. A. 1. The cause and extent of uncleanness (vv. 2–12)

I. A. 2. The duration and cleansing of uncleanness (vv. 13–15)

---

1. See Vonk, *Exodus*, 197, 220.

UNCLEANNESS THROUGH DISCHARGES OF MALES AND FEMALES

I. A. 1. *The cause and extent of uncleanness (vv. 2–12)*

1. The *cause* of defilement is described in verse 2 this way: When "any man" has a discharge "from his body," his discharge is unclean. Verse 3 says: Whether his body runs with his discharge, or his body is blocked up by his discharge.

What is meant by the expression "any man"?

Some think that this can mean "any human being." But in view of the outline of the entire chapter, the original meaning of the Hebrew word for man (*'ish*) must be in view here. In view here is the discharge that occurs with men, not women (dealt with in Part 2).

What is meant by the expression "from his body"?

Some think that this phrase could be referring to a discharge like dysentery. Indeed, the word "body" does not always refer to the male (or female) sex organ. Sometimes the Hebrew word used here for flesh (*basar*) does refer to "people" (Isa 40:6), sometimes to a (complete) individual person (in this very chapter, Lev 15:7), and sometimes to the human abdomen (Exod 28:42, unless there the word is referring to the male private parts of the priests).[2] But sometimes the word "body" is clearly referring to human private parts, especially those of the man (Ezek 16:26; 23:20). This latter meaning is apparently intended here in verse 2, in contrast with the female's private parts (v. 19).

We probably should not ask what kind of discharge from the male organ is being specifically referred to here. The expression is far too general to provide us an answer. But for Israelite men and boys the expression was adequate, enough to let them know under what circumstances their access to the sanctuary and participation in the sacred ceremonies were completely forbidden to them. We read nothing about medical assessments being made by the priests. Each person could, and had to, know for himself whether he was allowed to come near to the dwelling of Yahweh.

2. The *extent* of defilement was not limited to the man himself who had the discharge, but extended to the bed on which he lay, to every object on which he sat, and to everyone who touched him, or on whom he may have spit, or who had sat on something on which he had sat earlier. That person would also be unclean for a day, and would have to wash his clothes.

---

2. See Vonk, *Exodus*, 262–63.

I. A. 2. *The duration and cleansing of uncleanness (vv. 13–15)*

1. The *duration* of the uncleanness, namely, not only as long as the discharge persisted, but also seven days after it stopped, shows us again that in Leviticus 15 we are dealing with symbolic instruction. This means that we should not view the priests to be functioning as doctors and the declarations of cleanness as hygienic measures, but pay careful attention to God's pedagogical purpose with all of this. That was as follows. God took this opportunity of a man with a discharge as well to remind Israel once more what a holy God she was related to by means of the Horeb covenant. Anyone who kept such uncleanness a secret and nevertheless came near to the sacred dwelling of Yahweh, was risking his life (v. 31). Indeed, such unclean men should not remain within Israel's camp, just like lepers and persons who had touched a corpse (Num 5:2). You see here once again the allusion to death.

2. Pay careful attention also to the clear lines of similarity between the *cleansing* of a man with a discharge and that of a leper. In both cases, this lasted for a period of seven days, after which in both cases a sin offering and a burnt offering had to be brought. Though there were also dissimilarities. For the one with the discharge, the sacrificial animals need not include a sheep. He could suffice with two doves. In addition, no food offering was required. The "sin" of the discharge was not as serious as that of leprosy. But a (symbolic) crossing over the line between death and life had nonetheless occurred. This explains the need for "atonement."

I. B. NORMAL DISCHARGE WITH MEN (LEV 15:16–18)

Here the text discusses ejaculation, which could occur unintentionally as well as intentionally.

1. Verses 16–17: this can happen to someone entirely unintentionally, especially during sleep. When this happened to an Israelite male, he was supposed to bathe. Everything brought into contact with his semen, whether clothing or object, had to be washed. The male had to be unclean for a day, and therefore had to abstain from any cultic activities in the forecourt (v. 31).

2. Verse 18: but it could also result from sexual intercourse between the man and his wife. In that case, the specified regulations apply to both of them.

    With this, the woman is mentioned for the first time in our chapter. She will be the focus of attention in what follows.

II. A. NORMAL DISCHARGE WITH WOMEN (LEV 15:19–24)

Here the subject of menstruation is discussed. We wrote about this earlier, in connection with the initial period of uncleanness for the woman who had given birth. That lasted for seven days, at least if the woman had given birth to a boy. Leviticus 12:2 states: "as at the time of her menstruation," referring to the menstrual period. We observed that this was to be taken somewhat generally, apparently on account of the intention with the symbolic number seven, the number symbolizing covenant and holiness.

Here, the subject of menstruation is discussed in terms of the sequence of cause, extent, etc.

The *cause* of symbolic uncleanness was the flow of blood "in her body" (v. 19). We have here the same Hebrew word (*basar*) as in verse 2, though there it referred to the male organ, here to the female organ. For thereby the specific nature of this flowing of blood of the woman is being indicated. She was not (symbolically) unclean as a result of the loss of blood due to a wound or hemoptysis. Nowhere in Scripture will you read that someone was declared unclean because of these, even though these also consisted of a flowing of blood. Rather, with menstruation a sexual flowing of blood had occurred. And that was the focus of this chapter. All of these things are related to the procreation of the human race. And that was something lying very close to the line between death and life.

What is said about the *extent* of uncleanness is no less symbolic. For everyone knew enough to realize that anyone who touched a woman or girl who was menstruating would not acquire a dangerous infection. That was not the issue. Rather, as the Great Pedagogue of Israel, God was engaged in teaching his people to listen to the sounds of Easter. He wanted to make the Israelite "world" see how great was his love when his placed her on the life-foundation of his Horeb covenant. Therefore he could not tolerate anyone in Israel, man or woman, falling away from or sliding off that sacred basis for life, only then to fall prey to paganism and corruption. This explains all those (symbolic) warnings. Watch out for *death*! That is what is prowling beyond the line of the covenant. All of you must always stay close to me.

Indeed, God's fatherly care went a long way.

To reach his goal, he placed under his claim even the monthly discomfort of women and girls; and that goal was that Israel would constantly think about observing his covenant of Horeb. For their own good, for the sake of their lives, for the sake of their *eternal* life. For we have to, at this point, understand that much of the symbolic preaching of the tabernacle, that everyone will understand what God was intending here with verse 31: "Thus you shall keep the people of Israel separate from their uncleanness, lest they die in their uncleanness by defiling my tabernacle that is in their midst."

The tabernacle was a visible guarantee of God's promise, given already to the patriarchs, that they would once again arise and walk with him in a new world.

But it was being imprinted upon Israel again and again: People of death—pagans and covenant breakers—do not belong there.

This lesson is clear for us as well. Even though we no longer live under the Horeb covenant. Ours is far "better" (Heb 7:22; 8:6). Therefore the responsibility is that much greater as well (Heb 2:3; 10:29). How shall we escape if we deny Christ, who has bought us (2 Pet 2:1)?

If it ever happened that the wife began to menstruate while she and her husband were lying together, during the night, then the period of her husband's uncleanness did not last for only one day, just as for others who had come into contact with her, but for seven days. This may strike you as strange, because husband and wife "are one flesh" (Gen 2:24).

Once again we meet the number seven. After all, involved here was the covenant of Horeb.

At the same time we find here the second reason why our chapter was arranged as it is: first, concerning the man, then concerning the woman. And in dealing first with the man, starting with the "most serious." But that is not how the legislation started in connection with the woman, but rather how it ended. As a result, the man could be mentioned in connection with both ejaculation during sleep (v. 18) and with lying with his wife during her menstruation (v. 24).

So that the "most serious" discharge of the woman came up for discussion only at that point.

II. B. ABNORMAL DISCHARGE WITH WOMEN (LEV 15:25–30)

This last section of Leviticus 15 deals with the case of a woman flowing with blood apart from menstruating. The section proceeds almost parallel with the section dealing with abnormal discharges of men. Here as well three features are discussed: the *cause* of the uncleanness is mentioned (flowing); the *extent* of the uncleanness (everyone and everything with which the woman comes into contact); the *duration* of uncleanness (for seven days after the flowing had stopped and the woman would have been medically clean, she would be cultically unclean); and finally, the *purification sacrifices* to be brought (a sin offering and a burnt offering).

UNCLEANNESS THROUGH DISCHARGES OF MALES AND FEMALES

We are almost finished with Leviticus 15. Just this yet.

In our discussion of Leviticus 11–15, we have repeatedly drawn the attention of our readers to the Sinai covenant, as the life-foundation on which God had established the Israelite "world" at Horeb. We did that also in connection with the last chapter, Leviticus 15. We had a special reason for doing so.

Does our reader recall the command that God gave to the Israelites even before he began instituting the Horeb covenant, in terms of the announcement of the Ten Words of the covenant? At that time God wanted his people to sanctify themselves beforehand. They had to wash their clothes, etc. And then they heard: "*Be ready for the third day; do not go near a woman*" (Exod 19:15).

By means of that command, God was preparing his people Israel at that point for what would follow.

Israel's Great Pedagogue and Teacher was acting in these matters in the same way he did with respect to the Sabbath day. That had also been instituted before Horeb, on the occasion of the manna miracle. On the first day when manna fell, the people began to count, and on the seventh day, counted from the day when manna fell the first time. Israel was not allowed to gather manna, but on the seventh day(s) they would have to observe complete rest. We read about this in Exodus 16. That happened earlier on the route to Horeb, as similar preparation for what would later be said at Horeb about the Sabbath. Not only in the "Fourth Commandment," (remember the Sabbath day, etc.), but also in the Torah that God would give to Moses regarding the sacrifices, etc. The entire festival cycle of Israel was like an embroidered robe whose main motif was the Sabbath idea. Thereby Israel was constantly reminded of the establishment of the covenant at Sinai. We will return to this in due course.

So then, God did the same thing with respect to what was prescribed later in Leviticus 15. Regarding sexual discharges. Events in human life that were closely tied to the great contrast between being born and dying, between life and death. Very suitable, especially for an Eastern people with an appreciation for symbolism, to bind them to a lesson that constantly spoke of Israel being defined in terms of both Yahweh's holiness together with his dwelling, and in terms of the life-foundation on which Israel had been placed by Yahweh at Horeb, set by his side, and in terms of the defeat and corruption of every Israelite who forgot this covenant and slid down to the level of the pagans, over whom the devil ruled with his darkness and death.

19

"Zealots for the Law"[1]

WE MUST ALWAYS KEEP our promises. And this one is rather old. We had identified three enemies of the gospel of our Lord Jesus Christ as our complete Savior. These enemies were: (1) Judaizers,[2] (2) the Greek theory of an immortal soul, and (3) the Gnostic theory of new life-substance.

The latter two promises we have kept. But not the first one, at least not directly. Now and then we have devoted a word or two to this matter. But we have not yet focused our discussion on the matter of Judaizing. That was because we were looking for a more suitable opportunity, and we have found that here, in connection with our discussion of Leviticus 11–15, dealing with the food and the purification laws. Now is a good time for an excursus about Judaizing. For Judaizing was burdensome, and wanted to burden others, especially under the domination of the laws of Leviticus 11–15.

---

1. *Translator's Note:* the Dutch word appearing as the title of this chapter is *Wetticisme*, a word that most Dutch-English dictionaries render as *Legalism*. The English word *legalism* usually includes the theological notion of *synergism*, a teaching claiming that the human will cooperates with God in obtaining salvation. The Dutch word *wetticisme* lacks any notion of synergism, however. Therefore, in order to avoid the negative associations attached to the English word *legalism*, and to capture the somewhat positive force of Vonk's discussion, we have chosen the phrase "zealots for the law," based on Acts 21:20 and the actions of the apostle Paul.

2. *Translator's note:* the Dutch word *Judaisme* resembles the English word *Judaism*, and some might be inclined to render it that way. But in Dutch, the word *Jodendom* refers to the religion that is usually identified, in addition to Christianity and Islam, as one of the world religions, for which English uses the word *Judaism*. The field of biblical studies is familiar with the term *Judaizing*, referring to the phenomenon of Jews who had become Christians seeking to compel non-Jews who had become Christians to live like Jews, which is what we encounter in the New Testament. The *Judaizers*, then, were those Jewish Christians committed to *judaizing* the Gentile Christians.

"ZEALOTS FOR THE LAW"

But first this:

Family members can sometimes resemble each other in striking ways. Even distantly related family members. What should a person do, then, in order to avoid confusion? Not only pay attention to those features that such relatives share, but also and especially to pay attention to what they do not have in common, to their differences.

Well, the activities associated with Judaizing bears a family resemblance to those involved in being zealous for the Law, even though this resemblance is only on the surface. It displays far more points of difference than resemblance, however. So we would regret it if those two were confused. All Judaizers are zealous for the Law. But not everyone who is zealous for the Law is thereby a Judaizer.

We encountered an example of zeal for the Law when we looked at Leviticus 8–10. Moses was over-reacting when he demanded that Aaron and his two surviving sons eat the meat of the ram offered as a sin offering, after everything that had happened to their deceased sons and brothers, Nadab and Abihu. When Aaron drew attention to that, Moses fortunately agreed and wisely remained silent.

We encounter zeal for the Law in the New Testament as well, in connection with people we would not have expected. But it cannot be denied that the New Testament tells us about Christians who unfortunately were not free of a certain conservatism and zealotry when it came to the Law.

Consider, for example, the book of Acts.

We usually call this book the Acts of the Apostles, but the title "The Acts of the Ascended Christ" would have been more suitable. Early on in this book, we read that Christ had given his apostles the command to be his witnesses "in Jerusalem and in all Judea and Samaria and to the end of the earth" (Acts 1:8). But how much time and effort did it take before this command was carried out? And that did not occur particularly through the apostles themselves. The book of Acts is really not at all the kind of book that teaches us to expect the church's salvation from heroic people. Not even from apostles. Oh, of course, the twelve apostles did preach in Jerusalem (Acts 2–3, etc.). There were Jewish churches established in the region of Jerusalem (Gal 1:22). Nevertheless, the gospel was not preached to the Samaritans first by an apostle, but by the deacon Philip. Later, after that happened, two apostles went for the first time to Samaria (Acts 8:14). When it came to preaching the gospel of Christ to a *Gentile*, to someone from Nubia—someone to whom Christ was really referring when he sent out his apostles to "the end of the earth," for the eunuch served "Candace, the queen of the Ethiopians"—the first one to do that was that an apostle, but once again it was the deacon Philip. The persecution following Stephen's death scattered many here and there, but the apostles remained in Jerusalem (Acts 8:1). There, in the ancient city, they would have envisioned their field of labor. In fact, Philip seems initially to have thought it objectionable simply to accept the eunuch as a member of the Christian church. Certainly he did not think that way because of the eunuch's dark skin, for some ancestors of the Israelites also had dark skin. Joseph's wife was an Egyptian (Gen 41:45, 50). Moses took an Ethiopian woman as his wife (Num 12:1). The name Phinehas means Nubian. Rather, the issue with the Ethiopian was that he was a eunuch, someone who had been castrated. Such men whose genitals had been mutilated were not allowed *according to the Law* to enter the assembly of the Israelite church (Deut 23:1). But the eunuch himself had talked Philip out of that legalistic objection with the words: "See, here is water! What prevents me from being baptized?" (Acts 8:36).

It is true, subsequently the gospel of Christ was preached to Cornelius by the apostle Peter. But how much effort did it take before Peter decided to do so! The vision, thrice repeated, of the large sheet filled with clean and unclean animals were mixed together. After that lesson, Peter traveled with the Gentile men to Caesarea, he went inside "without objection" to talk with Cornelius, and he even lodged there (Acts 10:20, 48). But once again, Peter was not persuaded to baptize that Cornelius and his family apart from being compelled by divine facts. By the undeniable, visible gifts of the Spirit given to those people. When he returned later to Jerusalem, and was there called on to given an account, he honestly confessed to what had happened, but as justification for that he appealed to the gifts of the Spirit bestowed upon those Gentiles. At that point I could hardly refuse them baptism! Peter also fortified his argument by pointing his finger to "these six brothers" who had accompanied him to Caesarea (Acts 11:12, 17). At that point the Jerusalem leaders found peace in the situation. Everyone sensed the excitement that had been stirred up in the church by Peter's baptizing a Gentile family in Caesarea.

Certainly at that point the brothers were glorifying God. "Then to the Gentiles also God has granted repentance that leads to life" (Acts 11:18). Subsequently, however, among the Christians in Jerusalem who were Jews, everything had to remain as it had always been. They believed in the Lord Jesus, to be sure, but at the same time they continued going to the temple and participating regularly in the worship there. Everything was done according to the Law of Moses. And that occurred not only during the earliest period, but continued for years later.

We learn this from the episode of Paul's last visit to Jerusalem. As many people know, at that time the apostle was arrested in the temple. But how did he end up there? Earlier he had been visiting James. He occupied a position of leadership in the Jerusalem church. In the presence of all the elders Paul had narrated "what God had done among the Gentiles through his ministry" (Acts 21:19). At that point, the Jerusalem brothers had heartily rejoiced about that. "When they heard it, they glorified God" (Acts 21:20). But when Paul had finished his report, they made an urgent request of him. Here in Jerusalem there were thousands of Jewish converts to faith in Christ, although at the same time they had remained "zealous for the Law." Now those people had been hearing various nasty things about Paul. He had supposedly incited Jews living in foreign cities against Moses, "telling them not to circumcise their children or walk according to our customs" (Acts 21:21). For that reason, James and the elders requested Paul to help stop that slander by publicly participating himself once again in the ancient temple liturgy, namely, by joining several other Christians in a sacrifice ceremony associated with their Nazirite vow. Then those slanderers' mouths would be stopped. Then people could see how much Paul also loved the Law. "That you yourself also live in observance of the law" (Acts 21:24).

As we know, Paul granted that well-intentioned request. With the well-known tragic result: his arrest.

The question is understandable as to whether Paul acted properly in honoring the request of James. Indeed, we might ask whether his participating in the sacrifice ceremony in the temple could pass muster. Or whether he thereby committed treason against the gospel in terms of what he himself had been preaching, namely, that the shadows of the Law had been fulfilled by Christ and had thus come to an end (Col 2:16-17).

We would not answer those questions affirmatively.

We know very well that the apostle Paul loved his Savior so much that he did not refuse to die for him, let alone that he would have betrayed the truth of the gospel out of fear. The Judaizers discovered just how valiantly he stood up for the full gospel. But from Paul's conduct in Jerusalem in the episode of Acts 21 we can learn something very beautiful, namely, that we must first of all avoid confusing being zealous for the Law with Judaizing. Judaizers were bloodthirsty fellows. "False brothers" (Gal 2:4). "Enemies of the cross of Christ" (Phil 3:18). James, who led the church in Jerusalem, was not that. Despite his zeal for the Law, James was a faithful confessor of Christ. And stayed that way to the end. Until his own martyrdom. And James did not distrust his brother Paul. Nor was he out for Paul's life. Nor did he want to put him out of office. With deep-seated gratitude he listened to Paul's report of his official labor among the Gentiles. James was no persecutor. So then, we can afford to appreciate such brothers generously, especially during this time of transition. Paul was often very accommodating for such brothers (Acts 16:3; 18:18; 1 Cor 9:20-23). In fact, he himself did not bid an abrupt farewell to the Jerusalem temple ministry (Acts 22:17; 24:11, 17–18). The second thing we learn here is that we need not react fiercely and violently toward those who are zealous for the Law, making an extremely logical and straightforward appeal to the gospel in such a way that we in turn make this gospel into a Law so that with it we can slap down our neighbor in the church, such that we ourselves fall into ... excessive zeal for the Law, or worse yet, into Judaizing.

For Judaizing does in fact want to slap people down. To wound. To kill. To murder. But that is not the characteristic of zeal for the Law.

We can learn this from the letter to the Hebrews as well.

For centuries, the proper understanding of this epistle has been hindered by the misunderstanding that it was supposedly written by the apostle Paul. You find this misunderstanding in Belgic Confession, article 4. There is little in the epistle that argues for such a view, however, and much that argues against it. Its word usage and themes are clearly different from those epistles that definitely came from Paul. So much so that people who think they need to retain Paul as the author of Hebrews find themselves forced to take refuge in the assumption that Paul supposedly used a secretary who allowed himself great latitude in putting the finishing touches on this letter. This supposedly explains the great difference in the usage of terms and the line of argument. Even so, although the apostles did indeed use such secretaries occasionally (1 Pet 5:12), including Paul (Rom 16:22), the claim that the author of the letter to the Hebrews did so is nowhere to be found in the letter and cannot be inferred from its content.

In fact, the entire scope of this epistle argues against such an assumption. The epistle to the Hebrews does indeed combat a form of zeal for the Law, but it was not opposing Judaizing. Nowhere. Whereas in almost every letter that came indisputably from Paul, the latter danger was warned against.

Rather, the danger against which Hebrews is warning shows far greater resemblance to that threat we saw just a moment ago endangering the Jewish Christians in Jerusalem, in the episode of Acts 21, the episode of Paul's final visit to the temple.

Indeed, if we may be permitted to form a hypothesis regarding these things, then it would be this. The similarity between the local situation like this one that we can reconstruct from Hebrews, and the situation forming the background of the church in Jerusalem as that can be determined from Acts and from the church history written by Eusebius, seems to us so striking that there is reason to assume that the letter to the Hebrews was written to Jerusalem, at least to a specific part of the Lord's church in Jerusalem, apparently a Greek-speaking part of the church in that place (cf. Acts 6:1, 9).

When did this occur?

According to Eusebius, James, the brother of the Lord, was the leader of the church in Jerusalem, who died a martyr's death in the year 62. Did the author of Hebrews have in view the death of this James and others before him, from the time of Stephen on, when he wrote: "Remember your leaders, those who spoke to you the word of God. Consider the outcome of their way of life, and imitate their faith" (Heb 13:7)? In that case, Hebrews would have been written after AD 62.

But there is reason to think that Hebrews was written before AD 70, the year when the city and temple were destroyed. The basis for this can be found in Heb 9:6–10, among other places.

If you come across this passage as it is printed in some English Bibles, then it is easy to skip over it. In some versions, like the KJV, the translation the passage gives you the impression that the author had his eye on the worship that occurred in former centuries in the Israelite sanctuary. We will underline a few words (recall that in the KJV, words added to make good English sense are placed in italic; that is why we will underline):

> Now when these things were thus ordained, the priests went always into the first tabernacle, accomplishing the service *of God*. But into the second *went* the high priest alone once every year, not without blood, which he offered for himself, and *for* the errors of the people: The Holy Ghost thus signifying, that the way into the holiest of all was not yet made manifest, while as the first tabernacle *was* yet standing: Which *was* a figure for the time then present, in which were offered both gifts and sacrifices, that could not make him that did the service perfect, as pertaining to the conscience; Which *stood* only in meats and drinks, and diverse washings, and carnal ordinances, imposed *on them* until the time of reformation.

Compare the KJV above with the ESV below:

> These preparations having thus been made, the priests go regularly into the first section, performing their ritual duties, but into the second only the high priest goes, and he but once a year, and not without taking blood, which he offers for himself and for the unintentional sins of the people. By this the Holy Spirit indicates that the way into the holy places is not yet opened as long as the first section is still standing (which is symbolic for the present age). According to this arrangement, gifts and sacrifices are offered that cannot perfect the conscience of the worshiper, but deal only with food and drink and various washings, regulations for the body imposed until the time of reformation.

You will notice that the difference is between the past tense (KJV) and the present tense (ESV). The latter is more accurate in terms of the original Greek text. Following the ESV, we hear the writer to the Hebrews warning his readers against a danger that is threatening them in their own day, namely, the danger of Jewish Christians continuing to hold on to the old covenant, to the Horeb covenant, with its sacred places, sacred persons, and sacred actions. The significance of this passage becomes very different. Much more direct. Then in verses 6–7 the author is telling his readers about current priestly activities. And then what? Why was the author disapproving of the Jewish Christians holding on to the ordinances of the old covenant that were mentioned? Verse 8 tells us. There the author generously acknowledges that the Holy Spirit even today, in his day, was teaching a lesson by means of those ancient buildings belonging to the time of the old covenant. An ancient lesson. But then in the author's day that was a lesson of warning. "By this the Holy Spirit is indicating that the way into the holy place [here, this means heaven] is not yet opened as long as the first section is still standing (which is symbolic of the present age)."

That is how we would summarize verse 8. Notice that the sanctuary being referred to here is heaven, as in Heb 8:2, 9:12, and other passages in Hebrews. And we must reject any notion suggesting that access to that heaven would be opened to believers for the first time only in the time of Christ. Otherwise, what must we do with all those Old Testament prayers that testify to the opposite? In Ps 18:6: "He heard my voice out of his temple, and my cry came before him, *even* into his ears."

What then does the author of Hebrews mean?

He wants to encourage his readers toward greater confidence. For they were living in an oppressive situation (Heb 12:12). What explains that? They were Jewish people who had become believers in Jesus and who had endured a lot for the sake of that faith in Jesus as the Christ. The stealing of their possessions, to be sure. And yet they lacked nothing. Nevertheless, they were insufficiently aware of the finished work of Christ. Of what he had accomplished in his suffering and death. But especially what he was doing even now, at this moment, above our heads, in heaven—serving as our Advocate with the Father (Heb 5:1–10, 7:25). Oh, if only they paid more attention to that and had confidence in their wretched situation (Heb 4:16). But that is something they did far too little. What explains that? They were still too oriented toward the Old Testament. They lived far too much as though the Horeb covenant was still in force. The old covenant with its ancient worship, where sacrifices and offerings were constantly being brought, up to and including the present time. Proving that the one bringing the sacrifices was not being definitively helped. Otherwise those sacrifices, along with their accompanying washings, would not need to be repeated time and time again. So what was the lesson? Those sacrifices had been instituted by God back then as something temporary. Until the time when Jesus would come, who would bring a better covenant. And that had now happened.

That is the teaching of Heb 9:6–10.

Naturally, we do not want to force upon anyone our assumption that Hebrews was written to Jewish Christians in Jerusalem or its environs. It would not be fitting for us to bind someone to that conclusion. Our assumption has the value of a hypothesis only. But it does help us to read this epistle with flesh and blood people in mind. Jewish people, who, on the one hand, believed wholeheartedly that Jesus was the promised Messiah, but who, on the other hand, nonetheless thought they were not permitted to deny their own upbringing. What had been taught them from youth onward about respect for the Law, that respect required of them, so they thought, a faithful observance, even now, of everything, of all the commands of that Law, including those regarding temple worship.

We should not come down on them with wild fervor.

The author of Hebrews does not do that, either. He considered the conduct of his readers far from safe. They had themselves to blame for their oppressive circumstances. In such a serious way, they had lost sight of their beloved Lord. The lovely doctrine of his priestly ministry above, of his daily intercession with the Father for all those on earth who are his, had become far too much of a forgotten subject to them. How did that happen? Because they were far too busy walking to the temple and watching the priestly ministry of the old covenant.

Once again, the writer of this letter to the Hebrews admonishes his readers about this, not in a way that is harsh and sharp, but in a manner gentle and friendly. Does that perhaps explain why initially we were not irritated with that purpose of the epistle to the Hebrews? An admonition can be administered in a fashion so friendly that you "feel it" only later.

For Hebrews was intended as an "admonition," after all (Heb 13:22). And you'd have to be an angel of a person for an admonition not to make you feel stung just a little bit. On further inspection, that would also have been the case with the Hebrews.

Presumably the epistle was written rather early. We personally would be satisfied with the estimate of sometime between AD 62 and 70.

Although the author of Hebrews informs us that he did not personally receive the gospel from the Lord Jesus, but from one of his disciples (Heb 2:3). On this fact some have based the assumption that this person was someone who belonged to "the second generation," such that the letter was written rather late. But that is not necessary. Someone like Apollos did not personally hear the Lord Jesus, nor was he personally among the Lord's circle of original disciples. Nonetheless he was a contemporary of Paul.

In any case, you cannot date Hebrews all that late, for the author had to be able still to point his readers to the well-known miracles whereby our Savior had provided extra help to his church in its initial struggle (Heb 2:3; Mark 16:20; Acts 14:3). Timothy was still living (Heb 13:23). And, something we mentioned earlier, apparently the worship in the Jerusalem temple was in full swing and the temple was still standing. All of which points to pre-AD 70.

In those days the author of Hebrews wrote to the Christians who had been raised with the Law, that the Horeb covenant belonged to the past, and had gone away (Heb 8:13), and that the Law had been suspended (Heb 7:19). During those relatively early days. There had not been very much time to get used to this. Therefore the original readers of Hebrews would likely have felt deep pain in their hearts when they began gradually to understand this epistle better. In that letter, someone was coming to take something away from them, something that was intimately precious to them. But they also sensed that he was not writing as a tyrant, to strike and to wound, but to save. He did not accuse them of despising God's Son. But he made them feel that if they continued along this path, they could very well end up doing that (Heb 6:6; 10:29).

If you savor the letter thoroughly, you will encounter in Hebrews some terrifying admonitions. For example, these New Testament Hebrews are reminded of the sin that the Old Testament Hebrews, their ancestors, had committed when in the wilderness they faithlessly forsook God's gospel-of-that-time, but wanted to return to Egypt (Heb 3). They could sense very concretely the warning embedded in that admonition that the Hebrews' zeal for the Law—their holding on to the Horeb covenant, their walking to the temple with its sacrifices and altars, priests and earthly high priest—could lead to despising the High Priest in heaven and returning to the synagogue.

The author of Hebrews must have been an eloquent person. The Greek he uses is beautiful. His style is genuinely elegant. He must also have had a mastery of Scripture. What he brings up from the Old Testament is impressive to our eyes, to see that God's Son, our Lord in heaven, is greater than the angels (Heb 1–2), greater than Moses, the mediator of the Sinai covenant (Heb 3–4), and greater than Aaron, whose priesthood was so closely interwoven with that ancient covenant (Heb 5). Christ was a priest-king like Melchizedek (Heb 7–10).

But the writer of Hebrews used his wonderful gifts to protect his readers from a great evil, to which their zeal for the Law could have led them. He realized that among them there was living an inner bond with the very impressive worship activities of the Aaronic priesthood. Such worship, however, was far from harmless. This explains the "admonition." No matter that it was couched in careful language. For it was directed to brothers, holy brothers (Heb 3:1). And it was during a period of transition. Presumably between AD 62 and 70. In that kind of time, people needed to act calmly.

The interim period, when Hebrews was likely written, ended in the year that Jerusalem was destroyed, temple and all. At that time that earthly worship ceased, the worship that had so dangerously distracted the attention of the Hebrews from the daily work of their exalted Priest-King in heaven above. By means of such a shock, the true situation would at that point have become much more clear to them.

In fact, at that time there were more factors in play within Christianity, factors that would have helped clarify matters as well.

20

The Great Day of Atonement (Lev 16)

LEVITICUS 16 IS AN unfamiliar chapter about a familiar subject: the great Day of Atonement. You can hear that phrase used in popular lingo. For example, whenever people talk about someone who gets the blame for everything, they call him the "scapegoat." And when someone is fired from his job or excluded as a member of some group, people will be heard saying something along the lines of: "They sent him away to the wilderness."

Familiar expressions. But not used entirely correctly, as we will see in a moment. We will see that Leviticus 16, from which such expressions are drawn, is nonetheless really not so familiar as we may have supposed.

The subject of Leviticus 16 is familiar: the great Day of Atonement. Ever since we were young, we have heard people talk about this in connection with the tabernacle. Especially when the story got to the holy of holies. The teacher would be sure to tell us that the great Day of Atonement was the only day in the year when this most holy place was entered by a person. Only by the high priest. With incense and blood. And the teacher would immediately point to what the epistle to the Hebrews said, against the background of these shadows, about the work of our king-high priest, Jesus Christ. Correctly so.

But it is our task now first of all, and most importantly of all, to discuss Leviticus 16 and focus on the preaching of this chapter, in view of its content and in view of the place in the book where this material meets us today.

The reader would do well, for the sake of an overview, to place some Roman numerals in the margins of his Bible. Like this:

I. Preparatory commands (Lev 16:1–10)

II. The actual atonement (Lev 16:11–19)

THE GREAT DAY OF ATONEMENT (LEV 16)

III. Concluding actions (Lev 16:20–28)

IV. Concluding commands (Lev 16:29–34)

By means of this outline, we obtain an overview of the entire chapter. With the help of this outline we will dig more deeply into each of the four sections of this chapter dealing with the great Day of Atonement.

I. PREPARATORY COMMANDS (LEV 16:1–10)

In this first section, three things are in view:

A. The "prelude" of the chapter

B. The high priest's garments for the great Day of Atonement

C. The sacrifices for priesthood and people on the great Day of Atonement

I. A. The "prelude" (vv. 1–2)

Our chapter opens with the statement that God spoke with Moses about the great Day of Atonement, "after the death of the two sons of Aaron who died when they approached the Lord." This does not means that God would never have spoken about the great Day of Atonement if Nadab and Abihu would not have misbehaved in the way that we discussed earlier, but it does mean that these events provided an occasion to give Aaron a serious warning that whenever he entered the holy of holies, he was to do so only at the *time* and the *manner* stipulated by God. For otherwise it could cost Aaron his life as well, "because I appear in the cloud over the atonement cover." (Regarding that *kabod* or glory of Yahweh, see our commentary on Exodus, 184–85.)

One of our later concluding comments will deal with the *time* of the great Day of Atonement.

What God said about the *manner* in which Aaron alone was allowed to draw near, was related to the clothing and the sacrifices of the high priest that were stipulated for that day. We turn to these now.

I. B. The high priest's garments for the great Day of Atonement (v. 4)

Regarding the high priest's robe discussed in Exodus, we wrote the following:

> Strictly speaking we can distinguish three aspects to the uniform worn by Israel's high priest. First of all, there was the white

coat he wore on the great Day of Atonement (Lev 16:4, 23). We will not comment on that coat here.

Second, he wore the same items of apparel as all the other priests, although the bonnet he wore looked somewhat different.

Thirdly, there were certain items of apparel worn only by the high priest.[1]

That is what we wrote earlier. Now we want to supplement that, as follows. On the great Day of Atonement the high priest had to appear before God without wearing any of his usual ceremonial garb. That garb consisted simply of (1) a coat, and (2) breeches, along with (3) a sash around his waist, and (4) nothing but a turban on his head. All these articles of clothing had to be made of *bad*. Not *shesh*, (probably) referring to expensive Egyptian linen, and absolutely not with *shesh moshar*, stiff linen, embroidered with various adornments, no, but made simply of *bad* and nothing more.[2] On the great Day of Atonement, Israel's high priest wore simply a very plain white garment, made of the simplest of material. Only his cap had something striking. That did not have the shape of the priestly cap (*migba'ah*, presumably an upside-down cup), but it had the shape of his ordinary high priestly cap (*mitsnepheth*), presumably a turban. Perhaps this is so that Aaron would thereby have appeared somewhat higher and taller.

The assumption was expressed that this simple clothing "spoke" of humiliation and humbling before God's face. This was not said in so many words, however. It is true, though, that the great Day of Atonement was a day of humbling before Yahweh. This was the only prescribed day of fasting each year (Lev 16:29). The only thing that we read explicitly and repeatedly is that the articles of clothing mentioned were garments of *holiness*. That clearly pointed to the purpose of the day: to impress Israel thoroughly that she was to be a holy people, the people of Yahweh. Naturally this was also in view with the command that Aaron was supposed to bathe before putting on these sacred garments. And this was surely in view as well with the white color of the high priestly clothing prescribed for that special day.

I. C. *The sacrifices for priesthood and people on the great Day of Atonement (vv. 3, 5–10)*

Next, the special sacrifices for this day are mentioned. Special features are left out (accompanying grain- and drink-offerings, Num 29).

---

1. Vonk, *Exodus*, 265.
2. Vonk, *Exodus*, 257–58.

THE GREAT DAY OF ATONEMENT (LEV 16)

These sacrifices were twofold, namely, first, the sacrifice for Aaron himself, and second, that for the people.

1. The sacrifices for Aaron himself and for his "house," i.e., for the priesthood, would need to be a bull as a sin offering, and a ram as a burnt offering.
2. The sacrifices for the Israelite people would have to be two male goats as a sin offering and a ram as a burnt offering.

In this connection, we wish to make the point that the two goats are being identified here as a single sin offering. Not two, but one. We must store that in our memory for later. That those two goats together constituted a single sin offering (v. 5).

Finally, the last of all the preparatory commands.

When the slaughter of the requisite sin offerings is discussed, that slaughter had to occur in the following order. First, Aaron had to bring the sin offering for himself and his house. Next, the sacrifice for the people. Except, he was not to slaughter *both* goats, but he was supposed to slaughter one and release the other one into the wilderness. Which one? Which goat had to be slaughtered and which one spared? God himself would determine that by means of casting lots. Aaron was supposed to bring both goats into the presence of God, at the entrance of the tabernacle, and then cast the lot. "One lot for Yahweh and one for Azazel" (v. 8; lit., "the goal of removal," or the scapegoat).

What does the phrase "for Azazel" mean?

Nobody knows for sure. Many attempts have been made to explain the word *Azazel*. One person thinks it is a name for the goat itself, another person thinks it is a name for the wilderness, still a third person a term for the devil, and yet another thinks it means "departing" (for the departing goat), and someone else interprets it to mean "in order to remove" (the goat that removes).

If neither etymology nor ancient translations can help us, we will have to interpret the words "for Azazel" on the basis of what follows in the immediate context. Parts II and III will talk further about the *implementation* of the preparatory commands. Perhaps that will furnish more light.

II. THE ACTUAL ATONEMENT (LEV 16:11–19)

It is obvious that the implementation of the previously stated commands occurred in two phases. First, a bull was brought as a sin offering for Aaron and his house, and then a goat was brought as a sin offering for the assembly of the people.

At this point we would observe that beforehand, Aaron had to bring two handfuls of finely ground fragrant incense in a pan filled with burning coals that he had scooped from the altar of burnt sacrifice (on which fire was burning constantly), and had to set all of this down behind the second curtain. For what purpose? We read: so that "the smoke of the incense will conceal the atonement cover above the Testimony, so that he will not die" (v. 13). These words remind us immediately of the "prelude" to this chapter, the sin of Nadab and Abihu. Here Israel received instruction about the inaccessibility of God for people like those of whom Aaron was one, namely, not only a weak, mortal man, a man of "flesh," a child of Adam, but also a man who personally and specifically had grieved and saddened Yahweh more than once. Such people could not possibly approach God, who alone has immortality and dwells in unapproachable light; whom no man has ever seen nor can see (1 Tim 6:16). For that, they had to be made worthy, and to be called (Heb 5:4). And if they then came near to God, they still had to be protected, otherwise it could still cost them their life. This was stated symbolically by means of the aromatic curtain of incense. Aaron had to secure that, whenever he came near the *kabod* or glory of Yahweh above the atonement covering. (For the protecting power of the incense, symbolizing prayer, see Num 16:46–47.) Naturally we think in this connection of John 1:18: no one has ever seen God; the only begotten Son, who is at the bosom of the Father, he has made him known.

Only now could the commands regarding the actual atonement be implemented. By means of the sprinkling of blood. We will focus on the following four stages.

Stage 1

First, Aaron had to sprinkle the blood of the bull brought as a sin offering. With his finger, and not by throwing it. No, placing only a few drops on the golden disc, the atonement covering that lay "on the testimony, i.e., on the ark of the covenant, in which were stored the Horeb certificate, in double, both copies of the Ten Words of the covenant.[3] And he had to daub those droplets *on the front* of the atonement covering. We read literally: on the east side. This means that he was not supposed to proceed all too far into

---

3. Regarding the latter, see Vonk, *Exodus*, 95, 127–28, 228; and regarding the difference between sprinkling, spraying and throwing, see our earlier comments in the present commentary.

THE GREAT DAY OF ATONEMENT (LEV 16)

the holy of holies, but simply sprinkle with his finger the drops of blood on the front of the atonement covering.[4] Hereby again respect for the holiness of Yahweh would be bound upon his heart.

What did this action signify, however?

The reader needs to recall what we mentioned earlier about the altars of the tabernacle.[5] According to God's promise, those altars would be meeting places for him and his people (Exod 20:24). Those altars would represent his people to him, so that the blood on those altars would signify blood on the ones bringing the offering(s). Thereby the latter—the person(s) bringing the offering—would be covered (*kipper*) with the blood.

This time the sprinkling of blood on the ark pointed to the covering of Aaron and his sons, the priests, with the blood of atonement before the face of God. In connection with our earlier discussion of Lev 17:11, we explained what that covering of someone with blood signified. It signified his atonement.

That atonement of Aaron occurred this time on the ark, the most glorious of all the altars. Right under God's eyes. There was no place higher and more exalted.

At least at that time. This explains the annual repetition.

Later Jesus became the Surety of a better covenant, and the priest of a higher order. Had he been from the same order of priests as Aaron, then he would have had to suffer *often* since the foundation of the world (i.e., from Horeb, since the institution of the cult there). But now he appeared *once*, in connection with the end of the ages, in order to remove sin through his sacrifice (Heb 9:25–26).

This was followed by yet another sprinkling. This did not occur on the atonement covering, but in front of it. That must have occurred on the ground. On the ground between the ark and the inner curtain (v. 14). Presumably the sprinkling of the atonement covering that we just discussed pointed to the atonement of the persons of the priesthood, the people, whereas this second sprinkling, on the ground of the sanctuary between the ark and the curtain, gave assurance of the atonement for official sins whereby the priests had defiled the sanctuary. We must note, in this connection, the sevenfold repetition in connection with this second sprinkling. This spoke of the covenant. Apparently it had in view specifically God's covenant with Aaron and the rest of the priesthood. This covenant was certainly not kept perfectly, and thereby the sanctuary, especially the most important part, the

---

4. For a diagram of the forecourt and tabernacle, see Vonk, *Exodus*, 141; pay special attention to the various compass directions indicated.

5. Vonk, *Exodus*, 220–21.

holy of holies, was defiled. Those blemishes and shortcomings in observing the priestly covenant would now be (symbolically) covered by means of the second cleansing and thereby the most holy place would be cleansed.

Stage 2

After Aaron had brought the initial sacrifices for himself, he "shall then slaughter the goat for the sin offering for the people and take its blood behind the curtain and do with it as he did with the bull's blood: He shall sprinkle it on the atonement cover and in front of it" (v. 15). In verse 16a we receive the confirmation of the correctness of the explanation that we just furnished of the sprinkling of the blood of the bull. We stated that this was apparently first for the persons, and then for the defilement of the most holy place by means of their shortcomings.

That same thing happened again, but then with the blood of the goat and for the Israelite people. "In this way he will make atonement for the Most Holy Place because of the uncleanness and rebellion of the Israelites, whatever their sins have been" (v. 16a).

Stage 3

Now it was the turn for the "holy place." While the high priest was performing his atoning work there, no one else was allowed to go into that area (v. 17). His atoning work consisted in this, that in the holy place he would do what he had done in the most holy place. This is what verse 16b is talking about: "He is to do the same for the Tent of Meeting, which is among them in the midst of their uncleanness." The phrase "Tent of Meeting" should be understood to refer to the "holy place" (cf. v. 20). The atoning work in this area would have consisted in applying the blood to the horns of the incense altar one time (Exod 30:10), and sprinkling seven times the ground in front of this altar, between the altar and the curtain, in the direction of the ark behind the curtain. That blood would first have been the blood of the bull, and then the blood of the goat. First for Aaron himself, and then for the congregation.

Stage 4

Finally, the altar of burnt offering in the forecourt.

THE GREAT DAY OF ATONEMENT (LEV 16)

Here similar actions occurred. First, blood is applied (*natan*) to the horns of the altar, then it was sprinkled seven times on the altar itself. This time, however, not on the ground. This was certainly because this ground did not in that sense constitute the actual dwelling like the ground where the holy place and the most holy place stood, and thus no atonement function needed to be performed. Is it possible that "the blood" that needed to be handled here was a mixture of the blood of the bull and the blood of the goat? What perhaps argues in favor of this is the singular: "the blood," in verse 18. But a counter argument might be the fact that one will occasionally encounter a (presumed) mixture of blood and oil, and one of blood and water—although this was not in connection with a sacrifice—but nowhere one of blood with blood. We think that is not what is being referred to here in this passage. Otherwise, if the blood of the bull were to be mixed with the blood of the goat, the difference between the sacrifices for the sins of Aaron and for the sins of the people would disappear, a distinction on which Scripture places great emphasis, both here, in fact, already in Leviticus 8–10, and in Heb 5:3 and 9:7.

With the blood that belonged to the same blood and thus to the same *nefesh* that appeared in the most holy place and in the holy place, on the altar of burnt offering not only were the sins of the persons (of priests and people) covered, but also especially the purification was performed of the altar of burnt offering that had been defiled by the shortcomings associated with observing the covenant with the priests and with the people.

III. CONCLUDING ACTIONS (LEV 16:20–28)

When we study everything that had to be performed on the great Day of Atonement with respect to actions associated with atonement, if one thing has been observed very clearly, it is this: those actions associated with atonement were now ended. Finished. Almost unnecessarily this is stated in the opening verse of Section III of our chapter: "When Aaron has finished making atonement for the Most Holy Place, the Tent of Meeting and the altar, then he shall . . ." (v. 20). We need to register carefully the fact that among the "concluding actions" that follow, we must not expect any actions that bear a genuinely atoning character!

These concluding actions were five in number.

    A. Releasing the goat "for Azazel"

    B. Aaron changing his clothes

C. Aaron carrying the burnt offering for himself and the burnt offering for the people

D. The return of the man who had led away the goat that had been released

E. The final actions with the bull of the sin offering and the goat of the sin offering

III. A. Releasing the goat "for Azazel" (vv. 20–22)

These verses speak further about what had been stated briefly in verse 10, namely, that the live goat had to be placed before the face of Yahweh, i.e., before the door of the tabernacle (and this goat naturally had to stand in waiting during the entire time when the high priest was busy with his fellow goat), in order finally to perform a twofold action there. Verse 10 stated that an action of atonement had to occur on him, and then he would be "released for Azazel, into the desert."

We will discuss those two actions of verses 21–22 now.

1. First, the atonement actions (v. 21a).

We read in verses 21–22: "He is to lay both hands on the head of the live goat and confess over it all the wickedness and rebellion of the Israelites—all their sins—and put them on the goat's head. He shall send the goat away into the desert in the care of a man appointed for the task. The goat will carry on itself all their sins to a solitary place; and the man shall release it in the desert."

The first thing we observe about this atonement action is that it is not an ordinary action. It is not joined to any shedding of blood. And yet the rule tolerated no exception: there is no forgiveness without the shedding of blood (Lev 17:11; Heb 9:22). How was this possible now?

At this point we must recall that the two goats of verse 5 were presented to us together as one sin offering. The casting of lots as well, that is, the selection by God himself, of which goat had to die and which goat could remain alive, proceeded from that unity. At this point we must look back at the goat that had been slaughtered and whose blood had just covered the sins and had atoned, as if it had risen again and become alive again in order to fulfill its role still further. Now on this animal that had, so to speak, risen again and become alive again, the sins were once again confessed and laid upon it. Now no longer as unatoned sins, but as atoned sins. Actually this was supposed to happen with the dead (but made alive again) animal, but because this was not possible at this point, it happened with the second

THE GREAT DAY OF ATONEMENT (LEV 16)

animal, concerning which it is stated with repeated emphasis that it was alive, and that (in verse 5) it had just been introduced as being together with the other goat as a single sin offering.

(The fact that sins that are forgiven are nonetheless still confessed once more will not surprise the reader. In the same way, the great evil that Paul had committed again Christ and his followers had been forgiven for a long time [Acts 22:16], when years later he nonetheless confessed them once again [Gal 1:13; 1 Tim 1:13].)

Which sins of the Israelites were atoned, and laid on the (second) animal *as already atoned*?

People will answer: "Every sin," and that is correct, for that is what it says. But first of all, the sins of intention were naturally singled out, meaning thereby exclusively the sins committed without premeditation. Intentional apostates and traitors of God's covenant received no forgiveness. But then there was so much remaining, that could not exist before God's holy face. Various "iniquities," which would certainly have been included unnoticed transgressions against the sanctuary (*awonoth*, Num 18:1, 23). It could certainly happen that someone might come near to the tabernacle and altar without compunction who was not entirely pure. Further kinds of sins are mentioned: "all the iniquities of the people of Israel, and all their transgressions, all their sins" (v. 21). For "transgressions" a word is used (*pis'eihem*) that speaks for "falling away from Yahweh," and for "sins" a word is used that is used in connection with the sin offering, a word that can by itself mean sin offering (*hatta' t*), a word that we saw used with reference to the handling of the sin offering and also afterward, in close connection with God's covenant. All of these slips on Israel's part, no matter how unnoticed, away from the high plane of living, on which the people had been placed and exalted by God at Horeb, were forgiven. There was absolutely no further trace to be seen upon God's congregation.

2. Next, verses 21b-22 talk about what was supposed to happen with this live goat. We read that after first laying the aforementioned (atoned) sins on the head of the goat, the high priest was to hand over the goat to a man who had been appointed (or was readied) for this, and that man would bring the animal to the desert. In this way the goat would carry all their iniquities to a remote area. He was to release the goat in the desert.

The significance of this symbolic action seems no longer very difficult to identify. Obviously it was not intended to grant Israel atonement, but rather the assurance of atonement. For it embodied a sermon for the people. For whom else? For the entire people. For that purpose the sin offering had been brought to Yahweh (Lev 16:15). Perhaps connected with this was the instituted practice of having the live goat brought away by the most preeminent man among the people on whom the eye of the high priest happened to fall, after he had completed his task of bringing atonement in the sanctuary.

It is also clear why the live goat had to be led away and released in *the desert*. There, outside, was the place outside the camp of Israel, i.e., outside the area where the people of life had been arranged around the tent of the God of life. There was the place where the dead were buried. Out there, in that direction at least, outside the camp, everyone had to dwell who had leprosy, or a flow of bodily fluid, and all who had become unclean by touching a corpse (Num 5:2–3). There we find that altogether different terrain, the terrain of paganism and of Satan with his devils (Acts 26:18; Eph 2:2; 6:12). There it was no longer the power of the coming age that was at work (Heb 6:5), the Spirit of God with his saving gospel (Heb 4:2). Surely Israel did not yet possess as clear a knowledge of these things as we do, thanks to the New Testament. Although Satan and his devils were just as real and active then as now, and they fulfilled their terrible role in those days as they do now after Christ's coming. Therefore the manner in which God warned his ancient church against the danger of these spirits was different in Israel's time than now. It was symbolic then. Visual instruction. No less communicative. So communicative, in fact, that later the New Testament would be based upon it. Reformed Old Testament theologian B. Holwerda wrote:

> First of all there is repeated language about the *erēmos* [desert]; and that words possesses a gruesome ring. Think of the story about the possessed man from Gadara, who lived among the graves (!) and was driven by the devil to the deserts (!), whereas later the devils drove a herd of pigs into the water and made them drown. You find similar features in almost every story about the healing of someone who was possessed: the devils appear repeatedly like destructive powers. From this the connection is immediately clear between *desert, devil, and death*. But then by means of a long explanation this connection is illustrated by the apocalyptic portrait of the destruction of Babylon: this city then became "a dwelling place for demons, a haunt for every unclean spirit, a haunt for every unclean bird, a haunt for every unclean and detestable beast" (Rev 18:2), completely parallel with the portrait of the prophets). Also characteristic is what Christ says about an unclean spirit, when it has come out of a man: "it passes through waterless places seeking rest, but finds none" (Matt 12:43).[6]

---

6. Holwerda, *Voordrachten*, 376.

THE GREAT DAY OF ATONEMENT (LEV 16)

In this citation from Holwerda we placed in italic the words *desert, devil, and death*." You will recall that earlier we identified this trio in connection with the teaching of the sin offering and in connection with the unclean and dead animals. We believe we need to do that here as well. For on the one hand, the gospel of the great Day of Atonement was deeply shameful for Israel. After a year of slaughtering and sacrificing, Israel still had to be purified from various impurities and hidden errors that essentially were just so many slips away from the high place of life upon which God had place here, down to the level of the devil and of death. But that purifying had happened completely, so completely that the most prominent Israelite could take the visible and tangible proof of that (the goat) with him to the desert and release it there. That place to which Israel's eye could not look without her heart quivering about evil spirits. That region of God-forsakenness (Lev 17:7; Isa 13:21; 34:11–15; Jer 51:37; Rev 18:2). In the direction of that desert the cry was now being sounded (in the hearing of every Israelite): My people are pure. Keep your hands off them, you understand?

Two more comments.

Perhaps someone who has read the foregoing discussion will be inclined to suppose that we favor the view that the word *Azazel* referred to "a desert demon." This view was held by some rabbis, by Origen, and by later commentators in more recent times. This view fits easily with the idea that the live goat was sent into the desert as a testimony against Satan as Israel's accuser.

The temptation is great indeed, when it comes to Lev 16:8, where it talks about "one lot for Yahweh and one lot for Azazel," they think the word *Azazel* is a proper name, because the word *Yahweh* is also a proper name. And that proper name would then supposedly refer to the prince of the demons, Satan. But we think that there are many arguments against this view. (1) The oldest translations did not view Azazel as a person, but as a quality of the animal. (2) The rabbis we mentioned a moment ago were not among the earlier rabbis, so that the sentiments of the oldest rabbis could have been different. (3) Such talk about the devil would appear completely isolated within the entire Torah of Moses; even in Genesis 3 Satan is not mentioned explicitly, unlike, for example, Job 1:6 and Zech 3:1. (4) The notion that this Satan is being identified here as a kind of "desert demon" corresponding with Yahweh as more or less his partner does not at all sit well with us. Such an exaltation of a creature, let alone this kind of creature, to the position of a virtual anti-God strikes us as being in conflict with God's own command in the Law: You shall not mention the names of other gods or take those names upon your lips (Exod 23:23; cf. Ps 16:4).

So we do not see in the Hebrew word *la'azazel* a reference to the devil or a demon. But to what then does it refer? Although this question cannot be answered with complete certainty, we have the greatest affinity for translating the word in question as "to remove it." The first lot was then cast "for Yahweh," i.e., to be offered to him, and the second "in order to remove it," i.e., the animal itself that was led to the desert and released there (v. 21). Possibly the idea is related to this of the living animal at the same time taking along the (atoned) sins and putting them away (v. 20). But the main thing, in our opinion, is the contrast between "to be sacrificed" and "not to be sacrificed." *This* motive is mentioned *first*, in verse 10, and as we know, the Torah customarily mentions the most prominent item first.

Here is our second comment.

In the word *la'azazel* we see no name identification for Satan or one of his devils. Nonetheless we did see in the desert a symbolic identification of the world that was hostile to Israel, specifically, the world of evil spirits. If someone should now see in that leading away of the live goat to the desert, not only a symbolic testimony *for Israel*, unto the assurance of their complete purification, but simultaneously *against the world of evil spirits hostile to Israel*, we would not venture to reject such a interpretation as impossible. In the first place, having seen what Scripture says about the desert, as we explain earlier. Second, also having seen what it teaches about the hostile role of Satan and his subordinate spirits against Israel (Zech 3; Dan 10). And in the third place, having seen what happened with our Savior. For in his own person, he not only brought the sacrifice for our sins by means of his atoning death, and simultaneously received for himself and for us a testimony regarding the purification of our sins in his resurrection and ascension (Rom 4:25; Heb 1:3), but the Lord's exaltation was also a testimony against "the spirits in prison" (1 Pet 3:19), and following his exaltation, the expulsion of Satan and his angels from heaven (Col 2:15; Rev 12:7-9; cf. 1 Kgs 22:19-23; Job. 1:6).

We must take care not to simply accept the claim that in ancient times, in contrast to us, Israel had no more than a primitive knowledge about angels and devils. It may well have been just the opposite. Israel had certainly heard about this from their ancestors (Gen 18:22; 19:1; 28:12; 32:1). But probably via Moses as well. For even though we are told this for the first time in the New Testament (Acts 7:38, 53; Gal 3:19; Heb 2:2), it was certain, for example, that Israel (Moses) had received the Torah through the mediation of angels. Perhaps Moses told this to his contemporaries, but it simply was not written down (cf. Deut 32:8, 33:2 [lxx]).[7] In any case, even

---

7. Cf. Vonk, *Genesis*, 177-79.

THE GREAT DAY OF ATONEMENT (LEV 16)

if God would not have spoken extensively to Israel about the devils, these did exist in ancient times and did hold the Gentiles within their power. How they would have liked to have gotten their hands on Israel (again)! Something that did succeed all too often. Despite God's warnings against this that he gave in various ways (sin offering, food laws, etc.). Indeed, in the Book of the Covenant, Israel was warned about Canaanizing—becoming like the Canaanites.[8] But once more, perhaps Israel understood more about the dangerous spirit world that lay behind paganism, and about God's warning against that, than we think. How else can we explain that later that background is discussed as though it were an ordinary, well-known phenomenon?

Therefore, although in our reading of Leviticus 16 we would not wish to be guilty of recklessly placing equal signs (e.g., the death of the first goat = Christ's atoning death; the release of the second goat = Christ's exaltation; the desert = the world of devils; Azazel = Satan), we nonetheless consider the possibility to be rather great that the release of the live goat in the desert in Moses' day, is to be understood simultaneously as a testimony *for Israel* and as a testimony *against the spirit world that was hostile to Israel*, given the presence of abundant symbolism in the instruction of Israel throughout the entire book of Leviticus. So great is this possibility that we do not think it is improbable that in Peter's later words about Christ's ascension as being a blast of the victor's trumpet in the hearing of the (evil) spirits in prison (1 Pet 3:19), we can hear an allusion to the well-known symbolism of the great Day of Atonement. This first epistle of Peter contains not only the usual backward glances to the Law that we find in all the other New Testament writers (blood, sanctification, 1:2; lamb, 1:19; priesthood, 2:5, 9; etc.), but for us there is no doubt that we are being specifically and especially reminded of the symbolism of the ancient sanctuary by passages like 1 Pet 1:12 (angels who desire to look into something), 1:16 (be holy, for I am holy, Lev 11:44–45; 19:2; 20:7), 1:19 (the lamb without defect or blemish), 1:20 (the foundation of the world). If, with the release of the live goat, who was part of the single sin offering along with the goat that was slaughtered, God did indeed provide the symbolism of a demonstration, a triumphant declaration of purity for his people over against the army of spirits, concerning whose commander it would be said later in Israel that he was the accuser of God's own (Zech 3:1; Rev 12:10), then the assumption seems plausible that the apostle Peter was placing a tangible connection between this symbolic action of God in the Old Testament and his real exaltation of the once-dead and now-risen Christ at the ascension, before the eyes of Satan and

---

8. Vonk, *Exodus*, 116–21.

his wicked angels. In both instances we are dealing with a demonstration. (We are saving for later a comment about the place of Leviticus 16 and the significance of this chapter for the meaning of the release of the scapegoat as a demonstration.)

III. B.   Aaron changing his clothes (vv. 23–24a)

Another clear proof that the actual work of atonement was completed with the slaughter of the first goat is provided to us by what we read about the changing of clothes that Aaron had to perform. He had to do three things.

First, he had to take off the white garments of the great Day of Atonement. They had to be deposited in the sanctuary. They had to remain there. For that was holy (v. 4).

Next, he had to bathe. Perhaps this was on account of the work that had been performed earlier, even though the high priest would probably have been assisted by one or more priests in the slaughtering of the bull and the goat. But this bathing had already been prescribed for every priest who came near to the tabernacle or to the altar of sacrifice (Exod 30:19–21). Just so we don't suppose that the high priest had made himself unclean by touching the scapegoat who was being sent away. We read nothing of the kind.

Then Aaron had to put on "his clothes." That is, his usual decorative garment. Clothed in this manner, he had to perform the rest of his work. That was also priestly work. It was even atoning work, as we will see in a moment. But the *actual work of the great Day of Atonement* was now finished.

III. C.   Aaron carrying the burnt offering for himself and the burnt offering for the people (vv. 24b-45)

After Aaron had put on his customary high priestly clothing again, he had to go outside, i.e., to the forecourt, and prepare the burnt offering for himself (a ram, v. 3) and for the people (also a ram, v. 5).

We discussed the significance of the burnt offering earlier in this commentary. This was the preeminent sacrifice whereby God provided Israel with the assurance that she was his people and was to devote herself to him with all their heart and all their conduct. This sacrifice always functioned as a foundational sacrifice. In the literal sense of the word, it lay at the foundation of all the other sacrifices. On this day as well, it started off at the head of the daily sacrificial ministry.

Nevertheless, along with telling us about these two burnt offerings, the first for Aaron himself and then the one for the people, we are told that they administered atonement. This does not surprise us. When we discussed the burnt offering, we saw that the special meaning of this kind of sacrifice was related to sanctification, but the burnt sacrifice, just like every other bloody sacrifice, was also brought for the purpose of atonement, for justification (Lev 1:4). It is obvious that extra attention is being drawn here to this general purpose, in connection with these bloody sacrifices offered immediately after both of the sin offerings associated with the great Day of Atonement. The usual daily ministry of atonement was begun immediately once again. On what basis, after all, would the other sacrifices of that day supposedly have had to have been offered? For as the reader knows, the burnt offering was the indispensable basis of every other sacrifice.

Here the incompleteness of the Horeb covenant, specifically, of its ministry of atonement, is held up before our eyes. Annually, no, daily, the atonement sacrifices had to be repeated. Until Christ came "once for all into the holy places, not by means of the blood of goats and calves but by means of his own blood, thus securing an eternal redemption" (Heb 9:12).

We are reminded of that steady repetition of the (ancient, symbolic) ministry of atonement of the Law also by the precise prescription that the fat of the sin offering—namely, of both of the slaughtered animals of the sin offering, the bull and the goat—had to be burned on the altar. We will see in a moment what had to happen with the rest of the animal slaughtered for the sin offering.

III. D. *The return of the man who had led away the goat that was released (v. 26)*

While the high priest completed the last-mentioned activities, the man who had come to the high priest's attention for bringing the live goat out to the desert and release it there, completed the task assigned to him and returned to the camp of the people. But before he was allowed to enter the camp, he had to wash his clothes and bathe his body in water. Only then could he enter the camp.

It is very correct to explain these actions of the man as acts of purification. But it was entirely incorrect to suppose that the man had to purify himself because he had come into contact with the goat, the goat that had been sent out into the desert bearing the sins of the people. That interpretation arose because people did not correctly understand the intention of the symbolic action of releasing the live goat (see III. A. 2.). If what Jewish tradition reports is true, i.e., that the custom arose of throwing this goat over a cliff after it had been brought a couple hours distance away from Jerusalem, then neither did later Jews understand anything of that symbolic action. For why would the man have defiled himself by touching the goat? This goat, as we saw, had been designated to carry away into the desert sins that had been confessed and atoned, and was not sent away or chased off into that desert, but was released in the desert. That man was never given the assignment of killing the animal. That is exactly what God did not want. Otherwise the animal's life would not have been spared through God's own determination of the lot. Moreover, the live goat was united with the dead goat. A sin offering. Now, animals brought for a sin offerings were not unholy, but holy; not unclean, but clean. But this feature is lost from sight by exegetes and dogmaticians even in our day, so that they do not properly understand Heb 13:11–12.

No, the man had to purify himself because he had been *in the desert*. This was something that was not always demanded of someone who entered the camp of Israel from the desert, but it was required today, on the great Day of Atonement. That is very telling. Because on this day that desert had functioned as a symbol of the world that was hostile toward Israel, the world of Satan. Those mouths were stopped! Israel is my clean people!

Here again we would like to make two comments.

First, unfortunately, the action of the man who released the second goat outside the camp was understood entirely wrongly not only by the Jews, but also by the early Christians. (And if we are not careful today, then we too will allow ourselves to be duped by such translations like "chase away" with reference to the second goat, rather than "release" or "let go.") Tertullian, for example, wanted to persuade the Jews that Jesus was the promised Messiah by giving an explanation of the two goats, in which he provided this as his best argument:

> So, again, I will make an interpretation of the two goats which were habitually offered on the fast-day. Do not they, too, point to each successive stage in the character of the Christ who is already come? A pair, on the one hand, and consimilar (they were), because of the identity of the Lord's general appearance, inasmuch as He is not to come in some other form, seeing that He has to be recognised by those by whom He was once hurt. But the one of them, begirt with scarlet, amid cursing and universal spitting, and tearing, and piercing, was cast away by the People outside the city into perdition, marked with manifest tokens of Christ's passion; who, after being begirt with scarlet garment, and subjected to universal spitting, and afflicted with all contumelies, was crucified outside the city. The other, however,

offered for sins, and given as food *to the priests merely* of the temple, gave signal evidences of the second appearance; in so far as, after the expiation of all sins, the priests of the spiritual temple, that is, of the church, were to enjoy a spiritual public distribution (as it were) of the Lord's grace, while all others are fasting from salvation.[9]

He would have obtained such nonsense from writers like Pseudo-Barnabas, who also thought that the second goat was accursed and chased into the desert crowned with scarlet, again, as a "type" of Christ. Pseudo-Barnabas himself in turn had heard people in his surroundings tell about the mistreatment that the second goat endured at the hands of the Jews—the animal was pushed off a precipice. What damage a silly misunderstanding can do!

Second, if we may view the release of the second goat in the desert as a symbolic deed, that signified a challenge from Yahweh on Israel's behalf against the world of paganism and destruction outside her camp, then we may surmise why this chapter, which deals with the great Day of Atonement, Leviticus 16, was placed exactly at this point and not, for example, in the neighborhood of Leviticus 22, dealing with the feasts. The reason would have been because Leviticus 16, with this anti-pagan tenor, fit precisely between Leviticus 11–15 and Leviticus 17–20, with a similar, especially forceful anti-Canaanite thrust. We have seen this latter somewhat already, and will we see it further. As far as Leviticus 11–15 is concerned, those chapters preached: "Israel is my holy people." And in Leviticus 16: "Israel continues to be my holy people."

III. E. *The final actions with the bull of the sin offering and the goat of the sin offering (vv. 27–28)*

Finally, we have lying there in the forecourt those carcasses of the bull and the goat sacrifices associated with the sin offering, and we know from our earlier discussion of the sin offering what had to happen with dead animals associated with the sin offering. They were extremely holy. Ordinary Israelites were not allowed to eat of them. When it came to sin offerings that were brought for a (high) priest or for the people, and thus their blood was brought into the sanctuary, even the priests were not permitted to eat of them, but had to burn the animals in their entirety outside the camp. Therefore this certainly had to happen with the sin offering bull and the

---

9. Tertullian, *Answer*, chap. 14, 732–33 (italics original); cf. *Against Marcion*, chap. 7.

slaughtered sin offering goat on the great Day of Atonement. For their blood had been brought even further into the tabernacle than the holy place, namely, into the most holy place.

The reader will also recall how strong an emphasis we placed on the fact that some sin offerings were burned outside the camp, not because they were so *un*clean. Far from it. They were the exact opposite, extremely holy. No, simply in order to prevent confusion with the peace offering and burnt offering. That was all.

Well then, when we read that the man who had burned both of those dead sacrificial animals outside the camp on the great Day of Atonement was not allowed to return unless he had washed his clothes and bathed his body, then these actions must be interpreted in a way that corresponds with those pertaining to the man who returned after having released the (live) goat of the sin offering. That man as well, who had burned the carcasses, had not been defiled by the two dead animals of the sin offering, but by the *desert*. By which we mean the desert on the great Day of Atonement. For otherwise, this washing of clothes and bathing was not required for someone who had burned those sin offering animals outside the camp. In Leviticus 4 and 6 we read that on that day, the desert fulfilled a role of special importance, namely, to assure the Israelites that they were completely cleansed from all their sins. God had caused this to be sounded forth, for their comfort, in the hearing of death and of the devils. This explains why the man who returned from burning both of those (dead) sin offering animals on the great Day of Atonement outside the camp, that is, in the desert, had to submit to the command to wash his clothes and bathe. A fine feature as part of the symbolism of the great Day of Atonement.

IV. CONCLUDING COMMANDS (LEV 16:29–34)

The chapter about the great Day of Atonement ends with two commands relating mainly to:

    A. the fixed date for the great Day of Atonement; and

    B. the high priestly task on that day.

THE GREAT DAY OF ATONEMENT (LEV 16)

IV. A. Concluding command regarding the fixed date for the great Day of Atonement (vv. 29–31)

The actual atonement work of the great Day of Atonement occurred in all quietness. No one else was allowed in the tabernacle, not even a priest could be present in the holy place, when the high priest did his work in the holy place and the most holy place. No one saw it. And yet the entire people was involved in it.

Therefore God gave the command that this day would be a day of fasting from everyone. For "fasting" and for "humbling oneself," the Hebrew uses the same word. Perhaps the bejeweled garment worn by the high priest as he performed his task (vv. 4, 24) pointed in this direction. This was the only day of fasting in the entire year that God had prescribed in the Law for Israel. It is obvious that for the church of the new dispensation this command had become obsolete. Appointed fast days were not to be laid upon us by men, when God himself no longer does so. Nevertheless, (organized) fasting has occurred in Reformed churches. It is something different, of course, if we fast as a result of heavy sorrow, great sins, or dreadful fear. Then it is automatic that we are not hungry, when in such days we call to God for comfort, forgiveness, or deliverance. Then no one needs to lay upon us any ecclesiastical regulation, as Christians have unfortunately permitted to happen.

At the same time, God commanded that Israel had to spend this day like a Sabbath, indeed, like "a complete Sabbath." Thus, absolutely no cause or reason was allowed to distract Israel's attention from the great covenant events of this day. The person dwelling among Israel as a sojourner would not be permitted to do any work on that day. All attention had to be focused on what happened there in the sanctuary.

The great Day of Atonement would have to be celebrated every year on the tenth day of the seventh month. We will discuss this date more when we discuss Israel's feasts.

If we consult our list of dates, then we see that during Israel's stay at Horeb, she did not observe the great Day of Atonement. That must have occurred for the first time somewhere en route to Canaan.

IV. B. Concluding command regarding the task of the high priest on the great Day of Atonement (vv. 32–34)

The ordinance regarding the great Day of Atonement ends with a summary (just as do other parts of Leviticus, like 15:32–33). In that summary two

PART 4 | THE PEOPLE OF YAHWEH

things are pressed upon Israel's heart. First, that the work of the annual day of atonement was not to be performed by anyone other than Aaron, or after him, by the oldest son among his descendants. That matter would be governed "by bodily descent" (Heb 7:16). Second, this work on the day of atonement was not to be performed by the high priest in any other manner than in the sacred garments that we have already discussed, and would have the purpose of purifying the entire sanctuary. We directed the attention of our readers to this as well. The sanctuary was defiled by the sins of the priesthood and people. But there was relief for that, and *its* purification was at the same time a purification of priesthood and people.

Indeed, we think that this concluding command helps to focus even more clearly on the place of our chapter, Leviticus 16, in the entire book of Leviticus, and on the place of the priesthood together with the sanctuary and the sacrificial ministry in the midst of the people whom God had honored with the Horeb covenant.

At this point we have reached the center of the book of Leviticus. We have reached a point where we may perhaps place a rest stop. For we have now become aware of *the sacrificial ministry* (Lev 1–7), *the priesthood* (Lev 8–10), and *the possible means of defilement* (Lev 11–15). The chapter about the great Day of Atonement (Lev 16) fits automatically with all of these. That was the day when all possible uncleanness of the Israelites was removed.

Later, Leviticus will deal further with those possible means of defilement. Immediately in chapter 17 already. For the Horeb covenant was glorious, but it brought something with it. Israel was surrounded with warnings against forsaking the foundation of life on which Yahweh had placed her. For Israel, the Law, no matter how beautiful it was, was not so very easy. It had the quality of a disciplinarian, no matter how evangelical its purpose. Because of that, the sigh would have gone up on occasion: Who can do all these things! How easily our foot slips off the holy pathway!

So then, Leviticus 16 offered comfort. In no other chapter does the important task of Israel's priesthood come so clearly before us as in this chapter about the great Day of Atonement.

God wanted to bind the relationship between himself and his people of that time to this priesthood. Concerning this priesthood (of Leviticus) Hebrews 7:11 says: "for under it the people received the law." When at Horeb, "the foundation of the (Israelite) world" occurred, the new foundation on which the Israelite society would rest from that point forward, the priesthood with its mediating place and task constituted such a preeminent part that all the other laws were interwoven with those pertaining to this priesthood. They had their basis in those priestly laws, so much so that Hebrews 7 says: "For when there is a change in the priesthood, there is necessarily

THE GREAT DAY OF ATONEMENT (LEV 16)

a change in the law as well" (Heb 7:12). That meant: Since we, Christians, are now no longer directed to the mediation of priests, for us too the other ordinances and commands of the Horeb covenant no longer apply in their former manner. (Such a soft scolding appeared necessary for the Christians of that time. Recall what we wrote about the Jewish Christians in the time that approached the year of Jerusalem's destruction). But with all of this, the letter of Hebrews was definitely not speaking in unfriendly terms about the Horeb covenant. Nor of the Law resting upon it. Perhaps the Law has been "set aside" (Heb 7:18), i.e., declared void, but it always befits us to recall with gratitude what an excellent ministry it performed in order to arouse in Israel the hope of something better (Heb 7:19).

This excellent ministry we have seen described in Leviticus 16. For us as well, this chapter continues to hold great value. The sacrifice that the high priest had to bring on the great Day of Atonement, first for himself, causes our eyes today to look to "the Son, who has been made perfect forever" (Heb 7:28; 8:3). Whereas *we* may know everything about his coming in the flesh. How must this same Law of the great Day of Atonement have made the heart of the Israelite church long for the perfect High Priest. This is what Hebrews 7 is talking about. In the respect, it shows a similar emphasis as Galatians 3. Not only did the apostle Paul write in his letter to the Galatians (that was directed against Judaizing), that the Law for Israel was a *paidagogus* unto Christ (3:24), but also according to the writer of the letter to the Hebrews (that was aimed against the Jewish Christian zeal for the law), the Law "brought" the Israelite people to Christ (7:18).

What an impressive strengthening this hope-stimulating preaching by the Law with its visible instruction (on the great Day of Atonement as well) received later, during the time of king David, when this ruler received the promise that a successor would come forth from him who—an unheard of phenomenon is Israel!—would bear both the priestly as well as the kingly dignity. In the manner of Melchizedek (Ps 110).

21

Be careful with the blood! (Lev 17)

IN THIS CHAPTER WE will first say something about Leviticus 17–26, and then discuss the first of these chapters, Leviticus 17.

1. AN OVERVIEW OF LEVITICUS 17–26

According to some, Leviticus 17 is the first in a series of chapters that together form a kind of unit, an independent section that constitutes the conclusion of the book of Leviticus. Leviticus 27 supposedly follows as a supplement, but this main section of Leviticus 17–26 supposedly concludes the actual book of Leviticus. Because in this last large main section, so people thought, the holiness of Yahweh is discussed in such an unusual manner, as is the holiness of the priesthood and the people, it has acquired from many in the scholarly world a distinct name, the "Holiness Code."

Others refused to follow this line of thinking, however. Neither the claim that Leviticus 17–26 constituted an independent unit, nor the view that here the holiness of Yahweh and his people is being presented in an entirely unusual manner. They point out that in the other chapters of Leviticus, the holiness of Yahweh and his people is a constantly recurring theme. Moreover, one Reformed commentator (Gispen) has observed that the first of these chapters (Lev 17) can hardly be described as a heading or introduction for such an independent "Holiness Code." Our readers will admit the correctness of this comment, when in a moment they see in Leviticus 17 that here as well, Israel is being warned about defilement, and when they recall that on the Great Day of Atonement, sin offerings were brought in order "to purify" the Israelites (Lev 16:30). In other words, Leviticus 17 moves

BE CAREFUL WITH THE BLOOD! (LEV 17)

further along the same line as Leviticus 16, even as Leviticus 16 is joined to Leviticus 11–15 (see chapters 15–19, the clean people of Yahweh. Make a separation, then, between clean and unclean).

But is Leviticus 17–26 nonetheless perhaps a Scripture section that displays certain features of similarity with the kind of treaty documents that had been composed formerly in the pre-Asiatic world in connection with making covenants? Consider Leviticus 26, for example. Does not that chapter, with its sanctions of promised blessing and threatened curse, resemble such a covenant treaty document?

We discussed these treaties in our commentary on Exodus.[1] As we said there, it seemed that when at Horeb God entered his covenant with Israel, he apparently made use of certain customs that existed at that time in connection with establishing covenants. Correspondence in structure and wording between the documents that people drew up on those occasions in the world surrounding Israel, and the Ten Words of Exodus 20, is not to be denied. This applies, in fact, to other parts of the Old Testament, like Exod 19:3–6 (the very first words of God to Moses about the covenant to be established at Horeb), Exod 20:22–23:33 (the so-called book of the covenant), Exod 34:10–26 (repetition and underscoring of several matters from the book of the covenant), Joshua 24 (the covenant renewal at Shechem), 1 Samuel 12 (covenant renewal at Gilgal), etc.

Nevertheless, in this series of Scripture passages no room was made for Leviticus 17–26.

In the last chapters, matters arise that strongly resemble the form and content of the covenant documents we mentioned. We have already mentioned the sanctions of Leviticus 26, the blessing and curse of the covenant. Later we will obviously have to consider the customary reminders of God's saving deeds in Exod 19:3b, 4a; 20:2; 20:22; Josh 24:1–13; 1 Sam 12:6–12 (God's *tsidqoth*, righteous deeds, i.e., saving deeds, 12:7), when we will hear the words echo: "I am Yahweh, your God" (Lev 18:2, etc.). In addition, the place that Moses occupies in Leviticus 17–26 as the go-between, together with the commission given him (Lev 17:8, "and you shall say to them") leads us to think as well of the role played by Moses, Joshua, and Samuel, respectively, in the events of Exod 19:3–6, Joshua 24, and 1 Samuel 12, and of the commission of Exod 19:3 and 6 ("thus you shall say," "these are the words that you shall speak"). Nor will we later see the warnings against foreign gods omitted, warnings that are so characteristic of Scripture passages that indisputably demonstrate the ancient customary pattern of treaty

---

1. Vonk, *Exodus*, 96–101.

documents (Exod 20:3, 23; 34:14–17; Josh 24:14); you can see this starting already in Leviticus 17:1–7.

But all of this does not at all incline us to consider Leviticus 17–26 to be the entirety or part of a substantive treaty text. For that, this Scripture portion as a whole, and most of its sections, lack far too much the familiar usual structure of the documents mentioned (preamble, historical prologue, regulation of the future relationship between the parties of the treaty, stipulations, witnesses, depositing copies of the document, regulation for periodic reading of the treaty, curse- and blessing-formulae). Whereas what we just stated applies also to the first chapter, Leviticus 17, namely, that it can hardly be viewed as a heading or introduction, and certainly not of a treaty text.

How then must we explain the phenomena signaled in Leviticus 17–26, which strongly lead us to think of a covenant document?

When we reported in our commentary on Exodus the astonishing discovery achieved by scholars in connection with comparing excavated treaty documents (Assyrian and Hittite) with some parts of Holy Scripture, we mentioned the name of Professor Albright, universally respected as an expert in the ancient history and languages of the world of the ancient Near East, and we took special note of the widespread recognition of this scholar's adoption of the results of the investigation conducted by his students Mendenhall and Wiseman Jr., that until that time he had devoted too little attention to the place of the covenant in Israel's religious and political life. This investigation has subsequently been continued by others. We mentioned the name of Professor Meredith Kline. Now we could add the names of others in whose writings mention is made of the highly remarkable fact, which each person discovered independently of others, that we should speak not only of a certain influence of standard official covenant language around Israel upon such portions of Scripture as we enumerated (Exod 19:3–6; Exod 20; Josh 24), but also upon other parts of the Old Testament, e.g., the prophecies of Jeremiah and Ezekiel, indeed, that this influence can also be identified in certain Jewish writings discovered years later in the caves of Qumran, as well as in the literary form and content of the so-called Epistle of Barnabas, the Didache, and other early-Christian literature.

The covenant treaty practice appears to have left its traces all over. Covenant treaty language seems to have been universal.

Seeing this widespread influence of covenant ideas and covenant formulae, we need not be especially surprised by the phenomena in the book of Leviticus that we alluded to earlier, although the content of them came into existence quite sooner than a number of other biblical and extra-biblical writings mentioned above. For the Horeb covenant had been established shortly before. This Horeb covenant was the foundation beneath the commands and ordinances that constitute the content of Leviticus. No wonder, when we constantly hear the echoes of the covenant resonating in them. Just as that clearly happened with the teaching of the sin offering (Lev 4:1–5:13). And in chapters 11–15, dealing with the purity laws. And in the chapter dealing with the Great Day of Atonement. "You, paganism, and you, world of devils, keep your hands off my Israel!" Well, the same is true of Leviticus 17–26.

There is something else.

In Leviticus 17–26 we will see in addition the Israelite priesthood functioning once again. That was to be expected. The basis of the Horeb covenant was laid (Exodus). The sacrificial Torah and the priesthood, the purity laws and the Great Day of Atonement, had received their place (Leviticus). Later those two—covenant and priesthood—would function regularly in each other's company. Hereby the lesson of the epistle to the Hebrews addresses us even more clearly, namely, that the Horeb covenant (with its consequences for Israel's entire life; cultic, sexual, social life, etc.) even "rested" on the priesthood.

2. THEME AND OUTLINE OF LEVITICUS 17

This chapter consists of four or five sections. You can see this immediately when you take the trouble of underlining with a pencil the word "any one." Still better would be to underline, verse 3, "*any one of the house of Israel,*" in verse 8, "*any one of the house of Israel,*" in verse 10, "*any one of the house of Israel,*" in verse 13, "*any one of the people of Israel,*" and in verse 15, "*every person.*"

A single line runs through all these sections. The main subject is "blood" and the common rubric covering all these sections is the warning to be careful with blood.

We wish to draw the attention of our readers to the fact that all of these sections are dealing with *clean* animals. Unclean animals were dealt with earlier (our chapter 16 above). But these clean animals could be the kind that could, or could not, come into play with the sacrifices. By way of summary, we will use the (less attractive) phrase: suitable for sacrifice. All animals that were clean and could thus be eaten as food, were not thereby suitable for sacrifice. Oxen, sheep, and goats were clean and suitable for sacrifice. Deer and antelope were clean, but not suitable for sacrifice. Doves were clean and suitable for sacrifice. Partridges and quail were clean, but not suitable for sacrifice. Here is an overview:

	animals	
unclean	clean	
	suitable for sacrifice	not suitable for sacrifice

The reason God gave his ancient church the warning to be careful with blood will not be difficult for our readers to grasp if they are acquainted with the preceding chapters. Blood signifies death. Even though God himself wanted to make special use of blood and death—in order thereby to cover (symbolically) sins and sinners before his face—nonetheless, indeed, precisely all the more, Israel was supposed to abstain from every use of blood that was not scrupulously prescribed and permitted. For death did not fit with Israel. Death fit with pagans and devils. But Israel was the people of life.

The brief content of our chapter can be described this way.

The warning arising in all the sections is this: *Be careful for defilement with blood.* And the occasions when this defilement could occur are the following:

A. Lev 17:1–7: Idolatrous practices connected with slaughtering livestock

B. Lev 17:8–9: Self-directed sacrifices to Yahweh

C. Lev 17:10–12: Consumption of clean domestic animals suitable for sacrifice

D. Lev 17:13–14: Consumption of clean animals unsuitable for sacrifice

E. Lev 17:15–16: Consumption of clean animals suitable and unsuitable for sacrifice that are not properly exsanguinated

A. *Be careful for defilement with blood through idolatrous practices connected with slaughtering livestock (Lev 17:1–7)*

This heading will surprise many.

If only for this reason: many suppose that during Israel's stay at Horeb, there would not have been much talk about slaughtering animals. Did not God have to sustain his church in the desert by means of the daily manna miracle?

That is true. But we must not forget that on her trek from Egypt to Canaan, Israel did keep herds of oxen, flocks of sheep and goats, for which she would have procured food in various oases. When God appeared for the first time to Moses at Horeb, he was busy tending the flock of his father-in-law Jethro (Exod 3:1). So that scenario was possible.

But in addition, the warning against idolatrous practices would have generated among the Israelites at Horeb even greater amazement, because people had perhaps expected that a people so richly blessed would surely not quickly have been guilty of the sin of idolatry, and surely not in the days of "Horeb," the time to which we are transported by the content of Leviticus.

There is no reason to be surprised. On the contrary, even though Scripture does not speak often or extensively about it, Scripture gives us sufficient indication that not only did Israel commit idolatry during her stay in Egypt (Josh 24:14; Ezek 16:26; 20:7–8; 23:19),[2] but did the same on her travels from Egypt to Canaan (Deut 32:17; Jer 22:21; Amos 5:26; Acts 7:43). The view does appear worthy of commendation, as far as the time in the desert is concerned, not to think of pure idolatry, honoring another god than Yahweh, but of idolatrous manners, actions, gestures of a pagan derivation. These would have borne a particularly sensual character. As we have narrated earlier, people in the populated world surrounding Israel were pervasively guilty of worshiping fertility gods and goddesses.[3] This inherently included various sexual practices along with the use of sexual objects, whereby male and female genitalia were portrayed with more or less clarity. So then, such practices seem to have arisen among Israel as well, after her departure from Egypt, during the stay at Horeb. This was especially true when it happened once, though by way of exception, that people slaughtered for their own food an ox, sheep, or goat, and they seem to have thought such actions should not be omitted. Well, those filthy practices had to be eliminated. To put an end to them, God commanded Moses that the Israelites were no longer allowed to slaughter animals at just any place that they chose for themselves, but exclusively at the tabernacle. Then such an animal *would have to be sacrificed to him*. This explains why a priest had to be involved and the command was given: Speak to *Aaron and his sons* and to all the Israelites (17:2). Still, such an animal would not need to have been slaughtered as a burnt offering, of which, as we know, no one was to use any part, nor as a sin offering or guilt offering, of which only the priests were allowed to use some part, but as a peace offering. Of this sacrifice, the fat had to be burned for Yahweh on the altar. Presumably the priests also had obtained their share of this, though that fact is not included. But then enough was left over for the person who wanted to slaughter the animal for personal use. With this, the purpose would have been achieved, expressed

---

2. See Vonk, *Exodus*, 247–48, about the mirrors of the women.
3. See Vonk, *Exodus*, 106–108, 113–119.

this way in Lev 17:7a: "*So they shall no more sacrifice their sacrifices to goat demons [se'irim], after whom they whored.*" The Hebrew word for "goat demons" referred to objects in which people could see a representation of male and female sexual organs, such as a staff for the male organ and a vase or jar for the female organ.

We read further in 17:7b: "*This shall be a statute forever for them throughout their generations.*" Literally we read that it would have to be an "eternal" statute. But this word for "eternal" is not to be understood in the sense in which some people take it. In Scripture, "eternal" can often mean "very long time," but need not always mean "unendingly long." The statute under discussion here was suspended later. At least partially. Naturally not the prohibition it contained, namely, that with the slaughtering of an animal, pagan indecencies were not to occur. But the command was suspended, namely, that a person was not allowed to slaughter an animal unless it happened at the tabernacle. This could not be observed, of course, when they entered Canaan later. This explains why Moses later suspended this command, when Israel stood at the entrance to Canaan (Deut 12). We need to keep this in mind as we read Lev 7:22–27.

From this we learn that today as well, God cannot be pleased if we mix pagan ideas into our thinking and talking about him. For example, if we declare a few Scripture truths about him but sprinkle among them pagan inventions, like a god who looks down upon us from on high as one who is so unmoved that he could never experience sadness, or a god with whom some specially privileged persons would taste such intimate fellowship—even for a few moments, in those fleeting moments—that they would end up merging with the deity. Our service of the God and Father of our Lord Jesus Christ today may not be paired with such abhorrent paganism. Such admixture was charged against Israel as being defiled with blood, with death, with paganism, and with the devil. On such a transgressor there rested "bloodguilt," which means: he had to be put to death. This often happened by means of stoning. A terrible death. But that was the fault of the person himself (Josh 2:19; 1 Kgs 2:37), not of those who carried out the sentence. They remained clean.

B. *Be careful for defilement with blood through self-directed sacrifices to Yahweh (Lev 17:8–9)*

People are familiar with the distinction between transgressing the First Commandment, the first of the Ten Words of the covenant, and transgressing

BE CAREFUL WITH THE BLOOD! (LEV 17)

the Second Commandment. The first involves idolatry, and the preceding section dealt with that. No pagan admixture.

But if someone in the Israelite camp, whether Israelite or sojourner, honestly desired to bring Yahweh a sacrifice, out of respect toward him (a burnt offering), for example, or out of love and gratitude toward him (a peace offering), he was from this time onward no longer free to do this at just any place that he himself might select. Earlier that was permitted. But from now on, all sacrifices would have to be offered in the forecourt of the tabernacle.

In view of the context in which this brief section appears, its warning had the same direction as the preceding warning. Even though it was not warning directly against idolatry, we know from the subsequent history of Israel how easily the self-directed worship of Yahweh by Jeroboam could lead to the sheer idolatry of Ahab and Jezebel. It is also remarkable that the *sojourner* who was living among Israel was also included with the warning. In view here is not someone who was passing through Israel (the *nokri*), like a merchant, but someone who had taken up permanent residence and with whom people could be engaged more or less intimately (the *ger*). How easy it was for some with good intentions to mix something from paganism into the worship of Yahweh, and drag along this wrong pathway one or another Israelite. Such a danger of slipping away into paganism and death had to be prevented. Here we observe again the love-filled fatherly care that God exercised toward his ancient church, and we learn today that we must with hearty purpose remain faithful to the Lord (Jesus Christ) (Acts 11:23), who has saved us formerly from paganism. No carelessness. No weird, strange, unbiblical words about God, in books, conversations, and prayers. Rather we must talk about God and his worship as much as possible in a biblical manner. For self-directed piety is like a slippery slope. It leads a person from bad to worse. Scripture and experience teach that many descendants especially of self-directed religious people are eventually estranged from the worship of God.

C. *Be careful for defilement with blood through consuming clean domestic animals suitable for sacrifice (Lev 17:10–12)*

We have discussed this section earlier, at such length and so extensively that at this point we would hardly dare to add another word, if at that point we were not dealing with something that, no matter how important it was, was brought to remembrance here by God to the Israelites *only incidentally*. That had to do with the glorious ministry for which God had laid claim to the blood of clean animals suitable for sacrifice, namely, in order with that blood "to cover your souls." At that time, we mentioned Lev 17:11 as the key to the teaching regarding bloody sacrifice, and learned from it how necessary it is to hold on with might and mane *to the confession of the complete death of our Savior*. If we would not do that, we would not only be minimizing the work of our Savior, but also—and this would be even worse—the love of God our Father, who conceived of such a sacrifice for our sins and gave it to us, namely, the true and real death of one no less that his own Son. For Christ did not make God gracious for the first time, but he himself is a gift of God's grace and compassion for the covering, that is, the atonement, of our sins.

Even though that was a subordinate matter, at least in the argument of this little section, we can always learn from it *why* Yahweh was interested in specifying this further here. He definitely did not want his people to be defiled with death. That did not suit Israel. Blood signified death. Even though it was the blood of animals that may have been ever so clean and suitable for sacrifice.

From this little section we can see how incorrect it is for someone to write: "Because the life comes from God and belongs to God, it follows from this that the blood is holy, i.e., reserved unto God, and reconciling with God." In our opinion, here people are not distinguishing carefully enough. It is entirely untrue that all blood was holy. That was the case only with some blood, namely, with what was received by God in his sacred service, something that hardly occurred with all blood. Given that position, it would be far more correct to say that all blood was unholy. But it is better to say that Israel had to abstain from every defilement through blood, even through blood of slaughtered clean animals suitable for sacrifice, because all bloodshed naturally involved death. And in various ways, God impressed upon his ancient people that he had elevated them to be his covenant people, high above all paganism, where death and the devil exercised dominion. This chapter also occupies its own place in the great totality of the Torah, in which the gospel of resurrection of the flesh and eternal life was preached and certified through visual instruction.

Naturally, the eating of blood was the most offensive manner of defiling oneself with blood. Moreover, the sojourner (*ger*) was also included with this prohibition. Earlier we mentioned something about pagan customs in this respect. But by mentioning the most offensive, God certainly intended to provide the best possible clarity in connection with his warning against every defilement with blood. For blood signified death. Just how terrible that death was Israel could learn from the sacrificial Torah. By means of nothing less that the shedding of blood, that is, through death, soul for soul, could Israel's sins be covered, i.e., atoned. We know now that this visual instruction of the Law eventuated in the bitter and shameful—and complete!—death of God's Son on the cross. Let us not take anything away from that.

D. Be careful for defilement with blood through consuming clean animals unsuitable for sacrifice (Lev 17:13–14)

Gradually our chapter comes to speaking about cases that were not related to sacrifices.

According to the custom of the Torah, the most serious form of defilement with blood and death is placed first, namely, defilement through pagan usages in connection with slaughtering, practices that had an idolatrous character (vv. 1–7).

Next, *self-directed* sacrificial methods were prohibited. Those could easily lead and seduce people to paganism (vv. 8–9).

Next, consuming blood was forbidden, obviously (in view of what follows in vv. 13–14) on the occasion of consuming clean animals suitable for sacrifice (ox, sheep, or goat). That meant once again: no paganism!

But the case could arise where one shot a clean animal while hunting. A deer or a partridge. This kind of animal was then not suitable for sacrifice. But it was allowed to be used. There was no objection against that. At least, as long as one had allowed the animal to bleed out. Thus, if one allowed no blood to remain in the meat. Indeed, one was supposed to cover that blood with dirt. Then all consuming of that blood would certainly have been excluded. Notice that here again, the sojourner (*ger*) is included. Someone who lived among Israel, but remained a Gentile. We know how some Gentiles were accustomed to using the blood. That practice could easily be transferred to Israel. Perhaps something like this is reported to us in 1 Sam 14:32 (some soldiers of Saul ate the slaughtered animals "with blood and all"; that could have been done by a non-Israelite contingent among Saul's troops).[4]

---

4. Regarding such Hebrews, see Vonk, *Genesis*, 191.

E. *Be careful for defilement with blood through consuming clean animals that were suitable or unsuitable for sacrifice that are not properly exsanguinated (Lev 17:15–16)*

If we're not careful, we could encounter difficulties with the last section of this chapter, even though it is rather straightforward. It assumes the possibility that somewhere a clean animal died naturally or was killed by another animal, mauled, like a sheep by a lion or bear. How long ago? Was its blood drained out? Surely not, if it died naturally. The owner of the dead animal discovers it. What can be done now?

If he is an Israelite who fervently desires to maintain the ideal that Yahweh had provided his people at Horeb in the so-called Book of the Covenant (Exod 20:22–23:33), then he will not trouble himself any further with the dead animal. The (wild) dogs may eat it (Exod 22:31). No death was to be among Israel.

But if he is not that kind of Israelite, and thinks it is wrong and unfortunate that the animal would not be eaten by him, then the matter is different. He would not leave the animal to the dogs, but eat the animal himself. In that case, there is no mention of the fact that such a person would be culpable according to the Law. No. He was, however, unclean for one day. That had been stipulated already in Lev 11:39–40. And in the last two verses of Leviticus 17 it is stipulated that such a person, whether Israelite or sojourner (*ger*), had to bathe in water. Only if he neglected this would he "bear his iniquity."

Up to this point, no one need have any difficulty with this concluding section of Leviticus 17. Here as well, we have heard the voice of the gospel of the Law, whereby Israel was taught to remember that she had to be elevated by God above the level of the Gentiles, i.e., above death and the devil, because at Horeb Israel had been accepted as God's holy covenant people. Something that brought with it serious obligations. But in the last section we saw as well that Yahweh was not being more strict than necessary. For there happened to be stupid and insensitive people. Those people would also have belonged to the church in the wilderness. So stupid that they did not understand God's ideal: "no eating of carrion is suitable for members of my holy people." So insensitive that they out of avarice they would rather eat carrion than do what Yahweh had fixed as the ideal: "no blood, no carrion, no death among my Israel." But fine, if they nonetheless had eaten carrion, they at least had to bathe with water and be unclean until evening. Such people would not be allowed, for example, to participate in the meal of the peace offering. If they won't listen, then they'd better feel it.

BE CAREFUL WITH THE BLOOD! (LEV 17)

If we recognize the difference between the ideal and the real, then we will have no trouble seeing a particular passage in Deuteronomy as agreeing with the texts just mentioned (Exod 22:31; Lev 11:39–40; and Lev 17:15). We are referring to Deut 14:21, which says: "You shall not eat anything that has died naturally. You may give it to the sojourner who is within your towns, that he may eat it, or you may sell it to a foreigner. For you are a people holy to the Lord your God."

Is there a contradiction here?

Reformed Old Testament scholar B. Holwerda thought that the stipulation of Deuteronomy 14 is "broader" and this feature "was related to the fact that Deuteronomy was given with a view toward settled life in Palestine, whereas Exodus was directed primarily to the desert travels. As long as the people were nomadic, they had no *nokri* dwelling among them temporarily. The fact that the distinction between *ger* and *nokri* is very emphatic here emerges clearly from the difference between *natan* and *makar* (give and sell). The *ger* is someone involved with Israel, someone who has sought refuge among Israel, the displacedt person; the *nokri*, by contrast, is a foreigner who was passing through Israel temporarily." The *ger* was involved with Israel "in an entirely different relationship than the *nokri*. He belongs (cf. 10:18) to the category of the destitute and distressed, dependent on compassion, just like the widows and orphans." "Israel is obligated to have the *ger* share its various benefits of God's covenant (Sabbath rest, profiting from the triennial tithes, etc.)."

> The *ger* was subject to Israel's legislation, so to speak, in a negative sense: he might not commit any abominations whereby he would injure the God who has loaned him protection; he was not obligated to the positive worship of Yahweh, even though he enjoyed the profit of that worship. Therefore he was also permitted to eat carrion, and people had to provide it as a gift, on account of his destitute circumstances. But if he took it, then he would thereby be levitically unclean, so that, for example, he could not share in a sacrificial meal. The *nokri*, who was and remained a foreigner, and as such needed no protection as an indigent person (these people were traveling merchants, etc.), did not share the privileges of the *ger*: so they could pay for this meat. But Israel herself had to abstain from it.[5]

We too would look for the solution in this direction, but we would include at the same time Lev 11:40 and 17:15. Moreover, we would prefer

---

5. Holwerda, *Voordrachten*, 359.

not to speak of more or less "room" in connection with the desert travel or settled life in Canaan, but speak of a divine ideal and human behaviors.

It would have been ideal if no one in Israel had become involved with animal carrion, not even of clean animals. God had declared this ideal immediately at Horeb, and it was written down by Moses in the so-called Book of the Covenant (Exod 22:31). Throw such carrion to the dogs. Moses posited this same ideal in Deut 14:21. "You shall not eat anything that had died naturally. . . . For you are a people holy to the Lord your God." But because not everyone understood and practiced this ideal, God stipulated in Lev 11:39–40 and 17:15–16 the minimum that had to happen if a person did eat carrion. Unclean for the entire day. And bathe. We must remember: the Law was given by God as a pedagogue, for those lagging behind as well. Therefore, that was so in character for God, that patience with "the hardness of hearts." Just as with divorce, God actually had not wanted them at all. But if they occurred, at least a certificate of divorce was required. Now then, that same character, as far as possible, is what Moses was disclosing, when in Deuteronomy 14 he repeated the ideal with a view to living later in Canaan (members of the holy people of Yahweh, do not eat carrion!), but with an eye to the unfortunate and expected "hardness of hearts," he added: But if you lack the faith and love so that you throw it to the dogs, at least don't eat it yourselves, please—although that possibility was also considered in Leviticus 11 and 17—but leave it to the Gentiles; give it as a gift to the *ger* or sell it to the *nokri*. That's where death belongs. But not among Israel.

What, then, is the lesson for us?

By means of the commands contained in this chapter, God wanted to warn his ancient church against slipping from the high plane of life on which he had placed Israel at Horeb, slipping into the abyss of paganism and corruption. He no longer uses entirely the same means today with respect to the *Christian* church. (The friendly request of the Jerusalem church and the Lord's apostles, made to the brothers from the Gentiles, that they abstain from things that their fellow Christians from the Jews found reprehensible, was in force only for a short time. That was simply a regulation pertaining to a time of transition, not a command for all time.) Despite this being the case, these commands of Leviticus have not thereby lost all significance for us.

On the contrary, with this, it is just like with all the commandments of the Torah, for example, with the well-known Ten Words of the Horeb covenant. Even though in due course we would need to keep in mind as we explained them that they were given at a *particular* time to a *particular* people, and that they apply differently for us than for Israel, they apply no less for us, but even more, namely, as much more as the level of the covenant upon which they are placed lies higher than that on which Israel was placed at Horeb, namely, the level of the new and better covenant, of which Jesus had become the Surety. That covenant is not annulled. But for that reason, Christianity must be warned much more seriously than Israel was by means of a chapter like Leviticus 17; warned against falling back into paganism, for example, into pagan notions about God and about human beings. Despite this, how sad the history of Christianity has been on this score. In terms of the usual line of God's actions: Those who honor me I will honor, but those who reproach me will be esteemed lightly (1 Sam 2:30; Rom 1:28). The centuries-long pagan theologizing and philosophizing by Christians about God and about humanity[6] is being followed today by a period of godlessness and ungodliness, of atheism and perversion, that makes us shudder more each day for God's judgment.

There you see the penetrating preaching of Leviticus 17 for today. For a Christianity that had caused even far greater pain to the Spirit of God than the ancient people (Isa 63:10). The Spirit, who had immersed numerous nations in his evangelical bath (Eph 5:26). But people occupied themselves with all kinds of pagan prattle about their self-made god and about the "soul," that they had scarcely any time left for God's oldest textbook, his Torah. Including no time for Leviticus 17. Especially not for its flaming letters: No paganism any more!

In connection with the following chapters of Leviticus 18–20, the reader needs to be thinking along the same lines. No pagan perversion! We are stating this now already. These chapters make us shudder. For if at the end, we come to Leviticus 26, with its severe punishments threatened against Israel in cases where she despises God's Horeb covenant, who today would not be shocked, at least like king Josiah in 2 Kings 22, when we read in Heb 10:29: "How much worse punishment, do you think, will be deserved by the one who has trampled underfoot the Son of God, and has profaned the blood of the covenant by which he was sanctified, and has outraged the Spirit of grace?" Think as well of Peter's warning against false teachers who slip in those corrupting heresies, denying even the Lord who bought them, bringing upon themselves sudden destruction. Many will follow their licentiousness (2 Pet 2:1–2). With a view toward such a regression of Christians back to paganism, the apostle wrote: "What the true proverb says has happened to them: 'The dog returns to its own vomit, and the sow, after washing herself, returns to wallow in the mire'" (2:22). Oh, what is still coming our way!

---

6. On this, see Vonk, Genesis, 160–68.

22

No pagan lifestyle! (Lev 18–20)

OVERVIEW

Leviticus 18, 19, and 20 are three chapters that clearly belong together. That will appear not only from our discussion, but from our initial glance at the material. You need only compare the beginning and conclusion of Leviticus 18 and 19. In *both* of those chapters there is reference to certain "statutes and rules" of Yahweh (18:4–5; 19:37). The Israelites were supposed to observe them. But if they didn't? Then punishment would follow. Especially the third of these chapters discusses those punishments (Lev 20).

THE ANCIENT SONG WITH A NEW MELODY

In this portion of Scripture, issues will be treated that have the capacity to attract the attention even of people who find our Bible to be the most boring book in the world. We read here about forbidden marriages, and incest, and bestiality, sodomy, etc. These are choice morsels for a public driven by sensational subjects.

But to serious Bible readers we would offer advice in advance not to expect that they will be finding some tidbit or other that is shockingly new. On the contrary. The scope of this portion of Scripture is still the same as that of the chapters dealing with the teaching about the sin offering, leprosy, the food laws, the Great Day of Atonement, etc. *Here as well Israel is being warned against the danger represented by the paganism surrounding her.* When at Horeb the foundation of the (Israelite) world occurred, Yahweh

NO PAGAN LIFESTYLE! (LEV 18-20)

said to the Israelites: "And now you must never leave this high plane of living to which I have elevated you. For then you will tumble over the precipice of paganism and destruction. Abide with me, in the sphere and in the teaching of my Sinai covenant." God gave this warning to his ancient people at that time in many ways, as we have seen. He even used means that were extremely striking. For example, the distinction between clean and unclean foods was familiar to Gentiles as well. Among some Asiatics not only the mother of a newborn baby was viewed as unclean, but the entire family and house. Among the Persians a woman who had given birth was isolated for forty days, and among them, an involuntary nocturnal emission was also viewed as a cause of uncleanness. According to Herodotus, the Babylonians and Assyrians thought the same way about concubinage. So we have seen in what we have already studied that God even used things about which it is undeniable that similar practices appear among the pagans of antiquity, and he used these in connection with his visual instruction of Israel. In order to instruct his people constantly, even during the night, about his exalted noble character.

At least that was the chief purpose. A subordinate goal could have been to render such pagan parallels harmless for Israel by filling them with an entirely different content. But in all those ways, the lesson was impressed upon Israel that Israel was the people of Yahweh. Not pagan, but holy.

Achieving that same objective lies behind the laws of Leviticus 18-20. Except, they function largely in a different way. They too warn against the same danger of paganism, but for that, they use less the means of visual instruction, of symbols (compare Lev 11:44-45, for example, where we find symbolism, and Lev 19:2, where we find none). The song is certainly the same, but the melody sounds different. The tone here is often more direct. You can hear this already in the *introduction*. Israelites, you come from Egypt and you go to Canaan. Be careful: "You shall not do as people in the land of Canaan do" (18:3).

LEVITICUS 18

Nobility required (Lev 18:1-5)

We are calling Lev 18:1-5 the introduction. There we are immediately informed about God's intention with his commands in this portion of Scripture.

These commandments are addressed to "the Israelites" (18:2). Not to the priests, as in 17:2, in order to keep an eye on the slaughtering of livestock for food. In what follows, we will hardly hear anything about cultic matters. Human living involves more than our relationship with God. We are also related to people, wife, children, neighbors, and . . . animals.

Yahweh had the right to lay claim to every sphere of Israelite life, more than one right. First, he was allowed to stipulate the law among Israel because he had delivered Israel from Egypt. That right rested upon his *tsidqoth*, his "righteous deeds," his saving acts. Still another right flowed from his subsequent establishing of a covenant at Horeb. This explains why at Horeb, God introduced his Ten Words with the prologue: "I am Yahweh your God, who brought you out of the land of Egypt, out of the house of slavery" (Exod 20:2). So then, in this introduction an appeal is made to this with the formula: "I am Yahweh your God." We could translate that differently: "I, Yahweh, am your God." This translation better expresses the fact that Israel may not for a moment give any credence to the notion that Yahweh is an *elohim*, a god, like the other gods." In addition, if we recall in this connection that the rule applied everywhere: "as the people, so the god," then we must in any case, seeing what follows, hear already in these *very first words* of Yahweh a strong prohibition addressed to the Israelites against turning their life into the kind of abominable mess like the Gentiles, specifically, the Canaanites did. For the situation was supposed to be: As God, so the people! As Yahweh, so Israel. Be holy, for I am holy. I have an aversion to that filthy Canaanite mess. (We must remember that this, among other reasons, is why God had delivered Israel from Egypt, because the measure of unrighteousness of the Canaanites had meanwhile become full (Gen 15:16). But we will say more about this in connection with the book of Numbers.)

Already the introduction is anti-Canaanite.

It transports us in our thoughts to Horeb, where Israel is standing *between Egypt and Canaan*.

Now, in the previous chapter, Israel's conduct in Egypt was discussed. Scripture does not tell us very much, but enough to draw the conclusion that Israel had not remained pure while in Egypt.

Now Israel's face was turned toward *Canaan*. Within a short time, Israel would be able to enter the promised land. An entirely different land than Egypt, and with an entirely different population, but with a religion and therefore with a society that was no less perverse than those of Egypt. We have written about this earlier, when we discussed the so-called Book of the Covenant (Exod 20:22–23:33), that was read aloud by Moses to the people before the establishment of the covenant was completed. A land from where the aroma of death blew out to meet Israel. For death exists not only where a person is murdered, but also where sexual immorality, sodomy, and bestiality provide the atmosphere. And that happened in Canaan.

NO PAGAN LIFESTYLE! (LEV 18–20)

From ancient times it has been known from both biblical and extra-biblical reports. The latter sources have become more numerous in our day. In a word, it must have been gross.

In this reprehensibly filthy Canaan, Israel would now have to hold high his name and status. People of Yahweh! Not a God like other gods, but he is holy. Full of inner aversions against all those kinds of death in human society, including the death of sexual unchastity. If a father has sexual relations with his daughter, or a person uses an animal for that purpose, does that not actually mean the same thing as disgusting death?

So this introduction is anti-Canaanite! Although, seeing that the people groups of Canaan had been related in a variety of ways to those of the Near East, one could also say that in the following chapters, Israel was being warned indirectly against the dangers of infection that threatened them from their even wider environment. For example, one could identify this warning given in Leviticus 18–20 as being anti-Hittite and anti-Babylonian as well.

Indeed, just so we don't deduce from this line of reasoning, however, the claim that according to this portion of Scripture, there was absolutely nothing good among such nations as the Babylonians and the Hittites. For then we would raise our eyebrows in surprise later. Some stipulations in Leviticus 18–20 (to say nothing of other passages of Holy Scripture) appear to have been virtually cited from Babylonian and Hittite law books. The relationship between the covenant book of Moses and the Code of Hammurabi, between ancient Near Eastern jurisprudence and biblical jurisprudence, marriage, and other matters. Such similar kinds of stipulations circulated and were enforced throughout the world surrounding the patriarchs and their descendants.

How was this possible? That we can find so much good in Babylonian and Hittite law codes that reminds us of Leviticus 18–20?

We provided something of an answer to this question in our commentary on Exodus, under the heading, "The Great Annexation."[1] The power of the tradition of special verbal revelation has been so unspeakably great, from the earliest times until today, that no nation has ever existed without a certain kind of knowledge of God and his commandments, even though such knowledge was more or less defective. This explains why everywhere we find not only various forms of religion, in which, alongside much that is nonsense we nonetheless find something of value, but also various civil law codes, about which the same can be said. Anyone who does nothing but criticize the work of governments that demonstrate nothing other than

---

1. Vonk, *Exodus*, 293–304.

the same Christian faith he possesses, and refuses to look for what can be appreciated to some extent, does not find Scripture agreeing with him. Consider, for example, Leviticus 18–20. These chapters prove the truth of our earlier statement, that at Horeb God did not lay upon his ancient covenant people hitherto unknown novelties, notions that were part of no other religions. This pertains to both commands and prohibitions regarding sexual life. In fact, how else would Israel have understood God's intention?

With this, we have touched upon another subject.

Perhaps many Bible readers have been surprised that some things that, according to contemporary Christian standards, are impermissible, like slavery and polygamy (a man having more than one wife), are not explicitly forbidden but tolerated in Scripture, in the Old Testament.

Was such surprise fair, however?

With respect to these issues, we reject the dogma of evolutionism,[2] as though not only the religion of Israel would have arisen gradually from lower pagan religions, but in the same manner also the morality of Israel, indeed, of the Christian church. We do not believe that at all. Both what the church of the old dispensation and of the new dispensation was supposed to believe and to do, was and still is due to *revelation*. Divine revelation, from which the Holy Spirit has given us whatever was necessary to know by putting it in book form in Holy Scripture.

But this belief certainly does not lead us to close our eyes, on the contrary, to a certain kind of *gradualness* that has been used by God throughout the centuries in connection with making known his Word and commandments. Even though, for example, in connection with Abraham's faith in the promising God, nothing new in principle was added, whereby we today would not be able to stand along with him in the unity of true faith, nonetheless, Abraham never knew the name of Jesus Christ, and did not know as much as we do about God's work of redeeming humanity. The history of divine revelation has its periods and eras (Gal 4:4). This applies as well to what it tells us about God's will for human behavior. Abraham was married to his half-sister (Gen 20:12). But in Lev 18:8 entering such marriages was absolutely forbidden to Israel. That was a step in the direction of what we today find obvious. But whereas it is absolutely impermissible in terms of Christian standards for a man to be married to more than one wife at the same time, in the time of Horeb it was not yet absolutely forbidden. The same is true of slavery, with respect to the New Testament, even though everyone senses that owing to the apostolic preaching, the ancient slavery

---

2. For a discussion of this matter, see Vonk, *Exodus*, 297–304.

NO PAGAN LIFESTYLE! (LEV 18–20)

practices sooner or later had to disappear. But the gospel gradually displaced and dispelled those practices.

We must not be offended by this gradual divine work of restoring our human life with respect, for example, to polygamy and slavery. Rather we should be amazed at God's wisdom. Reformation is not revolution, not destructive but constructive, and building up goes more slowly than breaking down. If someone who is on the top floor of a house wants to get to the ground floor, he can choose the shortest way and *jump* down, but then he'll be giving himself some broken bones. It's better to take the stairs down. The more gradual and slower path.

Unless, of course, there is a fire. In order to postpone immediate death, then we need to act immediately, and to spare his life, that person will need to jump.

In the same way, God explicitly prohibited some things among Israel at the time of Horeb. There was no excuse for these things. In a moment we will learn what those were. Those were not only wrong and blameworthy, but they were dangerous, some of them definitely perverse, intensely bad.

Above all these commandments, with their sometimes very remarkable content, we find this divine statement:

"You shall follow my rules and keep my statutes and walk in them. I am the Lord your God" (v. 4).

One scholar translates the Hebrew word *mishpat* as "pronouncements" and the Hebrew word *chuqqah* as "laws" or "norms." To the degree that a distinction is made between these two Hebrew words, it would have consisted in this, that the latter word refers more to written law, and the former to the action of making a pronouncement (cf. the pronouncements of the Supreme Court, that have judicial import for other cases).

We would do well to understand *chuqqah* to refer to *written laws*, though without forcing the notion of writing. Perhaps the word is etymologically related to the word meaning inscribe, write, and hence pre-scribe. Another scholar associates this with "prescribed mores and customs." The pagan milieu, both in Egypt and in Canaan, would have prescribed these behaviors for people entering their world. "When in Rome, do as the Romans do." People had to adapt to them, for example, in terms of participating in their idolatrous and immoral festivals (cf. Exod 34:15–16). And that is precisely what Yahweh does not want the Israelites doing.

This hint regarding customs and mores seems highly plausible.

In connection with the terms "laws" and "pronouncements," we need not imagine each of the Israelites having a number of clay tablets or papyrus fragments or wooden or copper objects on which various commandments of Yahweh had been written, especially those of Leviticus 18–20. The Torah that did exist and had been fixed in written form would have been preserved by the priests, and from time to time instruction would have been given to the Israelites from this. But among the people over the course of time a certain body of practical knowledge of the will of Yahweh would have arisen. This introduction is placing heavy emphasis on that practical side of the law. Verse 3: "You shall not do as they do in the land of Egypt," which could be translated: "Don't act according to the *practices* of the land of Egypt." The same word is used to refer to *Canaanite practices*, followed then with: you shall not walk in their statutes (*chuqqah*) (v. 3b).

The power of unwritten laws is often greater than that of written laws. Every Christian discovers this when he has to resist the pull of a worldly custom. That can even make us momentarily shy and embarrassed. And then how much better we feel when we are among Christians once again, people whose practices of life are directed by God's Word and commandment. God would have intended such a fixed and fortified climate, when he said: My statutes and my rules (v. 5a; or "my laws and pronouncements").

The introduction to Leviticus 18 (vv. 1–5) ends with a promise. "*If a person does them, he shall live by them: I am the Lord*" (v. 5b).

Oh how this statement has been abused! When later the Jews discovered not one glimmer of God's pure grace in their beloved Torah, Moses' instruction had become for them a large chunk of paganism. It became a price list: by means of so many good works done here, people earned so much enjoyment later in Paradise. This Pharisaic line of thinking apparently became so dominant that virtually every Jew came to believe this as being thoroughly scriptural, to such an extent that Paul could use that to characterize the slavish Judaism of his day. After all, Rom 10:5 ("the person who does the commandments shall live by them") is a citation from Lev 18:5. But note carefully that with this statement, the apostle was not wishing to claim that God had given Israel two ways of salvation, the one being the way of faith, the other, the way of works, but he merely wished to say that the Pharisaic Judaism had allowed itself to turn a well-known passage from Leviticus 18, namely, verse 5b, into a slogan, a motto, for its theory. So they had perverted it into a false motto. (Paul fought against the same battle front in Gal 3:12.)

For the *good and true* meaning of Lev 18:5b ("*if a person does them, he shall live by them*") is quite obvious. These words contain a promise. Not a contract, like that used among merchants—so much for so much—but a covenant promise from a gracious God.

Of course God did not thereby promise that if the Israelites would behave according to the commands that followed, they would be accepted by God as his covenant partners and beneficiaries. (That is, in fact, how

Pharisaism in all its various forms has always thought, in every age.) That could not possibly be the case, however, for they were already God's covenant partners and beneficiaries.

No, the covenant had already been given, but the covenant had to be observed. The happiness of Israel had to be preserved. Not accomplished or achieved, but preserved and maintained. The heirs were being warned not to disinherit themselves. "Abide with me!" God is saying.

And if that happened? Then Israel would have it good with her God Yahweh, in Canaan. Life. Peace.

But if that did not happen, the same terrible punishment would come upon Israel, to which God had pointed Abraham centuries earlier as the future punishment awaiting the Canaanites (Gen 15:16), concerning which such dreadful things are stated here in Lev 18:24 and following. Then God would see to it that the land of Canaan would in turn spit out the Israelites, just as Israel would soon spit out and vomit and puke out the Canaanites, when Israel entered Canaan. For Israel, that would not mean *shalom*, peace and life, but defeat, destruction, and death. (This is indeed what happened later, with the captivities.)

People should interpret the words of Lev 18:5b, then, in terms of their own context here. Then you will hear the sound of *covenant blessing*, over against the covenant curse, which is what Leviticus 26 discusses further.

No incest among Israel (Lev 18:6)

People understand *incest* to mean sexual relations between close blood relatives. Incest was practiced in Egypt as well as in Canaan.

Regarding Egypt, the pharaohs lived in the illusion that they were gods. To preserve this level of divinity, some pharaohs married . . . their sisters. Their full sisters. Apparently the royal example incited the people to follow suit, so that it was not at all unusual for a young man to marry his sister. It seems that the Egyptians had no clue about what we call "incest." In their eyes, an incestuous relationship like that between father and daughter was not immoral.

Regarding Canaan's immorality, we have discussed this several times already. In this land, as in the entire ancient Near East, religion seemed in large measure to have borne the character of a fertility religion, that is, fertility played a large role in religious practices. This is understandable. For without progeny, the race would not survive. Especially true was that without sons, there was no masculine strength, no soldiers, no laborers, and no successors. This explains not only the presence of polygamy in Canaan, but also the phenomenon of "sacred marriage," whereby people thought they could stimulate the deity, represented by her temple personnel (priests and priestesses, as well as male and female "consecrated one," the well-known boy and girl prostitutes), to bless womb and soil with fertility. In addition to the disgraces committed in the temples, among the Canaanites there was also sexual relations between close blood relatives, something hardly avoidable given the fact that their gods provided them an example of such behavior. Their god El was married to his three sisters, Astarte, Asherah, and Baaltis, whereas the consort of Baal was his sister Anath.

Yahweh the God of Israel was entirely different. Against this background, the command recurring often in this section of Leviticus—"Be holy, for I am holy"—comes to have a very remarkable significance. Yahweh had an aversion to all these forms of filth that simply infected human life so fatally, and therefore he required corresponding conduct from the people that with word and deed he had chosen to be his people (I, Yahweh, am *your* God). Yahweh was holy. What would that have meant concretely?

The fact should strike everyone that the Old Testament nowhere speaks of Yahweh, in contrast to the gods of the nations, in any way that ascribed to him the least trace of sexuality. All the gods of the pagans mentioned in Scripture are male or female, and possess a marriage partner of the opposite gender. But nothing of this is stated about Yahweh. We should think about that when we read that this holy God, Yahweh, who was so completely averse to sexual loathsomeness, nonetheless demonstrated such great patience that in the time of ancient Israel, he tolerated things that today would be absolutely forbidden for us, such as polygamy.

Moreover, we think of the relationships that could arise in a large patriarchal communal Israelite family.

People did not get married as late as do the Europeans in our day, who must first travel everywhere and have furnished their homes fashionably before they reach thirty years old, only then finally to think about getting married. Such modern people have a hard time understanding God speaking in the Second Commandment about punishment to the third and fourth generation (thus, grandchildren and great-grandchildren). People today seldom see this. But in the ancient Near East people married for sure before their twentieth birthday, such that a man could be a grandfather before he was forty, a great-grandfather before he was sixty, and a great-great-grandfather by his eightieth birthday or sooner, and could therefore see *with his own eyes* the blessing or punishment of God's covenant upon his race. Remember that when you read the Second Commandment.

But what if an Israelite man of fifty or sixty years old would marry again? Assume that his new bride was twenty years old. Then he could have

NO PAGAN LIFESTYLE! (LEV 18–20)

had a son of thirty years or older with his first wife, in any case, someone close in age to his second wife. Suppose, however, that the man died shortly after his second marriage. Where would his second wife live, and who would take care of her? Among some nations, the son of the first wife was allowed to marry the widow of his father, at least if his father and second wife had not had any children. We know from our own culture, as well, how in "old-fashioned families," as a result of a sizable age difference between the oldest and youngest children born to one couple, the situation can arise where the children of the oldest child can be significantly older than the youngest brother or sister (a "tail-ender") of their fathers and mothers. Put another way, some uncles and aunts are younger than those who should actually call them by that title. In that situation, how easy it is for a nephew to cast his eye toward his (much younger) aunt, a sister of his father or mother. Such situations could arise in Israel, and as a result of polygamy they would occur far more often than among us. For example, Moses' own father, Amram, was married to his own aunt Jochebed (Exod 6:19).

We should read Lev 18:6 as translated this way: "*No one among you shall have carnal relations with his close blood relative. I am Yahweh.*"

There we see the principial regulation. Later this would be worked out further, though in a manner that was flexible and broad.

No pagan sexual defilement among Israel (Lev 18:7–30)

That outworking occurred in such a practical way that what follows in Leviticus 18 does not go on to list degrees of kinship for permissible marriage. We agree with Reformed Old Testament commentator Noordzij, who observed that Lev 18:6–18 is actually opposing not so much marriages and various kinds of sexual relations. As we know, especially in the Middle Ages, it was widely thought among Christians that Leviticus 18 was the chapter in which God supposedly provided us a list of prohibited *marriages*. But was that correct? Can we say, for example, concerning a prohibition like Lev 18:7—a son shall not have sexual relations with his (own) mother—that such a regulation was prohibiting a marriage? A son could hardly "marry" his mother, could he? He could certainly commit scandalous unchastity. Nor can we speak about a real marriage between a man and one or another woman who belonged to his father. Such a things was forbidden not as an example of a marriage, but it was condemned, to say it in the words of the apostle, "as a kind of sexual immorality that does not arise even among pagans" (1 Cor 5:1, referring to the pagans of Paul's day).

Rather, in the verses immediately following Lev 18:6, God was not forbidding his ancient Israel from entering certain kinds of marriages, but prohibiting frankly certain kinds of *pagan defilement in the sexual arena*. This explains the completely unremarkable transition to something else, when later, for example, in verse 19, sexual intercourse with a menstruating woman was forbidden. And when in verse 20 sexual intercourse was forbidden with the wife of one's neighbor. And when in verse 21 God forbids sacrificing their progeny to Molech.

Those are not marriage regulations. Not stipulations for our civic lawmakers.

Involved here is *pagan defilement in the sexual arena*.

The emphasis here is on *pagan*.

For other defilement in this arena was mentioned earlier. In Leviticus 15. In connection with male emissions and female flowing. At that point, such events that occurred in the sexual arena were used by God to instruct and to assure Israel about them, that Israel was the people of Yahweh and therefore she had to guard against slipping away from the sacred plane of living established with the Horeb covenant. For that purpose, washings were prescribed, and in serious cases, sacrifices. In order simply to impress upon Israel: Watch out for the boundary! Whoever comes close is risking danger. Be careful of the death on the other side, among the Gentiles, outside the covenant between me and you.

But here in Leviticus 18, Yahweh no longer reminds his people by means of symbolic instruction as he points to the Horeb covenant and warns about the boundary between Israel and paganism, but he emphatically observes that in this or that instance of sexual activity, one has already crossed the boundary, and has already entered the territory of paganism and death, and therefore deserves to be exterminated from among Israel. Indeed, should Israel unexpectedly ever become guilty of such pagan sexual defilements, then all of Israel will deserve being treated by Yahweh in the same way that God already now—albeit while speaking to Moses at Horeb—sees the Canaanites being treated in the future.

That is the theme of Leviticus 18. A prohibition of bad things. Of pagan sexual defilements! Which explains why in this chapter, nothing is said about possible purification by means of bathing or offering a sacrifice, as in Leviticus 15. Those were unavailable for the sins being explained here. Anyone guilty of these sins simply had to be *put to death*. Just like a murderer or adulterer. The latter was mentioned in verse 20. The capital punishment for the other sexual abominations mentioned here must have been very common. Whoever committed these sins had forsaken the covenant territory and had fallen into paganism and death.

NO PAGAN LIFESTYLE! (LEV 18–20)

Let's review the entire series.

Leviticus 18:7: an Israelite may not have sexual relations with his mother.

Leviticus 18:8: nor with another wife of his father (like Reuben and Absalom).

Leviticus 18:9: nor with his full sister (as we saw happen in Egypt) or with someone who is the daughter of his mother but who had been born from a marriage with another husband (thus, a half-sister; a sibling from the same mother, but not the same father).

Leviticus 18:10: nor with his granddaughter, whether this child belongs to his son or his daughter.

Leviticus 18:11: nor with the daughter of his father that he had with another wife. With this God prohibited from this time on a marriage like that between Abraham and Sarah, who had the same father but not the same mother (half-brother and half-sister). Seeing the great danger that one things leads to another, for this time on this was not allowed. Let's not forget that Israel was en route to Canaan, the land of perversion.

Leviticus 18:12: nor may anyone have sexual relations with his aunt, the sister of his father. For the same reasons, this too was forbidden any longer.

Leviticus 18:13: nor with his aunt who was the sister of his mother, the same was true.

Leviticus 18:14: nor with his aunt, the wife of his father's brother (naturally, after the death or divorce of the latter).

Leviticus 18:15: nor with his daughter-in-law, the wife of his son.

Leviticus 18:16: nor with his sister-in-law, the wife of his brother (assuming the latter did not die childless, for otherwise the ancient Near Eastern custom of levirate marriage applied, Deut 25:5–10).

Leviticus 18:17: nor with a woman and simultaneously with a daughter or granddaughter born to this woman from a previous marriage.

Leviticus 18:18: nor with a woman and simultaneously with a sister of this woman (thus, as Jacob was married with the sisters, Leah and Rachel).

Leviticus 18:19: nor with a menstruating woman.

Leviticus 18:20: nor with the wife of another Israelite. (One Reformed commentator offers the translation: "And to the woman of your fellow Israelite you shall not give the emission of your seed, so that thereby you become unclean." This translation makes more obvious the transition to the following verse, which also speaks literally about the "giving of seed.")

Leviticus 18:21: nor shall you give of your children (literally, of your seed) to allow them to go through the fire in honor of Molech. In doing this you would defile the name of your God. I am Yahweh.

We need to add three comments.

1. Regarding the name Molech, this would have derived from the Hebrew word for king (*m-l-k*), which was pronounced by the Israelites, out of aversion, with the vowels of the word *bōshet*, shame, so that it came out as *Molech*, but in the Greek of the Septuagint this was *Moloch*.

2. Regarding the *meaning* of this name, even though it would have been obvious that a Semitic people would have given their deity the name *m-l-k* or king—Yahweh also had this name in Scripture frequently—nevertheless in Mesopotamia already in the fourth century BC there was a particular deity with such a name; some theophoric names (i.e., personal names that included the name of a deity) appear in the Amarna tablets, combined with the name of an apparent Canaanite idol *m-l-k*; and in a later times known as the Ammonite Malech and Tyrian city deity Melqart.

3. Regarding the *evil* that is being forbidden here, some defend the view that this was referring to Canaanite child sacrifice (sometimes children were immured as construction sacrifices in the foundations of buildings or burned as firstborn, which explains that in Hebrew there is the idiom of making them pass "through the fire," 2 Kgs 23:10), whereas others are of the opinion that we should not think of actual sacrifices, but of symbolic occasions (where boys and girls were surrendered to the sanctuary for religious prostitution).

Leviticus 18:22: you shall not lie with someone from the human race as a man lies with a woman; it is an abomination.

(Although Scripture elsewhere condemns homosexuality in personal life [Gen 19:5; Judg 19:22-24; Rom 1:27; Jude 7], in view of verse 21, here specifically cultic prostitution of men would have been intended, men devoted to the Phoenician goddess Astarte; probably the same wickedness as Deut 23:17 has in view.)

Leviticus 18:23: you shall not have sexual relations with an animal (here as well, cultic bestiality is being condemned).

(This prohibition is addressed not only to men [probably the god Baal had sexual relations with a heifer before dying], but also to women. This sin occurred in Egypt, where women surrendered themselves in the worship of the goat of Mendes, who was thought to be a living manifestation of various gods.)

Following these verses we have the conclusion in Lev 18:24-30, whereby the intention behind the preceding becomes crystal clear. For there God says: But if Israel nevertheless lives in Canaan like the Canaanites, well, then she will undergo the same fate as they. Don't forget this when you have seen their defeat. That is how I deal with unclean pagans. And I will do the same even if they are Israelites.

NO PAGAN LIFESTYLE! (LEV 18–20)

LEVITICUS 19

Make a separation (Lev 19:1–2)

In a certain sense, Leviticus 18 and 19 are counterparts. In this sense, that the latter chapter deals with the same subject as the former, and similarly warns against a pagan lifestyle, but does so in a different way. That other way becomes evident in two ways. First, Leviticus 19 also contains prohibitions—Leviticus 18 contains nothing but prohibitions—but at the same time also contains commandments that state positively what God does desire from Israel. Moreover, there is also this difference, that whereas Leviticus 18 contains no symbolism, but only prohibitions contained in realistic and direct verbiage, such symbolism does appear in Leviticus 19. But not exclusively. There this chapter is so instructive in making us understand God's purpose with many of his shadowy ordinances for Israel. With and without symbolism, he bound the lesson upon Israel's heart: "You are my covenant people. Continue being so." For this reason, we think it is helpful to formulate the theme of this chapter in terms of a statement of Yahweh that he declared once in connection with distinguishing between clean and unclean animals (see chapter 16) and with which these three chapters, Leviticus 18–20, will be concluded later: *Make a separation* (between clean and unclean livestock, etc.) (Lev 20:25).

Israel would certainly have been obedient to the command when each one dealt faithfully and honestly with his fellow Israelite, but also, for example, when a farmer did not have two kinds of animals breed, and did not sow two kinds of seed in his field, and did not wear clothes made of two different materials. This latter (symbolic) ordinance is found in Leviticus 19, tucked between various other (non-symbolic) commands (v. 19). That was clearly possible. Yahweh's purpose with his symbolism was so striking for Israel, and in Israel's understanding, a symbolic ordinance and a non-symbolic commandment of Yahweh were very closely related.

If we have grasped the purpose of this entire chapter in the right way, then the purpose of both verses with which Leviticus 19 opens can be interpreted in a corresponding manner. These verses state: "And the Lord spoke to Moses, saying, 'Speak to all the congregation of the people of Israel and say to them, *"You shall be holy, for I the Lord your God am holy."*'"

Israel could know what kind of God she had. A God who in many respects detested the reprehensible conduct of Egyptians and Canaanites. Actually he had directly warned against that conduct in his Ten Words that he gave at Horeb (Exod 20). Next, he did so more broadly in his Book of the Covenant (Exod 20–23), then in more numerous (most symbolic) ways. He had just done so in the direct prohibitions of Leviticus 18. In contrast with the unclean Gentiles and their unclean gods, Yahweh was *holy*.

Well then, what else could he desire from the people whom he had honored with his friendship than that they be like him? *Holy* as well!

We automatically think here of a particular command that Paul also stated against a background of warnings against falling back into surrounding paganism: Be imitators of God! (Eph 5:1).

Notice the positive language of God in Leviticus 19. It was not enough to be warned against a dangerous *synthesis* with paganism, nor was it sufficient to be summoned to maintain the constant *antithesis* against paganism. The *thesis* is established here, that Yahweh is holy and Israel's lifestyle had to correspond with that holiness.

But that required *knowledge*. This explains why we read first of a command with the following design.

Abide in what you were taught (Lev 19:3)

This, in our view, is the design of both halves of this verse. The verse reads as follows:

> *Every one of you shall revere his mother and his father,*
> *and you shall keep my Sabbaths: I am the Lord your God.*

If you read these carefully, five features stand out:

1. Verse 3a resembles the Fifth Commandment.
2. Verse 3b resembles the Fourth Commandment.
3. The usual sequence of Commandments four and five is reversed.
4. Moreover, the mother is mentioned before the father here.
5. We read nothing about "Sabbath" (singular), but of "Sabbaths" (plural).

Regarding 1. and 2., we have intentionally said that verse 3a and 3b *resemble* the Fifth and Fourth Commandments. For the view that in Leviticus 19:3–4, 11–12, we are dealing with an abbreviated Decalogue (Ten Commandments), perhaps with a Decalogue in its more primitive form than that of Exod 20:1–17, is easier said than proven. In a rather arbitrary manner, one would need to isolate the intervening verses (5–8 and 9–10), treating them as later additions. But why would they be later additions? They fit very nicely here.

Regarding 3.—that the Fifth Commandment precedes the Fourth here—that difficulty (if indeed it is a difficulty) disappears when we

NO PAGAN LIFESTYLE! (LEV 18–20)

abandon the notion that the intention here was to present a repetition of the two commandments. The view seems far more obvious to us that God first said to Israel: Be holy as I am holy (v. 2); then he said: Therefore observe the teaching about me that you received from your parents (v. 3a); and then: Observe the teaching that I myself gave to you by means of my "Sabbaths" (v. 3b). For to be holy like Yahweh was holy, Israel certainly must have known a few things from her God.

Regarding 4., the fact that the mother is mentioned here before the father has led someone to suppose that here we are dealing not simply with an abbreviated Decalogue, but with a "children's catechism." Others explain the fact from the more intimate relationship that existed in a world of polygamy between mother and child than between father and child. But in our opinion, we need not think of the phenomenon of polygamy at all. Each child in every era is taught first of all by his or her mother. The Israelite children would have received their initial instruction about Yahweh from their mothers. Perhaps we are getting excited about nothing significant. For it could be that one or another scribe made a copyist error. The Hebrew words for "his father" (*abiw*) and "his mother" (*immo*) look very similar, and the Septuagint has the usual sequence (first, "his father," then "his mother"), a fact that should caution us, and could indicate that the usual sequence may well have been in the original Hebrew text. Let's not get excited about nothing.

Finally, we should pay attention to the fact that verse 3b speaks not of "Sabbath" but of "Sabbaths" (plural). We can explain this from the fact that at Horeb, the entire assortment of Israel's feasts (Passover, Pentecost, and Feast of Booths) rested upon the institution of the Sabbath day. By means of this weekly Sabbath, Israel was being continually instructed that no one less than the Creator of heaven and earth had become her Deliverer from Egypt and her Covenant God at Horeb. For the number *seven* recall both the creation (Exod 20:8–11) and the Horeb covenant, of which the Sabbath day was a sign (Exod 31:17). Here already we find a protection against paganism with its idols and its life full of immorality. But to this was added the preaching of the three feasts mentioned above. There were, so to speak, added as embroidery on the pattern of the Sabbath institution, which explains why the words "Sabbaths" in Ezek 44:24 can be used interchangeably with "feasts." We'll say more about this later, when we discuss the Israelite feasts. We have already noted how, already in the so-called Book of the Covenant, as God was pointing to these feasts, he was warning against the Canaanites (see Exod 23:13–33). After Israel's sin with the golden calf, God repeated that warning once again (see Exod 34:10–20).

Surely in Israelite families, the parents would have spoken to their children at a young age about Yahweh and his great works. At least they were supposed to (Exod 12:26; Deut 6:7; 11:19). The children constituted that part of the church that primarily needs instruction. But on the Sabbaths, at those times both old and young were instructed. For on those occasions, a sacred assembly was called (Lev 23:2–3; Num 10:10). Then Israel was instructed by the entire tribe of Levi, and blessed by the priests in the name of Yahweh. Faithful teaching in the Word of God offers the best protection against apostasy and paganism.

If only the Christian church had understood the meaning of Leviticus 19:3. Including the leadership of *parents*. Even before the "Sabbaths." Even the tribe of Levi (otherwise known as the teaching tribe) was not to take over, let alone usurp, the task of fathers and mothers to teach their children. That task was not to be taken away from parents, whether with or without their consent (see our comments on Lev 20:9 below) and handed over and left to schools and other groups. Is it not obvious that every creature provides for his own nest?

The first and great commandment is: Love God with all your heart (Lev 19:4–8)

We can now easily survey the beginning of chapter 19. The train of thought went as follows:

First God established the positive demand that Israel would be like him: holy (19:1–2).

But for that, correct knowledge of God and his commands was needed. Therefore, next came the command to abide in the sphere of father and mother and adhere to the teaching of the Sabbaths (19:3).

Once this basis had been laid, then Israel can be aroused to show her love to Yahweh in three ways.

1. No idols in place of me (19:4a).

2. No images in the worship of me (19:4b).

3. No carelessness at my altars (19:5–8).

1. *"Do not turn to idols."*

Rather than the translation of *idols*, perhaps it would be better to render it as "things of nothing." All those things the pagans trusted in were nothing more than rubbish. Not only did they turn to their idols for help, but they

NO PAGAN LIFESTYLE! (LEV 18–20)

also consulted "the spirits of the dead" and "spirits of divination," as we will read later in Lev 19:31. There the Hebrew uses the same words (for "turn to") as here. Perhaps here we should render them more broadly than, for example, with the First Commandment of Exodus 20 (*elohim*, idol gods), because here we have a Hebrew word with presumably a broader meaning (*elilim*, nothings).

Yahweh is not to be replaced by a *no one* and by a *nothing*.

He tolerates no competitor whatsoever.

2. *"Do not make for yourselves any gods of cast metal: I am the Lord your God."*

After first dealing with each kind of "idolatry," there now follows a prohibition against "image worship." Image worship in honor of whom? Apparently of Yahweh himself. That had already been forbidden in the Second Commandment of Exodus 20, as well as in the beginning of the so-called Book of the Covenant (Exod 20:23). Image worship was the wickedness committed in the episode of the golden calf (Exod 32), and therefore Yahweh warned specifically against it once more with extra emphasis, when he had the tabernacle constructed (Exod 34:10–26). We read in Exod 34:17: "You shall not make for yourself any gods of cast metal," and the same in Lev 19:4b: "You shall not make for yourselves any gods of cast metal." Why are images of deity made only out of metal mentioned here, since they could be made out of wood and stone as well? Presumably because condemnation of the most beautiful and most expensive included condemnation of the less attractive as well (Isa 40:19–20).

Nevertheless, as we know, such images—in honor of Yahweh, the God of Israel!—were later made by Israelites. Recall the episodes of Micah (Judg 17), and Jeroboam (1 Kgs 12:28).

3. *No carelessness at my altars*

So, then, was all paganism completely cut off in connection with the worship of Yahweh?

No, not at all.

Even when Israel did not look upon an *idol*, and did not make either a golden or a silver *image* in honor of Yahweh, Israel could still offend God by carelessness and indifference. Neither of those fits with loyal love. For love does not consist in clumsy, gross manners, but rather has an attentive eye for elegance and correctness.

As a teaching illustration God used the peace offering. Not because it mattered less with the other sacrifices whether they were offered according to the requirement of the Sacrifice Torah, but the peace offering would have been chosen as an illustration because with this kind of sacrifice, the laity played a much greater role than with any other sacrifice. The reader will recall that only the peace offering included a meal, one that included everyone, the one bringing the offering together with family and invited guests. God delighted in the fact that Israel could enjoy a festive meal in his presence. For example, he permitted in connection with that peace offering meal the use of leavened cakes. That fact spoke volumes. Yeast near the sanctuary of Yahweh! He even approved of the people eating from the peace offering animal for longer than a single day. In addition, consider this: at least in the case of a votive offering and a voluntary offering. But that was the outermost boundary, in view of the corrupting climate of Canaan; and perhaps also because the Canaanite pagans had a preference for "gamey meat." Still, everything that reeked of death was inadmissible near the altars of Yahweh. Here again we are dealing with that familiar symbolism with which God warned his ancient church against forsaking the life-territory of Horeb's covenant and falling back into the sphere of paganism and corruption. Symbolic and non-symbolic instruction easily overlap.

The second commandment is like it: You shall love your neighbor as yourself (Lev 19:9–18)

When our Savior was on earth, a lawyer asked him: Master, what is the great commandment in the Law? Christ answered: You shall love the Lord, your God, with all you heart and with all your soul and with all your mind. This is the great and first commandment. The second, like it, is: You shall love your neighbor as yourself. On these two commands depend all the Law and the Prophets (Matt 22:35–40).

The words, "You shall love your neighbor as yourself," appear literally here in Leviticus 19:18, so that our Savior was surely quoting them from this verse. For he wanted to say something about the Law, the Torah, didn't he? It is possible that in his answer he was providing a brief summary not only of the entire Torah that Israel had received via Moses at Horeb, but also of the entire first half of this chapter, Leviticus 19, especially verses 4–18. This explains, in any case, both of our headings, dealing with love for God and love for neighbor.

In five characteristic sections, that love for the neighbor is prescribed. Here is our outline:

NO PAGAN LIFESTYLE! (LEV 18–20)

1. Giving (19:9–10).
2. Not taking (19:11–12).
3. Surely not by force (19:13–14).
4. Or with a show of justice (19:15–16).
5. But treating each other with love (19:17–18).

When we read through these five sections attentively, we discover a climax in them.

1. In verses 9–10, Israel receives a command to employ gentleness in connection with gathering the harvest from the field and the vineyard. Israel was not to harvest the edges of the field, and in no case were the Israelites to go back to pick up the grain left behind. In the vineyard, Israelites were not allowed to pick the vines clean, down to the very last piece of fruit. Nor were they to gather what had fallen to the ground. That was designated for the poor and the sojourner.

Some argue that this command was adapted to a general custom existing in those days—leave something behind for those coming on behind—indeed, that to this pagan custom the religious purpose had been attached of making the spirits favorable with a view to the harvest of the following year. In Israel, that pagan purpose was then replaced with an entirely different and better purpose. On other occasions we have observed that God filled pagan forms with an entirely different content and meaning. We could believe without very much proof that gleaning by the poor occurred outside of Israel. And the fact that in connection with bringing in the harvest, the Canaanites appeared to have provided relief to the poor with a view to the next year, was evident as well in the prohibition of boiling a kid in its mother's milk. Furthermore, in view of the overall purpose of Leviticus 18–20, namely, to warn Israel emphatically against the lifestyle of the surrounding pagans, we would not be surprised if in both of these verses (Lev 19:9–10), God was wanting at the same time to set up a barricade against a pagan practice that was perhaps well-known among Israel.

But for us, that is not what deserves the most attention, and therefore should not get the most attention.

What is clear is *the evangelical purpose* of this command. The commands in the lovely Torah are numerous that Israel should care well for the poor. Yahweh had himself provided the example of that, by accepting as sufficient a lesser sin offering in his sanctuary in cases of poverty. The number of passages where gentleness is commanded specifically in connection with harvesting fields and orchards is not small (Lev 19:10; 23:22; Deut 24:19–22).

That evangelical purpose—that was especially Israelitish. Among the pagans, opportunity may well have been given to have the poor among their own people glean for their subsistence, but that this was allowed among Israel also for foreigners was something that surprised Ruth, the Moabitess, for one. For she said to Boaz: "Why have I found favor in your eyes, that you should take notice of me, since I am a foreigner?" (Ruth 2:10).

If later Christianity had only understood better that, although the commands of the Horeb covenant had lost their (mostly) symbolic form and binding, they apply *even far more* to us than to ancient Israel, since we have become participants in a covenant that is so much better, of which Jesus became the Surety. But as Christians, we now have the reputation among many pagans and apostates of being tight-fisted, harsh people. We should have been all the more generous than the Torah prescribed!

Fortunately, however, not all the rich were miserly people. Boaz was a man who not only took the name of Yahweh upon his lips, but at the same time told his harvesters, with an eye on Ruth: "Let her glean even among the sheaves, and do not reproach her. And also pull out some from the bundles for her and leave it for her to glean, and do not rebuke her" (Ruth 2:4, 15–16). In doing it this way, his generosity to Ruth was somewhat camouflaged. Entirely in line with the Spirit of Christ, who according to Paul, must have said once: It is more blessed to give than to receive (Acts 20:35).

2. Verses 11–12 deal with *taking*, rather than giving. The lead idea is: "You shall not steal." But phenomena or consequences that often accompany thievery are that people lie to one another and deceive one another. One another! Literally it says that someone is treating his fellow countryman that way. Someone who was just as much a covenant partner with Yahweh as he himself. Something the suzerain could not possibly allow. War between his vassals. Finally, because the one results from the other, the series ends with perjury by the one against the other, whereby he defiles the name of Yahweh by explicitly mentioning Yahweh's name, because he wants to cover over his deceit. That's the result.

3. People can steal from someone, however, also by misusing power (vv. 13–14). For example, by not paying the day laborer his wages at day's end. Often this would have been payment in kind. But if the poor fellow were to holler too loudly, the next day he would likely not get a chance to earn anything as an independent laborer. To oppress such a defenseless person was just as cowardly and unloving as if you treated a deaf person as though he were insane or would put a stumbling block in front of a blind person. This too was a misuse of power, of one's own privileged position (good eyes, etc.), and the other person's dependence. In the Book of the Covenant (Exod 22:21–27) we already learned that Yahweh despises such

violent conduct in Israel, against whomever—here in verse 13, it is against the "neighbor," a bit more general that in verse 11, "brother." There God had said: If you treat widows and orphans that way, then I will make your wives and children widows and orphans. Nor may you oppress sojourners, for you were sojourners in Egypt. Don't do that, out of fear for my wrath!

4. But the worst oppression always occurred with a show of justice. Whether on the part of judges (v. 15), or on the part of witnesses (v. 16). Or both, as happened with Naboth (1 Kgs 21). Then as well, it involved some possession of this world, as is often the case, including in this entire passage of Leviticus 19. A vineyard or field. Suddenly the miscreant faced a battlefront aligned against him, with the steely face that declared him guilty; judges and witnesses. How surprised Naboth would have been if every word on his part had hit a brick wall. Then you'd feel hands around your throat. That is really "going after your neighbor's life." You can kill someone in a direct manner, with knife or sword, but also in an indirect manner, by giving him such a bad reputation that no one trusts him for anything anymore.

Leviticus 19:15–16 warns against partisan class justice. This can consist of judges, with or without witnesses, showing partiality to the rich and prominent, perhaps allowing themselves to be bribed, or adjudicating the issue in dispute for those who are impressive in society, out of fear of people. But partisan class justice occurs also by currying favor with the crowd, or being guilty of Absalom's sin, attempting in a "democratic" manner to steal people's hearts in order to rebel against the lawful government. We don't fool ourselves, do we, into thinking such a thing cannot happen today?

5. The fifth section draws the conclusion.

The preceding sections dealt with the more visible arena of life. Everything involved the good of this world. Over this, quarrels arise most often. Although during those quarrels, people often suddenly discover that the parties couldn't stand each other for a long time already. Their hearts were hardened against each other. Now come verses 17–18: Don't let it get that far. Begin now already to guard against that.

Verse 17a: "*You shall not hate your brother in your heart.*" There you see the subject being brought up for discussion. Be on guard against an antipathy arising within you against your brother.

Verse 17b: "*but you shall reason frankly with your neighbor.*" The word "frankly" is not in the text, but rather it says: when you have something against your brother, you must *especially* discuss it with him, *whatever you do*. Don't keep it in, but talk it out. *Whatever you do.*

Verse 7c: "*lest you incur sin because of him.*" If you keep walking around with your (imagined or legitimate) complaint against your brother, continuing to let it fester, then eventually you'll end up hating him. And exactly that is what you must guard against. For then, even if you were perhaps completely right with regard to the issue itself, you would nonetheless be guilty of sin, the sin of hatred in your heart. And that is what Yahweh is warning against here.

Verse 18a: "*You shall not take vengeance or bear a grudge against the sons of your own people.*" A repetition in order to make crystal clear the purpose of the preceding.

Verse 18b: "*but you shall love your neighbor as yourself.*" That is the depth of Yahweh's concern. We are not yet finished when we simply do not hate one another, but we must love our neighbor.

Regarding the term *neighbor* we note the following. What does this term mean in general in the Old Testament? And what does it mean here? And how does the Lord Jesus use the term?

The Hebrew word used here for "neighbor" (*reaʿ*) is a very general word that can often be translated with our general phrase "an other person." One is involved with that "other person," then, either accidentally and temporarily, or by living next to him or something similar. We too talk in that very general way, for example, when we tell someone: "You have to show some regard for an other person." Who is that other person? That depends entirely on the situation in which the conversation is being conducted. In this way, the meaning of the Hebrew word *reaʿ* can be very broad. It doesn't always mean "pal" or "chum." It could refer even to someone's opponent, your mortal enemy. For example, Samuel told Saul: Yahweh has given the kingship to your *reaʿ*, to David (1 Sam 28:17). And when the twelve men of Joab and the twelve men of Abner fought against each other, each one grabbed the head of his *reaʿ* and stuck his sword in the side of his *reaʿ* (2 Sam 2:16). Here the word is being used in a very unfavorable sense. But in our previous passage, where we read successively of "your brother," "your fellow Israelite," and "the children of your people," it is being used in a favorable sense. How would you dare to hate someone who belonged, just like you, to the people with whom I, Yahweh, established by covenant here at Horeb, as the Supreme Ruler of all of you, indeed, as the God of all of you? Notice carefully that each of the five sections ends with those words. "I Yahweh" or "I your God Yahweh." That is *the constantly resonating echo of God's speaking.*

Moreover, in speaking this way, God did not intend to restrict the command to love "the other person" to the relationship between one Israelite and another Israelite. We will learn something quite different later, in verses 33–34. "When a stranger [*ger*] sojourns with you in your land, you shall not do him wrong. You shall treat the stranger who sojourns with you

NO PAGAN LIFESTYLE! (LEV 18–20)

as the native among you, and you shall love him as yourself, for you were strangers in the land of Egypt: I am the Lord your God."

The word *rea'*, which appears more than once in our chapter, was translated by the Septuagint with the Greek word *plēsios*, and this same word is used repeatedly in the New Testament. The Lord Jesus apparently interpreted it broadly. When the same lawyer that we spoke of earlier asked: "And who is my neighbor?," the Savior answered him with the parable of the compassionate Samaritan. In response to the man who had fallen into the hand of robbers, neither the priest nor the Levite, but the Samaritan, understands his obligation as neighbor and fulfills it (Luke 10:25–37). Our neighbor is the one with whom life brings us into contact. No matter what kind of contact. We must love "the other person."

By quoting Lev 19:18b in his conversation with the lawyer ("you shall love your neighbor as yourself"), our Savior simultaneously showed that he did not come to lay down brand new commandments. He never did that. Not in the so-called Sermon on the Mount, either (Matt 5–7). He returned repeatedly to what was said to "the ancients," that is, to the first Israel through Moses. Even earlier than Moses, to creation (the institution of marriage "in the beginning; Matt 19:7–8). Naturally, this gave Jesus' hearers the initial impression of something novel, but eventually the sheep listened to the good age-old voice of Israel's Shepherd. The Lord wanted to annul not one stroke or letter of the Bible of that time, nor add anything to it. Nevertheless some Christians later came up with the idea that in the Sermon on the Mount, the Savior came with brand new commandments. In this way, for example, people came up with the idea that the Ten Commandments applied to all Christians, but commands like not looking (at all) at a woman, applied only to "priests" and such people, to whom higher perfections had been granted. The "new law" applied to these people. But one cannot appeal to Scripture to justify such a dichotomy within the Christian church and for such a double morality. The commandments of the Torah, all its commandments, apply to us today as well. Not less, but more. (Even though they must be interpreted properly.) Because we belong to a new and better covenant, of which Jesus has become the Surety.

So make a separation (Lev 19:19a)

In the middle of our chapter we suddenly encounter the words: "*You shall keep my statutes.*" The Hebrew word for "statutes" is *chuqqoth*. We discussed this word earlier. The meaning of this little sentence is rather straightforward: Observe what I have prescribed for you. But in order to see what this little sentence is doing here, we must pay attention to the place where it appears in our chapter, to what precedes and what follows it.

The preceding verses (19:1–18) constituted a clear unit, in which the double command of love toward God and the neighbor was bound upon the hearts of Israel. They constituted a unity that closely resembled such Scripture passages as the well know Ten Words of Exodus 20. What strikes us about this is that the symbolic element is not entirely absent, but nonetheless appears rarely (Exod 20:8–11; Lev 19:5–8).

That is different in the subsequent verses in Leviticus 19, namely, verses 19–37. Perhaps the scope of those verses will be entirely the same as that of the first half of our chapter, namely: Remember that you are the people of Yahweh! But the manner in which this command is presented to Israel in the rest of Leviticus 19 is somewhat different. Making greater use of symbolism. For we may repeat this once more: God wants to warn his ancient Israelite church powerfully against falling back into the paganism of Egypt and Canaan, by forbidding her every kind of sliding toward the pagan lifestyle. But he did that either without symbolism, directly, by straightforward commands and prohibitions, or with symbolism, using various means of visual instruction.

This latter will occur again now, and with a view to that, the theme of Leviticus 18–20 is worth repeating once more—we almost wrote: worthy of polishing off once more. Not what paganism prescribes, but what I prescribe, with or without symbolic tools of instruction, that is what you shall observe.

So this little sentence serves to remind Israel of the one main thrust of these chapters: No intermingling! Make a separation! Otherwise you cannot continue as my covenant people.

The remaining content of verse 19 will confirm this.

You shall not allow two kinds of animals to breed, sow two kinds of seed in your field, and ear a garment made from two kinds of material (Lev 19:19b)

Here we have that section that we claimed gives the impression of having fallen smack dab in the middle of the commandments of Leviticus 19. But it certainly did not give Israel that impression, because the Israelite was thought to be so accustomed to the symbolism in the laws of Moses that he needed to hear but one single word, as here, for example, about not sowing two seeds in a field, in order to be reminded of the entire grand lesson of Horeb: You must be the holy people of Yahweh and therefore no element of the pagan lifestyle fits you. By way of comparison, you might think of

NO PAGAN LIFESTYLE! (LEV 18–20)

a child living in the city, who is warned by his mother not to play near the street. When he does play too close to the street, he turns around to see his mother standing by the window shaking her finger in warning. The child gets the message. By means of a single gesture the child is reminded of mother's whole sermon: "Be careful near the street, my boy; don't go near the street, understand? Because you'll get hurt." That brief but pointed language spoken with the upraised finger was the language being spoken to Israel by means of these commandments of Lev 19:19b regarding the breeding of two kinds of livestock, etc. Because that brevity could well be somewhat difficult for the Bible reader today, let's place a few other Scripture passages alongside.

1. Deuteronomy 22:5–12.
2. Leviticus 20:25–26.
3. Leviticus 19:19b.

1.   Deuteronomy 22:5–12

In that Scripture passage we read five commandments, whose common theme should be noted. Perhaps you'd like to open your Bible to that passage.

Part 1 forbids transvestitism, i.e., a man dressing like a woman, or a woman like a man (22:5).

Part 2 allows taking eggs or hatchlings from a bird, but forbids taking the bird (22:6–7).

Part 3 prescribes that when building a house, a railing must be put around the perimeter of the roof, a place for resting and socializing (22:8).

Part 4 forbids sowing two kinds of seed (in the soil between the vines) in the vineyard, or harnessing an ox and a donkey to a plow, or to make a garment out of two kinds of material, e.g., wool and linen (22:9–11).

Part 5 commands that one must wear tassels on the four corners of his garment (22:12).

What is the common purpose of all of these five sections of Deuteronomy 22? In answering that question, we will begin with the easiest part, the fifth part, because we read more often in Scripture (Num 15:37–41) that every Israelite had to wear a *tzitzit* (button, knob, knot, or tassel, with a dark blue thread woven through it). Thereby Israel would be constantly reminded that she was God's holy covenant people, and thus may not deviate from his commandments. It is rather certain that with this regulation, God was not introducing anything shockingly new to Israel, but was making use of particular Egyptian and Asiatic fashion customs. The pagan form was certainly filled with sacred content, namely, a daily reminder of the high privilege of being the holy covenant people of Yahweh. The word *tzitzit* was translated by the Septuagint with *kraspedōn*, and the same word appears in the New Testament. The woman who suffered from a flow of blood touched the *kraspedon* of Jesus' garment (Matt 9:20), and the scribes and Pharisees made their *kraspeda* extra large in order to show thereby how scrupulously they observed God's commandments (Matt 23:5).

When we look next at Part 1 (prohibiting transvestitism), then we see Israel being warned by this prohibition against transgressing God's command. We must understand this prohibition against the background of the pagan *cultus* that was fashionable among the nations around Israel, from ancient times until later periods of the history of the Near East. In the worship of the Sumerian city Uruk, the ritual honoring Anu contained a moment when the gods entered in procession and presented themselves; this was followed by the eunuchs changing clothes, since these men apparently wanted to look like women, clothed in the garments of the goddess. Among the Hittites the leader of the eunuch-priests who served the great goddess was a head priest who was clothed in an extravagant woman's costume. On Cyprus, sacrifices were brought to Astarte, a goddess with a beard, by men in women's clothes and women in men's clothes. Lucian of Samosata reports how in Syria a certain Kombabos was worshiped; this deity was represented as a woman in man's clothes. He reports further that the eunuch-priests of the goddess Cybele wore the clothes of the opposite sex. In regions where the male god Baal and the female Astarte were worshiped, the women wore men's clothes and the men wore women's clothes. All these examples justify the conclusion that in Deut 22:5, we are dealing with the prohibition of pagan worship. This verse describes transvestitism as *tho'avath*, an abomination, i.e., something that is absolutely incompatible with serving Israel's God. Just as incompatible as serving idols, who were also referred to with the word "abomination."

We come next to the intervening sections. Given the context, would it not be obvious that we should assume here as well that these sections 2–4 contained warnings against transgressing God's *commandments*? This assumption is confirmed immediately when we look at Part 3. For anyone who neglected to put a railing around his flat roof would be responsible if later someone fell to his death. He would then be guilty of manslaughter. The same goes for Part 2; if you come upon a bird with eggs or hatchlings, you may take the eggs and the hatchlings, but must let the bird go. In connection with this command of God to Israel, we should not start talking sentimentally about respect for life or for creation ordinances. It was just as

NO PAGAN LIFESTYLE! (LEV 18–20)

unpleasant for the young birds to be killed as for the older bird. Both were creatures. But this commandment was not at all given for the sake of birds, but for the sake of people, namely, the Israelites. We have the same as with the command: You shall not muzzle an ox treading the grain (Deut 25:4). Of course, an Israelite farmer was not allowed to prevent an ox treading the grain from eating some of it now and then, since he was working so close to his food. But if we remained at this level of understanding the command, and thought that we had exhausted the relevance of the commandment, we would be mistaken. Paul wrote later about this commandment: Do you perhaps suppose that with this command God was thinking simply about oxen? Of course not. He was thinking of people as well, indeed, especially of people. The laborer is worthy of his wage! That is what God intended to teach Israel with this commandment (1 Cor 9:9; 1 Tim 5:18). Well then, in the same way, in this section about the mother bird, God was giving Israel not a lesson in animal protection, but a symbolic pedagogical reminder of the Fifth Commandment: honor your father and your mother. The end of this section removes all doubt about the correctness of our explanation. For who would not think that the words, "that it may go well with you, and that you may live long" (22:7) were a direct allusion to the familiar conclusion of the Fifth Commandment: "that your days may be long in the land that the Lord your God is giving you" (Exod 20:12)?

We have yet to discuss Part 4 (Deut 22:9–11).

Here as well, we listen to the exegetical advice of Paul in 1 Corinthians 9. Do you suppose that with that prohibition of sowing two kinds of seed in one field, of yoking two kinds of animals to one plow, and making a garment from two kinds of material, God was concerned for the sake of the soil of the vineyard, with oxen, donkeys, woolen yarn, and pieces of linen? No, rather for the sake of people, of Israelites. In order with these various prohibitions to sharpen his command: You belong to me, so you shall keep my covenant and remember to do my commandments.

Yahweh set flags everywhere, across the entire surface of Israelite life, as it were, warning signs that were supposed to serve to remind Israel constantly that she had been received by him in a covenant and was his holy people. Israel couldn't turn around without running into such a sign. Caution! You're not walking about in a trance, are you? You're not crossing any forbidden boundaries, are you? Don't enter unsuitable friendships either! Don't enter any undesirable unions. Stay in my covenant territory! Remember the foundation of the (Israelite) world laid at Horeb!

2. Leviticus 20:25-26

These verses will form the close of the Scripture passage we are discussing in this chapter. This is what they say: "You shall therefore separate the clean beast from the unclean, and the unclean bird from the clean. You shall not make yourselves detestable by beast or by bird or by anything with which the ground crawls, which I have set apart for you to hold unclean. You shall be holy to me, for I the Lord am holy and have separated you from the peoples, that you should be mine" (Lev 20:25–26).

Twice already we have drawn the attention of our readers to this conclusion.

The first time was when we discussed Leviticus 11–15, and showed that by means of his commandments regarding clean and unclean animals, God impressed upon Israel through visual instruction that she was a people of "separated ones."

The second time we mentioned these verses was in the introduction of Leviticus 19. What Leviticus 18 accomplished without symbolism, we see Leviticus 19 doing with the use of symbolism. In every conceivable way, God was binding upon Israel's heart the requirement that she abstain from intermingling with "the nations."

3. Leviticus 19:19b

After discussing the preceding two passages, we come now finally to examine our verse a bit further.

The first thing that strikes us is that it shows a very strong similarity to Deut 22:9–11. Except, the latter is somewhat broader. But both have in common: (a) the prohibition against sowing two kinds of seed in the same soil, and (b) the prohibition against making a garment from two kinds of material. The only difference consists in a third feature, that Leviticus 19:19b forbids *breeding* two different kinds of animals together, whereas Deut 22:10 forbids *yoking in front of a plow* two different kinds of animals, like an ox and a donkey. But naturally, God's purpose is the same in both cases. That purpose did not consist in God obligating the Israelites to treat their animals well. People have understood something like that to have been God's purpose in forbidding the boiling of a kid in its mother's milk (Exod 23:19; 34:26; Deut 14:21). But we have come to think very differently.[3] People probably read something similar in the prohibition against yoking an ox and a donkey together to the same plow, namely, because the donkey would

---

3. See Vonk, *Exodus*, 118–119.

have had to shoulder greater responsibility, in view of its unequal size. But we believe, no matter how very obvious it would have been in Israel that a righteous man knew what was an efficient use of his animals (Prov 12:10), that it was not God's real purpose in Deut 22:10 (not plowing with an ox and a donkey) to give Israel a lesson in animal welfare. Nor when in Deut 22:6 (leaving the parent bird in the nest) and in Deut 25:4 (not muzzling an ox while it was threshing). With those commandments, God was not concerned for birds and oxen, but for people, as Paul has taught us (1 Cor 9:9; cf. 1 Tim 5:18). For Israelites. To remind them by means of the umpteenth visual lesson of the obligation to observe the Horeb covenant and to remember God's commandments to do them, rather than to become involved with Canaanite acquaintances and friends, young men and women, indeed, even with certain notions and views, mores and customs, with the faith and worship of "the nations" in Canaan.

So our verse is continuing the theme of Leviticus 18–20: No pagan lifestyle!

Some have pointed out that later the Israelites did possess mules. Indeed. The mule was a mix of a donkey and a horse, and appeared later not only in royal circles, with Absalom and his brothers (2 Sam 13:29; 18:9)—king David himself owned a female mule, 1 Kgs 1:33—but also among the ordinary people (2 Chron 9:24). But aside from the fact that it remains a question whether these mules had been bred by Israelites themselves or imported by Israelites, like people in Tyre had imported such animals from Togarma in Asia Minor (Ezek 27:14),[4] this still doesn't contradict our explanation of verse 19b. Indeed, a mule is a bastard animal, but how often don't the prophets complain about the Israelites consorting illicitly with Canaanites? If all the commandments of Yahweh that were later ignored would need to be scrapped from the Torah, then none would remain!

Except: unchaste kidnapping is not adultery (Lev 19:20–22)

People have been puzzled about this section appearing suddenly in Leviticus 19. It seems so out of character. It is dealing with an Israelite who had raped someone's female slave. In such a case, that person had to bring a *guilt offering* to Yahweh. This is why we discussed this section in connection with the Sacrifice Torah. At that time, we commented that when someone committed adultery with the wife of his neighbor, he had to be put to death (Lev 20:10), and as a matter of fact, even an Israelite who had had sexual relations with a young girl who was not yet married was similarly to be put

---

4. See Vonk, *Genesis*, 185.

to death (Deut 22:23). In both cases sexual immorality had been committed, and the Torah was certainly no less strict regarding punishment than the jurisprudence of the Babylonians, Hittites, and Assyrians. Throughout the ancient Eastern world, marital laws showed the very same features. The decisive moment in connection with entering marriage was the payment of the dowry to the father-in-law, whether this was done by the bridegroom himself or by his father. From that moment, the marriage was legally binding. If another person had sexual relations with the bride, even though she may have still been living in the home of her parents, that would be punished with death, since it was adultery. In Israel also, people were liable to death if they assaulted a "child bride." Just as when one had sexual relations with a woman who was no longer living in her parental home but was completely married to her husband. Whereas among Israel, in the case of adultery one never remained alive, nevertheless, outside of Israel that was possible. According to the laws of Middle Assyria, it was the case that a man whose wife was caught in adultery could demand that both his wife and the man with whom she had committed adultery would be put to death, but if he did not demand this, but was satisfied that his wife's nose was cut off, he also had to be satisfied that the one who had committed adultery with his wife was castrated and his face was scarred. Indeed, if the offended husband allowed his wife to go free, he also had to allow the man who had committed adultery with her to go free. From this we see that in ancient Near Eastern understanding, adultery was not first of all a sin against morality, but had to be seen as a violation of the offended husband's property rights.

Completely different was the instruction that Israel received in the Torah. The Torah was far more serious with regard to marriage. Accordingly, adultery was an entirely different sin than stealing, than violating someone's property rights. According to the Torah, adultery had to always be punished with death, but not stealing. A wife was not a female slave, not a piece of merchandise. But the reverse was also true: a piece of merchandise, a female slave, was not a wife.

Suddenly it becomes clear why in the middle of Leviticus 19 we find a section about raping the female slave of another man. In view of the opinion about slavery, which God still tolerated in Israel, we need not be at all surprised that the rape by Mr. A of the female slave belonging to Mr. B was not viewed by the Torah as adultery, but as the violation by A of the property rights of B (who owned the female slave). This is why a guilt offering had to be brought, as we discussed earlier.

Finally we have this remaining issue: Why was this section placed here? Answer: in order to warn against rigorism here, in the large Scripture passage of Leviticus 18–20, where God has been warning so sharply against

NO PAGAN LIFESTYLE! (LEV 18–20)

pagan sins and crimes, indeed, where later the death penalty would often be required for those committing such sins (Lev 20). Thereby people could easily have overlooked the significant difference between adultery with or violation of someone's spouse, and injuring someone by damaging his property, in this case, his female slave. The former was to be punished with nothing less than death, the latter not at all, in fact, never.

For purposes of comparison, consider what Moses says in Deuteronomy 19 about the cities of refuge. Whereas one would perhaps expect that in this connection he would be saying something about those who committed premeditated murder and how these persons would have to be punished, he instead binds upon Israel's heart care and provision for the one who killed without premeditation. That was the purpose of instituting cities of refuge. And that was the purpose for Moses' reminding Israel of this. Their attention was being drawn not to the guilt, but to the innocence involved in the situation, lest "the guilt of bloodshed be upon you" (Deut 19:10).

So too in Leviticus 19, a section is included that provides Israel with the lesson that she should not become guilty of adopting a pagan lifestyle, and therefore must stay far away from everything that came close to adultery. But in response to this warning, Israel should not become guilty of an all too severe strictness, for example, by treating a thief as they would treat an adulterer, even though that thief had had sexual relations with "the stolen goods," and his stealing thereby acquired an immoral and unchaste aroma. For that reason, it was precisely this case, as a boundary situation, that was brought up for discussion, and the warning is given that such a guilty party may not be classified with those who commit a crime worthy of death, such as adultery.

Adultery was serious.
But not everything was adultery.
Stealing was not adultery.
Not even unchaste stealing was adultery.

Later you shall not eat the fruit from the trees that you planted in Canaanite soil before those fruit trees are four years old (Lev 19:23–25)

When later Israel would take possession of the promised land, and would plant fruit trees there, for the first three years those trees were supposed to be for Israel like uncircumcised trees. They were supposed to throw away the fruit. Furthermore, they were to bring the fruit of those trees in the fourth year to Yahweh (who would have given them to the priests). And only then, that is, only in the fifth harvest year, could the Israelites consume the fruit of such trees.

The purpose of this ordinance is not hard to grasp, once we've read both of the preceding sections of the chapter. There the attention was on boundaries. Like our military personnel identify the boundaries of a dangerous territory by using red flags, so too God wanted Israel to be reminded in the middle of her busy daily life of the covenant to which God had exalter her, and of the commandments that Israel had to observe as a result.

The first section, verse 19, said: Take seriously the boundaries between you and paganism. No intermingling! No pagan lifestyle! Know that whoever is guilty of that is liable to be put to death.

(The second section, verses 20–22, said: But whoever violates the female slave belonging to his neighbor in not thereby liable to be put to death. I disapprove of his action, but atonement is possible. Do not fall into paganism.)

This third section, verses 23–25, says: Later in Canaan you shall be so attentive regarding the mores and customs of the pagans there that you may enjoy the fruit trees that you plant only after four years have passed.

We cannot determine that by this ordinance God wanted to drive out an ancient custom, according to which the first fruits had to be sacrificed to particular "field spirits." We are unacquainted with anything relating to such an ancient custom. We do read in the Code of Hammurabi that when someone had given a grower a piece of land for growing dates, only in the fifth year did he have the right that the grower would divide the harvest with him. Whether in this section, by referring to the fifth year God was intentionally adopting a particular known ancient custom, or whether we have here a pure coincidence, is difficult for us to determine. We are firmly convinced, however, that this prescription of verses 23–25 also belongs to that entire large complex of visual instruction whereby Israel is constantly being reminded of her holiness. In this ordinance regarding her fruit trees, Israel received once more a caution sign whose symbolic language was saying the same thing as that of the command regarding the breeding of different kinds of animals. Naturally, the children of the man who had planted such trees would have asked their father often enough why that delicious fruit had to be thrown away. "But father, throwing away such delicious fruit is a crime!" But then the instruction would come: This is how careful we must be with those Canaanites around us, my children. Be very careful for their idolatry and immorality.

(That we must understand these three sections in terms of their shared context is confirmed, in our judgment, by the words with which all of verses 19–25 are concluded: I am Yahweh your God.)

NO PAGAN LIFESTYLE! (LEV 18–20)

No pagan notions about death! (Lev 19:26–31)

This part of Leviticus 19 consists of three sections that at first glance are rather different from each other, but that nonetheless have one thing in common. All three warn against the dominant notion of death in paganism. Therefore we are grouping them together.

1. No pagan fear of death (19:26–28)
2. No pagan sacrifice for death (19:29–30)
3. No pagan concourse with death (19:31)

1. No pagan fear of death (19:26–28)

These verses read as follows: "You shall not eat any flesh with the blood in it. You shall not interpret omens or tell fortunes. You shall not round off the hair on your temples or mar the edges of your beard. You shall not make any cuts on your body for the dead or tattoo yourselves: I am the Lord."

Scripture commentators complain unanimously that these verses confront us with serious problems. For example, for many it is impossible to indicate precisely the distinction between the Hebrews words that in verse 26 are translated by "interpret omens" and "tell fortunes." In verse 27 we are certainly dealing with grieving customs that are universally followed, removing some hair from the head and beard. But it is assumed that originally pagans sacrificed some of their hair to the idols or on behalf of the dead. Something similar could have been the original purpose of tattooing, mentioned in verse 28. In fact, people would not only have sought to satisfy the powers of death by means of sacrificing hair and cutting their skin, but they would also have sought to protect themselves against the dangerous influence of death by using blood. People probably lived with the illusion that such use of life powers was a defense against death. That is, in fact, the first item discussed in this section. "You shall not eat any flesh with the blood in it" (v. 26a). For the umpteenth time we encounter in Leviticus the prohibition against using blood. But here it was being issued particularly in connection with pagan fear of death and with pagan grieving customs. Why?

Let's listen to what no one less than Moses said about this once.

When he later prohibited the Israelites from doing such things, in Deut 14:1–2, he did that with an appeal to the fact that they are children of Yahweh. Moses was there staying close to the Third Commandment. Recall what we wrote about the words: "I Yahweh" (in *Exodus*, 66–70). The entire gospel for that time was encapsulated in the name Yahweh. Yahweh had not delivered Israel from Egyptian death only to leave the matter at that point. His plans went further, to the complete vanquishing of death through our Lord Jesus Christ. Therefore the Israelites were not to manhandle themselves like pagans. For the same reasons the apostle Paul wrote later that we may of course grieve, when death takes a loved one from us, but we may *not grieve like the pagans* do. For the pagans had no hope. That pagan prattle over their dead brought them no comfort of a certain hereafter that was worth anything. Christians, however, are not only people of faith, but also and especially people of hope. The hope of eternal life, on the day of Jesus' return and our being gathered with him (1 Thess 4:12; 2 Thess 2:1).

2. No pagan sacrifice for death (19:29-30)

Next the Israelite is prohibited from handing over his daughter for sexual immorality. Given the context, we assume here as well the background of pagan fear of death.

On more than one occasion we have mentioned that the Easter world not only harbored the illusion that life and fertility came from their idols, but they also thought they had to stimulate these gods to grant their benefits, by sacrificing to them the most beautiful and beloved thing they possessed, their very own dignity, in concourse with temple prostitutes, along with the dignity of their own wives and daughters. The historian Herodotus reports that every night the sun god, Bel, received at Babel a virgin who sacrificed her virginity to him. In fact, every Babylonian girl had to surrender herself to a stranger one time in her life in honor of Mylitta, who was also called Ishtar and Astarte. For this reason, the poor wretches were not despised later on. After this encounter was past, they entered marriage all that much sooner. Therefore they sat in the forecourt of the temple waiting their turn. You can read about this in the apocryphal book of Baruch (6:42-43). This Mylitta was the heavenly queen who was the female partner of Bel. Her name, which was actually Moladta, meant Bearer. She represented procreative and reproductive nature. The days on which people paid her homage were presumably identified as specific feast days. This immorality occurred elsewhere as well, for example, on Cyprus and in the Canaanite city of Gebal or Byblos.

Although the Hebrew word for "committing unchastity" can refer to prostitution in general as well as to "sacred prostitution," i.e., in the sanctuary, here the latter would have been intended. This is in view of what we

NO PAGAN LIFESTYLE! (LEV 18–20)

read in verse 30: "You shall keep my Sabbaths and reverence my sanctuary: I am the Lord."

This last verse sets us to thinking.

In the first place, it leads us to think of verse 3 of this same chapter, half of which verse is identical. We have shown that there, Yahweh was pressing upon the hearts of his people that they must continue in what they had learned, that they must stand strongly against the temptations to wickedness discussed further in the chapter. Idolatry, etc.

Next, this verse leads us to think of Lev 26:2. That verse in Hebrew is fully identical to this verse, Lev 19:30. What kind of warning is added there with those words? Once again, a warning against . . . idolatry.

In the third place, this verse leads us to think back to the Book of the Covenant in Exodus (20–23), where Yahweh had already warned sternly against the religious and moral danger of Canaan. The Israelites would later not need to fear that the land would fail to yield a good harvest because they had not gone along with the celebration of the Canaanite agricultural festivals. They were supposed to celebrate the three festivals of Yahweh at the sanctuary of Yahweh, and nothing else. Those feasts were termed "my Sabbaths" (You shall not bow down to their gods . . . but you shall serve Yahweh, your God, then he will bless your bread and water, and I will drive sickness from your midst. No wife in your land will suffer a miscarriage or be barren. The number of your days I will make full [Exod 23:24–26]).

The conclusion of all of this is obvious, namely, that the Israelites received in these verses the warning not to allow themselves to be seized by the Canaanite idolatrous fear of dying nature and the dying season of the year, which fear would induce them, for example, to boil a kid in its mother's milk and sprinkle that milk on their grassland and field, and to sacrifice the honor of their own daughters to the fertility gods, in order to stimulate these deities to fill the land of Canaan with their blessings. Those were no blessings, but thereby the land was covered with *sexual immorality* and the land was filled with *zimmah*, something abominable, something inexpressibly shameful. This word is used for bloodguilt in 18:17. It appears in parallel with *tow'ebah*, which means abomination. Sometimes such a poor wretch of a girl was called a *kedeshah*, a consecrated one. But that was a euphemism, a nice word for an ugly reality. Just like the girls who put themselves at the disposal of the German soldiers also received the pretty name "honor bride" (*Ehrebraut*). But in reality it was prostitution. Such an Israelite girl was thereby no consecrated one, but an unconsecrated, defiled one, robbed of her dignity as a child of the people of the covenant of Yahweh.

3. *No pagan concourse with death (19:31)*

We read in this verse: "Do not turn to mediums or necromancers; do not seek them out, and so make yourselves unclean by them: I am the Lord your God." Much about this verse remains unclear. If we had only this verse in its context, we might legitimately think this verse involves dealing with the dead. Perhaps comparing it with Lev 20:27 might help: "A man or a woman who is a medium or a necromancer shall surely be put to death. They shall be stoned with stones; their blood shall be upon them." We would do well to associate Lev 19:31 with the dead, in light also of Deut 18:11. There Moses prohibited anyone among Israel being "a charmer or a medium [ʾowb] or a necromancer [*yiddeʿonî* or one who inquires of the dead."

From all these passages we learn at least two things: both that Israel is being warned against a particular *Canaanite* wickedness (Deut 18:9), and that the words "medium" [ʾowb] and "necromancer" [*yiddeʿonî*] place us in the realm of *inquiring from the dead*. In fact, Deut 18:11 explicitly mentions "the dead."

How this inquiring from the dead was done is unknown. The word for "medium" is feminine and for necromancer is masculine, so was it perhaps assumed that the former referred to the involvement of women and the latter the involvement of men? According to Lev 20:27, these could be men or women. Or is Scripture simply adopting pagan language here, such that in so doing, Scripture would not be claiming or teaching that such a medium or necromancer were at all dealing with realities? This latter seems to be the case. The Hebrew word for necromancer is etymologically related to the verb for "know" (*yada*). According to Canaanite superstition, the word for "necromancer" suggests that the dead knew a lot and therefore could be consulted by the living, whereas Holy Scripture explicitly denies this by teaching that the dead know nothing (Eccl 9:5).

By now our readers will naturally have thought of today's spiritist séances, whereby interaction occurs between the living and the dead. Is such a Canaanite spiritist séance being described for us in 1 Samuel 28?

There we read that Saul told his servants: "Seek out for me a woman who is a medium [*baʿalat-ʾowb*], that I may go to her and inquire of her." There was such a woman left in Endor. When he came to her, the king said: "Divine for me by a spirit and bring up for me whomever I shall name to you." This was a roundabout way of talking. But Saul did not want to mention the name of Samuel directly, in order not to make the woman even more suspicious. For she was already suspicious. We read, "When the woman saw Samuel, she cried out with a loud voice. And the woman said to Saul, 'Why have you deceived me? You are Saul.'" The king put her at ease, and

NO PAGAN LIFESTYLE! (LEV 18–20)

when he asked what she saw, she explained further by saying: "I see a god [*elohim*] coming up out of the earth." Here the word *elohim* would not have the meaning of a supernatural being (NASB: divine being; TNIV: ghostly figure), for this word is what the woman customarily used on occasions like this. Here *elohim* would mean government person, judge, as in Exod 21:6, 22:8, 28 (Masoretic text: 22:7, 27), and 1 Sam 2:25. This time, the woman did really see someone, in particular, a very prominent figure. Someone resembling a real magistrate official. Enough to frighten her, especially given that she was practicing something that had been strictly forbidden in Israel. When at Saul's request she described the figure more extensively, he mentioned that the apparition was clothed in a robe (*me'il*), or the garment of a prominent person.

Next it appears that a conversation occurred between Samuel and Saul. A face to face conversation. In this connection we read nothing about the mediation of the woman. In that conversation, Samuel continued speaking entirely as a dead person (vv. 15, 19). And that, when according to Scripture, the dead know nothing and no longer share in this life.

Therefore we believe that in 1 Samuel 28, what is being reported is no ordinary case of Canaanite consultation of the dead. That was nothing but deceit. Just as deceitful as sorcery, of which Ezekiel accused the prophets of Judah (Ezek 13:6–7). But in 1 Samuel 28 we are not dealing with pure deceit. At first, to be sure. But the woman was really frightened later. And the conversation between Samuel and Saul was face to face, something made possible either by means of Samuel temporarily and really coming back to life, or by means of God providing a vision to both the woman and Saul. The former option doesn't seem to fit with the actual speaking of Samuel: "Therefore tomorrow you and your sons will be with me." With this language, Samuel was not counting himself among the living, but among the dead. This leaves us with the second option. Just as occasionally we see and hear dead people in our dreams as though they were alive, in the same way Saul and the woman must have observed a shared visionary appearance of the deceased Samuel. In a terribly strict manner God then punished Saul's sin of forsaking God. When he had ultimately sunk so deeply along that path of forsaking God, such that he had fallen to the level of Canaanite spiritism, then certainly on that detestable path God did not preach the gospel (unto repentance) to him, but announced nothing but punishment. Death itself! Just as Leviticus 20 will do as well. Death without pardon (cf. 1 Chron 10:13–14).

PART 4 | THE PEOPLE OF YAHWEH

Practice obedience and justice (Lev 19:32–36)

Just like the preceding three sections, so too the following three portions belong together. All three are related to the Fifth Commandment.

1. Respect your parents (19:32)!
2. Love the sojourner (19:33–34)!
3. Be honest in jurisprudence and business (19:35–36)!

1. Respect your parents (19:32)!

When in Deut 16:17 Moses begins with an excursus about the Fifth Commandment, he does not open with saying this or that about our obligations as children toward our parents. Those parents are not mentioned at all. But Moses jumps into the subject with a command about appointing judges. For that too involves the Fifth Commandment. Respect for governments, including for judges.

In the conclusion of Leviticus 19, that also speaks about matters touching on the Fifth Commandment, the parents are not mentioned either. Older people are referred to, perhaps also governments and judges. For instead of translating it, "fear for *your God*," we could render it, "fear for *your judges*." Here again we have the word *elohim*, with the meaning of "government" and "judge" that we have encountered earlier. In that case, we would render it this way: "*You must stand up before old age, respect an old person and fear your judges. I am Yahweh.*"

To be sure, old age does not always represent wisdom. Not every old person in Israel would be equipped for governing and judicial matters. But leadership and order are nevertheless usually the safest when done by older people. In Exod 19:7, we saw how Moses was surrounded by a staff of elders. So then, even though not every older person is called to leadership and judicial service, gray hair does point in that direction, to the crown of government. When the word *elohim* is translated here not with "judges" or something similar, but with the word "God," then this command leads, by virtue of the outward appearance of the elderly in Israel, to remind the Israelites of Yahweh, who had tied to the commandment requiring obedience a long and blessed national existence in Canaan (Exod 20:12).

NO PAGAN LIFESTYLE! (LEV 18–20)

2. *Love the sojourner (19:33–34)!*

As we have seen earlier, the Torah uses especially two words for "sojourner" or "foreigner": *ger* and *nokri*. The former person lived permanently among Israel, the latter only temporarily. Naturally people came into more contact with the former. That is the one mentioned here: "*When a stranger resides with you in your land, you shall not do him wrong. The stranger who resides with you shall be to you as the native among you, and you shall love him as yourself, for you were aliens in the land of Egypt; I am the Lord your God.*"

Notice how frequently this appears in the Torah. Israel is repeatedly reminded of her own time of sojourning in Egypt. So Israel could know how such a person felt (Exod 23:9). And how he was often harassed, like someone with no rights. So that Ruth was surprised by her good treatment at the hands of Boaz.

That is what this warning seeks to oppose: violating rights.

Earlier Israel was commanded to leave behind some of the grain or fruit in the field or vineyard that was being harvested for the sojourner. That involved a donation, a gift.

But here Yahweh is opposing oppression, violating justice. Like cowards dare to do, against those who are weak, against widows and orphans. And sojourners. Often the latter are mentioned in the same breath, and we are told that Yahweh curses the man who "distorts" justice due to such defenseless people (Deut 27:19). Yahweh will "execute justice" for them (Deut 10:18).

3. *Be honest in jurisprudence and business (19:35–36)!*

First, then, attention was directed to young people and subordinates. You must show respect to those clothed with authority (v. 32).

Then a warning is given against violating justice. The example of those who are defenseless, those whom one can assault most easily and without being punished, was that of the sojourner.

But the final word is spoken to superiors. To those who are leaders in jurisprudence or in business. Little wonder that those two are grouped together. Not only because many issues are made to depend on the judge, by virtue of quarreling on account of differences in business life, but also because there is a certain correspondence between the judge's bench and the merchant's counter. Both have a scale. So then, things must be weighed honestly. Literally and figuratively.

You can sense the inner connection of these last passages. All three involve respect for justice, both toward those through whom and toward those before whom this ought to be maintained. Here again, each passage is underscored with the confession and warning: I am Yahweh.

Did God issue this *summons for respecting justice* to Israel especially with a view to her future dwelling in the land of *Canaan*? With a view to certain juridical abuses among the Canaanites? We simply don't know. No single concrete datum has come to us regarding the Canaanite judicial system, so that comparison with the ancient Israelite system is very difficult. We have no access to Canaanite law codes, as we do with respect to the Babylonians, Assyrians, etc. But wherever the Canaanite substratum shines through the covering of Israel's history now and then, there we do see abominable injustice. For example, Abimelech, king of Shechem, the seat of Baal-berith, slaughtered his seventy brothers (Judg 9). And Ahab learned from Jezebel, the daughter of the Phoenician king, how a king in Israel should exercise his governing authority. That is what poor Naboth and his sons discovered (1 Kgs 21; 2 Kgs 9:26).

The concluding verse of Leviticus 19 makes us reflect as well (v. 37). That conclusion of the large unit of Leviticus 18–19 points back, as we indicated earlier, to the warning against Canaanites manners in Leviticus 19:1–5. In opposition Yahweh posited the demand: "You shall observe *my* laws and decrees." Taken together, all of this leads us not to harbor high hopes regarding the moral quality of Canaanite rules of justice, which might yet be discovered.

Leviticus 20

Like the wrapping around a box, Leviticus 20 fits around Leviticus 18–19. Both of those chapters reach their climactic conclusion here. Here the sentence is pronounced for the terrible sins mentioned in those chapters. Pointedly pronounced. No other punishment is discussed here other than capital punishment. And the method of punishment is always stoning. A few times, burning. But always death. Real death. Because any compromise with Canaanitism was impossible.

Some think that Leviticus 20 fits only with Leviticus 18, and that Leviticus 19 fell entirely between the cracks. But the people were not seeing Leviticus 19 very clearly. This chapter has the same scope as Leviticus 18, except that its pronouncements are less symbolic and more positive. Because Leviticus 20 is also less symbolic, however, but strongly negative—Death! Put to death!—it gives the appearance of being a suitable counterpart of

NO PAGAN LIFESTYLE! (LEV 18–20)

Leviticus 18. But that is an optical illusion. If you take time to reflect on the character and goal of Leviticus 19, you will gladly acknowledge its legitimate place where we find it in Scripture.

By itself, Leviticus 20 is not longwinded. That characterization applies not just to the definitive rejection of any compatibility between water and fire. Nor to the constantly repeated sentence of death.

This section consists of three parts, which we would entitle as follows:

1. First of all: no pardon for those guilty of sacrificing to Molech and consulting the dead (Lev 20:1–7).

2. Main section: death for all Canaanite uncleanness (Lev 20:8–21)!

3. Closing declaration: So then, be separate (Lev 20:22–26)!

1. First of all: no pardon for those guilty of sacrificing to Molech and consulting the dead (Lev 20:1–7).

This introduction is organized somewhat different than we might be inclined to do it. According to the custom of the Torah, the discussion begins at the top level. The worst is placed first. For what could be worse than that Israel would sacrifice their children to Molech, no matter how that may have happened, whether they were alive or dead? What was worse than if this people of Yahweh, people of life, mind you, were to inquire of the dead? For these are the two subjects that are discussed first.

A. Concerning those who are guilty of sacrificing to Molech (vv. 1–5)

From the way in which the actual content of this section begins, in verse 2, you can see that it is closely connected to the preceding. In the preceding chapters, this or that sin was identified, but that was not sufficient. Now the punishment on all this wickedness had to be discussed. Therefore we should read the beginning of verse 2 this way: "Moreover, you shall say to the Israelites." That is the line of verses 2–5.

Verse 2: "Any man from the sons of Israel or from the aliens sojourning in Israel who gives any of his offspring to Molech, shall surely be put to death." With this the rule is firmly established and the punishment is stipulated. Such a thing may absolutely not be tolerated among Israel. "The people of the land," i.e., everyone who had any influence in the matter (2

Kgs 11:18-20), even though he might not be a priest, will see to it that the guilty party is stoned.

Verse 3 is discussing the situation, however, where this wickedness occurs in secret. That could happen with very small children. In that situation, Yahweh himself will find the guilty party. The word "I" that is often left unmentioned in the Hebrew, is used here, in a position of prominence in the sentence. "*I will also [in those situations not discovered by others] set My face against that man and will cut him off from among his people [by means, for example, of sickness or accident], because he has given some of his offspring to Molech, so as to defile My sanctuary [by, of all things, still participating in a sacrifice meal as a murderer] and to profane My holy name [if it came out later, people might suppose that Yahweh and Molech stood on the same line or were actually the same deities].*"

Verses 4-5. But what if the sin was known, but nobody did anything about it? Then Yahweh was also powerful enough to go after the guilty party. And his entire family, who had remained silent about the wickedness, would be included. For here something had occurred that a married man could no more tolerate in his marriage, than if his wife were to consort with another man. Adultery. Harlotry. That's the word used here. The background of the way of speaking is the covenant that Yahweh had established with Israel at Horeb. At that time, he had taken this people as his bride, his wife, as it were, and therefore the evil that Israel would be committing by surrendering to the service of one or more idols, was equivalent to the harlotry of a married woman (*zana*). We encounter this expression, "whoring after," frequently in the Old Testament, beginning already in the Book of the Covenant (Exod 34:15). From this expression we can learn that the covenant of Yahweh is and remains the starting point, even in connection with the admonitions and punishments of those who totally neglect that covenant. But God did not neglect that covenant. He calls their sin here "adulterous, harlotry, running after idols." In addition, what contributed to exactly this characterization was the fact that the religion of the Canaanites, as we have seen, bore such a hyper-sexualized character. That verdict of "whoring after" was thoroughly deserved.

B. Concerning those who are guilty of inquiring of the dead (vv. 6-7)

"*As for the person who turns to mediums and to spiritists, to play the harlot after them, I will also set My face against that person and will cut him off from among his people. You shall consecrate yourselves therefore and be holy, for I am the Lord your God."*

Once again we have the issue of consulting mediums and spiritists, something condemned here as harlotry, committing adultery. That inquiring of the dead is seen as belonging to that complex of despicably unclean Canaanite religion!

Just like sacrificing a little child to Molech—in the cemetery at Gezer, various jars have been found with half-burned skeletons of babies—so this inquiring of the dead, if this were done by Israelites, would have happened secretly. But here we read that Yahweh would know where to find those who committed such wickedness.

Here we would insert a few comments about the last verse of our chapter, verse 27. As we mentioned earlier, it says: *"Now a man or a woman who is a medium or a spiritist shall surely be put to death. They shall be stoned with stones, their bloodguiltiness is upon them."*

The difference between verse 6 and verse 27 is this, that verse 27 talks about people who are consulted, like the woman in Endor, for example, but verse 6 talks about people who go to such sources for advice, like king Saul. Both kinds of people must be put to death.

(Perhaps this latter verse was moved. Originally it could have been near verse 6, but a copyist may have initially overlooked it and later put it at the end of the chapter.)

Finally, the purpose of this introduction is expressed once more, in the words: *"You shall consecrate yourselves therefore and be holy, for I am the Lord your God [or: I, Yahweh, am your God]"* (v. 7).

We remember reading these verses earlier. That was at the end of Leviticus 11, in connection with unclean animals. A chapter full of symbolic instruction, whereby God impressed upon his ancient people: Make a separation! And we found these words also at the beginning of Leviticus 19, at the beginning of a chapter containing partly symbolic and partly straightforward instruction.

Here we encounter them once again, as the conclusion of this introduction pertaining to serving Molech and inquiring of the dead. When we compare these three passages, we are confirmed in our conviction that in Leviticus, in various ways, both with and without symbolism, God has given his people a harness of strongly relevant Torah, in order to arm Israel against the unspeakably dangerous paganism that she would encounter in Canaan.

2. *Main section: death for all Canaanite uncleanness (Lev 20:8–21)!*

PRELUDE: VV. 8–9

Verse 8. Now comes an entire series of punishments, all of them capital punishments. For there is no possible compromise with, or adopting of, anything that smells like Canaanite uncleanness. Israel will have to observe the laws and decrees of Yahweh (18:5). Period. Therefore yet one more reminder of that is given *first*. In verse 8: "*You shall keep My statutes and practice them; I am the Lord your Sanctifier.*"

We translated that last word as we did—your Sanctifier—in order that it would stand out. We must see clearly God's point of departure. His own historical work of redemption. At Horeb he gave Israel a place alongside himself. He thereby sanctified her. He placed her on the elevated level of the Horeb covenant. And that was a unique privilege. But for any reckless despising and transgressing of that privilege, there obviously was no pardon. This is why the familiar line is repeated once more: *Continue walking in my laws!!*

Verse 9. Therefore here as well we have first a reminder of the obligation to obey, provided to those in Israel who gave the initial instruction in the laws of Yahweh. To father and mother. "*If there is anyone who curses his father or his mother, he shall surely be put to death; he has cursed his father or his mother, his bloodguiltiness is upon him.*"

The word for "curse" in Hebrew can refer to the opposite of "honor" that we have in the Fifth Commandment. It means to "think light of" something or someone, to not ascribe weight or significance to something or someone, to mock, and thus to curse, someone. Abandoning the service of Yahweh naturally begins not directly with cursing one's parents, though it can lead to that, but it begins by ignoring the teaching and practice given at home. A person disregards the properly instructive guidance of father and mother. Later the instruction about the "Sabbaths" is also denigrated (19:3). And eventually . . . the way back to Canaanitism has been paved.

We would have preferred it if people would not be surprised that the text here "suddenly" speaks about father and mother. That is not happening "suddenly." Nor did it in 19:3. Without genuinely Christian families, the church has no future. The *parents* must make known to their children God's faithfulness (Isa 38:19). That "law" may not be set aside, whether in a friendly or an unfriendly manner, by various agencies or institutions that take over this task of the parents, to say nothing of taking it away from parents. In Lev 19:3 God mentions those parent before he talks about "the Sabbaths," and here in Lev 20:9 he mentions only the parents.

NO PAGAN LIFESTYLE! (LEV 18–20)

The Punishments: vv. 10–21

In Lev 20:10, men and women who committed adultery had to be put to death. There was no pardon for this, unlike among other nations. The addition that someone committed adultery "with another man's wife," can be intended as a way of emphasizing the cowardly nature of adultery. One deals more or less confidentially with another person, meanwhile committing adultery with his wife. Just so we don't deduce from this addition what appeared among the rabbis, namely, that therefore the marriage of a Gentile man and a Gentile woman was actually not a marriage. Marriage was instituted by God already in Paradise, and therefore, when it is entered by a man and a woman, it does not become a marriage for the first time through what a third party thinks may be required—for example, with or without a sacramental bestowal of a "marriage blessing." There is to be no despising of creation.

Leviticus 20:11: anyone who has had sexual relations with the wife of his father—mentioned also in 18:8—must be put to death.

Leviticus 20:12: anyone who has had sexual relations with his daughter-in-law (see 18:15) must be put to death.

Leviticus 20:13: anyone who has been guilty of homosexual intercourse must be put to death, as well as the person with whom this sodomy was committed (see 18:22).

Leviticus 20:14: what is in view here is the case discussed in 18:17, namely, where someone takes a wife and also her daughter whom she received from a previous marriage. All three must be put to death, the man and both women. Moreover, they must be burned. Surely on account of the abominable and wicked character of the evil that was committed. For the more customary punishment was stoning (20:1). But the burning had to be administered in special situations, as when the daughter of a priest had committed sexual immorality (Lev 21:9). This punishment of burning was also not unknown in the ancient Near East (Gen 38:24).

Leviticus 20:15: alternate translation: "a man who gives the emission of his seed to an animal shall surely be put to death, and you shall put the animal to death." Here the wickedness that was discussed in 18:23 is threatened with death. The next verse talks about this as well.

Leviticus 20:16: "If a woman approaches any animal and lies with it, you shall kill the woman and the animal; they shall surely be put to death; their blood is upon them."

At first glance, one might suppose that this wickedness (bestiality) was punished with death among the pagans as well. Among the Hittites, the person who committed sexual immorality with an ox, sheep, pig, or dog was put to death by the king. But this occurred only because those animals were consecrated to the deity. Sexual immorality with a horse or mule was not punishable. The matter was totally different with respect to the prohibitions that we find formulated in Scripture against bestiality (Exod 22:19; Lev 18:23; 20:15–16; Deut 27:21). They would have been given chiefly with a view to certain perverse practices that appeared among the Canaanites as well.

In Ugarit, for example, sexual intercourse with animals was not viewed as something to be rejected, as we see from the fact that Baal himself had intercourse with a heifer. In the religious texts of Ugarit this fact was celebrated, although people added that for this purpose Baal had altered himself into a bull. This cannot be said of his priests, who had turned this mythological fact into a ritual act. When the Bible emphatically forbids such acts, it adds, in so many words, that the Canaanites defile themselves by means of such conduct (Lev 18:24). From all of this, we see that the Ugaritic texts show that in this respect, the Bible is all too correct.

But why did the animals with which the sin had been committed have to be put to death as well? Not, of course, because there were equally culpable for the evil committed. That would never have been the reason why, according to Exod 21:28, a bull that had gored someone to death had to be killed. The foolishness of thinking that an animal had to appear before the judge would arise only in later Europe, in the Middle Ages. The primary reason why such a bull had to be killed would not even have been to prevent more people from being killed by that bull. Why was the prescription added that the bull had to be stoned and its meat was not to be eaten? Similarly, here in Lev 20:15–16, we should not think that these animals, with which sexual immorality had been committed, share culpable and punishable responsibility for that. For Israel, who in the Torah had been reminded by so many symbols, that it was and must remain a people of life and purity, would have found these stipulations obvious. The animal in question was not hygienically, but symbolically, unclean. Israel was supposed to see a (symbolic) danger in everything that hinted at fellowship with death and uncleanness. On the other side of the boundary of the covenant with Yahweh there lurked paganism and decay.

Leviticus 20:17: the man who has sexual intercourse with his sister, even if she is his half-sister (see 18:9 and 11), is worthy of death.

Leviticus 20:18: so too is the man who has sexual intercourse with a menstruating woman. If the Torah had intended to give Israel prescriptions of a medical nature, this would have been a suitable occasion to do so, since a menstruating woman, on account of her temporarily being unprotected, was exposed through intercourse to a serious risk of infection. But we read nothing about that. In this verse, where we find none of the symbolism

NO PAGAN LIFESTYLE! (LEV 18–20)

that we find in Leviticus 15, the purpose *remains* to focus Israel's attention on the danger of forsaking the covenant through contact with Canaanite practices. We need to ask how idolatrously people in Canaan thought about menstruation.

Leviticus 20:19: the man who has sexual intercourse with his aunt, i.e., the sister of his mother or the sister of his father, is worthy of death (18:12–13).

Leviticus 20:20: similarly, the man who has sexual intercourse with his aunt, i.e., the wife of his uncle.

When we try to comprehend the possibilities that existed in a society in which people married far younger than today, and in which polygamy was common, then we understand how easily it could happen that someone who was just as old as his uncle, as far as age was concerned, could easily marry his widow. But in Israel God would not bless such marriages with children; on the contrary, "they will die childless."

Leviticus 20:21: in Israel, marriage was also forbidden between a man and his sister-in-law, the wife of his deceased brother (18:18). God did not want to make use of such marriages for expanding his ancient church; on the contrary, "they will die childless."

3. *Closing declaration: So then, be separate (Lev 20:22–26)!*

A few comments about the last verse.

That verse in which capital punishment was required for someone who married the widow of his deceased brother. Parenthetically, perhaps there is such a person among our readers. What a burden he has perhaps carried when he read this verse in the Bible. Was he then worthy of death? Or do those decrees of Leviticus 20 no longer apply today?

In answering these and similar questions, you need to turn to Leviticus 20 itself. Especially to the concluding verses, verses 22–26. There we are supplied with a key with which we can open the lock very easily, the lock of the container that in many respects was artfully constructed, holding the preceding chapters of Leviticus. A container inlaid with beautiful pieces of symbolism. We cannot advise our readers strongly enough to read those verses carefully. Here they are:

> *You shall therefore keep all my statutes and all my rules and do them, that the land where I am bringing you to live may not vomit you out. And you shall not walk in the customs of the nation that I am driving out before you, for they did all these things, and therefore I detested them [recall what God had said already*

> to Abraham, Gen 15:16b, and how he punished Sodom already in Abraham's day, Gen 18:20; 19:24-25]. But I have said to you, "You shall inherit their land, and I will give it to you to possess, a land flowing with milk and honey." I am the Lord your God, who has separated you from the peoples. You shall therefore separate the clean beast from the unclean, and the unclean bird from the clean. You shall not make yourselves detestable by beast or by bird or by anything with which the ground crawls, which I have set apart for you to hold unclean. You shall be holy to me, for I the Lord am holy and have separated you from the peoples, that you should be mine.

In these verses, we receive, so to speak, a user manual for chapters 18-20. Actually, for all of Leviticus 11-20, to which not one chapter belongs—including the chapter about the Great Day of Atonement—that does not have in its background the dark shadow of paganism.

In these verses our attention is drawn to the light that God has placed behind those commandments given in both symbolic and non-symbolic form, whereby he warned Israel about Canaan. Through this light, those commandments become transparent and God's purpose with those chapters becomes evident. God has placed, as it were, flags and caution signs all across the landscape of Israel's life, all of them to remind Israel of God's Horeb covenant. Pay attention as to how, in addition, God reminds Israel repeatedly by means of such words as: "I am Yahweh" or "I am Yahweh your God" or "I, Yahweh, am your God." This reminder is repeated innumerable times.

Moreover, in the preceding discussion, we have seen as well that these chapters, with their commandments and symbols, do not in any way stand independently in the Torah. Recall that Israel was reminded of God's commandments by means of particular buttons or tassels on their clothes, along with a dark blue thread woven into them. And also by means of the command regarding emptying a bird's nest not to remove the mother bird along with the eggs or hatchlings.

All of these were means designed to lead Israel to observe Yahweh's (Horeb) covenant and (ten) words as her highest treasure. That is what all of this was about.

If we don't lose sight of the lesson contained in the concluding verses of Leviticus 20, then we too will obtain light on the questions people ask about those "forbidden degrees of kinship in Leviticus when it comes to marriage." Do these apply to us as well? Let's remember first of all: in Leviticus 18-20 no regulations for marriage are being given. In those chapters we find warnings against various kinds of Canaanite wickedness, including sexual wickedness. But God was not describing in broad strokes the various degrees of kinship allowed, nor the allowance of people to be married. In various passages nothing is being said about marriage, but about various disgusting, disordered expressions of sexual urges. And in other passages, not even that is in view, but rather things like inquiring of the dead.

Therefore, it is so regrettable that people have understood these chapters far too much in terms of their "sound," without first reading them in their context. How ignorant and uninformed people have been in arbitrarily carving out from these chapters a number of prohibitions and admonitions in the sexual realm, and laying upon the church of the New Covenant one, two, or three ironclad ecclesiastical rules. And then people added even more regulations about "impedimenta" or hindrances to marriage—such as: A could not marry B without receiving dispensation from on high, if A was a child of parents who had been the godparents of B and had presented B for baptism, for then A and B were "family" of each other—at that point the domination of the church was established for people's good, but it worked with the fatal misunderstanding that Leviticus contained a list of degrees of kinship that obstructed marriage.

That foolish misunderstanding must be eliminated first.

Leviticus 18–20 is not providing marriage regulations, but is forbidding Canaanitism. In this context God was including sexual crimes as well. And in this context, in order to warn his people not to go over the line, he also prohibited things about which we today might almost say: "Was that necessary?" For example, sodomy and bestiality, and that a man may not have sexual intercourse with his daughter or his mother or with someone who had been married to his deceased father. Thanks to the knowledge of God and of his commandments that had been transmitted down through the centuries, pagans too were disgusted by such things (Rom 1–2; 1 Cor 5), even though this was more evident among one nation than another, as a result of the suppression by many people of the transmitted truth of God (Rom 1:18, 21, 23, 25). Several times God also prohibited something in Israel about which we, for another reason, might say: "Was that really necessary?" For example, that someone was not allowed to marry the widow of his deceased brother (20:21). Today such marriages are entered among us without anyone raising a credible objection. And properly so, for this prohibition was not absolute even among Israel, as we see from the obligation that a man was required to marry the *childless surviving widow* of his brother (Deut 25:5–10). The reason why God prohibited such marriages among Israel should be explained on the basis of his concern that if his people were able to cross that relatively low threshold easily, then perhaps they would not have hesitated to cross an explicitly high threshold. Therefore we see that strictness, also with respect to a levirate marriage, always with the purpose of focusing Israel's attention on the boundary between life and death, between the people of Yahweh and the nations of Canaan. Be careful for intermingling. Already in terms of boundary situations that in themselves are innocent. Follow the certain rather than the uncertain. Don't take one step toward the edge.

This warrant has fallen away today.

Of course our chapters, Leviticus 18–20, retain their teaching for the New Testament church as well. For us they continue as part of Holy Scripture that is able to make us wise unto salvation (2 Tim 3:14–17). With this instruction, God intended to warn the Israelites against intermingling with the godless world of that time; and God commanded Israel to exercise great caution about that. And this warning has lost none of its power for the New Testament church. On the contrary, it applies to us all the more, since we have received a covenant that is so much better, of which Jesus has become the Surety (Heb 7–10). Listen to the apostles warn in their epistles against the impurities of pagan life (Gal 5; Eph 4–5; Col 3; 1 Pet 4; etc.). Our apostasy will be even more deserving of punishment.

If only medieval Christianity had not been so foolish by immersing itself in endless stipulations pertaining to marriage impediments, supposedly formulated in the spirit of Leviticus, while at the same time the church doors were opened wide for various pagan teaching and pagan practices. In fact, is our modern Christianity so careful that in its contact with the godless world, it prefers to choose the certain rather than the uncertain? That would surely have been according to the Spirit of Leviticus and according to the Spirit of the apostles of our Lord Jesus Christ. Be careful! No pagan lifestyle! Be careful of every movement leading toward the edge! For example, wicked conversations, not to mention wicked books and movies, corrupt good morals.

With this difference: today God's Spirit no longer employs former means of instruction with respect to the (adult!) New Testament church. Today we must suffice with his Word, together with baptism and the Lord's Supper.

23

Keeping priests and sacrificial gifts holy (Lev 21–22)

FOR EVERYONE READING LEVITICUS 21–22, it is immediately clear that these two chapters form a kind of unit. There is variety. The first chapter focuses more on the priests, the second on the sacrificial gifts (and their use by priests and possibly by non-priests). But even though the former chapter focuses more on persons and the second more on things, both of them bring us into the sphere of the priesthood and the sanctuary.

WHAT THE PURPOSE OF THESE CHAPTERS CANNOT BE

In these chapters we encounter things that are most remarkable, from which devoted Bible readers have perhaps often turned away in discouragement. What does all that mean, anyway? For example, that a priest may not be defiled by contact with death, even if the deceased were a member of his own extended family. Or that the high priest might not be defiled by contact with death, even that of his own father and mother. Indeed, that the high priest might not even marry a widow! Or that a priest's son who was born with a deformity, or a priest that had been physically mutilated, might not serve at the altar.

Some have pointed to the striking parallels between certain commandments for the Israelite priests and certain commands for pagan priests. To be sure, we cannot deny that among other nations, similar kinds of things were forbidden as with Israel. In Rome, a *flamen dialis*, or priest of Jupiter, was not allowed to marry a widow. The Romans followed the custom of placing a Cyprus bough in front of a house where a corpse was lying, out of fear that a priest might enter there. For he would thereby have become defiled. In Babylon, a priest's son who had a respectable appearance and was sound in body, could appear before the gods Shamash and Adad, but not someone whose fingers had been amputated or who had been castrated.

How are we to explain those undeniable similarities?

It won't do simply to assert that they were taken over. That would create even greater puzzles. If Israel inherited everything from their Babylonian ancestors, then how must we explain that Israel's priests were explicitly forbidden to render their service in the sanctuary naked,[1] whereas there is good reason to believe that exactly the opposite was true for Babylonian priests, who seem to have been required to appear unclothed before their gods? And if Israel is supposed to have taken over everything from Egypt, then how must we explain that Egyptian priests had to have shaved heads, whereas this was strictly forbidden for Israelite priests?

One could better explain such remarkable similarities that do exist from the fact that the Israelites were human beings just like the pagans, and they were Eastern people just like the nations surrounding them. Thereby the symbolism in the Torah of Horeb must be showing traces of similarity with those regulations of other nations, specifically, other Eastern nations. In this way we don't want to ignore for a moment the remnants of the original knowledge of God and his commandments that continued to exert influence, albeit in ways that were deformed, among the pagans in their religions. We have already spoken, in connection with the striking similarities between the religion of Israel and that of some pagans, of the "The Great Annexation."[2] Subsequently we were able to recall that phenomenon in connection with our further discussion of the institutions of the Law.

Nevertheless, such an explanation could not possibly be entirely satisfactory. It could lead us to suppose that at Horeb, God was looking at the Israelites like bothersome children who now also needed something to which their religious eye could look with enjoyment, lest otherwise they feel severely shortchanged when they looked at the nations surrounding them. With such an explanation, however, we cannot agree. For it would ignore especially the data regarding God's positive purpose with Leviticus 21–22 that the book of Leviticus provides us.

---

1. See Vonk, *Exodus*, 262–63.
2. See Vonk, *Exodus*, 299–304.

KEEPING PRIESTS AND SACRIFICIAL GIFTS HOLY (LEV 21–22)

THE PLACE OF LEVITICUS 21–22

To understand God's purpose with these chapters, we must first pay attention to the place where we find them in Holy Scripture.

That place is after a series of chapters connected by the constant unified symbolic pedagogical theme. In those chapters we find persistent discussion of means whereby God wanted to remind his ancient church of the Horeb covenant that he had established with her. Israel had been placed upon a foundation that, as it were, was set off with a hedge of flags and banners on which had been written: Therefore make a separation! Be holy, for I, Yahweh, your God, am holy.

We saw that anti-pagan theme everywhere.

In Leviticus 11–15, dealing with the clean nation, who was to have no fellowship with paganism and death.

In Leviticus 16 as well, dealing with the Great Day of Atonement. In the second goat, Israel's purity was demonstrated in contrast to the world outside of Israel. Keep your hands off Israel!

In Leviticus 17: be careful with the blood! Here too, the anti-pagan theme.

In Leviticus 18–20: no pagan lifestyle!

All of this applied, however, simply for all Israelites, because all of Israel had the calling to be a kingdom of priests before Yahweh (Exod 19:6).

So already for the *foundation* on which the Israelite pyramid rested in the middle of the sea of nations, the demand applied: "Be holy, for I am holy," and to that demand every Israelite man and every Israelite woman was reminded in thousands of ways.

But that symbolic-pedagogical line continues still further.

That antithesis with paganism and corruption returns here, in Leviticus 21–22. Along with the accompanying demands.

But here in Leviticus 21–22 both are strengthened. With an extra emphasis. For example, all Israelites had to see in death an image of paganism and corruption, and thus purify themselves after possible contact with a corpse. But priests were not allowed this contact except only within the immediate family. And the high priests not at all.

THE CONCLUSION OF LEVITICUS 21–22

This thread that we see running through the preceding chapters (Lev 11–20), as well as through these two (Lev 21–22), is tied off at the end of Leviticus 22. In a certain sense. For even afterward, we find a kind of continuation.

Something of this nature happened as well at the end of the preceding group of chapters, Leviticus 18–20. For there we read: "You shall therefore separate the clean beast from the unclean, and the unclean bird from the clean. You shall not make yourselves detestable by beast or by bird or by anything with which the ground crawls, which I have set apart for you to hold unclean. You shall be holy to me, for I the Lord am holy and have separated you from the peoples, that you should be mine" (20:25–26). That conclusion provided opportunity for very important commentary.

Well, the same sound echoes from the conclusion of these two priestly chapters of Leviticus 21–22. "*So you shall keep my commandments and do them: I am the Lord. And you shall not profane my holy name, that I may be sanctified among the people of Israel. I am the Lord who sanctifies you, who brought you out of the land of Egypt to be your God: I am the Lord*" (22:31–33).

"You shall not profane my holy *name*."

The reference to God's *name* must be understood to refer to familiarity with his accomplishments, with his great deeds. Where else had God performed greater miracles than in Egypt? And for what purpose had he performed them? Pay careful attention to this. The deepest reason why Yahweh delivered Israel from Egypt was this: because just as in Paradise, he wanted to enjoy concourse and fellowship with people. Toward that goal, the tabernacle construction was an important step. God wanted to dwell among his people Israel in a tent. That desire was the impulse lying behind God's mighty deeds of deliverance.

And how closely God's *name* was tied to that tabernacle!

And obviously to the tabernacle personnel as well.

But what a reproach for God's *name*, therefore, arose when the ministry of these tabernacle officiants did not proceed properly, the priests connected with that tabernacle. This explains why, at the conclusion of these two priestly chapters, we find the warning to all Israel to be on guard especially for that. In fact, repeated mention is made in these chapters of that *name* of God. That name was tied even more closely with the tabernacle and the priests than with all Israel.

GOD'S PURPOSE WITH LEVITICUS 21–22

If now someone were to claim that Israel's life, and especially that of the priests, was rather unenjoyable under all these regulations, then there would be some truth in that. As the apostle Paul said, while Israel was still a child, God "held her in custody under the law as a kind of protection," "under

KEEPING PRIESTS AND SACRIFICIAL GIFTS HOLY (LEV 21–22)

guardians and trustees" (see Gal 3:23; 4:2). But beware of infelicitous English translations of these verses that might give rise to mistaken ideas about the Law: the Law did not function as a jailor. By means of various regulations, God wanted first of all to instruct and assure the Israelites that they had been accepted as his children, and that despite all their sins and miseries, they were also permitted to continue in the path of the ministry of atonement conducted by the priests. For they had been given by God himself as mediators between him and the people. In various ways God guaranteed to the Israelites the reliability and veracity of his Horeb covenant. In this way, the Law of Horeb contained a beloved gospel! Fundamentally the very same gospel that is given to us today, although now without those regulations, because a better covenant has been granted to us today, of which Jesus has become the Surety. And because we received a High Priest who is not "beset with weakness" (cf. Heb 7:28). We have spoken about this so often that we can be brief at this point.

CONTENTS AND OUTLINE OF LEVITICUS 21–22

Although in these chapters, we find most prominently a discussion of regulations that the priest had to observe, they end with a conclusion in which God has all the Israelites in view. No wonder, for in that entire people, the priesthood found its meaning and reason for existence. Therefore we have entitled this chapter: *Keeping priests and sacrificial gifts holy*.

It is also the case that in connection with those priests and sacrificial gifts, God's name is repeatedly mentioned in these chapters. It would therefore have been more complete if we had formulated the theme of these chapters this way: *You shall keep my name holy by keeping my priests and sacrificial gifts holy*. But the clarity of such a chapter title would perhaps have been obscured by its length.

This Scripture passage is not difficult to outline. In Leviticus 21 we read about the priests, and in Leviticus 22 about the sacrificial gifts. Here is the outline:

I. Keeping my priests holy (Lev 21)
    A. Defilements for which the priests must be on guard (21:1–15)
        1. The priests (21:1–9)
        2. The high priest (21:10–15)
    B. Physical defects whereby the priests were excluded from service (21:16–24)

PART 4 | THE PEOPLE OF YAHWEH

II. Keeping my sacrificial gifts holy (Lev 22)

    A.   Concerning their use (22:1–16)

        1. By priests (22:1–9)

        2. By non-priests (22:10–16)

    B.   Concerning the gifts brought (22:17–33)

I. Keeping my priests holy (Lev 21)

A. Defilements for which the priests must be on guard (21:1–15)

If you have read our commentary on Leviticus 11–15, you know how many different ways God instructed his ancient church regarding the very special foundation upon which he had placed her at Horeb. God wanted to remind Israel of that so-called apartheid as his chosen people. By means of a book filled with pictures, filled with visual instruction. That book was Israel's everyday—and every night—life. For God laid claim to every possible thing in human life, in order thereby to warn Israel against forsaking the life-basis upon which he had placed her. For that purpose God placed his claim, for example, on the distinction between clean and unclean animals (Lev 11), on the birth of children (Lev 12), on the leprosy of people and houses (Lev 13–14), on emissions of men and women (Lev 15). All of these were letters and pictures in God's book that was filled with visual instruction. And there was still more: clothing, Sabbaths. And still more.

But if you followed all of this carefully, you will have observed that these two subjects played a very important role in connection with those innumerable warnings: (1) the contrast between death and life, and (2) what we customarily call sexuality, or sexual life.

Well now, on these two main subjects, God's commandments are focused both for the priests and for the high priest. Entirely in line with the method to which we have drawn attention earlier. The method of place the greater accent on something. This approach has become almost formulaic, so that we see the first half of Leviticus 21 constructed as follows:

1. Commandments for the priests (21:1–9)

    A. Regarding defilement through death (21:1–6)

    B. Regarding defilement in terms of sexuality (21:7–9)

KEEPING PRIESTS AND SACRIFICIAL GIFTS HOLY (LEV 21–22)

2. Commandments for the high priest (21:10–15)

   A. Regarding defilement through death (21:10–12)

   B. Regarding defilement in terms of sexuality (21:13–15)

1. COMMANDMENTS FOR THE PRIESTS (21:1–9)

(a) Regarding defilement through death (21:1–6)

These verses provide us with no great surprise. We have read earlier about Yahweh's aversion toward death. We recall the obligation for purification prescribed for every ordinary Israelite who came into contact with a dead person, a dead animal, or even with certain live animals whose mode of existence involved them being at home in what was filthy and stank (Lev 11). How much less would God be able to bear any defilement on the part of those who were allowed to approach him far more intimately than the people. In fact, we have seen earlier, on other occasions, that the priesthood and death formed an absolute opposition. For example, when we discussed the priestly garments, we observed at that point that the priest's robe was not allowed to be made like our garments of nobility, consisting of various sections sewn together, but that it had to be woven as one piece. Something similar was prescribed in connection with the priestly headdress. This had to rest securely on the priest's head. Tied to his head. Apparently to prevent it from falling off during his work. If it fell off, his head would be uncovered and this was a sign of mourning. We referred to this also in chapter 14, in connection with our discussion of the death of Nadab and Abihu.

The following two commandments were given to the priests in Leviticus 21:1–6:

1. Priests may not grieve (vv. 1–4); and
2. Priests may certainly not grieve in a pagan manner (vv. 5–6).

(1) Priests may not grieve (vv. 1–4)

With such absoluteness this section begins.

Moses had to address the priests emphatically—"Speak to the priests, the sons of Aaron, and say to them"—that a priest may not defile himself for a dead person (*nefesh*) among his relatives. That is verse 1. Perhaps verse 4, the last verse of this section, originally had a similarly absolute reach. All the commentators agree that this sentence as it stands is difficult to understand. The difficulty disappears, however, if we accept that a copyist wrote *ba'al* rather than *be'ebel*. If this is what happened, then verse 4 would have said: "He shall not defile himself by any grieving among his relatives and thereby profane himself."

That was the regulation.

Yahweh's priesthood and death were incompatible. Actually, that regulation applied for the ordinary priests as well. Later it would be placed definitively upon the high priest as an absolute prescription, since he was not permitted to be involved with anyone at all who was deceased. But for the ordinary priests, a few exceptions were permitted. An ordinary priest was permitted to be involved with a few instances of people who had died. But those would have to be of his nearest relatives. When the father or mother of a priest had died, he could mourn for them. Or for a son or daughter, for a brother or sister. At least if the sister was his full sister, instead of a half-sister, and as long as she was unmarried.

These were the only exceptions.

This hardly requires explanation. Yahweh was impressing upon all Israel that he was the God of life. Outside of the fellowship of the covenant with him there was only death. Among the pagans was only death. This explains God's use of every possible opportunity and occasion when death occurs in human experience, in order to teach and remind Israel of her exalted privilege. This explains the rule that men like the sons of Aaron, who came near to God on Israel's behalf with sacrificial offerings, were not allowed any contact with death at all. That spoke volumes.

Nevertheless, Yahweh was also merciful. He knew how frail a creature such an ordinary priest was. For this reason, he granted him on rare and exceptional occasions the privilege of mourning the death of a loved one from among his immediate family.

Was a priest permitted to grieve for his deceased wife?

In our view, one need not be surprised that a priest's own wife was not mentioned among those for whose death he was permitted to grieve (vv. 2–3). First, because the Israelite probably "heard" mention of her in the opening words introducing the exceptional cases in verse 2. The phrase, "except for his nearest kin," (literally, "his nearest flesh" [*se'er*]) included close family members, like mother, sister, etc. (18:6). But another Hebrew word for "flesh" (*basar*) is occasionally used together with the other word (see 18:6), which Scripture uses to indicate the unity of husband and wife (Gen 2:24). Second, we say in connection with our discussion of Leviticus 15:24 how in the practice of marital life, God proceeded on the basis of this unity between husband and wife as something that would have been most obvious. When a wife began to menstruate, if she and her husband were having sexual intercourse, not only what she unclean, but he was as well. And during the seven days. Thirdly, we read that God especially forbade the prophet Ezekiel to mourn over the death of his wife. Thus, this was apparently such a startling peculiarity that it could serve as a metaphor for the fall of Jerusalem, over which people were not to mourn later (Ezek 24:15–27).

The grieving of a priest over his deceased wife would have been a customary, natural matter.

(2) Priests may certainly not grieve in a pagan manner (vv. 5–6)

In these verses, the priests are forbidden to be guilty of following pagan mourning customs in their period of mourning. When we discussed Leviticus 19:27, we saw how some pagans mutilated themselves, driven to such acts by their fear of death. But for that very reason, such pagan manners were unsuitable for Israel. For Israel had nothing to do with death, and had nothing to fear from death, because Israel had been accepted as the chosen people of Yahweh, who had shown that he could overcome death.

So then, what was unsuitable among the ordinary Israelites was naturally entirely unsuitable for the priests of Yahweh. That is what verse 6 says: "They shall be holy to their God and not profane the name of their God. For they offer the Lord's food offerings, the bread of their God; therefore they shall be holy."

Let us take note of three things in this verse.

First, notice *God's name*. We observed that throughout Leviticus 21–22, that name of God is mentioned repeatedly. That is because the priesthood was so intimately connected to the sanctuary of Yahweh, the tabernacle, and because the name (the honor, the reputation and fame on the basis of his accomplished deeds of deliverance in Egypt, at the Red Sea, in the wilderness, etc.) was connected so closely with that tabernacle. For Yahweh had performed all those renowned deeds for the sake of Israel's liberation and deliverance and sustenance, because, just as in Paradise, he wanted concourse and fellowship with people, he wanted to dwell in the midst of people (see Lev 22:31–33).

So then, what a reproach it would be for Yahweh if not only his ordinary people, but even his priests—the saints among the saints—would behave as if they had not been completely delivered from paganism with its strange fear of death.

And we Christians must also see to it that people around us do not think that we are just as unbelieving as they. For we know much more about

God's name than ancient Israel. The God and Father of our Lord Jesus Christ has given us his beloved Son, who has conquered death and has brought life and immortality. No greater accomplishment has God performed until now than this (Eph 1:19–21).

Next we draw your attention to the phrase *the Lord's food offerings*. Those were the *qorbanim* (from *qereb*) or gifts of Israel to Yahweh that were designated for the altar of fire, entirely or partially, bloody or non-bloody. Here we are told those who were permitted to place these gifts of the people on the altars were the priests. They were the *qorbanim* par excellence, the one who approached. Naturally, such people could not appear before God with pagan symbols of death on their head or on their body.

Finally, these burnt offerings are called here the "bread" (*lechem*) of their God. We commented earlier on this expression. This is what, for example, the showbread was called. The sacrifices brought into the forecourt were also identified this way. These fire offerings naturally were not called "food" for Yahweh in order thereby to express some kind of divine dependence on human activity, but to indicate how much he delighted in Israel bringing him those offerings, although he did not need them for himself.

Just imagine that people, who were the only ones among Israel chosen to bring such gifts to their God in his sanctuary, had appeared before God during their period of mourning dressed like pagans. Trembling in fear of death. Would that not have been a mockery of the very name and reputation of Yahweh as the God of salvation and life for his Israel?

Earlier we point out the significance that such Scripture passages still have for us. All the more since as Christians, we have all been appointed to fulfill a priestly task (1 Pet 2:9). Of course, in periods of grieving we may indeed mourn, but we must not grieve as pagans do. Pagans and apostate Christians—these are people filled with fear of death, people filled with despair. They cannot see beyond the grave. But Christians ought to be those who confess the hope of eternal life that our Lord will grant us when, according to his promise, he comes to raise us on the last day.

(b) Regarding defilement in terms of sexuality (21:7–9)

Death is serious, but moral abuses can arise, of which we must say: this is even worse than death. We recall the urgent warning in chapters 18–20, against Canaanite immorality. As far as Israel was concerned, that had to lie on the same plane as death and corruption.

In the verses that follow, we read of women "with some kind of issue," probably an issue involving pagan immorality. That pagan element comes to

KEEPING PRIESTS AND SACRIFICIAL GIFTS HOLY (LEV 21-22)

mind first on account of the proximity of the preceding prohibition to the priests (vv. 5-6) not to be engaged in pagan grieving customs. But also in view of the content itself of these verses.

A priest was not allowed to marry three kinds of women (v. 7). (Indeed, verse 8 is apparently saying that all Israel must see to it that he comes into no contact with them.)

First, he may not marry an unchaste woman. In this instance we are dealing with a "public woman," a harlot or prostitute. Perhaps this is referring to pagan prostitutes.

Second, he may not marry a defiled woman, possibly referring to a girl like the one mentioned in Lev 19:29—a girl who, under pressure from, or at least with the approval of, her parents gave herself to so-called sacred prostitution.

Third, he may not marry a divorced woman. She could naturally have been divorced unjustly, but even then, a priest was not to marry her.

We would immediately add the stipulation of verse 9. If the priest's daughter committed sexual immorality, she thereby defiled not only herself—here the same word for "defiled" is used as for a girl who is violated, mentioned in verse 9 and 19:29—but her father as well. It is possible that the stipulation had in view common unchastity. But seeing the anti-pagan scope in the preceding context, perhaps we should think of a priest's daughter who brazenly gave herself to prostitution in an idolatrous Canaanite temple. Moreover, the wickedness would have to be punished symbolically, not by stoning, but by burning, just as in the case we read about in 20:14, where too we read of something just as brazen.

Such conduct would blaspheme and profane the sacred ministry of such a priest. For he was offering up the food of Israel's God. And the symbolic language would be obscured, the language spoken by the very existence of the priesthood, which rested on hereditary descent. We will discuss that language of symbolism below.

2. Commandments for the High Priest (21:10-15)

The most emphatic regulations applied to the high priest. This does not surprise us. He was *the* priest among all the priests. He was the only one who was allowed to enter the most holy place.

(a) Regarding defilement through death (21:10–12)

It was the case that all of Israel was actually supposed to understand themselves to be the people of Yahweh. Israel was reminded of that in all kinds of ways, such as by tassels on the corners of their garments. But it was obvious that the emblems of those permitted to enter the tabernacle—that paradisal place with its symbolic preaching of life for Israel with Yahweh—were even more imposing. The entire priestly wardrobe testified to that. We mentioned the priestly robe that was not to be made of parts sewn together, but woven as one piece.

But the high priest's garments took the cake. In addition to the usual priestly clothing, the high priest wore the dark blue outer robe. This too had to be woven, but in addition the neck had to be decorated with a seam. To prevent it from ripping. And to mention one more thing: a golden tassel had to be sewn on the headdress or headband of the high priest, on which the Hebrew words had been embroidered: "Holy to Yahweh."

It was evident that for this man, any and every form of contact with death was prohibited. As we saw, he was the priest who was actually anointed. This is being recalled here. "The priest who is chief among his brothers, on whose head the anointing oil is poured and who has been consecrated to wear the garments, shall not let the hair of his head hang loose nor tear his clothes" (v. 10).

This high priest was never to appear with an uncovered head. Even something that was permitted to the priests by way of exception, mourning for their close relatives, was absolutely prohibited for the high priest. He was not to be defiled not even by touching his father or mother. When we read immediately thereafter in verse 12: "He shall not go out of the sanctuary, lest he profane the sanctuary of his God," that regulation would surely have involved a particular mourning period for someone in the high priestly family who had died. This regulation entailed his entire lifetime. When someone in his immediate family died, then during the period when others were mourning and grieving, just to be sure that he didn't become defiled, he was not allowed to leave the area of the tabernacle and forecourt.

Why did things have to be this way?

Some have said: Because the sacred ministry was under no circumstances to be interrupted. We believe that such a practical answer deserves consideration, even though Scripture does not supply this explanation here. It points to the unique privilege of the high priest, that he had been consecrated to his God by means of the oil of anointing. To this prohibition is added: I am Yahweh (v. 12). The following section, which runs parallel to this one, ends with the words: For I am Yahweh, who sanctifies him (v. 15).

KEEPING PRIESTS AND SACRIFICIAL GIFTS HOLY (LEV 21–22)

That too leads us to think of the embroidery on the golden tassel: Holy to Yahweh.

Could the meaning of the absolute prohibition of the high priest's grieving have been symbolic-pedagogical as well? As a lesson for all Israel?

In the preceding context, we saw that Yahweh used the phenomenon of death frequently as a symbol of paganism that was disobedient toward him. Israel was being warned never to be engaged with that death, with that symbol of reprehensible paganism, indeed, for all that lurid outside world, the sphere of Satan and his evil spirits, as we express it nowadays.

But that warning was given to the priests with much more force.

And with absolute validity for him who represented the people to God and God to the people: the high priest.

Israel must have heard such symbolic language in these commandments. Israel would have received not only instruction, but also the strengthening of faith thereby. Israel would have been led to the confession: as surely as our high priest may approach God on our behalf, so surely are we, despite all our sins and defects, the people of Yahweh, his holy people, destined not for death and corruption, but for eternal life with him.

The high priest was, in our view, a walking sign and seal of the promise of Horeb: Israel, people of Yahweh. In a certain sense, all the priests were that already. But that is surely what the high priest was, completely and absolutely.

(b) Regarding defilement in terms of sexuality (21:13–15)

Anyone reading the following section should remember that we are dealing here with symbolism. Otherwise he might think that by stipulating that the high priest was never allowed to marry a widow, God was diminishing the pitiable women in comparison with others. And that is a definite falsehood. Recall how emphatically we are assured in Scripture that in general, God's eyes look down with compassion upon the distressed and needy, but also that in particular he desires to be a Father to the orphans and a Judge for the widows (Exod 22:22–24; Deut 10:18; 14:20; 16:11, 14; 24:19–21; 26:12; etc.).

Rather, the purpose was that all Israel should hear and see that Israel was allowed to be, and was supposed to be, the holy people of Yahweh. Even the commandment forbidding the high priest from marrying a widow taught this. We must not infer from this command that God was more or less despising widows, but we must learn to see how highly God valued Israel holding faithfully to the covenant foundation to which he had elevated her at Horeb.

For the sake of that lesson, he risked the tears of the widows.

The high priest was prohibited from marrying the same three kinds of women as the priests were. A divorced woman, a woman who had been defiled (a young girl who had been raped, possibly one defiled through sacred prostitution), and a harlot. But before all these, the widow is mentioned (v. 14). This helps us understand the purpose of the regulation. For it had just discussed defilement through death. What follows next is defilement in the area of sexual relationships The transition to that is formed by mentioning the widow. They head the list. Not because there was something wrong with the purity and honor of this woman, but because she had come into contact with death. For that reason she is listed first among the four prohibited kinds of women. Then came the other three—the divorced, defiled, and immoral women—because each of these were also characterized in some way by death. And that was in flagrant contradiction of the symbolic language that was supposed to be spoken by the priestly class among Israel, according to God's institution and purpose. Since whether one belonged to that priestly class depended on marriage or descent (Deut 18:5), God absolutely prohibited the high priest from marrying any woman associated in any way with death. The high priest was permitted to marry only a pure virgin, naturally, one *from Israel*. That emphasis was included as well. Now we understand why. A pure Israelite girl was a picture of life, an image of all Israel among the pagan nations. A holy people. People of Yahweh, the holy God.

B. Physical defects whereby the priests were excluded from service (21:16–24)

After the preceding discussion, it will be immediately clear that the scope of this portion of Scripture—involving physical defects of priests—was also symbolic.

Earlier we identified the striking similarity between the requirements the priests had to fulfill, and those established for the animals to be slaughtered. These also had to be without defect. Both the *qorbanim*, the gifts, as well as the *qerobim*, the ones who approached Yahweh with them to place them on the altar, had to be whole. Anything else would not have comported with the holiness of Yahweh.

As we have already explained, not all *qorbanim* were designated for the altar. These included firstfruits and tithes, for the support of priests and Levites.

KEEPING PRIESTS AND SACRIFICIAL GIFTS HOLY (LEV 21-22)

We should note that priests who had defects were not permitted to participate in the ministry of the sacrifices, but they were not excluded from enjoying the "food" of Yahweh. They were allowed to eat from both portions, coming from the most holy place and the holy place (v. 22). Here we would take note of God's gentleness. The son of a priest who was born with a deformity or who was no longer sound in body because of an accident, did not have to suffer deprivation. Our heavenly Father is merciful. He always has been.

But no matter how lovely that last regulation may have been, the emphasis fell in this section of the Law upon God's holiness. That divine perfection required that everyone who approached God as a "mediator" of his people, and that every gift brought to God, had to be whole and perfect. The New Testament directs us more than once to the fact that our Lord Jesus Christ fulfilled this divine requirement, both as Priest and as Lamb (Heb 7:26; 10:14; 1 Pet 1:19), and that his work is directed to the goal of presenting his church to the Father as a pure bride (2 Cor 11:2; Eph 1:4; 5:27; Col 1:22).

II. Keeping my sacrificial gifts holy (Lev 22)

It was obvious that after specific commands regarding priests who were allowed to appear before God, some commands would follow regarding the gifts that Israel brought to Yahweh through the mediation of the priests. A portion of those gifts could be enjoyed by the priests themselves. That is the first topic, followed by bringing those gifts by the people.

A. Concerning their use (22:1–16)

Since in the priestly dwellings, other persons could be present who did not belong to the priestly family, we read first about the use of the sacred gifts by priests, and then by non-priests.

1. By priests (22:1–9)

As we just observed, not all of the gifts that the Israelites brought to Yahweh were burned on the altar. A large portion of them was designated for the priests. But these men were not permitted to use them at just any time. They were not allowed to eat of them while they were unclean for a time. In such a case, they had to suffice with food that was permitted for use by every ordinary Israelite.

The reasons for such an inhibiting uncleanness whereby one of the priests (and this applied to his family members as well) was not allowed to eat from the gifts of the Israelites to Yahweh, the kinds that are mentioned are ones we have discussed before. For example, they were the same reasons that would have brought every ordinary Israelite into a situation of being unclean, into a situation of temporary uncleanness. This could be caused by leprosy or by contact with a creeping animal. In short, by one of all those reasons we investigated in chapters 16–19, dealing with Leviticus 11–15. Just as every ordinary Israelite was unclean until evening, and was obligated to purify himself, the same applied to everyone from the priestly families.

This is being discussed in verses 1–7.

To this, however, is added in verse 8 that someone from the priestly families was not permitted to defile himself by eating meat from a clean animal that had not been properly exsanguinated, because it had died naturally or had been torn apart by a wild animal.

This prohibition applied to every ordinary Israelite as well, but when we discussed Lev 17:15–16, we saw how the Law took into consideration—we almost wrote: had to take into consideration—the foolish members of the church. Not everyone possessed the desired capacity for discernment, and not everyone was prepared to submit wholeheartedly to God's will, even though that could mean experiencing harm. This often explains laziness and concessiveness. But something similar was not supposed to occur in a priestly family. This explains why precisely this instruction had to appear in the Law. The priests were supposed to give a good example. In verse 9, they are reminded once more of their duty not to bring bloodguilt upon themselves or upon the people.

2. By non-priests (22:10–16)

This class of persons is discussed in verses 10–13. The theme of this portion is stated emphatically with the words that appear at the beginning and at the end: "No lay person shall eat anything that is holy."

Only the priests were allowed to eat of the most holy things, and do so exclusively in the holy place, but the holy things could be eaten by their family members, their wives and daughters. This included a slave of the priest, whether he belonged to the family through having been purchased, or born into the priest's family through a female slave. A priest's daughter who had lost her husband or had been divorced by her husband, and had therefore returned to her father's house, was permitted to make use of the holy gifts. Unless she had children. Naturally we should understand that

KEEPING PRIESTS AND SACRIFICIAL GIFTS HOLY (LEV 21–22)

these were children fathered by a non-priest. Such a situation placed her family outside the priestly line. While her husband was alive—assuming, again, that he was not a priest—that was the case already. Only a priest's daughter who had become a widow or had been divorced and had no children from a father who was not a priest, was allowed to recover the rights of her youth. Otherwise the enjoyment of what was holy was prohibited for her, just as for anyone who was staying temporarily in the house of the priest, and a day laborer. Such people were lay persons, strangers.

This was the first stipulation, in verses 10–13.

But what was to happen if such a lay person did eat of the holy gifts? Naturally, this would have been unintentional, without premeditation. Such a thing could easily occur in a priest's home. But it was not permitted, and could not simply be ignored. First, what the person in question had taken had to be returned, and second, an additional one-fifth had to be paid as a fine. We recall encountering this one-fifth of a portion in the instruction regarding the guilt offering.

This is stated explicitly in verse 14. People were not to play around with the symbolism of the Law of Yahweh. Its scope was too serious for that. All Israel was actually the holy people of Yahweh. Therefore the sacrificial gifts that this holy people gave to Yahweh, and which he in turn gave back to his priests (with their families, as far as the holy things were concerned), had to be kept holy. If something else were done with them, then such a disrespectful disregard would be charged to the people and the priests as sin. That is what we read in verses 15–16. These verses underscore the preceding one more time, just as verse 9 had done.

The Law was indeed thoroughly evangelical, saturated with the gospel. But the disciplinary hand of the *paidagogos* (Gal 3:24), which compelled scrupulous observance, was not absent for a moment.

B. Concerning the gifts brought (22:17–33)

Not everything that the Israelites brought to Yahweh ended up on the altar, as we have seen. Just the so-called burnt offerings.

These burnt offerings were either bloody or non-bloody. Regarding the latter, the grain offering, nothing is said here. Therefore what is left is only the bloody sacrifices.

As we know, these were four in number. Here the last two, the sin offering and the guilt offering, are not mentioned. That is natural, since the element of voluntariness was completely absent. In connection with these sacrifices, there was nothing to choose or to specify. For those offerings, everything was regulated.

Two kinds of sacrifices remained, namely, the burnt offering and the peace offering. Regarding these sacrifices, God impressed the following instructions upon the heart of his people.

1. Regarding the burnt offerings (vv. 17–20)

Whereas there were numerous occasions when bringing a burnt offering was prescribed (for example, in combination with a guilt offering and a sin offering, when a cleansed leper was reinstated in the community, it could also happen that an Israelite wanted to bring a burnt offering to Yahweh entirely *voluntarily*. Even someone who had settled among Israel as a sojourner (a *ger*) was allowed to do this. But then the same requirements had to be followed in connection with such a voluntary burnt offering as at other times. We need not repeat them. The reader will understand why the burnt offering was being brought up once more in this passage. On account of the voluntary element that could occasionally play a role in connection with it.

2. Regarding the peace offerings (vv. 21–25)

Actually the same absolute rule—nothing other than a perfect animal on the altar!—applied to the peace offering as well. But we saw earlier that the requirements for this sacrifice were somewhat lighter. First, for all three kinds of peace offerings (praise sacrifice, votive sacrifice, and voluntary sacrifice), a female animal was to be used. Next, it was permitted not only to eat the meat of a voluntary sacrifice (thus, the third kind) on the day it was slaughtered, but also on the following day. Finally, it was not allowed for a peace offering, not even for a voluntary peace offering, to use an animal that had any kind of defect, such as an injury. But if an animal had parts that were merely too long or too short, like ears, for example, then one was allowed to bring it as a voluntary peace offering. But that was the only exception; otherwise, no animal that had any defect or deformity could be sacrificed to Yahweh.

In conclusion, the Israelites were given the following three very remarkable commands that they had to observe when bringing animals for sacrifice. It is striking that all these three prescriptions involved the issue of age. Let us look at the first and last prescriptions, and then the middle one.

First prescription (vv. 26–27): Israel was not permitted to bring as a sacrifice to Yahweh any portion of livestock, either sheep or goat, before

KEEPING PRIESTS AND SACRIFICIAL GIFTS HOLY (LEV 21–22)

such an animal was seven days old. The reason for this was obvious. A newborn calf and newborn goat would not have met the requirement of being perfect and complete. Everyone understands this. Something similar appeared among the pagans. The Roman author Plinius tells us that young pigs had to be at least five days old, sheep and goats at least eight days old, and calves at least one month old. The Torah of Yahweh stipulated the minimum required age of a sacrificial animal to be at least seven days old. This fit with the symbolic significance of the number seven, the number of the covenant and of holiness.[3]

Third prescription (vv. 29–30): When we discussed the peace offerings, we said that it was permitted to enjoy the meat of these sacrifices not only on the day of slaughter but also on the following day. Except if this peace offering was a praise sacrifice, whose meat had to be used only on the day it was slaughtered. Not later. Otherwise this would not have comported with the holiness of Yahweh.

If we look now at all these prescriptions together, we observe that both of them emphasize—in a symbolic manner—the holiness of Yahweh. Various means were employed to focus Israel's attention on that, including these two commands.

If we are correct in drawing this conclusion, then that will determine our choice among two explanations given about the *middle prescription*.

Second prescription (v. 28): With this stipulation, Israel was not allowed, and the priests were to ensure this, to sacrifice a young animal on the same day that its mother was sacrificed. People explain this in two ways.

The first interpretation assumes that here we find a similar prohibition as we find in the three Scripture passages that we discussed in our commentary on Exodus.[4] There Israel was forbidden to boil a kid in its mother's milk. Similarly, people suppose that our current passage is dealing with a strongly anti-Canaanite prohibition.

But the second interpretation assumes that here we are dealing with a similar prohibition as that given to Israel in Deut 22:6–7. In that passage, Israel was prohibited from plundering a bird's nest by taking the mother bird along with the eggs and baby birds. When we discussed that passage earlier in this commentary, we saw there one of the many symbolic-pedagogical measures whereby Israel was reminded that she had been placed by Yahweh upon the holy foundation of the Horeb covenant, to which the Fifth Commandment also belonged.

---

3. See Vonk, *Exodus*, 198–99.
4. See Vonk, *Exodus*, 118–19.

It is our judgment that the latter interpretation fits best in the series of the three concluding prescriptions.

In fact, it fits with the refrain that concludes this portion involving the bringing of sacrifices by Israel: I am Yahweh (v. 30).

Indeed, this interpretation fits within the entire context of Leviticus 21–22, in which the special character in verses 31–33 is underscored yet once more. We see how intimately God's name was involved with everything that happened in connection with his sanctuary on the part of all Israel—with the gifts to be brought, and especially by the priests, through whose mediation these gifts were offered to Yahweh.

Slaughtering a young sacrificial animal on the same day as its mother—one would have had to have been bereft of all sensitivity for symbolism if he did not understand that such an action would have sounded a discordant note in the harmonious music of Israel's liturgy according to the Law of Horeb.

24

Observe my Sabbaths! (Lev 23–25)

WE ARE NEARING THE end of the book of Leviticus. A big book, full of regulations whereby God wanted to focus Israel's attention on the foundation that he had laid beneath her society (her "world").[1] The foundation of the Horeb covenant.

We have been impressed with all the means he used for that purpose! What was left? What more could God do?

The portion of Leviticus that we are discussing in this chapter, Leviticus 23–25, focuses our attention on an instructional means about which we have written very little so far. For the sake of observing his Horeb covenant, God also wanted to make use of days, weeks, months, and years, that he would be giving to his people Israel to enjoy.

The key word of this portion of Scripture will be the word Sabbath (*shabbath*). And the key number will be the number *seven*.

We have met the word *shabbath* before, in Lev 19:3b. When we discussed that verse, we took the opportunity to point out the character of Israel's Sabbath days as genuine teaching days, instructional days, and we pointed ahead to the Scripture section that we are now discussing, and said that the Israelite weekly Sabbath days, as it were, formed a garment on which God embroidered the figures of Israel's feasts—Passover, Pentecost, etc.

We are going to develop that preliminary indication further here.

In the chapters we are now studying, we will see that God gave Israel a complete cycle of Sabbaths that spanned not just a single year, but more than one year. Not only a complete cycle, but also an *indivisible* cycle. We

---

1. Vonk, *Exodus*, 304–11.

want to point that out here and look at the consequences. Anyone who takes over and observes one part of the Israelite Sabbath cycle—for example, Sunday observance on Saturday, or strict Sabbath rest on Sunday—is unarmed and without any principled argument against various forms of sabbatarianism, and should be celebrating, in addition to the weekly Sabbath day, also Passover, Pentecost, and Feast of Booths. And why not the Great Day of Atonement and the sabbatical year and Year of Jubilee?

You know what happens when someone throws a pebble into a pond. On the surface of the pond you get ripples that expand like concentric circles further and further out. Now then, by means of such circles, Sabbath circles, Israel's entire life was divided and dominated, totally encircled and enveloped. All those circles had the feature of the number seven. Every circle involved a certain form of *shabbath*, whether the one with *shabbath*, rest, from this, another with *shabbath*, rest, from that. The extent of these Sabbaths differ widely. There was a Sabbath day, a Sabbath year, even a Year of Jubilee. But God had the same purpose with all of them: Remember my Horeb covenant!

When we keep in view this tenor or theme of all of Leviticus and especially of the chapters before us, we will not be surprised that between Leviticus 23 and Leviticus 25 another chapter was included that seems at first glance to be out of place. Leviticus 24 consists of three sections. First, it speaks about the daily provision of the golden chandelier, then about the weekly refreshing of the showbread, and finally, about the stoning of the man who had blasphemed the Name. We hope we can succeed in making clear the wisdom of the One who made room right here for these three sections. For this triad also calls out: Remember Yahweh's covenant!

OVERVIEW

To make things easier, we will supply an overview of all the "Sabbaths" that will be coming up for discussion. We should note that in this connection, we are sticking with the terms and names that have become standard.

0. *Introduction: regarding the weekly Sabbath day* (Lev 23:1–3)
1. *The Feast of Passover* (Lev 23:4–14)
2. *The Feast of Pentecost* (Lev 23:15–22)
3. *The Seventh New Moon day* (Lev 23:23–25)
4. *The Great Day of Atonement* (Lev 23:26–32)
5. *The Feast of Booths* (Lev 23:33–44)

OBSERVE MY SABBATHS! (LEV 23–25)

Intermezzo (Lev 24)

6. *The Sabbath year* (Lev 25:1–7)
7. *The Year of Jubilee* (Lev 25:8–55)

0. INTRODUCTION: REGARDING THE WEEKLY SABBATH DAY (LEV 23:1–3)

The first three verses of Leviticus 23 assume that everyone knows what Yahweh meant when he spoke to Moses about the weekly Sabbath day. Therefore we think that before going any further, it would be desirable to discuss several Scripture passages that are important for this subject. We will come to Lev 23:1–3 at the conclusion of this discussion.

0.1 Exodus 16 (manna from heaven)

It is true that in this chapter, *the Sabbath day* is not mentioned. That happens for the first time in Exodus 20, in the Fourth Commandment. But in order to understand this commandment, we must be acquainted with Exodus 16.

Notice first its context.

In Exodus 13–14, the passage through the Red Sea is narrated. In Exodus 15 we find that glorious song of Moses: "Yahweh is a warrior, Yahweh is his name." "You bring them and plant them on the mountain that is your inheritance." But after the Red Sea, the Israelites had to make a three-day trek through the wilderness of Sin. Our mariners know how warm it can get in the environs of the Red Sea. Moreover, the Israelites found no water in that wilderness of Sin. Other than "bitter" water. The place that was found is named accordingly: Mara. The people began to murmur against Moses: "What are we supposed to drink?" As if that poor man himself was not thirsty! In addition, he was worried about his physical safety in the company of all those exhausted people. So he cried out to Yahweh for help. He cried loudly.

Yahweh gave him a piece of wood that he simply had to throw into the water. Then the bad water would become good. The Israelites received more than enough to quench their thirst. But they also received something to think about. God had shown them that after the Red Sea he was just as mighty as before. And just as faithful.

That was the lesson of Mara. "*There the Lord made for them a statute and a rule, and there he tested them, saying, 'If you will diligently listen to the voice of the Lord your God, and do that which is right in his eyes, and give ear to his commandments and keep all his statutes, I will put none of the diseases on you that I put on the Egyptians, for I am the Lord, your healer'*" (Exod 15:25–26).

That was already covenant instruction.

Torah, instruction, about the covenant.

Perhaps the term "covenant" does not appear in this lesson of Mara, but the *style* of the covenant certainly does. Recall what we wrote about the shift between the first person and third person manner of speaking.[2] Typical, according to the pattern of covenants in those times, observed in the covenant made outside of Israel.

This lesson of Mara was in preparation for the establishment of the covenant that would occur later at Horeb.

It is true that Yahweh spoke in a very abbreviated manner. Like a highly placed ruler in those days would speak to a vassal, someone whom he had honored with a covenant treaty. That is how Yahweh spoke at Mara to his partners whom he honored with words containing the sound of a kind of treaty. "If you . . . then I will . . . ." But he was also beginning to nurture the Israelites for the real covenant partnership. Both parties would have to be, and remain, faithful and loyal to each other. Then the Israelites would see. Then all their suffering, of which they had received their fill in Egypt, would surely belong to the past. That is what Yahweh was guaranteeing them.

At that point, the episode of Exodus 16 followed, and in that event we see that the Israelites regrettably did not give to their God, who was so very mighty and faithful, the fidelity that he had required. For after they had broken camp at Elim, with its twelve springs and seventy palm trees, and entered the wilderness of Sin, that lay between Elim and Horeb, a new murmuring arose. This time because there was nothing to eat. The complaint went like this: "Would that we had died by the hand of the Lord in the land of Egypt, when we sat by the meat pots and ate bread to the full, for you have brought us out into this wilderness to kill this whole assembly with hunger" (Exod 16:3).

When we hear this complaint, or better said, this accusation, then we don't know what should surprise us more about God's reaction: his great patience or his great power. Did the Israelites complain about lack of meat and bread? Yahweh would supply them with both. On the evening of that very day they would receive meat, and on the following morning, it would

---

2. Vonk, *Exodus*, 77–78.

rain bread. And even though the first miracle happened only once, the second would be repeated anew each morning (16:4). Moreover, the Israelites would gather twice as much on the sixth day as on the other days (16:5). Yahweh wanted to see once if they would now walk according to his instruction (his Torah, 16:4), or not.

We know how God fulfilled his promise. On the evening of that same day, the Israelites got to eat the meat of quails. We will need to explain more about these quails, a kind of migratory bird, when we come to Numbers 11.

In Exodus 16, however, most of the attention is being devoted to the miracle of manna. When this manna lay on the ground the next day, Moses said: "It is the bread that the Lord has given you to eat. This is what the Lord has commanded: 'Gather of it, each one of you, as much as he can eat. You shall each take an omer, according to the number of the persons that each of you has in his tent.'" (Exod 16:15-16). An omer was one-tenth of an ephah. In addition, Moses commanded that people were not to store any of this manna for the following day. After what we have learned in Leviticus 11-15, we assume that hereby Israel was being prepared for the later Torah at Horeb. Israel had to know very well who Yahweh was. The God of life. Therefore Israel must not eat anything that was decayed and had the stench of death. And surely Israel was not permitted to treat this manna carelessly, but respectfully and properly. This explanation corresponds with God's own manner of action. After all, he caused the manna to descend not *within* the camp, where it could have been trampled, but outside the camp (v. 13; cf. vv. 4 and 29b, where it speaks of "going out"). Therefore Moses was angry when some Israelites so nonchalantly saved some of the manna for the next day. Had they done this because they lacked trust? Because they did not believe that Yahweh would provide for them again for the next day? In any case, the old manna was rotten and stank. Moses was angry about that. Did Yahweh deserve that?

This anger of Moses made an impression, as we see from what happened subsequently. To say it precisely: on the sixth day. At that point some Israelites had gathered not one, but two omers per person. One for that sixth day itself, and one to save for the seventh day. Those people had understood God's purpose very well. For from that time on, Yahweh had commanded, people were to gather a double portion on the sixth day (v. 5). But others appeared not to have understood very well. And these were not the cream of the crop. Various leaders—literally it says in verse 22, "all," but the Hebrew word can mean "many," as in Gen 50:7 and Exod 9:6—various leaders of the assembly came to Moses with the alarming report that some Israelites were busy gathering manna for two days. Was that allowed? Would Moses not be angry about this?

No. It was probably the first "sixth day" after the inauguration of the manna miracle. This explains why the one person understood and the other didn't, that on this day, they were allowed to gather double the amount—not only allowed, but required to, without fearing that the manna would rot and stink. God had already talked about this, before the first provision of manna (v. 5), and Moses had certainly communicated this to the people, for otherwise, how would those people who gathered double on the sixth day have known to do that? For the sake of clarity here, Moses tells us various things: "*This is what the Lord has commanded: 'Tomorrow is a day of solemn rest, a holy Sabbath to the Lord*" (v. 23). Therefore today you can do what you like with the manna, bake it or cook it, keep it for tomorrow. When people did so, this time there was no rotting or stinking.

Let's pause here to make two observations. First, regarding those numbers, six and seven. And second, regarding the words *shabbaton* and *shabbath*.

1. More than once in this chapter, mention is made of the sixth day. Beginning with verse 5, where we read God's command that the Israelites must gather a double portion of manna on the sixth day. Later again, at which point we find talk of the seventh day (v. 26). In this connection the question automatically arises: *According to which baseline* are those sixth and seventh days *being measured*?

In our opinion, the most obvious answer to this question appears to be that in Exodus 16, the counting begins with the first day that manna descended from heaven. At that point *the week* made its appearance in Israel's life. From that time onward, people would have divided the year into fifty-two weeks as well, following Egyptian custom, in terms of twelve months of mostly thirty days. At the same time, people would have adopted the Egyptian custom of not naming the months, as happened after the Babylonian captivity, under Babylonian influence, but to number the months. Except for the first month (*abib*).

2. In terms of the second observation, the Hebrew verb *shavath* meant: cease, stop, rest. From this came the noun *shabbath*, which meant rest. (Or was it just the reverse?) An extension of the noun is yet another word: *sabbathon*. This provided greater emphasis still.

Here we have the first place in Holy Scripture where it speaks about *shabbath* on the seventh day (v. 23). At the conclusion of the story, the word *shabbath* appears once more. For on the next day, the seventh day, Moses came back once more to this matter. He said that on this day people would not be finding any manna, but now, on this seventh day, they were supposed to enjoy what they had saved over from the sixth day. For now no manna would be falling from heaven. "Six days you shall gather it, but on the seventh day, which is a Sabbath, there will be none" (v. 26).

Nevertheless, on the seventh day several people still went out—the text uses the word that means "go out," indicating that they went outside the camp—to gather something. They found nothing, however. But their stubbornness did not go unnoticed. Did they not give the appearance as though Yahweh was not faithful and had forsaken his people? Whereas it was their own fault that they found nothing. Because they did not follow the declaration that had been given. Yahweh had said: "I will see once if the people will observe my "torah," or not (v. 4). Naturally with that word "torah" (note that it is not capitalized), God was not referring to that whole body of instruction that we read about in the rest of Exodus and Leviticus, but simply the teaching that he was giving at that moment, which he was tying to the instruction of Mara. We recall what kind of covenantal impact that episode had at the time. Yahweh would provide, but Israel would have to do what he said. And look, it's going badly already!

In the scolding that follows here, we observe again the remarkable shift from the first to the third person manner of speaking, that was so characteristic for covenant acts with which we have become acquainted from the ancient Near East. Are we not hearing the sounds of a prelude here? In the melody of the covenant that Yahweh was planning to establish with Israel later at Horeb. But then they would have to behave differently than they were now behaving. Listen to the tone of concern. *"How long will you [plural, referring to the Israelites] refuse to keep my commandments and my laws? See! The Lord has given you the Sabbath; therefore on the sixth day he gives you bread for two days. Remain each of you in his place; let no one go out of his place on the seventh day." So the people rested on the seventh day"* (vv. 28–30).

We should not twist these words. Naturally God was not demanding that from this day forward, the Israelites were supposed to sit absolutely still and quiet on the seventh day. He was not even demanding that they not set foot outside the camp. Healthy people would have had to use the latrine on the seventh day (Deut 23:12–14). No, they were simply not allowed to go outside the camp to look for manna. If they did that, this would prove their unsuitability for later entering into a new covenant with Yahweh. On account of stubbornness toward his "torah" (v. 4), his instruction, first at Mara and now here. And on account of a lack of trust in such a mighty, patient God.

Like a wise and understanding parent, Yahweh wanted in some sense to prepare the Israelites for entering the Horeb covenant. In the manna episode, he was focusing particularly on the institution of the Sabbath day. For after the requirement of relative rest on the seventh day in the manna episode, namely, rest from gathering manna, there follows the prescription about a complete rest on that day in the episode of Horeb. We turn to that now.

0.2 Exodus 20:8–11 (the Fourth Commandment)

This is the first place in Holy Scripture where we encounter the Sabbath commandment, which commands complete rest on the seventh day. It is the fourth of the Ten Words. Therefore we will first say something about these Ten Words in general, and then about the Fourth in particular.

0.2.1 The Ten Words in general

Scripture says that the Israelites "came to the wilderness of Sin, which is between Elim and Sinai, on the fifteenth day of the second month after they had departed from the land of Egypt" (Exod 16:1). That occurred in one month's time. For they went out of Egypt on the fifteenth day of the first month (Num 33:3). If we keep in mind that in the third month after the exodus from Egypt, they arrived in the wilderness of Sinai (Exod 19:1), where they camped at the foot of Mount Sinai, we can conclude (no matter which meaning the words of 19:1 "on the same day" may have—referring to the fifteenth day? or referring generally to: during the same time?) that what happened afterward at Horeb, namely, establishing the covenant, occurred rather shortly after the beginning of the manna miracle. How did things proceed then in connection with that covenant making?

Earlier we indicated repeatedly that when God made his covenants he apparently employed mores and customs that were observed by people in connection with such ceremonies. He had done that already when he made his covenant with Abraham. We know, for example, that on such occasions, the Greeks would divide their sacrificial animals in half, leaning the halves against each other, and then walk between them, thereby powerfully ratifying the oath-swearing that accompanied the covenant making. One would have been declaring that in the same way the gods were to cut asunder anyone who broke this covenant. A conditional self-malediction. From Genesis 15 we learn that God was willing to humble himself toward Abraham by means of such an oath-swearing. That is how faithful he would be, and that is the faithfulness he expected from Abraham (Gen 17:1). From now on, God would extend his faithfulness to Abraham's descendants, just like the kings who made treaties with each other were swearing fealty toward each other's successors (Gen 12:2–3). In connection with God's covenant making with Abraham, just as with covenant making among the kings of that time, there was even mention of the assignment of land. "To your offspring I give this land, from the river of Egypt to the great river, the river Euphrates, ..." (Gen 15:18).[3]

We observe something similar in connection with the covenant making of Exodus 20. The similarity between the making of God's covenant with Israel and the covenant makings of some kings during approximately the same period as the events at Horeb, such as the king of the Hittites with the pharaoh of Egypt, or those between the Hittite king and his Asiatic vassals, is very striking. (For more on this, see our commentary on Exodus 5, and on Lev 23.1 above). When a Hittite suzerain made a covenant with one of his subjects, two identical documents were drawn up, and one copy was deposited at the feet of the god of the sovereign in the temple of the deity, and the other copy at the feet of the god of his vassal, in his sanctuary. This was something that in many ways resembled (while still being very different from) what happened at Horeb. There Yahweh functioned as king over Israel, who made a covenant with his "vassal" Israel, had a document of this covenant drawn up, or rather drew it up himself, in duplicate, and had both copies of the covenant statute deposited not in two sacred places, for Yahweh alone was God and no one else, but deposited in the one ark of Yahweh, which then had to be constructed with this in mind, and which received the name of "ark of the covenant" or "ark of testimony."

In addition to this similarity regarding the *manner of depositing* both tablets of the covenant, there was also a striking similarity regarding the *content* of the treaty. This consisted in components that were very customary in that time. We would mention the following. First, a preamble or introduction, where the suzerain introduced himself to his vassal. God did this to Israel as well, when he said: "I am Yahweh, your God." Second, a historical prologue or introduction, where the suzerains customarily brought up for remembrance the efforts they had so generously expended on behalf of their subject vassals. Similarly, Yahweh recalled that he had delivered Israel from the house of bondage of Egypt. Next, a suzerain customarily laid on the heart of his vassal the obligation henceforward to show obedience to no other king than him. So too Yahweh declared the obvious expectation that Israel would have no other god or gods beside him, and that in serving him, Yahweh, they would use no images of any creature nor bow down to them. In addition, in connection with making covenant in the world in which Israel lived, there was regular calling upon gods as witnesses. With a certain similarity, but at the same time in tangible contrast to this, Yahweh required Israel never to use the name of Yahweh either for making covenants or on

---

3. See Vonk, *Genesis*, chapter 10.

other occasions, in such a pagan, foolish, and senseless manner (the Third Commandment).

And other components could be identified.

For example, the vassal was not only personally obligated to observe the covenant of his suzerain, but this obligation rested on his descendants as well, on his son and grandson. Similarly, God commanded Israel to keep his covenant throughout the coming generations. And to mention but one more feature of similarity, the suzerain could obviously not permit the vassals in his kingdom to wage war against each other, so that Yahweh also prescribed that good relationships should prevail among his Israelite covenant partners, rather than killing each other, stealing from each other, etc.

Descriptions of covenants like the one described in Exod 20:2-17 have been discovered in archaeological excavations throughout the Near East. Written on one tablet. Just like the tablets of Horeb, they were written on the front and the back (Exod 32:15). There is no reason to suppose, as people did in the past, including this author, that the words of the Horeb covenant were written in part on one tablet and in part on the other. There has been much disagreement on the question how many commandments were written on each of the two tablets. That conflict was unnecessary. The same commandments appeared on each stone tablet. All Ten Words were written on each. Yahweh had published the Ten Words in duplicate—Israel's beautiful covenant was lacking in nothing—and had the duplicates placed in the ark, whereby at the same time in a meaningful way he was excluding any and every notion that there was yet another God besides Yahweh.

The misunderstanding of the division of the Ten Commandments on two tablets—whether 3 + 7, or 4 + 6, or 5+5—has led in turn to another misunderstanding, namely, that the commandments of the first "table" supposedly involved the relationship between Yahweh and the Israelites, but the rest of the commandments of the second "table" supposedly involved the relationship among the Israelites themselves, and that these latter therefore bore a social character. But when the first misunderstanding disappears, this second misunderstanding loses any basis. It was not only the latter commandments of the Ten Words that possessed this social character, even though that feature may well come into view more easily, but this social feature was no less present in connection with the initial precepts of the Ten Commandments. Could an Israelite have rendered his brother any better service than to warn him against idolatry (First Commandment), against worshiping Yahweh with the use of images (Second Commandment), and against the pagan, foolish, empty, and vain use of the name Yahweh (Third Commandment)? (We will discuss the social dimension of the Fourth Commandment separately in a moment.) This social character pertained to all Ten Commandments, to such an extent that the apostle could write that whoever loved his neighbor had fulfilled the whole Law (Gal 5:14; cf. Matt 22:39; Rom 13:8).

0.2.2 The Sabbath command in particular

When we read the Fourth Commandment carefully, we see that it consisted in the following three parts. First, an introduction; second, the actual commandment; and third, the motivation of this commandment.

(A) THE INTRODUCTION

This reads: *Remember the day of the shabbath by reserving it.*

As you can see, we have left the Hebrew word *shabbath* untranslated. In so doing, we have probably immediately reminded our readers of something. Just as through this word, Yahweh would surely have reminded Israel of something that had just happened. The episode of Exodus 16. And of something that occurred regularly since then, namely, that every morning manna descended and was gathered by the Israelites. Except on the morning of the seventh day. Then the Israelites were not permitted to go out to gather manna. Then they would have to abstain from this, and this abstaining was "a *shabbath* for Yahweh," in honor of Yahweh. In connection with the institution of this abstaining from gathering manna on the seventh day—of this "rest," this *shabbath*—God made a forceful allusion at Horeb when he gave the introduction to the Fourth Commandment. The noun *shabbath* appears in the Bible for the first time in Exodus 16, and for the second time in Exodus 20.

But everyone understands that this recollection of something familiar was not the only purpose of the introductory words in the Fourth Commandment. They were designed also to prepare for something new. In his introductory words, God was speaking about both a "day" of *shabbath*, and of a command that people were supposed to reserve that day. The first meaning of the Hebrew verb used for this (*qdsh*) would have been: keep, designate, reserve. When this reserving was done for Yahweh, it obtained the meaning familiar to us: devote, sanctify. But in the episode of Exodus 16, however, there was not any mention yet of the designation of an entire day. Such an impression could be given by our modern English translations of Exodus 16:23: "This is what the Lord has commanded: 'Tomorrow is a day of solemn rest, a holy Sabbath to the Lord" (ESV). This rendering speaks of "a day of solemn rest," whereas the King James version has this:

"Tomorrow *is* the rest of the holy sabbath unto the Lord," which is more correct. Both Hebrew words, *shabbath* and *shabbaton* mean "rest," which is not yet the same as "a day of rest."

The new element in the introduction to the Fourth Commandment is that it prepares the Israelites for later mention of a day with the word *shabbath* in a more expanded sense, namely, not merely in terms of one specific activity (gathering manna), but every activity. We will see this in connection with the actual commandment.

(b) The actual commandment

The commandment reads as follows: "*Remember the Sabbath day, to keep it holy. Six days you shall labor, and do all your work, but the seventh day is a Sabbath to the Lord your God. On it you shall not do any work, you, or your son, or your daughter, your male servant, or your female servant, or your livestock, or the sojourner who is within your gates*" (Exod 20:8–11).

What is striking about this commandment?

First, that it does not say that there would be a *shabbath* on the seventh day, as it does in Exod 16:26, but that the seventh day as such would be a *shabbath* for Yahweh. Next, that not merely one activity is being prohibited, as in Exodus 16, namely, gathering manna, but every other activity as well. Or better: every other work. For what is intended is the activities connected with *serving*. We could translate verse 9a this way: "Six days you may *serve*." The Hebrew word for "serve" has the same three consonants (*'bd*) as the Hebrew word for "house of slavery" that appears in verse 2 (the prologue) and in verse 10 (for "servant"). Furthermore, what is striking is that it clarifies his intention with this prohibition, which is far more comprehensive than the that in Exodus 16, which was a general prohibition of work on the seventh day, by identifying an extensive series of persons or instruments through whom this work could be performed. He even mentioned animals. For God initially spoke of "you" singular, with emphasis, referring to the entire nation of Israel, but then as that was represented by the men, as we have seen from the use of the masculine pronoun. In view of the entire series, we believe the family head was being addressed, after whom various people are mentioned by whom one can be "served." Close relatives like a son or daughter, less close members of the household like male servant and female servant, terms that perhaps should be translated as "male slave" and "female slave." Next come the animals. Naturally those animals that people place in "service" in the field or on the road. The ox and the donkey. And the series is concluded with the *ger*, a kind of sojourner and foreigner that we discussed earlier. Yahweh was speaking about this matter as if Israel would have been settled in Canaan within a short period of time, something that would indeed have occurred if the wicked unbelief of the ten spies had not intervened (Num 13-14). We should always keep this in mind as we read Exodus and Leviticus.

As we mentioned above, we still need to discuss the social character that belonged to the Fourth Commandment.

Already at Horeb, we can observe a dual aspect. We need not say anything further about the first aspect. The Fourth Commandment instituted, in honor of Yahweh, an even further expanded rest than Israel had known up to this point since the manna episode. This prohibition forbade not only gathering manna on the morning of the seventh day, but every other activity characterized as work or service, throughout the course of the entire day. That entire day was to be "a *shabbath* in honor of Yahweh." Initially the only thing given, designated as "a *shabbath* devoted to Yahweh" involved gathering manna (Exod 16:23), but now the command came: "But the seventh day is a *shabbath* unto Yahweh, your God" (Exod 20:10), such that the entire day had to be reserved for Yahweh, and devoted to him (Exod 20:8). In the Scripture passages just referred to, the word "day" is emphatic. Initially the *shabbath* involved an hour, now it was an entire day, that had to be set apart in honor of Yahweh.

The content of that honoring of Yahweh, beyond simply abstaining from activities of work, will be seen when we discuss Lev 23:1-3 below.

But from the very beginning the Fourth Commandment had a social aspect. True enough, in his initial instructions at Horeb God did not emphasize this aspect in a special way. That happened later (as we will see below). But from the beginning, the Fourth Commandment displayed a social dimension. Notice the series of people who work in service, to whom a full day of rest had to be provided. In fact, even the animals, which people were otherwise used to using for service, were not to be put to work on the weekly Sabbath day.

(c) The motivation

This is the motivation: "*For in six days the Lord made heaven and earth, the sea, and all that is in them, and rested on the seventh day. Therefore the Lord blessed the Sabbath day and made it holy.*"

We are using a heading entitled "The motivation." We could also have used the heading, "The explanation." Precisely *what* is being explained we learn from the conclusion itself. The reason why Yahweh "blessed" and "sanctified" the day of the *shabbath*. What did this mean?

Let's rehearse the facts once more.

Israel could easily know which day Yahweh was referring to as the "day of the *shabbath*." Since the episode of the manna miracle, Israel was familiar with a day on which a certain *shabbath* had to be observed. On the seven day Israel was to abstain from gathering manna, to stop doing so, to cease that activity. Accordingly from that time on, that day could be called: "the day of the *shabbath*."

But later God gave this day a new and broader significance, through the Horeb covenant. At that time he laid claim to that day as an entire day of rest, and that with a dual purpose, namely, first, in honor of Yahweh himself, and second, for the enjoyment of every Israelite, young and old, poor and rich, indeed, even of the work animals.

This course of events is summarized at the close of the Fourth Commandment as a kind of summary. God had turned that day of partial *shabbath*, known since the time of the manna miracle, into a day of complete *shabbath*, and had "sanctified" it, i.e., reserved it for his honor, and "blessed" it, i.e., by making it a refreshing day for every Israelite, whether high or low.

Why did he do this?

Why, in order to accomplish his dual purpose, had his eye fallen on that "day of the *shabbath*," which was "given," that is, assigned, imposed, and established in the episode of the manna miracle (Exod 16:28)?

The answer is: He did that because that day was the seventh, and a specific remembrance was associated with that number seven. A remembrance of creation. At that creation, after six days God rested. That was the reason why his choice fell on the seventh day. Not on the fifth day or the sixth day, but on the seventh. By means of designating the seventh day, he wanted to say something like this: Just as I did, so too you must do. Like Father, like children. Like Yahweh, like Israel.

"Like Yahweh, like Israel."

As we wrote those words, we were gripped by a fear of being misunderstood. We must not connect any incorrect application to this explanation of the explanation (or motivation) of the Fourth Commandment.

The view has arisen through the writings of earlier and modern authors, that the essential, proper, and characteristic feature of the Fourth Commandment supposedly consisted in the fact that by it, God was imposing on the Israelites the obligation to behave in this world like image-bearers of God. A very familiar view. But in recent times it appears to have received archaeological support by virtue of the undeniable fact that tablets have been discovered on which the text of the treaty made between one potentate and another was punctuated with images of the deities who were being summoned as witnesses by those making a covenant together under oath.

We would make the following comments about this view.

To begin with the last claim, it is genuinely tempting to think, on the basis of this archaeological discovery, that not only in his declaration of the Ten Words was God taking into account the contemporary customs in the domain of making covenants, but specifically in connection with the Fourth Commandment he was following the custom of placing on the front side and the back side of the covenant tablet an image of the deities. This seems like such an attractive possibility, but it is far from likely. Even if we were to accept that God was following the specific custom with a polemical purpose, namely, by replacing the usual pagan image with the command that on the seventh day Israel was to display his image by resting on that day just as he had done at creation. The combination of these things strikes us as dangerous, not only in view of the immediately preceding Second Commandment that warns against any form of worshiping Yahweh using images of creatures of any kind, but also in view of what we find in the subsequent Torah as warnings against various forms of Egyptian and Canaanite paganism. We encounter such warnings not only later, as in Lev 18:1-5, but also immediately in the book of Exodus, in the Book of the Covenant that was given, mind you, immediately after the proclamation of the Ten Words (Exod 21-23; see 23:13-33, and 34:10-26). No, this idea strikes us as running counter to the whole thematic tendency of the Torah.

But there is more.

Is the viewpoint that we explained above really true? Was the most fundamental characteristic of the Fourth Commandment the requirement that the Israelites were supposed to display God's image on the seventh day of the week? We believe this claim is incorrect for two reasons.

In the first place, we would not wish to deny that today, the obligation rests upon all Christians to be imitators of God, and that this also rested upon the Israelites, to whom God had said so often: Be holy, for I, Yahweh, your God, am holy. The obligation that the doorways of the heart are not to swing open left, toward evil, but right, toward the good, dates back to Paradise. Therefore it was surely correct that people called regeneration the renewal of a person according to God's image. By regeneration we understand what our (original) liturgical form for baptism states: "First, that we, having genuine sorrow and penitence concerning our sins, deny our own understanding and various desires and submit to the will of God and hate every sin from our heart and flee from them; second, that we begin to have a desire and love for living according to God's Word in all holiness and

PART 4 | THE PEOPLE OF YAHWEH

righteousness." By means of this daily renewing of our lives, or regeneration, believers display God's image once again. They become imitators of God as his beloved children (Eph 5:1). This was something that the Israelites also experienced, since Moses also called them children of Yahweh, their God (Deut 14:1). So then, this renewing of life extended not merely over one day, but over every day of life. And this renewing of human understanding, words, and works was commanded not only by one of the Ten Words, namely, the Fourth Commandment, but by all ten.

For this reason we believe that the viewpoint explained above does not do justice to the essential content of the Fourth Commandment. It does not include enough, it is not specific enough.

But it falls short for yet another reason. When you trace the expression "image of God" back to the Old Testament, and read what Genesis understands by it, namely, that Adam was to function as God's substitute and the bearer of his authority,[4] then we prefer to argue that the Israelites received a command to display God's image in the Fifth Commandment rather than in the Fourth Commandment.

The following viewpoint strikes us as preferable.

The Fourth Commandment was, so to speak, super-covenantal. Of course, all Ten Words were covenant words, together constituting the statute of the Horeb covenant. But the Fourth Commandment was covenantal in a more particular way, because it imposed on the Israelites the obligation to reserve every seventh day as a day in honor of Yahweh. In this manner, they were being reminded of the Horeb covenant on this day in an extra way.

We will be taught more extensively about this entirely unique, this special essence of the Fourth Commandment later, in Exod 31:12–17. But we encounter an indication of this special essence here in the number seven. God commanded Israel to celebrate this day of rest not on the fifth or sixth day of the week, but on the seventh. Why? Because he himself, who was Israel's great covenant Partner, had rested after creating the world, on the seventh day. Therefore he wanted Israel, his covenant partner, to rest on the seventh day as well. The number seven was a number in which the Semitic ear more easily heard the sound of the covenant, its oath and holiness, than occurs in our ears with the number seven. The Hebrew word for "swear" was derived from this number. Its literal meaning was: "to seven oneself." This explains why at Horeb, God could immediately count on the Israelites having a certain understanding for the symbolic range of this number. He could count on this already when in Egypt he commanded Israel to eat

---

4. See Vonk, *Genesis*, 84–89.

OBSERVE MY SABBATHS! (LEV 23–25)

unleavened bread from the fifteenth through the twenty-first of the month Abib (Exod 12:18). Think as well of the seven lambs that Abraham had set apart when he made a covenant with Abimelech, offering them "as a testimony" (Gen 21:28–31).

There you hear the language of the number seven.

Consider and compare the following.

God used other means as well in order to remind the Israelites of his Sinai covenant. For example, he used the language of color. We know that each Israelite was obligated to attach to each of the four corners of his garment a tassel into which was woven a dark blue thread. For remembering the commandment of Yahweh. This dark blue color, which appeared in the tabernacle as well, spoke of God who had his dwelling in heaven above and among Israel. That color reminded Israel of her faithful God of the covenant.[5] This language of colors would have spoken more clearly to the Eastern heart of the Israelites, accustomed to symbolism and oriented to symbolism, than it does to us.

He did something similar with *number*.

Already from the time of creation, the number seven suited Yahweh in a special way. It characterized him as the only true God, as the Creator. For that reason he would have used the number seven at Horeb, when he made that covenant with Israel. But later he would use it countless times. Often in connection with Sabbath days. Such as at Horeb, by instituting an entire day of rest every seven days. This time he was not using a color, but a number.

With this number seven, which was recognized internationally as a symbolic number, which spoke of swearing an oath and of covenant, Yahweh was stamping his divinity more solidly on the Ten Words. It was, as it were, his signature, with which he, the only true God, the Creator of all things, was providing the document of his Horeb covenant with his divine stamp and seal.

If we understand the Fourth Commandment in this way, and then still wish to consider the possibility that God incorporated certain customs from Israel's environment into the redaction of the Fourth Commandment, as we find it in Exodus 20, namely, the custom of affixing the seal or stamp of the deity in covenant documents, we would have no objection. Because then at least every notion of imaging God would have been eliminated in advance. That is required. Because it is definitely incompatible with all of God's language in the rest of the Torah. What then survives is merely the idea that God made a refined and artful use, in connection with the Fourth Commandment, of a certain method associated with making covenants

---

5. See Vonk, *Exodus*, 209–211.

that was present in Israel's environment. Why would we object to that? We have written elsewhere about "The Great Annexation" of God at Horeb.[6]

Perhaps we should be thinking similarly in connection with the Fourth Commandment. But if this assumption is correct, then God was working very carefully in terms of the formulation of the Fourth Commandment at Horeb. He doesn't breathe a word about something like representing or imaging him. But neither does he say anything about any seal. Among Israel or others, this could perhaps have generated an association with other figures. What is known is that the pagans were accustomed to affixing various figures to their seals. Figures of gods, people, animals, trees, flowers. That's what archaeology teaches us. But we find nothing of this in the Fourth Commandment. Not even the word "sign." At least not here in Exodus 20, in the Fourth Commandment itself.

Only the number seven.

That is the imprint that Yahweh, in his capacity of Divine Covenant Maker—as Creator!—placed at the very heart of the covenant text of Horeb, as his very meaningful, but at the same time, extremely restrained monogram and signature.

We will bump into it more often. For it is present in every part of the cycle of Israel's Sabbaths.

0.3 Exodus 23:12 (Sabbath rest for those rendering service)

Unfortunately, when people in the past discussed the Ten Commandments, they did so in the same way they talked about man. They divided a person into two parts, calling the first part the soul and the second part the body, although Scripture leads us in using each of these two to refer to the entire person. In Scripture, the phrase "my soul" can mean *I*, or *I myself*, just as the phrase "your bodies" can mean *you*, or *yourselves*. Often the difference is more a question of aspect. For example, in Rom 12:1, by means of the word "body," the emphasis is being placed on the person's visible and tangible side.

Unfortunately, people in the past regularly divided the Ten Commandments into two parts. They though that the first part, made up of Commandments 1–4, though others divided it differently, involved Israel's relationship to God, and the second part involved the relationships among the Israelites themselves.

We have identified that strange and arbitrary division as a illegitimate child, fruit of a misunderstanding, as if the Ten Words would have been

---

6. Vonk, *Exodus*, 299–304.

distributed on the two stone tablets, on which God had written them with his own finger. We saw at that time as well that we can speak of two aspects in connection with not one or a few, but with all of the Ten Words, aspects important for our perspective on the Ten Words. All Ten Words were related to Israel's covenant with Yahweh, to the Israelites' relationship to Yahweh and to their relationships with each other.

The same was true of the Fourth Commandment.

From this time forward, the seventh day was not only supposed to be reserved for honoring Yahweh, being thereby sanctified, but was also supposed to be a joyous day of rest for all Israel, thereby being a blessed day. A day for everyone to catch their breath. For master and servant. Even for the work animals.

This was expressed at Horeb already, when these words were proclaimed by Yahweh. But shortly thereafter, God had paid special attention to that second side of the Fourth Commandment, to its social side. You can read about this in Exod 23:12.

As we saw earlier, this Scripture passage forms part of the so-called Book of the Covenant, which was written down by Moses after prior consultation with Yahweh on Sinai. Initially Moses brought to Israel's elders an oral report of that consultation, and then he put that report in writing, after which this document played a role in connection with the formal establishment of the covenant. The reader will recall all of this. This Book of the Covenant occupies about three chapters in our Bible, namely, Exod 20:22–23:33. To recall just one feature of what we mentioned earlier, we noted in that connection God's demand in Moses' Book of the Covenant, that the Israelites were supposed to treat each other like people who knew what *mercy* was.

That Book contained Exod 23:12.

And that demand for mercy is heard very clearly here.

The verse appears in a genuinely "social" context. The Israelites were not to spread false reports about one another (23:1). They were not to pervert justice for the poor (23:6). They were not to condemn the innocent to death (23:7). The judges were not to accept bribes (23:8). The sojourner was not to be oppressed, "for you were sojourners in the land of Egypt" (23:9).

And then we read this.

Just as Yahweh was the God of the number seven, so too Israel was supposed to be the people of the number seven. The people of the Horeb covenant. Naturally this would have to be shown daily in observing God's commandments and in the concourse of the Israelites with each other. But even more so on some occasions. On every seventh day and in every seventh year. "For six years you shall sow your land and gather in its yield, but the seventh year you shall let it rest and lie fallow, that the poor of your people may eat; and what they leave the beasts of the field may eat. You shall do likewise with your vineyard, and with your olive orchard" (23:10–11). That was referring to the sabbatical year, which we will discuss below.

Immediately following this commandment about the sabbatical year we read our verse (23:12): "*Six days you shall do your work, but on the seventh day you shall rest; that your ox and your donkey may have rest, and the son of your servant woman, and the alien, may be refreshed.*"

How lovely this sounds, both our verse as well as its entire context. In fact, how lovely was the opening of the Book of the Covenant, in 21:2, which proclaimed the thoroughly evangelical purpose of the entire Book of the Covenant in the ordinance that an Israelite had to allow someone who had come upon hard times and therefore had to enter into the service of another Israelite as a slave, to leave as a free man after working for six years. And Moses (who would surely have understood God's purpose) later added to this: and do not allow such a man to leave empty-handed! That is how Moses later viewed the character of the Fourth Commandment (Deut 15).

We should not suppose that the element of friendliness and social compassion appeared for the first time in the Fourth Commandment, according to the version Moses gave the Israelites later. With this conclusion: "*. . . that your male servant and your female servant may rest as well as you. You shall remember that you were a slave in the land of Egypt, and the Lord your God brought you out from there with a mighty hand and an outstretched arm. Therefore the Lord your God commanded you to keep the Sabbath day*" (Deut 5:14–15).

There you see the motivation of the Fourth Commandment. As people have observed, there is no mention here of God's creation of heaven, sea, and earth, unlike in the version of the Fourth Commandment that we find in Exodus 20. There, the social aspect was not emphasized nearly as strongly as in Deuteronomy 5. Admittedly so. But that does not mean this aspect was absent in Exodus 20. No one would make such a claim, if they take into account the mention made there of rest for everyone, including animals and personnel, so that exhausted servants could heartily bless that day designed for catching their breath, saying to one another: O how glorious a day Yahweh has given us in his weekly Sabbath day. What a day of blessing for us!

From the outset, God wanted the seventh day to be a joyful day for all his people. Any possible doubt about this would be removed by reading what comes rather shortly after the Book of the Covenant that came into existence with the proclamation of the Ten Words. We have no better commentary.

The Fourth Commandment certainly bore an extra strong covenantal character. It preached Yahweh as God of the number seven and Israel as the people of the number seven. It repeatedly reminded Israel of her exalted status since Horeb. And to the Sabbath day was added later the Sabbath year. And something far more beautiful still, about which we will speak in a moment. But let no one think that God imposed his Sabbaths on Israel in order to oppress her. On the contrary. The pattern of the number seven, so artfully woven into Israel's daily garments, obviously reminded people constantly of their obligations toward Yahweh, their Suzerain, but just as much of the covenant duties of every covenant member toward each other. Especially this, that they must do good toward each other. That they should care well for each other. Naturally most of all for those with the greatest need.

0.4 *Exodus 31:12–17 and Exodus 35:1–3 (Sabbath rest and tabernacle construction)*

In the past, people referred to both of these Scripture passages to prove that the Sabbath day had been a very strictly commanded day already in the wilderness, a day on which Israel was not only not permitted to perform any work, but not even to prepare any meals and light any fire. Nor gather any wood. We will come back to this latter item below.

Talking about the prohibition of preparing meals makes us think of Exodus 12. In Egypt God gave the statute that on the first and seventh days of the weak of unleavened bread, not only was all work forbidden, but also this was commanded: "But what everyone needs to eat, that alone may be prepared by you" (Exod 12:16). So it is mistaken to appear to this statute as the basis for the alleged total prohibition of preparing meals on the Sabbath day. To say nothing about the fact that Exodus 12 is not talking about the Sabbath day.

Nor do we read about such a strict prohibition in Exodus 16, the episode of the manna miracle. Regardless of how one concludes anything from the commanded double gathering of manna on the sixth day with respect to baking or cooking on the seventh day (Exod 16:23), one thing is clear: in this passage we read nothing prohibiting people from preparing a meal on the seventh day.

We must also be careful when we talk about occupational labor. In the wilderness, various kinds of work needed to be done on the Sabbath day. For example, people had to care for and guard the livestock. People were supposed to abstain from unnecessary daily work. Not even a slave, presuming that Israelites already possessed slaves in the wilderness, was allowed to sense on the Sabbath day that he was a slave.

But what about lighting a fire? Here as well, we should recall Israel's circumstances. They would have had to keep a fire going regularly and carefully among the embers, in order to be able to stoke a fire when needed, such as when fire was needed to prepare a meal. Would that kind of "lighting a fire" have been forbidden in the two passages mentioned above? Let's see.

We will first look at these two passages together, and then at each passage separately.

(a) The two passages together

When we commented on these two passages in our commentary on Exodus, we pointed out that we must not lose sight especially of the *location* where we find them in the Bible.[7]

The first passage appears before, and the second appears after, the "intermezzo" involving the golden calf (Exod 32–34). Stated another way: the first passage forms the conclusion of Exodus 25–31, the chapters about *the mandate* to construct the tabernacle. And the second passage opens Exodus 35–40, chapters dealing with *the execution* of that mandate.

We may not ignore this remarkable fact.

The *location* where a portion of Scripture appears can be very significant. And here that definitely appears to be the case. At first glance one can see that the first passage must definitely be read as part of Exodus 25–31, dealing with *the mandate to construct the tabernacle*. Just read it for yourself, and you will agree that this is obvious. But just as obvious is the fact that the second passage, if it is to have any meaning, must be read in connection with *the execution of the mandate for constructing the tabernacle*, described in Exodus 35–40. What other reason could Moses have had to begin talking suddenly about the Sabbath days, evidently to all the people—"the entire assembly of the Israelites"—than this, that the entire people was involved in connection with the manufacture of the tabernacle (35:1). Men and women were involved (35:20, 22, 25, 29). A lot of work was accomplished in very little time. Many items were spun and woven, stitched and embroidered, melted and forged! The first ones would probably have required illumination during the evening hours, the second would have required fire during the day, and rather large fires at that.

So then, it is simply obvious that we should read these two passages *in connection with the construction of the tabernacle*, and explain the

---

7. Vonk, *Exodus*, 304–305.

instruction about resting on the Sabbath days in both passages as referring to various *work-related activities associated with constructing God's sanctuary*. That was surely beautiful work. But it was not supposed to lead Israel to forget the Sabbath day. Something that can happen among enthusiastically industrious people whose inner drive can limit their perspective somewhat. (Compare this with just such a commandment in Exod 34:21: During those labor-intensive times of plowing and harvesting, you shall rest.)

The prohibition of "lighting a fire on the Sabbath day" in Exod 24:3 was not supposed to have been so universalized throughout the course of time, into a prohibition against cooking a meal and the like. Given the context, that prohibition was not about that at all. Preparing meals on the Sabbath day was nowhere forbidden in Scripture.

(b) Each passage separately

(1) Exodus 31:12–17.

This passage is by far the largest and most important for our purpose of getting to know the character of Israel's weekly Sabbath day.

In the name of Yahweh, Moses was supposed to say to the Israelites (plural, since everyone participated in constructing the tabernacle): "*Above all you [plural] shall keep my Sabbaths, for this is a sign between me and you throughout your generations, that you may know that I, the Lord, sanctify you*" (v. 13).

The Hebrew word for "above all" (*akh*) is emphatic. Here it has a restrictive meaning. This rendering as "above all" is like a father giving his children permission to go out for the evening, but calls out as they are leaving: "Above all, be home on time!" So with God who, after telling Moses about everything needed for constructing the tabernacle, adds in conclusion: the heavy and busy work being done for the tabernacle must not lead his people to forget his Fourth Commandment. This was a suitable opportunity to make Israel sense how important his Sabbath days were to God. Why? That is what comes next.

For the Sabbath day is next called *a sign*. The Hebrew word for "sign" (*oth*) is also used to refer to circumcision (Gen 17:11, recalling God's covenant with Abraham), to the stones in the Jordan river (Josh 4:6), recalling the wilderness trek, etc. Thus, the word referred to a means of instruction. That meaning is obviously present here as well, for we read next: "... for this is a sign between me and you throughout your generations, *that you may know* that I, the Lord, sanctify you" (v. 13). Therefore, the Sabbath day is here being called a sign whereby Yahweh *gave instruction to the Israelites about the new relationship between him and them, namely, that of the Horeb covenant*. When he made this covenant with the Israelites, he had set them apart from all the nations of the world and chosen them. Thereby he had sanctified them. And at the same time he had called them to faithful honoring of that deed, that sanctification. It was supposed to be evident every day that the Israelites were different people than the pagans, but on the Sabbath days this was supposed to be even more evident. By their general abstaining from all daily labor, and by exempting everyone from rendering service on that day. The Gentiles knew nothing like this. Thereby the Sabbath day was all the more a sign of remembrance and a sign of distinction for Israel.

The great value that God assigned to his Sabbath days is expressed also in the punishment that he required for defiling the Sabbath: capital punishment. Anyone in Israel who on the Sabbath days did not lay aside his daily activities, but performed them as usual, would be demonstrating by his despising of that day that he was despising the Horeb covenant and therefore wanted nothing to do with the two parties with whom that covenant had been made: with Yahweh and with Israel. Therefore, "everyone who profanes it shall be put to death. Whoever does any work on it, that soul shall be cut off from among his people" (v. 14). Such a person was unfaithful, a covenant breaker. Because he had despised Israel's election as the people of Yahweh.

To provide every necessary clarity and because of the great importance of this matter, several features were expanded and repeated. The Israelites were supposed to observe the Sabbath day *from generation to generation*. "As an eternal covenant." Here again we encounter that word "eternal" (*olam*).[8] If we use the word "eternal" biblically, then no one will be stymied by the question as to how the epistle to the Hebrews can say later about this Horeb covenant that it was now annulled and has become obsolete.

At the very end of this passage, the explanation is repeated once more that had been given in the Fourth Commandment (Exod 20:11), as to why at Horeb God had assigned exactly that seventh day as the Sabbath day for Israel. In Exod 31:17 we read: "It is a sign forever between me and the people of Israel that in six days the Lord made heaven and earth, and on the seventh day he rested and was refreshed." The Bible reader should not stumble over that last phrase ("was refreshed"), nor explain it as an anthropomorphism, a kind of human-like description of God. For people violate Scripture with that disrespectful term. God does nothing in a human-like manner, but always in a God-like manner, including "being refreshed" and

---

8. See the discussion of this word in Vonk, *Genesis*, 130–31.

"resting" (along with having sorrow, coming down, etc.).[9] That we do not comprehend this is no wonder (Job 36:26).

(2) Exodus 35:1–3.

This passage contains nothing new, but does not that fact testify to the greatness of this minor Scripture passage? For where is it located? It comes after that great interruption of Exodus 32–34, the so-called intermezzo with the golden calf. What happened there? Israel had very quickly broken that beautiful Horeb covenant just made by God and just accepted by the elders. Under the leadership of Aaron, no less.

It was not accidental that both tablets were smashed by Moses. For they were the covenant! That covenant was broken. Moses understood that very well.

God's wrath, because of what happened, was terrible. Directed against the people, but also against Aaron. We know this, not from Exodus, but from later information given by Moses, preserved in Deut 9:20. Yahweh wanted to destroy Aaron as well.

But in response to Moses' intercession, this did not happen. Aaron was not put to death. (We know what a glorious office this man was later assigned. Purely from grace!) But the people of Israel were also spared, as a covenant people. For the Horeb covenant was maintained from God's side. He renewed it, by once again engraving the same Ten Words with his own hand on other tablets (Exod 34:1). "Yahweh, Yahweh, a God merciful and gracious, slow to anger, and abounding in steadfast love and faithfulness," as Moses cried out (Exod 34:6). Indeed, the tabernacle plan of God—that he would come to dwell among Israel in a tent, something he had initially rejected and refused even to accompany Israel—that original plan remained in place.

Therefore following the chapters about the "intermezzo with the golden calf" (chapters 32–34), we find those wonderful concluding chapters of Exodus about *the execution of the mandate for constructing the tabernacle* (chapters 35–40).

We read immediately in Exodus 35 that Moses announced "the charge." Everyone was permitted to participate in building God's palace.

Moses preceded that charge with a repetition of the prohibition against working on the Sabbath days (Exod 35:1–3). What was intended, of course, was working on constructing sections of the tabernacle.

---

9. See Vonk, *Genesis*, 160–68.

Although he did so briefly, Moses repeated the Sabbath commandment one more time. There was good reason for doing that. For the Sabbath day was, as it were, the Horeb covenant in miniature. It was given by God as a sign of that, and served as a striking means of instruction. Clearly remembering the divine seal that Yahweh had imprinted on the top of his Ten Words, by means of the Fourth Commandment.

Moses would have thought: "If the Horeb covenant were to be broken once again by Israel, for example, by neglecting the Sabbath day, I would not know what would be left for me to do." He had more than one reason to think this way. God's own hint given after the mandate for tabernacle construction: "Do not work on this on the Sabbath day!" As well as what had happened during the sad intermezzo.

0.5 Numbers 15:32–36 (the wood gatherer)

In connection with this Scripture passage as well. We must pay careful attention to its context. We will say something first about what precedes this passage, and then about what follows it.

(a) In *the preceding context,* God had taught Israel what she had to do when his command was transgressed unintentionally (*vishgagah*). That was not permitted, but there was forgiveness for such a sin. It was stipulated in great detail what kind of sacrifice had to be offered if the entire assembly had sinned, and what kind of sacrifice had to be brought if an individual member of the congregation had sinned. But whoever transgressed God's commandments insolently, intentionally, with premeditation (literally, "with a high hand"), had to be cut off. Why? Because he had mocked no one other than Yahweh. He had demonstrated his despising of the covenant through word or conduct, the covenant that Yahweh had given to Israel, and that he knew very well he was doing so. "Because he has despised the word of the Lord and has broken his commandment, that person shall be utterly cut off; his iniquity shall be on him" (Num 15:31; cf. Num 15:22–31).

(b) In *the subsequent context,* Num 15:37–41, we read about the cord or tassels that each Israelite had to wear on the corners of his garment. A blue thread was supposed to be woven into the tassel. We have discussed this several times, so we can be brief here. What was the purpose of this ordinance? This thread was to serve as a reminder of God's commandments, so that Israel would remember that she was the holy people of Yahweh.

As we can see, both of these Scripture passages have the same scope. Israel was a highly privileged people. At Horeb, she was taken up by God into a special covenant, concerning which she was instructed, and would be instructed daily, in many and sundry ways. Tassels on garments, Sabbath days, forbidden foods, uncleanness through leprosy, etc. But now the people must also behave accordingly. As a set apart, unique, holy people of Yahweh. For unto that purpose Yahweh had rescued Israel from Egypt.

(c) *Between* these two sections we find our passage about the wood gatherer (vv. 32–36). What had he done? Simply pick up a stick from the ground, like a child at play or an adult on a walk might do? No, he was really busy collecting firewood. He thought that was needed for preparing his food, whether manna or meat. Now this latter was not forbidden on the Sabbath day, as we have seen. But on the Sabbath day, one was not allowed to conduct himself as though it were not a Sabbath day, let alone, to neglect the very day on which God had imprinted the signature of his Horeb covenant in a special way, by plugging away and lugging materials, by toiling and hauling things. No, something this insolent had dismayed the entire assembly (the elders?). What was supposed to happen with such an intentional transgressor of God's commandment, in this case, the Sabbath commandment? Surely such a person had to be put to death, as we learn from Exod 31:14. But how? Yahweh had not yet made that known. Something like this had never happened before. Therefore Moses inquired of Yahweh. (Here again we see the special place among Israel that God had assigned to Moses. Yahweh talked with him "mouth to mouth" [Num 12:8]. He could simply go to God with his questions on behalf of the people, and he received an immediately answer [Exod 25:22; 33:11; Num 7:89; 9:8; 27:5].)

To the question about what punishment that man had to undergo for gathering firewood on the Sabbath day, Yahweh answered Moses that he had to be stoned. So Israel stoned him. Outside the camp, of course.

As we can see, the three passages fit completely with each other. All three have the same scope, namely, to imprint upon Israel the need for respecting the Horeb covenant. All of the commandments imposed through that covenant had to be honored with respect. Including the Sabbath commandment. Especially that one. For if there was one commandment that was intended to remind Israel of the Horeb covenant, it was that one. With extra force. In that institution was concentrated the entire covenant between God and the Israelites, and between them mutually.

That wood gatherer committed sacrilege covenant breaking against Yahweh and his people. When you grasp that, you will no longer consider his punishment barbaric.

Conclusion: Genesis 2:3: the Sabbath day is not a creation ordinance

From the Scripture passages we have discussed, we learn that observing the Sabbath day was imposed upon Israel at the time of "Horeb." We have also seen that a particular preparation occurred for that assignment at the beginning of the manna miracle (Exod 16), but that the institution of celebrating the weekly Sabbath day occurred at Horeb, with the proclamation of the fourth of the Ten Words of the covenant (Exod 20).

Whoever agrees with this conclusion will have no difficulty understanding the next Scripture passage that we will now discuss before we return to Leviticus 23.

This passage reads as follows: "*And God blessed the seventh day and made it holy, because on it he rested from all the work of creating that he had done*" (Gen 2:3, NIV).

In the past, people appealed to this verse as proof that the celebration of the Sabbath day after six days of work was imposed upon humanity already at creation. This has become a rather general sentiment, spread by way of study books and popular writing. All people are supposedly "bound in their conscience by God" to "the observance of a holy day." This supposedly shows the foundation of this celebration in creation, thus, as an act of God that is valid for the whole world, as long as it exists. This is supposedly a "universal ordinance of God over all creatures."

Even though this opinion is advocated in our day as well, the insight is gaining ground that this was incorrect. We agree with that insight. First, because it rests on a misunderstanding regarding Gen 2:3, and second, because it does not fit with other facts.

We begin with the latter reason. People insist with conviction that an "after effect" of such an institution of the Sabbath day existed by means of an alleged Paradise-tradition among pagan nations. But the opposite appears to be the case. The "Sabbath" was a Hebrew institution. The Israelite celebration of a Sabbath day was entirely unique in the ancient Near East. With this fact we find a corresponding reality that we never hear the Old Testament prophets, who announce judgment to the pagan nations, accuse them of not observing the Sabbath day. Every appeal and summons to repentance and return to observing such a commandment that supposedly dates from the time of Paradise is absent. In fact, any report of a kind of celebration of a Sabbath day by believers in the time of Enosh, by Noah, by Abraham and his household, and by the Israelites before "Horeb," is similarly absent. This latter fact gives us pause.

But more important is what Scripture teaches positively. Whoever takes the Pentateuch in hand does well to open it at the book of Exodus.

OBSERVE MY SABBATHS! (LEV 23–25)

There the great history of "Horeb" is narrated for us, how Yahweh made the Sinai covenant with the Israelites.

And *the books of Leviticus and Numbers* provide us now with the sequel to Exodus, when they tell us about the extended Torah under which the Israelites were placed with regard to the sacrificial ministry and the priestly ministry, the purity laws and food laws, etc. (Leviticus), and how, armed in this way against the dangers of Canaanite religious practice, Israel marched onward from Horeb (Numbers).

And *the book of Genesis* was the prologue to that book of Exodus. In that former book, Israel received a description of what God had already done for Abraham, Isaac, and Jacob. How God had already made a covenant with them. Earlier, how God had saved Abraham from the corrupted post-Flood world. Still earlier, how God had saved Noah from a corrupted pre-Flood world. And how sin and death had come into the world. And earliest of all, how good God had created everything.

The account about this creation is thus the first passage included in Holy Scripture for the people of Israel. That conclusion follows directly from our overview. We can see that as well in the introduction, in Scripture, of the name Yahweh. That occurred for the first time in Gen 2:4. When first, the creation of heaven and earth by God—at that point we read only of *elohim*, God, the divine name used universally in the Semitic world—is narrated, it is then said: and this *elohim* is now Yahweh. He is the same God who is known among us, Israelites, as Yahweh. This was a privilege that was given to none of our ancestors, not even to Abraham, Isaac, and Jacob. God said to Moses: I appeared to Abraham, Isaac, and Jacob as God the Almighty, but I was not known to them by my name Yahweh (Exod 6:12).

This introduction of the use of the name Yahweh in the book of Genesis—translated into English by means of the not-so-felicitous term Lord—is inaugurated precisely in the verse following our passage, i.e., in Genesis 2:4. There the instruction begins that is sustained throughout the rest of Genesis, from which the Israelite readers and hearers would discern that this almighty *elohim* was none other than the God of the burning bush, of "Horeb," namely, Yahweh.

So then, this inaugurated usage found in Gen 2:4 is preceded immediately by our text, Gen 2:3: "*And God blessed the seventh day and made it holy, because on it he rested from all the work of creating that he had done*" (NIV).

If we would narrowly fixate on the sequence of Bible chapters, and say: "Now, in Genesis 2—far earlier than Exodus 20, therefore—we read that God had set apart the seventh day as a day for himself," then we would be grasping at straws. In Holy Scripture, we find "proleptic reports" more often. To give but one example: in Num 21:1–3, we read that the king of

Arad, from the Negev region, fought against the Israelites and took some of them prisoner, but the Israelites killed the Canaanites of that region with the ban of total extermination. "So the place was named Hormah." This name comes from the Hebrew consonants *ḥrm*, the word for "ban." If we were not alert, we would easily think that this Israelite punishment expedition had occurred *immediately* after the appearance of that king of Arad. But further investigation shows that Israel had applied the ban to that region only later (Judg 1:17). Therefore we do well occasionally to add the word "later" at least in our thinking as we read something like this. For example, in Numbers 21, we should understand that the king of Arad from the Negev had taken some Israelites prisoner, but the Israelites—later!—applied the ban of extermination to this place, and called the place Hormah. At that time, that earlier reproach was erased.

If we agree that the author of Genesis permitted himself in 2:3 to speak in a proleptic manner, then every objection falls away. We then read Gen 2:3 simply with the word "later" in our mind, understanding the author of Genesis to be explaining merely this: And this is now the reason why God *later, at Horeb, by means of proclaiming the Fourth Commandment*, made the seventh day a blessing for us, Israelites, and a holy day for himself, devoted to his service and praise. "Because on it he rested from all the work of creating that he had done" (NIV). The same reference that we find at Horeb, in the Fourth Commandment (Exod 20:11).

The author of Genesis permitted himself such a pastorally explanatory addition not only in Gen 2:3 (for which reason we now receive at Horeb the Sabbath day on the seventh day), but also in Genesis 2:4 (introduction of the name Yahweh), as well as in Gen 2:24 (therefore a man shall leave his father and mother and cleave to his wife and they shall be one flesh).

LEVITICUS 23:1–3: INTRODUCTION TO THE CHAPTER ABOUT THE FEASTS

Looking back, we can observe that God had accustomed the Israelites little by little to recalling the Horeb covenant by means of special days, weeks, months, etc., in which the number seven regularly appeared.

He began doing that already in Egypt. The Passover was instituted there, as an annual memorial. "Seven days you shall eat unleavened bread." "On the first day you shall hold a holy assembly, and on the seventh day a holy assembly. No work shall be done on those days. But what everyone needs to eat, that alone may be prepared by you" (Exod 12:14–16).

OBSERVE MY SABBATHS! (LEV 23–25)

He continued with that in the wilderness, by instituting a kind of rest on every seventh day (after the first appearance of manna). At that point it was simply a partial and very specific rest, namely, from gathering manna (Exod 16).

He went still further at Horeb, by prescribing, in connection with making the covenant there, general rest on that seventh day (Exod 20:10–11).

And he moved much further in Leviticus 23–25, when he gave Israel an entire cycle of Sabbaths occurring at various times, but all of the same nature. All governed by the notion of rest, whether from this or that activity. All of them bore the same signature: they all bore the number seven as God's divine stamp.

We come now to Lev 23:1–3.

By way of introducing his commands regarding Passover, etc., that will follow, in the first three verses of this chapter, Yahweh established the day of the weekly Sabbath as a model. For the rest, he did not say all that much more about that weekly Sabbath day itself. More instruction was unnecessary. He was now interested in those broader sabbatical circles. With those in view, he said in verse 2: "*These are the appointed feasts of the Lord that you shall proclaim as holy convocations; they are my appointed feasts.*"

We must discuss the word "feast." We have a good opportunity for doing that in connection with the Hebrew word that is translated as "feasts." We should translate the Hebrew word *mo'ed* more accurately as "time" (and the plural *mo'edim* as "times"). For a "feast" in our sense of the word, the Israelites used the word *chag*, a cognate of the verb *chagag*, to dance. But a *mo'ed* like the Great Day of Atonement was not an occasion for dancing, but especially for fasting (see chapter 22). The Hebrew word *mo'ed* meant simply a fixed time, as we see from Ps 75:2, where God declared in his sovereignty: "At the set time that I appoint I will judge with equity." We express it this way: God comes in his own time. Genesis 1:14 and Ps 104:19a teach us that God used heavenly bodies to indicate fixed times (days, months, seasons) for people.

Strictly speaking, the translation "times" would be the best, since it is the most neutral. Nevertheless, in view of the practical usage (the word "feasts" has become standard) and in view of the joyful occasions that will be discussed in Leviticus 23 (Passover, etc.), we believe it is helpful to continue rendering *mô'ĕdîm* as "appointed feasts."

In somewhat paraphrastic translation, Lev 23:2 says: "*The appointed feasts for Yahweh, to which you will be summoned, will be convocations that are to remain reserved for him. They are the following. My feasts.*"

From the frequently mentioned Book of the Covenant, we know that at Horeb Moses wrote that shortly after announcing the Ten Words to the

Israelites, God spoke about three annual feasts. The first time before the intermezzo with the golden calf (Exod 23:14–17), and the second time after that episode (Exod 34:18–26). In what connection did he do that, in each instance? In connection with Canaanitism. The conclusion of the Book of the Covenant was clearly anti-Canaanite. The repetition of that conclusion appeared to have been very necessary, given the episode of the golden calf. We must remember that the Canaanites would also have had their sanctuaries with altars and sacrifices. And most likely their feasts as well, which they celebrated at fixed times in connection with phenomena of nature. Apparently during the harvest of one year they saw to ensuring a good harvest in the following year by means of the ceremony of boiling a kid in its mother's milk. God would have had his wise reasons for prescribing at that point three feasts for Israel, who stood at Horeb ready within a short time to enter the land of Canaan.

So then, it appears that God was looking back to those earlier mentioned three feasts and recalling their tangible anti-Canaanite secondary purpose when here at the beginning of Leviticus 23, a chapter dealing with the same three feasts, he issued the explicit demand that these were feasts for him, Yahweh. Reserved for him, and thereby holy. When the Israelites were summoned to the feasts by the priests of Yahweh with their silver trumpets (Num 10:1–10), they were in fact to celebrate those feasts simply and only as people of Yahweh. In faithfulness to his Horeb covenant. Here again we should notice the shift from the third person to the first person, so characteristic for covenantal language. Notice as well the great urgency with which Yahweh is speaking. With all due respect, it seems as if Yahweh were stumbling over his words, as though he were interrupting himself. After the words, "as follows" (or: "these are those feasts"), we would actually have expected a summary. That does come later, but first we get another reminder: "My feasts!"

From this we learn God's purpose in instituting his feasts. The same as with the institution of his weekly Sabbath days. To drill into them his Horeb covenant! The same purpose behind those other means of instruction about which the Torah speaks and through which it functioned as a *paedagogus* (Gal 3:24) to keep Israel close to Yahweh and to preserve Israel for his service. The same purpose as the prohibition of certain foods, the commands regarding purification, instruction about tassels or cords on the corners of their garments, the same as the prescription about animals pulling a plow, seed in the field, etc. Observe my Horeb covenant!

That is what God intended, also with the instituting of his feasts.

The reminder of Israel's weekly Sabbath day had to serve to bind this upon the hearts of the Israelites as well. For then the Israelites could understand that much better what kind of character those feasts would have to demonstrate, and what divine intention lay behind them. For they had heard frequently about the weekly Sabbath days, and they were being observed faithfully already by this time. Therefore these are used now as a teaching tool. We read in verse 3: "*Six days shall work be done, but on the seventh day is a Sabbath of solemn [better: complete] rest, a holy convocation. You shall do no work. It is a Sabbath to the Lord in all your dwelling places.*"

Everyone would have recognized in these words the description of a weekly Sabbath day. On that day, complete rest had to occur as though during the midday heat or during the evening hours of darkness. Literally it says: "rest of the rest" (*shabbath sabbaton*). This was the Hebrew way of expressing the superlative grade. For example, the most beautiful song was "the songs of songs" (Song 1:1). We would translate the phrase in Lev 23:3, "complete rest."

In this way it is being indicated once again what kind of character those feasts were to exhibit on account of their days of complete rest as occurred on the Sabbath days, and what purpose they had, namely, to focus attention on Yahweh and his Horeb covenant. For in a thousand and one ways God was summoning his ancient church: Abide with me!

1. THE FEAST OF PASSOVER (LEV 23:4-14)

As we know, this feast was instituted in Egypt. But the celebration of this feast would have come into its own later. Therefore we will discuss first the original institution of the Passover, and second, its later celebration. And thirdly, we will attempt to understand the symbolic significance of the Passover.

1.1 *The institution of the Passover*

We can read about this in Exodus 12, immediately after the tenth plague was announced in Exodus 11. The institution of the Passover is described in Exod 12:1-28, followed by the story in Exod 12:29-42 about the execution of the punishment announced earlier, namely, the death of the firstborn. The large chapter of Exodus 12 is concluded with several regulations about the Passover. To this was added Exod 13:3-10, regarding eating unleavened bread.

In this connection we are immediately reminded of the deep distress in Egypt from which Israel was delivered. And in what an impressive manner this occurred. When it was really God's time to act, his arm appeared strong and powerful, unlike ours, and his hand mighty and effective, unlike ours. He delivered Israel "by a mighty hand and an outstretched arm, and by great deeds of terror" (Deut 4:34). Terrible. This is talked about all the way to the last book of the Bible, Revelation to John.

Israel was led out in the month of Abib. You can find the meaning of this name in Exod 9:31 and Lev 2:14: the barley was "in the ear." After the captivity, people used the name "Nisan" (Neh 2:1; Esther 3:7), the Babylonian name of the harvest month.

From the time of Egypt on, the Israelites were to count the months of the year from this month on as the first (Exod 12:2).

On the tenth day of the month they were to set apart a male animal from their livestock (a sheep or a goat), one without defect and one year old. The characteristic feature was that of perfection or completeness, including the number ten. Later it appears to have become customary for people not to slaughter little goats on the occasion of the Passover, but exclusively lambs.

The prescription was: one lamb per family. Was the family too small to eat a lamb, then they were to join together with a neighboring family.

The lamb had to be slaughtered on the fourteenth day of the month. The number fourteen is, of course, 2 x 7, and thus twice the number characteristic of the subsequent Horeb covenant. The slaughtering had to occur "between the two evenings," as we read literally in the Hebrew. Some versions speak of "twilight," and in view of Deut 16:6, this is entirely correct.

The blood of the lamb had to be collected in a bowl, and some of it was to be smeared on the lintel and both posts on either side of the door of the house, using a bundle of hyssop. Not on the threshold, of course, otherwise people might have walked on that blood. Due to the blood, those in the house would be spared when Yahweh struck all the firstborn in Egypt.

When people prepared the lamb for the meal, they were not to cut it in pieces, but leave it whole. Therefore it was not to be boiled in water, which would have required it to be cut into pieces, but it had to be roasted long enough so that the meat was done.

People were supposed to eat their lamb in their own houses. None of it was to be left behind in the house. If any meat remained, then it was to be burned up.

No uncircumcised person was permitted to participate in the meal.

Along with the lamb's meat, they were to use bitter herbs and unleavened bread. And finally, the Israelites were to eat the Passover with their loins girded, which means with their upper garment tied up at the waist with a belt, with shoes on their feet, and with their staff in their hand. In other words, ready to travel with haste.

1.2 Later celebration of the Passover

It is obvious that there was a difference between the first celebration of the Passover in Egypt, and the celebration that occurred later. For example, during the departure from Egypt, people could certainly not have observed the prescribed rest on the first and the seventh days. And later the smearing of blood on the lintel and side posts of the door of the house would have been omitted, as was the celebration of the Passover in travel uniform.

More important is the alteration that occurred later with respect to the slaughtering of lambs. At that time, this was not allowed to happen anywhere else than in connection with the sanctuary. Moses had commanded this before he died, with a view to the future when Israel would be living in Canaan (Deut 16:5–8). In fact, at the time Israel was staying at Horeb, God commanded that the three feasts—Passover, Pentecost, and Booths—were later to be celebrated "before the face of Yahweh." For that purpose, all men were to appear before him three times each year. We read this already in the Book of the Covenant (Exod 23:14–17). So the Passover was supposed to be a pilgrim festival, and was not able to be celebrated by the entire congregation, including mothers and children.

Exodus 12 remains fundamentally significant, therefore. Indeed. But whereas some things mentioned there appeared later to have been temporary, other things were later given their full due. And new things were added. Especially the latter is in view in our current passage, Lev 23:5–14, when it not only prescribes that on the fourteenth day of the first month the Passover was supposed to be held, and that for seven days thereafter, a great burnt offering—which you can find described in Num 28:16–25—would have to be brought each day, but also that later, in Canaan, "on the day after the Sabbath," "the sheaf of firstfruits of the harvest" was to be brought to the priest, and he was to wave the sheaf before Yahweh (Lev 23:10–11; for the grain offering).

1.3 The symbolic significance of the Passover

The Passover also held before Israel the lesson that Yahweh wanted to be a God of life for his people. Passover was a real festival of life. Note the following.

1.3.1 You can see this already in both of the *names* used for this feast: Passover and the Feast of Unleavened Bread. For the feast is called each of these. The former name is indeed used more frequently especially to designate the first day—although the Passover meal was accompanied by unleavened bread—and the second is used to identify other days.

The former name, Passover, comes from the Hebrew word *pesach*, that probably meant to leap over, and later to pass over, to spare. This latter meaning fits very well with Yahweh's promise given in Egypt: When I see its blood, I will pass by (Exod 12:13; cf. 12:27). God gave the blood of the Passover lamb to the Israelites so that they would by protected by it, against the terrible tenth plague. This plague involved the death of every male firstborn among people and livestock belonging to the Egyptians. "And there was a great cry in Egypt, for there was not a house where someone was not dead" (Exod 12:30). Simply by means of recalling this event, the annual Passover proclaimed that Yahweh had been a God of life for his people.

The second name for the feast was "the Feast of Unleavened Bread." This bread was called in Hebrew *matstsah*, from which the familiar Jewish term *matzot* comes. Here as well, the symbolic meaning is not difficult to identify. We have discussed frequently the divine command that at specific occasions, Israel was supposed to prepare only unleavened bread, and that the clear intent of this was that death and decay had no place in connection with Yahweh and the people of Yahweh. The institution that in the month of Abib Israel was to eat nothing but unleavened bread for seven days, in fact, that no yeast was permitted in their houses, had a clear pedagogical purpose (Exod 13:8), namely, that God had saved his own people out of Egypt, out of the power of death and destruction, so that she would be his holy people and therefore would not commit sin at pagan altars and carved images (Deut 7:5–8). Israel had risen from the dead, as it were. Therefore no pagan grieving practices were suitable for Israel (Deut 14:1).

1.3.2 Take note, next, of the *Passover lamb*, and what was supposed to happen with that: first, slaughtered, and second, eaten.

Regarding the first, we cannot deny that the slaughter of the Passover lamb bore the character of a sacrifice. This was at one time disputed among Roman Catholics and Protestants. According to the former, the mass was a repetition of Christ's sacrifice on the cross. To show the Scriptural character of this teaching, they appealed to, among other things, the Passover lamb that was repeatedly slaughtered after Egypt, not only for a meal but also as a sacrifice of atonement. If only their Protestant opponents at that time had specifically pointed to the symbolic and inadequate nature of the Old Testament Passover sacrifice, which means that this sacrifice, together with all the others since "the foundation of the world"[10] had to be slaughtered by necessity again and again, and if only in this context they had pointed to the

---

10. For the meaning of this phrase, see Vonk, *Exodus*, 304–311.

fulfillment of this shadow by Christ's "once for all" sacrifice, his "one time" sacrifice (Heb 7:27; 9:28), this would have been sufficient. But in their zeal to remove every Scriptural basis for the aforementioned Roman Catholic doctrine, unfortunately various Protestants went so far as to deny that the slaughter of the Passover lamb, both in Egypt and later, had any sacrificial character at all. To be honest, this was a mistake. For not only was the slaughtered Passover lamb called a sacrifice offering (*zebach*) both in Egypt and later (Exod 12:27), but the Israelites in Egypt were, as we say, spared by the blood that was smeared on the lintel and on the posts of the door, from the wrath of God and from the death of their firstborn. That was due to the (symbolic) atonement and covering of the Israelites through the lamb's blood. Whereas it cannot be doubted that in what followed, the slaughter of the Passover lamb bore the character of an atonement sacrifice, since, first of all, this lamb was called a sacrificial gift (*qorban*) in Num 9:7; second, it had to be slaughtered in connection with the sanctuary (Deut 16:5–6); and thirdly, its blood had to be thrown (*zaraq*) against the altar—unlike the sin offering, but nonetheless like a burnt offering, peace offering, and guilt offering (2 Chron 20:16; 35:11). Whereas here, finally, we may recall the word of the apostle: For our Passover has also be slain (*thuein*), namely, Christ (1 Cor 5:7), and this was done according to God's manifest will that our Savior would die "at the feast," something that despite every counter move by the Jewish leaders, did indeed happen (Matt 26:5; John 19:14, 36; Acts 2:23).

The preaching of the gospel of atonement was certainly present in the Passover sacrifice. This feature is certainly shared with all the other peace offerings, to which class the Passover sacrifice belonged, in view of the meal that must be seen in connection with it.

Nevertheless, this atonement sermon, no matter how improper it would be for us to neglect it, was not the characteristic element of the Passover sacrifice, just as it was not characteristic of all other peace offerings that we discussed in connection with the Sacrifice Torah. That chief mark was rather the assurance that the Israelites received by means of the meal, that there was peace and communion between Yahweh and them. God had rescued them from death in Egypt, so that they would enjoy a paradisal future with him. Therefore, Passover was a feast in connection with which the Hallel (Pss 113–118) was joyfully sung (Matt 26:30; 1 Cor 10:18), as though it were a feast of thanksgiving, which in truth it was.

As they ate, the Israelites were not only being assured through the Passover meal of their peace and communion with God, but also of the same blessings with one another. The meal pointed to that, but so did eating the lamb that had to be left intact as much as possible. This was something relevant not to the eating, but to the preparing of the lamb. It was not permitted to be divided into pieces, not even boiled, but it had to be roasted. And when a family was too small to eat the entire lamb, it had to share it with a neighbor. At the same time, no bone of the lamb was to be broken. This pertained to its preparation. The lamb had to be presented whole. No part of the lamb was to be taken outside the house. All of this would have been related to strengthening the mutual fellowship of the Israelites. Compare this with the word of the apostle. Because we eat one bread, we who are many are one body; for we all share in the one bread (1 Cor 5:7).

Let us remember in this connection, finally, that no single Israelite was permitted to abstain from eating the Passover lamb, on pain of death. For those who on account of uncleanness were prevented from sitting at the Passover meal at the usual time, there was a second opportunity a month later for celebrating the Passover (Num 9). No uncircumcised person was permitted to share in the meal. Only members of Israel.

It is clear that by means of instituting the communal eating of one Passover lamb, as it were, God was binding upon the heart of his ancient church in a powerful way the command for exercising mutual fellowship and peace.

1.3.3 In addition to the meat of the Passover lamb, *unleavened bread* and *bitter herbs* were eaten in the Passover meal (see Exod 12:8).

Regarding the symbolism of eating bread without yeast, we need say nothing further. The same divine intention lay behind the *bitter herbs*. The Hebrew word used for these herbs (*merorim*), would have reminded the Israelites immediately of Exod 1:14: the Egyptians made their lives bitter (*yemorru*). Compare, in this connection, the statement of Naomi: "Do not call me Naomi; call me Mara, for the Almighty has dealt very bitterly with me" (Ruth 1:20), and note as well the phrase "bread of affliction" in reference to unleavened bread (Deut 16:3).

What should we understand by these bitter herbs? We know that it was customary among the Egyptians to dip bread in a mixture of fresh herbs and vinegar in connection with their meals. Clearly the Jews adopted this custom. Bitter herbs are used with Jewish meals and are eaten by many Jews in the East along with morsels of bread. Chicory (*Cichorium intybus*), endives (*Cichorium endivia*), watercress (*Nasturtium officinale*), garden lettuce (*Lactuca sativa*), and sour weed (*Rumex acetosella*) were among the bitter herbs that people usually associate with the Passover meal of the Jews. Most of them grow wild in Egypt and in the Near East.

1.3.4 We also mentioned God's command that later in Canaan, Israel was to bring the firstfruits sheaf of harvest to the priest in connection with the Passover feast (Lev 23:10–11). This ceremony fit entirely with the beautiful month of Abib. You can count on the fact that when they left Egypt, the Israelites walked among the anemones and the lilies. Later as well, no month was more beautiful for celebrating the first feast of the year than the month of Abib. Even the barren places in the wilderness of Palestine were for a brief time renewed as a blooming Paradise. The flax was blooming at that time. And the grain, at least the barley, which was the earliest grain of the year, earlier than wheat, was ripening. Passover Feast, Feast of Booths! At that time the firstfruits sheaf of the new harvest was offered to Israel's good God. This was actually the consecration of the entire future harvest, placed with gratitude in the hands of Yahweh. According to the rule: if the firstfruits are holy, then so is the dough, and if the root is holy, then the branches are as well (Rom 11:16).

In connection with this sacrificing of the firstfruits sheaf, it was most fitting to remember with thanksgiving the preservation of Israel's firstborn in Egypt. When the Israelites walked out of Egypt, all the Egyptians were busy burying their dead (Num 33:3-4). When in Exodus 12 the institution of the Passover is narrated for the first time, immediately following we find in Exodus 13 the law of the firstborn.

No wonder that God commanded Israel from that time on to number the months of the year from the month of Abib as the first (Exod 12:2).

1.3.5 We conclude with a few comments about *the times* of the Passover feast.

As has been said, on the tenth of the month a perfect one-year old male lamb was supposed to be selected from the flock. How young and strong such an animal was! We already pointed to the correspondence of the symbolism of the number ten and that of the youth and perfection of the whole one-year old male lamb. That is what our Savior was, when he offered himself in death for us. In the strength of his years (1 Pet 1:19).

Why was this lamb to be held for exactly four days in isolation? Some have answered: because four generations of Israelites had lived in Egypt (Gen 15:16). This strikes us as artificial. The issue appears to us to have been simply this. In order to move from the symbolic number ten to the other symbolic number fourteen (2 x 7, very holy), four days had to be added to the ten. (Compare this with the calculation of the [symbolic] times of uncleanness for a mother who had just given birth. In order to move from the symbolic number seven to the symbolic number forty, thirty-three days had to be added, and in order to move from the symbolic number fourteen [2 x 7] to the symbolic number eighty [2 x 40], sixty-six days had to be added.

The number ten symbolized perfection, while the number seven is the number of the covenant and of holiness. The Passover feast was identified thereby as a genuine covenant feast. Although it was instituted already in Egypt, it was completely included later in the Torah of Horeb, just as the feast of Pentecost and of Booths (Exod 23:14–17; 34:18–26; Lev 23:5–44). These were feasts that belonged to the Horeb covenant. Therefore the number seven was involved with each of them.

The number seven as the signature of covenant and holiness was stamped upon the Passover feast in yet another way.

On the fifteenth day of the month of Abib, the seven days of unleavened bread began. Even though in connection with the Passover meal, on the fourteenth, nothing but unleavened bread was eaten. But those seven days were often identified especially by that phrase. They were counted from the fifteenth, the day on which Israel was kept alive and came forth out of Egypt, and the Egyptians were busy with their dead.

That week began with this fifteenth day, when the great sacrifices were brought each day, about which you can read in Num 28:19–25. The first day of this week, the fifteenth, was a complete Sabbath day. So was the last day of this week (Lev 23:7–8).

On the second day of Passover week, on the sixteenth of Abib, the presentation of the firstfruits sheaf occurred. Naturally not by themselves, but on the perpetually required basis of a burnt sacrifice. This is prescribed extensively in Lev 23:12.

We have already commented that the firstfruits sheaf consisted of barley, because the barley ripened before the wheat (Ruth 1:22; 2:23).

With this, we have said enough about the Passover feast of the Israelites. The Israelite fathers were supposed to explain it to their children as well (Exod 12:26; 13:8).

It was instituted already in Egypt, but later we see how through this Passover feast God had prudently prepared the Israelites for the establishing of the Horeb covenant. This feast was therefore explicitly identified with this covenant by our Savior. When Christ instituted the Lord's Supper, he said that the cup associated with this meal was the cup of the new covenant, of which he was the Surety (Matt 26:28; Mark 14:24; Luke 22:20; 1 Cor 11:25). Through his suffering and death, the old covenant—the covenant of Horeb—became obsolete. Today it would no longer be fitting for us to celebrate Passover. For instruction in the new covenant, of which Jesus has become the Surety, the Holy Spirit today no longer uses lambs and their blood, nor unleavened bread with bitter herbs, nor any of the symbolic numbers seven, ten, fourteen, and twenty-one, nor Sabbath days and festival weeks, to say nothing of the presentation of firstfruits sheaf. All that old symbolism and practice, no matter how beautiful it was, is past. Now we may know the gospel of Christ, who died for our sins and through his resurrection has brought us life and immortality.

2. THE FEAST OF PENTECOST (LEV 23:15-22)

The feasts of Passover and Pentecost were intimately connected. Both were genuine festivals of life. Except that with Passover, more emphasis fell on the *beginning* of life—think of the deliverance from Egypt and the initial gift of the grain harvest—while with Pentecost, more emphasis fell on the *progress and sustenance* of life.

For purposes of illuminating the similarities and the differences between Passover and Pentecost, we will look first at the time of the feast of Pentecost, second, at the names, and thirdly, the sacrifices that were to be brought on the occasion of this feast.

2.1 The time of the Pentecost feast

In contrast to the feast of Passover, the feast of Pentecost was celebrated for one day. It concluded the time of the grain harvest. This lasted for seven weeks, a period that might seem somewhat long to us, but we should not forget that the threshing of the grain occurred during the same time (Ruth 3:2).

The time began with that day of the week of Passover when the firstfruits sheaf was brought to Yahweh. From that day people counted fifty days, during which there were seven "complete Sabbaths" (Lev 23:15). That is how they came up with the day for celebrating the feast of Pentecost, by counting from Passover. From this we see clearly the dependence of the feast of Pentecost on the feast of Passover.

The reader will have noticed by now the covenant signature that this feast bore as well, with the number 7 x 7. Consequently, in this way ancient Israel was reminded again of God's Horeb covenant. Indeed. But the Jewish custom of recalling on Pentecost the proclamation of the Ten Words at Horeb arose much later, after the turn from BC to AD. You read nothing about that in Holy Scripture.

2.2 The names of the Pentecost feast

Actually the name "Pentecost," which we have maintained for ease of reference, is not very suitable. For it comes not from the Hebrew, but from the Greek (*pentekostē*, fiftieth day). This Greek word leads us to think automatically of the event in Acts 2, the outpouring of the Holy Spirit, which would not be suitable. The passages in the Torah, where the Hebrew name for this feast is used, are the following.

Exodus 23:16: the feast of harvest, of the firstfruits of your labor

Exodus 34:22: the feast of weeks, the firstfruits of the wheat harvest

(Leviticus 23 does not mention a specific name, though it discusses this feast in verses 15–21)

Numbers 28:26: the day of firstfruits; your feast of weeks (literally, your weeks)

Deuteronomy 16:10: the feast of weeks

Here as well, we see once again the correspondence and difference between the feasts of Passover and Pentecost.

Both were harvest festivals and they spoke of God's delight in Israel's life and well being.

But whereas the feast of Passover opened the grain harvest, the feast of Pentecost concluded the harvest. At the feast of Passover, only a sheaf of barley was brought to Yahweh as firstfruit, while at the feast of Pentecost, bread was offered, baked bread. And at the feast of Passover Israel was supposed to present to Yahweh only something of the earliest ripened grain, namely, of barley, while at the feast of Pentecost something of the last ripened grain was brought, namely, wheat.

Between them lay forty-nine days, or seven weeks. The feast of Pentecost was, namely, after that. In this manner God definitely wanted to focus attention on himself as the God of the number seven, of the covenant that he had made at Horeb, where he showed Israel that he wanted not only to deliver Israel from the death of Egypt, but also to care faithfully for her and protect her.

To protect her especially from the lurking danger of Canaanite paganism where it confronted Israel precisely at those points of life, eating, and food.

Let us consider carefully the *passages* where we saw the feast of Pentecost mentioned. There were three of them.

1. Exodus 23:16. This appears in the conclusion of the Book of the Covenant, which warned vigorously against Canaanitism.

2. Exodus 34:22.

3. Leviticus 23:15–21. This belongs to that part of a book in which, from chapter 11 onward, the command is laid upon the heart of Israel: Be separate!

Whereas the pagans surrounding Israel ascribed their weal and woe, including their harvests, to (impersonal) natural forces, Israel's harvest was enclosed by God between Passover and Pentecost and thereby Israel's attention was being claimed by means of Pentecost for Passover, and by means of Passover directed back to a verifiable *history, to a genuine historical fact, to the redemptive deed* of their (personal) God, to Israel's deliverance from Egypt by Yahweh.

The pagan feasts with their cultic dramas were obnoxiously annoying mythological reenactments of their deity fantasized as annually dying and resurrecting.

In direct contradiction, the feast of Passover with its related feast of Pentecost supplied memorial instruction regarding Yahweh, the Deliverer from Egypt, the Covenant Maker of Horeb.

2.3 The sacrifices at the Pentecost feast

The feast of Pentecost concluded a period that had begun with the feast of Passover. That connection was visible everywhere.

For example, in the relationship between barley and wheat, as between earlier and later kinds of grain. Only a *sheaf* of the former was to be presented to God, while *a loaf, even two loaves, of bread* were to be presented. In addition, these Pentecost loaves were not unleavened, but leavened. Deliciously prepared. Ready to be eaten. Moreover, they were not laid on the altar (after all, they were leavened!), but after being "waved" they were given to the (ministering?) priest. The relationship between the feasts of Passover and Pentecost was evident from something else as well, namely, as the beginning and end of the following phenomena. The barley of Passover was called in Hebrew an *omer* (Lev 23:15). And the second tithe of an ephah of fine flour, from which the two Pentecost loaves were to be baked, could similarly be called two *omers*. The word *omer* could be the term for both sheaf and for a unit of weight (Exod 16:36; an *omer* was 1/10 of an ephah). Again we have the ratio of 1:2, of less to more, of single to double (Lev 23:17).

This same relationship, between beginning and end, less and more, was present in the (bloody) sacrifices accompanied by the sheaf of Passover and the loaves of Pentecost. In addition to the firstfruits sheaf of Passover, *one sheep as a burnt offering* had to be brought, but in addition to the two firstfruits loaves of Pentecost *two sheep* as a *peace offering* had to be brought, although no one other than the priest was permitted to eat from this (Lev 23:19-20). Not only in the ratio of 1:2, but also in the peace offering that, as we saw earlier, was accompanied with psalms of praise and thanksgiving, the concluding character of the feast of Pentecost came to expression.

The extent to which the feast of Pentecost was to be seen as the conclusion of a period that began with the feast of Passover appears, finally, from the fact that both on all seven days of the Passover week and on the single day of the feast of Pentecost, two young bulls, one ram, and seven (notice this number again!) one-year old sheep had to be sacrificed (Lev 23:18; Num 28:19-21, 27). (In addition, one goat as a sin offering [Lev 23:19;

Num 28:22, 30]. In addition, at the feast of Pentecost the two sheep already mentioned as a peace offering; at the feast of Passover one sheep as a burnt offering.) The line with regard to the sacrifices was obviously extended from Passover and tied off at Pentecost.

We need to return for a moment to discuss the two wave loaves.

The Israelites were supposed to bring these from their "dwelling places," as Lev 23:17 says. From this people infer that each Israelite family had to bring two loaves from their fresh harvest to the sanctuary. But that does not seem very likely. The priests would have been buried under the loaves. And because these loaves were not permitted to be burned on the altar (for they were leavened!) not to be thrown away (for they were sanctified unto Yahweh), they would certainly have become moldy and inedible. Therefore, it seems best to understand the words "from your dwelling places" in Lev 23:17 to be referring to the future when Israel would be living in the promised land. We repeat it once more: the laws of Horeb were given from the viewpoint that in a short time Israel would be entering the land of Canaan. The forty-year wandering was not supposed to have happened at all. "From your dwelling places" would mean: when you have later settled in Canaan. At that time, two Pentecost loaves were to come from somewhere. The honor of delivering of those loaves would have been given one time to this locale, another time to a different locale.

Even though only two loaves were to be offered to Yahweh on Pentecost, namely, as a symbolic representation of the entire harvest—for if the firstfruits were holy, then so too was the entire harvest (cf. Rom 11:16)—nevertheless each Israelite had the right to honor Yahweh on Pentecost with a voluntary offering in addition (Deut 16:10). It was a festival of thanksgiving and honor to Yahweh. Because the relationship to Yahweh and the relationship to the neighbor were indissolubly bound together, the poor also had to be remembered with liberality and generosity. This explains the prescription: "When you reap the harvest of your land, you shall not reap to the very edges of your field, or gather the gleanings of your harvest; you shall leave them for the poor and for the alien: I am the Lord your God" (Lev 23:22). Later, when Moses had spoken in a similar vein about the voluntary gifts given on Pentecost—except that he mentioned at that point the Levite in addition to the widow and the orphan—he concluded this way: "Remember that you were a slave in Egypt, and diligently observe these statutes [of Passover and Pentecost]" (Deut 16:12). That was yet another point where attention was paid to the social side of God's institution of the feast of Pentecost.

Must we also still celebrate the feast of Pentecost? As a day with no "servile labor" (Lev 23:21)? As a Sabbath day?

We have seen that the feast of Passover, to which our Savior pointed emphatically, belonged to the old covenant. The same is true of the feast of Pentecost that occurred during the harvest season and began with the feast of Passover. In the rabbinic literature, the feast of Pentecost was usually called *atseret*, or closing feast.

Nevertheless, Christians have thought it important to continue to celebrate these feasts. Already in the second century there was a serious dispute about the futile question whether they were supposed to celebrate the feast of Passover on Friday or on Sunday. Once again, such superfluous contention.

Finally the council of Nicea (325), under pressure from the government—emperor Constantine wanted visible unity throughout his empire—took up the matter of regulating the celebration of the feast days, and assigned the feast of Passover to Sunday. And the feast of Pentecost, forty-nine days later, was also put on Sunday. But the celebration of various feasts was not prescribed for us by the Lord's apostles—quite the contrary, in fact, if you read Gal 4:10 and Col 2:16-17.

3. THE FIRST DAY OF THE SEVENTH MONTH (LEV 23:23-25)

In this context we would like to follow the same procedure as we did with Pentecost, and pay attention to the following: first, the time of this day; second, the names for this day; and third, the sacrifices given on this day.

3.1 The time of the First Day of the Seventh Month

God gave Israel the Torah at Horeb, whereby they would be reminded moment by moment of the covenant that he made with them. Also by means of the obligation to give to Yahweh the first of everything, the first of the barley harvest on Passover, and the first loaves of the wheat harvest on Pentecost. He did the same thing with the months of the year.

Every first day of each month was not a Sabbath day, but it was nonetheless a special day. That came to expression in the sacrifices that were supposed to be brought on such a day (Num 28:11). Originally it was certainly not a Sabbath day, in view of the sacrifices for that day (compare Num 28:9-10 with 28:11-15), but later it was mentioned in the same context as the Sabbath day (2 Kgs 4:23; Isa 1:13; Hos 2:13; Ezek 46:1), at a time when the day was (occasionally?) free from business activity (Amos 8:5), and when a sacred meal was held (1 Sam 20).

In any case, however, the seventh new moon day was a very special day. For this was the first day of the seventh month. Notice again the number seven, the number of the covenant. Moreover, this day marked the beginning of the month when most of the holy days of the entire year occurred: the Great Day of Atonement, the Feast of Booths, and the Closing Feast. In that month, after 7 x 7 years, the year of jubilee was announced.

We will not discuss this any further. Later Judaism adopted the custom of celebrating New Year's Day on this seventh new moon day, but you will find no clear trace, if any at all, of this in Holy Scripture.

3.2 The names of the First Day of the Seventh Month

The First Day of the Seventh Month was identified with more than one name. A general term for it is the term *shabbaton*. But the special meaning of this day was expressed in the phrases *yom teruʿa* and *zikron teruʿa*.

1. The phrase *yom teruʿa* is translated as day of gladness or day of the blasts. *Yom* means day, and *teruʿa* must be explained in such a way that we take into consideration God's command that at certain times, the priests were to blow on the two silver trumpets that Moses had made (Num 10:1–10). Various signals could be given with these trumpets, such as a signal calling the entire congregation to assemble at the entrance to the tent of meeting. So it was expected that the people would listen to such a signal. But it was also expected that God would listen to such a signal, for example, in a time of war. For then as well, the priests had to blow the trumpets and thereby the Israelites would be brought to remembrance in the presence of Yahweh their God, and be saved from their enemies.

This institution probably strikes us as strange, because we run the risk of thinking that a simple prayer is acceptable to God and is heard by God, when it is uttered aloud. But that opinion is not entirely Scriptural. The stones on Aaron's shoulder- and breast-pieces served to bring Israel to God's remembrance (Exod 28:12, 29). So too the silver trumpets of the priests in times of distress due to enemies (Num 10:9). So too the daily incense sacrifice, every morning and evening, was offered as a continual prayer of the priests who served as Israel's "mediators." With this in view, Gabriel could say to Zechariah: "Your prayer has been heard" (Luke 1:13). With these words, the angle was not referring to the prayer of the multitude in the forecourt, for he said: "*Your* [singular] prayer." Nor did he have in mind certain words spoken aloud by Zechariah. We read nothing about such words.

But we do read that as priest, Zechariah was to offer up the incense sacrifice (v. 9), that he was to bring scoops of fire to the incense altar and scatter the incense on the altar. That was Zechariah's priestly prayer. "Your prayer." That is how God wished to receive prayer in the old covenant.

So then, the same was true with respect to that blowing by the priests on the silver trumpets. In days of threatening war, God would listen to that (Num 10:9). But also when the priest blew on the trumpet in connection with joyful occasions. Then the promise would be honored: also on your days of gladness, at your feasts, and at the beginning of your months, you shall blow the trumpets in connection with your burnt offerings and peace offerings. They will serve to bring you to remembrance before your God. I am Yahweh your God (Num 10:10).

When the trumpets mentioned (*chatsotseroth*, Num 10:2) were used to summon together the people or the rulers over the "thousands" of Israel, the trumpets were simply blown, yielding a simple long blast. That was intended for the people. But in connection with impending war or with feasts, short blasts were sounded, simulating the sound of alarm or excitement. That series of short trumpet blasts was for God, serving to "bring Israel in remembrance" of God.

2. The same verb, "to bring into remembrance," or "cause to remember" (*zkr*) is part of the second phrase for the Seventh New Moon Day, namely, *zikron teru'a*, which the King James Version renders as "a memorial of blowing of trumpets," which seems to us to be an accurate translation. This phrase is clear, in light of Exod 28:12, 29, and Num 10:1-10. The seventh month was a very important month, since it contained most of the special feast days, including the Great Day of Atonement. For this reason, on the first day of this month God received prayers of special intensity that he would sanctify and bless this month for his people. It was, as was explicitly stated, a special Sabbath day, a *shabbaton*, when a holy convocation was held, all servile labor was forbidden, and special sacrifices had to be brought, which were scrupulously prescribed (Lev 23:24-25).

3.3 The sacrifices on the First Day of the Seventh Month

The special character of a day came to expression in various ways, among them in the number and size of the offerings that had to be sacrificed on that day.

Take the Sabbath day, for example, when the sacrifice that had to be brought every day was supposed to be doubled (compare Num 28:1-8 with vv. 9-10).

The same feature characterized the first day of the seventh month. On that day, not only the sacrifice brought on every other ordinary first day of the month—about which you can read in Num 28:11–15—but an extra festival sacrifice—about which you can read in Num 19:1–6—was added.

It would be unnecessary to point out that we are not supposed to observe the First Day of the Seventh Month. By this celebration, Israel was forcefully reminded of their Horeb covenant. Think of the number seven. But we no longer live under that covenant. For us all the feasts of the seventh month—the Great Day of Atonement, the Feast of Booths, and the Closing Feast—fall away, together with the prelude to them, namely, the First Day of the Seventh Month.

4. THE GREAT DAY OF ATONEMENT (LEV 23:26–32)

Despite the importance of this day for Israel, we may be brief here. In chapter 22 we discussed this extensively.

4.1 *The time of the Great Day of Atonement*

This occurred on the tenth day of the seventh month.

Two numbers whose symbolic purpose is familiar.

Seven was the number of the covenant, and ten was the number of perfection or completeness. The measurements of the holy of holies were ten. On the tenth of the month Abib, the perfect gift of the Passover lamb had to be separated from the flock. On the tenth day of the seventh month, there was a *abbt* or rest, for the covenant people, for the priests, for the high priest, indeed, even for the sanctuary itself with all its accessories, from all purification. (And during the Year of Jubilee, on the Great Day of Atonement the trumpet was to be blown everywhere [Lev 25:9].)

4.2 *The names of the Great Day of Atonement*

1. The first name was *shabbath shabbaaton*, or rest of rests, a Hebrew manner for indicating the superlative degree (cf. *qodesh qoddeshim*, or holy of holies, or most holy; and *shir hashirim*, or song of songs, the highest song). This terminology pointed to the unique character of the Great Day of Atonement. Later Jews spoke of *yoma rabba*, the great day, and currently they often speak simply of *yoma*, the day.

2. Related to the covering of impurities, the day was also called *yom hakkippurim*, literally: day of atonements (Lev 23:27-28; 25:9). *Kippurim* is plural: atonements. This plural occurs, however, not only in connection with the Great Day of Atonement, but also on other occasions that involve atonement (Exod 29:36; 30:10, 16; Num 5:8, 29). Apparently, this plural was a Hebrew way of simply expressing what we would call "the atoning."

We studied the manner in which this atoning (*kipper*) occurred, namely, by covering with a dead *nefesh* that God supplied as a substitute, in connection with our discussion of the Sacrifice Torah. At this point we should recall the Hebrew word for the atonement covering, namely, *kapporeth*, derived from *kipper*, to cover, to atone. It was the golden covering on the ark of the covenant, Israel's most holy place of sacrifice, upon and in front of which the high priest sprinkled the blood of the animals sacrificed as the sin offering, both for himself and for the people, on the Great Day of Atonement.[11]

4.3 The sacrifices on the Great Day of Atonement

Everyone in Israel had a job to do on this day.

1. First, the high priest. He approached Yahweh in order to cover the sins of the priesthood and people (symbolically) on the highest place of sacrifice in Israel. Recall what we wrote about this in chapter 22.

2. But in addition to the sacrifices that had to be brought on that day by the high priest, still others had to be brought. For example, the daily burnt sacrifice with everything associated with it. This is recalled emphatically in Num 29:11. But in addition, on this day the same great sacrifice had to be brought that belonged to the First Day of the Seventh New Month, along with the usual daily and new month sacrifices, namely, the food and blood sacrifices (compare Num 29:8-11 with Num 29:2-6).

Now, when we consider the large number of animals that had to be slaughtered on this occasion, and all the work that went along with that, including the preparation of the accompanying food sacrifices, then everyone will realize that all of this could not have been performed by one single person, such as the high priest. Therefore in connection with this second kind of labor we think of the priests, and perhaps also the Levites, as having been enlisted.

3. A task was assigned to the entire people as well. First, the people were to abstain from all work. This would have begun already on the evening of the preceding day, or the 9th of the month (Lev 23:32). Moreover,

---

11. See Vonk, *Exodus*, 227.

on the Day of Atonement itself there was to be a holy convocation (Lev 23:27). And in the third place, throughout that day people were supposed to "humble" themselves. Everyone. Anyone who omitted this would be liable to death (Lev 23:27, 29–30).

The question arises as to what this humbling consisted in.

Surely fasting would have been part of this. For we read literally that the Israelites had to *anah* their "souls," that is, press themselves down (Lev 16:29; 23:27). The word "souls" can be a general reference here to people or persons, but probably refers at the same time to people's desires, probably for eating and drinking. We find this in Ps 35:13, for example. What the ESV renders as "I afflicted myself with fasting," is literally, "I humbled my soul with fasting" (as in the KJV).

But it is not out of the question that God's intention was that on the Day of Atonement the Israelites would abstain from other things as well, things that people usually desire. According to Jewish tradition, on the Great Day of Atonement it was also forbidden to bathe, to anoint, to tie one's sandals, and to have sexual relations. We do not read the latter prohibition in Holy Scripture, but it does lead us to recall God's command preceding the proclamation of the Ten Words at Horeb, that the Israelites were to sanctify themselves by washing their clothes and by not approaching a woman (Exod 19:10, 14–15). It also reminds us of the custom that God had established, in light of Leviticus 11–15, not only with respect to people's food, but also involving such matters as sexual emissions, in order to make his Israelite church aware of the holiness of Yahweh and of the covenant that he had established with her at Sinai. This holiness was so great that Israel could not stand before Yahweh if she had not been covered (symbolically) by God himself with the blood of atonement. Every day. And that was not even sufficient. Every year anew on the Great Day of Atonement.

The divine commandment that on this day, Israel was to abstain from everything desirable to the soul, eating and drinking and whatever else, would certainly have sought to focus attention especially on God's holiness, on the repeatedly recurring distresses and deficiencies of his people, and on the rule that with God, there was no forgiveness without the shedding of blood.

For the truth of this rule can quiet us as well. And it does that despite the fact that we are living in the new covenant, of which Jesus has become the Surety.

In sharp contrast to the high priests of the old covenant, the Horeb covenant, our Lord Jesus Christ did not render his atoning sacrifice many times, daily, or even annually. He was not a high priest like Aaron. "For then he would have had to suffer *repeatedly* since the foundation of the world," says Heb 9:26. How clearly we see here that with the expression "foundation of the world," we must understand: Horeb. Hebrews 9:26 goes on to say of Christ: "But as it is, he has appeared once for all at the end of the ages to put away sin by the sacrifice of himself."

Therefore it was so foolish that people within Christianity introduced something like a Great Day of Atonement once again. In our own youth, we witnessed the custom in some towns of closing the shutters on so-called Good Friday, which was the well-known sign of mourning.

Was this simply a Roman Catholic leftover?

No, this goes back to a tradition that existed long before the Roman Catholic custom. Back in 1880, we read Rev. Johannes Krull talking enthusiastically, in his work on "The Christian Church Year." He noted that Good Friday, as the day of suffering, together with the day of the Lord's resurrection, constituted a festival in the early church, and was celebrated with just as much interest. From the time of Constantine this entire celebration lasted for fourteen days, and Good Friday enjoyed high priority as a feast of suffering. All the ornaments and decorations usually covering the altar and the walls were removed, so that people's spirits and hearts could be more genuinely united with the dying Savior. People abstained from all earthly activities, and spent the day in strict fasting. On this day, the penitents prepared for this occasion were gathered together in the fellowship of the church.[12]

That is how Christianity entered the Middle Ages.

Then God granted the blessed church reformation. As we know, our Reformed ancestors originally wanted nothing to do with feast days. They tried to eliminate them, but the government resisted that. This was a story of suffering, a real tug-of-war, with compromises, and the church was forced to back down. All the decisions involving the issue of the feast days were concessions by the ecclesiastics to the state. In principle people opposed them, but the government fought tooth and nail for them. Why? They didn't want to let go of their "vacation days."

Initially our Reformed ancestors wanted nothing to do with Good Friday. In the Church Order of Dort (art. 67) this feast day was not even mentioned. During that time, people did begin observing Good Friday here and there, but this custom was fiercely opposed and was not universal.

In our view, the observance of something like a Great Day of Atonement feast in this New Testament period was not laid upon us by any apostle. Nor Easter or Pentecost. On the contrary. We are warned against

---

12. Krull, *Kerkjaar*, 46, 174.

any appearance of going back to the old covenant. See the epistles to the Galatians and to the Colossians.

We are to remember the death of our Savior when we celebrate the Lord's Supper (1 Cor 11:25–26). We are to give expression to his death and resurrection as events that occurred once for all time, and do so in our conduct and our walk. "Do you not know that all of us who have been baptized into Christ Jesus were baptized into his death? We were buried therefore with him by baptism into death, in order that, just as Christ was raised from the dead by the glory of the Father, we too might walk in newness of life" (Rom 6:3–4).

5. THE FEAST OF BOOTHS (LEV 23:33–44)

Permit us to begin our discussion of this feast with a warning against possible misunderstanding.

There is remarkable difference between the feast of Passover and the Feast of Booths.

For what were the Israelites being reminded about by the feast of Passover? Of the rescue of their ancestors out of Egypt.

And what were they being reminded about by the Feast of Booths? Of the sojourn of their ancestors in the wilderness.

Those answers are correct. The latter one as well. But what do people understand in terms of that *sojourn of Israel in the wilderness*? Would we not be seriously mistaken if we said that some Bible readers understand this to refer to the entire, long wandering of forty years that Israel endured between Egypt and Canaan? Yet, this view is not correct.

Indeed, the Feast of Booths did remind the Israelites of the sojourn of their ancestors in the wilderness. But in that connection people should not be thinking of the second part of Israel's travel to Canaan, namely, from Horeb to Canaan, but of the first part of that journey, namely, from Egypt to Horeb. Once again, there is a big difference between these two.

The journey from Horeb to Canaan was severe. Not only for geographical reasons. Later, and the end, that journey was characterized by Moses as a journey through "all that great and terrifying wilderness" (Deut 1:19; 8:15). But also for pedagogical reasons. That trek was largely a punishment.

But the first portion, the trek from Egypt to Horeb, must not be viewed this way, in the first place, because during that part of her journey, Israel visited some rather pleasant rest areas. These places featured virtually tropical, fertile plants that we can still find in oases between Egypt and Horeb. Even more important is what we learn from the first three Scripture passages that

OBSERVE MY SABBATHS! (LEV 23–25)

mention the Feast of Booths. First, Exod 23:16b. This verse is part of the familiar Book of the Covenant that Moses wrote shortly after the proclamation of the Ten Words and before the making of the Horeb covenant. In other words, before—long before—Israel's departure from Horeb. The same is true of the second passage, where the observance of the Feast of Booths is commanded, namely, Exod 34:22b. This passage is part of Exod 34:10–26, a brief supplement to the Book of the Covenant, provided after the golden calf incident. The third time when the Feast of Booths is mentioned is in Lev 23:33–44—still in the book of Leviticus, a book in which we find the prescriptions for Israel's living before God and living together, prescriptions that Moses had received at Horeb, after the construction of the tabernacle, within a month's time. In other words, this was given before the departure from Horeb for the second portion of Israel's journey to Canaan.

People need to keep in mind as well that this forty-year wandering of Israel actually should never have happened. All the more so, since the institution of the Feast of Booths had definitely occurred before that wandering. Therefore it could not have envisioned the second portion of Israel's journey, namely, from Horeb to Canaan, but rather the first portion, from Egypt to Horeb. And that portion was completed in an entirely happier period. For at that point, Israel was free! Saved from the bondage of Egypt, rescued by God near the Red Sea from the terrifying claws of Egyptian despotism. Now Israel was traveling freely and safely to the promised inheritance, under the wide-open heaven of Yahweh, the God who had acted powerfully on Israel's behalf.

This is what we must recall when we read Lev 23:43: "[so] that your generations may know that I made the people of Israel dwell in booths when I brought them out of the land of Egypt: I am the Lord your God."

The Feast of Booths was not designed to remind the Israelites about something they endured—punishment—but about something God did. Not about something for which they had to be ashamed—after all, is that appropriate for a feast?—but about something for which they could be heartily grateful.

The Feast of Booths was a feast, a genuinely joyful feast. Everyone admits that. But then especially this: a freedom festival.

We need to add something else.

What good is freedom if someone is dying of hunger?

Freedom must be accompanied by life.

The instituting of the Feast of Booths—and we have already seen that this definitely happened at Horeb!—signified for Israel simultaneously a guarantee, based on the promise that Yahweh would later lead Israel into a land flowing with milk and honey.

A land in which life would be good.

Indeed, this kind of guarantee-character was already enjoyed with the institution of the feast of Passover. This had been instituted already in Egypt, but had been re-commanded at Horeb (Exod 23:15; 34:18–21; Lev 23:6–14). As a feast of harvest!

The same can be said about the feast of Pentecost. This was the second feast of harvest (Exod 23:16; 34:22; Lev 23:15–22).

But the third feast of harvest, the Feast of Booths, was the crown jewel. Easily so. We will see this when we now discuss the time, the names, and the sacrifices associated with this feast.

5.1 The time of the Feast of Booths

This feast occurred in the seventh month. It began on the fifteenth day and ended on the twenty-first day of the month.

That it occurred in the seventh month was not without reason. Seven was the symbolic number of God's Horeb covenant, and the entire journey from Egypt to Horeb had been focused on the making of that covenant now under construction (Exod 3:12; 20:2; 29:46). Therefore what Jeroboam did later was so wicked. Driven by the urge to compete with Jerusalem, he invented a feast "from his own heart" and assigned its observance to the eighth month, perhaps also on the fifteenth day of that month (1 Kgs 12:33). In other words, a counterfeit Feast of Booths.

The Feast of Booths was supposed to begin on the fifteenth day of the seventh month and end on the twenty-first day. Once again we have seven days. The beginning of the feast had to occur on the fifteenth, after 2 x 7 = 14 days of the months were past. This feast thus occupied the third seven-day period of the seventh month. That signified a strong emphasis on the covenant number of seven.

The feast was supposed to begin with a Sabbath day. On that day no servile labor was to be performed, and a holy convocation was to be held (Lev 23:34–35). But the fact that people had to cut branches from trees on that day in order to build booths (Lev 23:39–40) was not a violation of the Sabbath-character of that day any more than the fact that the priests were always supposed to bring double sacrifices on the Sabbath day (Num 28:9–10), any more than the fact that on this first day of the Feast of Booths, the priests were supposed to bring very extensive sacrifices. We will return to this below, and we will see that after the conclusion of the festival week, from the fifteenth to the twenty-first of the seventh month, yet another feast day was supposed to be observed, on the twenty-second of the month, but strictly speaking this closing feast did not belong to the Feast of Booths (Lev 23:36b).

5.2 The names of the Feast of Booths

This feast was identified with three names.

1. Occasionally it was simply called "the feast." This is what we find in Lev 23:39, although there it is called "the feast of Yahweh"; and in Deut 16:14 Moses speaks to the Israelites about this as "your feast." Later it is simply called "the feast" (1 Kgs 8:2, 65; 2 Chron 5:3; 7:8; Neh 8:15; Ezek 45:25). This proves just how popular this feast was.

2. When God spoke at Horeb for the first and second times about this feast, he called it "the feast of ingathering" (Exod 23:16; 34:22; *chag ha' asiph*). It was supposed to be the harvest feast par excellence. Israel was supposed to have gathered in especially the fruit, oil, and wine harvests. For this feast was supposed to conclude such a harvest of the entire year that it would incorporate even the harvest of grain that had been celebrated in the feasts of Passover and Pentecost. On one occasion, with a view to the Feast of Booths, Moses had said: "You shall keep the Feast of Booths seven days, when you have gathered in the produce from your threshing floor and your winepress" (Deut 16:13). This feast surpassed all the preceding feasts, to the extent that grain was needed for the essential maintenance of life, but fruit, oil, and wine testified to a degree of luxury and abundance. How powerfully God was guaranteeing that he would honor his promise faithfully, and would lead Israel into the promised land of Canaan. He provided already at Horeb a glimpse of an autumn feast, in celebration actually of the harvest of the entire year.

3. Another name that God provided at Horeb for this feast, though a bit later, was the name "Feast of Booths" (Lev 23). This name was used later by Moses as well (Deut 16:13; 31:10).

The Hebrew phrase for this was *chag hassukkoth*, or feast of *sukkoth*, the plural of *sukkah*. You could translate the phrase *chag hassukkot* as either Feast of Booths or Feast of Tents. Hebrew uses two words for tent or hut, *ohel*, referring to what we usually mean by "tent"—which is also what the tabernacle was called—and *sukkah*, referring to an enclosure for animals (Gen 33:17), or for soldiers (2 Sam 11:11), and for guards in a vineyard (Isa 1:8; Job 27:18). This term was also used for Jonah's little hut (Jonah 4:5). But the enclosures that the Israelites would have used on their trek from Egypt to Canaan, which we should not imagine to have resembled the elegant tents of experienced nomads who used to live from generation to generation in the wilderness, but to have been like the primitive contraptions for protecting a person from the sun, were identified with the same word. In Leviticus 23 they are called *sukkah* (vv. 42–43), but in many other passages they are called *ohel* or the plural, *ohelim* (Lev 14:8; Num 16:26; 24:5; Deut 1:27; 11:6; Ps 106:25).

By itself, the word *sukkah* means hut, but not quite booth. In the wilderness, the Israelites would initially have made use of branches and twigs and leaves, whereas only a few would have had at their disposal a more solid kind of tent. But they were free. And having arrived at Horeb, they received a command whereby this living in primitive tents was to be recalled as a matter of great joy. Once they had arrived in the promised land, they were to replace their tents with palm branches, willow branches, and other kinds of branches. The fruit would still have been attached to the branches they were using. They were to leave that fruit attached, and live beneath these structures for a week. "You shall celebrate it as a feast to the Lord for seven days in the year. It is a statute forever throughout your generations" (Lev 23:41).

It was supposed to be a feast.

The Feast of Booths was not supposed to commemorate what happened during the second portion of the journey, from Horeb to Canaan. There had been no mention of this when the feast was instituted at Horeb. And Israel was supposed to be ashamed of that, anyway.

No, the Feast of Booths was instituted at Horeb, and looked back to the first portion of the journey, from Egypt to Horeb, and to the lovely stay at Horeb, when the tabernacle was constructed and dedicated, and when God had given Moses all those instructive laws that we now have gathered for us in Leviticus. It was a good time. Thinking of that time, people were to celebrate the most joyful feast of the entire year (Deut 16:14). A sad harvest feast was unimaginable. When living in Egypt, with its little huts honoring Osiris, the Israelites had not witnessed anything like this, and later in Canaan, they would not see anything like this in honor of Baal. Would not the service of Yahweh far surpass these examples, in terms of displaying festive joy?

We must be careful that we do not inadvertently turn the Feast of Booths into a funeral gathering. Something like what Dutch people do with their custom of commemorating the hunger winter of 1944–45 every year with a day or a week of eating nothing but sugar beets and potato peels. A feast of voluntary poverty. The Feast of Booths definitely did not have that character. Israel was never obligated to commemorate a terrible time by living in impoverished dwellings during one week each year. For that would not be a feast "to Yahweh" (Lev 23:41). During her journey from Egypt to Sinai, when it came down to it, Israel never lacked the necessities of life, even though God tested Israel to teach her to depend upon him

(Deut 8:3). On the contrary, Israel had had it good. Israel could live so freely and joyfully under God's protection, that Hosea could later characterize this period as a time of Israel's first love (Hos 2:13-14). The Feast of Booths was definitely supposed to be celebrated by the Israelite "joyfully" (Lev 23:40). And that is what they did. We learn that not only from Scripture (1 Kgs 8; Neh 8; John 7), but also from Jewish and pagan tradition.

5.3 The sacrifices at the Feast of Booths

The unique character of this feast can be discerned from the sacrifices that were to be offered throughout the seven days. It was to be a feast of great thanksgiving for all the blessings bestowed by God upon his people in the land of the fathers.

On each of the seven days, of course, the prescribed daily sacrifices had to be offered (Num 29:16). In addition, however, were the festival sacrifices. We provide the following overview of these. In order to place on one line everything that had to be sacrificed each day, we will use abbreviations: G = goat, B = bull, R = ram, S = sheep, SO = sin offering, and BO = burnt offering.

Day 1: 1 G as SO, 13 B as BO, 2 R and 14 S
Day 2: 1 G as SO, 12 B as BO, 2 R and 14 S
Day 3: 1 G as SO, 11 B as BO, 2 R and 14 S
Day 4: 1 G as SO, 10 B as BO, 2 R and 14 S
Day 5: 1 G as SO, 9 B as BO, 2 R and 14 S
Day 6: 1 G as SO, 8 B as BO, 2 R and 14 S
Day 7: 1 G as SO, 7 B as BO, 2 R and 14 S
Totals: 7 G as SO, 70 B as BO, 14 R, and 98 S
Impressive numbers!

And every total figure is a multiple of seven. The total number of bulls even equals 10 x 7. So in addition to the covenant number seven, we have the number of completeness or perfection, the number ten. This was apparently because the bull was the most exalted and perfect sacrificial animal. It is also remarkable that the number of bulls that were sacrificed during this week had to be decreased by one each day, until on the seventh day exactly seven bulls had to be sacrificed. By means of this gradual decrease, attention was being focused on the number seven, the number associated with the covenant.

So in a very abundant manner, Israel would later be reminded of the faithfulness of Yahweh, who would have fulfilled his promise and would have brought his people into the land of promise, where he would have blessed them with the fruit of Canaan's soil, the fruits of field, meadow, and orchard.

5.4 The Closing Feast after the Feast of Booths

After the Feast of Booths, there was to be a Closing Feast (*atsereth*) as well. Actually, this was no longer exclusively part of the Feast of Booths, like the end of the seventh day of Passover week still belonged to the Feast of Passover. The Closing Feast that was to follow the Feast of Booths was supposed to be commemorated on the eighth day. Not on the twenty-first day, but on the twenty-second day of the month. It served to conclude not just one feast, the Feast of Booths, but all the feasts of the "festive" half of the year. We learn this from the number of sacrifices that were to be offered. On account of the sabbatical character of this day, these sacrifices must have been rather numerous, but yet significantly fewer than those of the last or seventh day of the Feast of Booths, namely, one goat as a sin offering, one bull as a burnt offering, one ram and seven sheep. Quite a bit less. Exactly as many as were sacrificed at the beginning of the seventh month, on the First Day of the Seventh New Month.

Are we still supposed to commemorate the Feast of Booths? In the autumn? In a kind of arbor hut? As far as we know, nobody has ever answered these questions in the affirmative. Of course, we too thank God for food and drink, sustenance, clothing, and houses. But it would be the best if we did this daily and not at separate hours or "times." In order to avoid any appearance of returning to the time of the Horeb covenant.

INTERMEZZO (LEV 24)

Between Leviticus 23 and Leviticus 25 we find a chapter that seems incongruent. It consists of the following three sections:
1. The golden lamp stand (Lev 24:1–4)
2. The showbread (Lev 24:5–9)
3. The person who blasphemed God's name (Lev 24:10–23).

The question automatically arises why attention is being given to these matters. To this question Scripture offers no direct answer. So we will have to be satisfied here with an assumption, for which we will provide our reasons.

Let us consider the larger context of the entire book of Leviticus, within which these sections are placed.

In our preceding discussions, we were able to observe repeatedly that God was pleased to remind the Israelites in innumerable ways of his Horeb covenant. Exodus shows us how he did that by means of his beautiful tabernacle. Leviticus shows us first of all the divine tool of altars, sacrifices, and priests (Lev 1–10). Then we read how God also wanted to make use of numerous items in daily life, such as the distinction between clean and unclean animals, the impurity of mothers who had given birth, leprosy, etc. (Lev 11–20). This is followed by two chapters related especially to the priests (Lev 21–22), but where we discover again the very same purpose as we found in the preceding chapters, namely, to direct Israel's attention to honor the covenant. We saw that same theme continued in Leviticus 23, dealing with various feasts. So that now we dare to assert confidently that this will also be the case with Leviticus 25, dealing with the sabbatical year and the Year of Jubilee, and with Leviticus 26, dealing with the blessing and curse of the Horeb covenant.

In view of this larger context, is it not reasonable to assume that these three sections are placed here because each of them has the same theme?

Investigation of each of these three sections separately will confirm this assumption.

1. *The golden lamp stand (Lev 24:1–4)*

In our commentary on Exodus, we discussed this lampstand, which was also called candlestick.[13] This was one of Israel's most sacred places of sacrifice, in the forecourt where oil was offered to Yahweh on the altar of burnt offering, as well as with the grain offerings. But the most exalted offering of oil, consisting of oil from "crushed" olives that were not yet ripe, occurred with the golden lamp stand.

Similarly, the sacrifice was not to be brought to Yahweh by just anyone in Israel, but exclusively by the priests. It occurred in the holy place, in front of the curtain "of the testimony," namely, the curtain behind which the ark was placed that contained the certificate (in duplicate) of the Horeb covenant (Lev 24:3). Only the priests had access there. In God's covenant they had been assigned, together with Aaron, to fulfill within Israel a certain mediatorial task between Yahweh and his covenant people. Among other things, they were supposed to keep the lamps of the lampstand burning from evening until morning. This was their nightly watch (Ps 134:1, "who stand by night in the house of Yahweh").

The meaning of that priestly task would have been this.

Without a continually ascending prayer for Israel's illumination by God's Spirit, the people would not be in a position to observe God's

---

13. Vonk, *Exodus*, 236–41.

covenant. In this connection, we must not forget especially that in terms of the Law, persons and objects possessed their significance and value before God only because they had been assigned that significance and value by God beforehand. This was the case regarding the blood on the altars (Lev 17:11), and this was the case with the sound of the trumpets. But this was also the case with the priests and the high priests (Num 17; Heb 5:4).

The Horeb covenant was supposed to be honored daily. By all Israel. But with her priests in the lead, functioning as mediators of the Horeb covenant, through whose ministry Yahweh was pleased to bless his people. Particularly to enlighten his people by means of instruction, by means of "Torah."

2. The showbread (Lev 24:5–9)

In our commentary on Exodus, we also discussed these loaves of bread,[14] and earlier in this volume, and we saw that the golden table of showbread belonged to Israel's most highly exalted "altars." The task that the priests had to perform at this table of showbread as those who stood as mediators between Yahweh and his people, is being emphasized once more in this section. For in actuality, this depositing of the twelve loaves of bread on every Sabbath day, the day that was especially identified with the Horeb covenant, was the covenant duty for every Israelite, as we read in verse 8. But this duty was to be performed in the sanctuary by those who had been assigned to that duty by God himself, namely, the priests.

So we find the following. The Horeb covenant was to be honored daily. And every night. By everyone. With Israel's priests in the lead. By tending the lamps in the sanctuary throughout the night. Lamps that stood immediately in front of the ark in which the covenant had been deposited, written down on the tablets, "black on white."

And every week, the Horeb covenant was to be honored. On every Sabbath day. By all Israelites. With the priests in the lead. And then as well, directly in front of the innermost curtain, behind which the covenant lay deposited in the ark. On every Saturday—the day marking the Horeb covenant—they had to bake twelve loaves of bread, placing the new loaves in two stacks of six each—recall the twelve names placed six on each shoulder of the high priest—and atop the stacks of loaves they were to place the incense, which was a symbol of prayer.

---

14. Vonk, *Exodus*, 229–34.

OBSERVE MY SABBATHS! (LEV 23–25)

Both of these passages bound upon the heart of both people and priesthood the requirement never to forget Yahweh and his covenant that he had bestowed at Horeb.

3. *The person who blasphemed God's name (Lev 24:10–23)*

We read in Leviticus 24:10–11: "Now an Israelite woman's son, whose father was an Egyptian, went out among the people of Israel. And the Israelite woman's son and a man of Israel fought in the camp, and the Israelite woman's son blasphemed the Name, and cursed. Then they brought him to Moses. His mother's name was Shelomith, the daughter of Dibri, of the tribe of Dan."

This was the situation. An Israelite woman, Shelomith, the daughter of Dibri, of the tribe of Dan, became involved while in Egypt with an Egyptian man. Perhaps she was married to him. In any case, she had a son with this man. These verses are about this son.

Whether the Egyptian father of this son had gone along from Egypt, we don't know. He is not mentioned in the story. But the son of that Egyptian and Shelomith had gone along from Egypt. Because of his mother? Though he remained a true son of his father, a real Egyptian, a sojourner. Just as there were more sojourners who left Egypt along with Israel (see Exod 12:38; Num 11:4; and recall how often we learned about the *ger* earlier in Leviticus). God definitely wanted the Israelites to treat each other well, but also these sojourners.

This Egyptian lad—or was he perhaps already grown up?—got into a fight with one of the Israelites. Very likely it came to physical blows in front of witnesses all around, for it happened in the camp. People heard that the Egyptian tried to attack his opponent in a violent manner, namely, by invoking God's name. We read: "The Israelite woman's son blasphemed the Name, and cursed" (v. 11). From verse 16, we learn that this "Name" referred to the name of Israel's God, or Yahweh. "Blaspheming" and "cursing" came down to the same thing; the first word likely meant something like "piercing" or "puncturing" by reproaching, and the second referred to swearing.

The spectators considered those words so abominable that they overpowered the son of the Egyptian woman and brought him to Moses. Moses faced the question as to what now had to be done with such a person. His difficulty was this, that they were not dealing with an Israelite who had profaned the name of Yahweh. Earlier we saw that for members of the covenant people who had intentionally abandoned the covenant basis of Horeb, for example, by committing sexual immorality with another man's wife, or by committing intentional murder, there was no pardon.

But this person was not an Israelite. It appears that from his Israelite mother he has acquired sufficient knowledge about Israel's God to know that his name was Yahweh, but the Horeb covenant had been made not with sojourners but with Israelites. Thus, this son of an Egyptian father and the Israelite woman, Shelomith, could not be treated as an Israelite covenant breaker. For that reason, he could not be punished with death. The case was possibly even more sensitive for Moses because Yahweh had so often commended the sojourners specifically as objects of Israel's protection.

This explains why Moses laid the matter before Yahweh himself. As we know, Moses had the right to do this. He was allowed to bring his problems involving official matters directly to God in order to receive a direct answer.

And what was God's decision?

Yahweh commanded that the man had to be taken outside the camp, that the witnesses had to lay their hands on his head—as a sign that they refused to have any fellowship with the evil of which they were accusing him—and that they must then stone him to death.

Why? Here comes the *deliberation*.

In this connection, Yahweh proceeded on the basis of a principle universally recognized at that time: "Whoever curses his God shall bear his sin" (v. 15).

This word *elohim* (god) had more than one meaning. In general, it pointed to everything that people considered to be elevated above the ordinary human level. People used the word *elohim* to refer to judges and rulers (Exod 20:28), and to angels (Ps 82:1; 89:7). But it is also well-known that in Scripture, idols were also identified with this word (Exod 18:11), as well as Yahweh himself.

So then, according to a general sense of justice, it was not fitting for anyone to curse his *elohim*, or what he considered to be *elohim*.

Even less appropriate was it to injure Yahweh so severely within his own camp, as this person had done. Even though he was no Israelite, but someone who as a sojourner enjoyed many privileges among Israel.

This explains the subsequent *conclusion*.

"The sojourner as well as the native, when he blasphemes the Name, shall be put to death" (v. 16).

If we recall the Egyptian ancestry of the guilty party in our story, then we will certainly understand this verdict.

In addition, God provided more by way of response to the question put before him. Entirely in line with the tenor of that time, though not according to the style of our law books today. Eastern jurisprudence tended to be more practical, proceeding from examples with which the judges themselves could function further. Thereby it did not happen often that a judge faced a case that his law had not considered, as can often happen among us today.

Such examples and such a principle is supplied in the commentary that Yahweh coupled to his response to Moses.

When someone injured his neighbor, must he not be punished with the same injury? According to the principle of "eye for eye, tooth for tooth." All of ancient Eastern jurisprudence recognized that standard as being fair. So then, according to that universally recognized standard, should not everyone who murdered his neighbor be liable to death? And did not a sojourner, who had pierced Yahweh, the God of Israel, and had taken his life (if such had been possible), similarly deserve to be put to death?

Looking back at these three sections of Leviticus 24, we see that they are linked by a single theme. A theme that echoes throughout the entire context of this chapter.

Israelites, remember the covenant that Yahweh made with you!

Priests, pay attention to your place and task!

Pay scrupulous attention to the honor of Yahweh in your relationships with one another! But also in your relationships with sojourners who dwell among you.

Finally, when we recall how emphatically anti-pagan the laws of Leviticus are, then we might ask whether perhaps with an eye to that emphasis, this third section was placed here. Because every sojourner among Israel represented a possible doorway for paganism. But we must acknowledge that in this respect we cannot go beyond positing the question. We find no certain answer in the text.

6. THE SABBATH YEAR (LEV 25:1-7)

God's promises do not fail.

We learn that again in Leviticus 25.

This chapter talks about the Sabbath year and the Year of Jubilee, both of which subjects relate to possessing the land. For the Israelites this meant, of course, the land of Canaan. Leviticus 25 is introduced with the report that already on Mount Sinai, Yahweh gave the command to observe the Sabbath year and the Year of Jubilee. This was when the Israelites had travelled only half the distance between Egypt and Canaan. Nevertheless, the promise that God would later actually grant them the promised land was reliable. Except for the strange episode of Numbers 13-14, the episode of the ten spies, these promise would have been fulfilled in who knows how short a time. God was busy already at Horeb with the fulfillment of this promise. For there he mentioned in the Fifth Commandment, "The land that Yahweh your God is giving you" (Exod 20:12). This was repeated many times subsequently. "When you come into the land of Canaan, which I give you for a possession . . ." (Lev 14:34). "When you come into the land that I give you . . ." (Lev 23:10). And as the introduction to this very chapter: "When you come into the land that I give you . . ." (Lev 25:2). We may certainly summarize all of this to say: the land I am giving you, or the land that I am about to give you.

God's promises are as pure as silver purified seven times (Ps 12:6).

The Bible reader must be careful not to consider every passage that talks about serving six years followed by the granting of freedom as a passage dealing with the Sabbath year.

Consider, for example, Exod 21:2–6.[15] We saw how, in the Book of the Covenant, Yahweh had emphatically bound upon the heart of Israel the command especially to be merciful. Already at Horeb. Already at the beginning of the Book of the Covenant. For example, it might happen that an Israelite had become so impoverished that he had to become the servant of a fellow Israelite, then after a period of six years service, the latter was supposed to release the former Israelite. And Moses later added (see Deut 15:12–18): Don't let him go away with empty hands!

This was to occur, then, in the seventh year.

But was this the Sabbath year that is being discussed here in Leviticus 25? No. At least it need not have been. The question as to whether a year was a Sabbath year was simply calculated with a calendar, and automatically applied to everyone. But the question as to when the seventh year began, the time when an Israelite recovered his full freedom after having served for six years, was calculated of course in terms of the date when that service began, and was therefore a matter between no one other than those two Israelites, the boss and his servant.

We don't wish to argue that the numerical signature belonging to the Horeb covenant was completely absent here, especially since 7 = 6 + 1. A reminder of the number seven, belonging to the Horeb covenant, was definitely present here. "Israelites, keep my covenant, also in your relationships with each other!" But this passage is not about the actual Sabbath year.

That occurred for the first time in Exod 23:10–11, already in the Book of the Covenant. That passage states this: "For six years you shall sow your land and gather in its yield, but the seventh year you shall let it rest and lie

---

15. Regarding this, see Vonk, *Exodus*, 110–11.

OBSERVE MY SABBATHS! (LEV 23-25)

fallow, that the poor of your people may eat; and what they leave the beasts of the field may eat. You shall do likewise with your vineyard, and with your olive orchard."

It was only a short time ago that we discussed the verse following these verses. This involved the command to observe the weekly Sabbath day. "Six days you shall do your work, but on the seventh day you shall rest; that your ox and your donkey may have rest, and the son of your servant woman, and the alien, may be refreshed" (Exod 23:12). At that time we pointed out that this command appeared in such a "social" context. The command resounds repeatedly: "Treat each other well!" Now then, in the two verses dealing with the seventh year, we hear the same note sounded, where people are supposed to leave the land untilled. "So that the poor of your people may eat; and what they leave the beasts of the field may eat."

Already in the Book of the Covenant God was indeed preparing the Israelites for observing the Sabbath year. Just as he did with the Feasts of Passover, Pentecost, and Booths (Exod 23:14-17). But he saved his additional commands about both the one and the other for later. We are informed about the Sabbath year most extensively in Lev 25:1-7.

Before we discuss these verses, consider these observations.

This initial portion of Leviticus 25 deals with the Sabbath year (and the following verses about the Year of Jubilee), but we should avoid disconnecting these verses from the chapter in its entirety. Otherwise we will forget to think here of verse 21, where God promised that in the sixth year, he would bless those Israelites who were faithful, so that they would be able to live for three years from the harvest of that sixth year—namely, for the sixth, seventh, and eighth years. This is especially true so that we do not lose sight of one of the most important themes of this chapter. For later we will read that the land of Canaan that Israel would be entering would actually not become the possession of Israel, but be the possession of Yahweh. "For the land is mine" (v. 23). This entire chapter, including the portion about the Sabbath year (vv. 1-7), should be read in light of this special property right of Yahweh whereby he laid claim to Canaan.

Next, consider something relating to Canaan's climate and soil.

There were two seasons when it rained in this land. In the autumn, after the harvest was completed, the early rains fell in late autumn and winter. For us, this is around November through January. This torrential rainfall was needed for softening the soil so that farmers could plow the land and sow the seed. Then came the late rains from March until around the beginning of April. For Israel that was the month of Abib, when Passover was celebrated. Around the second half of April, the harvest would begin in the warmer valleys, and a month later, on the hillsides, until the harvest was completely finished in the second week of June.

That was the order of nature. That was also how people regularly spoke, first about sowing, then about harvesting (Lev 25:3–4, 11, 20). This was the language borne of practical experience. Although Israel was not supposed to begin her year in the autumn, but with the month of Abib (Exod 12:2; 13:4).

Israel never had a problem when it came to fertilizing the fields, just as today, the inhabitants of Syria have no problem with this. They never fertilized the grain fields as we are familiar with on our farms. In general the land was very fertile. The regular heavy rains and the severe heat constantly led to a constant supply of gravel and limestone from the rocky bluffs. In the autumn, the flocks were pastured in the fields where the harvest had left food behind. In this way, the farmland received sufficient supply of needed nutrients for the next year.

God permitted the Israelites to use this land for six years in a row. For six years they were allowed to plant their fields and prune their vineyards and gather the harvest from these. But during every seventh year they were to give the land a *shabbat shabbaton*, that is, a complete rest. For what purpose? As "a Sabbath to Yahweh" (v. 4).

We must understand this properly. It was not forbidden for an owner to set foot in his own field. He was permitted to walk through his own vineyard and eat a bunch of grapes. But he was not permitted to harvest, to gather in the fruit or grain, to store the produce. Everything that the field and vineyard produced "by itself" (v. 5) would be for everyone. The owner himself could eat it, with his employees. But so could everyone else. The day laborer and the sojourner. Even the livestock and the animals of the field. Regarding what field and vineyard produced "by itself," we are reminded that even today, in many grain fields the produce can come from the previous year.

Naturally this institution brought with it a number of consequences. In the seventh year nothing was going to be earned by such an agrarian people as Israel. As a result, in the Sabbath year one was not to go after a person to whom one had loaned seed corn; he was not to come collecting his debt in that year. That is what we read in Deuteronomy 15. In the Sabbath year the debts were to be "released." Some interpreters disagree with this translation and interpretation, others agree with it. The former point out that the Sabbath year—this term actually does not appear in Scripture— in Deut 15:9 is called *shenath hashshemittah*, the year of the release, and that the verb that is translated "release," whose noun is used here and in Exod 23:11 (the latter with respect to the field, "but the seventh year you shall let it rest and lie fallow") is not intending to say that the field is released for all time, but only temporarily released. According to this view, Deuteronomy 15 is talking only about a *resting* from debt, a moratorium, a postponement, but not a total elimination. Others by contrast are of the opinion that in Deuteronomy 15, Moses had in view not merely the stopping of payment for debt, but a *complete forgiveness* of the debt. They can appeal to Deut 15:9, where Moses warns about not permitting the base thought to enter one's heart: my brother is in need, but I will not lend him anything, because soon the Sabbath year will come and then the debt will be wiped off the books, so that I will not get back what I might otherwise lend. Perhaps our Savior was also thinking of this in connection with a passage in the so-called Sermon on the Mount. For we know how he loved to quote Deuteronomy. For example, in connection with his temptations, he answered Satan three times with quotes from Deuteronomy (Matt 4:4, 7, 10), and directed the scribe who asked him about the great commandment in the Law to a saying from Deut 6:5 (cf. Matt 22:37). Perhaps, then, our Savior had this book in view, namely, Deut 15:9, when he said: "And if you do good to those who do good to you, what benefit is that to you? For even sinners do the same. And if you lend to those from whom you expect to receive, what credit is that to you? Even sinners lend to sinners, to get back the same amount. But love your enemies, and do good, and lend, expecting nothing in return, and your reward will be great, and you will be sons of the Most High, for he is kind to the ungrateful and the evil" (Luke 6:33–35).

Finally, we wish to answer the following three questions.

1. People have been preoccupied with the question: When did the Israelites observe the Sabbath year for the first time? Holy Scripture provides no answer to this question. According to Jewish tradition, the law of the Sabbath year and the Year of Jubilee came into force for the first time fourteen years after entering Canaan, or after to conquering and dividing of the land. The twenty-first year was the first Sabbath year, and the sixty-fourth year was the first Year of Jubilee.

2. Another question: Which day of the seventh year signaled the start of the Sabbath year? To this question as well, Scripture provides no direct answer. According to some, it seems obvious that we should not think of the first month, the month of Abib, also known as the beginning of the year, but of the seventh month, the tenth day of that month, the Great Day of Atonement. Not only because the Year of Jubilee was proclaimed on that day (Lev 25:9), but especially because the new year of sowing and harvesting began in the eighth month, and only at that point could the resting of the land commence. We will return to this matter in connection with the Year of Jubilee.

3. More important is the final question, concerning God's intention with instituting the Sabbath year.

What is his intention of a social character?

Undoubtedly for a people that was busy primarily with agriculture, in addition to animal husbandry, as Israel was, the rest for the land of Canaan brought with it significant rest for the population. For everything lay untouched. Fields and gardens. There was no work going on in the vineyards. This universal cessation of labor must have included a year of rest for people and for animals. Nevertheless, people cannot argue that the Sabbath year was instituted with that specific goal in mind. That rest of people and of animals is mentioned nowhere as God's intention. Not even in Deuteronomy 15. Moses did command that in the Sabbath year nobody was to go after the payment of debts owed to him, whether that command is to be understood as a *complete forgiveness* of debt, or as a *temporary relief* from paying the debt. This command, however, was of a secondary nature, the result of the fact that Israel was an agrarian people.

We would make a similar comment in connection with Exod 23:10–11: "For six years you shall sow your land and gather in its yield, but the seventh year you shall let it rest and lie fallow, *that* the poor of your people may eat; and what they leave the beasts of the field may eat. You shall do likewise with your vineyard, and with your olive orchard." We italicized the word *that*. People could infer from this word that the Sabbath year was intended by God ("so that") as a gentle outreach to the poor (and the animals). But that goes too far. The phrase "so that" is not in the Hebrew; rather, we read simply "and . . . and . . . and." The command simply calls for giving the land rest. The commentary accompanying the command insists that what grows on the land shall be for everyone. Naturally, the poor would benefit the most from this. Such would have been an automatic consequence. Therefore, in Exodus 23 the Sabbath command is emphatically included. But the claim that the Sabbath year would have been *instituted* specifically with the intention of caring for the poor (and for animals) cannot be argued on the basis of Exod 23:11.

Was the purpose perhaps an economic one, then?

One view is that the institution of the Sabbath year was an economic measure to teach the Israelites thriftiness, and in that way to protect them in times of famine. Another view is that Moses was not yet familiar with the composting of the land, as well as that by observing the Sabbath year, when Israel would have to save all her grain for herself, she would be freed from merchandising relationships with pagan, idolatrous nations. But we read nothing about this in Scripture. Moreover, the institution of the Sabbath year did not come from Moses, but from God. The wise intentions that our good and wise God may have had for Israel's economy and Canaan's soil when he instituted the Sabbath year are probably seen in this truth: the Sabbath year for the land of Canaan, for a nation that lived as Israel lived, is an agricultural regulation that has not found an equivalent anywhere else. However, even if we paid careful attention to Canaan's climate and soil conditions, to the organic fertilizing of the fields by Israel's cattle, sheep, and goats, and to the blessing that the earth enjoyed during that year of rest, when it could be reconstituted with very desirable humus and trace minerals like barium, manganese, copper, etc.—even then we would need to acknowledge regarding the possibility of such secondary intentions that God may have had for Israel's land of inheritance, that these too are not explicitly mentioned anywhere in Scripture.

No, God's purpose with the Sabbath year was also a symbolic-didactic purpose.

By means of this institution, Yahweh wanted to instruct Israel about himself and his Horeb covenant.

We see this already in Lev 25:2, where the rest of Canaan's land is called "a *shabbat* to Yahweh." By interrupting the annually recurring cycle of sowing and harvesting, reaping and threshing, picking grapes and treading them, Israel's attention was being drastically focused on Yahweh, from whom this sit-down command had come.

But this is seen even more clearly in Deuteronomy 31.

Here, the book of Deuteronomy is coming to a close. A book that displays so thoroughly and pervasively the form of a covenant tract. We will say more about this later. In Deut 31:9–13, we read that Moses commanded that the Torah which he had written down was to be read to Israel in the Sabbath year at the Feast of Tabernacles.

It seems obvious that with this, Moses was adapting a contemporary custom. The covenant documents that were drawn up between kings and their vassals also customarily included instructions regarding their periodic public reading. Sometimes this happened only once annually, sometimes it happened thrice annually.

In order to prevent misunderstanding, we would point out that we are not for this reason describing God's purpose behind the Sabbath year as didactic, instructional, simply because Moses' Torah, given in Deuteronomy, was supposed to be read publicly in every Sabbath year at the Feast of Booths. That single reading every seven years was far too little when it came to inculcating the required knowledge. Instruction both at home and in the gatherings on the Sabbath days was needed first of all (Lev 19:3). The reading of Moses' Torah, referred to in Deuteronomy 31, was in addition, not so much for increasing knowledge as for the purpose once again of pointing officially to the foundation on which Israel had been placed by Yahweh, namely, the Horeb covenant. The official character of this public reading appears from the fact that it was assigned to priests and elders (Deut 31:8).

With this we see the Sabbath year set in the entire series of symbolic-didactic means that God wanted to use for fixing Israel's attention on his Horeb covenant, the laws regarding clean and unclean animals, emissions and washings, etc. In that series the Sabbath day received a place as well. As did the Sabbath year.

Here is one final proof that the Sabbath year was intended by God to function as a signal for directing attention to the Horeb covenant. In the chapter immediately following, we read how at Horeb God promised all the blessings of his Horeb covenant to those who kept that covenant, and threatened with his curse those who transgressed the covenant (Lev 26). The punishments that Yahweh would bring upon his people would become all the more severe as their hardness increased. Ultimately even captivity would result. And that captivity would then last as long as needed for the land to have received the "Sabbath years" that it had coming (Lev 26:34–35, 43).

Must we today also observe the institution of the Sabbath year?

Yes and no. Not by giving rest every seventh year to fields, trees, and vineyards on the basis of any divine command given to us in the Law of Horeb. This is not necessary any longer, because the Horeb covenant belongs to the past (Heb 7:18; 8:13; 10:9). Therefore we are free from observing "days, months, fixed times, and years." For us, these are all equivalent (Rom 14:5; Gal 4:10; Col 2:16).

But we are now obligated to a far greater obedience than Israel was, to *the gospel-saturated command* that the law communicated through its institution of the Sabbath year, because we have received such a better covenant. We must give that much more attention to this new covenant than Israel did to the old one. For example, drawing the attention of each other and especially of our children to that covenant. To its obligations as well, that flow forth to all people, but especially to our fellow believers. When we help the distressed and impoverished in their need by, for example, forgiving their monetary debts altogether, then this would surely be as pleasing to God as it was in ancient times. Christians must be known as gentle people (2 Cor 9:7). But woe to us if we should denigrate God's new covenant. Then we would deserve even more severe punishment than Israel (Heb 10:28–31). God our Father no longer makes use of Sabbath years in order to focus our attention on the foundation of our lives, the new covenant. But he does make use of baptism and the Lord's Super as helps alongside his Word. Because of her despising of such means, Israel was ultimately punished very severely, with captivity. What then awaits Christians who despise the covenant whose

Surety is Jesus, and who are no longer mindful of their baptism and the Lord's Supper? Or who profane these?

7. THE YEAR OF JUBILEE (LEV 25:8–55)

The cycle of Sabbaths is concluded with the Year of Jubilee. In the Law, it is only in Leviticus 25 that we receive information about this. The Year of Jubilee is merely mentioned in Lev 27:14–23, and once in the books of Numbers (36:4), but only incidentally, when it deals with an application of the prescription involving the Year of Jubilee to a particular inheritance question (viz., the daughters of Zelophehad).

So then, even though Leviticus 25 is practically the only chapter where the Torah talks about the Year of Jubilee, this discussion is so extensive that we can outline it this way:

1. The institution of the Year of Jubilee (Lev 25:8–12)
2. The application of the Year of Jubilee to various matters (Lev 25:13–34)
3. The application of the Year of Jubilee to persons (Lev 25:35–55)

7.1 The institution of the Year of Jubilee (Lev 25:8–12)

Under this heading we will consider two matters, the time and the name of the Year of Jubilee.

7.1.1 The time of the Year of Jubilee

Two question arise in this connection.

First, when did the Israelites observe this for the first time? Scripture provides no solution or answer to this puzzle.

The other question concerns which year the Year of Jubilee was to be celebrated. Some think it was in the forty-ninth year, others believe it was in the fiftieth year.

The latter view seems untenable, in our opinion. This position requires that the Year of Jubilee would fall after the seventh Sabbath year. Several objections can be registered. If this were the case, then in the sixth year God would have had to provide a grain production that would last not for three years, as verse 21 says, but for four years, for the sixth, seventh, eighth, and ninth years (that is, for the sixth year itself, plus for the two years when they were not allowed to sow and reap, which were the Sabbath year and the Year of Jubilee, plus for the year immediately following when there would have been nothing to harvest, since no sowing was permitted during the Year of Jubilee, v. 11). In addition, especially this objection can be raised, that verse 22 states most emphatically: "When you sow in the eighth year," whereas according to the second view mentioned above, that would definitely not have been permitted in the Year of Jubilee, since this view construes it always to have been an eighth year.

In view of these objections, we believe that the Year of Jubilee occurred repeatedly in the seventh Sabbath year. To be sure, the Year of Jubilee is called "the fiftieth year" in verse 10, but this could easily have been an Israelite manner of speaking, simply a way of counting that surfaced already in connection with Pentecost, a manner of speaking that God himself adopted. This method of counting and speaking is known in other languages, similar to the Dutch phrase "vandaag over een week," for example, which means something like "the day after a week," or the eighth day from now.

7.1.2 The name of the Year of Jubilee

Our phrase "Year of Jubilee" comes straight out of the Vulgate, the Latin Bible of the Middle Ages, which speaks of *annus jubileus*. The phrase comes indirectly from Scripture. The Hebrew term for the Year of Jubilee was *yovel*, or "Year of Jubilee." This term *yovel* refers first to a ram, but also to a ram's horn. The term is occasionally used in such a way that there is reason to see the term *yovel* as practically synonymous with *shophar*, trumpet (Exod 19:16; Josh 6:5–6). Just like the Day of the Seventh New Moon was named according to the sound heard on that day, so too the Year of Jubilee.

The sound according to which this year was named was also supposed to be made on the Great Day of Atonement (v. 9). The fact that the Year of Jubilee was only then to begin, as some claim, is not stated. The word *then* with which many Bible versions begin verse 9 ("Then you shall sound the loud trumpet on the tenth day of the seventh month") could lead readers to that conclusion. But the Hebrew has nothing more than *and*. Israel had received a command from God to begin her year not with the seventh month, but with the month Abib (Exod 12:2; 13:4). God's purpose would have been that the Year of Jubilee would begin like an ordinary Sabbath year. Moreover, it would always be a year that signified glorious liberation for many. But after about halfway into the seventh Sabbath year, this year was to turn into a Year of Jubilee, because on the Great Day of Atonement, held in the seventh month, (still more) freedom was supposed to be proclaimed. "Each of you shall return to his property and each of you shall return to his clan."

Was this proclamation of freedom accompanied with a trumpet blast to be performed by the priests? Scripture doesn't say. Nor does the text use the special Hebrew word for the instrument that must be blown which we find in Numbers 10, that we discussed above in connection with the Day of the Seventh New Moon, namely, the term *chatsotserah*. Because it states that the freedom must be proclaimed on the Great Day of Atonement "throughout the land to all its inhabitants," practical objections could be dealt with already at the institution of this day. Therefore we do not dare to answer this question with certainty in the affirmative. Or perhaps we should understand that the priests were supposed to be busy with public proclamations not only on one day but on many more days, so long as they did this from the Great Day of Atonement onward. We need not take a narrow and wrangling approach to the Law regarding this point. Perhaps it was even allowed for the priests to be assisted by the Levites.

7.2 The application of the Year of Jubilee to various matters (Lev 25:13–34)

The matters to which the Year of Jubilee was applicable were simply the kind that we usually describe with the term "real property." Fields, vineyards, and houses. When a person lost possession of these for one or another reason, he received it back in the Year of Jubilee. The rule was this: "In this year of jubilee each of you shall return to his property" (v. 13).

It was obvious, however, that the institution of the Year of Jubilee brought with it consequences for the Israelites in their relationships toward God and toward one another. This explains what the following fourfold sections have in view:

1. Buying and selling property (vv. 14–17)
2. Leaving fields lie fallow (vv. 18–22)
3. Buying back property (vv. 23–28)
4. Selling houses (vv. 29–34)

7.2.1 Buying and selling property (vv. 14–17)

God took into account the possibility that a person could fall so deeply into distress that he would have to sell his field. At that point people were supposed to remember that the land of Canaan was actually not for sale, because it remained Yahweh's property, who had stipulated that all real property was to be returned in the Year of Jubilee to the original owners (vv. 13, 23). So then, if someone was forced by poverty to sell his field, he would actually be selling not the field itself, but the produce of that field that would be grown between the year of sale and the next Year of Jubilee. Only the produce. In connection with the sale, or as we would say, the leasing of those harvests, all kinds of fraud was possible. In order to profit from someone's need, the tenant or lessee could set the price of the coming harvest far too low. But the tenant could abuse the sympathy of another person and set the price of the coming harvest far too high. This explains the warning against afflicting and oppressing one another in such a situation. God is speaking here like a father to his children, like a suzerain to his vassals, whom he has honored with his covenant. "You shall fear your God, for I am the Lord your God."

7.2.2 *Leaving fields lie fallow (vv. 18–22)*

The Year of Jubilee was supposed to be first of all a Sabbath year, when the usual work in the fields and in the vineyards was to cease. How easily could one's concern about daily bread lead one to forget the command of Yahweh. This accounts for the encouraging promise: If you do what I am saying, you will see how I can bless you. "I will command my blessing on you in the sixth year, so that it will produce a crop sufficient for three years" (v. 21).

7.2.3 *Buying back property (vv. 23–28)*

When God spoke to Moses at Horeb about the inheritance that the Israelites would be entering in the near future, the land of Canaan, he simultaneously indicated the conditions under which that would happen. First, the land would remain his, and the Israelites would be allowed to use it strictly out of his favor. "The land shall not be sold in perpetuity, for the land is mine. For you are *strangers and sojourners* with me" (v. 23). We have encountered both of those italicized words earlier. When Abraham purchased a grave for Sarah, he called himself a "stranger and sojourner" with respect to the Hittites at Hebron (Gen 23:4). For at that point he did yet not possess one square foot in Canaan (Acts 7:5). Later such people lived among the Israelites, people who were allowed as a favor to live on Israelite soil. "Strangers" (*ger*) would have been the more general term, and "sojourner" (*toshab*) would have been the term for those who had a fixed residence. So then, the

OBSERVE MY SABBATHS! (LEV 23–25)

Israelites in turn were allowed as a divine favor to use the land of Canaan. For Yahweh would remain the actual owner of the land (in fact, Canaan was later conquered by Yahweh, Josh 5:14–15; 6:2; Judg 2:1).

A second condition was this, that each Israelite who had lost control in one way or another over the plot of land assigned to him was supposed to receive it back. That could occur in three ways.

1. By having another person buy back what had been sold. Such a person would usually have been a close relative, and was called a "redeemer" (*go' el*; vv. 48–49). This manner of redemption was found outside Israel as well.

2. By the person who sold the property buying it back himself, when he was in a position to do so. In such cases the seller was not permitted to obstruct the purchase, even though honesty would naturally require that the purchaser would pay back the seller the money that he received for the annual harvest that would occur after the Year of Jubilee.

3. The third possibility was the Year of Jubilee. For then each one received back his original property.

7.2.4 Selling houses (vv. 29–34)

Houses were also part of the real property to which the institution of the Year of Jubilee applied (along with the right of redemption). But with distinctions.

Regarding the houses in villages, the same rule would apply as for the land on which they stood and on which they had been built in order to work the surrounding field. Village houses that had been sold were to be returned to their original owners in the Year of Jubilee. Before that time, however, people would also have to be allowed to purchase them back.

Regarding the houses in the cities, the same rule did not apply. They did not automatically revert back to the original owners in the Year of Jubilee. A person who had sold his house in the city had the right to buy it back or to redeem it, but this right lasted only for one year after the sale.

An exception was made to this rule pertaining to houses in a city, however, with respect to the houses of Levites. For the tribe of Levi would not have received an inheritance in the land of Canaan. They would be spread throughout all of Israel and dwell in forty-eight levitical cities, as we learn from Numbers 35. And the pastures surrounding those cities would be for the livestock belonging to the Levites.

The exception was twofold. First, a Levite who had to sell his house in one of those levitical cities would have the right to buy it back not only during that single year, but he would have it permanently. Second, if such a house of a Levite had been sold to a non-Levite, and thereafter it was purchased by another Levite other than the initial seller, this latter Levite would receive his house back in the Year of Jubilee. Thus, it would not be sufficient that the house was returned to just any Levite so that it remained within the tribe of Levi, but in the Year of Jubilee the house was supposed to return to the possession of that Levite who had originally sold it. Finally, it was stipulated that the pasture around the levitical cities was to remain permanently unsalable.

7.3 The application of the Year of Jubilee to persons (Lev 25:35–55)

It could also happen that an Israelite lost his independence and personal freedom on account of poverty. The last part of our chapter deals with this. It is continuing to teach about the Year of Jubilee. Anyone who lost their personal freedom on account of poverty was to receive it back in the Year of Jubilee. But it would be even better to prevent matters from going that far. For that reason, there is something of a prelude in this section. The actual subject—release in the Year of Jubilee—is then treated very practically. Intimations are given in that connection with a view to various possibilities that could arise. Finally, the matter is discussed regarding what must be done if an Israelite had to sell himself to a foreigner.

This explains the following three sections:

1. What to do when your brother becomes poor (vv. 35–38)
2. What to do when your brother has sold himself to you (vv. 39–46)
3. What to do when your brother has sold himself to a non-Israelite (vv. 47–55)

7.3.1 What to do when your brother becomes poor (vv. 35–38)

It is desirable that people properly construe the circumstances in which Israel lived while at Horeb and thereafter. We should not imagine these folk to have been primitive. Even though Israel was delivered from dishonorable forced labor and death in Egypt, she nonetheless departed from Egypt triumphantly, loaded down with loot, or perhaps better stated: with honestly deserved back wages (Exod 3:22; 12:36). Otherwise in the wilderness

OBSERVE MY SABBATHS! (LEV 23–25)

Israel would not have been able to present gifts for the construction of the tabernacle and its accessories (Exod 35:5, 22; 38:8, 21–31; Num 7). They also would not have been able to purchase the needed material for the tabernacle from passing caravans, or been able to offer the Edomites payment for drinking water needed on the journey through their land (Num 20:17; cf. 21:22). Just as there must have been a number of Israelites who learned their skills for gold- and silversmithing while in Egypt, surely some Israelites also became skilled in agriculture (Deut 11:10). Occasionally we read about Israel in the wilderness that they were living in tents like nomads, and they had probably become familiar with this from earlier times. When we discussed the Feast of Booths, we indicated that a lot of these assumptions are not credible. The journey from Egypt to Canaan could have taken a short time, and Israel could have been taken quickly from a land where it had hardly led a nomadic life, to another land where it could have continued its orderly lifestyle of agriculture, animal husbandry, and several forms of manual labor without having to adapt very much. That journey took longer than expected, on account of unexpected circumstances, but even so, in forty years the life of a people would not have changed all that dramatically, such that relationships known earlier, in terms of culture and finance, would have been completely forgotten.

So, then, the Bible reader should not be surprised to read that at Horeb, God gave prescriptions of an economic, or specifically, of a financial scope, to govern Israel's life at that time and later. On the contrary, if such prescriptions had been omitted entirely from the Book of the Covenant (Exod 20:22–23:33), this would have been a far more surprising gap. Since the institutions of Sabbath year and Year of Jubilee included social relationships, it could be expected that we would find traces of that in Leviticus 25 as well. This appears to be the case, in fact.

For proper understanding of the passage under discussion, we would like to make a few comments about what the Law that God gave at Horeb stipulates concerning (1) loans, (2) repayments, and (3) monetary interest in Israel.

1. Already in the Book of the Covenant, it seems that God was assuming that Israel would experience what every society faces, namely, that one person would loan something to another person, including money (Exod 22:25). The Hebrew word used for *lend* has the primary meaning of assisting someone in an honorable manner.

2. It was obvious that the borrower was supposed to repay the lender when he was able to do so. Not to do so was wicked (Ps 37:21). But on the other hand, the Israelite who had loaned to another was not to

act unmercifully toward the borrower, by, for example, not returning before nightfall the latter's coat that he had given as collateral for the loan (Exod 22:26–27). Nor was the lender permitted to pressure the borrower to repay the loan before the Sabbath year (Deut 15:2); in fact, perhaps he would have to forgive that loan altogether in that year (Deut 15:1, 3). Later, not every Israelite creditor acted according to the Law toward his debtor, as we may infer from 1 Sam 22:2 (regarding David gathering Israelites, among others, who were indebted to creditors), and definitely from 2 Kgs 4:1 (the creditor had come to take away both children of the prophet's widow to make them his slaves).

3. It was absolutely forbidden for one Israelite to lend to another Israelite at interest or profit (the words *neshek* and *tarbit* have similar meanings). Not that taking interest was in itself forbidden, but that could be done only with a foreigner (*nokri*), not with a fellow Israelite (Deut 23:19–20; 28:12). The prohibition was particularly strict against taking interest from a poor fellow Israelite (Exod 22:25; Lev 25:36–37). Back in the Book of the Covenant, a person who would dare do that was termed a *nosheh* (moneylender), a term referring to the occupation practiced especially by Assyrians and Canaanites. We recall just how anti-Canaanite the Book of the Covenant was.

But note well that the Torah did not simply forbid an Israelite from charging excessive interest from another Israelite, what we today might call "usury." No, the taking of any interest at all was permitted only for foreigners (the *nokri* was a nomadic merchant); taking any interest from a fellow Israelite was completely forbidden. That was to act in a pagan manner toward one's brother.

It is well-known that the medieval church, legalistic as it had become, prohibited taking interest (based on Aristotle, but afterward seeking support with an appeal to Scripture), and called this a mortal sin. That position arose because people continued to view the New Testament church as being subject to the Horeb covenant and to the Torah, without taking into account our liberation by Christ.

Here is the passage: "If your brother becomes poor and cannot maintain himself with you, you shall support him as though he were a stranger and a sojourner, and he shall live with you. Take no interest from him or profit, but fear your God, that your brother may live beside you. You shall not lend him your money at interest, nor give him your food for profit. I am the Lord your God, who brought you out of the land of Egypt to give you the land of Canaan, and to be your God" (Lev 25:35–38).

As we can see, this is directed ultimately to all Israelites, without distinction. It was as though God had already seen this occur, that a rich Israelite would treat his poor brother, who was in desperate need, mercilessly by profiting from that need, taking interest from him. It is as though God were speaking to both of them: Is that why I delivered you both from Egypt? And then especially to the rich person: If I showed you such great mercy, why have you not shown your fellow Israelite mercy that by comparison is far less? (See Matt 18:32–33.) The Suzerain cannot tolerate his vassal partners treating each other this way.

Don't let your brother perish on account of his distress. You may not do that even to a "stranger and sojourner" living among you (Lev 19:33–34).

Perhaps this was stated because no war is waged more fiercely than a war between brothers. Some Christians find it rather easy to be nice toward strangers, but very difficult to respect the Blood, which is worn by their fellow Christians on their foreheads.

As was stated, this passage serves as an introduction to the next section, dealing with the Year of Jubilee. Prevention is better than treatment, isn't it? It was glorious when someone in Israel regained his freedom in the Year of Jubilee, but it was even better when people saved him from slavery. "Keep him alive" would mean: keep him on his feet economically and socially.

7.3.2 What to do when your brother has sold himself to you (vv. 39–46)

We could say that the Scripture passage that is now before us consists of two parts: (1) about people who may not be treated as slaves (vv. 39–43), and (2) about people who may be treated as slaves (vv. 44–46). We must not forget, however, that the purpose of *both* parts is to bind upon the hearts of the Israelites the command not to hound each other with harshness in cases of servitude.

(1) People who were not allowed to be treated as slaves (vv. 39–43)

Even when an Israelite reached the position of having to sell himself to a fellow Israelite, the latter was not permitted to view and treat him as a real slave.

Already in the Book of the Covenant, at the very beginning, something similar was stated in Exod 21:2–6. There we read about an Israelite who had become a "Hebrew," that is, one who had fallen into such misfortune, for some unspecified reason, like unemployment, and rented himself voluntarily as a servant to a fellow Israelite. After six years, the latter was to let him go free; later Moses added this: don't let him depart with empty hands! (Deut 15:12–16). But if that Israelite servant had received a wife from the hand of his master, then that woman and their possible children had no right to freedom after those six years. Then it could happen that for the sake of his wife and children, such a servant would remain voluntarily with his master. Of course, the Year of Jubilee put an end to such relationships, for then everyone returned to his own property and to his clan (Lev 25:10).

In the Scripture passage we are discussing here, a specific cause of impoverishment is being assumed. For in the immediately preceding context Israel is warned against charging interest. Evidently that situation is being discussed further. It can happen that someone cannot repay the loan. Instead, he offers himself. He "sells himself." This would not be voluntary at this point, but out of necessity, on account of debt.

Two things needed to be kept in mind.

First, in the Year of Jubilee the man was to be completely freed, together with his family, and he would receive back the property of his ancestors.

Second, during his time of service, the man was not to be treated like a real slave, like a serf, but like someone who was coming to a boss to work voluntarily, and would receive his wages each day or regularly. Such a day laborer did not become a serf. The serving Israelite could never become that, for he already had an Owner. No one less than Yahweh. In the same way in which Yahweh remained the owner of Canaan's land, he would also remain the Owner of the Israelites who would one day come to live on that land. This explains the requirement that in the Year of Jubilee every Israelite was to receive back both his ancestral portion of the land inheritance in Canaan and free independence for himself and his family. Whoever neglected that, by, for example, forcing his fellow Israelite during his period of service to complete humiliating slave chores—according to Jewish tradition, this would include foot washing, removing another's shoes, carrying the master around in a sedan chair, carrying the master's accessories while walking a little behind him en route to the bath house—would be forgetting not only his own background, his own rescue from the house of bondage in Egypt, but also Yahweh's rights as Owner of Canaan and Israel, Owner of the land and of the people. Especially this latter reality supplied the deepest motive behind the warning against harshness by one Israelite toward the other.

Could we not compare this with the admonition of the apostle: "By what you eat, do not destroy the one for whom Christ died" (Rom 14:15)?

(2) People who were allowed to be treated as slaves (vv. 44–46)

Israel had slaves. Real slaves. They were allowed by God to have slaves. In this respect as well, God let his people live in their cultural context as an ancient Eastern people.

But Israelites were not permitted to have any brothers from their own people as slaves, and if an Israelite came into circumstances of servitude, it was not allowed to be genuine slave labor. That is repeated once more!

What kind of slaves, then, was Israel permitted to have?

Not slaves from among the Canaanites, for that would have been too dangerous. She was allowed to have slaves from the nations surrounding Canaan, and from descendants of the sojourners.

Moreover, in his Law to Israel, God commanded Israel not to behave unmercifully toward these real slaves. You can find something about this in the Book of the Covenant. For example, an Israelite was not permitted to kill his male or female slave with impunity (Exod 21:20), and if someone injured a slave's eye or knocked out a slave's tooth, the slave had the right to be set free (Exod 21:26–27). You will not find such mild stipulations of gentleness in any ancient Near Eastern law code. Here is one more example. Later Moses commanded that Israel was not allowed to capture and return a fleeing slave to his master (Deut 23:15–16), but in the code of Hammurabi, anyone who allowed a male or female slave to leave the city or hid such a person was threatened with death. How much more mercifully God treated the (real) slaves among Israel! The Sabbath applied also to them (Exod 20:10; 23:12), and together with their entire family they were allowed to participate in the religious feasts (Deut 12:12; 16:11). The difference was that they were not set free in the Year of Jubilee. That regulation was in force among Israel by virtue of "Horeb."

7.3.3 What to do when your brother has sold himself to a non-Israelite (vv. 47–55)

The last situation that Yahweh discusses involves the possibility that an Israelite fell so far into debt to a prosperous non-Israelite who was living among the covenant people. That would not have been a good sign. It might possibly have signaled apostasy, and its associated punishment. For Moses had later threatened Israel: If you forsake Yahweh, then the sojourner among you will become prosperous, but you will fall into poverty. "He shall lend to you, and you shall not lend to him" (Deut 28:44).

But if something like this occurred, and such an impoverished Israelite "sold" himself to his creditor, then the following regulations must be observed among Israel.

First, in such a situation, an Israelite must continue to have the right of release. Whether this release occurred with the help of a relative, or whether he obtained it himself because in one way or another he had regained some economic independence. Nevertheless, such a release had to proceed fairly. They were to calculate how long the debtor had been with his creditor; how much he could have earned during that period if he had worked as a day laborer; that amount would be subtracted from what he owed; but then the sojourner would also have the right to payment of the remaining balance.

Second, as has already been stated, the impoverished Israelite was not to be treated by the sojourner as a real slave, but as someone who was voluntarily working for a wage. The sojourner was not to dominate him with the use of force or harshness. The text says: "He shall not rule ruthlessly over him in your sight" (v. 53). The phrase, "in your sight," refers to Israel, and teaches us that God's covenant people were not to permit such a thing to happen to a member of their own. Every Israelite was to see to that.

Thirdly, if before the Year of Jubilee no release had occurred, then the Israelite who had landed in servitude on account of his debt to a non-Israelite was to be set free in the Year of Jubilee. Even though his master was a sojourner.

Why? It is repeated once more with a view both to the previous situation and to the entire chapter, because Yahweh had not redeemed Israel from Egypt in order thereafter to deliver them into another slavery. They already had an Owner, and they continued to keep him as Owner: "I am Yahweh your God."

Are we still supposed to celebrate the Year of Jubilee?

It is remarkable that later Christians immediately understood that some of the "Sabbaths" from the Law did not need to be observed any longer. No one spent a week in the autumn living in a garden hut in order to celebrate the Feast of Booths, as a kind of *Christian* Feast of Booths. Unlike what they did with the Feasts of Passover, Pentecost, and the Great Day of Atonement. Fortunately, this never happened with respect to the Sabbath year and the Year of Jubilee.

Christianity was vexed with the question whether it was permissible to charge interest. We mentioned already that people answered that in the negative, on the basis of Aristotle, the teacher of the Middle Ages. This philosopher-ethicist reasoned as follows. A cow can bring a calf into the world, whereupon the calf is the property of the cow's owner. But money is dead and cannot give birth. Therefore, charging interest for money loaned is morally impermissible. This teaching is one of so many examples of foolish argumentation on the part of pagans. But it held wide sway over people's thinking. In Shakespeare's *The Merchant of Venice*, the merchant asks: "Or is your gold and silver ewes and rams?"[16] (such that they can reproduce). Later, charging interest was sanctioned by the Christian church with an appeal to God's prohibition to the Israelites against charging interest from a fellow Israelite. But this appeal was entirely worthless. For not only was charging interest not forbidden as such by God, but exclusively the charging of interest to the brother, whether poor or rich. Moreover, God gave this prohibition "under the Law" with the goal of instructing Israel regarding the foundation that he had placed beneath Israel's society (or world), by means of his great deeds in Egypt (by leading the people out of the house of bondage) and by means of Horeb (the number seven repeatedly told Israel about the covenant God had made there). The time of the pedagogical purpose was now past, as the New Testament has taught us. The apostle Paul explicitly testifies to his readers that they are no longer "under the Law." God no longer uses such means to each us about the new covenant, of which Jesus has become the Surety.

So a Christian may confidently loan his money at interest, and take that interest for himself.

But the demand of the gospel, that echoes for us in the Law's prohibition of taking interest, remains valid for us in view especially of the commentary on that prohibition in Leviticus 25, the chapter about the Sabbath year and the Year of Jubilee. It remains valid especially with respect to our treatment of fellow believers (Gal 6:10). Today as well, we could very well be called upon to help someone without necessarily counting on interest, indeed, perhaps even without any hope of repayment. You may wish to reflect further on the beautiful manner in which Isa 61:1–3, by using figurative language borrowed unmistakably from the institution of the Year of Jubilee, proclaims the gospel to the church that was redeemed from the Babylonian captivity, and how the Lord Jesus applied Isaiah 61 to himself when he announced his appearance in the synagogue of Nazareth and to John the Baptizer (Luke 4:17–21; 7:22). The Spirit of God had anointed him to bring the gospel to the poor. He had been sent to proclaim release to the prisoners and give sight to the blind, to send the brokenhearted away in freedom, and to proclaim the acceptable year of the Lord. You will understand, of course, that this was spoken in figurative language.

---

16 Shakespeare, *Merchant of Venice*, 154.

PART 4 | THE PEOPLE OF YAHWEH

REVIEW

When we look back now over Leviticus 23–25, dealing with the Sabbaths whose observance God had required among ancient Israel, we find a garment for ourselves whose material was fashioned from the weekly Sabbath days and upon which God himself had embroidered seven special Sabbath scenes. With fine thread and sharp colors he embedded these in the garment. The background was formed by the weakly Sabbath days. All work was forbidden on those days. The Great Day of Atonement was just such a Sabbath day, even though it did not necessary occur on a Saturday (Lev 23:3, 31). But on the other days of the festival weeks that were connected to the Feast of Passover and the Feast of Booths, only "servile work" was forbidden. So there was a difference between the command of absolute rest and the prohibition of servile labor. The Feast of Passover and the Feast of Pentecost differed from each other in color, just like the green firstfruits of the barley of Passover and the golden yellow grain from which the Pentecost loaves were baked.

What has the Christian church done with this artwork?

She has messed it up royally.

She has taken her scissors and cut off from the garment of the weekly Sabbath days the embroidered threads of the seven special Sabbaths, and hidden them in the rarely opened museum box so that hardly any minister dares to preach a sermon about the Day of the Seventh New Moon or the Feast of Booths, and she has kept one thread for the Christian celebration of Good Friday, Easter, and Pentecost. Without any connection or significance drawn from the fullness of Scripture. Nevertheless, with the meager leftover of her vandalism, she has turned the rag known as the weekly Sabbath days into a Sunday frock.

But she has forgotten that the one was closely connected with the other. For in the entire Law of Horeb has been cut up in a striking manner. The division of the Torah into, for example, moral, civil, and ceremonial laws has become commonplace. Although, fortunately, not without protest. Nowhere in Scripture can you find any basis for this kind of dividing up of the Law. Scripture always presents the Law to us as an indivisible entity, in which we can certainly make distinctions but no separation. Without any rhyme or reason it was decreed that the primary laws, or the "moral" laws, reduced in practice to the Ten Commandments, remain binding for us. Although the Synod of Dort put the scissors to the Fourth Commandment by explaining it as consisting of a moral and a ceremonial element.

This is terribly dangerous, simply making a separation between a portion of the Law that remains binding and a portion that does not. Recall

OBSERVE MY SABBATHS! (LEV 23–25)

in this connection that a man of such prestige as Gomarus identified the so-called Covenant of Works with the Sinai Covenant, and recall what an epigone like Witsius defended in this regard.[17]

This was a gateway for Legalism. And an opportunity for Judaizing, for boasting once again in the flesh (Gal 6:13), for trusting in the flesh (Phil 3:3–4), just as Paul did before his conversion (Rom 7:5: "while we were living in the flesh"), as did Israel when they opposed Christ, and the Judaizing Christians who did not genuinely obey him (Israel "according to the flesh," 1 Cor 10:18) with its "regulations for the body" (Heb 9:10). The result of this separation within the Law was to render meaningless the struggle between religion-according-to-the-flesh and religion-according-to-the-Spirit, against which Paul had so urgently warned the Roman Christians (Rom 8:5–9). The kingdom of God does not consist in (quarreling about) eating and drinking (or nowadays things with the same subordinate value), but in righteousness, peace, and joy through the Holy Spirit (Rom 14:17).

Moreover, this kind of fanaticism for the Law was entirely in conflict with the Law itself, as we see from the fact that the apostle Paul could cite from the Law to his heart's content in support of the gospel that he was preaching, as we learn from Rom 3:21 and Romans 4–5. Witness the Law itself, which provides time and again a glimpse of God's accommodation. One Dutch Reformed Old Testament scholar has written about "The Flexibility of the Mosaic Law." He insists that neither legalism nor rigorism are genuine fruits of the Torah or of the Mosaic Law. Here are some examples. Passover was to be celebrated in the first month, under penalty of death. But if a person was prevented from doing so, it could also be celebrated in the second month (Num 9:1–14). This was permitted not only in cases of uncleanness, in connection with which the hindrance had arisen, but also, as God himself gently added, if someone was gone on a long trip. Later, during the time of Hezekiah, people made widespread use of this divine gentleness (2 Chron 30:2–4, 13, 15). That godly king of Judah displayed no trace of literalism. When in the episode of Leviticus 10, Aaron did not act according to the letter of the Law and had angered Moses in that regard, he had to admit his error later. Aaron dared to deviate somewhat with regard to a particular case of cultic prescription. The priest Ahimelech gave the showbread to David and his men, because there was no other bread (1 Sam 21:1–6), and the Lord Jesus appealed to that to justify his own conduct (Luke 6:3–5). Recall how flexibly Yahweh dealt with the daughters of Zelophehad with regard to their complaint. When there was no son to inherit, the daughters were allowed to receive the inheritance (Num 27).

---

17. See Vonk, *Genesis*, 132–35.

The Law of Horeb was definitely a "law of the Medes and the Persians," one that could never be appealed (see Esth 1:19; 8:18). The possibility of setting it aside once its essence had been fulfilled, was built into its structure.

But people have acted brazenly against the Law of the Sabbaths. People have mutilated them, scarred them, and gutted them.

Scarred them by recklessly ripping them from the body, the entirety of the Law. For example, no one insisted that Christians had to observe the command that a person was to wear on the four corners of his garment tassels or cords containing a dark blue thread in remembrance of God's commands (Num 15:37–41; Deut 22:12). Nor are people embarrassed before God when men wear articles of women's clothing or women wear clothing resembling men's garments, or when people wear garments made of mixed material, all contrary to Lev 19:19 and Deut 22:9. Christian farmers have never objected to sowing a field with two kinds of seed, contrary to Lev 19:19 and Deut 22:9. Nor have people sent lepers, those with a flow of blood, etc. from the church on the basis of Num 5:1–4. And people have paid so little attention to the food laws of Leviticus 11–15, that there was a time when every farm worker, no matter how God-fearing, grew his pig and slaughtered it in November for his winter supply. Yet, from the entirety of these commandments people have boldly cut out that piece of the Sabbath days.

In order then to put the scissors yet once more into that cloth. They carved it up.

The Feast of Booths and the Day of the Seventh New Month were cut off.

The Feasts of Passover and Pentecost? Well, to be sure, they were Christianized, but nonetheless also torn off. The Great Day of Atonement was separated so radically that it has been moved from the autumn to the spring, promoted to Good Friday.

This feature and that were scrapped.

All except the weekly Sabbath day. Not that one. Precisely not that one. What logic!

What an irrational, destructive impulse with regard to the one indivisible entity of the beautiful cycle of Israel's Sabbaths.

Then this sad remnant of the Sabbath Torah was Christianized as well. The weekly Sabbath day was viewed as having been moved from Saturday to Sunday. And behold, the Christian church had thereby opened her doors to all those woes of Legalism with regard to "the Christian Sabbath."

She delighted in that, also in the Netherlands. Such quarrels as we see nowadays in modern Israel turned the Sabbath rest into a source of unrest for our ancestors as well. The airplanes of El Al airlines may not fly on Shabbat in Israel today, and they must depart from a foreign terminal with enough time to land in Israel before Shabbat begins. Electricity has been introduced to remote parts of Israel, but the householder still used oil lamps on Shabbat, because he does not wish to make use of the services of other Jews who work on Shabbat in the electricity plants. Such practices are familiar to our ears. One of the many issues that has soured church life in the Netherlands was the issue of "the Christian Sabbath." A phrase, by the way, that contains an inner contradiction. For Sabbath days were signs of the Horeb covenant (Exod 31:17), and that Horeb covenant belongs now to the past (Heb 8:13).

It is unfortunate that people continue to speak of a Sabbath day for Christians, since that no longer exists. The Horeb covenant no longer exists. Nonetheless, the sabbatistic spirit succeeded in making Sunday a tortuous experience for some Christians. One well-known Dutch Reformed minister, long before automobile transportation was common, when asked why he did not use public transportation on Sunday when he went to preach a long distance away, said: "My Father approves of it, but my brothers have problems with it."

All such narrowness arose because of misunderstanding. People acted as though the Horeb covenant still existed. Of course, in a renewed, sublimated form in the new covenant, of which Jesus had become the Surety. Instead, as Heb 8:13 teaches us, it has passed away.

When in his epistle to the Romans, the apostle Paul indicated that he would be traveling to Rome in the near future, he knew full well that he would be greeted by some of his readers as an apostate, as one who had rejected what had always been viewed as holy and sacred. Including the Sabbaths!

Indeed, the apostle deeply regretted that the Galatian Christians allowed themselves to be subjected to "days and months and seasons and years" (Gal 4:10). He wrote to the Colossians as well: "Therefore let no one pass judgment on you in questions of food and drink, or with regard to a festival or a new moon or a Sabbath" (Col 2:16). Such demands never appeared in Paul's preaching of the gospel. Now that Christ had come, he viewed all days in the same way (Rom 14:5). We read nowhere that he chased people to church on Sunday with a stick made with wood from Horeb.

Some (Jewish) readers would have viewed him as rather superficial on this account, and his preaching rather liberal.

From Romans 1, it appears that the apostle was of the view that they could think of him what they wished. He would be coming to Rome, for, as he put it: "For I am not ashamed of the gospel" with respect to you. Even though it was a gospel without a Sabbath day (Rom 1:16).

Therefore it is regrettable that the custom arose of saying to the church of the new covenant every Sunday morning: "Remember the Sabbath day to keep it holy." No wonder, then, that synods and church assemblies speak incorrectly even today about Sunday as "Sabbath."

25

Conclusion and transition to Numbers (Lev 26–27)

As we bring our discussion of Leviticus to a close, we will take the last two chapters, Leviticus 26–27, together.

In so doing, we are not following a contrived approach.

These last two chapters belong together, something you can see from their final verses. Leviticus 26 closes this way: "These are the statutes and rules and laws that the Lord made between himself and the people of Israel through Moses on Mount Sinai." And the last verse of Leviticus 27 states this: "These are the commandments that the Lord commanded Moses for the people of Israel on Mount Sinai." As you can see, the similarities are many. Both are genuine closing verses, and both draw our attention to what happened on Mount Sinai between the construction of the tabernacle at Horeb and the numbering of the Israelite men who were twenty years or older, with a view to the march from Horeb.

There is no objection against taking these two chapters together, especially in terms of the *location* and the *content* of these chapters. On the contrary, we will see this clearly when we consider the following:

1. The content of Leviticus 26
2. The place of Leviticus 26
3. The place of Leviticus 27
4. The content of Leviticus 27

PART 4 | THE PEOPLE OF YAHWEH

1. THE CONTENT OF LEVITICUS 26

1.1 Introduction (Lev 26:1–2)

May we review once more, very briefly, the latest events? All of them are facts related to what Scripture calls the foundation of the (Israelite) world.[1] Facts surrounding Horeb!

First, on that very mountain of Horeb Moses was called as savior, when he was tending sheep. God promised deliverance for his oppressed people in Egypt. As guarantee he revealed his new name, Yahweh, the One Who Is Near, and he promised that the Israelites would one day worship him at this very place.

Then followed the Israelites being led out of Egypt, and being led to Horeb. Great works!

Then God established a covenant with Israel at Horeb, entirely in line with the requirements of that time. The certificate of the covenant was given in duplicate in Moses' hands, and Yahweh spoke about it with Moses in an extended conversation, explaining how he wanted his covenant people to conduct themselves toward him and toward each other. Moses initially provided an oral account of this conversation to the elders, and later put it into writing. This became the Book of the Covenant.

Next, after declaring himself king over Israel and having taken Israel as his priestly kingdom, Yahweh informed them of his desire to come dwell in the midst of his people in a tent. With that in view, the tabernacle was constructed and employed by Yahweh as his dwelling.

All of this occurred within a year's time.

From that point forward, this tabernacle was the place where Yahweh spoke to Moses from the ark of the covenant. Over the course of a month, he gave Moses further instructions regarding Israel's concourse with him and with each other. Moses would have written this down immediately. Today they constitute the contents of the book that we know as Leviticus.

We now know, from this book, in how many different ways Yahweh wanted the Israelites to recall his covenant. By means of sacrifices, altars, and the priesthood. But also by means of many and sundry regulations that affected their lives day and night.

We could summarize all of this under one command: Israelites, observe my Horeb covenant!

Nevertheless, it is striking that we find nowhere in Leviticus such formulations of God's further statutes and ordinances. That is, such a positive formulation. We do find many prohibitions and many warnings of a

---

1. See Vonk, *Exodus*, 304–11.

CONCLUSION AND TRANSITION TO NUMBERS (LEV 26–27)

negative cast that were given to the Israelites, such as never getting involved with pagans and their practices. Examples galore. Don't eat the blood! Don't consult the dead! No scurrilous sexual relationships!

How must we explain this?

In this fact, the most exalted relevant character of Leviticus is manifested. If it is true of any portion of Scripture that we must constantly seek to read it in the context of its time of origin, then this certainly goes for Leviticus. We should never read it as some timeless document. When reading Leviticus, we should always be thinking of that month of divine activity. Horeb was nothing more than a rest stop. The trek was toward Canaan. A beautiful land, to be sure, but inhabited by terribly filthy people.

It was for this reason that earlier, we compared the commandments and statutes that we now find in Leviticus with a harness with which God yoked his people to himself before he let them march off to Canaan. "For God did not want his Israel to go into battle unprotected" (as we wrote near the beginning of this commentary).

So then, the introduction found in Leviticus 26 fits completely with this sharply antithetical formulation of the single covenant requirement (vv. 1–2). These verses also bear a situational character. We must recall that after receiving the revelations of God to Moses, known to us now from Leviticus, Israel broke camp a few weeks later and began the second, or final, stage of the trek to Canaan. This evidently explains this very special, highly relevant and exceedingly concrete opening of Leviticus 26.

Let's read through it.

Verse 1: You shall not make idols for yourselves. Here, the word *elohim* is not used, a word that could be used even for Yahweh and that we translated as *images of gods* and *gods of silver/gold* when we discussed Exod 20:23.[2] Rather, the denigrating word *elilim* is used, that can be translated as *rubbish*, or *things of nothing*, as we indicated in connection with Lev 19:4. It is a deeply disapproving word. We need to hear the warning that it contains!

Or erect an image or pillar. Here is expressed what is explicitly forbidden. First, making a *pesel*, an idol of a deity. The word itself indicates that this would have been hewn from stone, but it could also have been crafted from clay, wood, or metal. The second Hebrew word used here, translated as *figured stone*, is *matstsevah*, referring to a stone that people would erect as a memorial (Gen 28:18 [Jacob], 35:20 [Rachel], 2 Sam 18:18 [Absolom]). So the word could be used also in an entirely favorable sense, for a stele or pillar. In connection with the establishing of the covenant at Horeb, Moses

---

2. Vonk, *Exodus*, 105.

erected an altar "of twelve *matstsevoth*" or twelve pillars (Exod 24:4a[3]). But here, as in Exod 23:24 and 34:13, the word is used to warn against Canaanite symbols of honor for Baal.

And you shall not set up a figured stone in your land to bow down to it, for I am the Lord your God. The meaning of the first Hebrew word, *maskit*, is not altogether certain. Various scholars translate it as "stone with emblems," or as "sculptured stone," or as "figures of stone." The idea involves stones that represent pagan figures, before which or over which or on which people bowed down. From Num 33:52 it appears that something like this was present in Canaan.

Verse 2: You shall keep my Sabbaths and reverence my sanctuary: I am the Lord. This verse will be familiar to our readers. Here once again, the Israelites receive the same command as in Lev 19:3–4. Earlier, the positive element came first—observe the teaching of your parents and your priests regarding the Sabbaths—and then the negative: no idolatry! Here the warning against pagan worship is joined directly to the summons to observe what Israel learned at the sanctuary on the Sabbaths (the weekly Sabbath days plus the seven special Sabbaths).

Indeed, the longer we look at this introduction to Leviticus 26, the more familiar it sounds. It makes us think of the Book of the Covenant, whereby in its strongly anti-Canaanite conclusion, Yahweh summons the Israelites: Later in Canaan, you may not visit any sanctuaries of the idols, but faithfully celebrate my feasts! (See Exod 23:13–33, repeated in Exod 34:10–26.)

1.2 The promise of God's blessing in connection with observing the imposed obligations (Lev 26:3–13)

We have drawn attention to the fact that the word *covenant* does not appear in the introductory verses of Leviticus 26. But we explained why that happened. The word *covenant* did not appear in the previous chapters, with one single exception, Lev 2:13, although no one would deny the explicitly covenantal character of those chapters. Simply recall the repeated warnings against intermingling with paganism.

The same feature characterizes the rest of our chapter here.

In the bulk of this chapter the word *covenant* does appear. Three times, in verses 9, 15, and 25. That is not frequent. Nevertheless, the character of that main content is thoroughly covenantal. For this portion deals with the promised covenant blessing (vv. 3–13) and the threat of the covenant curse (vv. 14–45).

---

3. Vonk, *Exodus*, 123.

CONCLUSION AND TRANSITION TO NUMBERS (LEV 26–27)

The first of those two portions is short enough for us to read in its entirety with a few explanatory comments interspersed.

Verse 3: If you walk in my statutes and observe my commandments and do them, [4] then I will give you your rains in their season [the early rains after sowing, from October through December, and the late rains in March, Deut 11:14], *and the land shall yield its increase, and the trees of the field shall yield their fruit. [5] Your threshing* [which begins near the end of April] *shall last to the time of the grape harvest* [which begins in September], *and the grape harvest shall last to the time for sowing* [October—November]. *And you shall eat your bread to the full and dwell in your land securely. [6] I will give peace in the land, and you shall lie down, and none shall make you afraid* [a metaphor borrowed from the tranquil lying down of a flock]. *And I will remove harmful beasts from the land, and the sword shall not go through your land.* [You shall not need to fear either predatory animals or enemies.] *[7] You shall chase your enemies, and they shall fall before you by the sword [8] Five of you shall chase a hundred, and a hundred of you shall chase ten thousand, and your enemies shall fall before you by the sword* [since God would bring a spirit of cowardice upon Israel's enemies, Exod 23:8]. *[9] I will turn to you* [be concerned for you, 2 Sam 9:8, Ps 25:15, 69:17] *and make you fruitful and multiply you* [especially by bestowing the blessing of children] *and will confirm my covenant with you* [I will honor it, by granting you offspring]. *[10] You* [even though you are so numerous] *shall eat old store long kept, and you shall clear out the old to make way for the new* [due to lack of storage space]. *[11] I will make my dwelling among you* [perhaps with a view to 2 Cor 6:16, this could be translated more generally: By blessing you in this way, I will show clearly the blessing that I am not willing to forsake you], *and my soul* [or *I*] *shall not abhor you* [as can happen in a marriage, Ezek 16:45]. *[12] And I will walk among you* [continue dwelling, of which promise the tabernacle was a seal] *and will be your God, and you shall be my people. [13] I am the Lord your God, who brought you out of the land of Egypt, that you should not be their* [the Egyptians'] *slaves. And I have broken the bars of your yoke and made you walk erect* [in connection with the exodus; there was an Assyrian relief clearly showing prisoners sweating under the yoke of dragging heavy burdens under the watchful eye of a supervisor; the part of the yoke resting on the shoulders was called the *shoulder bar*].

1.3 Threat of God's curse in connection with not observing the imposed duties (Lev 26:14–15)

This portion is far larger. It deals with the punishments that God would visit upon the Israelites if they broke his covenant. Naturally this has the intention of warning them. But if the one warning did not help, then the others would follow, and if Israel went from bad to worse, Yahweh would intensify his punishments. This explains why in verses 14–33, we can observe different stages in God's wrath.

In *verses 14–17*, the situation is not yet at its worst. There is covenant breaking on the part of the people. Not on the part of individuals, but on the part of the majority of the people. Nonetheless, the punishments are not yet very serious. The Israelites would have to deal with sicknesses and endure the invasions of plunderers who would rob Israel of their valuable harvest.

Verses 18–20 presuppose, however, that this would not help. At that point, Yahweh would punish Israel sevenfold, which means, even more severely. For at that point he would hold back the rains, so that the sky would be like iron and the land like copper. Not a cloud in the sky, not a drop of dew on the soil. That was very serious in a land like Palestine!

Verses 21–22 presuppose that this too did not help. At that point, Yahweh would punish even more severely. For at that point, he would release the predatory animals against the children of the Israelites, in order to rend them asunder, and upon their livestock in the meadows, and upon the travelers on the roads, so that people would just as soon not travel.

Verses 23–26 presuppose that this punishment was not enough, either. At that point, Yahweh would avenge his covenant even more severely, the covenant that the Israelites had dared to violate, and he would visit them with war. And when people would retreat from their enemies into fortresses, he would send a pestilence among the people who were piled into those fortresses. Whoever survived the plague would fall into the hands of the enemy as a prisoner of war. Great scarcity would spread everywhere. Whereas otherwise every housewife baked her own bread in her own oven, now ten would have to make do with a single oven. A tiny ration would be distributed to each person, so that he or she would not get even half the food he needed.

Verses 27–33 presuppose the last stage of hardening, and talk about the terrible punishments that Yahweh would visit upon the Israelites. Desperately hungry, people would eat their own children. Seething with anger, Yahweh would allow the sanctuaries of the Israelites to be destroyed where they came to beseech their pagan idols for help with their burning of incense sacrifices. In an ironic way he would have the pillars of their

CONCLUSION AND TRANSITION TO NUMBERS (LEV 26–27)

idol gods defiled by having the corpses of their own worshipers thrown on them (v. 30). The Hebrew word used here for *idols* is an insulting word that means *pile of dung*. Furthermore, city and country would be given over so thoroughly to destruction that the enemies who had come to live in Israel's land would be shocked. For the Israelites themselves would be led away into captivity. Moreover, that would happen in a harsh manner, with the sword of Yahweh's anger chasing them.

Verses 34–39 paint the situation where the land and the people would end up. The land would receive payment for its shortage of sabbatical years. Those were years when the land was to lie fallow. And the captives would die off in a foreign land, their nerves shot, as scared as a hare, trembling at the slightest danger.

Verses 40–45 answer the question: But would Israel be destroyed completely?

That would be impossible.

When Yahweh once turned in terrible rage against Israel at Horeb, on account of the sin with the golden calf, and he spoke with Moses about destroying them all, he wanted to spare Moses and make him into a great nation (Exod 32:10). You read later about something similar (Num 14:12). In this way, through Moses the promise given to Abraham about a numerous posterity would be fulfilled.

So already at Horeb, God had predicted that the Israelite people would never disappear entirely from the face of the earth. Not even if he would have to visit the people with the most extreme punishment of captivity. In that case, there would always remain a remnant of those converted to Yahweh, to whom Yahweh would show himself faithful to his covenant, which lay deeper than the Horeb covenant and that was immutable, namely, his covenant with Jacob, with Isaac, and with Abraham. Notice how the chronological sequence is reversed, in order to express God's unbreakable faithfulness to his covenant with Abraham.

Yahweh would remember land and people again with compassion.

But the land would have to catch up with its Sabbath years. God's threats were not empty threats. With the statutes given at Horeb, including those involving the Sabbaths, he would not permit them to be violated with impunity.

1.4 Concluding verse (Lev 26:46)

This verse reads as follows: *These are the statutes and rules and laws that the Lord made between himself and the people of Israel through Moses on Mount Sinai.*

We have already discussed several words in this verse. For example, regarding the word "between," Israel was supposed to know that God was not a filthy *ba'al*, but the holy Yahweh. People were not allowed simply to come near to him. Just like during the time of God's descent on Sinai, a protective railing had to be constructed for protecting people and animals, so too the laws of Leviticus would, as it were, form a protective fence of isolation between Yahweh and his people. And regarding the words "on Mount Sinai," we observed that they appear more often in Leviticus (7:38). They have in view especially the Sacrifice Torah, as that was given by God to Moses at Horeb. These words appear in Lev 25:1 as well, and there refer specifically to the provision of Sabbath year and Year of Jubilee. But here in Lev 26:46, they refer to everything that God had declared to Moses from the ark of the covenant that had been placed in the recently constructed tabernacle, in the second month of the second year. In view of the extensive list of "statutes, ordinances, and laws." Indeed, in view of this very extensive list, and in view of its very ordinary and extremely generalized character, this conclusion of Leviticus 26 could very well have been designed to draw the attention of the Israelites to the recently mentioned sanctions of covenant blessing and covenant curse, affixed by God, as a kind of culmination, to all the words that he had spoken at Horeb in connection with, and after, establishing his covenant there. Including his Ten Words, Moses' Book of the Covenant, and the institution of the tabernacle with everything connected to its ministry.

2. THE PLACE OF LEVITICUS 26

Anyone familiar with Leviticus 26 will not be surprised that this chapter has been located here.

First, on account of the special content of this chapter. It contains the sanctions of the Horeb covenant. Promise of blessing with an eye to observing the covenant bestowed upon Israel, and the threat of wrath with an eye to not observing the covenant. People do not position such a chapter before, but after the mention of that covenant and everything connected to it.

But that also apparently involved a custom of that time. For nowadays we have become acquainted with so much about the covenants established in the world of the ancient Near East that we may consider it commonplace that such covenants were concluded with particular sanctions that were added to the agreed-upon covenant stipulations. Yahweh obviously employed this custom in this situation, already somewhat in terms of the Ten Words of Horeb. But more explicitly in the conversation he had with Moses afterwards, from which the Book of the Covenant originated (see

CONCLUSION AND TRANSITION TO NUMBERS (LEV 26–27)

Exod 23:13–33, as well as Exod 34:10–26). And Moses did similarly later in connection with the renewing of the covenant on the plains of Moab (Deut 28). Here, then, we seem to be dealing with a permanent standard.

It is to this that Leviticus 26 owes its location at the end of the book. For it was not fitting that covenant sanctions would be at the beginning, but at the end.

With this we are not arguing that the one who assigned our chapter this location was, by this action, declaring that he had seen a formal covenant structure in the entire preceding book of Leviticus. No, but he did see a document that was thoroughly covenantal. Something that in our discussion of those preceding chapters, we have observed repeatedly. We mentioned earlier that in the laws of Leviticus people have constantly heard the sounding board of the Horeb covenant.

To that we would add the following.

The fact that a document that in its entirety does not display the shape of a formal covenant treaty, but contains little more than a collection of laws, nonetheless ends with a chapter that contained sanctions, is without parallel in the extra-biblical history of the ancient Near East. When Hammurabi concluded his famous law code, then he expressed a benediction with respect to those who would observe what he had written on his memorial stones (the law stipulations). But if that person failed to observe his words, then may Anum rob him of his royal splendor, and break his scepter. And then follow columns filled with curses, whereby Anum, Ellil, Ea and other gods and goddesses are summoned.

Two more comments.

First, concerning Leviticus 26 and the subsequent history of Israel.

Anyone reading Leviticus 26 cannot help but think repeatedly of various events told to us from Israel's subsequent history. How carelessly the warnings of Horeb were later ignored.

Indeed, in the time of Gideon, it happened that the Israelites sowed, and their seed grew, but plundering tribes from other nations came to steal their harvest (Judg 6:3–6).

Worse still was when in the days of Ahab and Elijah, God held back the rain and the dew, which were so indispensable in Palestine (1 Kgs 17:1).

Under Jeroboam the prophet from Judah, who had prophesied to the king the defilement of his altar with burned human bones but who himself was disobedient, discovered how dangerous the roads had become with predatory animals. He was killed by a lion (1 Kgs 13:24).

In the time of Elisha, the famine was so severe in besieged Samaria that women were eating their children (2 Kgs 6:25, 29; cf. Lam 2:20, 4:10).

Before this, Israelite children had been led away as slaves (2 Kgs 5:2; cf. 2 Chron 21:16–17; Joel 3:3, 6; Obad 11, 20). This was a proof that it had already become very late on the clock of God's patience. Finally, first the ten tribes and then the two tribes went away into captivity. At that point the promised land lay there, depopulated, to say nothing of being inhabited by foreigners (2 Kgs 17:24), and the land received the Sabbath years due to it (2 Chron 36:21).

But repentance and conversion among those led away did come, in view of the wonderful prayers in Daniel 9 and Nehemiah 9, and God brought a remnant back to the land of the fathers, and the size of the exilic church was made even larger than that of the church that had been led away into captivity (Isa 54). The apostle Paul pointed out that the glory of the post-exilic church consisted especially in the bringing forth of our Lord Jesus Christ and the inclusion of the Gentiles by faith in him (Gal 4:27). Thereby God's covenant promise to Abraham was fulfilled (Gen 12:1–3; Gal 3:14).

There is no clearer commentary on Leviticus 26 than the subsequent history of Israel and what we read in the New Testament about the engrafting of Gentiles into the ancient, though still preserved Israelite church proceeding from the blood of Abraham (Rom 11:17–36).

It is an altogether different question whether we who are Christians should still read a chapter like Leviticus 26 as having been written for us and as something still applicable to us.

Of course, the book of Leviticus remains for us a part of Holy Scripture of the old covenant, given to us as well as to Timothy in order to make us wise unto salvation through faith in Christ Jesus (2 Tim 3:15). How often did we not see in the Sacrifice Torah the entire suffering and death of our Savior portrayed before our eyes, together with the benefits that he has obtained for us, namely, our justification, sanctification, and glorification! For this reason alone Leviticus is an indispensable book for readers of the New Testament. It provides the foundation for the doctrine of Christ and his apostles. Even though we know very well that that Sacrifice Torah no longer mandates us to bring various sacrifices with everything connected with them. There, too, we see clearly that the Horeb covenant belongs to the past.

In still another sense, Leviticus plays an important role in the New Testament. How often don't those who speak and write in the New Testament—Christ and his apostles, as well as many of their contemporaries—allude to that book, even quote literally from it at times? We can see this from the following list:

CONCLUSION AND TRANSITION TO NUMBERS (LEV 26–27)

Lev 7:6 → Rom 10:18
    7:12 → Heb 13:15
    7:15 → Rom 10:18
    8:15 → Heb 9:21
    8:19 → Heb 9:21
    9:7 → Heb 5:3
    11:2 → Heb 9:10
    11:44 → 1 Pet 1:15
    12:22 → Luke 2:22
    13:2, 49 → Matt 8:4, Mark 1:44, Luke 5:14, 17
    14:4 → Heb 9:19
    15:8 → Heb 9:10
    16:2 → Heb 6:19
    16:6 → Heb 5:13, 7:27
    16:12 → Heb 6:19, Rev 8:5
    16:13 → Rom 3:25; Heb 9:13
    16:14 → Heb 9:13
    16:15 → Heb 7:27
    18:5 → Rom 10:5, Gal 3:12
    18:16 → Matt 14:4, Mark 6:18
    19:2 → 1 Pet 1:15
    19:15 → Luke 20:21, Jas 2:9
    19:16 → Jas 4:11
    19:18 → Matt 22:39, Mark 12:31, Jas 2:8
    19:32 → 1 Tim 5:1
    20:9 → Matt 15:4
    20:10 → John 8:4
    20:19 → 2 Cor 6:14
    20:25 → 2 Cor 6:17
    23:15 → Acts 2:1
    23:34 → John 7:12
    23:36 → John 7:37
    24:5–9 → Mark 2:26
    24:16 → Matt 26:66, Mark 11:64, John 19:7
    24:19 → Matt 5:39
    25:10 → Luke 4:19
    25:35 → Luke 6:34
    25:43 → Eph 6:9, Col 4:1
    25:53 → Col 4:1
    26:11 → 2 Cor 6:16b
    26:21 → Rev 15:6, 8; 21:9
    26:41 → Acts 7:51
    27:30 → Matt 23:23

It would be foolish indeed if Christians were to neglect such an important book of the Bible. They would suffer voluntary impoverishment. They would not be walking in the footsteps of the apostles. Note, for example, how the apostle Peter uses Lev 19:2 to direct his (former) Gentile readers to God's holiness (1 Pet 1:15), and how the apostle Paul alludes to Lev 25:43, 53, when he commands Christians who had believing slaves not to act harshly and unjustly toward them (Eph 6:9; Col 4:1). Even though we need not bother with the (symbolic) command to separate clean from unclean animals (Lev 20:25–26), with an obvious allusion to that command, the apostle commands the Corinthians not to intermingle with the wicked (2 Cor 6:17).

The entire Law, including Leviticus, teaches us how holy our heavenly Father is even now, and how we are covered only by the blood that he has supplied for us (Lev 17:11), and how we must walk now before him and before all people.

And *this* pertains especially to Leviticus 26.

Here as well it is true that now we need no longer fear God's punishment and wrath because we no longer observe his statutes and ordinances of Horeb, dealing, for example, with the Sabbaths (Feast of Passover, etc., Sabbath years, etc.; see Lev 26:34, 43). We don't want Judaizing. Nobody has the right now to subject the church of the New Covenant to such laws that belonged to the fading Horeb covenant. But from this it does not follow at all that the church of the New Covenant today no longer needs to be warned about *the wrath* of this New Covenant. The New Testament teaches us differently. For the same passage that we just quoted from Paul's letter to the Romans warns the Christians from Gentile background that God would punish them in the same way if they fell away from Christ as he punished the Jews who in Paul's time had rejected Christ (Rom 11:21). An identical warning is directed by the author of Hebrews to Christians who were of Jewish background. Indeed, he goes so far as to write that unfaithfulness toward the gospel of the High Priest who was more than Aaron would be punished even more severely than the arrogant transgression of the Law of Moses. For we read in Heb 10:29–31: "How much worse punishment, do you think, will be deserved by the one who has trampled underfoot the Son of God, and has profaned the blood of the covenant by which he was sanctified, and has outraged the Spirit of grace? For we know him who said, 'Vengeance is mine; I will repay.' And again, 'The Lord will judge his people.' It is a fearful thing to fall into the hands of the living God."

Just as the later history of Israel offers the clearest commentary on Leviticus 26, with respect to the promise and wrath of God's Horeb covenant, so too, it is to be feared, the later history of Christianity, about which such somber woes have been expressed in these recent times and which feels threatened today by apocalyptic horrors, can also offer a poignant commentary on the two passages of Romans 11 and Hebrews 10, which we have mentioned.

Anyone who does not see this will lay aside our comment. There have been those who absolutely refused to hear any talk of covenant wrath toward the church of the new dispensation.

Anyone who does see this will be like Josiah. When this king heard the words of the Law, he tore his clothes (2 Chron 34:19), because he understood how great God's wrath had to be on account of Judah's forsaking of his covenant. This was something that later was all too justified. At that point, God would know nothing of forgiveness (2 Kgs 24:4). May it not be that late for Christianity.

On the other hand, however, it is also the case that the New Testament, far from lumping together the righteous with the wicked, makes a similar distinction between those who serve God and those who do not serve him (Mal 3:18). Just as the latter are threatened with God's punishment, so God's promise is given to the former. For example, with words like these: "For 'Whoever desires to love life and see good days, let him keep his tongue from evil and his lips from speaking deceit; let him turn away from evil and do good; let him seek peace and pursue it. For the eyes of the Lord are on the righteous, and his ears are open to their prayer. But the face of the Lord is against those who do evil'" (1 Pet 3:10-12). The apostle took these words from the Old Testament, from Ps 34:12-16. He could do that because Scripture is one, even though it must be read with skills of discernment.

3. THE PLACE OF LEVITICUS 27

The book of Leviticus ends not with chapter 26, concerning the sanctions of the Horeb covenant, but with chapter 27, concerning vows and concerning buying back people, houses, etc. And that has been a thorn in the flesh, for people have felt that that should never have happened. The book of Leviticus should have ended with chapter 26, with the sanctions of the covenant. That would have been a fitting conclusion, also in view of its final verse: "These are the statutes and rules and laws that the Lord made between himself and the people of Israel through Moses on Mount Sinai" (26:46). But now comes yet one more chapter after that, dealing with an entirely new subject, namely, the paying of vows. And the final verse of that chapter also functions as a conclusion: "These are the commandments that the Lord commanded Moses for the people of Israel on Mount Sinai" (27:34). Who did this? Who would end a book this way?

For this reason people have identified Leviticus 27 generally as an appendix, and claimed that this was a supplement added to Leviticus later, in the time of the kings.

What must we say about this?

We must first determine the question.

In our opinion, the question here is not *who* wrote down and collected into one entity what Moses received in terms of divine revelation at Horeb in the month mentioned earlier, nor is the question *when* this occurred. We discussed this in the early pages of this commentary on Leviticus. We simply don't know.

Nor does the question involve the dating of the content of Leviticus 27. We know all about that. The concluding verse (27:34) tells us. "These are the commandments that the Lord commanded Moses for the people of Israel on Mount Sinai."

No, this is the question: Do we have the right to describe Leviticus 27 with such a denigrating term as an appendix, a supplement?

There are actually two questions involved here. First: Would people have a right to this description even if Leviticus 26 were the formal conclusion of a covenant document? Second: Would people have this right if they did not view Leviticus as a covenant document but simply as a book, an Israelite book, and nothing more?

Regarding the first question, let's suppose for a moment that the preceding chapter, Leviticus 26, with its covenant sanctions would constitute the conclusion of the covenant document. We don't believe this, for reasons made clear in the preceding section. But let's suppose this were the case. Would it have been so incredible if such a formal conclusion had still been added to that document?

In that case, what we find in Leviticus 27, which we are discussing now, would not have been discussed in a way that is unprecedented. Something similar happened in a time other than the time of "Horeb," regardless of its date, but in any case not many centuries later. We are thinking of the famous treaty made in 1284 [1259?] BC between pharaoh Ramses II and the Hittite suzerain Hattusili III.

It appears that after the conclusion of the prior negotiations in the Hittite capital of Hattusa, this treaty was inscribed on a silver tablet and brought by a Hittite delegation to the residence of Ramses. The scene of the arrival of the delegation at Pi-Ramses (Tanis) was reproduced in great detail in sculpture and inscriptions on the walls of the great hall of pillars at Karnak and in the Ramesseum. The text was originally composed in

CONCLUSION AND TRANSITION TO NUMBERS (LEV 26–27)

Babylonian, the diplomatic language of the time, but was translated into Egyptian and published, while Ramses in turn had the text of the Egyptian version of the treaty translated back into Babylonian, and gave it to the Hittite delegation to take back with them. In connection with the modern excavations at Hattusa (modern Boğazkale, Turkey), this Babylonian translation of the Egyptian versions was recovered, and people have found the Egyptian translation of the Hittite version written on temple walls in Egypt. So people were very familiar with this treaty.

Well, this treaty mentioned the following matters: (1) the contracting parties; (2) the former relationships between these parties; (3) the function of the treaty; (4) the validity of the treaty for posterity; (5) the non-attack clause; (6) renewal of the previous treaty; (7) a defensive alliance; (8) promise of assistance against domestic rebellion; (9) reciprocity of defensive alliance; (10) reciprocity of assistance against domestic rebellions; (11) specification of legitimate succession; (12) extradition of prominent Egyptian fugitives; (13) extradition of ordinary Egyptian emigrants; (14) extradition of prominent Hittite fugitives; (15) extradition of ordinary Hittite emigrants; (16) call upon the gods of Hatti and Egypt as witnesses to this treaty.

These were the main elements of the treaty, as we have outlined them briefly.

Next followed something that one might call the usual concluding section of treaties, namely, *curses and blessings*. This section reads in its entirety as follows:

> *Curses and Blessings for this Treaty*
> As for these words which are on this tablet of silver of the land of Hatti and of the land of Egypt—as for him who shall not keep them, a thousand gods of the land of Hatti, together with a thousand gods of the land of Egypt, shall destroy his house, his land, and his servants. But, as for him who shall keep these words which are on this tablet of silver, whether they are Hatti or whether they are Egyptians, and they are not *neglectful of* them, a thousand gods of the land of Hatti, together with a thousand gods of the land of Egypt, shall cause that he be well, shall cause that he live, together with his houses and his (land) and his servants.[4]

What would people have expected to follow next?

Surely that the document ended at this point. But this was not the case. After this section containing sanctions, we find two more sections, one

---

4. *Ancient Near Eastern Texts*, 201; italics original.

dealing with amnesty for extradited Egyptian fugitives and another dealing with amnesty for extradited Hittite fugitives. In short: each side would extradite each other's fugitives, but each side promised that those returned would not be punished, nor would their wives and children, and they would not be mutilated in terms of eyes, ears, lips, or legs.

If someone might assume that these two sections were possibly added later to the original treaty, then they need to note that these sections belonged to the document that the Hittite delegation brought to Egypt. They were original!

This provides proof of the possibility that in ancient times, certain stipulations in a document could follow the sanctions, *without disrupting the literary or formal unity of such a document*. On the basis of this proof, we think that would be somewhat premature if people treated Leviticus 26 as something like the formal conclusion of a covenant document and would then call Leviticus 27 an "appendix."

Regarding the second question, we simply do not accept that for a moment. We view Leviticus 27 lying before us not as the last part of a covenant document, but of a book; a book that forms part of the Pentateuch.

Elsewhere we noted several features concerning the arrangement of the Pentateuch.[5] At that point we indicated that the books of the Pentateuch as we now possess them never ended abruptly, but rather with a gradual transition to the following book, in such a way that the subject that is to be continued in the following book is in a certain sense introduced in the conclusion of the preceding book. According to Reformed Old Testament scholar, Benne Holwerda, such a gradual transition and coupling can be shown in connection with other books of the Old Testament.

So then, how does this transition between Leviticus and Numbers occur?

To answer that question, we must be permitted a double excursus, one dealing with the beginning of Numbers, and the other dealing with the content of the (definitive) conclusion of Leviticus, Leviticus 27, in order finally to draw our conclusion.

a. Numbers 1

We would mention the following points.

1. At the beginning of the book of Numbers, the departure of the Israelites from Horeb is described. Israel will be going up against Canaan, in order to execute punishment upon the inhabitants of this land, which was

---

5. See Vonk, *Genesis*, 24–28.

CONCLUSION AND TRANSITION TO NUMBERS (LEV 26-27)

mentioned in passages like Gen 15:16 and Lev 18:24-30. But in that holy war, the Israelites would run the grave danger of defiling themselves with the corpses of their victims. That fact meant that the people of Yahweh, who had defiled themselves in war, were not permitted to return to the holy camp at the center of which was the tabernacle (Num 31).

2. With a view to this possible military defilement through death, God had already earlier given a command to Moses, even before the tabernacle came into use, that every Israelite, when at twenty years of age he joined the ranks of able-bodied men, had to pay a half-shekel as ransom (*kofer*) for his person (*nefesh*). This money would be assigned to the sanctuary (Exod 20:12-16).

3. This instruction from Exodus 30 was implemented. The first time, of course, en masse. We are told about that in Exod 38:25-26 and Numbers 1. (We hope to look at the difference between the two Scripture passages in our commentary on Numbers.)

4. The intention of this is clear. Israel was actually far too holy to become involved with death in her later conflict against Canaan, because the tabernacle of Yahweh was in her midst. Therefore Israel could not simply march out to war, but for doing that, every person in Israel had to pay out at Horeb an amount of compensation, head for head. And for every young Israelite who would later enter the army (of potential "killers"), that payment was supposed to be made at the moment he became a warrior, i.e., when he reached the age of twenty. Israel was the people of life!

b. Leviticus 27

In previous chapters in Leviticus we also encounter the idea of compensation. In connection with the guilt offering. The Israelites were not permitted to infringe upon the rights of Yahweh and those of their neighbor. Whenever a violation of these rights did occur, forgiveness was possible for that. But not until restitution had been made. In addition to that, one-fifth of the value was calculated as additional compensation. The calculation of that value was assigned to the priest. Payment had to occur with consecrated shekels, and without arbitrariness.

The intention of Leviticus 27 is to sound a similar warning. When anyone had made a vow to Yahweh, but later regretted making that vow, it was possible to annul the vow, but to do so in an orderly, legitimate manner, along the path of compensation. Suppose that a father had promised his son to Yahweh, to render service, for example, in connection with the sanctuary, but later he wanted to be released from his vow, because he wanted his son back, then this was permitted as long as the value of this son was paid to Yahweh as compensation. Again, according to the estimate of the priest. And again, paid with consecrated shekels. We will return to this in a moment.

c. Conclusion

So we cannot deny very clear lines of correspondence between the end of Leviticus and the beginning of Numbers, specifically, between Leviticus 27 and Numbers 1. Both passages are dealing with certain rights belonging to Yahweh. Both are dealing with a particular infringement of those rights. And both deal with compensation that was to be paid for such infringement. In both cases we read very specifically about compensation for souls, or persons. We most certainly should not think here of a "contingency" (an accident in the canon). Instead of this contemporary fashionable theological locution, we should speak of appreciation for fine composition.

Hereby, therefore, Leviticus 27 demonstrates the same character as the ending of other books of the Pentateuch, and of books outside the Pentateuch. This character has to do with a transitional section leading the reader into the next book.

We are therefore of the opinion that no reason at all remains for any surprise about the location of Leviticus 27. Calling it an "appendix" or a supplement is possible only for someone who has closed his eyes to the facts we have mentioned. Whoever does not do this, but rather acknowledges these facts, will join us in paying tribute to the divine revelation given to Moses at Horeb, which we have in Leviticus 27, in view of the apparently customary and at the same time fresh and compelling manner in which this was done. He will henceforth appreciate Leviticus 27 as a properly enchanting transition to the beginning of the book of Numbers, especially Numbers 1, about which we hope to say more later.

4. THE CONTENT OF LEVITICUS 27

The story of Hannah, found in 1 Samuel 1–2, is well-known.

Hannah received no children, no matter how much she wept and prayed. At one point she made this vow: "O Lord of hosts, if you will indeed look on the affliction of your servant and remember me and not forget your servant, but will give to your servant a son, then I will give him to the Lord all the days of his life, and no razor shall touch his head." Almost one year later, Hannah gave birth to a son. She called him *Samuel*, for, she

CONCLUSION AND TRANSITION TO NUMBERS (LEV 26–27)

said, I have prayed for him from Yahweh. As soon as possible, she gave her boy permanently in service to Yahweh. She fulfilled her vow.

But if Hannah had regretted her vow, would she have been permitted to keep her boy?

Yes, indeed. But not just like that. For in Israel it was forbidden to infringe upon the rights of Yahweh. One could receive a dispensation from a vow one had made, but that was to occur according to good order and careful regulation. For no one in Israel was permitted to violate the rights of another person. Not those of other people, but also not those of Yahweh.

Leviticus 27 is dealing with such cases. With release from obligations toward Yahweh, whether on account of vows that had been made, or on account of something else.

The obligations being discussed in this chapter can be divided approximately in terms of those that could receive an exemption and those that could not. The following overview describes them.

A. Obligations for which exemption could be obtained (Lev 27:1–25)

    A.1. Obligations with respect to people (vv. 1–8)

    A.2. Obligations with respect to animals (vv. 9–13)

    A.3. Obligations with respect to houses (vv. 14–15)

    A.4. Obligations with respect to land (vv. 16–24)

B. Obligations for which exemption could not be obtained (Lev 27:26–34)

    B.1. Obligations with respect to firstborn animals (vv. 26–27)

    B.2. Obligations with respect to what is banned (vv. 28–29)

    B.3. Obligations with respect to the tithe of the produce of the land and orchards (vv. 30–31)

    B.4. Obligations with respect to the tithe of cattle and livestock (vv. 32–33)

    B.5. Signature (v. 34)

A. *Obligations for which exemption could be obtained (Lev 27:1–25)*

We have made this observation frequently. When God established a covenant with Israel at Horeb, and carefully prescribed the manner in which Israel was supposed to observe this covenant, he did not prescribe for them all kinds of novelties. On the contrary. In connection with the basis of Israelite society—that is, in connection with the foundation of the world—he made explicit use of things with which Israel was more or less familiar. Such explicit use that we may speak of a Grand Annexation.[6] We find examples of this in Leviticus 27. The phenomenon occurred in connection with other religions in the Semitic world, namely, that someone would consecrate a person in service to the sanctuary by means of a vow, a person like a son or a daughter or a slave. We find in connection with other religions that people gave tithes of produce of livestock and field to the sanctuary. Or that people made a particular vow to the deity and later wanted to be released from that vow, but had to provide compensation for that release.

God also paid attention to all such matters at Horeb, and discussed them with Moses, so that later Israel would not need to feel shortchanged and go looking to pagan advisors for counsel, but could get advice for everything from the priests of Yahweh. All of this, in order to keep Israel safely at his side and to preserve Israel until the day of Christ (Gal 3:23–25).

A.1. Obligations with respect to people (vv. 1–8)

The first verse relating to this matter reads as follows: "*If anyone makes a special vow to the Lord involving the valuation of persons . . .*" (v. 2). This formulation is very brief and concise. It omits quite a bit that, in view of its generality, seems to be assumed. If we were to diagram this sentence, and in our diagram were to include everything assumed but omitted, that diagram would look something like this: If anyone makes a special vow to the Lord, but he wants to obtain release from that vow, then that is surely permitted, but then he must purchase the fulfillment of his vow in terms of the amount that the priest will assign; then that amount shall be for the sanctuary of Yahweh; and then that valuation, if it involves *souls* (i.e., *persons*), must be according to the following amounts:

For a man	20–60 years old	50 shekels of silver
Woman	20–60	30
Young man	5–20	20
Young woman	5–20	10
Boy	1 month—5 years	5
Girl	1 month—5 years	3
Man	60+	15
Woman	60+	10

---

6. See Vonk, *Exodus*, 299–304.

CONCLUSION AND TRANSITION TO NUMBERS (LEV 26-27)

If this dispensation tax could not be applied to someone who had made a vow, because he was too poor, then the valuation of the payable exemption cost was left entirely to the priest.

From the last stipulation, it is obvious for whom this schedule of substitution tax was actually provided. For the priests. For it was conceivable that someone who had made a vow but wanted to retract it, had some money left over for this transaction. In this connection there was danger of arbitrariness on the part of the priest, especially if there was profit to be made. With a view to that, God prescribed as careful a list of required payments as possible. In the case of poverty, the danger of demanding excess payment was less likely, since one could hardly expect payment in silver from a poor person.

Several comments can be made regarding the list above.

The costs were not altogether low. For if it happened that someone's ox gored his neighbor's male or female slave, the compensation was only thirty shekels of silver, according to the Book of the Covenant (Exod 21:32). But here we read that for releasing a man from his vow, fifty shekels of silver was required. People sensed the intention very clearly. Making a vow had to be viewed as a sacred obligation (Eccl 5:3).

In this and other cases, remarkable difference was made between the male and female genders, according to the rule that we have encountered before, when we discussed the duration of the (symbolic) impurity of women who had given birth.

It is also striking that the costs of exemption for someone making a vow varied according to age. Someone who was sixty years old was apparently viewed as a person whose power had decreased significantly. Children who were younger than a month old were not assigned any cost at all (cf. Num 18:16).

We discussed the weight of a shekel earlier as well.

A.2. Obligations with respect to animals (vv. 9-13)

As we saw, not all animals were able to be sacrificed. Of the clean animals, only oxen and smaller livestock, and none of the unclean animals.

In verses 9-10 we read about the first class of animals, and in verses 11-13 about the second class.

1. If by means of a vow someone had devoted to Yahweh an animal that could be sacrificed, such as an ox, sheep, or goat, then that animal could not be exchanged. Certainly not for a (clean) animal of lesser quality, something that would have been attempted by dishonest Israelites. If someone

nevertheless attempted that, then both animals had to be given to the sanctuary, including the less valuable animal, like an animal with a physical defect (Lev 22:22-24). The first animal was to be sacrificed, and the second would have been for the priests' consumption, for it too had become holy.

2. If someone had devoted an unclean animal to Yahweh by means of a vow, like a donkey, such a vow was also supposed to be kept, but that could happen in two ways. First, the owner could bring it to the priest and sell it for the value assigned by the priest, with the money going to the priest. Or if the owner wanted to keep the animal for himself, he would pay the replacement value assigned by the priest plus one-fifth of that value as the additional premium. The first amount covered the vow and the second the compensation for retracting the vow. (For the symbolic significance of the number five, see our commentary on Exodus, 196-98.)

A.3. Obligations with respect to houses (vv. 14-15)

If the cases involved something of this nature, then the procedure was exactly the same as for vows involving devoting a donkey to Yahweh. If someone did not wish to keep his house, then it was to be sold for the value assigned by the priest. The priest was to speak the decisive word. But if the owner of the house which had been devoted to Yahweh wanted to keep the house, he could do that, but would have to pay one-fifth of its value in addition to the value of the house.

A.4. Obligations with respect to land (vv. 16-24)

One could come into possession of land either by way of inheritance or by way of purchase. Verses 16-21 involve the former, while verses 22-24 involve the latter.

1. When we discussed the Year of Jubilee, we saw that the right to own property inherited from one's ancestors was inalienable. If someone gave to Yahweh his field or a part of his field by means of a vow, this land that had been devoted to Yahweh returned to the person's ownership in the Year of Jubilee, or to the ownership of his descendants, so that by means of that vow a person was not actually giving the field but only its produce, during those years between the vow and the subsequent Year of Jubilee. With this in view, the priests were to follow these prescriptions.

First, with respect to the *standard* for calculating the value of the produce of the land that had been consecrated to Yahweh, the priest was to use a field of the same size that had been sown with a homer of seed (about ten ephahs), and for the produce of this amount he could ask fifty shekels of silver. If the field was smaller or larger, then the produce to be given to the sanctuary was valued accordingly. With the number *fifty* it was assumed that the vow had been made near the beginning of the new Year of Jubilee period, such that the owner was required to pay one shekel per year as (part of) the produce of the field. If he paid that amount, he could have a clear conscience and be assured that he had fulfilled his vow appropriately. He would have cared for the field as if it were his very own property, and he would be able with a clear conscience to enjoy the rest of its produce himself (v. 16). That was the norm.

There were, however, always *two options*. If between the date of making the vow and the next Year of Jubilee, there were fifty years, then one would pay fifty shekels of silver. We discussed that option (v. 17) already. But if there were not fifty years between these two dates, for example, perhaps only forty years, then the ten years that had lapsed since the last Year of Jubilee were subtracted, and the produce could be required from the field only for forty years. In other words, only forty shekels of silver was the required amount for such a field (v. 18).

This, then, was the regulation governing the person who had made a vow, without making use of a dispensation for release.

But what if he wanted a release from such a vow? Because he wanted free use of his field, perhaps to sell it, or for another reason?

Then once again he had *two options*, namely, acting honorably or dishonorably toward Yahweh.

If he acted *honorably*, then he would not seek to escape Yahweh's right to his field, but traveled the orderly path of release by paying the obligatory amount plus one-fifth of this amount. Then everything would be well and he could do with his field as he wished (v. 19).

But if he acted *dishonorably* and tried to escape Yahweh's claim to his field, without paying the required redemption amount, but sold his field to someone else (v. 20), then what?

At that point, this inappropriate reneging of a vow, and this offensive violation of Yahweh's right was to be punished severely. Apparently they would have allowed the buyer—who surely would not have known that the field in question had been consecrated to Yahweh by means of a vow—to retain possession of his new field until the next Year of Jubilee. But as soon at that year dawned, the field in question would not return to the former owner, as otherwise required (Lev 25:28). For that person had not honored his vow to Yahweh and therefore his inheritance fell entirely to Yahweh, i.e., to the use of the sanctuary. For at that point, such a field was viewed as lying under the "ban" and such property came into the possession of the priesthood (Num 18:14). This was a severe and embarrassing punishment (v. 21; see our comments about the "ban" below).

2. But someone could come into the possession of a field in other ways as well, not by inheritance, but by purchase. What must happen in that case, if someone had consecrated such a field to Yahweh be means of a vow (v. 22)?

In that case, the priest must take two factors into consideration. First, he must assess not the field itself, but the produce of the field, throughout the years that would occur between the date when the vow was made and the next Year of Jubilee. But second, *on the very day* when the assessment of value occurred, he was to receive the determined amount as income for the sanctuary ("as a holy gift to the Lord") (v. 23). This latter procedure was based on very understandable reasons. This field was not inherited property, but merely purchased property. The chance was always present, therefore, that the original (heir) owner might want to buy back the field or to have it sold, according to his rights described in Lev 25:25–27, whereupon not only the field, but also the produce of the field—and this latter is what is in view—would not be able to be given to Yahweh. In that circumstance the vow would not be fulfilled, and the right of Yahweh would be violated. This explains the prescription "on that day." Immediately, at the time of assessment, the amount was supposed to be paid.

A.5. *Postscript (v. 25)*

Due to the seriousness of the matter—the right of Yahweh and maintaining his sanctuary—the priest is told once more that every calculation and payment must occur in terms of the sacred shekel, i.e., that nothing illegitimate must be occur with such a standard of value. In the Law the value of the sacred shekel is repeatedly indicated as being the value of twenty gerahs (Exod 30:13; Num 3:47; 18:16), whereas according to Exod 38:26, a half-shekel was called a *beqa'*.

B. *Obligations for which exemption could not be obtained (Lev 27:26–34)*

We indicated that our classification of duties into two, according to whether or not exemption was obtainable, was an approximate classification. For in the first category, we encountered several duties from which there was no exemption, such as with animals to be sacrificed (B.1.) that had been devoted to Yahweh by means of a vow (vv. 9–10). Similarly here, we encounter

CONCLUSION AND TRANSITION TO NUMBERS (LEV 26–27)

obligations from which exemptions can be obtained (e.g., v. 31), but this is an exception. In general our classifications are accurate.

B.1. Obligations with respect to firstborn animals (vv. 26–27)

We read more than once in the Bible that someone had made a vow to God—frequently in the Psalms, for example. "I will pay my vows to the Lord in the presence of all his people" (declared by someone who had been very near unto death and had prayed that he might be kept alive, Ps 116:14). Under the pious appearance of making such a vow, Absalom hid his rebellious assembly at Hebron. He asked permission from his father David to repay a vow there, a promise he had made to Yahweh during his captivity in Geshur, when he had prayed to be allowed once more to return to Jerusalem (2 Sam 15:7–8). In such cases, people would promise Yahweh that if such a prayer would be answered, they would present a particular thank offering.

In the verses we are studying, it is stated that when a person made good on such a vow, he was not allowed to promise to Yahweh animals that were already due to him by virtue of the law of the firstborn.

This law dated back to the exodus of the Israelites from Egypt.

When at that time in history, the pharaoh had repeatedly and hardheartedly broken his promise to allow the Israelites to depart, God finally broke his resistance by killing every male firstborn among people and animals throughout the entire land of Egypt. Only the Israelites were spared this terrible assault. But for that reason, God instituted the requirement that henceforth all male firstborn of either people or animals in Israel were to be devoted to him, in remembrance of the exodus and of the change that he had shown Israel in connection with the tenth plague. This consisted of the requirement that every male firstborn clean animal would be sacrificed to God, and every male firstborn unclean animal (donkeys and camels) were to be redeemed with an animal from the livestock (a sheep or a goat) or put to death; and that every firstborn male child was to be redeemed. You can read about this is Exodus 13. Later at Horeb God emphasized this institution once again, when after the episode of the golden calf he repeated the strongly anti-Canaanite conclusion of the Book of the Covenant (Exod 34:10–26). At that time, in connection with the renewal of the covenant, he bound upon Israel's heart the three annual feasts, and when speaking about the Feast of Passover, the feast commemorating the exodus, he repeated especially this statute of the law relating to the firstborn (Exod 34:19–20).

These two verses of Leviticus 27 have this institution in view. The first relates to clean animals, the second to unclean animals. Both intend to say, of course, that people should never make a firstborn male animal the object of a vow, for the simple reason that such an animal already belonged to Yahweh.

Verse 26 prescribes what was to happen with such a firstborn male animal if it was a clean animal, such as an ox, sheep, or goat. It was and remained devoted to Yahweh and therefore had to be brought to the sanctuary to be sacrificed there. At least the blood and the fat of the animal. All the rest of this sacrificial animal was designated for the priests (Num 18:17–18).

Verse 27 prescribes what had to happen if the animal was unclean, for example, a donkey. Earlier the obligation had been assigned that one was either to kill such an animal or let it go, after which one probably continued to own the animal. In any case, this regulation would probably have been easily applicable during the wilderness travel. But when Israel would later come to live in Canaan, such an animal could probably have been used very easily for various tasks. With an eye to that situation the possibility was now being afforded of not killing such an animal—likely by breaking its neck—and also not to let it go by exchanging it for a sheep or a goat, but to let it go for money. But in that case, the priest was to be paid not only the value (assessed by the priest) but one-fifth of that value in addition. If the owner was unwilling to pay that, then the animal was to be sold for the assessed amount. The profit was for the sanctuary, of course. Perhaps the last two regulations were instituted for the purpose thereby of supplying a cash reserve for the priesthood later in Canaan.

B.2. *Obligations with respect to what is banned (vv. 28–29)*

In the immediately preceding, we read about an unclean firstborn male animal, which one could either release or sell. The latter, of course, for the benefit of the sanctuary, or practically speaking: the priesthood. In emphatic contrast with that, these verses prescribe that such a thing was never to occur with something that was banned.

The word "ban" has a thoroughly frightening meaning, but it also has a meaning that is not at all scary. We find both meanings of the word in this Scripture passage, though with more attention to the latter, and less to the former.

The phenomenon of the "ban" appeared among other peoples as well, but for Israel, God made use of this for the purpose of protecting Israel from Canaanitism (Deut 7:2; 20:17). That is to say, Israel received the prohibition against keeping alive any of the Canaanite inhabitants of the cities that Israel would conquer. The intention of this prescription was to keep the Israelites

CONCLUSION AND TRANSITION TO NUMBERS (LEV 26–27)

free from contamination through Canaanite idolatry and immorality (cf. Exod 23:24–25; 34:11–17). This ban, however, was not yet complete. We find mention of a total ban in connection with entering Jericho (Josh 6:17). In connection with that event, Israel was not only supposed to put to death the inhabitants, except for Rahab and her family, but they were also not allowed to keep for themselves any objects made of silver, gold, copper, and iron, because those were to be consecrated unto Yahweh (Josh 6:19). When Achan nevertheless did keep some of those objects, he together with his wife and offspring, along with the gold and property, were stoned and burned.

In addition to this *prescribed* military ban, the *voluntary* military ban could also be applied (Num 21:1–3). The place named Horma reminded Israel of that (from *cherem*, also written as *herem*, or ban).

In addition to the prescribed ban *outside* of Israel, there was also a prescribed ban *within* Israel. In the Book of the Covenant we read that the Israelite who sacrificed to the idols was to be punished with the ban (Exod 22:20). That person had lowered himself to the level of the Canaanites, and therefore deserved to perish in the same way as those wicked people (Gen 15:16). This would have meant that he together with his entire family would be put to death, and all his possessions would have been burned with fire. Just as happened later with Achan, and as was supposed to happen, at Moses' command, with the entire Israelite city where idolatry was tolerated (Deut 13:12–18).

This was the ban in its terrifying sense.

But we are dealing with an entirely different kind of ban in this section of Leviticus 27. At least for the most part. It could happen that someone wished to devote some part of his possessions to Yahweh permanently, such as a field. Then such a field could never again be redeemed. Nor could it be sold so that the money from it went to the sanctuary, but its produce to someone else. No, that was not possible. Just as the field mentioned in verse 21 remained the permanent possession of the priesthood. This rule would apply also for livestock that had been placed under the ban. Everything under the ban with Israel was for the priests (Num 18:14). It was "most holy" (just as the leftovers of the food offerings, Lev 2:3).

Nevertheless, as we just mentioned, in these verses we find *for the most part* the term *ban* being used in the non-terrifying sense of the word. It could happen, you see, that people came under the ban. At that point such people were put to death without the possibility of pardon, we read in verse 29. And verse 28 prepared us for that with the summary classification of "people, livestock, or field."

The intention of this, of course, was not that if someone gave a son or a slave to the sanctuary, such people first had to be put to death. That would have been in conflict with the commandment, "You shall not murder" (Exod 20:13). For in Israel, people could not put their own slave to death with impunity (Exod 21:20). The intention here was surely this, that livestock and land that was under the ban would never end up outside the possession of the sanctuary, either through redemption or through sale, and that people (who on account of idolatry within Israel or on account of military action outside of Israel had come under the ban!) would have to be put to death. Without the possibility of pardon, redeeming such people was impossible. Here too the manner of expression is somewhat abbreviated, but for Israel's priests it was clear enough.

B.3. Obligations with respect to the tithe of the produce of the land and orchards (vv. 30–31)

We should not view these two verses (and the next two, verses 32–33) as an expanded regulation covering the tithe in Israel. You find that elsewhere, for example, in Num 18:21–32, where we learn that the tithe was assigned to benefit the tribe of Levi. No, here we must keep in mind the scope of the entire chapter, which serves as a transition to what follows in the canon, namely, Numbers 1. No one may violate Yahweh's rights! Including his right to the tithe.

The tithe of the produce *of the land* should be understood to refer to one-tenth of the *grain harvest*. Later the Pharisees would make use of this regulation to require people to give a tenth part of garden produce like dill and cumin, the so-called "soup vegetables" (Matt 23:23), but our Savior mentioned that example in order to denounce their legalistic showing off.

The phrase "the fruit *of the trees*" would have referred to wine and oil, the produce of vineyards and olive trees.

We are not surprised that within Israel, God laid claim to this tithe for himself. That belonged to him, because he could claim it, so to speak, as Israel's landlord: "For the land is mine" (Lev 25:23), and he could deal sovereignly with the tithe by, for example, giving it to the tribe of Levi, or by allowing the redemption of one kind of product and forbid it for another. At least, that's what we read, namely, that God allowed the redemption of this tithe of the produce *of the land and of the trees*. That must have meant that instead of grain, wine, and oil, people were allowed to bring money to the sanctuary. But in that case, one-fifth of the value would have to be added to its amount.

CONCLUSION AND TRANSITION TO NUMBERS (LEV 26–27)

B.4. Obligations with respect to the tithe of cattle and livestock (vv. 32–33)

It is striking that the tithe of this livestock, however, could not be sold. We think automatically here of the firstborn male clean animals that were similarly unable to be exchanged (v. 26).

With this tithing of the flock, we should not think of something done annually with the entire flock, but only with the young livestock born that year. For this constituted the "produce" of the flock, just as the grain harvest constituted the produce of the land. With this tithe of young livestock, then, something occurred that happened with all the livestock every morning and evening. The animals were counted with a stick when they left the fold and when they returned. Except in connection with the annual tithe, the young animals were not led past the stick for counting, but every tenth animal was segregated, in order to be devoted to Yahweh. Whether it was a good animal made no difference. One was not to exchange the segregated animal for another. If this happened, then both animals, both the initially segregated animal and the animal used for exchange, were holy. That is how precise and exact people were to be with regard to Yahweh's rights.

B.5. Postscript (v. 34)

In the postscript supplied to Leviticus 27, we learn that these concluding commandments were given for the Israelites by Yahweh to Moses will they were still at Mount Sinai. Apparently in the same month in which all the laws contained in our present book of Leviticus were given by God to Moses (Lev 26:46). The final verse of Leviticus 27 is obviously looking back to this Scripture passage, and is undoubtedly connecting to it. Looked at in this way, Leviticus 27 could also have been placed before Leviticus 26.

We have already discussed why this did not happen. The person who wanted to put Leviticus 27 precisely here did so because he not only saw afterward, but also beforehand, that he wanted the book of Leviticus to be connected to Numbers 1 and to the book of Numbers, not only formally and chronologically, but also substantively. For both chapters, Leviticus 27 and Numbers 1, embody the sermonic message that Israel had to deal faithfully with the rights of Yahweh.

Indeed, now that we have studied the content of Leviticus 27 carefully, we can say a bit more about the striking similarity between Leviticus 27 and Numbers 1.

We have already noted that the initial implementation of the command of Exod 30:12–16 (a half-shekel of silver as redemption price for each one numbered) in Exod 28:25–28, and the definitive implementation of that command (putting the names of those mustered on lists) in Numbers 1, is reported. Also, that this money for redeeming the men who would be called up was assigned for the furnishing of the tabernacle (see Exod 38:25–28), for the sanctuary.

Well then, anyone reading through Leviticus 27 will certainly be struck by the fact that there as well, we read constantly about income for the priesthood. Once again: for the sanctuary!

So that we could simply say that for this reason as well—the close relationship with the sanctuary—these two chapters, the last chapter of Leviticus and the first chapter of Numbers, are so close in terms of content that there was every reason to place Leviticus 27 where we now find it.

People should stop talking about an "appendix," then. We believe such a characterization of this chapter is definitely undeserved.

Rather, we should speak of a beautifully crafted *transition*.

CONCLUSION

We conclude with the following comments about the significance of Leviticus 27 for us as Christians today.

Leviticus 27 deals with the faithfulness of God and the faithfulness of people.

We see this already when we notice generally that this chapter forms part of the entire Law whereby God desired to preserve his ancient people and lead them to the coming of Christ (Gal 3:23–24). The book of Leviticus is no exception to this rule. On the contrary. Whereas the books of Exodus and Numbers deal in part with matters that did not occur at Horeb, Leviticus is from beginning to end devoted to describing what God has done in connection with "the foundation of the world."

As our readers have learned, this is an expression that appears in Holy Scripture at various times. They know as well what is intended with this fixed expression in Scripture. Simply put: Israel's coming into existence as the people of the Horeb covenant. Or to put it more accurately: we should understand the expression "the foundation of the world" to refer to the establishment of the priestly kingdom of Israel under Yahweh as King and Lawgiver. This establishment occurred at Horeb.

Regrettably, the knowledge of the correct meaning of this fixed expression has been lost among Christians. In that respect, we have come to lag behind not only the Israelites but presumably also some of their pagan contemporaries. Certain Egyptians with whom Moses had dealings would have understood it correctly. We learn this from the episode of the seventh plague, the plague of hail. God had given Moses the assignment to go tell the pharaoh that it would hail so heavily "as never has been in Egypt from the day it was founded until now" (Exod 9:18). Then too what was in view was the founding of a nation, as is clear from what follows: "There was hail and fire flashing continually in the midst of the hail, very heavy hail, such as had never been in all the land of Egypt since it became a nation" (Exod 9:24). God would have assumed that the pharaoh and his court would have understood this way of speaking. So too, the author who wrote down this history for later Israelites would have assumed that such a way of speaking was clear to them.

But it did not remain clear for the church after Christ. The knowledge of the correct meaning of the fixed expression "the foundation of the world" got lost among Christians, evidently early on. What was the meaning that this expression came to have?

Apparently based on the sound of the word "world," understanding this to refer to "heaven and earth," people took the phrase "foundation of the world" to refer to the creation of heaven and earth. This was far from correct. For the word "world" as it appears in Scripture does not always mean the same thing, and does not always refer to "heaven and earth." We can see this clearly in one and the same verse, John 1:10: "He was in the world, and the world was made through him, yet the world did not know him." Sometime in the Gospel of John, the word "world" (*kosmos*) can refer to the Jews (1:10; 7:7; 8:26; 15:18–19; 17:14).

The consequence of this misunderstanding of the expression are obvious. By means of this inaccurate understanding, a fog has descended not only on certain Scripture passages where the phrase "foundation of the world" appears literally, but also on other passages where it does not appear literally but nonetheless points in the direction of that phrase.

With the first class of Scripture passages, we have in mind New Testament passages like Matt 13:35, 25:34; Luke 11:50; John 17:24; Eph 1:4; Heb 4:3, 9:26; 1 Pet 1:20; along with Rev 13:8 and 17:8. Here already we can see that a mishap like this seldom occurs in isolation. One misunderstanding leads to another. We can see this, for example, with respect to Ephesians 1:4, where the apostle writes: "... even as he chose us in him before the foundation of the world." Because people mistakenly interpreted the expression "the foundation of the world" to refer to the creation of the world, this erroneous widespread understanding came to mean that people saw God's election as mentioned in Eph 1:4 to refer to something eternal in the sense of something pre-temporal, from before the creation of the world. Although it is not at all obvious that in Scripture, the word "eternal" must always mean this. When the same apostles speaks, for example, in Rom 16:25, 2 Tim 1:9, and Titus 1:2, about God's compassion upon the Gentiles—Timothy and Titus each had a Gentile father—in or before "eternal ages," by that phrase he means the same as what could be expressed with the Hebrew word *olam*, namely, lasting a long time or from the ancient past. Similarly, in Eph 1:4 Paul simply had in view something whose beginning was before the foundation of the world, that is to say, before God established his covenant with Israel at Horeb. Already then, in the time of the patriarchs, or more accurately, during the time of Abraham, God had set in motion the plan and began to implement it by means of Abraham's greatest Descendant, Christ, the plan to save from destruction not only people like Paul, who was from Israelite ancestry, but also such people as the original readers of Eph 1:4, among whom were some of Gentile blood, including us. The apostle could have had in view passages like Gen 12:3.

This describes the first group of passages, from the New Testament. But the inaccuracy we mentioned has brought fog to lie also over various Old Testament passages. In these passages, the phrase "foundation of the world" does not occur literally, but they contain allusions to and recollections of the phrase. The most clear example is found in Ps 93:1 and 96:10, along with 1 Chr 16:30. Three passages that sound remarkably similar, which we earlier translated this way: "Yes, he has given the world firm foundations so that it would not be shaken."[7] At that time we also said that these passages are not obviously talking about the creation of heaven and earth, but about what happened at Horeb, when God equipped his people to be his priestly kingdom and placed the entire Israelite society upon the foundation of his Torah. We were not alone in holding to this interpretation of the passage we have mentioned. Those holding another view also acknowledged that they were hazarding a guess regarding the establishment of a *moral order*. We used to share this view, though we preferred to speak of a *religious-ethical order*. At Horeb, God gave Israel commandments regarding how they were to interact with him and with each other, indeed, with the sojourner as well.

On this foundation God set the Israelite world at Horeb. No one was to abandon this basis. And if this nevertheless did occur, then this signaled the end of everything. The end of God's love relationship toward the Israelites. If they rejected his Torah and Testimony (Covenant), what else was left for them?

As we know, there have been times like that.

---

7. See Vonk, *Exodus*, 308.

CONCLUSION AND TRANSITION TO NUMBERS (LEV 26-27)

Of course, we do read of a man like Boaz, who walked steadfastly in the Torah of Yahweh. He specifically saw to it that Ruth, the foreigner, found something for herself and her mother-in-law to read (compare Lev 19:22 with Ruth 2:15-16), and he faithfully observed God's commandment regarding redeeming one's family (compare Lev 25:24-25 with Ruth 3:10-15, 4:1-12). God made him a forefather of Christ.

But there were also times when the Law and the Testimony were not honored in Israel. When widows and orphans were oppressed. When innocent people were murdered. When justice faltered in the streets of Zion. When both God and the few remaining righteous ones had to complain that the foundations were being destroyed (Ps 11:3; 82:5).

In our discussion of Leviticus, we often had the opportunity to show the reader what *content* was given to the phrase "foundation of the world" by means of the book of Leviticus. So often, in fact, that we saw no chance of executing our original plan of covering Leviticus together with Numbers and Deuteronomy in a single volume. This explains why the title of this volume is not altogether correct. You must forgive us. If anyone has a problem with this, then he needs to realize not only what content the phrase "foundation of the world" must have had for Israel in view of Leviticus, but in addition, what a rich content this book continues to supply for our Christian teaching of doctrine and morality even today.

Leviticus must be one of the most familiar of Bible books rather than one of the least familiar. It is indispensable for understanding both Old and New Testaments. It teaches us what reconciliation with God consists of. It teaches us what kind of death "according to the Scriptures" our Savior had to die; the kind that required of him not a partial death (no matter how great), but a complete and entire death, becoming a dead *nefesh*. It teaches us to speak with discernment about the covenants. It teaches us, even as we heartily appreciate the good intentions, to reject all that talk about "coming to Jesus," which completely ignores the historical fact that we have belonged to Christ's church for a long time. It teaches us today what it still means to keep God's (new) covenant as Christians. It teaches us to talk Scripturally about the faithfulness of God and the faithfulness of people.

Leviticus 27 does that, too.

Behold how Yahweh focuses the attention of the Israelites by means of the Sacrifice Torah on the foundation of the Horeb covenant under their feet. How he warns them by means of various ordinances against forsaking that covenant and slipping into paganism. In that connection we think not only of God's commands with respect to foods, washings, etc., but also of his institution of the Great Day of Atonement—the leading out of the second goat, signifying an antithetical action over against the world of the demons and of paganism—and of God's warnings against the use of blood, idolatrous abominations, etc. Indeed, by means of the final laws of Leviticus, Yahweh wanted as it were to tether his people to his sanctuary (with the emphatic holiness prescriptions for the priests, observing the Sabbaths, and providing for the sanctuary and for the priesthood).

When we read Leviticus 27 as constituting part of this larger context, then we discern in this chapter the same general warning for us today, which we received in the preceding chapters as well, namely, that today we not forsake the force-field of Christ's Spirit, so that on account of our unfaithful forsaking of the New Covenant we do not receive an even more severe punishment (Heb 10:29).

But in our view, the unique and special significance of Leviticus 27 for Christians today appears to be that we be faithful people not just in general, people who honor their obligations toward God and neighbor honestly and uprightly, but very particularly toward what today may be called God's sanctuary and tabernacle, that is, the church of our Lord Jesus Christ. That sector of our Christian living is what receives the accent here. *The church!*

We have explained, with a fervor bordering on excess, that we may not place an equal sign between a building used for Christian gathering and the tabernacle, or between (certain) office-bearers in Christ's church and Israel's Levites and priests. The reader can discern adequately that we are deathly afraid of this kind of "application." We may not confuse the Horeb covenant and the New Covenant.

But a symbol denoting parallelism is entirely different than an equal sign. Similarity is altogether different from identity.

In the day of the apostles, none of the tiny Christian churches had its own building for meeting together, but they would meet at this or that home (Rom 16:5, 10, 15; 2 John 10). Nevertheless, these Christians were called, head for head and all of them together, the temple and house of God (1 Cor 3:16–17: "For God's temple is holy, and you [plural] are that temple"; 6:19–20; 2 Cor 6:16; Eph 2:21; 1 Tim 3:15). Recall how faithfully Christ watched over these little churches (Rev 2–3).

Well then, we are not being faithful toward God and his sanctuary if we feed those churches of our Lord Jesus Christ with food other than the heavenly teaching contained in Holy Scripture. If we play upon the churches a foreign yoke, and bind them to commandments other than those laid upon us by Christ and his apostles. If we do not pursue love, because we are seeking ourselves, and resemble a prating Diotrephes, who wanted to be first (3 John 9–10). But God's dwelling is built when Christians walk according to their calling (namely, according to the promise glory of the new earth), with all humility and meekness, as our Savior has shown us when he

CONCLUSION AND TRANSITION TO NUMBERS (LEV 26–27)

himself was silent before the most horrible and unfair accusations. When Christianity lived from this Spirit, it conquered the world.

Indeed, Leviticus 27 presses upon our hearts so concretely the care for God's sanctuary that we dare not even omit recalling the words of the apostle in 1 Corinthians 9: "Do you not know that those who are employed in the temple service get their food from the temple, and those who serve at the altar share in the sacrificial offerings? In the same way, the Lord commanded that those who proclaim the gospel should get their living by the gospel" (vv. 13–14).

No one will suspect that the apostle Paul wanted to see the entire Law regarding priests and Levites bluntly applied to the office-bearers of the New Testament churches. He was not stupid enough to place an equal sign there. But when he spoke about the duty of Christians to care for those burdened with preaching and teaching, he dared to cite, without fear of being misunderstood, the command given to Moses: "You shall not muzzle an ox when it treads out the grain." Twice, in fact: in 1 Cor 9:9 and 1 Tim 5:18.

From this we learn that it is God's will that like Israel of old, we today may not withhold from the sanctuary of Christ, that is, his church, our money and our goods. So that the preaching of the Word may be advanced. Leviticus says little or nothing about caring for the poor, widows, and orphans. For that, you must go to Deuteronomy. That obligation to provide in this manner for God's house exists today as well. But in view of the unique character of Leviticus 27, in the light of the apostolic warning just mentioned, we believe that this chapter lays upon us today particularly the obligation of opening our hearts and our wallets for the proclamation of the gospel. Recall the great sacrifices made by our pious ancestors in the sixteenth century! But soon enough, the increasingly distressing Judaizing spirit took over with regard to Sunday observance, together with the poor provision for preachers and especially for their widows and orphans. Rather often. And shamefully so. Did something change? For where the Spirit of Christ governs, there the wallets fall open for the House of God, which today is the church of our Lord Jesus Christ (Acts 2:45; 4:37).

Bibliography

Ancient Near Eastern Texts Relating to the Old Testament. Edited by James B. Pritchard. 3rd ed. Princeton, NJ: Princeton University Press, 1969.

Apostolic Fathers. Edited and Translated by Bart D. Ehrman. Vol. 1. Loeb Classical Library 24. Cambridge, MA: Harvard University Press, 2003.

Bähr, Karl Christian Wilhelm Felix. *Symbolik des Mosaischen Cultus.* 2 vols. Heidelberg: J.C.B. Mohr, 1837–1839.

———. *Die Lehre der Kirche vom Tode Jesu: in den ersten drei Jahrhunderten vollständig und mit besonderer Berücksichtigung der Lehre von der stellvertretenden Genugthuung.* Sulzbach: J. E. v. Seidel, 1832.

Eusebius. *Eusebius' Ecclesiastical History.* Translated by C. F. Cruse. Repr. Peabody, MA: Hendrikson, 1998.

Holwerda, B. *Oudtestamentische Voordrachten.* Vol. 3: Deuteronomium. Kampen: Copieerinrichting v. d. Berg, 1971–72.

Köhler, Ludwig. *Hebrew Man.* Translated by Peter R. Ackroyd. New York: Abingdon, 1956.

Köhler, Ludwig and Walter Baumgartner. *Lexicon in Veteris Testamenti Libros.* Grand Rapids, MI: Eerdmans, 1951.

Krull, Johannes. *Het Christelijk Kerkjaar. Eene handleiding tot de evangelieprediking op de hooge feesten, de vast terugkeerende heilige tijden en gedenkdagen, en bij andere plechtige gelegenheden in de Hervormde Kerk.* 2nd ed. Sneek: J. Campen, 1880.

Kurtz, J.H. *Sacrificial Worship of the Old Testament.* Translated by James Martin. Clark's Foreign Theological Library. Third Series 20. Edinburgh: T. & T. Clark, 1863.

———. *Der Alttestamentliche Opferkultus nach seiner gesetzlichen Begründung und Anwendung.* Bern: University of Bern, 1862.

Ridderbos, J. *Schriftuurlijke Anthropologie?* Aalten: De Graafschap, 1939.

Shakespeare, William. *The New Cambridge Shakespeare: The Merchant of Venice.* Edited by M. M. Mahood. Cambridge, England: Cambridge University Press, 2003.

Tertullian. *An Answer to the Jews.* Vol. 3 of *The Ante-Nicene Fathers: Latin Christianity: Its Founder, Tertullian.* Translations of the Writings of the Fathers Down to A.D. 325. Edited by Allan Menzies. Translated by S. Thelwell. Christian Classics Ethereal Library. Eugene, OR: Wipf and Stock, 2022.

Vonk, C. *Exodus.* Edited by Jordan J. Ballor and Stephen J. Grabill. Translated by Theodore Plantinga and Nelson D. Kloosterman. Opening the Scriptures. Grand Rapids, MI: Christian's Library, 2013.

———. *Genesis.* Edited by Jordan J. Ballor and Stephen J. Grabill. Translated by Theodore Plantinga and Nelson D. Kloosterman. Opening the Scriptures. Grand Rapids, MI: Christian's Library, 2013.

Subject Index

Aaron
    anointing of, 152
    carrying burnt offerings, 260–61
    compared to Christ in Hebrews, 150
    entering the holy of holies, 247
    first blessing of the people, 162–63
    first entrance into the holy place, 163–64
    living from the Spirit of Christ, 174
    ministry of accepted by God, 164
    not allowed any bereavement for his sons, 170, 171
    not letting Miriam be as one dead, 203
    ordained as high priest, 54
    robing of, 151
    role of leader assigned to, 168
    sacrifices for, 160–61, 249
    sacrifices for the people, 159–62
    sons of, 8, 153
    sprinkling the blood of a sin offering, 250
Aaron and his sons
    ate meat of the peace offering, 157–58
    chosen by God, 51
    "inauguration" of, 159–65
    sons suddenly killed, 104
    sprinkled with both blood and oil, 157
Aaronic priesthood, 113, 245
Abel, 16
Abib, month of, 391, 392, 417
Abihu, 9, 104, 166–75, 250
Abimelech, king of Shechem, 322

abnormal discharge
    with men, 230–32
    with women, 234–35
abomination (*tho'avath*), transvestitism as, 308
Abraham
    built an altar at Shechem, 18
    covenant established with, 186
    covenant with Abimelech, 369
    God saved, 199, 381
    God took into his covenant, 93
    God's faithfulness to descendants of, 360
    God's new and immense beginning with, 101
    God's unbreakable faithfulness to, 447
    married to his half-sister, 286, 293
Absalom, 465
abstinence, on the Day of Atonement, 402
Achan, kept objects from Jericho, 103, 467
Adam, 207, 368
Adam and Christ, Paul on, 26
Adam and Eve, 17, 101
admonitions, 243, 244
adultery, 98, 311–13, 327
Ahab, learned from Jezebel, 322
Ahimelech, gave the showbread to David, 437
altar(s)
    blood of the sin offering placed on, 154
    of burnt offering, 112–13, 252–53

SUBJECT INDEX

altar(s) (continued)
    God coming to Israel via, 111
    of incense, 113
    Moses performed atonement for, 30
    no carelessness at, 299–300
    as a promised place of meeting with God, 112
    representing God's people, 251
    rights to eat from, 120
ambition, Nadab and Abihu drunk with, 168
Amram, married his own aunt Jochebed, 291
"an aroma pleasing to Yahweh," 71
Ananias, on sins committed in ignorance, 104
ancient Near East, marriage age in, 290
angels and devils, Israel's knowledge of, 258
animal(s)
    allowing to bleed out, 277
    bodies of burned outside the camp, 120
    clean and suitable for sacrifice, 271–72
    distinction between clean and unclean, 182
    on eating clean and unclean, 188–201
    general procedure for sacrificing, 46–59
    killing for eating, 38
    no sexual relations with, 294
    not allowing two kinds to breed, 306–11
    obligations with respect to, 461–62, 465–66
    putting to death, 327, 328
    requirements for sacrificial, 42–45
    sacrifice of, 17, 171
    for the sin offering, 108–10
    without defect, 346
animal blood, 47, 142
animal sacrifice, names used for, 64
animal welfare, God not giving Israel a lesson in, 311
"anointed" cakes, prepared with oil, 75
anointing oil, 152

anti-pagan theme, in Leviticus, 335
antipathy, being on guard against, 303
apostasy, 18, 115, 342
apostles, 143, 332
apparel, worn only by the high priest, 248
"appendix," Leviticus 27 not serving as, 458
"approachers," to God on behalf of Israel, 149
Aristotle, on taking interest, 430, 434–35
ark of the covenant, 113, 114, 361, 401
"army of life," army of the Israelites as, 217
Assyria, adultery laws of, 312
Assyrian relief, showing prisoners under a yoke, 445
Astarte, 294, 308
atonement
    the actual, 249–53
    covering by daubing droplets of blood, 250
    by the death of another soul, 41
    happening soul for soul, 30–33
    means of not death, but blood for Bähr, 22
    necessity for after childbirth, 206
    not completely foreign to the peace offering, 92
    path of in the period of the shadows, 52
    proceeding from God, 29, 30
    sacrifices, 39, 123, 209
    of sins, 98
    through blood, through death, 50, 58
    usual daily ministry of, 261
atoning (*kipper*), 401
atoning work, of the high priest, 252
augury, 142
aunts, no sexual intercourse with, 293, 329
authority, showing respect to, 321
Azazel, 257
azkarah, "memorial offering," 82

Baal, 290, 308, 328, 444

SUBJECT INDEX

babies
    deaths of, 207, 325
    as not unclean, 208
baby girl, 205
Babylon, destruction of, 256
Babylonian priests, appearing
    unclothed, 334
Babylonians, good among, 285
Bähr, K. C. W. F., 21, 22, 23, 24–25, 26,
    27–28, 32, 38, 68–69
baked bread, at the feast of Pentecost,
    394
the "ban," protecting Israel from
    Canaanitism, 466–67
baptism, focusing on the new covenant,
    422
barley, ripened before wheat, 392
Baruch, apocryphal book of, 316
bathing, prescribed for priests, 260
Bel, received a virgin at Babel, 316
bestiality, 327–28
Biblias of Lyon, 143
biblical leprosy. *See* leprosy (biblical)
birds, 189, 191, 196, 307, 351
bitter herbs, eaten in the Passover meal,
    390
blessings
    of the people by Moses and Aaron,
    163
    promised through covenant, 444–45
blood
    on altars, 251
    applying to certain objects of the
    sanctuary, 51
    applying to the cleansed leper, 226
    applying to the horns of the incense
    altar, 252
    of atonement, 25
    atoning through the soul
    [*bannefesh*], 28
    of a bird, 223
    care of, 268–81
    as the chief gift laid upon Israel's
    altar, 39
    clean from the flow of, 208, 209
    commands for priests regarding,
    140–43
    effecting atonement on behalf of
    the life, 36
    ending up in the required place,
    50–51
    everything done with as the work
    of the priests, 50
    of the guilt offering, 132
    Israelites abstaining from using, 25
    of Jesus, 47
    of the lamb, 386
    life of the flesh in, 21
    making an atonement for the soul,
    22
    priests bringing to the altar, 54
    prohibition against eating, 32
    prohibition against using, 315
    replacing with blood atones, 29
    respect for, 38
    role of, 27–28
    sacrifice of as central, 19–21
    shedding of required for
    forgiveness, 17
    signifying death, 142, 272, 276
    for the sin offering, 97
    of the sin offering, 110–17
    soul of the flesh in, 33–34
    sprinkled upon people, 156–57
    used for atonement, 35, 72
bloodguilt, *zimmah* meaning
    abomination, 317
bloodguiltiness, of cursing father or
    mother, 326
bloodless sacrifice, as incidental, 19–21
bloody burnt offerings, kinds of, 349
bloody sacrifice, 21–27, 68
blue color, spoke of God, 369
blue thread, as a reminder of God, 378
Boaz, 302, 321, 473
bodies, of believers, 55
body, 75, 231
"bond of fellowship," covenant forming,
    92
Book of the Covenant
    anti-Canaanite conclusion of, 465
    covenant of Yahweh and, 324
    evangelical purpose of the entire,
    372
    in Exodus, 269

SUBJECT INDEX

Book of the Covenant (continued)
    Israel warned about Canaanizing, 259
    by Moses, 371, 442
    on a *nosheh* (moneylender) taking interest, 430
    on observing the Sabbath year, 417
    read aloud by Moses to the people, 284
    on three annual feasts, 383–84
    on treatment of slaves, 433
    warning in, 295, 297, 317
borrower, repaying the lender, 429
boundary situations, identifying, 313, 314
breach of faith, by deceiving a neighbor, 130
bread, two loaves of presented at Pentecost, 395
bread and wine, tied together inseparably, 72
"bread for Yahweh," fire offerings as, 58–59
"the bread of his God," designated for the priests, 57
the breast of a sacrificial animal, 89, 90
brother, 430, 431
brush or broom, using hyssop as, 224
"buck." *See* male goats
bull
    for guilt brought upon the entire people, 109
    as a sin offering, 97, 249–50, 263–64
    slaughtered for Aaron and his sons, 153–54
burning
    administered in special situations, 327
    of incense, 76
    occurred after the atonement, 53
    as the punishment for a priest's daughter, 343
    of a sacrificial animal, 52, 53–54
burnt offering(s)
    for Aaron and his sons, 154–55
    Aaron and his surviving sons finished, 171
    Aaron carrying, 260–61
    altar of, 111
    assurance of surrender to God, 160
    atoning character of, 74
    brought daily for all of Israel by the priests, 65, 137
    burned up on the altar, 118
    called "bread" (*lechem*) of their God, 342
    for the cleansed leper, 226
    emphasizing sanctification, 112
    fundamental position of, 63–67
    God delighted in, 55
    no one received anything to eat from, 139
    presented by Moses, 18
    priority of, 137
    regarding, 350
business, honesty in, 321

Cain, 16, 18, 101
calf, as a sin offering for Aaron, 160–61
camel, only partially cloven hooves, 190
camp, keeping holy, 181
Canaan
    child sacrifice in, 294
    climate and soil of, 417–18
    God warned Israel about, 330
    incest practiced in, 289
    Israel's face turned toward, 284
    judicial system as unknown, 322
    languages of, 6
    Leviticus given with a view to, 7
    not walking in their statutes, 288
Canaanites, 284, 289, 326–29, 384
candlestick. *See* golden lamp stand
cap, of the high priest, 248
capital punishment, 292, 322, 329, 376
captives, dying off in a foreign land, 447
carcasses, incense driving out the smell of, 224
carrion, 278, 280
cast metal, not making any gods of, 299
casting of lots, as selection by God himself, 254
casuistry, 184
cattle and livestock, on the tithe of, 469
cedar wood, durability of, 223–24
ceremonial garb, of the high priest, 248

SUBJECT INDEX

ceremony, of a leper being declared clean, 223, 226
childbirth, 202–10, 312
children
    no sexual relations with, 293
    people eating their own, 446
    of a priest's daughter fathered by a non-priest, 349
    retaining what their parents do, 167
    taught first of all by his or her mother, 297
    of wrath, 207
Christ. *See* Jesus Christ
Christian church, 435, 436
"the Christian Sabbath," in the Netherlands, 439
Christianity, 212, 281, 434, 452–53
Christians
    on historic acts of redemption, 187
    as imitators of God, 367
    in Jerusalem following the Law of Moses, 238
    on the Law, 142
    in northern climates allowing sprinkling, 155
    participating in pagan sacrificial events, 46
    as people of hope, 95, 316
    reputation of being tight-fisted and harsh, 302
    significance of Leviticus 27 for today, 470–75
church of the New Covenant, needing to be warned, 452
church of the New Testament, protected by the apostles, 199
circumcision, 183, 195, 205, 375
cistern, dead animal in, 193
cities of refuge, Moses on, 313
civil law codes, 285
class justice, 303
classes, of animals, 461
clean
    meaning of, 181
    separating from the unclean, 295, 310
clean animals, 42–43, 44, 198, 271, 275–77, 278–81

clean birds, no specifications for, 191
clean livestock, defilement through, 194
cleansing of a leper, 222–27, 232
cleansing of a man with a discharge, 232
Closing Feast (*atsereth*), after the Feast of Booths, 410
clothing
    Aaron changing his, 260
    infected with *tsara 'ath*, 218
    leprosy on, 217
    made out of two kinds of material, 183
code book, sacrificial Torah nothing like, 173
Code of Hammurabi, 285, 314, 433
color, of wine, 73
colors, language of, 369
commandments
    about the Sabbath day, 364–65
    for the priests, 339–43
    remembering to do, 309
    of the Torah, 305
    warnings against transgressing God's, 308
compensation, 127, 457, 458
complaint, festering against your brother, 303–4
complete rest, giving the land every seventh year, 418
concluding commands, on the Day of Atonement, 264–67
confession, 49, 276
consecration, anointing oil for, 149–50
consecration offering, mentions of, 145
Constantine, 397
consulting the dead, no pardon for, 323–25
continual burnt offering (*tamid*), 137
cookware, for the meat of the sin offering, 118
corban, 19, 20
corbanim, or the gifts of Israelites, 58
cord or tassels, wearing on the corner of a garment, 378
corpse, becoming unclean by touching, 106
corruption, allowing to slip in, 105

SUBJECT INDEX

counting, beginning with the first day of manna, 358
covenant(s)
    with Abraham, 102
    concluded with sanctions, 448
    establishing, 66–67, 153–58, 269, 360
    God not neglecting, 324
    lesson of Mara and, 356
    in Leviticus, 209, 444
covenant blessing, 289, 444–45
covenant curse, threat of, 446–47
covenant language, in other parts of the Old Testament, 270
covenant of Horeb, 183, 392
covenant of salt, 77
covenant treaty, 269, 270
covenant wrath, in the new dispensation, 453
covenant zone, 110
covering with blood, 28–29, 389
creation, 18
creeping animals, Peter's vision including, 201
creeping insects, 192, 194
crime, guilt of not bringing to light, 106
cultus, God's commands regarding, 102
"curse," referring to the opposite of "honor," 326
curses and blessings, as the concluding section of treaties, 455

dabbed blood, with the sin offering, 110
daily labor, fruit of Israel's, 72
dassie, not a real ruminant, 190
daughter
    of an Israelite's father with another wife, 293
    of a priest committing sexual immorality, 327, 343
daughter-in-law, sexual relations with, 293, 327
daughters of Zelophehad, 423, 437
David, 106, 145, 267, 311
Day of Atonement. *See* Great Day of Atonement
day of atonements (*yom hakkippurim*), 401

day of judgment, for apostate Christians, 187
Day of the Seventh New Month, 438
deacon Philip, preaching of, 237–38
the dead, 256, 318, 324–25
dead animals, 193, 196, 203
dead person (*nefesh*), 339–40
Dead Sea, salt mining near, 77
death
    atonement through, 38
    blood signifying, 272, 276
    of Christ, 41
    Christ delivered up for, 27
    contrast with life, 338
    defilement through, 192, 339–42, 344–45
    of the firstborn, 385
    God's warning sounded against, 195–96
    incompatible with rich promises, 142
    as irrevocable if outside God's communion, 229
    Leviticus 13–14 containing a warning against, 222
    no pagan notions about, 315–19
    reconciliation through, 15–41
    as Satan's companion, 198, 284–85
    soul departing as a description of, 40
    swallowed up in victory when Christ returns, 200
    as a symbol of paganism, 345
    watching out for, 196, 233
    Yahweh abhorred, 182, 339
debts, 418–19, 420, 432
Decalogue, 296
defects, in sacrificial animals, 10, 43
defenseless persons, oppressing, 302
defilement
    with blood, 272
    in connection with slaughtering, 277
    extent of not limited to the man himself, 231
    possible means of, 266
    sacred prostitution and, 343
    for which priests must be on guard, 338–46
"deposition," of Nadab and Abihu, 166–75

SUBJECT INDEX

desert
  defiled the man who burned dead sacrificial animals, 264
  live goat released in, 256
  as a symbol of the hostile world, 262
desert, devil, and death, from Holwerda, 256, 257
devil, wanting to rob us of our freedom, 186
"differentness," priests teaching Israel on, 180
Dionysian orgies, eating ram animals, 142
discharges, of males and females, 104, 228–35
disobedience, to father and mother, 102
dispensation tax, for someone who made a vow, 461
divided heart, prophets warned against, 67
divination, liver of a sacrificial animal used for, 87
divine revelation, history of, 286
divorced woman, priest could not marry, 343
domestic animals, clean, 190
domesticated animals, for sacrifice, 42
doron, meaning gift, 20
dough, putting an old portion with new, 78
dove(s)
  gender of for sacrifice, 63
  mentioned frequently in the Sacrifice Torah, 191
  not allowed for the peace offering, 88
  for one with a discharge, 232
  the only bird identified as a sacrificial bird, 223
  replacing sheep for a cleansed leper, 227
  sacrificing of, 43, 50
  as a sin offering, 97, 106, 108
  two slaughtered for Mary, 208
drink offering, 71, 72, 73, 74
Drogendijk, A. C., 212
"dry" part, of the grain offering, 74
duration, of uncleanness for women, 234

dying, of one soul for the atoning of another, 40
ear, needing to learn to know God's will, 155
early Christians, would meeting at homes, 474
earthen vessel, dead animal in, 193
eating of blood, 276
Edomites, 429
Egypt, 244, 288, 289
Egyptian ka, 197
Egyptian priests, having shaved heads, 334
Egyptians
  Joseph's wife as, 238
  not eating meals "with the Hebrews," 92
ejaculation, 229, 232
El (god), married to his three sisters, 290
El Al airlines, not flying on Sabbath in Israel, 438–39
Eleazar (son of Aaron), 104, 170, 172
elephantiasis Graecorum, as Hansen's disease, 214
Elisha, threw salt into a well, 77
elohim (god), 319, 381, 414
Elzaphan, nephew of Aaron but not a priest, 169
entire nation, sin offering for, 111, 113
Ephraim, eating unclean food in Assyria, 200
"eternal," in Scripture meaning "very long time," 274
"eternal" (*olam*) covenant, Fourth Commandment and, 376
"eternal ages," 472
eternal life, 58
eunuch, Ethiopian as, 238
evangelical (gospel-filled) character, of the Torah, 131, 135
Eve, punishment of, 229
evil, 125–26, 129, 135
evil spirits, world of hostile to Israel, 258
exemption
  not obtainable, 464–70
  obligations for, 459–64
Exodus, 3, 15

SUBJECT INDEX

extent, of uncleanness of a woman, 233, 234
"eye for eye, tooth for tooth," 415
Ezekiel, 87, 341

face of Yahweh, pointing to the ark of Yahweh, 113
faithfulness of God and people, 470
falling asleep, as real death, 41
falling into the hands of the living God, 452
fallow, leaving fields as, 417, 426
fanaticism, observing regulations of, 200
fasting, 265, 402
fat
    commands for the priests about, 140–43
    of the land for God, 87
    of sacrificial animals, 64, 117
    of the sin offering, 261
father and mother, honoring, 309
fatty tail, of a sheep in Palestine, 88–89
Feast of Booths, 404–10
    celebrated "before the face of Yahweh," 387
    closing Feast after, 410
    cut off by Christians, 438
    as a genuinely joyful feast, 405
    names of, 407–9
    not commemorating Horeb to Canaan, 408
    as a reminder of the sojourn of ancestors, 404
    sacrifices at, 409–10
    time of, 406–7
feast of harvest, 393
Feast of Passover, repeated the law relating to the firstborn, 465
Feast of Tents. *See* Feast of Booths
"the Feast of Unleavened Bread," 78, 388. *See also* Passover
"the feast of Yahweh." *See* Feast of Booths
feasts, 382–85, 392, 394, 406
Feasts of Passover and Pentecost, Christianized, 438
feet, needing for doing God's will, 155

fellow citizens, intentional offenses against, 130–31
fellowship of God's sanctuary, readmission into, 225–27
fellowship with God's people, readmission into, 222–25
female animals, for the peace offering, 88
female gender, as weaker, 204–5
female sheep, as a guilt offering, 225
female sheep or goat, as the sin offering, 108
female slave
    as not a wife, 312
    sexual relations with, 134
fertility gods and goddesses, worshiping, 273
fertility religions, in Canaan, 289
festivals of Yahweh, celebrating, 317
fidelity, salt representing, 77
"field spirits," first fruits sacrificed to, 314
fields, 418, 464
Fifth Commandment, preceding the Fourth, 296
fire, on the altar, 54–55, 374
fire offerings, 58, 74
first and great commandment, Love God with all your heart, 298–300
first day of each month, as not a Sabbath, 397
First Day of the Seventh Month, 397–400
First Day of the Seventh New Month, 401
firstborn, being redeemed as, 208
firstborn clean animals, 127, 465
firstborn male animal, 466
firstborn male child, to be redeemed, 465
firstborn unclean animal, 466
firstfruits, not intended for the altar, 58
firstfruits sheaf, 391, 392
fish, 190, 191
fixed date, for the great Day of Atonement, 265
fixed times, heavenly bodies indicating for people, 383

SUBJECT INDEX

flesh, in reference to people and animals, 34
fleshly piety, with which God is not at all pleased, 174
flour, as a sin offering, 97, 98, 106
flow of blood, as the "sin" that had to be atoned, 209
flying insects, going on all fours, 192
food
    given to the priests, 82
    oil used for preparing, 75
    sacrifices as for Yahweh, 55
    setting apart from pagans, 183
food for Yahweh (*lechem le Yahweh*), 56, 342
food offerings
    for the cleansed leper, 226
    portion of Aaron and his sons from, 144
food or drink, dead animal into contact with, 193
foods, distinction between clean and unclean, 283
"for Azazel," meaning of, 249
forecourt, 73, 118
foreign gods, warnings against, 269
"foreigner." *See* sojourner(s)
foreigners, gleaning allowed for surprised Ruth, the Moabitess, 302
forgiveness
    for the (intentional) transgressor of God's commandment, 131
    obtaining along the path of the sin offering, 107
    requiring death, 26
    of sins, 94, 112
fornication, abstaining from, 143
fortunes, not telling, 315
forty, unique significance of, 205
forty-year wandering of Israel, 405
foundation of the Torah, God placed the entire Israelite society upon, 472
"the foundation of the world"
    content given to the phrase, 473
    at Horeb, 109, 121, 403
    identified with creation, 117

Leviticus devoted to describing, 470
    referring to the creation of the world, 471
    the Torah and, 105
four-footed animals, clean, 190
Fourth Commandment, 365, 368, 372, 373
freedom, proclamation of, 425
freedom festival, Feast of Booths as, 405
freewill offering, 85–86, 88, 91
"the fruit of the trees," referring to wine and oil, 468
fruit trees, in Canaan like uncircumcised trees, 313
full sister, not having sexual relations with, 293
funeral gathering, turning the Feast of Booths into, 408

Gabriel, to Zechariah: "Your prayer has been heard," 398
"gamey meat," Canaanites preferring, 300
garment(s)
    of the high priest, 344
    not wearing from two kinds of material, 306–11
    of the person declared clean, 226
    wearing tassels on the four corners of, 307
Genesis, 380, 381, 382
genitalia, discharges from male and female, 229
Gentile Christians, 143
Gentiles, 450, 472
gentleness, of God, 135, 347
the *ger*
    living permanently among Israel, 321
    as sojourners or strangers, 277, 304–5, 426
    subject to Israel's legislation, 279
gift, or *corban*, every kind of sacrifice as, 55
"gifts and sacrifices," to God, 20
giving, as more blessed than receiving, 302
gleaning by the poor, outside of Israel also, 301

gleanings, for the poor and for the
    alien, 396
glorification, 86, 112, 132
glory of God, 164–65
Gnostics, 116
goat(s)
    carrying all iniquities to a remote
        area, 254, 255
    released in the desert, 262
    as a sin offering, 97, 249, 250, 252,
        263–64
goat demons, sacrifices to, 274
goat "for Azazel," releasing, 254–60
goat of Mendes, 294
God. See also Yahweh (the One Who
    Is Near)
    approaching with thanksgiving, 93
    approved of Aaron and his sons, 173
    atoning us to himself through
        Christ, 30
    commanded Israel to keep his
        covenant, 362
    created people and animals as
        "living souls," 38
    detested conduct of Egyptians and
        Canaanites, 295
    disapproving the smallest
        stumbling movement, 116
    divided the peace offering animal, 87
    doing nothing in a human-like
        manner, 376–77
    established a covenant with Israel at
        Horeb, 18, 442
    esteemed the value of blood, 39
    as the God of the number seven, 394
    on the Great Day of Atonement, 247
    hated the world of death, sin, Satan,
        paganism, 199
    as host at the peace offering meal, 57
    identified animals that resembled
        human beings, 43
    laid claim to every possible thing in
        human life, 338
    on listening to the sounds of Easter,
        233
    lived in the tabernacle, 102
    no longer appointing fast days, 265
    not being served by human hands,
        55
    not permitting service without
        compensation, 139, 150
    not restricting the command to
        love, 304
    not wanting anyone to violate the
        Torah, 107
    not wanting rote obedience from
        his servants, 173
    not wanting to see any pagan
        grieving rituals, 197
    nurtured Israel, 186
    oath-swearing to Abraham, 360
    permitted use of the land for six
        years in a row, 418
    placed Israel on a special
        foundation at Horeb, 92
    pleasure in Israel's keeping his
        covenant, 83
    preaching life in the covenant with
        him, 222
    predicted that the Israelites would
        never disappear, 447
    prohibited some things among
        Israel at the time of Horeb, 287
    provided for the covering with the
        blood, 29
    purpose of with Leviticus 21–22,
        336–37
    requisitioned animals from people's
        property, 43
    rested after creating the world, 368
    right of to Israel's whole heart, 65
    seeking Israel's life and happiness,
        197
    as the source of the fire on the altar,
        54
    stench and decay incompatible
        with, 140
    as too pure to look on evil, 101
    used similar practices from the
        pagans, 283
    wanting the seventh day to be a
        joyful day, 372
    wanting to dwell in the midst of
        people, 101, 336, 341

warning against falling back into
paganism, 306
on what is sinful, 105
God of life, Yahweh as, 340
gods, stimulating to grant benefits, 316
"God's beloved sick ones," "lepers"
called, 214
God's blessing, promise of for observing
imposed obligations, 444–45
God's curse, threat of, 446–47
God's face, humiliation and humbling
before, 248
God's glory, appearance of, 164–65
God's name, connection to the
tabernacle, 336, 341
God's Spirit, 207, 227
God's wrath, stages of, 446
golden calf, as image worship, 299
golden lamp stand, 411–12
golden tassel, on the headdress of the
high priest, 344
Good Friday, 403
gospel
of the Great Day of Atonement, 257
of the old covenant, 202
redemptive benefits of, 49–59
those proclaiming getting their
living by, 144
gospel of Christ, 238, 392
government
fought for feast days as "vacation
days," 403
respecting, 320
grace, continuing in God's, 187
gradualness, used by God, 286
grain harvests, 74, 468
grain offering, 68–83
Aaron and his surviving sons not
finished with, 171
accompanied each bloody sacrifice,
53
commands for concerning the
priests, 137–38
designated for the officiating priest,
139–40
devoted to Yahweh, 82
of the high priest, 138
main component of, 74–75

prepared with oil, 76
for the priests as their honorarium,
81
prohibition against leaven being
used with, 79
as a sacrifice with a unique
character, 69–70
symbolized good works, 75, 76
Gramberg, K. P. C. A., 212
Grand Annexation, 460
granddaughter, no sexual relations
with, 293
grasshoppers, belonging to the diet of
poor people, 192
"The Great Annexation," 180, 285, 334
Great Day of Atonement, 400–404
blood sprinkled on the ark, 111, 114
fixed date for, 265
focusing attention on God's
holiness, 402
freedom proclaimed on, 425
high priest's garments for, 247–48
institution of, 473–74
promoted to Good Friday by
Christians, 438
a Sabbath day, 436
as the subject of Leviticus 16, 246
task of the high priest on, 265–67
Greeks
covenant making by, 360
eating bread with salt, 77
grieving, in Israel, 170, 217, 339–42
grudge, not bearing against your own
people, 304
guilt, brought upon the entire people,
109
guilt offering, 123–35
bringing to Yahweh, 311
commands for the priests
concerning, 139–40
compared to sin offering, 97, 98, 132
for the leper, 135
making restitution in, 457
one-fifth of a portion in instruction
regarding, 349

hair, leprosy initially detected in, 225

half-sister, no sexual relations with, 293, 328
Hammurabi, law code of ending with sanctions, 449
hands
    of Aaron and his sons "filled," 156
    needing for doing God's will, 155
Hannah, story of, 458–59
Hansen's disease, 213, 214, 216
"the hardness of hearts," God's patience with, 280
hare, not a real ruminant, 190
harvest, 301, 394
harvest festivals, 394
head
    of the animal severed from the torso, 64
    uncovered as a sign of mourning, 339
headdress, of the priest, 339
healed leper, dabbed with blood and oil, 185
healing, of possessed persons, 256
health, playing a role in the Law, 181
heart, strengthened by grace and not by foods, 120
"heartfelt zealot," Paul had been, 201
hearts, opening for the proclamation of the gospel, 475
"heave offering," 90
Heavenly Father, goodness of, 94, 115–16
Hebrew language
    of Moses' day having Egyptian influence, 5
    repetition of an idea in poetry, 166
    uses of *nefesh*, 31–32
    word for "swear," 368
Hebrews (book of)
    author of received the gospel from one of Jesus's disciples, 243
    dating, 244
    emphasis on Christ's priesthood, 52
    encouraging readers toward greater confidence, 242
    on the Horeb covenant, 244
    original readers of felt deep pain in their hearts, 244

word usage and themes different from epistles of Paul, 240
Heidelberg Catechism, 93
hell, punishment of, 53
Herodotus, on the sun god Bel, 316
Hezekiah, 437
high priest
    anointed and consecrated, 344
    approached Yahweh on the Great Day of Atonement, 248, 401
    commandments for, 339, 343–46
    garments for the great Day of Atonement, 247–48
    holy, without guilt or stain, 45
    installation of Aaron as, 149
    Israelite church longing for the perfect, 267
    Jesus as, 158
    never to appear with an uncovered head, 344
    not allowed contact with a corpse, 335
    not permitted to be involved with death, 340
    permitted to marry only a pure virgin, 346
    rendering sacrifice "for himself," 160
    sin committed by, 109
    sin offering brought blood into the holy place, 111, 113
    sin offering for, 97
    task of on the great Day of Atonement, 265–67
high priesthood, only Aaron called to, 153
high priestly blessing, words of Aaron's, 162
high priestly grain offering, daily, 138
Hittite suzerain, making covenants with subjects, 361
Hittites, good among, 285
holiness
    as "calling," 7
    garments of, 248
    of God, 8, 174, 347
    of priests and sacrificial gifts, 333–52
    of some blood, 276

SUBJECT INDEX

"Holiness Code," in Leviticus, 268
holy, meaning of, 7–8
holy convocation, on the Day of
    Atonement itself, 402
holy fire, became "strange fire," 168
Holy of Holies, 114, 246
Holy One, God revealing himself as, 7
holy people, 185, 349
holy place
    Aaron's first entrance into the,
      163–64
    in front of the curtain "of the
      testimony," 411
holy shekel, weighed about ten grams,
    128
Holy Spirit. *See also* Spirit of Christ
    blaspheming not forgiven, 103
    indicating the way into the holy
      place, 242
    leading us out of the power of
      Satan, 186
    oil symbolized, 76
    symbolized by fire, 54
holy things, eaten by priests' family
    members, 348
holy things of Yahweh, sinning
    unintentionally against, 126–27
Holy to Yahweh, on the golden tassel,
    344, 345
homosexual intercourse, 327
homosexuality, condemning, 294
honesty, in jurisprudence and business,
    321
honey, forbidden from the grain
    offering, 78, 79
honey and leaven, not symbolizing
    purity and life, 79
Horeb. *See also* Mount Sinai
    covenant foundation at, 105
    Feast of Booths instituted at, 408
    foundation of, 145
    institution of the weekly Sabbath
      day, 380
    Israel standing between Egypt and
      Canaan, 284
    laws from the viewpoint that in
      a short time Israel would be
      entering the land of Canaan, 396
    on the mountain of Moses called as
      savior, 442
    not to risk slipping off the life-
      foundation of, 117
    as nothing more than a rest stop, 443
    on slaughtering of animals, 141
    unique place in the history of
      redemption, 199
    warnings of later ignored, 449
Horeb covenant. *See also* Law of Horeb
    as antiquated and obsolete, 183
    applying differently for us than for
      Israel, 280–81
    to be honored daily, 412
    established shortly before Leviticus,
      270–71
    events at the establishment of, 156
    financial scope governing Israel's
      life, 429
    gave *shabbath* a new and broader
      significance, 366
    imprinting upon Israel the need for
      respect, 379
    Israel's coming into existence as the
      people of, 470
    made not with sojourners, 414
    maintained from God's side, 377
    no longer existing for Christians,
      400, 439
    not confusing with the New
      Covenant, 474
    "rested" on the priesthood, 271
    same commandments on each
      stone tablet, 362
    shortly after the manna miracle, 360
    sprinkling with oil not occurring,
      157
    visual lessons of the obligation to
      observe, 311
horns of the altar, 97, 111, 112
house mold, removing, 218
houses
    in cities not reverting back to the
      original owners in the Year of
      Jubilee, 427
    Law for cleansing leprous, 227
    leprosy on, 217, 218
    obligations with respect to, 462

houses (continued)
   placing a railing around the roof, 307
   selling, 427–28
   in villages returning to original owners in the Year of Jubilee, 427
human nature, depravity of, 206
"humbling oneself," same Hebrew word as fasting, 265
husband's uncleanness, during menstruation of the wife, 234
hyper-sexualized character, of Canaanites, 324
hyssop, Syrian oregano (*origanum maru*) of the species *Labiaten*, 224

"I am Yahweh," God reminding Israel repeatedly, 330
idolatrous abominations, clamping down on, 141
idolatrous practices, defilement with blood through, 272–74
idolatrous sacrifices, having fellowship with demons, 46
idolatry, 100, 273
idols, 143, 298–99, 324, 443
"image of God," tracing back to the Old Testament, 368
"image worship," prohibition against, 299
impoverished Israelite, not to be treated by the sojourner as a real slave, 434
impurity, color of as the color of death, 217
in the desert, purification for being in, 262
"inauguration," 159–65, 170
incense
   altar of, 111
   burned continually, 70
   for consecration, 150
   quantity of, 81
   smoke of, 250
   symbolized prayer, 76
incense sacrifice, every morning and evening, 398

incest, 289
indigent person, sin offering for, 97
indivisible cycle, of Sabbaths, 353–54
infectious diseases, 228
infectiousness, of the leper as not that serious, 212–13
iniquities, of the people of Israel, 255
insects, 189, 191–92, 194
"installation," of Aaron and his four sons, 149–58
instructional capacity, of Israel's priests, 180
intentional indirect offenses (*ma'al*), against Yahweh, 133–34
intentional offenses, 129–33
intentional sins
   cannot be atoned, 98
   committed directly against Yahweh, 130
   examples of, 106
   no forgiveness for, 126
   worthy of death, 99–100
interest, taking only with a foreigner (*nokri*), 430
intermezzo chapter, of Leviticus 24, 410–15
intestines, of the animal, 64
Isaiah 61, Lord Jesus applied to himself, 435
isolation, of lepers from the camp, 217
Israel
   abstaining from defilement through blood, 276
   all male firstborn devoted to God, 465
   all summoned to know Aaron and his sons had been chosen, 150–51
   as but one nation among others, 8
   departed from Egypt loaded down with loot, 428
   feasts rested upon the institution of the Sabbath, 297
   Horeb covenant broken under leadership of Aaron, 377
   obligated to have the *ger* share various benefits of God's covenant, 279

SUBJECT INDEX

as a people bearing a priestly character, 113
people of called holy, 7
as the people of life, 272
as a people of "separated ones," 310
as the people of the number seven, 371
prescribed ban within, 467
privilege of being Yahweh's covenant people, 114
prohibition against using blood, 25, 272
repeatedly reminded of her own time of sojourning in Egypt, 321
separated from the peoples, 330
surrounded by nations strangled by Satan, 102
times when Law and Testimony were not honored in, 473
as too holy to become involved with death, 457
warned against paganism, 282
warned against the dangers of infection, 285
worship orbiting times associated with sun and moon played an important role, 132
would not be destroyed completely, 447
Israelite(s)
agrarian diet of, 42
allowed to slaughter animals only at the tabernacle, 273
bringing animals for sacrifice, 350
children led away as slaves, 450
complaining about lack of meat and bread, 356–57
continuing to have the right of release, 434
danger in Canaan of defiling themselves with the corpses, 457
in Egypt loved to eat fish, 191
fate if living in Canaan like the Canaanites, 294
God's command to not eat any blood, 25
honoring Yahweh on Pentecost with a voluntary offering, 396
led away into captivity, 447
marrying again, 290–91
not permitted to have any brothers from their own people as slaves, 433
objects as representatives of, 51
observing the Sabbath day from generation to generation, 376
sacrifices for on the great Day of Atonement, 249
sacrificing to the idols punished with the ban, 467
selling oneself to a fellow Israelite, 431–32
transferred to the Levites the obligation that firstborn sons should serve Yahweh, 49
at twenty years of age paid a ransom (*kofer*) for his person (*nefesh*), 457
Yahweh laying claim to every sphere of life, 284
Ithamar (son of Aaron), 104, 170, 172

James (brother of the Lord), 238–39, 241
Jericho, total ban on entering, 467
Jeroboam, invented a feast "from his own heart," 406
Jerusalem temple, 244, 245
Jesus Christ. *See also* Savior
appearing at the end of the ages, 403
arose "from the dead," 41
ascending the path as our substitute, 9
assaulting ancestral doctrine, 201
died in his prime at thirty-three years of age, 44
enemies of the gospel of, 236
entering heavenly sanctuary by means of his own blood, 52
gave his life as a ransom for many, 41, 43–44
as God's gift for the covering, the atonement of our sins, 276
God's Son as greater than the angels and a priest-king like Melchizedek, 244

493

SUBJECT INDEX

Jesus Christ (continued)
    as a High Priest not "beset with weakness," 337
    historical Word-bath of the gospel of, 210
    Law fulfilled by, 95
    met requirement of wholeness, 44–45
    not cast outside Jerusalem like an unclean sacrificial animal, 119
    as our Savior to our good God, 30
    permitted to enter into the holy of holies, 9
    as the priest of a higher order, 251
    readiness to include individuals in his life-communion, 23
    reproach of, 121
    serving as our Advocate with the Father, 242
    slain for us, 27
    suffered outside the gate, 119, 121
    suffering and death of portrayed in the Sacrifice Torah, 450
    as the Surety of the new and better covenant, 158, 281
    those turning their backs on returning to paganism and to death, 210
    "types" of, 174
    whole and perfect as Priest and as Lamb, 347
Jewish Christians, holding on to the old covenant, 242
Jewish converts, remaining "zealous for the Law," 239
Jewish people, who believed that Jesus was the promised Messiah, 243
Jewish scribes, neutralizing the simple word and command of God, 20
Jewish worship, continuing to be practiced in Jerusalem, 121
Jews
    not eating meals with Gentiles, 92
    used the term leprosy in a broad sense, 212
John, 41, 116
John the Baptist, food of, 192
Jonathan, 174
Joshua, 269
Josiah, 453
journey, from Egypt to Canaan, 429
joyous sacrifice, peace offering as in every respect, 91
Judaizers, 142, 236n2, 239
Judaizing, 184, 236–45, 437, 452
judgment, expectation of for sinning deliberately, 116
jurisprudence, being honest in, 321
justice, 320–21, 322
justification, 27, 49–52, 112, 132

kavod (glory), Yahweh making visible, 164
kedeshah, a consecrated one, 317
Keil, Carl Friedrich, 27
kid, boiling in its mother's milk, 384
killing someone, in an indirect manner, 303
king of Arad, from the Negev, 382
kingdom of God, 437
"a kingdom of priests and a holy nation," as God's desire for Israel, 184, 186
kings and priests, "worshiping" the Holy One, 9
Köhler, L., 214–15
kpr, usage of in Holy Scripture, 28–29
Kurtz, J. H., 24, 26, 40, 69

labor, 68, 420
laborer, as worthy of his wage, 309
"laity," sin offering to be brought by, 108
lamb
    for the guilt offering for the cleansed leper, 227
    for Passover, 390, 391
    slaughtered on the fourteenth day of the month, 386
lamps, of the golden lampstand, 70, 75, 76
land
    assignment of to Abraham, 361
    under the ban, 468
    giving rest, 420
    leaving untilled every seventh year, 417

obligations with respect to, 462–64
receiving payment for shortage of
    sabbatical years, 447
tithe of the produce of, 468
land of Canaan, Yahweh remained
    owner of, 417, 426, 427
language
    of the Israelites not remaining
        unaltered, 5
    as living and undergoing change, 33
the Law. *See also* Law of Moses
    arousing in Israel the hope of
        something better, 267
    church today free from, 9
    fanaticism for, 437
    as God's own Word, 201
    as "holy, righteous, and good," 132
    learning from nurture and
        instruction, 187
    no basis for dividing up found in
        Scripture, 436
    as not an irritating anchor, 185
    as not easy for Israel, 266
    not functioning as a jailor, 337
    on priests not permitted to eat of
        the sin offering, 120
    sacrifices of as shadows, 41
    sighing under as under a yoke that
        was hard, 200
    teaching us how holy our heavenly
        Father is, 452
    zealots for, 236–45
Law of Horeb, 337, 438. *See also* Horeb
    covenant
Law of Leviticus 11, 200
Law of Moses, 47, 198, 208. *See also*
    the Law
law of the firstborn, animals due to
    Yahweh by, 465
Law of the Sabbath, 438
law of the Sabbath year, 419
laws
    of Leviticus, 7, 8, 283
    walking in, 326
lawyerism, not at all related to the Old
    Testament, 184
lay persons
    eating of the holy gifts, 349

not eating anything that is holy, 348
represented by the altar of burnt
    offering, 51
laying on of hands, by the one bringing
    the sacrifice, 49
laying upon with blood, on the altar,
    28–29
Lazarus, disease or sickness of, 214
leadership and order, usually safest
    done by older people, 320
leather, infected with *tsara'ath*, 218
leaven, 78, 217
leavened cakes, with the peace offering
    meal, 300
legalism, 236n1, 437
lender, not acting unmercifully toward
    the borrower, 430
lenience, of God in regard to
    unintentional sin, 101
leper homes, 214
lepers
    bringing a sin offering for
        purification, 104
    identified as those symbolically
        dead, 217
    not allowed to approach God's
        sanctuary, 182
    purification of, 220–27
    re-inclusion into the community of
        Israel, 184–85
lepra, did not refer to Hansen's disease,
    214
leprosy
    bringing a sheep as a guilt offering
        when healed, 135
    course of events in a case of,
        219–20
    kinds of, 217
    as a metaphor of the consequences
        of sin, 222
    as a symbolic death, 203
    Torah instruction with regard to
        uncleanness of, 211–27
leprosy (biblical), 211–18, 222, 227
leprous disease, teaching for any case
    of, 180
Levi, 57, 90, 427
Levites, 44, 127, 427, 428

levitical cities, pasture around, 428
Leviticus
    connecting to the book of Numbers, 458, 469
    given before the march against Canaan, 6–7
    last chapter of added to the book, 5
    laws of, 448
    role in the New Testament, 450
    special place among the first five books of the Bible, 2
    style of, 9–11
    time of, 3–6
    understanding Old and New Testaments via, 473
liars, 18, 99
liberated people, we are just as much as Israel was, 186
life
    cedar wood as a symbol of, 224
    ceremony declaring a leper to be clean on, 223
    God's greatest desire and love for our, 211
    of the living being is in the blood, 36
    Passover as a real festival of, 387
life-communion with Christ, being included in, 23
live bird, dipped and released, 223, 225
liver, of sacrificial animals, 87, 88
livestock, 467, 468, 469
living water, 223
loans, Law that God gave at Horeb stipulating, 429
loaves of bread, 70, 92
locusts, 192, 196
log of oil, 225, 227
loneliness, of lepers, 212
the Lord's food offerings, *qorbanim* (from *qereb*) or gifts of Israel to Yahweh, 342
Lord's Supper, 404, 422
love, for the neighbor prescribed in five sections, 300–301
love of God, as resourceful, 228–30

ma'al
    translating in Lev 5:15 as "injure," 126
    against Yahweh, 130
male animals, 63, 65
male goats, 109, 161
male lamb, replaced for Mary with a dove, 209
males and females, uncleanness through discharges, 228–35
mammals, in Palestine, 188–89
man
    with abnormal discharge, 230–32
    ejaculation during sleep and with lying with his wife during menstruation, 234
    giving the emission of his seed to an animal, 327
    with normal discharge, 232
    releasing from a vow, 461
    taking a wife and also her daughter, 327
    who led away the goat, 261–63
manna
    institution of the Sabbath day and, 359
    miracle of, 235, 357
    not allowed to be gathered on the seventh day, 235
manner, for entering the holy of holies, 247
Mara, lesson of, 356
marriage
    entering with payment of the dowry, 312
    entering without a list of sins, 114–15
    forbidden between a man and his sister-in-law, 329
    God always highly esteeming, 229
    God not forbidding Israel from entering, 292
    instituted by God, 327
    misconduct eroding the foundation of, 115
    regulations not provided for, 331
"marriage blessing," 327
Mary, purification of, 208
mature animals, as sacrificial animals, 4

SUBJECT INDEX

meals, 91, 373, 375
meat
    of the animal used for the sin offering, 118
    of the guilt offering eaten by the priests, 132–33
    Israel not eating every day, 74
    never sacrificed within the holy place and within the holies of holies, 70
    of the sacrificial animal handled only by priests, 54
mediation, 20
medieval church, prohibited taking interest, 430
mediums, 318, 324–25
member of the congregation, sin offering for, 97, 108, 111
menstruating woman, not having sexual relations with, 293, 328
menstruation
    beginning while lying with her husband, 234
    discussed in terms of sequence, 233
    number seven having no medical relevance to, 204
    uncleanness of, 209
    with women and girls, 229
The Merchant of Venice (Shakespeare), 435
mercifulness, 340, 347
Messiah, Israel crucifying "in ignorance," 103
Middle Ages, afflicted with epidemics, 200
mildew, kinds of known in Palestine, 218
military bans, prescribed and voluntary, 467
military camp, lepers excluded from Israel's, 203
minchah, as the name of the grain offering, 71
ministry, of blood, 1
Miriam, 203, 212
Mishael, nephew of Aaron, 169
mo 'ed, meaning simply a fixed time, 383
Moladta, partner of Bel, 316

mold spores, preventing the spread of, 218
Molech, 294, 323–25
monetary debts, forgiving altogether, 422
monetary interest, Law stipulating, 429, 430
money, given as security, 131
months of the year, 386, 391
moral abuses, as even worse than death, 342
moral order, establishment of, 472
mortal sin, taking interest as, 430
"Mosaic system," corresponded with pagan religions, 23
Moses
    on capturing and returning a fleeing slave, 433
    command to cover excreta outside the camp, 228–29
    communicated commands regarding Aaron, 159
    connection with Yahweh, 197
    dabbed blood of the sin offering for Aaron and his sons, 154
    on the drink offering, 71
    functioned temporarily as priest, 150
    instructed in all the wisdom of the Egyptians, 5–6
    laid the matter before Yahweh himself, 414
    meetings between God and, 3–4
    over-reacting on Aaron and his two surviving sons eating the sin offering, 237
    prohibition against working on Sabbath days, 377
    reminded Aaron a high priest was never allowed to grieve, 171
    responsibility for the proper course of events, 171
    restrained Aaron and his sons, 104
    role played by, 269
    on the sin offering as not to be burned, 172
    took an Ethiopian woman as his wife, 238
    zeal for the letter of the Law, 173

SUBJECT INDEX

"most holy," grain offering as, 171
most holy place, 163, 252, 343
most holy things, only priests allowed to eat of, 348
"most holy" wages, to the priests, 82
mother
    not having sexual relations with, 293
    who had just given birth as unclean, 208
mother of Jeroboam, called Zeruah meaning Leper, 216
mother's milk, Israel forbidden to boil a kid in, 351
motivation or explanation, for the Sabbath, 365–70
Mount Sinai. *See* Horeb
"on Mount Sinai," meaning at Horeb, 5
Mount Sinai, Lord commanded Moses on, 4
mourning, prohibited for the high priest, 344
mourning clothing, worn by lepers, 221
mourning customs, priests forbidden to follow, 341
mules, Israelites did possess, 311
murderer, 98
mycelium flakes, developing from rot, 218
Mylitta, also called Ishtar and Astarte, 316

Naaman, Bible story about, 212
Nadab, 9, 104, 166–75, 250
Naomi, said "call me Mara," 390
Nazirite, 104, 135
Nearby One, Yahweh as, 197
necromancers, not turning to, 318
nefesh, 31, 32, 36–37, 111
neighbor, 240, 300–305
nephew, eyeing his (much younger) aunt, 291
nesekh, as the Hebrew term for drink offering, 72
new covenant, 117, 185, 422
New Testament
    allusions to Leviticus, 450–52
    doctrine of as even more strict, 115
    formulations borrowed from the Old Testament, 117
    on those who serve God and those who do not, 453
New Testament church, teaching for, 332
newborn calf, or goat as not being perfect and complete, 351
Nicea, council of assigned the feast of Passover to Sunday, 397
no pagan concourse, with death, 318–19
no pagan fear, of death, 315–16
no pagan sacrifice, for death, 316–17
Noah, 101, 199, 381
Noahic distinction, between clean and unclean, 195
the *nokri*, 279
non-bloody sacrifice, 68
non-priests, use of sacrificial gifts, 348–49
normal discharge
    with men, 232
    with women, 233–34
the North, representing night, darkness, and death, 50
Numbers (book of), transition between Leviticus and, 456–58
numbers (symbolic). *See* forty; seven; ten

oath, swearing a, 106
obedience, 174, 320–21, 326
objects
    called holy, 7
    leprosy on, 217
    significance and value assigned by God, 412
obligations
    to animals, 461–62
    to houses, 462
    to land, 462–64
    to people, 460–61
    with respect to what is banned, 466–68
    to the tithe of cattle and livestock, 469
    toward Yahweh, 459
    for which exemption could be obtained, 459–64

SUBJECT INDEX

for which exemption could not be obtained, 464–70
occasions, of defilement with blood, 272
occupational labor, done on the Sabbath day, 373
offense, committing against Yahweh, 125
offerings, 80, 83
official sins, atonement for, 251
officiating priest, precedence with the eating of the meat of the sin offering, 138
oil
    added to the grain offering, 69, 75
    for anointing, 152
    for consecration, 150
    from "crushed" olives, 411
    represented the work of the Spirit, 226
    symbolizing the Holy Spirit, 76
old age, not always representing wisdom, 320
Old Testament, being too oriented toward, 242
olive oil, 75
omens, no interpreting, 315
omer, as the term for both sheaf and for a unit of weight, 395
oppression, Yahweh opposing, 321
ordained leaders, lifting up hands, 163
"ordination offering," 145
original sin, 207, 209, 229
"other person," as your neighbor, 304
"the other person," loving, 305
oven, dead animal in, 193
ox, not muzzling treading the grain, 309

pagan defilement, God forbidding, 292
pagan derivation, idolatrous manners, actions, gestures of, 273
pagan feasts, 395
pagan figures, stones representing, 444
pagan ideas, 274
pagan lifestyle
    Leviticus 18–20 not allowing, 282–332
    making a separation from, 295–96
    no element of fitting for holy people, 306–7

not becoming guilty of adopting, 313
pagan manner, priests not grieving in, 341–42
pagan practices, liver of sacrificial animals and, 87
pagan priests, 89, 333–34
pagan sanctuaries, parallels with the tabernacle, 19
pagan sexual defilement, not allowed among Israel, 291–92
pagan sorrow, not permitted, 197
pagan theologizing and philosophizing, by Christians about God and about humanity, 281
pagan worship, 79, 444
paganism
    allowing to slip in, 105
    avoiding the dark shadow of, 330
    boundaries with, 314
    danger of slipping away into, 275
    God called us out of, 94
    regression of Christians back to, 281
    sin placing into the sphere of, 115
    terrain of, 256
    Yahweh abhorred, 182
pagans
    affixing various figures to their seals, 370
    aligned with the devil and with death, 198
    filled with fear of death, 197, 341, 342
    having no hope, 316
    idolatrous drinking of blood among, 38, 142
    only death among, 340
    sacrificed hair to the idols, 315
    superstitious practices among, 229
Palestine, rainfall in, 188
Paradisal element, of the peace offering, 86
Paradise of God, that will descend one day to earth, 56
parents, 298, 320, 326
partisan class justice, 303
Passover
    celebrated "before the face of Yahweh," 387

SUBJECT INDEX

Passover (continued)
  celebrated in the first or second month, 437
  compared to Feast of Booths, 404
  feast of, 385–92
  instituted in Egypt as an annual memorial, 382
  institution of, 385–86
  symbolic significance of, 387–92
Passover feast, 392, 393
Passover lamb, bore the character of a sacrifice, 388–89
Passover Lamb, Jesus of Nazareth appeared as, 27
Passover meal, participating in, 183
patience, of God toward the pre-Flood world, 101
Paul
  acted in ignorance persecuting the church of God, 103
  appealed to divine care for Israel's priests, 144
  on being imitators of God, 296
  commanding Christians with believing slaves not to act harshly and unjustly toward them, 452
  confessed his sin once again, 255
  on the death of Christ, 26–27
  on the duty of Christians to care for those burdened with preaching and teaching, 475
  on before the foundation of the world, 472
  on God holding Israel in custody under the law, 336
  on the inclusion of the Gentiles by faith, 450
  last visit to Jerusalem, 238–39, 240
  on not grieving like the pagans do, 316
  on not muzzling an ox treading out the grain, 475
  participating in a sacrifice ceremony in the temple, 239
  protected against Judaizing Christianity, 199
  on sanctification, 55
  testifying to his readers that they are no longer "under the Law," 435
  viewed all days in the same way, 439
  warning Christians from Gentile background of God's punishment, 452
  on without a Sabbath day, 439
payment of debts, in the Sabbath year, 420
peace (*shalom*), much wider meaning in Israel, 85
peace offering(s), 84–95
  for Aaron and his sons, 155
  atoning character of, 74
  brought with a clear conscience, 93
  commands for the priests concerning, 140
  emphasizing glorification, 112
  kinds of, 91, 350
  not confusing with a sin offering, 119
  not fully completed by Aaron and his surviving sons, 172
  for the people as a cow and a ram, 161
  portion of assigned to the priests, 144
  "portions" of, 91–95, 144
  presented by Moses, 18
  referred to an entire group of sacrifices, 85
  regarding, 350–52
  spoke of atonement to an extent, 86
  as a teaching illustration, 300
  teaching of remaining valid for us, 95
peace offering meal, 56, 86–87, 91, 300
peace with God, 24, 94
Pentateuch, endings of books of, 456
Pentecost, 387, 393–97
people of Israel
  Aaron's first blessing of, 162–63
  abstaining from all work, 401–2
  by the atonement covering in the holy of holies, 51
  under the ban were put to death, 467
  keeping separate from their uncleanness, 234

SUBJECT INDEX

leprosy in, 219–20
obligations with respect to, 460–61
permitted to repay God, 55
received the clearest proofs of God's love, 67
represented by the altar of incense, 113
sacrifice for on the Day of Atonement, 248–49
people of life, 8, 203, 221
people of Yahweh, as holy people, 345
perfection, number ten symbolized, 391
Persians, isolated a woman who had given birth for forty days, 283
personal freedom, receiving back in the Year of Jubilee, 428
personal sin, babies committing no, 207
persons
    application of the Year of Jubilee to, 428–35
    blaspheming God's name, 413–15
    buying property back, 427
    consecrating in service, 460
    divided into two parts, 370
    as the object of the atonement, 30
    possessed significance and value, 412
pesach, meaning to pass over, to spare, 388
pestilence, Yahweh sending among people, 446
Peter, 201, 238, 452
pharaohs, some married full sisters, 289
Pharisaic line of thinking, characterizing slavish Judaism, 288
Pharisaism, 289
Pharisees, 201
Phinehas, meaning Nubian, 238
physical defects, excluding priests from service, 44, 346–47
piety, self-made punished, 174
pigs, 190–91, 200
plague of hail, in the land of Egypt, 471
Plinius, 351
plot of land, receiving back, 427
plow, not harnessing an ox and a donkey to, 307
polygamy, 286, 289, 290
the poor, 97, 396, 428–31

poor and the sojourner, leaving something for, 301
pork, 182, 200
possessions, devoting some part of to Yahweh, 467
power, misusing over one's neighbor, 302
praise of God, burnt offering related to, 66
praise offering, 85, 91
praise songs, psalms of thanksgiving, 94
praising and exalting God, never exceeding any limits, 66
prayer, 76, 137, 250, 399
preamble or introduction, to a covenant, 361
predators, forbidden to be eaten, 196
predatory animals, 446, 449
"prelude," of Leviticus 16, 247
premeditation, transgressing God's commandments with, 378
preparatory commands, for the Day of Atonement, 247–49
priest(s)
    allowed to eat meat of the sin offering for the laity, 118, 120
    assessing the produce of a field, 464
    blowing trumpets, 398
    bodies anointed with oil, 76
    caught blood and sprinkled it on the altar, 50
    commands for, 338, 339–43
    commands for concerning guilt offerings, 139–40
    commands for concerning peace offerings, 140
    commands for concerning the grain offering, 137–38
    commands for concerning the sin offering, 138
    commands for involving the daily morning and evening sacrifices, 136–37
    commands to see that Israelites not use any fat or blood, 140–43
    with defects not excluded from enjoying the "food" of Yahweh, 347

priest (continued)
- depositing twelve loaves of bread on every Sabbath day, 412
- estimating the expense of the ram, 128
- forbidden to render their service in the sanctuary naked, 334
- God demanding respect for holiness, 167
- God desired exemplary conduct from, 166, 170
- keeping holy, 338–47
- keeping the lamps of the lampstand burning, 411
- manual for as they instruct Israel, 179–81
- as mediators, 29, 113, 337
- not allowed contact with a corpse, 335
- not allowed to eat meat of the animal of the sin offering slaughtered for the (high) priest or the entire people, 118–19
- not allowed to marry three kinds of women, 343
- not functioning as doctors, 221, 228, 232
- not permitted to use alcohol during duties, 180
- physical defects excluding from service, 346–47
- placing sacrifices on the altar, 20
- pointing the way in complicated situations, 181
- portion of the peace offering designated for, 89–91
- publicly identifying Aaron and his sons as, 156
- as *qorbanim* par excellence, 342
- requirements for, 44
- in Rome could become defiled by death, 334
- as the saints among the saints, 341
- sin offering for, 97, 109
- sprinkled blood, 64
- sprinkling, dabbing, and smearing of blood performed by, 51
- sprinkling the blood as exclusively the work of, 22
- task and place of in the Old Testament, 175
- use of sacrificial gifts, 347–48
- "worshiping" the Holy One, 9

priest of Jupiter, in Rome in allowed to marry a widow, 333–34

priesthood (of Leviticus)
- by the altar of incense in the holy place, 51
- Horeb covenant rested on, 271
- income for, 470
- opposition to death, 339
- people received the law under, 266
- sacrifice for on the Day of Atonement, 248–49
- Torah or Teaching of Israel rested upon, 150

priestly character, of the conclusion of the sacrificial Torah, 136
priestly covenant, 252
priestly families, 348
priestly garments, robe woven as one piece, 339
priestly kingdom of Israel, "the foundation of the world" referring to, 470
priestly wardrobe, life for Israel with Yahweh testified to, 344
priest's daughter, burned with fire for committing immorality, 169
"the prince of this world," as death, 222
produce of the land, 462–63, 468
program schedule, sacrificial Torah nothing like, 173
"proleptic reports," in Holy Scripture, 381
promised land, 284, 415–16
"proof of access," not throwing away, 9
property, buying and selling, 425–27
property rights, injuring, 127
prostitution, sacred, 294, 316–17
Psalm 100, as "a psalm for giving thanks," 94
Pseudo-Barnabas, on the second goat, 263

SUBJECT INDEX

public reading, of covenant documents, 421
punishment
    of death by fire, 169
    on the Israelites, 289, 446–47, 449–50
    for stealing, 130
    viewing the killing of the animal as an act of, 26
pure Israelite girl, as a picture of life, 346
purification
    duty of, 199
    by fire as an obvious notion, 54
    of God's people, 259
    of Israel, 257
    of lepers, 220–27
    not mentioned in Leviticus 18, 292
    of our sins in Christ, 258
    of priesthood and people, 266
purification sacrifices, 208, 234
purifying work, of salt, 78
purity laws, number seven appearing in, 204
putting to death, distinguished from sprinkling blood, 22

quails, Israelites got to eat the meat of, 357
quantities
    of flour, oil, and wine depending on the size of the animal, 81
    of the ingredients of the drink offering and the grain offering, 80
    of wine, 73, 80
quarrels, indicating hearts hardened against each other, 303
Qumran, Jewish writings discovered in, 270

rabbinism, not at all related to the Old Testament, 184
rainfall, 188, 446
ram
    as a guilt offering to Yahweh, 127–28, 131, 133
    slaughtered as a burnt offering for Aaron and his sons, 154

"ram of ordination," or "consecration," sacrificed for Aaron and his sons, 155
raping, of a female slave of another man, 312
"raw flesh," translating as "healthy skin," 220
"real property," Year of Jubilee applicable to, 425
reconciliation, 15–41
"redeemer," buying back land that had been sold, 427
redemption, eternal secured by the blood of Christ, 261
reformation, as not revolution, 287
Reformed ancestors, wanted nothing to do with feast days, 403
Reformed churches, fasting in, 265
regeneration, 367, 368
regulations, about "impedimenta" or hindrances to marriage, 331
religious feasts, slaves allowed to participate, 433
religious-ethical order, establishment of, 472
remembrance, coming to God's, 83
remnant, brought back to the land of the fathers, 450
remorse, a thief filled with, 100
repayments, Law that God gave at Horeb stipulating, 429–30
repentance and conversion, among those led away, 450
reptiles, in Palestine, 189
rest, on the Sabbath, 370–73
rest of rests (*shabbath shabbaaton*), indicating the superlative degree, 400
"rest of the rest," expressing the superlative grade, 385
restitution, 127
restored concourse between God and people, as the goal of God, 165
resurrection, no real apart from real death, 41
resurrection chapter, Leviticus 11 as, 200
revelation, beliefs due to, 286
Ridderbos, J., 36

SUBJECT INDEX

right foot, dabbing blood on the big toe of, 155
right hind quarter, shank as, 89
right side, as a person's most important side, 155
rings, exchanging in a wedding, 185
robbery, punishment for, 130
robing
    Aaron, 151
    Aaron's sons, 153
Roman Catholic Church, struggle with, 93
Roman soldiers, salt payment of, 77
roof, putting a railing around, 308
ruler, sacrificing a male goat for, 109
Ruth, 302, 321

Sabbath (*shabbath*)
    applied also to slaves, 433
    extent of, 354
    as key to Leviticus 23–25, 353
    spending the great Day of Atonement like, 265
Sabbath circles, dominated Israel's entire life, 354
Sabbath commandment
    of complete rest on the seventh day, 360
    three parts of, 363–70
Sabbath day(s)
    all work forbidden on, 436
    as genuine teaching days, 353
    getting to know the character of Israel's weekly, 375–77
    as the Horeb covenant in miniature, 378
    Israelite celebration of as entirely unique, 380
    no longer exists for Christians, 439
    as not a creation ordinance, 380–82
    not mentioned in Exodus, 355–60
    observing, 353–440
    regarding the weekly, 355–82
    violating, 102
Sabbath idea, as the main motif of the festival cycle of Israel, 235
Sabbath violator, 99, 102
Sabbath year, 415–23
    added to the Sabbath day, 373
    calculated with a calendar, 416
    fixing Israel's attention on the Horeb covenant, 422
    informed about in Lev 25:1–7, 417
    institution came from God, 420–21
    land receiving, 450
    observation of, 419
    relating to possessing the land, 415
Sabbaths
    entire cycle of occurring at various times, 383
    God not permitting to be violated with impunity, 447
    keeping, 444
    overview of all, 354
    using interchangeably with "feasts," 297
sabbatical year, as the seventh year, 372
"sacred marriage," phenomenon of, 290
sacred obligation, making a vow had to be viewed as, 461
sacred shekel, 464
sacrifice, 16–19, 22
"sacrifice for sin," "sin offering" as, 98
"sacrifice of filling," 156
sacrifice offering (*zebach*), slaughtered Passover lamb called, 389
Sacrifice Torah, 450
sacrifices
    of Aaron for himself, 160–61
    of Aaron for the people, 161–62
    giving too narrow a meaning to, 58
    of Horeb instituted by God as temporary, 243
    instructing Israel in the Gospel, 46–48
    kinds of, 20
    Leviticus 1–7 dealing with, 10
    mediating character of, 21
    as not automatic instruments, 47
    offered in the forecourt of the tabernacle, 275
    at the Pentecost feast, 395–97
    for priesthood and people on the great Day of Atonement, 248–49

SUBJECT INDEX

relinquishing to God something that one owned and valued highly, 42
  required from the cleansed leper, 225
  for a woman following childbirth, 206–10
sacrifices of the Law, as symbolic teaching tools, 47
sacrificial animal(s)
  Bähr trivialized the death of, 24
  blood of sprinkled on the altar by the priest, 21
  bringing with one's own hands, 49
  determining the kind and size of, 80
  inadmissible defects in, 10
  representing Christ, 27
  requirements for, 42–45
  something burning from every, 53
sacrificial automatism, warnings against, 47
sacrificial blood, 28, 51, 110
sacrificial ceremony, concluded with a meal, 56
sacrificial gifts, keeping holy, 347–52
sacrificial Torah
  assuring Israel of God's veracity and good intentions, 48
  beginning anew with the burnt offering, 63
  burning as delightful bringing pleasant aroma before Yahweh, 53
  conclusion of the second section of, 144
  Leviticus 1–7 as, 2, 39
  postscript in connection with, 144–45
  second section of, 136–45
  understanding via the Holy Spirit now called the Spirit of Christ, 145
salt, 76–77, 78, 81
salt fellowship, 92
salvation, 49, 187
Samaritan, parable of the compassionate, 305
Samaritans, gospel preached first to, 237

Samuel, 269, 318–19
sanctification, 52–56, 86, 112, 132
Sanctifier, God's point of departure as, 326
sanctions, 448, 456
sanctuary
  defiling by participating in a sacrifice meal as a murderer, 324
  income for, 470
  purifying the entire, 266
  reverencing, 444
  unnoticed transgressions against, 255
sanctuary and cultic personnel, publicly connected to each other, 149
sanctuary of Christ, not withholding our money and goods from, 475
Satan
  attempting to turn the Christian church into a Jewish church, 142
  keeping people stupid, 186
  life and death battle against, 198
  pushed into retreat by apostolic preaching, 115
  scriptural mentions of, 257
  terrible role of, 256
satisfactio vicaria, rendering a substitutionary satisfaction to God, 22
"satisfaction theory of the atonement," Bähr's antipathy toward, 25
Saul, 277, 318, 319
saving deeds, of God, 269
Savior, 93, 389, 391. *See also* Jesus Christ
scarlet yarn (*sheni thola 'ath*), as crimson, 224
Schleiermacher, F., 23
sealing function, of the sacrificial meal, 57
Second Commandment, on punishment to the third and fourth generation, 290
second great commandment, from Christ, 300
security deposits, widespread among Israel, 131
seed, not sowing two kinds of, 306–11

505

SUBJECT INDEX

seed grain, dead animal fell or lay in, 193
self-directed sacrifices, 274–75, 277
Sermon on the Mount, 305
servile labor, prohibition of, 436
serving Israelite, as a day laborer and not a serf, 432
servitude, not hounding with harshness in cases of, 431–33
seven
　as the imprint of Yahweh, 370
　as the number of the covenant, 398
　remembrance of creation associated with, 366
　suited Yahweh in a special way, 369
　as a symbolic number, 114, 221, 400, 406
seven "complete Sabbaths" counting from Passover, 393
seven times, leper being cleansed sprinkled, 225
sevenfold sprinkling of blood, pointing in the direction of the Holy of Holies, 113
seventh day
　people rested on, 359
　reserved for honoring Yahweh, 371
　as the Sabbath day as a sign forever, 376
　shabbath on, 358
seventh month, most of the holy days of the entire year in, 398
seventh Sabbath year, Year of Jubilee occurred repeatedly in, 424
seventh year, 418–19
sexual defilement, not allowed among Israel, 291–92
sexual discharges, as events in human life, 235
sexual flowing of blood, 233
sexual immorality, 184, 312, 316, 317
sexual intercourse, 202
sexual matters, near the boundary between death and life, 229
sexual relations
　between close blood relatives among the Canaanites, 290
　flow of blood connected with, 209
　forbidden, 293–94
　with the wife of his father, 327
sexuality
　defilement of priests in terms of, 342–43
　defilement of the high priest in terms of, 345–46
sexuality or sexual life, as a main subject, 338
shabbat shabbaaton, giving the land every seventh year, 418
shabbath, 358, 363–64
"a *shabbath* in honor of Yahweh," for the entire day, 365
shabbaton, as the First Day of the Seventh Month, 398
shallem, 84
shalom or peace, 85, 162
the shank of the sacrificial animal, for the officiating priest, 89
shanks, of the animal as both hind legs, 64
shavath, meaning cease, stop, rest, 358
shedding of blood, 26, 40
sheep
　brought as a guilt offering, 135
　given as security, 131
　as a peace offering animal, 88
　sacrificing of three, 227
　as a sin offering, 97
　treatment of the fatty tail of, 88–89, 117–18
　two as a peace offering at Pentecost, 395
shekels of silver, amount for types of persons, 460
shekels of the sanctuary, payment in, 128
Shelomith, the daughter of Dibri, of the tribe of Dan, 413
shophar, trumpet, 424
showbread, golden table of, 412–13
a sign, Sabbath day as, 375
silver, as the usual means of payment, 128
Simon the Leper, 216
sin(s)
　committed without premeditation atoned for, 255

SUBJECT INDEX

covered and atoned, 48
covered by blood and sprinkling, 22
forgiveness of, 23–24
forgiving unintentional, 105
of hatred in your heart, 304
"with a high hand" as intentional, 98
of the Israelites putting on the goat's head, 254
as the object of the atonement, 30
our death as retribution for, 26
removal of through God and God alone, 47
sin offering spoke of the covering of, 206
unintentional, 98
wages of as death, 49
for which the guilt offering was brought, 123
for which the sin offering was brought, 123
for which the sin offering was instituted, 114–15
for which there was no pardon, 99–100
sin offering, 96–122
for Aaron, 160
actions connected with, 117–22
actions related to the blood of, 110–17
bringing not indicating guilt, 202–3
burned outside the camp, 119, 264
for a cleansed leper, 135, 226
as a closed book for many people, 117
commands for the priests concerning, 138
compared to the guilt offering, 123–24
emphasizing justification, 112
Jesus as a genuine, 121
kinds of animals used for, 108–10
Moses found something had gone wrong, 172
never joined with a peace offering, 118
not from committing a crime, 206
not suited for leprous houses, 227
preached atonement with God, 160
prescribed about unintentional sins, 103
reason for bringing, 65
separate section regulating bringing a sheep, 89
for a woman who has given birth, 206
Sinai covenant, God reminding the Israelites of, 369
sinners, 133–34, 184
sinning once, as a slip up, 116–17
sister, sexual intercourse with, 328
sister-in-law, not having sexual relations with, 293
sixth day, 357, 358
skin, of the animal used for the burnt offering, 63, 139
skin disease (vitiligo), as the disease described in Leviticus, 215
slaughter, of the sacrificial animal, 49–50
slaughtered animals, meat of spoiling quickly, 91
slavery, as impermissible, 286–87
slaves, 432, 433
slaying of an animal, 26
smoke, from Israel's forecourt, 137
social character, 362–63, 365
social context, 371, 417
Sodom, God punished in Abraham's day, 330
sojourner(s)
having a fixed residence, 426–27
loving, 321
oppressing, 303
prosperous if Israelites forsake Yahweh, 433
representing a possible doorway for paganism, 415
some accustomed to using blood, 277
as well as the native who blasphemes shall be put to death, 414
who left Egypt along with Israel, 413
Solomon, meaning prince of peace, 85
song of Moses, in Exodus 15, 355
sons of Aaron, as priests, 149

SUBJECT INDEX

soul (*nefesh*)
    as the best choice for translating *nefesh*, 37
    in the blood, 28, 33–34, 39, 40
    as eating and drinking, 33
    making atonement for, 30
    putting up as ransom for another, 40
    translating as life, 36
"soup vegetables," Pharisees requiring a tenth part of garden produce, 468
Spirit, gifts of bestowed upon Gentiles, 238
Spirit of Christ, 116, 173, 174. See also Holy Spirit
spiritists, turning to, 318, 324–25
"the spirits of the dead," consulting, 299
spring, dead animal in, 193
sprinkled blood, with the sin offering, 110
sprinkling of blood (*zaraq*), 22, 50, 64
sprinkling with oil, 227
stages, of the actual atonement, 250–53
"statutes," keeping, 305
"statutes, ordinances, and laws," extensive list of, 448
stealing, 130, 302, 312
stillborn child, as colorless, 217
stoning, 274
story, role in Leviticus, 11
stove, dead animal in, 193
"strange fire," 168, 169
stranger [*ger*] sojourning, with you
    treating as the native among you, 304–5
"strangers" (*ger*), as a more general term, 426
strangled animals, abstaining from, 143
strictness
    not becoming guilty of too severe, 313
    with respect to marriage, 331–32
style, of Leviticus, 9–11
substantive treaty text, in Leviticus, 270
substitutionary atonement, Bähr's antipathy toward, 25
substitutionary death, idea of, 40

sukkah, meaning hut, but not quite booth, 408
Sunday as "Sabbath," as incorrect, 440
sweep or sweep away, as the meaning of *kpr*, 28
swimming insects, 192
symbolic deed, release of the second goat in the desert as, 263
symbolic meaning, of the numbers seven and forty, 205
symbolic-didactic purpose, of God with the Sabbath year, 421
Symbolik des Mosaischen Cultus (Bähr), 21
symbolism
    ancient Eastern peoples having feeling for, 195
    of the application of blood, 51
    in Leviticus, 11, 182, 259
    of the tabernacle, 48
    in the Torah of Horeb, 334
    using various means of visual instruction, 306

tabernacle
    anointing, 152
    defiling through improper grieving, 170
    God's accepting of, 15
    mandating for constructing, 374, 377
    one month between the completion of and the census of the fighting men, 3
    as the place where Yahweh spoke to Moses, 442
    purchasing needed material for from passing caravans, 429
    symbolism of, 48, 56
    work done for not leading people to forget the Fourth Commandment, 375
tablets, smashed by Moses were the covenant, 377
tame animals, as sacrificial animals, 43–44
tassel, 183, 307–8, 369
tastiness, of salt, 77
tattooing, original purpose of, 315

SUBJECT INDEX

teachers, 221
teaching, 180, 298
teaching and practice given at home, ignoring, 326
teachings
 of Leviticus, 473
 not being led away by diverse and strange, 120
ten, symbolized perfection, 391, 400
Ten Commandments, 362, 370
ten spies, episode of, 415–16
Ten Words
 all related to Israel's covenant with Yahweh, 371
 announcement of, 235
 day of the proclamation of, 166
 prologue of, 284
 reading in Sunday worship gatherings, 184
 written on each tablet, 362
tent of meeting, 3, 4, 252
tenth day, of the seventh month for the Great Day of Atonement, 400
tenth plague, 388
tents, living in recalled as a matter of great joy, 408
Tertullian, explanation of the two goats, 262
"thank offerings." *See* peace offering(s)
thieves, 99, 100
thigh
 heaving of, 90
 for the priest, 91
things
 called holy, 7
 leprosy on, 217
"things of nothing," idols as, 298
thrown blood, resembling sowing, 110
thumb, dabbing blood on the right, 155
times
 of the Passover feast, 391
 of the Pentecost feast, 393
Timothy, 244
tithes, 57, 58, 127, 468
"torah," as simply the teaching that God, 359
Torah (Instruction, Knowledge, Law)
 altar fire and altar salt of, 77

 on clean and unclean animals, 188–201
 commands to care well for the poor, 301
 evangelical (gospel-filled) character of, 131, 135
 filled with warnings, 115
 fixed in written form, 287–88
 God gave to Moses for Israel at Horeb, 199
 harness arming Israel against paganism in Canaan, 325
 on how to interact with God, 8
 indirectly connected to Israel's health, 181
 laws of sacrifice in, 132
 minimum required age of a sacrificial animal, 351
 as not a burdensome straightjacket, 173
 protecting Israel, 105
 read publicly every Sabbath year at the Feast of Booths, 421–22
 received through the mediation of angels, 258
 serious with regard to marriage, 312
tow 'ebah, meaning abomination, 317
transference, laying on of hands as, 49
"transgressions," of the people of Israel, 255
translations, using more than one, 31
translators, omitting the word soul (*nefesh*), 35
transvestitism, 307, 308
treaty, between pharaoh Ramses II and the Hittite suzerain Hattusili III, 454–56
trees, 189, 313–14
trek from Egypt to Horeb, 404–5
tribal head, sacrificing a male goat for, 109
tribal leader, sin offering for, 97, 111
trumpets, priests blowing on two silver, 398
truth, as indispensable for liars, 18
tsara 'ath, 213, 214, 218
twelve tribes, representing the atonement of, 156

SUBJECT INDEX

"types," of Christ, 174
tzitzit (button, knob, knot, or tassel, with a dark blue thread), every Israelite having to wear, 307–8

Ugarit, sexual intercourse with animals, 328
ulcerations, of *tsara 'ath* could heal, 213
unchaste kidnapping, as not adultery, 311–13
unchaste woman, as a "public woman," 343
"unclean," not a synonym of dirty or messy or unhygienic, 181
unclean animals, 43, 465
unclean dead animals, defiling a person, 192–93
unclean insects, 196
unclean large animals that have died, 192–93
unclean meat, giving to pagans, 198
unclean men, not to remain within Israel's camp, 232
unclean person, not permitted to approach the sanctuary, 180
unclean small animals, defilement through, 193
unclean spirit, passing through waterless places, 256
"Unclean! Unclean!" loud cry of, 217
uncleanness
    for abnormal discharge of a man, 231, 232
    of males and females, 228–35
    from the monthly blood flow, 204
    priests keeping people of Israel separate from, 180
    priests not allowed to eat from the gifts of the Israelites to Yahweh, 348
    of a woman following childbirth, 203–5, 207
unfaithfulness, 125, 452
unintentional direct offenses *ma'al*, against Yahweh, 134–35
unintentional offense, against Yahweh, 125–29
unintentional sins, 98, 101, 104

unleavened bread, 388, 390
unwritten laws, power of, 288
use, of sacrificial gifts, 347–49
king Uzziah, Bible story about, 212

valuation of persons, vowing to the Lord involving, 460
value, of the sacred shekel, 464
vegetative fire offerings, smelling of Israel's labor, 59
vengeance, not taking against the sons of your own people, 304
vicarious atonement (*satisfactio vicaria*), according to Kurtz, 25
vicarious death, 38
visual instruction, constantly reminding of holiness, 314
"vitiligo and related diseases," 213, 216
voice of the Lord your God, listening to, 356
voluntary poverty, fest of, 408
votive offering, 85–86, 91
vow to God, paying as a votive offering, 85
vow to Yahweh, annulling, 457–58
vows, 135, 453, 463
Vulgate, 125, 214, 424

wallets, opening for the proclamation of the gospel, 475
war, visiting the Israelites with as punishment, 446
washing with water, before installation, 151
wave offering, 90, 226
weak gender, as more vulnerable to death, 205
the week, making its appearance in Israel's life, 358
weekly Sabbath day, 438
what is banned, obligations with respect to, 466–68
white, Scripture about in connection with leprosy, 216–17
white coloring of the skin, of *tsara 'ath*, 213

SUBJECT INDEX

white garments of the great Day of Atonement, Aaron taking off, 260
whole animals, as sacrificial animals, 44–45
whole congregation, sin offering for, 97
wickedness, of Canaanites, 7
widow, 345, 346
wife, priest grieving for his deceased, 340–41
wife of another Israelite, not having sexual relations with, 293
wife of his father, not having sexual relations with, 293
wild animals, not suitable for sacrifice, 42
wilderness of Sin, three-day trek through, 355
wilderness travels, prohibition on eating fat, 141
will of Yahweh, body of practical knowledge of, 288
wine, 69, 72, 73
wine or strong drink, prohibited for the priests, 167
winged insects, not to be eaten by Israelites, 192
witchcraft, not practicing, 142
woman, who suffered from a flow of blood, 308
woman a sister, not having sexual relations with, 293
women
    abnormal discharge with, 234–35
    after giving birth bringing a sin offering, 104
    approaching any animal, 327
    eating their children in besieged Samaria, 449
    with an issue involving pagan immorality, 342–43
    normal discharge with, 233–34
wood, piece of to turn bad water into good, 355
wood gatherer, committed covenant breaking against Yahweh, 379
wooden piece of equipment, dead animal in, 193

work, clarifying regarding the Sabbath, 364
work-related activities, associated with constructing God's sanctuary, 375
"world," not referring to heaven and earth, 471
worship in the temple, continuing as obsolete, 120
worst, placing first, 323
wrath, of God, 9, 377

Yahweh (the One Who Is Near). *See also* God
    abandonment of, 115
    abusing the name of, 102
    appearing in the cloud over the mercy seat, 164
    atoned by means of the blood, 29
    aversion to all forms of filth, 290
    aversions against all kinds of death, 285
    called Aaron as Israel's high priest, 164
    commanded that a man be stoned to death, 414
    committing offense against, 125
    covered and effected atonement, 29
    declared Israel would have no other god or gods, 361
    delivered Israel from the house of bondage of Egypt, 361
    desire to come dwell in the midst of his people, 442
    direction to Israel on the use the name of, 361
    executing justice for defenseless people, 321
    finding the guilty party, 324
    focusing attention of the Israelites on the Horeb covenant, 473
    forbidden to infringe upon the rights of, 459
    functioned as king over Israel at Horeb, 361
    as the God of life, 198
    God revealed his name as, 381, 442

Yahweh (continued)
  gospel for that time encapsulated in the name, 316
  as holy and Israel must correspond, 296
  indirectly offending, 131
  injuring the property rights of, 127
  intensifying punishments, 446
  intentional indirect offenses (*ma'al*) against, 133–34
  intentional offense against, 129–33
  as Israel's Landlord, 19, 57
  laid claim to Canaan, 417
  ma'al against, 130, 134–35
  meeting his people at the altar, 57
  as merciful, 340
  name signifying "Savior of life," 197
  as not an *elohim*, a god, like the other gods, 284
  now known to us as our God and Father in Christ, 185
  Old Testament ascribing to him no trace of sexuality, 290
  portion of the peace offering designated for, 87–89
  prepared to save his people at any cost, 19
  preparing the Israelites for entering the Horeb covenant, 359
  remaining the owner of the Israelites, 432, 434
  spoke in a very abbreviated manner, 356
  spoke to Moses and Aaron, 180
  talked with Moses "mouth to mouth," 4, 379
  tethering his people to his sanctuary, 474
  tolerating no competitor, 299
  tolerating no confusion, 167
  unintentional direct offenses *ma 'al* against, 134–35
  unintentional offense against, 125–29
  as very holy, 8
  wanted to destroy Aaron, 377
  ways of showing love to, 298–300
Year of Jubilee
  application to various matters, 425–28
  beginning like an ordinary Sabbath year, 424
  cycle of Sabbaths concluded with, 423–35
  debtor receiving back the property of his ancestors, 432
  each receiving back his original property, 427
  first came into force, 419
  institution of, 423–25
  land returned to the person's ownership in, 462
  names of, 424–25
  regaining freedom in, 431
  relating to possessing the land, 415
  "years of discretion," reaching, 207
  yom teru 'a, as day of gladness or day of the blasts, 398
  young animal, not to be sacrificed on the same day as its mother, 351
  young livestock, as the "produce" of the flock, 469
  "your feast." *See* Feast of Booths
  yovel ("Year of Jubilee"), referring to a ram's horn, 424

zeal for the Law, 237, 240, 244
Zechariah, 76, 398–99
king Zedekiah, sin committed by, 126
zikron teru 'a, as "a memorial of blowing of trumpets," 399

Scripture Index

OLD TESTAMENT

Genesis

	2, 5, 18, 21, 42, 381
1:14	383
1:20–21	37
1:24	37, 38
2	381
2:3	380, 382
2:3 NIV	380, 381, 382
2:4	381, 382
2:7	36, 37
2:16–17	26
2:17	49
2:19	37
2:22	229
2:24	234, 340, 382
3	257
3–4	19
3:6	26
3:15	17, 18
3:16	229
3:19	49
4	16
4:4	17, 71
6:14	28
6:17	34
7:2	182, 195
7:4	205
8:20	17, 65
8:21	53
9:2–4	17
9:3	195
9:4	38, 40
9:10	37
9:12	37
9:15	37
9:16	37
12:1–3	450
12:2–3	360
12:3	472
12:7	18
15	360
15:12	93
15:16	289, 391, 457, 467
15:16b	330
15:18	93, 361
17:1	360
17:11	375
18:20	330
18:22	258
19:1	258
19:5	294
19:24–25	330
20:12	286
21:28–31	369
22:2	65
23:4	426
28:12	258
28:18	75, 443
32:1	258
33:17	407
35:20	443
37:34	217
38:24	327
41:45	5, 238
41:50	238
43:32	92

SCRIPTURE INDEX

Genesis (continued)

45:18	87
48:14	89
49:6	32
50:7	357

Exodus

	2, 3, 15, 17, 20, 24, 69, 149, 150, 151, 158, 180, 183, 247, 269, 271, 279, 285, 351, 359, 365, 367, 380, 381, 412, 462, 470
1:14	390
2:10	5
3:1	273
3:12	135, 406
3:22	5, 428
4:6	216, 217
5	361
6:12	381
6:19	291
9:3	386
9:6	357
9:18	471
9:24	471
10:25	65
11	385
12	373, 385, 387, 391
12:1–28	385
12:2	386, 391, 418, 424
12:8	78, 390
12:13	388
12:14–16	382
12:16	373
12:17	3
12:18	369
12:22	224
12:25–26	135
12:26	298, 392
12:27	388, 389
12:29–42	385
12:30	388
12:36	428
12:38	413
12:43–49	183
13	391, 465
13:2	208
13:3–10	385
13:4	3, 418, 424
13:5	135
13:7	78
13:8	388, 392
13–14	355
15	355
15:11	7
15:25–26	356
15:26	181
16	235, 355, 356, 357, 358, 363, 364, 380, 383
16:1	360
16:2	364
16:3	356
16:4	357, 359
16:4, 29b	357
16:5	357, 358
16:10	164, 364
16:13	357
16:15–16	357
16:22	357
16:22–30	99
16:23	358, 365, 373
16:23 ESV	363
16:23 KJV	363–64
16:26	358, 359, 364
16:28–30	359
16:29b	357
16:36	395
18:11	414
18:12	65
19:1	3, 360
19:3	269
19:3–6	269, 270
19:3b	269
19:4a	269
19:5–6	186
19:6	7, 67, 184, 185, 199, 226, 269, 335
19:7	320
19:10	402
19:14–15	402
19:15	235
19:16	424

SCRIPTURE INDEX

19–24	185	22:31	278, 279, 280
20	269, 270, 295, 299, 306, 355, 361, 369, 372, 380, 381	23	420
		23:1	371
		23:6	371
20:1–17	296	23:7	371
20:2	269, 284, 406	23:8	371, 445
20:3, 23	270	23:9	130, 321, 371
20:8	365	23:10–11	372, 416
20:8–11	99, 297, 306, 360, 364	23:11	418, 420
20:10	365, 433	23:12	370, 371, 372, 417, 433
20:10–11	383		
20:11	376, 382	23:13–33	297, 367, 444, 449
20:12	309, 320, 416	23:14–17	384, 387, 392, 417
20:12–16	457	23:15	406
20:13	468	23:16	393, 394, 406, 407
20:22	269	23:16b	405
20:22—23:33	269, 278, 284, 371, 429	23:19	310
		23:23	257
20:23	270	23:24	444
20–23	295	23:24–25	467
20:23	299	23:24–26	317
20–23	317	24	156
20:23	443	24:3	375
20:24	57, 58, 251	24:4	6
20:24–26	111	24:4a	444
20:28	414	24:5	18
21:2	372	24:8	51, 157
21:2–6	416, 431	24:9–11	169
21:6	319	24:11	161
21:10	202, 229	24:18	205
21:20	433, 468	25:2	90
21–23	367	25:22	379
21:26–27	433	25:29	72
21:28	328	25–31	374
21:32	461	27:20–21	76
22:1	130	28	82
22:2–3	100	28:1	150
22:7	130, 319	28:12	82
22:8	319	28:12, 29	398, 399
22:19	328	28:25–28	470
22:20	467	28:29	82
22:21–27	302	28–29	145
22:22–24	345	28:29	398, 399
22:25	429, 430	28:42	231
22:26–27	430	29	149, 159
22:27	319	29:14	119
22:28	319	29:22	76
22:30	198	29:23	75

SCRIPTURE INDEX

Exodus (continued)

29:26	150
29:32–33	158
29:36	401
29:38–46	137
29:40–41	71
29:41	53
29:42	3
29:44–46	165
29:46	197, 406
30	457
30:9	71, 73
30:10	252, 401
30:12–16	470
30:13	464
30:16	401
30:17	76
30:19–21	260
30:22–23	149
31:12–17	368, 373, 375
31:13	375
31:13–17	99
31:14	376, 379
31:17	183, 297, 376, 439
32	299
32:10	447
32:15	362
32:30	30
32:30–33	51
32–34	374, 377
33:11	379
34:1	377
34:6	377
34:10–20	297
34:10–26	269, 299, 367, 405, 444, 449, 465
34:11–17	467
34:13	444
34:14–17	270
34:15	324
34:15–16	287
34:17	299
34:18–21	406
34:18–26	384, 392
34:19–20	465
34:21	375
34:22	394, 406, 407
34:22b	405
34:26	310
34:28	205
35	377
35:1	374
35:1–3	99, 373, 377
35:5, 22	429
35:20	374
35:22	90, 374, 429
35:25	374
35:29	374
35–40	374, 377
37:16	72
38:8	429
38:21–31	429
38:25–26	457
38:25–28	470
38:26	464
40	2, 152
40:2, 17	3
40:15	157
40:17	3
40:35	164

Leviticus

	2, 3, 4, 7, 8, 10, 11, 16, 21, 39, 66, 105, 265, 381, 408, 413, 443, 449, 450, 453, 456, 457, 458, 470, 473, 475
1	2, 59, 66, 68, 71, 136
1:1	3, 4, 164
1:2	20, 42, 43, 55, 136
1–3	2
1:3	20
1:4	30, 49, 261
1:5	52, 64, 110
1–7	2, 10, 15, 16, 25, 34, 39, 149, 266
1:9	53, 58, 64, 162
1–10	411
1:11	52
1:13	53, 162
1:15	53
1:17	162
2	59, 68, 71, 73, 75, 77

SCRIPTURE INDEX

2:1	20	5:1	106
2:2	73, 76, 82	5:1–6	106
2:2–3	71	5:1–13	96, 100, 106, 107
2:3	467	5:2–3	106
2:4	20	5:4	106
2:5	75	5:5	49
2:5–10	75	5:6	29
2:8	90	5:7–10	106
2:9	82	5:9	97
2:11	79	5:11	69, 98
2:11–12	77	5:11–13	106
2:12	20, 79	5:14	125, 129
2:13	77, 79, 444	5:14—6:7	59, 123, 124, 125, 129, 133
2:14	386		
2:14–16	75	5:14–16	129, 130, 134
2:16	82	5:14–19	125, 128, 134
3	56, 59, 88	5:14–26	124
3:1	20, 87	5:15	125, 126, 128
3:1–5	88	5:17–19	128, 129, 130
3:2	110	5:19b	129
3:3–4	87	6	264
3:5	63, 65, 88	6:1	129
3:6–11	88	6:1–7	125, 129, 130, 133, 134
3:7	20		
3:10	9	6:2	130
3:11	55	6:5–6	54
3:12	20	6:8—7:38	136
3:12–15	88	6:8–13	65, 136
3:17	34	6:12	65
4	96, 100, 101, 104, 106, 124, 264	6:12–13	63
		6:14–18	137
4:1—5:13	59, 100, 271	6:16	82
4:2	98	6:19–23	138
4:3	96, 109, 113	6:24–30	138
4:6–7	113	6:25	119
4:10	63	6:26	118, 138
4:11–12	119	6:29	118, 138
4:13	20, 96, 98	6:30	119
4:14	20	7:1–10	139
4:17–18	113	7:2	110, 132
4:22	96, 98	7:3	20
4:23	20	7:6	451
4:27	96, 98	7:7	139
4:27–31	89	7:8	63, 139
4:28	107	7:9	139, 140
4:32–35	89	7:10	140
4:35	117	7:11–12	85
5	124, 125	7:11–21	140

Leviticus (continued)

7:11–27	56	8:24	157
7:12	75, 92, 451	8:25–28	157
7:13	85	8:28	157
7:14	92	8:29	150, 157
7:15	85, 91, 451	8:30	156
7:16	86, 91	8:31–32	157
7:17	53	8:33–36	158
7:18	91	9	150, 159, 168
7:19–20	91, 140	9:1	150, 159
7:20–21	180	9:2	159
7:22–23	140	9:3	43
7:22–27	140, 274	9:3–4	159
7:23, 25	141	9:4	159
7:23–24	144	9:5	159
7:24	141	9:6	159
7:25	141	9:7	29, 159, 160, 451
7:26–27	34, 142	9:7a	160
7:28–34	140	9:7b	160
7:30	89, 90	9:8	160
7:31	89	9:8–14	160
7:32	89	9:12–13	54
7:33	90	9:15–21	160, 161
7:35–36	136, 144	9:18	85
7:37–38	5, 144	9:22	162
7:38	4, 448	9:22a	162
8	149, 150	9:23	161
8:1	4	9:23a	163
8:1–3	150	9:23b	165
8:3	150	9:23b–24a	164
8:5–6	151	9:24	54, 169
8:6	151	10	150, 166, 167, 180, 437
8:7–9	151	10:1	168
8–9	168	10:1–7	8, 167, 168
8–10	2, 15	10:2	169
8:10	76	10:3	8, 51, 166, 167
8–10	104, 145, 149, 150, 237, 253, 266	10:6	217
		10:6–7	104
8:10–12	152	10:8–11	167, 168
8:13	153	10:9	73
8:14–17	153	10:10–11	180
8:14–36	153	10:11	166
8:15	30, 451	10:12–20	167
8:18–21	154	10:17	30
8:19	451	10:18	279
8:21	53	10:19	170
8:22–29	155	11	5, 42, 106, 179, 188, 190, 192, 194, 195,

SCRIPTURE INDEX

		196, 199, 200, 201,	11:44–47		194
		203, 210, 229, 280,	11:46–47		194
		325, 338, 339, 394	12		179, 202–3, 204, 206,
11:1		4, 180			207, 208, 209, 210,
11:1–3		190			221, 338
11:1–8		190	12:2		204, 209, 233
11:2		451	12:4		208
11:4–8		190	12:6		43, 104, 206
11:9–12		191	12:7		30, 206, 208, 209
11:10		192	12:8		209
11–12		222	12:22		451
11:13–19		191	13		5, 213, 215, 216, 229
11–14		229	13:1		180
11–15		2, 91, 94, 142, 179,	13:1–46		211, 219
		181–82, 184, 185,	13:2		216, 219, 451
		187, 195, 210, 217,	13:2–8		219
		222, 228, 229, 235,	13:3		219, 225
		236, 263, 266, 269,	13:4–5		219
		271, 310, 335, 338,	13:6		219
		348, 357, 402, 438	13:7–8		219
11:20		192	13:9		220
11–20		330, 411	13:9–17		214, 220
11:20–23		191, 192	13:10		213
11:24		192, 193	13:10–11		220
11:24–25		192	13:12–13		220
11:24–28		192	13:13		222
11:24–40		192	13–14		135, 179, 203, 211,
11:25		192			212, 213, 217, 218,
11:26		193			222, 338
11:26–28		192	13:14–15		220
11:27		193	13:14–16		220
11:29–31		193	13:16–17		220
11:29–38		193	13:18–23		220
11:32		193	13:20		225
11:32–38		193	13:24–28		220
11:33		193	13:29–37		220
11:34		193	13:38–39		220
11:35		193	13:40–44		220
11:36		193	13:45		217
11:37		193	13:45–46		220
11:38		194	13:46		180
11:39		194	13:47		216
11:39–40		194, 278, 279, 280	13:47–59		218, 219
11:40		194, 279	13:49		451
11:41		192	14		5, 216, 223, 224, 229
11:41–43		194	14:1–32		211, 219, 220, 227
11:44		451	14:2–9		222
11:44–45		194, 259, 283	14:3		180

519

SCRIPTURE INDEX

Leviticus (continued)

14:4	224, 451	16:1–10	246, 247
14:6	221	16:2	164, 451
14:8	408	16:3	248, 260
14:10–31	222, 225	16:4	248, 260, 265
14:12	20, 135	16:5	160, 249, 254, 255, 260
14:14	185	16:5–10	248
14:16	110	16:6	29, 451
14:16–17	111	16:8	249, 257
14:17	185	16:11–19	246, 249
14:19	104	16:12	168, 451
14:32–53	218	16:13	250, 451
14:33	180	16:14	251, 451
14:33–53	219, 227	16:15	252, 255, 451
14:34	416	16:16	30, 36
14:54–57	180, 219	16:16a	252
14:57	180	16:17	252
15	5, 179, 204, 209, 228–29, 232, 234, 235, 292, 329, 338	16:18	253
		16–19	348
		16:20	252, 253, 258
15:1	180	16:20–22	254
15:2	231	16:20–28	247, 253
15:2–12	230, 231	16:21	49, 255, 258
15:2–15	230	16:21–22	254
15:2–18	230	16:21a	254
15:3	231	16:21b–22	255
15:7	194, 231	16:23	248
15:8	451	16:23–24a	260
15:13–15	230, 232	16:24	265
15:15	104	16:24b–45	260
15:16–17	232	16:26	261
15:16–18	230, 232	16:27	119
15:18	225, 232, 234	16:27–28	263
15:19	204, 231, 233	16:29	248, 402
15:19–24	204, 209, 230, 233	16:29–31	265
15:19–30	230	16:29–34	247, 264
15:24	230, 234, 340	16:30	268
15:25–30	230, 234	16:32–34	265
15:30	104	17	25, 26, 32, 34, 36, 38, 39, 40, 141, 142, 266, 268–81, 335
15:31	180, 229, 230, 232, 233		
		17:1	4
15:32–33	230, 265	17:1–7	141, 270, 272, 277
16	2, 36, 114, 223, 246, 259, 260, 263, 266, 269, 335	17:2	283
		17:3	271
		17:7	257
16:1	4	17:7a	274
16:1–2	247	17:7b	274

520

SCRIPTURE INDEX

17:8	269, 271	18:19	292, 293
17:8–9	272, 274, 277	18–19	322
17:10	32, 33	18–20	281, 282, 284, 285,
17:10–12	272, 275		286, 287, 295, 301,
17:10–16	25, 32, 40		306, 312, 330, 331,
17:11	22, 25, 26, 27–29, 30,		332, 335, 336, 342
	32, 33–34, 36, 37, 38,	18:20	292, 293
	48, 51, 52, 69, 111,	18:21	292, 293, 294
	142, 251, 254, 276,	18:22	294, 327
	412, 452	18:23	294, 328
		18:24	289, 328
17:11 KJV	21	18:24–30	294, 457
17:11a	39, 40	19	142, 143, 282, 295,
17:11c	40		310, 311, 312, 313,
17:13	38, 271		315, 320, 322, 323,
17:13–14	272, 277		325
17:14b	40		
17:15	194, 271, 279	19:1	4
17:15–16	272, 280, 348	19:1–2	298
17–20	263	19:1–5	322
17–26	268–71	19:1–18	306
18	282, 283–94, 295,	19:2	259, 283, 297, 451,
	296, 310, 322, 323		452
18:1	4	19:3	296, 298, 326, 421
18:1–5	283, 288, 367	19:3–4	296, 444
18:2	269, 283	19:3a	296, 297
18:3	7, 283, 288	19:3b	296, 297, 353
18:3b	288	19:4	443
18:4	287	19:4–8	298
18:4–5	282	19:4–18	300
18:5	288, 326, 451	19:4a	298
18:5a	288	19:4b	298, 299
18:5b	288, 289	19:5–8	296, 298, 306
18:6	289, 291, 292, 340	19:9–10	296, 301
18:6–18	291	19:9–18	300
18:7	291, 293	19:10	301
18:7–30	291	19:11	303
18:8	286, 293, 327	19:11–12	296, 301, 302
18:9	293, 328	19:13	303
18:10	293	19:13–14	301, 302
18:11	293, 328	19:15	303, 451
18:12	293	19:15–16	301, 303
18:12–13	329	19:16	303, 451
18:13	293	19:17–18	301, 303
18:14	293	19:17a	303
18:15	293, 327	19:17b	303
18:16	293, 451	19:17c	303
18:17	293, 317, 327	19:18	300, 451
18:18	293, 329	19:18a	304

Leviticus (continued)

Reference	Pages
19:18b	304, 305
19:19	183, 295, 314, 438
19:19–25	314
19:19–37	306
19:19a	305
19:19b	306, 307, 310
19:20–22	134, 311, 314
19:22	473
19:23–25	313, 314
19:26	38, 142
19:26–28	315
19:26–31	315
19:26a	315
19:27	315, 341
19:29	343
19:29–30	315, 316
19:30	317
19:31	299, 315, 318
19:32	320, 321, 451
19:32–36	320
19:33–34	304, 320, 321, 431
19:34	130
19:35–36	321
19:37	282, 322
20	282, 313, 319, 322–23, 329, 330
20:1	4, 327
20:1–5	323
20:1–7	323
20:2	323
20:2–5	323
20:3	324
20:4–5	324
20:6	325
20:6–7	324–25
20:7	259, 325
20:8	326
20:8–9	326
20:8–21	323, 326
20:9	298, 326, 451
20:10	134, 311, 327, 451
20:10–21	327
20:11	327
20:12	327
20:13	327
20:14	327, 343
20:15	327
20:15–16	328
20:16	327
20:17	328
20:18	328
20:19	329, 451
20:20	329
20:21	329, 331
20:22–26	323, 329
20:23	7
20:24–26	43, 182, 183
20:25	295, 451
20:25–26	199, 307, 310, 336, 452
20:26	7
20:27	318, 325
21	170, 199, 337, 338
21:1	4, 339
21:1–4	339
21:1–6	338, 339
21:1–9	337, 338, 339
21:1–15	337, 338
21:2	340
21:2–3	340
21:4	339
21:5–6	339, 341, 343
21:6	341
21:7	343
21:7–9	338, 342
21:8	55, 343
21:9	327, 343
21:10	344
21:10–12	339, 344
21:10–15	337, 339, 343
21:12	344
21:13–15	339, 345
21:14	346
21:15	344
21:16–24	44, 337
21:17	51, 55, 57
21–22	333, 334, 335, 336–37, 341, 352, 411
21:22	57, 347
22	199, 263, 335, 337, 338, 347
22:1	4
22:1–7	348
22:1–9	338, 347

SCRIPTURE INDEX

22:1–16	338, 347	23:21	396
22:8	348	23:22	301, 396
22:9	348, 349	23:23–25	354, 397
22:10–13	348, 349	23:24–25	399
22:10–16	338, 348	23–25	353, 383, 436
22:11	33	23:26–32	354, 400
22:14	349	23:27	402
22:15–16	349	23:27–28	401
22:17–20	350	23:29–30	402
22:17–25	10	23:31	436
22:17–33	44, 338, 349	23:32	401
22:20–22	43	23:33–44	354, 404, 405
22:21–25	350	23:34	451
22:22	88	23:34–35	406
22:22–24	462	23:36	451
22:23	88	23:36b	407
22:24	88	23:37	71
22:26–27	350	23:37–38	85
22:27	43	23:39	407
22:28	351	23:39–40	406
22:29–30	91, 351	23:40	409
22:30	352	23:41	408
22:31–33	336, 341, 352	23:42–43	408
23	71, 354, 380, 383, 384, 407, 410, 411	23:43	405
		24	354, 355, 410, 415
23:1	361	24:1–4	410, 411
23:1–3	354, 355, 365, 382, 383	24:3	411
		24:5–9	410, 412, 451
23:2	383	24:7	76
23:2–3	298	24:10	5
23:3	385, 436	24:10–11	413
23:4–14	354, 385	24:10–23	102, 410, 413
23:5–14	387	24:11	413
23:5–44	392	24:15	414
23:6–8	78	24:16	413, 414, 451
23:6–14	406	24:19	451
23:7–8	392	25	354, 410, 411, 415, 416, 417, 423, 429, 435
23:10	71, 416		
23:10–11	387, 390		
23:12	392	25:1	4, 448
23:13	71	25:1–7	355, 415, 417
23:15	393, 395, 451	25:2	416, 421
23:15–21	394	25:3–4	418
23:15–22	354, 393, 406	25:4	418
23:17	79, 395, 396	25:5	418
23:18	71, 73, 395	25:8–12	423
23:19	85, 160, 395	25:8–55	355, 423
23:19–20	395	25:9	400, 401, 419, 424

523

Leviticus (continued)

25:10	424, 432, 451
25:11	418, 424
25:13	425
25:13, 23	426
25:13–34	423, 425
25:14–17	425
25:18–22	425, 426
25:20	418
25:21	417, 423, 426
25:23	57, 127, 417, 426, 468
25:23–28	425, 426
25:24–25	473
25:25–27	464
25:28	463
25:29–34	425, 427
25:35	451
25:35–38	428, 430
25:35–55	423, 428
25:36–37	430
25:39–43	431
25:39–46	428, 431
25:43	451
25:43, 53	452
25:44–46	431, 433
25:47–55	428, 433
25:48–49	427
25:53	434, 451, 452
26	5, 162, 269, 281, 289, 411, 422, 441, 442, 444, 448–49, 450, 452, 453, 454, 469
26:1	443
26:1–2	442, 443
26:2	317, 444
26:3	445
26:3–13	444
26:9	444
26:11	451
26:14–15	446
26:14–17	446
26:14–33	446
26:14–45	444
26:15	444
26:18–20	446
26:21	451
26:21–22	446
26:23–26	446
26:25	444
26–27	441
26:27–33	446
26:30	447
26:34	452
26:34–35	422
26:34–39	447
26:40–45	447
26:41	451
26:43	422, 452
26:46	5, 8, 447–48, 453, 469
27	5, 268, 441, 453–54, 456, 457, 458, 459, 460, 465, 467, 469, 470, 473, 474, 475
27:1–8	459, 460
27:1–25	459
27:2	460
27:2–3	128
27:9–10	461, 464
27:9–13	459, 461
27:11–13	461
27:14–15	459, 462
27:14–23	423
27:16	463
27:16–21	462
27:16–24	459, 462
27:17	463
27:18	463
27:19	463
27:20	463
27:21	464, 467
27:22	464
27:23	464
27:25	464
27:26	466, 469
27:26–27	459, 465
27:26–34	459, 464
27:27	466
27:28	467
27:28–29	459, 466
27:29	467
27:30	57, 127, 451
27:30–31	459, 468
27:32–33	459, 468, 469
27:34	4, 5, 454, 459, 469

SCRIPTURE INDEX

Numbers

	2, 3, 7, 8, 381, 441, 456, 457, 458, 469, 470, 473
1	456, 458, 468, 469, 470
1:1	3
1–4	217
1:9	399
3:4	168, 173
3:47	464
4:7	72
5	217
5:1–4	180, 438
5:2	217, 222, 232
5:2–3	256
5:5–10	133
5:8	401
5:29	401
6:6	37
6:12	135
6:14	104
6:15	71
6:20	127
6:22	162
6:24–26	162
6:27	162
7	429
7:3	19, 58
7:15–16	66
7:89	379
8:7	225
8:10	49
9	390
9:1–14	437
9:7	389
9:8	379
10	425
10:1–10	384, 398, 399
10:2	399
10:9	398
10:10	298, 399
10:11	3
11	357
11:4	413
11:5	191
12:1	238
12:8	379
12:10	216
12:12	203, 221
13–14	365, 415
14:12	447
14:33	205
15	71, 80, 99, 102
15:2	72
15:8	84
15:22–31	98, 378
15:30	98, 100, 129
15:31	378
15:32–36	99, 378, 379
15:37–41	183, 307, 378, 438
16:26	408
16:46–47	250
17	412
18	58, 127
18:1	255
18:12	87
18:14	464, 467
18:15	208
18:16	461, 464
18:17–18	466
18:19	77, 153
18:21	57
18:21–32	468
18:23	255
18:24	57
19:1–6	400
19:6	221, 224
20:17	429
21	382
21:1–3	381, 467
21:22	429
24:5	408
26:61	173
27	437
27:5	379
28:1–8	137, 399
28:2	59
28:9–10	397, 399, 406
28:11	397
28:11–15	397, 400
28:15	160
28:16–25	387
28:19–21	395
28:19–25	392

SCRIPTURE INDEX

Numbers (continued)

28:22	160, 396
28:26	394
28:27	395
28:30	396
29	248
29:2–6	401
29:8–11	401
29:11	401
29:16	409
29:39	85
30:3	85
31	457
31:50	19
33:3	360
33:3–4	391
33:52	444
35	427
35:11	98
36:4	423

Deuteronomy

	2, 279, 419, 421, 473, 475
1:19	404
1:27	408
4:34	386
5	372
5:14–15	372
5:28	166
6:4	65
6:4–5	137
6:5	55, 65, 419
6:7	298
6:14	102
7:2	466
7:5–8	388
8:3	120, 409
8:15	404
9:20	377
10:8	162
10:12	55
10:18	321, 345
11:6	408
11:10	429
11:14	445
11:19	298
12	141, 274
12:6	85
12:12	433
12:23	40
12:27	84
13:12–18	467
14	197, 279, 280
14:1	107, 368, 388
14:1–2	315
14:1–21a	197
14:3–21a	199
14:4–5	190
14:11	191
14:20	345
14:21	198, 279, 280, 310
15	372, 418, 419, 420
15:1	430
15:2	430
15:3	430
15:9	418, 419
15:12–16	432
15:12–18	416
15:13	102
16:3	390
16:5–6	389
16:5–8	387
16:10	394, 396
16:11	345, 433
16:12	396
16:13	407
16:14	345, 407, 408
16:17	320
16:18–17	102
17:2–7	100
17:8–13	5
18:3	84
18:5	346
18:9	318
18:11	318
19	313
19:4	98
19:10	313
20	102
20:17	466
21:16–24	346
22	307
22:5	307, 308
22:5–12	307

526

22:6	311	6:5-6	424
22:6-7	307, 351	6:17	467
22:7	309	6:19	467
22:8	183, 307	7	129
22:9	438	7:1	103
22:9-11	307, 309, 310	8:31	85
22:9-12	183	24	269, 270
22:10	310, 311	24:1-13	269
22:12	307, 438	24:14	270, 273
22:23	312		
23:1	238	**Judges**	
23:12-14	181, 229, 359		162
23:15-16	433	1:17	382
23:17	294	2:1	427
23:19-20	430	3:29	87
23:22	85	6:3-6	449
24:19-21	345	9	322
24:19-22	301	9:13	72
25:3	205	17	299
25:4	309, 311	17:2	106
25:5-10	293, 331	17:7	144
26:12	345	19:22-24	294
27:7	84	20:26	84
27:14	180	21:24	84
27:19	321		
27:21	328	**Ruth**	
28	449	1:20	390
28:12	430	1:22	392
28-29	162	2:4	302
28:44	433	2:10	302
31	421	2:15-16	302, 473
31:8	422	2:23	392
31:9-13	421	3:10-15	473
31:10	407	4:1-12	473
32:8	258		
32:14	87	**1 Samuel**	
32:17	273	1-2	458
33:2 LXX	258	2:25	319
33:9	153	2:30	281
33:10	64, 180	2:36	144
		6:20	9, 103
Joshua		7:9	64
	162	10:1	75
2:19	274	12	269
4:6	375	12:6-12	269
4:14-15	427	12:7	269
6:2	427		

1 Samuel (continued)

13:9	84
14:32	277
15:22	47
16:13	75
18:4	174
20	398
20:13	174
20:26	180
21:1–6	437
22:2	430
25	106
28	318, 319
28:15	319
28:17	304
28:19	319

2 Samuel

1:22	87
2:16	304
9:8	445
11:11	407
13:29	311
15:7–8	465
18:9	311
18:18	443
24:24	42

1 Kings

1:33	311
2:37	274
8	409
8:2	407
8:63	85
8:65	407
11:4	67
11:26	216
12:28	299
12:33	406
13:24	449
17:1	449
17:12	75
18:21	67
19:16	75
21	303, 322
22:19–23	258

2 Kings

2:20–22	77
4:1	430
4:23	397
5:2	450
5:7	221
5:27	216
6:25	449
6:29	449
9:26	322
11:18–20	323–24
12:16	128
17:24	450
22	281
23:10	294
24:4	453

1 Chronicles

10:13–14	319
16:30	472
24:2	173

2 Chronicles

5:3	407
7:1	54
7:8	407
9:24	311
13:15	77
15:3	180
20:16	389
21:16–17	450
29:24	50
29:34	50
30:2–4	437
30:13	437
30:15	437
30:16	50
30:17	49, 50
31:5	79
34:19	453
35:6	50
35:11	50, 389
36:21	450

Ezra

4:14	77

SCRIPTURE INDEX

9:4–5	137

Nehemiah

2:1	386
5:19	82
8	409
8:15	407
9	450
13:14	82
13:22	82
13:29	153
13:31	82

Esther

1:19	438
3:7	386
8:18	438

Job

1:6	257, 258
6:6	77
27:18	407
36:26	377

Psalms

7:5	32, 36
11:1	31
11:3	473
12:6	416
16:4	257
16:9	32
18:6	242
19:12	105
20:3	83
23:5	75
25:15	445
26	93
34:12–16	453
35:13	402
37:21	429
40	145
40:1–10	145
40:8	145
44	93
44:17–18	93
50:12–13	55
50:14	84, 85
51:5	206
51:6	47
51:7	217, 224
51:16	47
51:21	64
56:12–13	94
57:4	31
69:17	445
75:2	383
78:31	87
81:16	87
82:1	414
82:5	473
86:11–12	67
89:7	414
93:1	472
96:10	472
100	94
104:14–15	120
104:15	72
104:19a	383
106:15 KJV	37
106:25	408
113–118	389
116	85
116:4	93
116:9	94
116:12	85
116:14	85, 465
119:176	93
124:5	31
126:4	188
134:1	411
141:2	76
141:8	40

Proverbs

6:30 KJV	33
11:30	99
12:10	311
28:9	174
29:24	106

SCRIPTURE INDEX

Ecclesiastes

5:3	461
7:16	173
9:5	318

Song of Solomon

1:1	385

Isaiah

1:6	75
1:8	407
1:11–17	47
1:13	174, 397
1:18	217
6:3–4	76
9:6	95
10:6	87
13:21	257
29:13	67
32:30	64
33:14	9
34:11–15	257
35	95
38:19	326
40:6	231
40:18	7
40:19–20	299
53:12	40, 41
54	450
60:6	77
61	435
61:1–3	435
63:10	281

Jeremiah

6:20	77
7:22	47
18:23	28
22:21	273
33:21	153
51:37	257

Lamentations

2:12	40
2:20	449
3:33	94
4:10	449

Ezekiel

4:14	200
13:6–7	319
16:26	231, 273
16:45	445
17:20	126
20:7–8	273
20:41–42	7
21:21	87
23:19	273
23:20	231
24:15–27	341
24:17	217
24:22	217
27:14	311
43:26	145
44:10–11	50
44:24	297
45:25	407
46:1	397

Daniel

1:8–9	200
8:11–13	65
9	450
9:7	125
10	258
11:31	137
12:11	137

Hosea

2:13	397
2:13–14	409
9:3	200
11:1	187

Joel

1:9	71
3:3, 6	450
3:6	450
4:17	95

Amos
5:22	84
5:25	47
5:25–27	75
5:26	273
7:17b	200
8:5	398
9:13	95

Obadiah
11, 20	450

Jonah
4:5	407

Habakkuk
1	191
1:13	101

Zephaniah
2:9	77

Zechariah
3	258
3:1	257, 259

Malachi
2:4	153
2:6–7	180
3:18	453

ANCIENT NEAR EAST TEXTS

Code of Hammurabi
	285

DEUTEROCANONICAL BOOKS

Baruch
6:42–43	316

2 Maccabees
6–7	200

Sirach
45:14	138
45:15	153

NEW TESTAMENT

Matthew
2:11	20
3:4	192
3:11	54
4:4	419
4:7	419
4:10	419
5–7	305
5:39	451
8:4	451
8:11	57
9:13	201
9:20	308
10:10	82
11:30	200
12:7	201
12:31	103
12:32b	103
12:43	256
13:33	78
13:35	471
14:4	451
15:4	451
15:8	67
16:1–29	27
18:32–33	431
19:7–8	305
20:28	41, 44
22:1	57
22:10	57
22:11	57
22:35–40	300
22:37	55, 419
22:39	363, 451
23:5	308
23:23	451, 468
25:3	75

Matthew (continued)

25:34	471
26:5	389
26:6	216
26:28	185, 392
26:30	389
26:66	451

Mark

1:44	216, 451
2:26	451
6:13	75
6:18	451
7	20
7:5	201
7:8	201
7:9	201
7:11	20
9:49	54, 77
11:64	451
12:31	451
14:24	185, 392
16:20	244

Luke

1:13	398
1:20	76
2:22	451
2:22–29	207
2:22a	208
2:22b–23	208
2:22b–24	208
2:24	208
4:17–21	435
4:19	451
4:27	216, 222
5:14	451
5:17	451
6:3–5	437
6:33–35	419
6:34	451
7:22	435
7:46	75
10:25–37	305
10:27	55
10:34	75

11:46	201
11:50	471
14:15	57
17:15	221
20:21	451
22:20	185, 392

John

1:4	211
1:10	471
1:18	250
1:29	30
3:12	184
3:16	30
5:46	6
7	409
7:7	471
7:12	451
7:37	451
8:4	451
8:26	471
8:57	44
12:3	216
12:31	211, 222
12:42	103
14:30	222
14:30–31	211
15:18–19	471
16:11	211, 222
17:11	9
17:14	471
17:19	174
17:24	471
19:7	451
19:14	389
19:35	41
19:36	389

Acts

	237, 240
1:5	54
1:8	237
2	393
2:1	451
2:3	54
2–3	237

SCRIPTURE INDEX

2:23	103, 389
2:31	41
2:38	104
2:45	475
3:17	103
3:19	104
4:37	475
6:1	240
6:7	52
6:9	240
6:13	201
7:5	426
7:22	5
7:38	258
7:42–43	75
7:43	273
7:51	451
7:53	258
7:53–54	201
8:1	238
8:14	237
8:36	238
10:4	83
10:13	142
10:15	43
10:20	238
10:48	238
11:12, 17	238
11:17	238
11:18	43, 238
11:23	275
13:35	41
13:43	187
14:3	244
15:1	142–43
15:20	143
15:28	143
16:3	239
17:25	55
18:18	239
20:35	302
21	239, 240
21:19	239
21:20	236n1, 239
21:21	239
21:24	239
22:16	104, 255
22:17	240
24:11	240
24:17–18	240
26:16	105
26:18	18, 43, 117, 186, 198, 222, 256

Romans

	58, 439, 452
1	439
1–2	331
1:16	439
1:18	18, 331
1:21	331
1:23	331
1:25	331
1:27	294
1:28	281
3–5	55
3:21	437
3:25	451
4–5	437
4:25	27, 258
5	207
5:2	94
5:8	30
5:12–14	26
6	55
6:3–4	116, 404
6:22	58
6:23	26, 49
7:5	437
7:12	132
8:4	170
8:5–9	437
8:23	26
8:32	30
9:11	207
10:5	288, 451
10:18	451
11	453
11:13–24	94
11:16	82, 391, 396
11:17–36	450
11:21	452
12:1	55, 370
13:1 ESV	33
13:1 KJV	33

Romans (continued)

13:8	363
13:10	132
14:5	422, 439
14:15	432
14:17	437
15:17	143
16:5	474
16:10	474
16:15	474
16:18	183
16:22	240
16:25	472

1 Corinthians

	57
2:8	103
3:6	174
3:11	54
3:16–17	474
5	78, 184, 331
5:1	291
5:6	79
5:7	389, 390
5:10	184
6:19–20	474
9	81, 309, 475
9:9	309, 311, 475
9:13	63
9:13–14	82, 144, 475
9:20–23	239
10:18	46, 57, 389, 437
10:21	57
11:25	185, 392
11:25–26	404
15	41
15:12	41
15:13	41
15:18	41
15:54	200
16:13	66

2 Corinthians

2:11	186
3:6	185
4:4	43
5:18	30
5:19	30
5:21	9, 30
6:14	451
6:16	445, 474
6:16b	451
6:17	451, 452
9:7	422
11:2	347

Galatians

	132
1:13	255
1:14	201
1:22	237
2:4	239
2:11–21	201
2:12	92, 143
2:21	201
3	267
3:8	186
3:12	288, 451
3:14	186, 450
3:19	258
3:23	337
3:23–24	470
3:23–25	460
3:24	105, 267, 349, 384
3:28	182
3:29	186
4	185
4:2	337
4:3	132
4:4	286
4:9	132
4:10	397, 422, 439
4:24–26	184
4:27	450
5	332
5:9	79
5:14	363
6:10	435
6:13	437

Ephesians

1:4	198, 347, 471, 472

1:19–21	342	**2 Thessalonians**	
2:2	18, 43, 222, 256	2:1	316
2:21	474		
3:10	198	**1 Timothy**	
4–5	332		
5:1	296, 368	1:12–16	103
5:8	187	1:13	201, 255
5:22–33	229	3:15	474
5:26	187, 210, 281	5:1	451
5:27	347	5:18	309, 311, 475
6:9	451, 452	6:14	44
6:12	142, 184, 186, 187, 256	6:16	101, 250

Philippians

2 Timothy

2:3	174	1:9	198, 472
2:5	174	3:14–17	332
3:3–4	437	3:15	450
3:18	239	3:15–16	95
3:19	183		
3:19–20	184	**Titus**	
		1:2	472

Colossians

Hebrews

	132		142, 175, 240, 241, 243, 245, 267, 452
1:12–13	187	1–2	244
1:13	105, 117	1:3	258
1:13–14	186	2:2	258
1:22	347	2:3	234, 243, 244
2:8	132	2:14	198, 211, 222
2:11	185	2:14–15	44
2:15	258	2:17	47
2:16	422, 439	3	244
2:16–17	199, 239, 397	3:1	245
2:20	132	3–4	244
2:23	174	4:2	256
3	332	4:3	471
3:1–2	184	4:16	170, 242
3:11	182	5	150, 244
4:1	451, 452	5:1	20
4:6	77	5:1–10	242
		5:3	160, 253, 451

1 Thessalonians

2:14–15	184	5:4	250, 412
2:15	186	5:5	52
2:18	142, 184, 186	5:13	451
4:12	316	6:5	210, 256

Hebrews (continued)

6:6	244
6:10	83
6:19	451
7	266, 267
7:1—10:18	150
7–10	244, 332
7:11	150, 266
7:12	267
7:16	266
7:18	267, 422
7:19	244, 267
7:22	158, 185, 234
7:25	242
7:26	45, 158, 347
7:27	114, 160, 161, 389, 451
7:28	160, 267, 337
8:2	242
8:3	20, 267
8:6	185, 234
8:13	120, 183, 186, 244, 422, 439
8:15	158
9:6–7	242
9:6–10	243
9:6–10 ESV	241
9:6–10 KJV	241
9:7	52, 160, 253
9:8	242
9:9	20
9:10	437, 451
9:12	51, 52, 261
9:13	242, 451
9:14	45, 54, 174
9:15	185
9:19	224, 451
9:21	451
9:22	17, 26, 254
9:24–26	1
9:25–26	251
9:26	403, 471
9:28	389
10	453
10:1	27
10:4	46, 47
10:9	422
10:10	47
10:14	347
10:19	51
10:22	111
10:24	187
10:26–31	116
10:28–29	187
10:28–31	210, 422
10:29	185, 210, 234, 244, 281, 474
10:29–31	452
10:33	121
10:34	52
10:35	9
11:10	121
11:14	121
11:15	185
11:26	121
12:12	242
13:7	241
13:9–14	119, 121
13:9a	120
13:9b	120
13:9c	120
13:10	120
13:11	120
13:11–12	261
13:12	121
13:12–13	121
13:13–14	121
13:15	95, 451
13:18	95
13:20	185
13:22	243
13:23	244

James

1:6	93
1:27	44
2:8	451
2:9	451
4:11	451
5:14	75

1 Peter

1:2	259

1:11	145, 174
1:12	259
1:15	451, 452
1:16	259
1:19	44, 45, 259, 347, 391
1:20	471
2:5	54, 83, 259
2:9	185, 186, 259, 342
2:9–10	137, 187
2:10	94
2:24	121
3:7	204
3:10–12	453
3:19	258, 259
3:21	48
4	332
5:12	240

2 Peter

1:11	117
2:1	117, 234
2:1–2	281
2:22	210, 281
3:14	44

1 John

1:3	116
1:5	101
1:7	47
2:1	117
2:11	116
2:19	116
2:28	116
3:15	116
4:7	116
4:9	30
5:3	200
5:16	116, 117
5:19	18

2 John

1:10	474

3 John

1:9–10	474

Jude

1:7	294

Revelation

1:5–6	187
2–3	474
2:7	9
3:20	57
5	76
5:6	27
5:8	76
5:9	27
5:12	27
8:3	76
8:5	451
11:10	20
12:7–9	258
12:10	259
13:8	27, 471
14:5	45
15:6	451
15:8	451
17:8	471
18:2	256, 257
21	56
21:2	9
21:9	451
22	56
22:3–4	9

APOCRYPHA (NEW TESTAMENT)

Epistle of Barnabas

270

Pseudo-Barnabas

263

EARLY CHRISTIAN WRITINGS

Didache

270

Eusebius
240, 241

Church History
V.1.25–26   143

Origen
257

GREEK AND ROMAN LITERATURE

Aristotle
434

Herodotus
283, 316

Plinius (Pliny the Elder)
351

Tertullian
262

Answer
Chp. 14, 732–733   263n9

Against Marcion
Chp. 7   263n9